CAIN

ROY HOOPES

HOLT, RINEHART AND WINSTON
NEW YORK

Library of Congress Cataloging in Publication Data
Hoopes, Roy, 1922–
Cain.
Bibliography: p.
1. Cain, James M. (James Mallahan), 1892–1977.
2. Novelists, American—20th century—Biography.
1. Title.
PS3505. A3113Z69   813'13.52 [B]   81-16133
ISBN 0-03-049331-5   AACR2

First Edition

Designer: Joy Chu
Printed in the United States of America
1 3 5 7 9 10 8 6 4 2

ISBN 0-03-049331-5

Grateful acknowledgment is given to the following:
Liberty Library Corporation for use of illustration by
James Montgomery Flagg, from Liberty *magazine, Copyright*
1936 Macfadden Publications, Inc., Copyright © 1982 Liberty
Library Corporation. Reprinted by permission. The poem "Auld
Lang Syne" by James M. Cain is reprinted by permission.
Copyright 1930, Copyright © 1958 The New Yorker, Inc. The
cartoon by Stan Stamaty, Copyright 1946 by the New York
Times Company. Reprinted by permission. Drawing by Richard
Decker, Copyright 1936, Copyright © 1964, The New
Yorker Magazine, Inc. Reprinted by permission.

Letters quoted and reprinted in this book are by kind
permission of the following: Estate of Oscar Hammerstein II;
George A. Raftery; Andy Logan; Allan Nevins Papers, Rare
Book and Manuscript Library, Columbia University; William
Morris Agency (for Edith Haggard); Estate of Jerry Wald;
Estate of Raoul Fleischmann; Alfred A. Knopf; William
Koshland; Leo Tyszecki (for Elina Tyszecka); Ruth
Goetz; Max Gissen; William Blair (for Arthur Krock);
Enoch Pratt Free Library (for H. L. Mencken); Yale
University Library (for Walter Lippmann); and Helga Greene
(for Raymond Chandler).

FOR CORA,
whose many and varied contributions
to this project were beyond
the call of duty

C O N T E N T S

PREFACE   The Writer's Writer   *xi*

PART ONE
ANNAPOLIS, CHESTERTOWN, BALTIMORE, FRANCE (1892–1919)

1   "A Midget Among Giants"   *3*
2   Consolation Prize   *30*
3   Doughboy Editor   *60*

PART TWO
BALTIMORE, NEW YORK (1920–1931)

4   "Treason" Did Not a Novel Make   *83*
5   Deep Water at Last   *102*
6   Bombing Out in Stamford and Worcester   *126*
7   The Corporate Awfulness   *159*
8   The Literary Life   *178*
9   End of the *World* and the Twenty-sixth Jesus   *195*

PART THREE
HOLLYWOOD (1932–1948)

10   Murder on the Love Rack   *217*

11   The "Unlaydownable" Book Launches a Strange Career   *244*

12   "How You Write 'Em Is Write 'Em"   *273*

13   Finney Pylorectomy—"A Very Great Event"   *298*

14   In War, They Have to Spell "Mother"   *316*

15   Raising Cain with the Hays Office   *341*

16   AAA—"The Brand of Cain"   *389*

17   Pleasant Harbor   *413*

PART FOUR
HYATTSVILLE (1948–1977)

18   Two Trials and Many Tribulations   *441*

19   "A Kind of Mouse Is Born"   *456*

20   Twilight Time   *478*

21   Resurrection   *509*

22   End of the Rainbow   *522*

AFTERWORD   The Newspaperman Who Wrote Yarns on the Side   *545*

CHRONOLOGY   *557*

ACKNOWLEDGMENTS   *560*

SOURCES AND NOTES   *563*

PUBLICATIONS BY JAMES M. CAIN   *645*

CAIN FILMOGRAPHY   *650*

INDEX   *655*

Photo sections follow pages 40, 140, 354, and 488.

THE WRITER'S WRITER

In February 1975, the *Washington Post* published a fine, beautifully written tribute to the late Walter Lippmann by—of all people—James M. Cain, author of *The Postman Always Rings Twice* and other controversial, best-selling novels of the 1930s and 1940s. Cain, much to my—and many other Washingtonians'—surprise, was not only still alive and well, he was living in Hyattsville, Maryland, just thirty Beltway minutes from my home, then in Potomac. Not only that, he was still writing; a few months after the Lippmann article appeared, Cain published his seventeenth novel—at the age of eighty-two! It was titled *Rainbow's End*, and the reviews were mostly favorable, with many critics saying that the old Cain was back, just as tough and lean in his writing as ever.

The Lippmann article also prodded from my memory a favorite James M. Cainism: When a reporter asked him if he deplored what Hollywood had done to his best-selling novel of the 1930s, *The Postman Always Rings Twice*, he said: "They haven't done anything to my book. It's right up there on the shelf." It was still right up there on my shelf too, along with nine other Cain books, including *Serenade, Mildred Pierce, Past All Dishonor, Three of a Kind* (which included "Double Indemnity," "The Embezzler," and "Career in C Major"), *The Moth,* and *The Butterfly.* In short, although Cain had always been a favorite author, dating back to my college days, it came as a surprise to me that he had also been an editorial writer for Walter Lippmann. And, with a little research, I learned a few more things about him that I did not know: that he considered it a "consolation prize" when he made his decision to be a writer, after voice lessons confirmed that he would never be an opera singer; that he contributed at least a dozen articles to the original *American Mercury* and was a close friend of its editor, H. L. Mencken, who said "the only author I ever knew who never wrote a bad article was James M. Cain"; that during the most exciting literary decade in American history— the 1920s—Cain was writing in New York, trying unsuccessfully to become a playwright, drinking and talking into the night with the Mencken crowd of Sinclair Lewis, Phil Goodman, W. C. Fields, and Alfred A. Knopf, among others, and bantering and feuding during the day with the *New York World* gang, which included Arthur Krock, Laurence Stallings, Morris Markey, Allan Nevins, Franklin P. Adams, and Heywood Broun. At the *World*, he became one of the most respected editorial writers in New York, and his first book, *Our Government*, published by Knopf in 1930, was a collection of satirical dialogues. Then he was briefly on Harold Ross's fledgling *New Yorker*, before abruptly leaving New York for Hollywood to spend the next seventeen years trying to become a screenwriter, a job at which, by his own confession, he was a miserable failure.

From 1934 to 1948, however, he did manage to write eight best-selling novels while also achieving the reputation with which many people still identify him—as one of Hollywood's most celebrated and successful writers, despite the fact that he never wrote a single successful, first-rate, original movie script. Yet nine of Cain's novels and stories were adapted by others for the screen, and two of them—*Double Indemnity*, and *The Postman Always Rings Twice*—were big controversial hits of the 1940s, films that forced the Hays Office to accept conspiracy to murder an adulterous woman's husband as a subject suitable for movies. In addition, his *Mildred Pierce* won an Academy Award for Joan Crawford in 1945. While in Hollywood, Cain divorced his second wife, Elina Tyszecka, and married movie star Aileen Pringle. Then, at the height of his fame, when he could command $2,500 a week from the studios, he abruptly left Hollywood to "make something" of himself as a writer. He and his fourth wife, the former opera star Florence Macbeth, went east, where Cain wanted to do research in the Library of Congress for what he considered his major work—a trilogy of novels of the Civil War. The couple settled in Hyattsville, Maryland, and Cain spent the next twenty-nine years writing continuously, eventually publishing five more novels, none of which had the originality and impact of his big best sellers of the 1930s and 1940s.

It is a long time before a writer's place in his country's literature is decided, and Cain's is still undetermined. He was undeniably one of the most provocative and popular novelists America ever produced. His books have been published in more than seventeen languages around the world, and they are continually being reprinted and read, here and abroad. But some critics still consider him little more than a commercial phenomenon, corrupted by Hollywood, whose only contribution to our literature was to give us a glimpse of life and morality among an unattractive and insignificant class of Americans. Others feel Cain is a major American writer whose place in literature is secure. Edmund Wilson, for example, in his famous essay "The Boys in the Back Room," thought Cain the best of a group of writers he called "poets of the tabloid murder," which also included John Steinbeck, John O'Hara, and William Saroyan. Max Lerner wrote, "More than any other contemporary writer, Cain has become the novelist laureate of the crime of passion in America." And David Madden, himself a talented novelist, said in his study of Cain (*James M. Cain*, Twayne Publishers, 1970) that Cain wrote the "pure novel," one that "takes us through experiences whose special quality is found in no other writer's work. . . . Cain's art, more than anything else, moves even the serious reader to almost complete emotional commitment to the traumatic experiences Cain renders."

Still others have had even higher praise. In a review of one of Norman Mailer's novels, Tom Wolfe advised Mailer to study Cain to learn how to write a novel; Stephen King, author of several thrillers, including *Carrie* and *Salem's Lot*, said of Cain: "Everyone should study him in writing class, instead of the marsh gas they put out for us to admire." Mystery writer Ross Macdonald called *Postman* and "Double Indemnity" "a pair of native American masterpieces, back to back." And another mystery writer, Thomas Chastain, says: "Cain is one of the few writers who, when you read him, if you wanted to be a writer, showed you the potential of what writing could be." Gertrude Atherton, a turn-of-the-century American author, called *Postman* "a work of art." Marcia Davenport, author of *Valley of Decision*, said, "*Serenade* is inexplicable except as pure genius." And Rebecca West wrote Cain: "You seem to me one of the few modern novelists who know what you mean to say when you start a novel, and end up by saying much more because you let the thing grow in good imaginative soil as you write it. You were a fool not to be born a Frenchman. The highbrows would have put you with Gide and Mauriac if you had taken this simple precaution."

There is considerable truth in Ms. West's observation. Even in criticizing *Past All Dishonor*, Malcolm Cowley recognized that Cain was an important literary figure abroad: "From Helsinki to Melbourne by way of Paris and

Buenos Aires, he is regarded as a type, a symbol, a trend in American letters." André Gide was a great admirer of Cain, as were Jean-Paul Sartre and Albert Camus, the latter having used *Postman* as a model for *The Stranger*.

As I read over the reviews of Cain's books and the appraisals and comments on his writing, one fact struck me as consistently significant: As a rule, the conventional literary critics put him down while *writers* praised him, sometimes almost in reverence. James M. Cain, I decided, was clearly a writer's writer. And this, it seems to me, is why he is studied in colleges today primarily in writing courses and workshops rather than literary classes . . . as Cain himself would have preferred.

Whether or not James M. Cain will eventually become established as a major American author will be left to the only critic Cain himself felt was competent to judge—Posterity. But there is little doubt that he is the perfect subject for a biography. He enjoyed three careers—as a journalist, novelist, and screenwriter—wrote seventeen books, and had four wives and a long life that spanned the first seven decades of the twentieth century. As far as "golden ages" go, he was invariably in the right place at the right time: New York in the 1920s, Hollywood in the 1930s and 1940s, and Washington in the 1950s. It was a life dedicated to and supported solely by writing, from that memorable day in 1914 when, sitting across from the White House on a bench in Lafayette Park, he arbitrarily decided to become a writer.

But surely, I thought, after reading his tribute to Walter Lippmann, someone must be working on a biography, or, more likely, Cain was writing his own autobiography. I decided the best way to establish contact was to arrange to write a magazine profile of Cain, and the editor of *The Washingtonian* agreed. So I called up Cain and, after a few nervous, introductory remarks, in which I attempted to present some sort of credentials, told him of my desire to write a profile and, eventually, a full-length biography. I also said I assumed he was working on his autobiography, in which case I would abandon my hopes for the larger project.

"No," he said in a voice still gruff, though weakened somewhat by age, "I don't believe in 'em. I don't believe any man should write his autobiography unless he can give it the same subtitle Booker T. Washington gave his: *Or, Up from Slavery.* Unless you can say that, you've got no story to tell."

There was also the question of whether someone else was working on a biography. He assured me there was no one. Would he cooperate with me on a biography if I could find a publisher? "Yeah, if we hit it off all right and I like the article you do on me. But the interviews will have to be after dinner. I work and rest in the daytime."

That was my introduction to James M. Cain. I did the profile, and he liked it. He agreed to the biography and, in fact, gave me two boxes of his papers and persuaded the Library of Congress to lend me ten more he had put on deposit there.

As I looked a little more into his life, a disturbing fact emerged: James M. Cain was an authority on biography. His interest in the subject had begun early in his childhood, when he was carried away reading his father's edition of *Who's Who in America*, and his lifelong preoccupation with biography culminated in his last published novel, *The Institute*, about a University of Maryland professor who starts an Institute of Biography to assist biographers in every way—including grants-in-aid. Not a bad idea, I thought, given the fact that the writing of biography today has become an overwhelming proposition, what with the mass of accumulated papers and research most biographers face—to say nothing of the inherent challenge of compressing into a single book the total life of a man . . . especially one who lives eighty-five years and is active in his profession to the very end.

It was Mark Twain who argued that the real biography of a person is in his or her head and is known to no one else. Furthermore, if you did know it, you could not record it. "Every day," said Twain, "would make a whole book of 80,000 words—365 books a year. Biographies are but the clothes and buttons of the man—the biography of the man himself cannot be written." Twain's observation has not prevented some writers from trying to write the complete story, which has resulted in several monumental biographies in recent years that are easier to put down than to pick up. This, in turn, has led to a mild protest against what Peter Prescott in *Newsweek* called these "overlong and graceless biographies." Complaining about such a biography of Evelyn Waugh, he said he could not shake his "wish for a trim and elegant book about this man who wrote trim and eloquent novels."

I tend to sympathize with Prescott's wish, although I quickly found it would be impossible to write a biography of James M. Cain that would come out the size of one of his own trim little novels. There was simply too much in Cain's long life to compress into a small book, although I have done my best to hold it down, aided by my instinct to follow Cain's wishes and *not* write a "critical biography." As Cain once suggested in a review of a book about O. Henry, the biographer should focus on the man and "where stories inevitably figure concern himself with origins rather than worth." It was Posterity's business to determine a story's worth.

During my interviews with Cain, I was struck by a curious paradox. Despite his remarkable career and his seventeen books, several of them highly acclaimed worldwide best sellers, he said he did not have a sense of accomplishment in his life; it was, he maintained, one of the reasons he had no inclination to write an autobiography. When I told him I thought he had led a fascinating life, he replied: "It may be to you, but it's never been interesting to me. There's something very peculiar about me that I don't understand. I cannot write in the third person—and it seems to have something to do with this sense of a lack of accomplishment. I have written three books in the third person and they came off all right, but did not have the bite of the others. And the reason is that I simply can't imagine why I know what the character is thinking of. What am I, God or something? Now, when I write in the first person, that's different. But to write anything, I have to pretend to be somebody else."

In the following years, as I tried to pull the story of his long, unusual career together for this biography, that thought stuck with me and, in a sense, became my guiding light: Why did a man who had accomplished so much feel he had done so little—and why, in his writing, did he have to pretend to be someone else? What was wrong with being James M. Cain?

—ROY HOOPES
Washington, D.C.
August 6, 1981

PART ONE

ANNAPOLIS,
CHESTERTOWN,
BALTIMORE,
FRANCE

1892 – 1919

"A MIDGET
AMONG GIANTS"

In 1938, forty-six-year-old James M. Cain, having decided that many of his views as a writer were the result of being Irish—on both sides of the family—went to considerable effort to learn as much as he could about his roots. He and his wife, Elina, even took a trip to Ireland and hired a retired sergeant from Dublin Castle, the Irish Scotland Yard, to find all he could about his origins. But the only sure thing Cain found on his 1938 trip was: "I hated Ireland, hated every piece of it, hated everything it stood for."

However, this much he did know: All four of his grandparents came over from Ireland in the 1850s and settled in New Haven, Connecticut. He did not know why they came, but apparently not because of the potato famine, as family legend had it. His grandfather on his father's side, P. W. Cain, as the family and *Who's Who in America* called him, was superintendent in the shops of the New York, New Haven, and Hartford Railroad in New Haven. "A massive, handsome man, obviously of great physical strength," Cain said. He knew very little of his father's mother, Mary Kelly Cain, except that she was a woman of charm and beauty. In 1860, P. W. and Mary had a son they named James W. Cain, and whom everyone then called Jim. When he was sixteen Jim came down with typhoid fever and lay one whole summer in a state of delirium. Once he'd recovered, he was told that his mother, who also contracted the fever, had died. It was a shattering blow and seems to have been the dominant factor in his boyhood. Three years later, P.W. remarried and young Jim Cain could not accept his father's new wife. He felt lonely and estranged in his own house and began to spend more and more time across town in the home of friends named the Mallahans, where there were always lots of young people around. The senior Mallahan was an invalid, and the household was taken care of by the oldest son, Edwin, who was the manager of the New Haven office of a financial firm, Bradstreet's. There were also three Mallahan girls, Margaret, Mary, and Rose, the last a very attractive young girl with a beautiful singing voice.

Jim Cain went to the public schools in New Haven, graduated from Hillhouse High School, and entered Yale in 1880. He was the prototype of the late-nineteenth-century Yale man—handsome, articulate, intelligent, and athletic. He majored in economics, under William Graham Sumner, and was satisfied with a "gentleman's C" in his studies. He rowed on the class crew; and the cup he won and oar he used, when the Yale freshmen beat Harvard in 1891, were Cain household relics for years, both prominently displayed over the fireplace. Jim Cain also played football under Walter Camp, and although it is not clear whether he was ever on the varsity, his knowledge of football was extensive and he would later coach the team at St. John's College. He believed football built character and that all sports should be played for competition, not money.

Jim Cain graduated from Yale in 1884, having decided to be a teacher. By now he was principal of an evening school in New Haven, where he had been teaching at night since 1880, to help pay his tuition. After graduation from Yale, he spent two years in Lewiston, Pennsylvania, as head of the Lewiston Academy. Then he moved down to Annapolis, Maryland, as a professor of mathematics and acting professor of English literature at St. John's College. He was soon made superintendent of the Preparatory School and college treasurer. Clearly, he was moving along in his career well enough to consider marriage, and in 1890 he married Rose Mallahan, the singing daughter of the Mallahan family, with whom he had spent so many of his boyhood years.

By all accounts, Rose Mallahan Cain was a striking woman. About her father, Matthew Mallahan, very little is known. Her mother, Brigid Ingoldsby Mallahan, was small, pretty, and very distinguished-looking. Her grandson was certain she was related to the Irish pirate William Ingoldsby, who seized the city of New York in 1691 and created a brief but remembered reign of terror. Rose Cain was born and grew up in New Haven, where she was taken care of by her older brother, Edwin. Early in life, it was obvious that she had a big, beautiful, lyric soprano voice, and she spent seven years with the best music teacher in New Haven, at her brother's expense. After her musical training, she started an opera career in New Haven, but according to her son, she lacked the one thing a singer must have: "An obsessive desire to be a singer. What she wanted was to be a wife to a good-looking Yale man she knew and have five children by him," which she eventually did. In 1890, she married Jim Cain and went to live in Annapolis, where he had been appointed superintendent of the St. John's College Prep School. Two years later, she bore the first of their five children, and he quickly became known as "Jamie," partly because of her husband's Irish habit of bestowing nicknames on everyone and partly to help distinguish him from her husband.

Jim Cain was rapidly becoming a big man on the campus, and apparently headed up the academic ladder. In addition to his classroom duties, he was college treasurer, coach of the Prep School's football team, and chairman of the Annapolis Board of Education.

The move to Annapolis and St. John's was an important step for the young educator. The college, although small and not noted for its academic achievements then, was a historic landmark, having been started in 1696 as King William's School. In 1784 it was chartered by the Maryland legislature as St. John's College. The petition for the charter and the original Board of Governors contained the names of four Maryland signers of the Declaration of Independence: William Paca, Samuel Chase, Thomas Stone, and Charles Carroll. The charter was also the first in America specifically to prohibit religious discrimination.

Jim Cain arrived at St. John's the same year that Dr. Thomas Fell, a young Englishman, was appointed president of the college. Fell gave the school an enlightened and progressive thirty-seven-year administration, adding, among other things, a library, gymnasium, and dormitory to the campus, which was only a few short blocks from the Maryland State House. St. John's was also a military school, considered among the top half dozen of its kind in the country, and the U.S. government gave direct commissions to its graduates. However, the military program eventually led to conflicts between the faculty and its officers, and was abolished in 1924.

Although a military school, St. John's emphasized the classic liberal arts curriculum: exposure to the great Greek and Latin writers and thinkers, and work not only in mathematics, logic, and philosophy, but also chemistry, astronomy, geology, American history, political economy, natural theology, and, most important, English composition. As a result, the children of Jim and Rose Cain, who lived in a house on the campus of St. John's, grew up in an environment that stressed the importance of knowledge and literature—

into which the mother blended a rich portion of classical music. There was also heavy emphasis on sports.

The Cains were a very popular couple in Annapolis. Jamie once described his father as the most handsome man he ever saw. "He was a bit over six feet, and slender, but with a rugged, raw-boned look that proclaimed he had inherited his father's great strength. He had the large, soft blue eyes that his whole family had, regularly formed features, and a fair, pinkish, and deeply bronzed skin. But his hair was the most arresting thing about him. It was straight, thick, and black, but by the time he was thirty it had turned completely white. He wore it, in the fashion of the eighties, parted in the middle, so the total result, tall, lanky, and graceful, with a distinguished cut to his jib, and crowned by this gleaming silver chrysanthemum, was really something to see. . . . He never alluded to his good looks, but everything he did betrayed that he was aware of them: he loved to play tennis for a feminine gallery, to wear his scholastic robes, to make speeches, to dance at state balls in full clawhammer regalia."

Jamie's mother, whom he especially doted on, was equally striking. She was small, pretty, spoke beautiful English, and was often asked to sing at parties. "In her adolescent pictures," Cain said, "she is a pretty Irish cutie with an exciting figure, but I never thought of her as pretty. There was always something heroic about her, to me at least, that went beyond frivolous implications; the Brünnhilde voice, no doubt, had a great deal to do with the way I thought of her. It is inextricably woven into the memories of my childhood: racing up and down scales, popping up into *alt*, cascading down into a middle section that was as big and deep as a contralto. Its agility was amazing."

The year 1892 was an important one for Jim Cain. That was the year he stroked the Severn Boat Club's first crew, which defeated the United States Naval Academy's crew stroked by Winston Churchill (later to become a distinguished American novelist, *not* the Prime Minister of England). It was also the year his first son was born. The birth was a difficult one for Rose, who was thirty, but she recovered quickly and James Mallahan Cain was baptized at St. Mary's Catholic Church on Duke of Gloucester Street in Annapolis. The Cains were Catholic, but it was an intellectual rather than a religious atmosphere that dominated their home.

Annapolis was an exciting place for a young boy to be born and raised. As the capital of one of the nation's thirteen original colonies, the city was steeped in colonial lore and tradition, and Maryland, as a state, had played an important part in most of the nation's early history—the Revolution, the War of 1812, the Civil War, and the Gilded Age of commerce and great fortunes. Anne Arundel County is geographically the northernmost edge of Dixie, and during the Civil War the industrial leaders in Baltimore managed to keep Maryland in the Union for commercial reasons, though the state's sympathies were with the South. A regiment of Massachusetts troops was attacked by a mob while marching through Baltimore during the war, and John Wilkes Booth fled into Maryland after assassinating President Lincoln, feeling that he was escaping into friendly territory.

Annapolis was also just south of what at the turn of the century was the nation's second most important transportation center—Baltimore, then a city of 434,000 people. Great clipper ships could still be seen sailing up or down the bay headed for or leaving Baltimore, and the Chesapeake was already developing as the most important steamboat center of the country. Over the years, the Chesapeake and Delaware, the Great National Road, and the Baltimore and Ohio Railroad all played a part in linking the spectacular Baltimore Harbor with the rest of the nation, just as the harbor itself had linked the nation to the rest of the world. Five years after Cain was born, the clipper ship *Josephine II*, a coffee trader, set the record for the Rio de Janeiro–Baltimore run—twenty-four days and thirteen hours, wharf to wharf.

Jamie's home in Annapolis was an ivy-covered brick duplex building. It was restored in 1955, again in 1981, and is something of a historic landmark, now known as the Paca-Carroll House, after the signers of the Declaration of Independence. Today it is a St. John's dormitory, but in 1892 it was a faculty residence and Jamie's home for the first eleven years of his life.

The Cains lived on the north end of the double house, and, of course, it was haunted. "The colored help, who knew its history, said it was," Cain recalled, "and I am under the impression some bloody episode had taken place in it some time in the seventies. My father would get very angry at such tales, for one of the things he had convictions about was the frightening of children, which he held was wrong and likely to produce unfortunate results later in life. He said there were no such things as ghosts, and with my head I suppose I believed him. But my heart was a different matter. The front room in the cellar, where a pale gray light filtered in from under the front steps, certainly looked like a place that a ghost would like. And my room, which was on the third floor and had dormer windows, I was always a little frightened to go up to, and left the door open when I had gone to bed, so I could see the friendly light and hear the reassuring talk from down below."

Jamie was soon joined by three sisters and a brother, all born in Annapolis. The best description we have of them comes from Cain himself: "Virginia was next to me, a very beautiful child, with a delicate face that didn't resemble the rest of us; years later, seeing it all over Dublin, I realized it was a classical, and not at all uncommon Irish type. She is the only one in the family who inherited her mother's gift for words, and is capable of true wit. Next to her came Rosalie, a pretty little thing, a replica of her mother. Next to her came my brother Edward, who even in the cradle showed a heavy endowment of his father's beauty, which he never lost and never forgot. Genevieve was the youngest, the smallest of the family, another Irish girl, with high color and vivid black hair. All four of the others, indeed, had their fair share of good looks, but I didn't, and I imagine this has had its effect on my life. I have none of the high, ruddy color that the rest of them have; to most eyes, I don't even look Irish, but rather Jewish."

Jamie's earliest recollection was of a beautiful luna moth which appeared near their house one dark day in summer, when "the sky was about the color of a wet slate shingle." He was so impressed by this color that he ran in the house to call his mother, so she could see the moth, too. When they went outside, a boy was chasing it with a stick, whacking at it. Jamie screamed, the boy turned toward him, and the moth escaped through the lower limbs of the tree. Cain's sense of relief and joy was so vivid it stayed with him all his life; fifty-four years later, he opened his novel *The Moth* with a slightly altered version of the incident. That beautiful green thing, all filled with light, fluttering through the trees alive and free, stirred in Cain "a feeling I imagine other people have when they think about God in church. . . . A few times in my life, when something was happening inside of me, I could tell what it meant by the pale blue-green, all-filled-with-light color the feeling had."

The same evening that he saw the moth, Jamie's mother recalled his boast that he could beat his father running, and a footrace was immediately organized from the house, which is on a slight rise, down the hill to the foot of the campus. Jamie was off and running—but his father did not run; he strode, looking back with a grin, not even bothering to put out his cigarette, as gales of laughter came from the spectators' bench. Jamie collapsed in a torrent of tears.

It was a bad day, one that left an imprint on him for years. The boy beating the moth with his stick, he said, reappeared many times, mostly in the form of censors beating a book. The footrace had an even greater impact. Before long, he came to believe his defeat in the race was not necessary. It seemed to Cain that a man six feet tall might have held back and let the child have the illusion of victory. But that was not Jim Cain's way. Later, in his writing, Cain says he put the reader in the place of the child in a footrace, not forgetting that he hopes to win. No matter what the reader is enticed with— sex, violence, or whatever—he must be indulged and not put off; he must win. "This, rather than any penchant for violence as such," he said, "is the reason for much that is in my novels . . . where indirection might have been used by other writers . . . for plunging the action along at the bull's eye without any flinching, for giving the reader what he came for."

When Jamie was six, he developed a friendship with young Henry Hopkins, later a famous Baltimore architect who probably designed more buildings in the state of Maryland than anyone else. They remained friends to Cain's death in 1977; and Hopkins still remembers their playing around the St. John's campus with Jamie's old Civil War sword, found in the basement of his house. Jamie, as Hopkins recalls, was slow-speaking, quiet, friendly, wholesome, kind, and considerate. Both boys had what Hopkins recalls as a normal childhood and played all the games of that time. And, of course, being on the river, they did a lot of swimming—mostly at the Severn Boat Club. The river was deep, and in all the years of swimming and diving around there Jamie only once remembered touching bottom, while swimming around to the shorewall side of the float. It scared him to death. It was the first time it ever occurred to him that a river had a bottom. They also did a lot of high diving, whenever they could find something high enough, but how much Jamie really enjoyed it is questionable. Two of his short stories evolve around incidents of a young boy terrified at high diving.

When he was six, Jamie also entered school in Annapolis, and he remembered his father walking him to the bottom of the hill on Green Street, where the school was located then. It was easy for him to gauge his height now because he could reach up just far enough to hold his father's hand. His first teacher was Miss Harriet Luhn. She was kind to him and he doted on her, even though she did something on the first day that had a shattering impact on the young boy. She came in with some lined cards, and in the lines on each card she had written a child's name. The tall letters touched the top line, the dangling letters the bottom line, and the others fitted into the middle lines. But when Jamie saw his name, "James M. Cain," he raised his hand and told Miss Luhn she had made a mistake. "My name," he said, "isn't James, it's Jamie." "Well," she said, with a little smile, "your father will explain it to you." Years later, Cain wrote: "I realized, in that moment, that I'd been, as they say, had. I was called something I was not. It may seem I was making a mountain out of a very tiny molehill, but from that day on, for years, I couldn't say Jamie. I didn't mind being called that, and in fact rather liked it, but I couldn't say it myself. Over the phone, to my sisters, I would say, 'This is your brother,' or 'This is you-know-who,' or something equally silly, but I wouldn't say 'Jamie.' "

Another incident he was to remember occurred in the second grade on a day the whole school was called to the assembly hall. The children waited nervously, a little afraid, not knowing what to expect. Suddenly, from a side door, Mr. Smith, the principal, appeared, carrying a boy so that his feet did not touch the ground. The boy was a good friend of Jamie's. Mr. Smith stopped in the middle of the stage, obviously in a rage. So was the boy, who was on the verge of tears. Then Mr. Smith began to shout: "Apologize! Did you hear what I said, Bushrod? Apologize."

But Bushrod Howard did not apologize. Instead, he began banging his heels on the principal's shins. Mr. Smith had to let him drop, and Bushrod ran off the stage. Jamie was not sure what "apologize" meant, but that night he looked up the word in the dictionary and was convinced he would have apologized.

Jamie was impressed with Bushrod's courage in defying Mr. Smith. Years later, when Cain was in his eighties and pondering the incident, he suddenly was inspired to call Bushrod in South Carolina and ask him just what he *had* done to arouse Mr. Smith's wrath. He called, but Bushrod Howard had died six years earlier. The friend who answered the phone said that Bushrod had, indeed, mentioned the incident several times, but had never said what he'd done. Cain went to his grave never knowing. But he had learned what courage meant and said that whenever, throughout his life, "I was in some spot where I was tempted to do some clammy thing just because it was convenient, I think of those heels crashing against the principal's shins and they sustain me."

Jamie was very precocious in class, which made him something of a pest to those who did not appreciate bright young pedants. And one reason for this precociousness was his omnivorous reading at home. Professor Clarence W. Stryker, a member of St. John's faculty, lived in Humphreys Hall, just across the lawn from the Cains, and he and his wife took an interest in young Jamie's reading and introduced him to *Alice in Wonderland*, which, to the end of his life, remained his favorite novel. The Strykers also introduced him to Kipling and *The Jungle Books*, which Jamie read and reread. "Mowgli, Shere Khan, and Bagheera became a reality to me, almost as though they existed." When he did his homework, he would surround himself with *Alice*, *The Jungle Books*, *Tales of Peter Rabbit*, and *The Adventures of Sherlock Holmes*. These were his favorites, and he would read them over and over again. His father thought he was a little nutty and kidded him about it. Jamie, on the defensive, finally agreed it was silly, but later decided maybe it was not. Of all the books he read when he was young, these early favorites were the ones that lived.

Another great world opened up to him one summer when he was nine. He was in his father's study, supposedly boning up on square roots, when he discovered a fascinating book, *Who's Who in America*. It told all about "Roosevelt and Sampson and Schley and Dewey and McKinley and Bryan and other worthies of the era, as well as George W. Cable and James Whitcomb Riley, Joel Chandler Harris and others lying closer to my heart, and transformed them from fabulous newspaper figures into flesh-and-blood human beings."

Jamie was continually coached at home in speech, grammar, and the proper use of language. He recalled his childhood as "one long series of corrections," with the corrector being his father, something of a demon on how people should talk.

"Not sort of a, but a sort of."

"Not those kind—that kind—those kinds."

"Not preventative, preventive."

"Not so that! So means that, so that is one word too many."

"Not bring, brought."

His mother also spoke very proper English and had a more instinctive feeling for words and phrases. In her writing, she had the capacity to say what she wanted with that "one perfect word," and could "make the remark you remember the rest of your life." But despite the fact that he eventually became an expert at it, good grammar bored Jamie, and gradually he developed what he called "a profane, streety lingo of no eloquence whatsoever." He always thought this was part of his Annapolis heritage, where the men swore with appalling wantonness, vivid intention, and noble pride, some even cussing "in meter." But whenever he was upset, Cain said, "my atavism is to the impeccable grammar of the household in which I grew up."

Jamie's precocious reading and obvious aptitude for words and language marked him as a very bright boy, so much so that he later suspected his father had succumbed to parental vanity and was excited at the idea that he might have brought a *wunderkind* into the world. By the time he had finished the third grade, it was obvious he was a whiz kid, every bit as bright as his friend Bushrod Howard. Bushrod (the grandson of the Bushrod Howard whom President Ulysses S. Grant mentions in his *Memoirs* as the mayor of Galena, Illinois) was a couple of years older than Jamie. His father was a naval officer, stationed at the Academy. Before that, he had been stationed in China, and Bushrod had spent a good deal of his early life on the Yangtse River. As a result, his education had been interrupted; so when he arrived in Annapolis at the age of ten, he was placed in the third grade, where the other kids were eight. As soon as it was discovered that he was smart enough to do the work, he was skipped ahead two grades—and when Bushrod was promoted ahead two grades, Jamie began teasing his father that he was as smart as Bushrod and why wasn't he being promoted? The more he thought about it, the more he liked the idea of a "double promotion," as he put it.

Jim Cain, no doubt proud of his little *wunderkind*, was not difficult to convince. By now head of the Annapolis School Board, it was easy for him to arrange that Jamie move ahead from the third grade to the fifth. Everyone was very proud of little Jamie, but Cain later thought the move was possibly the worst thing that ever happened in his childhood, and he regretted all his life that his father did not have enough sense to veto it.

In the fifth grade, he quickly found what it was like to be a little *wunderkind* among older kids—especially the girls. His fifth grade teacher, Miss Wells, was the first female to have a physical effect on him. She was very good-looking, with an attractive figure, and one day when Jamie was out on his bicycle and saw her walking with a naval officer, he was struck with jealousy. In class he felt more and more like a little boy; he was nine and some of the girls were at least eleven. The boys were bigger, too, and Jamie now had to get used to being pushed around. The gang—the Annapolis Tough Team, the A.T.T.—was always picking on him and never asked him to join in any of their activities. Jamie was a deceptive-looking boy. Physically he was large for his age, but a weakling with, as he said, "soft, squashy muscles." He was awkward and usually made people laugh when he ran.

So, suddenly, school became bewildering, and by the time he entered Bessie Tate's sixth grade class he was a miserable young boy. "Those eleven-year-old girls were now twelve," he wrote seventy years later, "and twelve, regardless of what you may hear, knows all that's worth knowing, without any sex education, and doesn't mind showing it knows. It shows its legs, the contents of its blouse, and its underthings, with no detectable diffidence. Most frightening to a ten-year-old boy was that woman smell."

Jamie was growing up, maybe too fast. He was also intellectually precocious: Miss Tate's methods of teaching included writing on the blackboard words which the students had to copy in their composition book, adding each word's definition, to be found in the dictionary. From his vast reading, Jamie knew the meaning of most of the words without looking them up in the dictionary, so he would just write his own definition in his composition book. Once the word was "membrane" and Jamie defined it in his book as the "brain you remember with"—over which Miss Tate marked a large red exclamation point! This led Jamie to think that maybe his definition was wrong, and when he looked up the word that night he realized what a fool he had made of himself. "I suddenly got cured and became the best definer in the class, listing the words, one under the other, with red lines, done with a ruler, under each, and the definitions all honestly looked up."

Translating "membrane" into the "brain you remember with" suggests that little Jamie had a flair for language even at the age of nine. But despite his interest in books and words there was still no indication that he was moving toward a writing career. In fact, there was only one incident in his youth that might have foreshadowed his literary bent, and it centered on the momentous decision of what to do with all the cigarette coupons he had collected from his father. In those days, smoking was not only considered safe, but was thought by some people, such as his father and their neighbor, Professor Stryker, both of whom smoked steadily, to be intellectually stimulating. Cain always remembered watching his father smoke and counting the smoke rings he could exhale. At first, his father rolled his own cigarettes, with a mixture he made in a special tobacco jar, but then he switched to the new Turkish Trophies in a black and red box. The package included a coupon, and these coupons, when saved, accumulated, and sent to Mr. S. Anargyros at 70 Fifth Avenue in that fabulous city to the north, could be traded for valuable prizes.

What young Jamie should get with the coupons was a matter of some discussion between Jamie and his mentor, Professor Stryker. They considered baseball mitts, air rifles, tennis rackets, and sleds, but finally decided on a fountain pen, complete with an eyedropper for filling it with ink. Looking back years later, he decided that his preference for a fountain pen over more exciting prizes reflected an early interest in writing, although he confessed that, at the time, he was more intrigued at loading the pen with the eyedropper without spilling the ink all over the place.

By the summer of 1903, Jamie was eleven and not very happy. But suddenly, a reprieve from his life in Annapolis appeared on the horizon. By now, his father was vice-president of St. John's but, more important, was becoming recognized, if not around the country, at least all over Maryland, as the man responsible for building St. John's into a respectable and substantial small college—for which he was awarded an honorary LL.D. in 1903. The professor—now "Dr. Cain"—was obviously a young man on the rise, and his spreading reputation had come to the attention of the Board of Governors of Washington College across the bay in Chestertown. As former Maryland Senator Clarence W. Perkins put it years later in an address at the dedication of the James W. Cain gymnasium:

> Due to prevailing conditions prior to 1903, Washington College had been drifting toward a crisis which called for heroic action to avoid irretrievable disaster. The old school . . . had fallen upon parlous times. After having had upon its roster of students the names of many of Maryland's most illustrious citizens, the student body had practically dwindled to the vanishing point and many troubles lay just ahead. To avoid disaster, the Board of Visitors and Governors made a searching survey of the field for a suitable man for the emergency. Across the Chesapeake Bay at Annapolis, the College management had noticed evidences of aggressive life, ceaseless energy and success at St. John's College. Investigation disclosed that the Annapolis institution was

drawing a large portion of its inspiration and success from the management of one James W. Cain. . . .

Dr. Cain was receptive to overtures from Washington College, and this led to several train trips to Baltimore to discuss the possibility of assuming the presidency. Washington College was older and more historic than St. John's, but what was even more exciting, Chestertown was a long way across the huge Chesapeake Bay, and the Eastern Shore was a different world from the Western Shore.

As a result, nervous anticipation dominated the Cain household all during the summer of 1903. Then came the big news: the Cain family was moving to Chestertown, where Dr. Cain was going to be president of Washington College. The prospect of the move must have given Jamie that mothlike pale, blue-green feeling, all filled with light.

"I think we all felt the same way about it," Cain said years later, recording his first visit to Chestertown in an article for the *American Mercury*.

It had, to be sure, certain agreeable features. There were rose bushes in our yard, and pear trees, and a walnut tree, and a grape arbor; there were neighbors with horses, who came with grins on their faces and invited us to take a ride; there were farmers with peach orchards, who told us to help ourselves, and apparently meant it. But . . . there were other entries in red which gave us great uneasiness, and which struck at parts of our natures much deeper than could be reached by flowers, horses, or the freshest of fruit.

There was, for example, the matter of the lower campus. At St. John's, to say nothing of the Naval Academy, the grass was mown to the semblance of green velvet. But here it grew as high as your knees. . . .

Then there was the windmill, with an auxiliary engine in its basement. The college was perched high on a big hill, so high that it couldn't make use of the town water-supply. This explained the windmill, but it didn't dispose of the windmill's bucolic appearance. Nothing could dispose of the boardwalk that led down the campus to town. Even the smallest of us children knew that a college walk should be of brick. . . . Then there were queer things about the town itself. It had no saloons. My father seemed to understand but the rest of us had never heard of local option. . . .

There were also the people and their strange customs. Although Chestertown was only thirty miles from Annapolis, and north at that, the Cains were moving into a new sort of country where the people not only showed "the familiar symptoms of yokelry," as Cain put it, but were different in ways Jamie did not then understand. As Dr. Cain explained it to Jamie: "They all pride themselves on their fine Southern Blood." And if there was one thing Dr. Cain detested, it was fine Southern Blood. Thirty years later, his son felt the same way: "It gives me the pip."

That first trip to Chestertown may have dampened their enthusiasm somewhat, but the Cains were still excited about moving, especially Jamie. In the first place, he knew it was an important step up for his father's career, and naturally they would be very important people in Chestertown. Then there was the hope he would be more in step with other children, once across the bay.

Cain remembered the move vividly. Their furniture was carted down to the wharf and loaded on a bugeye, a common Chesapeake Bay boat (essentially an overgrown canoe) around the turn of the century. The family rode to Baltimore on the Short Line and boarded the steamship *Emma Ford* for the trip down the bay and up the Chester River.

The new Cain home was a large frame house on College Lane, facing what was then called the Public Road, today Washington Avenue. It was a pleasant domicile with a dining room, library, parlor, kitchen, and pantry on the first floor. The second floor had four bedrooms, and there was also an attic. The three sisters shared one bedroom; Jamie and his brother, whom everyone called Boydie, were in another; their father and mother had one; and the fourth, which was designated a "guest room," would often be occupied. But the thing Jamie remembered most vividly about his first days in Chestertown was the telephone. They had "hello girls," known as "Central," who greeted you when you picked up the receiver and chatted while they rang your number. There were not many numbers: Jamie's home number was 88 and his father's office, 123.

In 1903, Washington College was a small, nondenominational, coeducational school with an enrollment of 106. It was founded in 1782, two years before St. John's, and was named for George Washington, the first of many colleges to be so named (though it has the distinction of being the only college named after him with his permission). The real founding father of Washington College, however, was the Reverend William D. Smith, who, with Benjamin Franklin, had organized the College of Philadelphia (now the University of Pennsylvania) and was for twenty-four years its provost. After the Pennsylvania college's charter was revoked, the Reverend Smith came to

Chestertown as rector of the Emmanuel Church and was soon appointed to the principalship of the Kent Free School, a flourishing little academy with 140 students and 100 acres of land. In 1782, the Kent School was enlarged by charter and renamed Washington College.

Later, James M. Cain, a budding writer, influenced no doubt by the iconoclasm of his mentor, H. L. Mencken, did some research on the good Reverend Smith and decided he was not quite the sterling character that emerges in the college catalog. Cain always wanted to do a play about Smith, who, he said, "was the most celebrated drunk of his time and wanted to be the first Anglican Bishop (the colonies not having a bishop being one of the minor causes of the Revolutionary War not mentioned in the Declaration of Independence). So, having quarreled with Benjamin Franklin, who took exception to his personal morals (now there was a pot for you, hollering at a nice organized kettle), he plied on down to Maryland, founded a college, and began rolling his logs to be nominated bishop from Maryland at a convention the church was holding in New York in 1783. It worked. He sewed the delegates up and then, in New York, invited his friends to Fraunces Tavern to celebrate his triumph. . . . But he got so drunk at his own party that in the morning he knew his hopes were gone."

Dr. Daniel Gibson, president of Washington College in the 1960s, to whom Cain sent the above interpretation of history, did not acknowledge Cain's version as accurate. But he did write Cain, as he sat staring at a Gilbert Stuart portrait of Smith, with its reddish flush on the Reverend's face, that he recalled how most of the faces painted by Stuart had reddish flushes and wondered whether they might not all have been painted this way for the same reason.

Although there were 40 students making up the first class (1907) under Dr. Cain's new administration, there were only 106 in school, most of them enrolled in either the Preparatory School or the Normal School for Women, where the ladies, as the saying went, were there "to learn to teach young ideas how to shoot." Six professors taught at the college, and its physical plant consisted of West Hall, Middle Hall, East Hall, and Normal Hall, plus a small gymnasium, an athletic field, three faculty houses, and of course a windmill and the boardwalk.

Washington College was not to remain a little hick academy for long. Dr. Cain was a builder, and he had been hired—at an annual salary of $2,000—to build! Furthermore, he wanted to be president of a real college, not a sleepy little school primarily concerned with preparing young men for college and young women for teaching children. But dropping the prep and normal schools would come later. First there was the problem of a new building or two—and that boardwalk, which reminded Jamie's father of a western frontier town. Dr. Cain decided that the campus needed a brick walk, of the kind found at most eastern colleges, and this led to another memorable episode in young Jamie's development.

Dr. Cain knew a bricklayer named Ike Newton who could do the job, and soon alternate piles of white sand and bricks were placed along the route the walk was to take. Then one day Ike Newton appeared. Ike was a stocky, powerful man in jeans and boots, who would squat on the ground as he chipped the bricks with the edge of his hammer—and talk and talk and talk. And there was always one person who could be counted on to listen—the president's son, Jamie Cain.

What fascinated Jamie, who had been coached continually by his father and mother to use proper language, was *the way* Ike Newton talked. Not what he said, but how he said it. For the first time, Jamie was hearing the language of an uneducated but articulate person. Just as Jonathan Swift liked to sit in taverns and on the greens listening to the talk of teamsters and coachmen, and Stephen Crane would sit by the hour listening to Bowery bums, Jamie Cain listened to Ike Newton and was spellbound by the rhythm and tempo of his speech. He began speaking like Ike at home, to the horror of his mother, who called such talk "low." But Jamie was carried away by the beautiful bounce and rolling cadences of Ike Newton's speech. He hung on his every word as "brick by brick and sandpile by sandpile, the brick walk got built. It was a miracle of perfect slope, grading and crown." Ike Newton's brick walk, sometimes called "lovers' lane," is still there on the Washington College campus—a monument to the development of one of the finest writing styles in American literature. "Later," wrote James M. Cain, "my dialogue would be praised off and on by critics, and I would save myself argument by acknowledging debts to various experts on the 'vulgate,' as H. L. Mencken called it. But actually, if a writer owes a debt to what his ears pick up, mine would be to Ike."

Jamie did not realize it then, but Dr. Cain was primarily an academic politician rather than a scholar or teacher. What he liked to do most was sit around with people and talk—beautiful talk about big ideas and grand concepts. His principal talent was an ability to persuade others, especially legislators, that his dreams were possible. Not that he disregarded his students or learning. In fact, he was later to get into a major fight with the Board of Governors on the question of academic standards over athletics. Dr. Cain appreciated the importance of sports to the individual, but felt a boy should be a good student before being permitted to represent Washington College on the athletic field.

Dr. Cain had been brought to Chestertown to save a small rural college that appeared on the verge of disaster, and this meant spending time in Annapolis lobbying the state legislature for school appropriations. The first objective on his Annapolis forays was to raise money for a new administration building, which would, among other things, enable all the college classes to be taught under one roof. Everyone in the Cain family knew what Dr. Cain was trying to do in Annapolis, and there was the same kind of excitement in the house that had accompanied his trips to Baltimore early in the summer. Then came the news that Jamie's father had persuaded the legislature to appropriate $100,000 for a new administration building. The February night when they walked over to inspect the site for the new building—to be called William Smith Hall—was etched in Jamie's memory: all across the western sky was a strange orange glow. The next day, when the papers came in on the morning train, the *Baltimore Herald* headline told them what it was: HEART OF BALTIMORE WRECKED BY GREATEST FIRE IN CITY'S HISTORY. The head was written by the young city editor, H. L. Mencken.

In addition to traveling back and forth to Annapolis seeking money, Dr. Cain was trying to put together a football squad. And Jamie naturally became a faithful fan of the team in Chestertown, although football on the Eastern Shore was not quite the same caliber as what they played in Annapolis. He remembered going down to the field to watch Washington's first practice, and it was a dreadful shock: "Only two or three of the candidates were what I considered the proper size, and even these didn't have the right look on their faces."

Soon, Dr. Cain came down to the field, and he concurred with Jamie's estimate of the team. That night, at dinner, he said: "They're a sad lot. St. John's will murder them." But he added, "Still, there is one boy out there that might be a footabll player.

"Which one is that?" asked Jamie.

"His name is Moore. I like the way he goes about it."

There were no stands on the football field at Chestertown; the crowd watched on foot and moved along with the ball. A team had three downs to make five yards, which it tried to do mainly by plunging the line. "Unexpectedly," Cain recalls, "a wild-eyed quarterback would head for the sidelines and the crowd, which always encroached on the field, would scurry for cover in panic, ladies screaming, gentlemen helping them run, and small boys whistling between their fingers. It was an event to remember."

There were no forward passes in those days—at least not as we know them today. One time, Jamie's father came back from a Yale game talking about Tim Coy throwing an end-over-end pass, "skying it up in the air," though Cain always thought it was a Washington College player named John Meegan who actually threw the first spiral pass.

That first year of football was a bad one for Washington, and Dr. Cain's prediction proved right—St. John's did murder them. The following year was not much better, although Jamie was beginning to have a much higher estimation of Moore and recalled a tackle he made in the game with Western Maryland as "the hardest tackle I ever saw." Both players were knocked out.

It is not surprising that, if anything, life in Chestertown for Jamie was worse than in Annapolis. Jamie did not like swimming in the Chester River, although he once swam across it and back (it was a mile wide at Chestertown) "to get on the same side as my clothes." But the river seemed all bottom. The local boys teased him, and the girls gave him even more of a problem. When he entered the Chestertown public school, he was in the seventh grade, which, on the Eastern Shore, was part of high school. This threw the eleven-year-old boy in with girls who seemed even older than in Annapolis and made him horribly uncomfortable. "They never saw me at all, looking through me, around me and past me, as though I wasn't there."

After one year, Jamie pleaded with his father to let him enter the prep classes at the college. Most Maryland colleges at that time had prep schools, designed to bridge the gap between college and the not-very-good high schools. Jamie had continued his voracious reading and, by now, was into Poe, Thackeray, Cooper, and Dumas; his favorite books included *The Three Musketeers, The Count of Monte Cristo, The Last of the Mohicans, The Deerslayer, The Adventures of Sherlock Holmes, The Virginian, Vanity Fair,* and *Treasure Island.*

It was not very difficult to persuade his father to permit him to move into prep school, where the work was easy. But now the age gap was worse than ever. At twelve, he was still a boy, but his new classmates were sixteen, young men. As a result, Jamie retreated somewhat into family life, which was dominated by Friday night fudge-making parties and musical evenings, in which one of the Cain girls would play the piano, Boydie and Jamie would play violins, and Dr. Cain turned the pages of the music. Strangely, Jamie's mother, though the most musically gifted of all the Cains, did not take part.

Around this time, Jamie was also introduced to another important part of his life—alcohol. Drinking in Kent County was governed by "local option," which meant the county was dry. Alcoholic beverages had to be imported from Baltimore, and one or more of the Cain children were usually on hand at Pier 16 when the *Emma Giles* arrived from Baltimore with its weekly supply of five-gallon demijohns containing the family liquor. The wooden box was protected by two pieces of wood, nailed at an angle to form a little tent. Virginia thought this looked like the hands of the priest as he stood ready to dispense the blessing. Hence, any large quantity of liquor in the Cain household was referred to as "Dominus Vobiscum." The Cains were very liberal about letting the children have liquor, and Jamie was given his evening "toddy" regularly while still in his teens. Dr. Cain, of course, was very liberal about his own imbibing, which eventually would cause him considerable trouble at the college.

As at Annapolis, religion did not play an important part in Jamie's development. The family practiced what Cain called *"Feinschmecker"* Catholicism, meaning the Cains were gourmets of religious ritual. While they had attended Mass regularly in Annapolis—in part, Cain said, because "the services were mounted in a manner worthy of Ziegfeld"—in Chestertown, High Mass was "a farce painful to behold. The priest was tone-deaf and did nothing but harangue the congregation about money. The choir did not sing and was always muffing its cues." One time in church at Chestertown, when the organ started the introduction to the offertory, the woman who was to sing it whispered in panic to Jamie's mother that this was not the score she had learned and she could not sing it. Rose Cain adjusted her glasses and sang it at sight—and it was at this moment that Jamie became aware that his mother was an accomplished vocalist.

By the time he was thirteen, Jamie was ready to break with the Catholic Church. Not only was it a "hick operation," at least in Chestertown, but he could not agree with a doctrine that forbade him to marry "a beautiful Methodist girl." Much deeper, he found he did not believe one word of the "whole mumbo-jumbo, especially the confessional, where I was faking and suddenly knew that the priest knew it." In later years, he came to regard the Church as one of the most ominous factors in all human history, and he worked out his own views on life and God. In Chestertown, his mother persuaded the church to let him continue singing in the choir, but eventually the whole family shifted to the Episcopal Church.

In second prep, Jamie continued to find the work easy and devoted most of his time to following football. It was a particularly bad year for the team because James Garfield Moore, the player Dr. Cain liked, had decided to give up the game. Some thought this all for the best, because he was said to be a demoralizing influence on the team. Jamie had even heard some say he was "yellow," but when he reported this to Dr. Cain, his father replied: "You tell them to find me ten more men as yellow as he is and I'll beat Yale." Dr. Cain said Moore's real problem was that he did not like football and was a "voluptuary"—which he explained was someone who would rather sit with the girls on an Indian summer afternoon than be out there on the field taking it on the shins.

That year, the big game, which Jamie would later immortalize in an article for Mencken's *American Mercury*, was with Maryland Agricultural College (now the University of Maryland). Not only had the Aggies trounced most of the teams they had played, they had beaten mighty St. John's by the unbelievable score of 27–5. The team came to Chestertown on a special boat, and, to Jamie, "they looked like giants" compared to the Chestertown squad. One especially "terrifying apparition" was left end Curly Byrd.

There was some hope now for Washington, however, because James Moore had finally consented to play in the big game. But when Jamie went to the upper terrace, where the team assembled, he saw that Coach Halbert's face was white with rage. Something was wrong with Moore, who was slouched against a tree, his mouth literally foaming as he mumbled: "I can't do it! I can't play!" Jamie went down to the field miserable, prepared for the worst. But, all of a sudden, just before the kickoff, there was Moore, running through the signals with all his old fretful impatience. Something had happened up there on the terrace, which Jamie did not learn about until much later. It seems Moore had continued with his act of self-pity, waiting for Dr. Cain, who he knew would understand and send him to the showers. But when Dr. Cain arrived, he took one look at the fullback and said: "Well, goddammit, Moore, make up your mind. Don't stand there slobbering like a baby." That was all it took.

Washington received the kickoff and brought it back to around the twenty-yard line, where it was first down and five to go. Washington lined up, but there were problems on the field because Moore had not practiced with the team much that year. As a result, the signal-calling was sounding like this:

Wilson: "Eighty-five, ninety-seven, forty-one, sixty-two."

Moore: "Signal."

Wilson: "Eighty-five, ninety-seven, forty-one . . ."

Moore: "Quit yelling them goddamn numbers and gimme the ball! I'm going through right guard."

They gave Moore the ball—and he went through right guard as if the Maryland line were made of paper. He made ten yards on his first plunge, and then right halfback McGinness picked up ten yards on two carries. Then Moore gained, only this time he didn't go down—he burst through the tacklers and suddenly was in the open field. The Maryland quarterback dived for him and missed, and Moore was through the goalposts for a touchdown: 5 points, and then left tackle George White kicked the extra point to make it 6–0 Washington (that was the way they scored it in those days).

The defense also played well, holding Maryland, and when Washington took the ball again it marched down the field with McGinness scoring a touchdown. On this drive, Moore hit Curly Byrd so hard with a block that Byrd was out for the rest of the game. McGinness scored a third touchdown, but White missed the extra point and the first half was over, with Washington leading 17–0. And that was the score at the end of the game.

It was a momentous day and, years later, Cain wrote: "A great man had come through, had proved he was really great . . . it is like nothing else in this world. It can only happen when you are young, for when you get older, there are no more great men."

Despite being absorbed in football, Jamie breezed through his studies in prep school and was allowed to enter Washington College as a freshman at the age of fourteen. Neither Jamie nor his father had learned much from the misery Jamie suffered in Annapolis, when he was so out of step with his fellow students. Now he was thrown in with boys who were anywhere from four to six years his senior. During his entire four years in college, he felt he was "a midget among giants."

In his freshman year, his father let him go along with the football team to Westminster, Maryland, to see one of the big games. Jamie also wanted to see Kent Greenfield, a friend in Chestertown who had moved to Westminster when his father, a Methodist minister, was transferred there. When he got off the train, Jamie was met by Kent and invited to stay at the Greenfield house. The night before the game, Kent suggested they take in the picture show, at a place called the "nickelodeon," explaining to Jamie: "It's not really good entertainment, but it's the best the town affords." Both boys were bright (Greenfield later became chairman of the history department at Johns Hopkins and an official army historian), a couple of "intellectual snobs," as Cain said, in their attitude toward going to a movie house.

The bill included a comedy which featured an actor named John Bunny, playing a chiropodist removing a bunion, which brought screams of laughter from the audience at Bunny's pantomine of the smell of the foot the bunion was on. But the two boys were disgusted and utterly appalled at the main feature—*The Great Train Robbery*. It never occurred to either one of them that the film was movie history. They thought it so bad as to be beyond belief—the proper subject of scorn for two young intellectuals.

As a college student, Jamie was erratic. Bright and well read as he was, he found his studies easy, but still he felt that he learned very little in the four years he was in college, primarily because he was so young. "You can't take a seventeen-year-old and put him with a lot of twenty-one-year-olds and expect him to get anything out of the experience." Some who attended college with Cain thought he was an exceptional student; others thought he was fair. "He was kind of devilish in class and pretty smart," says Ethel Gibbs ('11), who knew Jamie very well. "But we had several real bright boys in class who were brighter than Jamie. He was not as outstanding as they were—but, of course, he was younger than the rest of us." (Cain remembered that "Ethel used to put her feet on the crossbar of the chair in front of her, but nobody minded at all, as she had the most beautiful legs, and if a little elevation improved the view, so much the better.")

The only course Jamie flunked was speech, or "elocution," as it was called, and he once lost a debate to classmate Bob Gill, who made the simple point that "the reason the Torrens System of Land Registration is superior in all ways to the one we've got now is that it's better" (Cain said this became a standard mode of argument in his house). Jamie did not worry much about flunking speech at the time—"a humorous toe-stubbing"—because he was doing well in so many other classes. But later, he decided maybe this failure was one of the more significant things that happened to him in college: "I simply don't have the capacity to stand up on my hindlegs and bark," he once wrote a college professor who was trying to persuade him to give a lecture.

Jamie did not do well in Greek either, but he excelled in German and French, primarily, he thought, because he liked the head of the department of modern languages. He also liked Dr. J. S. William Jones, head of the mathematics department, although not enough to do very well in Dr. Jones's classes. Jamie was not interested in math, and he remembered one conversation he had with Professor Jones about this. Jamie had had *la grippe*, as it was called then, on the occasion of the examination in analytic geometry, and he learned of the makeup exam only the night before it was to be given. He had not so much as opened a book the whole year, and flipping through his text, he thought: "Don't befuddle yourself with trying to memorize too much. Be sure you're clear on the definitions of these curves, and trust to luck, and your own ingenuity."

He took the exam, feeling it was much too easy. A couple of days later, he asked Dr. Jones whether he had marked the exams yet.

"Yes, I have," the professor answered. "Your mark was ninety-three—you made a mistake on one original problem, and under the rules I had to take off seven and a half points. But if I could have, I'd have given you one hundred, perhaps more."

"You would?" Jamie asked. "Why?"

"You had a deduction of the equation of the parabola I'd never seen, that's why."

"Well, neither had I, if I have to tell you the truth," said Jamie. "There was a reason . . ."

"I know the reason," Dr. Jones interrupted. "You had no more idea of the usual deduction, the one there in the book, than the man in the moon.

You did your deduction yourself. But I'd rather have that one deduction, by a pupil with his own ingenuity, than a hundred learned-up deductions out of the book."

Dr. Jones went on to tell Jamie that he had a remarkable mathematical mind and asked why he did not apply himself and really learn the subject. "I'm sorry, it doesn't interest me," replied Jamie, who also confided in Dr. Jones that he had really not made up his mind what he wanted to do in life.

Dr. Jones was upset, but sixty years later Cain felt he had been right in not continuing with mathematics. "In all those years, though just as gifted at math now as I ever was, I haven't once had a use for it, or felt any interest in it. It's just a leftover talent, like Woodrow Wilson's ability to wiggle his ears." Which was not to say that Cain's mathematical mind was unimportant to his writing—he always maintained that plotting was just a matter of getting your algebra right.

Jamie also took science, chemistry, and Latin, but his favorite subjects were literature and history. At one time, he even entertained the idea of being a historian but decided he did not have the talent. Later he would become something of a crusader for history, urging young people at every opportunity to study history and make the reading of history a regular thing in their lives.

It is significant that in all Cain's papers and writings about his early years, there is no evidence that Jamie was especially concerned with what was going on in the rest of the world, even while in college. He grew up during a very exciting period in America's development. During the time he was in Annapolis, the country had been drawn out of its isolation by the Spanish-American War, and when Theodore Roosevelt became President in 1901, after the assassination of President William McKinley, the exuberant Teddy embarked on a program to make the United States a world power. At home, Roosevelt turned his incredible energies against the industrial trusts that had been developing since the Civil War. Reform was everywhere, and young men in the universities were debating the evils of the big trusts, the huge fortunes being amassed in business, and the faults of a capitalist system that exploited not only the working man, but even women and children. At Washington College, however, there did not appear to be much interest in public affairs, at least as far as Jamie Cain, considered one of the bright students on the campus, was concerned. Of course, at the turn of the century, there was no radio, and although by 1910 movie houses had opened here and there, some of which showed newsreels, there were not many on the Eastern Shore. In fact, Chestertown's only link with the outside world was the Baltimore press, and there is nothing to suggest that the school's young intellectuals either read these papers religiously or debated the issues of the day. Nor is there evidence that many people in Chestertown read *McClure's* magazine, which had achieved fame in the early 1900s when the muckraking articles of Lincoln Steffens, Ida Tarbell, Finley Peter Dunne, and Ray Stannard Baker were waking up the social consciousness of the nation. In fact, it is questionable how many people over there even read H. L. Mencken, whose column was appearing in the *Baltimore Sun*. Jamie did not discover him for nearly twenty years.

Jamie's classmates knew he had a lot of ability, but they made fun of him, calling him "Pedro" for some unexplained reason. The 1909 *Pegasus* (college yearbook) said that "Pedro, the awkwardest man of the class, runs the track like a turkey, with both wings broken." Cain maintained he never took part in college athletics, although *Pegasus* reported that he "once had the distinction of playing on the third football team." It is difficult to imagine Washington fielding thirty-three players in the years 1908–10, but there were some of those alumni whose most vivid memory of Dr. Cain was that of a tall, white-haired gentleman standing on the sidelines at a football game, yelling: "Run, Jamie, run!"

Cain maintained that as a student, and despite his father's disapproval, he had "complete indifference to campus affairs." But the yearbook shows that he was a member of the Adelphia Literary Society, vice-president of his class in 1907–1908, a member of the Glee and Mandolin clubs, class historian in 1909 and 1910, literary editor of the *Pegasus* in 1909 and 1910, and class poet in 1910.

Jamie also gained a reputation as a good teacher and was usually friendly about helping the other students with their work. At the end of his junior year, he was hired to tutor a girl named Louise Crane, who wanted to pass the exam for first prep. "So, for two dollars a morning, and feeling quite important, I put on white ducks and blue coat and marched myself down to tutor Louise. She was quite pretty, but we did nothing about that at all. For the better part of two months we made with the books, so she passed with flying colors, and I had a triumph, secondhand."

The $80 Jamie earned tutoring was the only money he earned in college. Some of the other boys held summer jobs, and a few worked in the academic year, but Jamie spent his summers swimming, reading, fishing, boating, and visiting friends. The truth is, there were not many jobs for a boy growing up in Chestertown, and neither of his parents ever put pressure on him to find work.

Jamie's main concern in college lay in looking and acting older than he was. In his freshman year, he started wearing his father's derby; by his sophomore year, he was rolling his long pants up at the cuff—"an audacious act proclaiming a certain raffishness of character." *Pegasus* also reported that he was a "self-supporting pool shark," but Cain recalled that his main pastime was poker. The game: penny-ante, five-card show, in which Jamie usually lost. Cain thought his poker-playing reflected on the college: "If I and the other players had had something better to do with ourselves, we wouldn't have been at it morning, noon and night."

There were, of course, the girls, but sociable contact was limited and strictly regulated. Most communication was through an underground system of note- and parcel-passing at mealtime in the basement of Normal Hall, the college dining room for the student body. The ladies were expected to stay home on Friday nights and make candy and were not permitted into town after dark—even to meet the evening mail—unless accompanied by an adult. "Social intercourse" between gentlemen and lady students was strictly forbidden except in the presence of one or more teachers, which prompted one member of the faculty to comment that a duet on the piano would not be permitted without a chaperone. Cain said there was some "sociable shacking" going on (completely undercover and strictly against the rules), which he thought was a good thing: "It's natural for young people to seek a bed together and much better for them than poker."

Early in his college years, Jamie met Mary Rebekah Clough, who was a little older than he was and a very striking young woman, as Cain described her: "Though of no more than medium size, she had even in middle age . . . a simply beautiful figure. She carried herself with distinction, aggressively, perhaps, but with head up, shoulders back, and feet square on the ground. Her hair was blond, but ashy blond, not golden blond, her skin fair, clear, and soft. Her eyes were blue, and so big they were somewhat startling. Her features, however, were a bit on the thick side, and the set of her jaw and the way she carried her head were all somewhat pugnacious . . . as a student, I was insane about her."

Mary Clough came from Church Hill, Maryland, a little village about eight miles across the river in Queen Annes County. She was born on February 1, 1891, which made her about a year and a half older than Jamie. She went to the public schools in Church Hill and entered Washington College in 1905, when Jamie was in second prep. Mary must have been in second prep, too, because she had to make up some high school credit at Washington (there was no high school in Church Hill) and did not graduate until 1910, the same year as Jamie.

Jamie did not have his first date with Mary until 1907, when he asked her to attend a school affair. Grace Riggin, Mary's roommate in Normal Hall, recalls that Mary asked her opinion of Jamie and whether she should go out with him. "If you can look at him for the entire evening, accept," Grace replied.

Cain was, in fact, not very good-looking. He had a pockmarked face and unruly hair. However, despite his ugliness, most women were curiously attracted to him. Mary finally consented to go out with Jamie because he was the president's son, said Grace. She also said Mary reported her "smart" remark to Jamie, and the first time Jamie and Grace met on the campus, he said, "Grace, you are a girl of great integrity, you know the truth when you see it. I know I am as ugly as the devil and there is nothing I can do about it"—which may have been why *Pegasus* commented that "Pedro" was "always ready to criticize someone's good looks."

For most of their college years, Jamie and Mary "went steady," says Ethel Gibbs. Jamie took Mary everywhere—to the dances, the open meetings of the literary societies, and all the receptions. Every Friday night the girls living at Normal Hall would sit in a large room on the first floor with their backs to the wall, the boys in chairs, pulled up, knee to knee, facing them. Sometimes Mary would spend the weekend with Ethel Gibbs, who lived about a mile out of town, and Jamie would go out to see her. Ethel recalls that Mary was crazy about Jamie, although for some reason his family did not seem to approve of her. At the same time, some of Mary's friends did not approve of Jamie. "I was amazed that she was interested in him," says another classmate, Ethel Cooper. On the other hand, Suzi Frazier says: "Everybody thought it was a very nice match."

In the summers, Jamie would rent a horse and buggy from the livery stable and drive out to Church Hill to see Mary. But it was a peculiar relationship. Mary was more intellectual than emotional, recalls Ethel Cooper. Cain said later that she had "a taste for highbrow things, and in our college conversations we talked mostly about books." From all he had observed, "it's natural for youths and girls in their teens to be fairly contactual about it, to do a lot of necking, and often to go even further. No such intimacies took place between Mary Clough and me. In the four or five years that we dated, while going to college, I doubt if I kissed her more than a half dozen times. I certainly had normal impulses, but with her, they never even got started."

By Jamie's senior year, the other boys thought he had lost his head over Mary and were disgusted with the way she treated him. The 1910 *Pegasus* reported that "Pedro" was deeply in love and "never tires of hearing that song, 'Mary had a little lamb, his name is Jamie Cain.' " The same yearbook had this comment about Mary, probably written by Jamie: "Rather whimsical and uncertain. Can put on the high and mighty air, too, at times. No one has ever ventured to say that they thoroughly understand her. She doesn't understand herself. She'll turn up her nose when she reads this."

Jamie certainly did not understand her. Mary seemed to like him, but also had a compulsion to put him down. And Jamie took it. But at no time, Cain wrote years later, "did she ever show signs of loving me, or of being 'in love' with me—which isn't quite the same, but important to marriage, too. And yet, though I never seemed to possess her, she seemed obsessed by a compulsion to possess me. So, there we were, two squirrels caught in a trap"—a trap that eventually led to marriage.

As graduation day approached, the class started thinking about the yearbook for 1910, but Dr. Cain intervened. He said there would be no *Pegasus* unless the parents of every member of the graduating class would sign a letter pledging responsibility for any debts the editors might leave behind. "My father . . . knew a bit about such projects," said Cain. Naturally Dr. Cain's stand made the students angry, and in their resentment Jamie was the only class member not elected to the board of editors. However, when Jamie's friend Eddie Crouch, the editor in chief, saw the galley proofs he was horrified. There was very little in them in the way of reading matter—apparently the editors thought the printer, or someone, would take care of that. So Jamie, who by now had gained something of a reputation as a writer, mostly for his work on term papers and the *Pegasus*, was called in by Eddie for some last-minute editorial work—including the writing of a class "Prophecy," supposed to suggest what some members of his class would go on to do.

The "Prophecy" was well written and gives us just a hint of the developing writer. It opened with a provocative sentence: "I had been out of this country since the week after I graduated from college, being a foreign agent for Henizerling Bros. banking establishment." It had an even punchier ending provided by the "unfortunate death of Mr. Cain," who was run over by an automobile in New York. Jamie was, in fact, not a bad prophet: he was almost killed by an automobile in the 1920s in front of the *World* building in New York, but was saved by his boss—an editor named Walter Lippmann. He predicted as well that Mary Clough would get her Ph.D., which she did thirty-one years later.

Jamie was also the class poet, although there was little evidence of his poetry in the *Pegasus*. But twenty years later, he did have a poem about his Class of 1910 published in *The New Yorker*, and very few class poets can claim that distinction:

> *AULD LANG SYNE*
>
> In the year 1910,
> On the campus of Washington College,
> Chestertown, Md. (founded in 1782),
> On a night in May,
> A few days before our impending graduation,
> Four of us took a vow.
> Twenty years from then, we swore,

To the month, to the day, to the very hour,
We should reassemble,
Provided all, by the grace of God, still lived,
And sing another song,
Harmonized for tenor, second tenor, baritone, and bass.

I was the bass
Of that quartet

Twenty years have passed:
The year 1930 marches to its close.
Have I received memo, tag, or ticket,
Note, letter, call, or telegram,
Or return post card,
Clipped along the edge and perforated down the middle,
Calling me to that reunion?
I have not.
Nor have I sent any.

It is not that the day has slipped into the mists,
For it could easily be ascertained
By making certain calculations;
Nor is it that I lack the addresses
Of those who took this vow with me.
I do, but of itself that would be no obstacle,
For I am in the newspaper business
And adept at all enterprises dark and sleuthy:
Were it merely a matter of streets and numbers,
I could find them in an hour.

No, I fear the trouble
Is more serious than that.
I have flogged my mind in a diligent manner,
Consulted diaries, notebooks, old picture albums;
Yet I cannot seem to remember
Who any of these gentlemen were.

—James M. Cain

2

CONSOLATION PRIZE

In his unpublished memoirs, Cain wrote: "At last on June 15, 1910, I became *Artium Baccalaureus*. I was not quite eighteen years old." To all appearances, Jamie Cain was a college graduate. He had been shaving for five years and wore a derby and long pants with the trousers turned up at the cuff; he stood nearly six feet tall and sang in the chorus with a deep, impressive bass voice. But inside, he was still very much a boy, and he knew it. Except for family chores and tutoring, he had never held a job in his life. Furthermore, he did not even comprehend that he was supposed to work for a living. "Never once, in our house, was there so much as a hint that life was hard, that work was the lot of all, that the night was coming." And never once did Jamie's mother and father sit down with him and have a serious talk about what he wanted to do with himself, what he wanted to become. Now and then, at the dinner table, his father would remark what a fine career "the law" was for a young man, but whether he felt Jamie should enter law school and who would pay for it were conceptions conveniently ignored— along with the fact that Jamie took no interest in law whatever. All Jamie knew was that he wanted to "be somebody" and maybe one day appear in *Who's Who.*

So, at an age when most boys were preparing for college, where they would likely decide what career they would follow, Cain was graduating from college with absolutely no idea of what he wanted to do. He was not interested in law or mathematics or medicine or business or politics. His bent was academic and intellectual, which would seem to point to teaching. But apparently there was never any discussion in the Cain household about Jamie's going to graduate school, despite the fact that his father was a teacher and had done graduate work at Yale. And no consideration was given to making a career of his writing, which Dr. Cain considered "a harmless aberration."

After the commencement ceremonies, Eddie Crouch came over to shake hands before going off to take a job with the State Roads Commission. Mary Clough, still Jamie's girl friend, returned to Church Hill to prepare for a teaching job that fall in Crumpton, a little village up the river from Chestertown. All the students went home, or somewhere, but Jamie was already home. When Mary began teaching in Crumpton, he went up to visit her, but he noticed an odd change: "The girl who had been so friendly that day in June, when we took our diplomas together, was cold and somewhat disagreeable. I was baffled, but little by little came to realize that whereas to a girl student in college, being dated by the president's son was a bit of an honor, to a teacher in a small country town being called on by a boy who had no job or any idea what job he might try to get for himself was just a nuisance." Jamie drove home that night feeling bleak and a little sick.

Then, quite by accident, Jamie had a job. In the course of an evening at the Rennert Hotel in Baltimore "with the boys," Dr. Cain told Charles Cohen, manager of Consolidated Gas and Light of Baltimore, about the plight of his son. Cohen offered Jamie a job copying totals from one set of ledgers to another, and for this work Jamie would be paid $8 a week. His father helped by sending extra money, but Jamie hated the job and sometimes thought it would drive him insane. He stuck it out for six months, then came down with the mumps, and the people with whom he boarded tactfully suggested that it might be better if he took the steamer to Chestertown. He went home for a while, but when he returned to Baltimore he found the gas company had forgotten him, which did not break his heart. He applied for a job with the State Roads Commission and was hired. The new job paid $60 a month and took him out of town during the week, inspecting roads, but allowed him the weekends in Baltimore.

Things were looking up. Jim Cain—as he was now called away from home—was beginning to feel a little more like a man. He dressed in corduroy suits and took great pride in working for Chief Engineer Walter W. Crosby, an elegant man who wore a coat with an astrakhan collar and made the unheard-of sum of $5,000 a year.

While working for the gas company Cain shared a room on Carney

Street with a classmate from Washington College. His friend, who was much older than Cain, took it for granted that on Saturday nights all young men-about-town should go down to the whorehouses. This friend invited Cain to come along, but Cain was not sure he was ready. When he declined, his friend said he did not have to do anything; he could just wait downstairs while he went upstairs. "It'll be O.K., so long as you set up a beer."

So Cain agreed to go along to the whorehouses, then on Raborn, Pine, and Josephine streets between Baltimore and Fayette streets, a few blocks from the center of town. The way it worked was that you went in to appraise the girls and could look as long as you wanted if you ordered a round of drinks for fifty cents. This bought one beer served by a black girl ("often better-looking than the white girls the customers came to look over," said Cain), in a glass so tiny that "small as a whorehouse beer" was a popular phrase of the time. You were also free to invite a girl to dance without going upstairs, as long as you kept putting nickels in the electric piano. You barely had one turn around the room before it was time to put in another nickel, hence, "short as a whorehouse dance."

"I set up so many beers you couldn't count them and got to know most of the girls by name," Cain said. But he did not go upstairs. Once, a girl who had very pretty legs put them in his lap and he felt tempted, but he was afraid of disease and resisted. Another time, the "most celebrated girl on Raborn Street," after pushing her last customer out, turned to Cain and said: "Jim, come on up with me, darling, I want you and I want you bad. I've just turned forty-nine tricks tonight and there's time for one more before my friend gets here. Come on, Jim, help me make it an even fifty." The invitation turned his stomach.

Jim Cain was not ready to be a whorehouse trick. But he was ready for the real thing. Before going out into the state to inspect roads, he spent a week in the Baltimore headquarters, and one day a woman (identifiable from Cain's papers only as "Sallie") who worked in another state office dropped in. When she heard Cain's name she asked if he was related to Dr. James W. Cain, president of Washington College. He said he was his son, and she exclaimed: "But of course—I should have known it, you look so much like him," which could hardly have been true. She said she had a picture of Dr. Cain she had cut out of the paper because "he looked so handsome."

One thing led to another, and the woman gave Cain her address and said if he would come around that night she would find the picture and show it to him. By the time Cain arrived at her apartment on North Howard Street she had found the picture of his father, one he hadn't seen, and they looked at it, on the sofa. "I began reacting at once," Cain wrote, "and presently screwed up my courage to slide my arm around her. She didn't seem to mind, but caught it as though to control it, so it didn't wander. But that just made it want to, and suddenly we were in the same old wrestling match human beings have engaged in since before they were even human. Then we were sliding down on the floor. Then we were consummating, my very first time—but not hers, it was easy to see."

For many weekends thereafter, Cain would come into town from inspecting roads, check in at the New Howard Hotel, and hurry around to see her. But never once did she ask him to bed, always entertaining on the floor because "someone might come and I have to be dressed if they do—and you have to be, too." In between sessions, as they lay on the floor, she would say: "I don't see how two people could *help* having children—if they really loved each other."

Jim Cain, who was growing up in a hurry, concluded his friend wanted him to marry her—an idea that filled him with horror. Then, one day when his job took him to western Maryland, he received a telegram in Hagerstown: SORRY TO BREAK OUR DATE BUT I'M GETTING MARRIED TOMORROW—SAL-LIE. Cain was shocked at first and sick for three days. But then he found himself relieved—off the hook.

Soon he would be in love again, having two brief affairs, one with an older woman, another with a very young girl, "from neither of whom did I collect so much as one kiss." The woman was beautiful, twice his age, and lived in southern Maryland. She found him amusing, and he was infatuated with her. The girl was fourteen years old and Cain was "insane about her." Much later, he confessed to still being in love with her and that he had put her hair, especially its "corn husk color," and her "stubby features" in heroine after heroine in his novels. (*The Moth* is about a twenty-two-year-old man falling in love with a twelve-year-old girl. *Kingdom by the Sea*, an unpublished novel written in his seventies, is about a young man who marries an older woman.)

Cain was doing well in his new job and was soon raised to $75 a month. But he had to admit he was bored, and he thought he was in the wrong work. "I became the worst engineer the state of Maryland ever had." Still, he was making new friends. One day he was coming out of Ryon's General Store in Waldorf, Maryland, when a man introduced himself and offered to help him with his packages. His name was John R. Monroe, and he was a pianist, organist, and voice teacher in Washington, D.C. He seemed to know who Cain was, and he invited him over to his place that night, a farm near Waldorf. Cain accepted, and that evening, as he started out for the Monroe house, about a mile and a half out of Waldorf, he met a girl, Grace Robey, who lived over the same saloon Cain did. She was also going to Monroe's, as was her friend, Aleta Hannon. So Jim and Grace stopped by for Aleta, and the three of them walked out together.

It turned out to be a musical evening with Monroe, his three aunts, the two girls, and Jim Cain playing Chopin and singing opera arias. That night and Monroe were to have a tremendous impact on Cain. "For the first time in my life," he wrote in his memoirs, "I was living. Don't ask me why." Suddenly, he felt something inside he had never felt before. He had been going to recitals and concerts in Baltimore, but this was something different, sitting right in the same room with people making music.

A few days later, Cain saw Monroe at the Waldorf station, waiting for the train, and stepped over to say hello. Monroe was meeting a lady, who presently arrived and was introduced to Cain as Mrs. McPherson. She lived at Bryantown, a few miles to the east, was handsome, vivacious, and friendly, and when Cain told her he was with the state government, she asked where he was staying. He pointed to his room over the saloon and she said that wouldn't do. "You're moving down to our house—isn't he?" She said this to her husband, a big handsome man named Bill (who later became principal of the Charlotte Hall Academy). He said: "Yes, Mary—if you say he is, then he is."

Cain was delighted, and next day Bill McPherson drove him over to their house in his buggy. Thus began a memorable summer for young Jim Cain, in a house that was always open to visitors. Not only John Monroe, Grace Robey, Aleta Hannon, and other local people came, but singers from Washington, pianists, newspaper people, and even Cain's mother, dropping over for a weekend.

Cain's love of music was increasing, but he did not know what to do about it. Nor did he know what to do about something else stirring inside. In the fall of 1913 he had been transferred to the Eastern Shore office in Easton and he had to write more and more reports to the home office. He began to admire them, knowing they were readable and taking pride in the writing. For the first time in his life, he started to feel he had talent as a writer, although he had not the least idea how to make a living at it.

One day it was announced that the Commission had chosen a new chief engineer, and that the man had picked two new assistants. All the inspectors were summoned to Baltimore to meet their new superiors and, no doubt, be inspected themselves. The meeting was to take place on a Saturday morning. *Manon Lescaut* was playing the preceding Friday night at the Lyric Theatre in Baltimore, so Cain decided to invite John Monroe to accompany him, in return for all his hospitality in Waldorf. Cain wired Monroe and he came to Baltimore, sharing Cain's room Friday night at the New Howard Hotel. The next morning, Cain went to the meeting and all seemed well. He returned to Easton and mailed in his expense account, charging the state for half of the room—$1.75. Then, to his astonishment, he received notice that he had been laid off for the winter. He wondered why, and when he reported back to Baltimore on his last day, he asked one of the new assistants to the chief engineer. With an odd look in his eye, the man said: "If, as, and when you sleep with a woman, we prefer to know nothing about it."

"Woman?" Cain asked him. "What woman?"

The engineer found a folder in his file, took out Cain's receipted hotel bill, and said: "Well, there it is, a room for two!"

"It was a room for two," Cain replied, "but the other person was a man, a friend. We went to the opera that night, *Manon Lescaut*, at the Lyric. I invited him, he was my guest, and I put him up for the night."

"You being funny or what?" the assistant replied.

So Cain was unemployed and looking forward to a grim winter. But then, through a friend, a lawyer in Cambridge, he landed a job as principal of the high school in Vienna, Maryland, a little village halfway between Cambridge and Salisbury on what is today Route 50.

The job paid $800 a term and it gave him experience and confidence in teaching, which would help later. But the most important thing that happened to Cain in Vienna was caused by a young woman, a pianist. She encouraged him to sing for an audience. He tried it a few times and appeared to make a big hit—at least he drew applause and was asked to sing an encore. Cain decided that he had finally found something he really enjoyed. Near the end of the school year, early in June 1914, he determined he would be a singer.

Cain quit his teaching job in Vienna and could hardly wait to tell his family. When he did, his mother was horrified. All one day she lectured him, arguing that he did not have one single qualification to be a singer: "Not one! You have no voice, no looks, no stage personality. You have some musical sense, but it's not enough." Cain conceded she could be right but stuck to his decision to be a singer—"At least I'll give it a try."

Despite his mother's vote of no confidence, Cain headed for Washington to enroll in John Monroe's singing class—and was deflated again. His friend was not very enthusiastic about Cain's singing either, although he did accept him as a pupil. There was also the question of how to finance his career. One day, through Monroe, Cain met a man named J. Harris Franklin, who owned an insurance agency called the General Accident Company. Franklin offered Cain a job selling insurance, "office to office," as he put it. Cain thought this sounded like a good opportunity primarily because it would enable him to arrange his own working hours, leaving time to work on becoming the next

Caruso . . . and maybe, someday, even sing with one of his divinities—the Chicago opera star Florence Macbeth, whose career he was following in the music magazines.

But the summer slipped by and Cain did not sell one insurance policy. Worse, he gradually found out why his mother had hit the roof and his friends did not take his singing seriously: although he had a good barroom bass, he could not really sing! Furthermore, he did not like the endless practice at the piano that seemed to go with a singing career. Finally, deciding that maybe his mother was right, he quit his music lessons.

Cain was flat broke by September, and went looking for a job at Kann's department store in Washington, D.C. He was hired at $12 a week to sell Victor records and Victrolas, his specialty being Red Seal records. For a while it was an interesting job. He liked meeting some of the famous Washingtonians who came in—Jack Bowie, the town's leading tenor; his wife, Mary Sherrier, Washington's "dream girl," who was a soloist with the United States Marine Band; Tom Greene, the grand opera tenor and Washington's leading impresario, and his wife. Cain began to branch out and show some initiative. He watched for meetings of various groups in the evenings, where there might be dancing, and would offer to furnish the music—with a Victrola and Red Seal records, all available at Kann's. The store was enthusiastic and did everything it could to cooperate with its young promoter—except to pay him what he thought he was worth. Mr. DeNeal, his boss, said he had been impressed with Cain's initiative and offered to recommend him for a $3 a week raise, to $15. But Cain held out for $25, deciding he would probably quit if he did not get it.

Actually, he was being stirred in another direction. Cain had not forgotten how proud he had been of his written reports for the State Roads Commission, and again he was wondering just how one went about being a writer. His favorite contemporary author was a novelist by the name of Henry Sydnor Harrison. After graduating from Columbia in 1900, Harrison had decided to go into journalism. He quit when he found "it was nothing but newspaper work." He then started writing novels with intriguing titles such as *Captivating Mary Carstairs*, *Queed*, and *V.V.'s Eyes*. Cain devoured them all, remembering whole passages by heart. (He later learned that H. L. Mencken thought Harrison a "merchant of mush.")

Harrison was living in Richmond, so Cain went down to ask him for some advice about following in his footsteps. Unfortunately, the author was not home, and Cain returned to Washington. Then Mr. DeNeal told him Kann's would go no higher than a $3 raise, and Cain quit. He walked west up Pennsylvania Avenue, soon finding himself sitting on a bench in Lafayette

Park across from the White House. He was twenty-two years old, broke, out of a job, and had no better idea of what he wanted to do in life than the day he had finished college four years earlier. And then, suddenly, he heard his own voice. It said: "You're going to be a writer!"

"I've thought about it a thousand times," Cain wrote later, "trying to figure out why that voice said what it did—without success. There must have been something that had been gnawing at me from the inside. . . . Nor did I have any realization that the decision I'd made wasn't mine to make. . . . [It] would not be settled by me, but by God."

Cain had finally awakened to what was inside him—and the decision would affect him the rest of his life. It came, he said, at the lowest point in his woe at having found he would never be a singer. "But it was no clarion call. Writing to me was distinctly a consolation prize."

He also decided later that his arbitrary decision to be a writer had not been the right approach, that it "was looking at the thing from the wrong end of the telescope, a procedure from the general to the particular, instead of the other way around! If I had had an idea, some story idea that had come to me, that I meant to write up in secret, then send to some magazine—if I had had this notion, and then sprung the grand surprise on my family and friends and well-wishers when the magazine accepted it—if it had happened that way, and then after three or four acceptances, I had decided to be a writer, then it would have made sense."

So once again, Cain went home to tell his parents he had failed at something and was headed in still another new direction. But this time, his mother, vindicated in her judgment about his singing, was delighted and said writing "is what you were born for." Even his father was enthused (possibly relieved), and instead of coming up with another job suggestion, he began giving Jamie his ideas about what good writing should contain—mostly "a good stock of quotations," such as Dr. Cain used extensively in his own writing.

Cain's unhappy years of searching were over. They were not, however, quite as misspent and aimless as he thought. Having graduated from college at an age when most boys are just beginning, he had gone out into a graduate school of perhaps the only kind that means anything to a novelist. Almost everything he experienced in those four years of drifting around southern Maryland, Baltimore, and Washington, D.C., played a part in his future fictional works: his frustrating job with the insurance company contributed to "Double Indemnity"; construction work, which he learned about on the Road Commission, played an important part in *The Moth*, *Mignon*, and *Past All Dishonor*; his brief music career contributed to his understanding of the sing-

ers in *Serenade*, *The Moth*, *Career in C Major*, and *Mildred Pierce*; his Baltimore whorehouse nights were moved out to Virginia City, Nevada, and put
info *Past All Dishonor*, and his knowledge of southern Maryland and its people contributed background to *Galatea* and *The Magician's Wife*. They may
have been four aimless years for the young Cain, but they were not wasted.

B y the time Jamie returned home, the Cain family
had become very popular in Chestertown. And his brother and sisters, now
growing up, had developed their distinguishing characteristics.

Virginia was beautiful, easygoing, sociable, and gifted with words. Cain
said that if anyone in the family was destined to be a writer it was she, and he
spent a lifetime trying to persuade her to write, but without success. She
taught for some years in Western High School in Baltimore, then became an
assistant purchasing agent for Johns Hopkins Hospital. She never married.

Rosalie was pretty, rather than beautiful, the "*practico* of the family,"
as Cain put it, and the one he was closest to. She could do things, and she
did them right. In her twenties, she married Robert Glenn McComas of Baltimore and had one son by him, Glenn. She also taught for a few years before
becoming executive secretary at radio station WFBR in Baltimore.

Edward, or "Boydie," was growing into a handsome boy—tall, lean,
and graceful. He could do all the physical things Dr. Cain admired and understood: catch a forward pass, grab rebound basketballs, and serve cannon-
ball aces in tennis. He could also use his fists, or play Beethoven on the
violin, and he was the apple of his father's eye. He was killed, tragically, in
an airplane accident at the end of World War I.

"Baben"—the youngest sister, Genevieve—was the intellectual of the
family and the sibling Cain always thought he was most like. She was withdrawn, literary, and widely read, but did not get along too well socially. She
did a little writing, and Cain once helped her with a novel. Baben never married, and eventually she went to work for Rosalie at station WFBR.

Cain never felt close to his parents, which he later said was "one of the
blights of my life." Apparently, his mother thought he had no sense, and he
claimed there were only two things she taught him that ever stuck: "(1) Don't
stay too long; and (2) if a lady says she's been ill, do *not*, *not*, ask for any
details—get off the subject quick." However, he loved his mother and remembered fondly the little things about her, such as the birthdays when the
children would punch holes in a shoebox and fill them with daisies, laurel,
and honeysuckle as a present for her. And he could not forget his mother's
remark when they learned that her husband was out on a boat in a storm:

"We didn't worry about him *nearly* enough." Cain was always amazed at her musical ability, which to him was "black magic." But he was annoyed at her fear of what a musical career would have meant. Cain thought his mother wanted to remain a little girl all her life, with someone to take care of her. She used to try to appeal to Jamie's indignation when someone did not treat him right, and Jamie would "get so furious, wanting to sock somebody, and then would tell myself: Calm down, it's only your mother, making polite conversation." She had a gift for language, and Cain always felt that any writing talent he had, as well as his interest in music, came from her. In later years, he said many times that the novels he wrote in which music or a singer played an important part were "wreaths laid at my mother's grave." It is probably significant that his first ambition was to be a singer, following his mother's talent, rather than go into teaching or academia, his father's career. And psychiatrists might find something in his preoccupation with incest between parent and child in at least two of his books—*The Butterfly* and *Kingdom by the Sea*. In the latter, an unpublished novel, a young boy comes home to live with his family after being away for a while, and considerable importance is attached to the physical attraction of the youngish mother, a singer and dancer, to the son.

Dr. Cain was a convivial man who liked to sit around and talk. It always annoyed Jamie that he never once heard his father praise his mother for her singing ability, a lapse that drew Cain to the conclusion that, despite his academic credentials, his father was "a philistine, having no comprehension of music or anything—even writing." However, Dr. Cain did fancy himself something of a writer, though his daughter Virginia would usually put him down, saying all he could write were "pretty thoughts—with quotations."

Cain thought his father had a bad case of ergophobia—fear of work. Chores like mowing the lawn, raking the leaves, shaking the furnace, or driving a car bored him. But he could rise to an occasion. One time in Annapolis little Virginia was burned (when Jamie suggested they run through a fire) and Dr. Cain nursed her through much of the crisis, relieving her mother and changing bandages with some skill.

There were barriers between Jamie and his father, which Cain eventually decided went back to his difficult birth and what his father must have thought during those hours when Rose's life was in danger. Dr. Cain was disappointed in Jamie's disinclination to be an athlete or a leader on campus. Jamie, in turn, was aware of his father's wishes and wanted very much to have a career his father would respect: "To amount to something."

The truth is, Jamie was afraid of his father. He remembered an incident once when his brother Boydie, glancing through the proofs of the college catalog, found his name listed in the sophomore class as "Edward Joseph Cain." Boydie marched into his father's library and said: "My name is Edward Cain—you can take that Joseph out."

Dr. Cain said: "Your name is Edward Joseph Cain, it was given to you, and . . ."

Boydie interrupted: "It was without my consent or even my knowledge. But not to argue with it, it's either out, or *I* am."

"You are? What do you mean by that?" Dr. Cain replied.

"I mean, I'm offered a job by Du Pont in Wilmington, Delaware, and unless Joseph comes out of this catalog I'm taking it and quitting this college."

The "Joseph" came out, but Jamie always knew that he would never have defied his father as Boydie had. In fact, he never once stood up to his father.

Cain's own portrait of his father, sketched in his memoirs, is significant: "So far, add him all up, you might say the man God created was destined for a rake—a handsome, gabby, likable rake, but a rake just the same. And you could be right, except that he got into the act himself, going on from where God left off, to mold all three of his weaknesses, his love of drink, his love of talk, and his fear of work, into one pillar of massive strength, and an adroitness at politics that transformed the anemic character of academic life into something meaningful, difficult and very well worthwhile."

Whether Dr. Cain's love of drink affected relations with his son is not clear. But it was obvious that, by now, it was affecting Dr. Cain's standing at the college.

How his father and the rest of the family looked on Jamie is also uncertain, but there is some evidence that they saw him as a "mama's boy," a term he sometimes used to describe himself. And we can draw some conclusions from a comment he once wrote Rosalie: "Remember, I'm the one the rest of you counted out as being so helpless. I wouldn't even be asked to help out in an emergency." A curious observation, considering he was the oldest son.

When he arrived home in 1914 to launch his literary career, James M. Cain's writings consisted of a class "Prophecy," reports to the State Roads Commission, and a brief travel sketch, written about his trip to Richmond to see Henry Sydnor Harrison. Now that he was going to be a writer he had to write something—but what? He finally decided on fiction, and within a few weeks he had written several short stories and sent them off to various magazines. They came right back.

But he learned three things from the experience—the only things, he always maintained, you could teach a writer: grammar, punctuation, and how to use a typewriter.

Portrait of Cain's father,
James W. Cain, that hangs at
Washington College.

Cain's mother,
Rose Cain.

The Paca Carroll House on the St. John's campus where Cain was born in 1892. M. E. Warren.

The 1909 editorial staff of Pegasus, *the Washington College yearbook. Cain is on the left, second from the front; Mary Clough is across the table from him.*

The 1910 Washington College Glee Club. Cain is in the middle row, second from the right.

James M. Cain

Chestertown, Md.

"Pedro," the awkwardest man of the class; runs on the track like a turkey, with both wings broken. Always ready to criticise some one's good looks. Has recently fallen deeply in love, and never tires of hearing that little song: "Mary has a little lamb. His name is Jamie Cain."

Cain's entry in the 1910 Pegasus.

The house on the Washington College campus where the Cain family lived from 1903 to 1918.

Photographic portrait of Cain around 1915. Christhill Studio

Cain's brother "Boydie" in his World War I aviator's uniform shortly before his death in 1919.

The brick walk built by Ike Newton
on the Washington College campus.
It is still there today, a monument
to the unique literary style of James
M. Cain. Roy Hoopes

Christmas party, 1918, the Headquarters Group of the 79th Division. Cain is unidentified, but is possibly the soldier with the moustache seated two men to the left of the post. The Infantry Journal, *National Archives*

The battlefield where Cain's story, "The Taking of Montfaucon," took place. The Infantry Journal, National Archives

OPPOSITE: *Cain (left) in France, 1918–19, with his buddy Drexel Truitt.*

Cain's World War I buddy, Gilbert Malcolm. The photo was taken in 1959 at the time Malcolm, then 66, was made president of Dickinson College.

THE LORRAINE CROSS

PUBLISHED BY THE 79TH DIVISION

VOLUME 1	FRANCE, THURSDAY, MAY 8, 1919	NUMBER 14

79TH ALL READY FOR LAST LONG MOVE TOWARD HOME; RECEPTION STILL UNSETTLED

DIVISION WILL HAVE VETERANS' ORGANIZATION

Preliminary Meeting Was Held At Headquarters On Monday

GENERAL KUHN PRESIDENT

Board Of Directors Will Represent Each Unit; Philadelphia Named As Temporary Headquarters In The United States.

At a meeting of representatives from the various organizations of the division held Monday at Division Headquarters, preliminary arrangements were made for the formation of a divisional organization after demobilization.

Officers Nominated

It was decided that the proposed organization should have one president, one first vice-president, five second vice-presidents, a treasurer and such assistants as he should select. For these offices the following were nominated: President—Major General Joseph E. Kuhn.

1st Vice President—Brigadier General William J. Nicholson.

2nd Vice President—Five officers or enlisted men to be elected by the Board of Directors.

Treasurer—Captain David E. Williams, 315th Infantry.

Secretary—Lt. Col. J. H. Steinman, Division Adjutant.

Representation Planned

There will be a board of directors, on which representation will be allowed on the basis of two per thousand, one officer and one enlisted man, based on tables of organization strength. On this basis, each infantry regiment will be allowed eight; each artillery regiment four; each train, two; each machine gun battalion, two; engineer regiment and train, four; signal battalion, two; each brigade at large, two; the division at large, eight.

This board of directors will be selected by the respective organizations. Philadelphia was named as the temporary headquarters of board of directors.

THANK YOU!

Headquarters, 79th Division,
American E. F.
30th April, 1919

Private James M. Cain,
Editor, The Lorraine Cross
Sir:

Since its appearance, I have been an interested reader of our divisional paper, "The Lorraine Cross." It has not only lived up to my expectations, but has far exceeded them. But, after all, it is a Seventy Ninth affair, and could therefore not possibly have been a failure.

If all members have enjoyed The Lorraine Cross as much as I, and I feel sure they have, then all must have benefitted. It has uniformly maintained a clean, wholesome, and inspiring tone, claiming credit only where credit is due, and exhibiting malice to none.

I wish to not only thank you and your fellow workers of The Lorraine Cross for your excellent camp paper, but to congratulate you on having contributed in no small degree to the maintenance of good feeling within the division during the long and trying period waiting, now so nearly at an end.

Very sincerely,
JOSEPH E. KUHN,
Major General, U. S. A.

GOES TO STATES ON JOB CAMPAIGN

Lieut. Frank A. Gale Proceeds Division On Employment Mission.

In order to start a widespread publicity campaign to get jobs for the men of the Seventy Ninth Division, Lieut. Frank A. Gale, of the 158th Infantry Brigade, has preceded the division back to the states.

Lieut. Gale, before entering the army, was a newspaper man, and for the past two months has been acting as supervising editor of The Lorraine Cross. His going is part of the campaign announced some time ago in this paper, when it was stated that everything would be done to get back for the men the jobs they left. Lieut. Gale will work through the medium of the large newspapers in the East, and it is expected that his efforts will meet a ready response from employers.

Before going, Lieut. Gale said: "I have no doubt that everywhere *Continued on Page Four*

79TH OFFICERS ARE PROMOTED

Recent Order Advances Grade Of Many To Fill Existing Vacancies

Many Seventy Ninth officers received promotions under Special Orders No. 122-A, G. H. Q., dated May 2. The appointments fill existing vacancies in rank.

Those promoted are as follows:

Infantry: From Major to Lt. Col: Gerald P. Murphy; From Captain to Major: Kenneth Mayo, Thomas H. Stilwell, John W. Feeney, Harry C. Duncan; From 1st Lt. Captain: Lincoln S. Godfrey, Jr., James D. Judson, Charles A. S. Keeley, Norman L. Wymard, Frederick R. Clark, Carl W. Wentzel, William P. Cole, Jr., Robert M. Laird, George L. Bliss, Spencer S. Large, John Cahill, From and Lt. to 1st Lt.: Herbert W. Pritchard, Miles C. Morrison, William Y. Fillebrown, William H. Blandy, Stanley C. Butler, Alfred Johnston, Charles T. Blanchard, William C. Longstring, Fred A. Conrad, Benjamin T. Dillard, Thomas E. Blake, Frank H. Graham, Raymond L. Young, Warner R. Dixon, William P. Berry, Thomas C. Main, Joseph F. Murphy, Paul Esling, Horace A. Cannon, Charles E. Miller, George J. Evans, Carl W. Andrews, Russell M. Willard, Louis Golden, David A. Wiley, John J. Canahan, Charles F. Baer, James McGee, Harry T. Mitchell, Bryan Beckwith, Norris S. Barratt, Alfred Bower, John G. Griffin, Colley E. Williams, John G. Kerlin, Benjamin S. Harris, Daniel J. Dougherty, William L. Adcock, Walker M. Taylor, Jr., Patrick V. Doyle, Karl G. Goedel, Harrison H. Mayhew, Frank J. Callahan, William N. Johnson, William R. Mount, John W. Converse; From 1st Lt. to Captain: Frank B. Fox, Frederick M. *Continued on Page Four*

SAILING STARTS SATURDAY

Last Man Will Be Out Of France May 17—Parades In Eastern Cities To Depend On Desires Of Men Themselves.

The Seventy Ninth is ready for the last move that will be made before demobilization in the United States.

Ships that are to carry the division across the water are now arriving at St. Nazaire. The tentative schedule calls for the departure of the first boat Saturday; the last on May 17. The schedule, as it stands at present, with the names of the boats and the capacity of each, is as follows:

May 10; Matsonia; 3340 men; arrive Newport News.

May 12; Virginia; 4150; arrive Newport News.

May 13; Orizaba; 3780; arrive Newport News.

May 14; Shoshone; 1750; arrive Newport News.

May 14; Siboney; 3300; arrive Newport News.

May 14; Antigone; 3050; arrive Newport News.

May 15; Princess Matoika; 3750; arrive Charleston.

May 17; Aeolus; 3540; arrive Newport News.

At present there is no information obtainable as to the camps at which demobilization will take place, or whether the division will be held in service for a parade. Unofficial rumors are that most of the men will be demobilized at Camp Meade. A previous sailing schedule, giving New York as one of the ports at which boats would land, made it seem likely that some of the men would be discharged at Camp Dix, but the schedule given above does not make this probable.

As to parades, nothing definite has been decided upon. Papers arriving from the United States tell of plans for receiving the 158th Infantry Brigade in Philadelphia, and the 313th Infantry, and possibly the whole 157th Infantry Brigade, in Baltimore. As to whether any effort is being made to have the whole division parade in any of the Eastern cities little or nothing can be learned.

Unofficially, it might be stated that the parades and kind of reception to be given the division depend very largely upon the disposition of the men themselves. It might help speed up decisions and arrangements if the men of *Continued on Page Four*

Final issue of
The Lorraine Cross.

He was also learning more about human nature and the young mind. About the time he started writing short stories in Chestertown, a professor who taught English and math in the preparatory school became ill and his father asked Jamie, as everyone still called him around Chestertown, if he would take over his classes. He agreed—but was determined to continue writing stories when he had the time. To prepare for his English classes, Jamie studied his subject thoroughly, and as time went by and the professor did not return to his job, Jamie became a walking encyclopedia of grammar, syntax, rhetoric, and especially punctuation. It also quickly became obvious that he was good at teaching, and when the ill professor recovered and accepted a job elsewhere, Jamie's father not only asked him to stay on permanently at Washington College but enlarged his responsibility. In addition to teaching English and math, Jamie would be in charge of the prep school students, which meant living in the dormitory and maintaining discipline. He accepted the job.

When he moved into his new quarters he was confronted with chaos—months of accumulated orange peels, water marks, and other refuse accompanying boyish pranks and general sloppiness. So on his first night in the dorm, he assembled his charges and told them: "I intend to live in a place that my mother, my sisters, or any woman can drop in on any time, and find a place fit for them to visit. I assume you do too, that that's the kind of place you would maintain if it weren't for a few clowns trying to be funny. Well, that's the kind of place we're going to have!"

The students quickly complied, and the incident taught Cain something about young men that would stick with him the rest of his life. "Apparently," he said, "they like the iron mike—being told what they have to do lets them know where they're at, and they get the point without resentment. At the same time, being allowed to participate . . . seems to stimulate their pride."

George Bratt, who took courses under him, recalls that Jamie Cain was not exactly a fashion plate and that he taught class with an open collar and no tie. But he was "a very efficient teacher and very popular. His face was pock-marked and he did get a little high on whiskey every now and then." And everyone on the campus knew that Jamie was primarily interested in being a writer and that he was writing short stories all the time.

While teaching at prep, Jamie became friends with Washington's professor of French, Charles L. Townsend, who convinced him that as long as he was there, he might as well work for his master's degree. Cain agreed, a decision he later considered "a big mistake." The experience turned out to be a one-year "ordeal," during which Cain earned his M.A. in English drama and the American short story. It seemed a logical step, considering Cain's ambition, but he said that in fact the studies did not interest him and the year taught him a lesson: "Unless you have an honest interest in something, lay off."

Townsend knew of Cain's interest in writing and would take long walks with him across the bridge over the Chester River discussing stories. One in particular, the only real story idea Cain had in these early years, would stick with him for a long time. Its central idea was that a famous male singer would commit a crime, escape, and then discover that he dared not open his mouth or he would identify himself to the whole world. Townsend liked the idea, and then it occurred to Cain that someone else, perhaps a woman, would commit the crime instead, and they would both realize he could not open his mouth—because it would lead the police to her. The story "hung in dead center" for years, but Cain would eventually develop it into one of his most famous novels, *Serenade*.

In his English class, Cain had come to the conclusion that writing cannot be taught. What can be taught is grammar, syntactical soundness, the general principles of rhetoric, and finally, interlaced with all these and depending on them, punctuation. "When you learn how to punctuate," he told his students, "you'll be free to be yourselves. Instead of being in a straitjacket of what can be put between commas with a period at the end, you can write as freely as you talk, and know that you can set it up so it reads."

He drilled the boys on punctuation "until it ran out of their ears," and, in justification, assured them: "Writing, in one respect, is like football: It's all fundamentals, there are no higher branches."

To arouse interest in their writing, he had them arrange for jobs as college correspondents with their local papers, covering the college athletic games and following the hometown boys. It worked well, and most of the students took it seriously.

Cain's prep school was on the far side of the main road running through the campus, and the students were known as "rats." When they invaded the gymnasium on journalistic assignments, some of the upperclassmen complained: "Who the hell's running this joint, Jake or them rats?" Jake was a nickname for Cain's father, and this sort of talk around the campus must have proved especially difficult for Jamie at that time, because all was not going well with Dr. Cain. His troubles had begun several years before, in 1910 according to Cain, when Marion DeKalb Smith, perhaps the most powerful member of the Washington College Board, died. Smith had given Dr. Cain more or less a free hand to rebuild the school, and the other members of the board would not challenge him. With Smith gone, Dr. Cain began to feel pressure from the board, and his son recalled that the politicians began looking to the college for patronage jobs.

Dr. Cain's first real conflict with the board occurred in 1911 and concerned his lifelong passion, football. That year, Washington (for the first time in its history) beat St. John's, 11–0, but the game had been played in Baltimore rather than Annapolis or Chestertown. This helped the team run up a debt of over $800 for the year. The board agreed to appropriate some money to alleviate the debt, but was obviously irritated. It ordered that football games would be played only on the campuses of one of the two schools involved in a game and reprimanded the school's Athletic Committee, under Dr. Cain. However, two years later, for some reason, Dr. Cain again agreed to games being played in Baltimore against St. John's and Western Maryland. The board rescinded its ban on the Baltimore games, but also reprimanded Dr. Cain. This time, St. John's defeated Washington 16–6, and that did not help matters.

By 1914, interest in athletic competition at the little college was so intense that the faculty became alarmed; it appeared as if sports were becoming more important to the athletes than their studies. To counteract this, the faculty adopted a set of rules governing the eligibility of students taking part in sports. The board, wanting Washington to do better—not worse—on the athletic field, ordered the faculty to rescind its action. The faculty refused, and a major confrontation developed. Dr. Cain, despite his intense belief in competitive sports as a means of building character in young men, supported his faculty.

The board responded by insisting the eligibility rules be revoked and ordered that meetings of the board be attended only by "duly elected" members. Dr. Cain correctly interpreted this as being directed at him, and submitted his resignation. He won this round when the board finally passed a resolution rescinding its actions, and in April 1915 he withdrew his letter of resignation. But there now existed considerable tension among Dr. Cain, the faculty, and the Board of Governors.

The following year another crisis developed. On the night of January 16, 1916, William Smith Hall burned down. Everything inside was destroyed—historical records, the library, students' records, Dr. Cain's private papers. The only thing to survive was the Gilbert Stuart portrait of William Smith, saved by a student named Donald Tydings. Cain always felt the board blamed his father for the fire, possibly because of his drinking (in fact, on the night Smith Hall burned, the faculty and Dr. Cain held a meeting there until 11:00 P.M. discussing the eligibility rules). If Dr. Cain had had a few the night Smith Hall burned down, it would naturally have been held against him. His drinking had long been acknowledged and tolerated, but now it was becoming a problem; the students knew about it, and it was a subject of much comment. "Of course, his father liked to drink," says Ethel Gibbs, a friend of Jamie's, referring to Dr. Cain. "He would go away on these weekend trips and Monday morning he would not be at school and they would say he had a hangover." Another former student who was there when Jamie was teaching in prep school remembers being called on the carpet by Dr. Cain, who had obviously been drinking quite a bit. "Everyone in Chestertown knew Dr. Cain had a drinking problem," the former student says.

Jamie was also developing problems—but of a different kind. Although he was now twenty-five years old, he still did not have a steady girl. There was one romance, but he could hardly talk about it: "I remember the night of the eclipse," he wrote of the girl many years later, "and how all of a sudden, by some magic, I was palpably close to this little fourteen-year-old, with her Mona Lisa smile."

He had also started seeing Mary Clough again. She still had the "hex" on him, as he put it, but he was not sure what attracted her, unless it was his confiding that he wanted "to be a writer." Mary was an intellectual, and her mother's side of the family was related to Stephen Crane. Often they discussed *The Red Badge of Courage* (which he thought one of the most dreadful novels ever written) and other books.

Meanwhile, Jamie was hard at work on his short stories, though still without success. "In the afternoons I played the typewriter, on which I was becoming a virtuoso," he said, "writing short stories in secret, sending them off to magazines, and getting all of them back. In a year or more of trying, I didn't make one sale, until the thing became ridiculous and I was horribly self-conscious about it, to the point where self-respect, if nothing else, demanded that I quit."

By then, Cain's success in taking over the prep school had become known in academic circles, and in the spring of 1917 he received an offer from a high school in Easton, Pennsylvania, to teach math. His father thought it was a good idea to "deal yourself a fresh hand," and Cain agreed, particularly given the fact that the new job would pay more money. In addition, Cain felt the time had come for him to think about leaving home—for good. He was twenty-five, the oldest child in the family and still very much tied to his parents. Maybe, he thought, it was time for Uncle Sam to come to the rescue.

In April, America declared war on Germany, and shortly thereafter Cain registered for the draft. But he was not enthused about the war. "Bleeding Belgium" was, to be sure, a horrible thing, but he also realized that much of what he heard was propaganda. He also knew about what had gone on in the Belgian Congo, which the muckraking press had exposed as anything but idealistic, and he was among those who suspected that the country was being used as a cat's-paw to salvage the financiers' investments. He wondered if the march of history did not point to Germany as the wave of the future, rather than to the southern European countries with their archaic industrial systems.

His new teaching job did not start until the fall, and after his own classes were over, suddenly, one day early in the summer, he decided he would find a job in one of the many war factories in Baltimore. But when he went to the city and saw, out of the window of his streetcar, a long lineup of men beside an iron fence topped with barbed wire, he stayed on the car and went back to his boardinghouse. Then, annoyed at his timidity, he delivered himself an ultimatum: "The first possible place that might have a job you're going in there and get it." He went back downtown and spotted Swift and Company, on Pratt Street. He jumped off the streetcar, went into Swift, and in two minutes had a job paying $25 a week as weightmaster in the cold room. In his brief time there, he made some good friends and picked up valuable research contacts for future novels dealing with the meat-packing industry. But reporting for work at 3:00 A.M. got him down, and after a week he was on the lookout for another job.

He was wandering around downtown Baltimore when he saw a big sign on the side of a building: THE BALTIMORE AMERICAN. He had no idea what qualifications one needed to get hired on a newspaper, but he decided to go in and find out. He ended up talking with William Kines, the city editor, and must have impressed him, because Kines offered him a job as a reporter at $10 a week. It was a momentous day. For the next fourteen years Cain would be primarily employed in journalism, and all of his life he considered himself "a newspaperman," a profession he preferred to list in *Who's Who in America* rather than "author" or "novelist."

For his first two days on the *American*, Cain traveled with a veteran police reporter named Holmes, learning the business. Then he was assigned the southern police district, and his first story was a drowning. He went back to the city room to type his story, at around 10:00 P.M., and dropped it in the "in" basket. Back at his desk, he watched the night city editor, Raymond Hoblitzel, pick the story up and study it. Hoblitzel was a fine, experienced editor, who talked with a slight stammer. Cain noted that something seemed to be wrong as Hoblitzel fingered the story, until finally he came over to Cain's desk and stammered: "Mr. Cain, you've b-b-been in the newspaper business bef-f-fore? May I ask where?"

"No," said Cain, "I'm new at it." And then, as Hoblitzel stared, he added: "Matter of fact, that's the first story I ever wrote—the one you have in your hand."

Still Hoblitzel stared, and then finally said: "I—compliment you on it. I would say—you're in—the right business. I predict—you'll go far."

Cain remembered this prophetic comment the rest of his life, but he had no idea what there was about the story that caught the night editor's eye.

The next day, Mr. Kines called Cain to his office, gave him a $5 raise, and asked if he could cover some big stories about the war mood developing in the country. Excited over having made an impression, Cain said yes and was soon attending Liberty Loan drives, parades, rallies, meetings, training camps; he was also writing thousands of words every day, six to eight columns of copy a night, and employing the principles of rhetoric he had taught himself.

One interview from this period was with John Philip Sousa. Sousa had come to Baltimore with his Great Lakes Training Band—250 sailors who went around the country with him selling Liberty Bonds. Cain was impressed with Sousa—a handsome man, above medium height and compactly put together. "His manner was quiet and courtesy itself," wrote Cain. "Not once, in spite of all the inane things a newspaper reporter must ask, did he show impatience, or in any slight degree seem pompous. And yet, when he mounted the podium and lifted his baton, something steely got into his stance and every gob in the band felt it."

The summer slipped by with Cain interviewing, reporting, and writing. Then all of a sudden it was September and he had to go up to Easton, Pennsylvania, to teach. He did not mind teaching algebra to the high school kids, but some of them wanted to act a little older than they were, which created problems. In his unfinished memoirs, Cain tells the story as if it were written for one of his novels:

"And then in one of those classes she appeared. She was, I would say, twelve, and her second day in class she showed up in black silk stockings. . . . The pair of legs were the most beautiful I've seen on a twelve-year-old, who folded them in her seat in such a way as to let me glimpse Honolulu, as Zsa Zsa Gabor called it—then let her eyes lock with mine.

"She was pretty, and meant business I knew, from the stab I kept getting from the area of my heart. Then suddenly she was at my desk, pressing her stomach against it. 'Mr. Cain,' she said, half whispering, 'I know where you're staying. I found out. You're just up the street from me—here's my address on this slip.'

"When I looked, a slip of paper was there, which I tried not to put in my pocket, but did. 'So,' she went on, 'if you were to stop by after school, say around four thirty, we could go up to my room, where I could stretch out on the bed and you could explain me quadratics, which I don't at all understand.'

" 'I'll think about it,' I told her.

"But what I actually did think about was how well I was going to like it in the Pennsylvania State Penitentiary for Men."

Cain immediately called Kines at the *American* to see if his newspaper job was still available. Kines said it was, and Cain told the high school superintendent he was going back to the newspaper business. Although the superintendent was furious, Cain was on the four-thirty train to Baltimore. Later, the young lady came to Baltimore and phoned Cain at the *American*, saying she wanted to see him. But Cain "avoided her like poison."

Cain worked at the *American* until the end of 1917, then was offered a job with the *Baltimore Sun*, for $3 a week more than the $20 he was making at the *American*. The *Sun* was considered the best paper in Baltimore, and Cain accepted the offer.

He went to the *Sun* the first week in January 1918 and was soon back at his old assignment in the southern police district, with occasional forays into the western and northern districts. The northern district was the affluent section of town where not much went on, but it contained a lot of hotels where visiting celebrities stayed, so Cain interviewed a number of opera singers there, including Madame Schumann-Heink and Geraldine Farrar. He eventually concluded he did not have much talent at interviewing. But over in the western district, a disturbing incident occurred, which Cain would remember all his life. A man had dropped dead in a woman's apartment. He was an Army colonel, unquestionably married, and obviously having an affair with the woman, who was a nurse. The police would not give the *Sun* her name for fear it might result in her losing her job. When Cain was in the station, he happened to hear the clerk mumbling the number of a telephone. He jotted it down. When he returned to the office, he called information to find out who the number was listed under and learned it was in a woman's name. He also obtained the address, and not knowing whether this was *the* woman or not, he went to her apartment. He knocked on the door, and when a woman's voice answered he said, "Cain's my name and I want to ask you some questions about what happened up here last night with the colonel."

The woman said, "I don't want to discuss that matter at all. I don't know how you got my name. You didn't get it from the police. I know that because they protected me."

That was all Cain needed to know. He went back and told what had happened to the city editor, Clarke Fitzpatrick, adding that he was the only one who knew about it and that there was no need to print it.

"What the hell," said Fitzpatrick, "it's what everyone wants to know." Reluctantly and very disturbed, Cain put the woman's name in the story— and was convinced for the rest of his life he had made the wrong decision.

Despite such incidents, Cain was enjoying his job at the *Sun*. And now that he was regularly employed, Mary Clough began to pay him even more attention. Cain also had begun to think that perhaps his antiwar and anti-Allies positions were just an elaborate psychological smokescreen to justify his staying out of the fray, so he tried to enlist in various branches. He had already been rejected at least once by the draft board, and now he was turned down again. The problem was something in his right lung. Cain did not take it seriously, even when his case came up for review again in the spring of 1918 and the Army doctor in Baltimore said: "I don't like the sound of that lung—it may not mean much, but I'm supposed to turn you down."

After the man had gone on with his head-shaking for a minute or two, Cain asked: "You can send me down, can't you? I'm not a total cripple. I don't have TB, do I?"

"Well, I shouldn't," said the doctor. "But—I can so far as that goes. No, you don't have active TB, at least as my examination shows. But don't be surprised if you get sent back."

When he arrived home, from where he was to report to his Kent County draft headquarters, Cain immediately noticed something wrong. There was a change in everyone's manner, as though his family was hiding something from him. His father was reluctant to talk about it, saying the most important thing was the possibility that Jamie was going to war. But it did not take Jamie long to find out what had happened: His father had been fired from Washington College. Even today it is not clear precisely why. The records show that he "resigned" on June 19, 1918. But Cain remained convinced that his father was forced out by a cabal of "politicians" and anti-Cain members of the board, principally over the issue of control of the new gymnasium, built in 1912. The gym gave the college and the town the opportunity to have dances, balls, and social functions as well as basketball, and a fierce struggle had developed for control of these activities. Also, despite the board's having backed down on the issue of scholastic requirements for athletes, friction still persisted between Dr. Cain and the college board on the question of scholastic requirements. And then, of course, there was the continual problem of Dr. Cain's drinking.

His dismissal was a terrible shock and tragedy for Dr. Cain, coming as it did after he had truly built the school from nothing to a respectable little liberal arts college. Eventually his contribution to the college was acknowledged when, in 1925, Dr. Paul Titsworth, then president, wrote him: "Without the good work which you put in here for 15 years, Washington College would not be today where it is. This fact impresses me more and more as I know the history of the institution and get in contact with alumni." But this did not help Dr. Cain in 1918. His dismissal was "a catastrophe," said his son, "that would have destroyed most men." Dr. Cain was fifty-eight years old, had been in education all his life, and the circumstances under which he was leaving his job suggested that his academic career was over.

So Jamie's return to Chestertown to join the local draftees, say good-bye to his family, and embark on the greatest adventure yet in his twenty-five years was an unhappy, emotional experience. And as the young men of the Eastern Shore were shipped off to Camp Meade on a journey to help make the world safe for democracy and from which many would never return, Jamie was much more concerned about what would happen to his father in Chestertown than his own fate in France.

3

DOUGHBOY EDITOR

When Cain left Chestertown in early June 1918, he was sent with a hundred or so other draftees from the Eastern Shore to Camp Meade, Maryland (now Fort Meade), about fifteen miles south of Baltimore. On Cain's first morning in camp, when his group lined up for injections, the sergeant bellowed: "All college men, one step forward, ho!"

Cain and twenty or thirty others "ho'd" one step forward and were instructed to fall out. The noncollege recruits were dismissed and Cain's group was told to give their names and skills to the company clerk. Then came a period of standing around waiting, during which they huddled to discuss what their separation from the herd might mean. Various conjectures were offered, such as a bid to officers' school or special high-toned work, but nothing developed that morning. In the afternoon, all the new recruits were assembled again and marched into the woods where a group of men were chopping down trees, trimming and sawing them into lengths suitable for fence posts. Their job was to carry the trimmed trees to the place where the fence was being built. Cain quickly noted that when a log was ready to be carried, the sergeant would look up and motion to the first two men he saw, who would get up off the grass and carry the trimmed tree on their shoulders to its destination. Cain was not enthused about log-toting, so he figured the smart thing was to shift his position on the grass so as to avoid the sergeant's eye. Then he decided it might be wise to drift into a clump of bushes nearby. As he parted the ferns and slipped out of sight of the sergeant, he was startled to see twenty or thirty men sitting in the shadows. He heard a high, cackling laugh and looked around to see a tall, raw-boned, redheaded man with "a face from the Firth of Forth." It was Cain's first meeting with Gilbert Malcolm.

The men called him "Red" because of his hair, but not liking nicknames, Cain always called him Gilbert. The man motioned Cain to survey the others sitting among the trees, which he did, and noticed that, by odd coincidence, they were the college men who had been asked to step forward and give their names that morning. They never learned why they had been singled out, but Cain realized "at one fell swoop the value of a college education."

Cain did not see Malcolm again for a while after being assigned to the camp's psychological division—the "nut house"—where he graded Alpha and Beta tests given new recruits. Before long, he heard of an outfit going overseas that needed men. He went to the unit's captain, Edward O. Madeira, who asked Cain about his horsemanship, ability to speak French, and other aspects of his background. Cain exaggerated his accomplishments in both French and horsemanship and thought he had impressed Madeira when he was asked to wait outside while his qualifications were discussed.

Cain wandered around the rows of tents, and in front of one was Gilbert Malcolm, carefully cleaning a rifle. He remembered Cain from the fencepost gold-bricking and motioned him to sit down. Malcolm said he was curious about what Cain was doing up at Madeira's tent—and Cain was equally curious about Malcolm. After a bit of verbal sparring, Cain finally confessed he had not been 100 percent truthful with Madeira. "I can tell the front end of a horse from the hind end," said Cain, "and have had some experience staying on top—but that about lets me out. As for French, I had four years of it in college, but beyond that couldn't ask for a doughnut in it." Malcolm laughed and said he had given Madeira the same lies. "But if challenged I intend to brazen it out. I figure there's a difference between a man lying to be taken in and one lying to get out." Then he asked Cain why he had lied.

"What the hell," said Cain, "France is where the war is."

"That's right," Malcolm agreed. "I didn't put on this suit to sit up in the balcony somewhere and watch other guys give the show. I'd like to be in it."

So the two men shook hands. Malcolm was already "in it," having been accepted by Madeira despite his lies, and soon Cain was also assigned to Madeira's unit—the Headquarters Troop of the 79th Infantry Division. It had originally been known as the Joan of Arc Division, but this was before General Joseph Kuhn, the division's commander, had been in France reconnoitering and learned that Joan of Arc had been a saint. Figuring the French would not appreciate seeing Saint Joan on the shoulder patch of several hundred American doughboys, Kuhn vetoed the idea just in time to cancel the division's christening ceremony, to which Miss Geraldine Farrar had been invited to sing and break a bottle of champagne over something. So the division went to France without an insignia. But then General Kuhn solved the problem when he saw a Cross of Lorraine on a bottle of beer in Bar-le-Duc, and soon enough the 79th had its name and an insignia: the Lorraine Cross Division, symbolized by a gray cross on a field of blue.

Gilbert Malcolm and Cain were about the same age. Malcolm had graduated from Pennsylvania's Dickinson College and Dickinson's law school, and like Cain he had worked briefly for a newspaper—the *Harrisburg Times*. The two men became buddies, in the classic World War I tradition, with Cain seeming always to look up to Malcolm and defer to his judgment. He admired the Scot for his practical wisdom and common sense, which he was beginning to think were much more important than book learning, especially in the Army.

Within a week they were to board ship. Cain's father and mother came to camp to see him off, his mother bringing a French Grammar and, more important, the good news that Dr. Cain had been offered a job by the United States Fidelity and Guaranty Company in Baltimore, at a salary much higher than he had been making at Washington College. It was a great relief for Cain, who had been deeply concerned about his father.

Mary Clough also came to Camp Meade to see Cain off. By now they had become quite close, although the details of their courtship are still sketchy. Whether it was the emotion of the moment, with Jamie going off to save the world for democracy, or some other factor is not certain, but Cain said that when he left Camp Meade there was no doubt that he was "pledged" to marry Mary Clough.

On July 6, the Headquarters Troop took the train for Jersey City and the next morning boarded the U.S.S. *Leviathan* at Hoboken, scheduled to sail for France that evening. There were no torpedo attacks by the German submarines on the trip over, and the days, one like another in the middle of the ocean, slipped by very fast for Cain and Malcolm. Most of the voyage was spent studying French. "And then, one gray and overcast morning," Cain wrote, "I was staring out at the waves, when suddenly above them, hanging it seemed in midair, a fairy castle appeared, with turrets and windows and trees. It was actually there, however, a château in France." Cain was startled because with all the zigzagging at sea he had been sure they were still in the middle of the Atlantic. Soon they were heading into the harbor of Brest, and after the men piled into a barge and went ashore, they were marched three miles to the Pontanzen Barracks, which they were told had been built by Napoleon.

The first troops of the American Expeditionary Force, under General John Pershing, had landed in France in June 1917 and been rushed to the front in time to repel a German attack at Château-Thierry. The winter of 1917–1918 had been relatively quiet, but by the spring of 1918, the Germans had decided the time for a final major effort to defeat France had arrived—before the full impact of American troops could be felt. On March 21, General Paul von Hindenburg, promising he would be in Paris by April 1, launched a massive offensive along a fifty-mile front. The Allies held, however, and by May 31, the Germans had penetrated only as far as Belleau Wood on the road to Paris, where they met the 4th U.S. Marine Brigade and were turned back in one of the bloodiest battles of the war.

The momentum of the war then shifted, as the Allies, under French Marshal Ferdinand Foch, launched a broad offensive along the western front. This drive was just getting under way as Cain's 79th Division landed at Brest. Then the Germans staged a major counterattack, which resulted in the critical Second Battle of the Marne.

On July 19, Cain's Headquarters Troop packed up to travel by train to Prauthoy, a village in the east of France. They arrived on July 27, set up Division Headquarters, and stayed at Prauthoy nearly six weeks as the Allies, after defeating the German counterattack at the Battle of the Marne, pushed forward in a broad, massive offensive all along the western front. On August 8, Canadian and Australian troops won a tremendous victory at Amiens, with the Canadians moving ahead 14,000 yards, one of the longest one-day advances in the whole grueling three years of trench warfare. By August 26, the Germans were retreating to the Hindenburg line and the stage was set for the last major allied offensive on the western front—the Meuse-Argonne campaign.

At Prauthoy, Cain and his troops slept in lofts above the stone barns, where, as the Headquarters Division *History* (written by Cain and Malcolm) put it: "the rats run races on moonlight nights." It was hard duty for the Headquarters men. Not only were they on the verge of going into battle, but the 79th was scattered over an area the size of a small American county, which meant that Cain and his buddies were spending hours taking messages back and forth on motorcycles, automobiles, and trucks.

But there was time to visit a few cafés in the towns around Prauthoy, and there Cain learned about French peasant girls. They were having lunch at one café where a young lady near their table was serving *poilus*. She was very pretty and causing a lot of excitement as the men slapped her bottom and explored other places. She took it all right, Cain thought, but did not seem especially flattered. Cain said: "Well, there she is, the immemorial symbol of France in war," and began to sing a French ditty.

The girl looked over and waved, and Malcolm said: "She heard you. Now you have a thing on your hands."

In a moment, the girl came over. "Alors?" she said.

Cain replied, "Allo, allo," a little nervously.

Then he learned "the secret of French country girls," which he described many years later: "As she waited for our order, something hit my nose indescribably horrible, a foul, unwashed smell so bad you could hardly believe it." Cain suddenly lost all interest in the flirtation, and Malcolm started to laugh. When the girl left, Malcolm said: "Well, you've just encountered one of the tragedies of the French nation. That girl has probably never had a bath in her life."

It was about this time that the Army solved what might be called the Great American Bunion Problem. Cain always maintained that the prevalence of so many corns on American feet was due to the fact that around the turn of the century America associated small feet with gentility, and to have small feet, one had to wear small shoes—as many people did, whether their feet would fit in them or not. The small, tight shoes produced a nation of corns, and comedians like Johnny Bunny (who had so repulsed Cain and his friend at the movies in Westminster) made a career mimicking the "chiropodists" who had to remove America's bunions.

As a result, sometime in 1918, the Army decided it marched on its feet, not its stomach, and the best way to avoid corns would be to put soldiers in shoes that fit, with room to spare. So, as they were getting ready to go to the front line, the supply sergeant handed Cain a new pair of shoes he could not believe. "Sergeant," said Cain, "I'm sorry to inform you that a pair of cockroaches could run a race, without bumping, between the sides of these shoes and my foot."

"O.K.," said the sergeant, "I'll take the gray, you take the black. I'll give you even money—what do you say to five dollars?"

"I say I want other shoes."

"You don't get them. You're taking these or standing a court."

"I don't like no court."

"Then—"

"I'm taking the shoes."

"Now you've got it," said the sergeant.

"They look more like beer kegs," muttered Cain.

"Something wrong with that?"

"Not that I know of."

Orders finally came sending Cain's outfit to the front, and on a rainy Sunday night, September 8, they marched to Vaux-sous-Aubigny and boarded a train, which left at 3:00 A.M.

The next afternoon at Revigny, the men labored in the rain unloading the Division Headquarters equipment, piling it in the middle of a big field. They were then ordered to sleep by the pile in the rain. Cain and Malcolm tried to bed down on the edge of a tarpaulin, and soon Captain Madeira came along and folded the tarp over them so they would keep dry. Then it stopped raining, and from the north every so often there would be orange flashes like heat lightning—the guns of the western front. Next to Cain, a trooper was weeping.

Three days later, the group joined the rest of the Headquarters outfit, which had set up camp at a place called Dugny, just south of Verdun. The 79th went into the lines on September 12, in Sector 304, west of Verdun, and held this sector for about two weeks, during which there was very little fighting.

When Cain arrived at the front, he was assigned duty in an observation post, and about that time he ran into a reporter he had known on the *Baltimore Sun*. He had not shaved for three weeks and was beginning to look like a wild man. The reporter suggested that a sure way to end the war would be for Cain simply to stick his head out of the trenches and "scare the Germans to death." Cain eventually shaved, but he did leave a mustache, which he wore until 1922.

The observation post was a sturdy wooden structure (which included an iron box men could crawl into when the shelling got heavy) built on top of "the tallest tree in France." Cain found the duty exciting. He could see the whole battlefield in all directions, and across the dreary brown field he would occasionally see a German. He came to know the terrain thoroughly, but the monotonous duty soon got to the others. One observer began to mumble about the desolate, bleak battlefield. "Ha, ha, ha. Listen!" he burst out on one occasion, then stopped and looked at Cain with a crazy light in his eye: "Listen, you know it's alive, and it breathes."

Cain said he never noticed, and the soldier said, "That's because you ain't got that two o'clock watch."

Cain insisted he was imagining things, that his trouble was lack of sleep, so he volunteered to stand the watch the next time.

That morning Cain took the 2:00 A.M. watch and was not up there very long when he knew what the soldier meant. It was eerie: all of a sudden, "I felt my lips go numb and my heart began pounding like it would jump out of my throat. I was just looking at my watch, and it was 3:28 and I was getting ready to make my 3:30 entry in the book, when I heard it, just like he said . . . it gave kind of a sigh and then went right quiet again."

Apart from its early morning breathing, the front remained quiet until the night of September 25, when the Allies began an artillery barrage in preparation for the Meuse-Argonne offensive. The next morning, at five-thirty, the attack began, and the 79th went into battle. The first target was Malancourt, which was captured on the afternoon of the twenty-sixth. Next came Montfaucon, which led to what Cain called "the nightmare of September 26," the worst six-hour experience of his life.

It was a time for heroes: At Montfaucon, Colonel George S. Patton, Jr., in command of a light tank brigade, abandoned his damaged tank and, leading a group of men, stormed a German machine gun nest with both ivory-handled .45s blazing. He was wounded and would receive the Distinguished Service Cross. Near Saint-Mihiel, Captain Harry S Truman would soon be cussing and swearing at a message to turn his artillery from northeast to northwest, before he broke up a German counterattack by firing his cannons directly into a host of Germans charging across an open field carrying machine guns strapped around their necks. On the first morning of the Meuse-Argonne offensive, Lieutenant Sidney Howard, an ex-ambulance driver turned bomber pilot, led a bombing attack against the Germans in one of seven de Havilland-4s, described by Howard as "the very worst airplane between the North Sea and the Swiss border." He survived to write two Pulitzer Prize–winning plays and most of the film script for *Gone With the Wind*.

Private First Class Cain also survived the night of September 26, and he too had a brief moment of heroism—though it did not end in glory. It all began quietly enough when Captain Madeira summoned Cain and another Headquarters Troop soldier named Shepler to his dugout and ordered them to go to General William Nicholson's Post of Command (P.C.) for the 157th Infantry Brigade, then report back. Nicholson's P.C. was about a thousand yards west along the same row of trenches, and the mission was to establish liaison with Nicholson so that 79th Headquarters could find his P.C. after nightfall. Cain and Shepler found General Nicholson—just as he was moving on to another position. So they followed the general and his party for about two hours, until he set up a new P.C.—marked by a piece of corrugated iron in the middle of a road. Fortunately Cain had some idea where they were because of his weeks in the observation tower.

Cain and Shepler finally found their way back to Division HQ, where General Kuhn congratulated them and said he was glad to see them because Nicholson had again broken liaison and he had an order for him: "Attack Montfaucon and take it."

Kuhn wanted to know if they could find their way back to Nicholson's P.C. and Shepler said no, but Cain said he could. So they issued him the best horse they had and he set off to again find General Nicholson. He finally made his way back to the piece of corrugated iron in the road, where he had last seen General Nicholson's P.C., only to discover that the 157th had moved on. Cain began wandering around the battlefield in the dark with everyone he talked to giving him smart answers when he asked for the location of the 157th P.C. "I swear, Bud, I wouldn't know about that—somewhere around, I bet." It turned out that GHQ had passed an order down, before the offensive began, that no one at the front should answer any questions about unit locations because they might be talking with a spy.

Cain suddenly felt like he was in a madhouse. He stumbled around until dawn trying to find General Nicholson, then admitted defeat and went slinking back to his own HQ. Reporting to General Kuhn that his message was still undelivered, Cain felt himself "shriveling to nothingness" with the look the general gave him. Then, suddenly, who should come striding up but General Nicholson.

"Where have you been?" bellowed General Kuhn. "And what do you mean, breaking liaison that way?"

"Been?" answered General Nicholson, bellowing even louder. "I've been taking that hill, that's where I've been—I moved on Montfaucon and took it! And what do you mean, 'breaking liaison'? Two of your own couriers knew where I was—and I posted guides for them, every foot of the way."

Cain was miserable. It turned out the general had, indeed, posted guides, but no one had told Cain. Moreover no one had told the guides, who were new men, of the new position to which the 157th had moved; they did not themselves know where the P.C. was.

Cain stood there for some moments while the generals cussed at each other, then Captain Madeira whispered: "It's been one hell of a night." Cain saluted in the generals' direction, then withdrew. The captain stayed with him and tried to console him: "You did your best to carry out orders, and if you didn't succeed, it wasn't at all your fault. Relax. Better luck next time."

The Headquarters Troop stayed around Haucourt for a few days. Then, on September 30, the day Bulgaria surrendered, the 79th was temporarily relieved by the 3rd Division and pulled out of the line. Cain and his troop moved back to Jouey-en-Argonne, and as they sloshed through the mud a plane flew over and dropped newspapers on the column. They were copies of *Echo de Paris*, which were quickly brought to Cain by some soldiers who knew he read French. After translating the story proclaiming Bulgaria's request for an armistice, Cain shouted: "Hey, this things's almost over. We're in sight of the end!"

But a soldier named Bryan interrupted to say, "Us and who else? Read what it says—and leave out all them damned yelps." But the other soldiers wanted to hear more of Cain's theorizing about the possible end of the war, and when Bryan continued to interrupt, one of them said: "Why don't you shut his mouth for him, Cain? Tell him to say it with money. Tell him why don't he bet?"

Bryan took up the challenge and said if Cain knew so much why didn't he name the date and back it up with some money. Cain said O.K., and picked December 1 for 10 francs. By the time his troop had reached Jouey-en-Argonne for a few days of rest and rehabilitation, Cain was the primary subject of conversation as the first man to see the end.

After a few days, the 79th went back in the line and HQ was moved to Thillambois. On October 8, it was advanced to Troyon-sur-Meuse and was charged with holding the Troyon Sector, which it did for three weeks. The front was relatively quiet now, with rumors of German surrender beginning to filter in regularly. On the twenty-sixth, the P.C. was moved to Dieue-sur-Meuse, then, three days later, to Vacherauville on the Meuse River. At Vacherauville, Cain and his troop came under heavy artillery fire, but he remained confident that the end was near. On October 30, in a dugout at Dugny just south of Verdun where rear-echelon headquarters were set up, Cain got in another argument about the end of the war and bet 10 francs it would be over by noon on November 10. The shelling continued, along with gas attacks, which sent Captain Madeira, Bryan (the soldier with whom Cain had made his first bet), and about twenty other men off to the hospital, blinded, many permanently, by mustard gas. Although exposed to the gas, which would later cause him serious problems, Cain escaped blindness by finding for what he described as his "extra-big face" an extra-large mask, which he kept on for two hours during the attack. A few days later, Headquarters was moved to a dugout at Moleville Farm that had just been evacuated by the Germans.

They were at Moleville Farm the morning of November 11, and everyone knew something was up. All eyes were on the Division P.C., where General Kuhn and his men were assembled. An announcement was expected momentarily. It was a sunny, mild autumn day. Contrary to legend, the guns on the front were not firing. All was deathly still, although once, in the distance, there was a burst of machine gun fire, which Cain would later find signaled tragedy for one of the men in his division. (A few days before, Supply Sergeant Henry Gunther had been busted to private. Determined to show he was a good soldier so he could win back his stripes, he set out on the morning of November 11 to take a German machine gun position, despite the efforts of the men in his company, who begged him to stay in the trench.

Everyone knew the war would be over soon. But Private Gunther persisted even though the Germans were also shouting at him not to advance. He kept coming until the Germans fired their machine guns. Private Gunther died at one minute of eleven, having convinced everyone in his company and the division he was a good soldier.)

The men were glancing simultaneously at their watches and the group of officers clustered in front of the P.C. At eleven o'clock on November 11, General Kuhn stepped forward, looked at his watch, nodded, and turned around and walked back into his dugout.

The war was over.

A few minutes later, Cain was standing in a chow line where he gladly paid off his second 10-franc bet, which he had missed by twenty-three hours. The other bet—for the war to be over by December 10—could not be paid because Bryan was still in the hospital.

Despite the legends about the wild celebration at the front on the night of November 11, 1918, it was very quiet at Moleville Farm. For one thing, it rained; for another, the cynical doughboys did not believe the war was over: "Just one more Headquarters rumor." Mostly, the soldiers simply sat on their packs and argued, recalling Cain's bet and claiming it could not be true.

The next night, however, was different. On the morning after the Armistice, Cain was included in a contingent sent to Thionville to clean up a German P.C. General Kuhn was scheduled to use. The German headquarters were on a high bluff looking down on the pastoral valley of the Moselle, still green in the daytime despite the constant shelling. Knowing that Corporal Friebel, in charge of the detail, was a slave to his stomach, Cain approached the corporal and said, "Friebel, my lofty intellectual soul is revolted by the idea of shovel and broom, so why don't we do this: I, in return for being excused from such labor, will hustle myself out and by dint of larcenous skill get possession of flour, syrup, lard, all the makings of first-class flapjacks, be back by mess time, and then we'll have ourselves something to eat. How about that?"

Friebel was reluctant, but the troop had not had a good meal for days and a lot of the men were in favor of Cain's offer. So Friebel put the matter to a vote, and it was agreed that if Cain would come back with the goods, all would be well and they would do his work for him; if he failed, Cain would be lynched.

Cain accepted the directive and went down into the Moselle valley with a big empty gunnysack, playing on the sympathy of mess sergeants, explaining that his outfit had really been in the thick of things and had not eaten a good meal in weeks, which was mostly true. He filched flour from one regiment, syrup from another, lard from another. He also begged bacon, cookies and cakes, preserves, condensed milk, and, most important, a huge can of George Washington Coffee.

He returned to Thionville around 3:00 P.M. and spent the rest of the afternoon loafing and telling the men what a fine job they were doing cleaning up after the Germans, and laughing when they yelled, "Go to hell, Cain!"

But he had delivered the goods, and that night Friebel cooked the flapjacks, carved the bacon, and made the coffee—"extra strong," as everyone agreed they were sick of the dishwater they had been drinking for six months. But what no one realized was that the coffee mix was almost pure caffeine and when made extra strong became a near-lethal stimulant. Loaded with sugar cubes and colored with condensed milk, its strength was camouflaged, but as Cain said, they were drinking "instant dope." As a result, shortly after dinner, they were all "higher than a kite," dancing around the edge of the bluff while down in the valley the infantry regiments that had provided the food, now reinforced by their band instruments which had been trucked up from the rear echelons, were beginning the real Armistice celebration. All over the valley in the bright moonlight, the bands were striking up, the men were singing "Lil Liza Jane," "K-K-K-Katy," "Mademoiselle from Armentières," "Over There," "There's a Long, Long Trail A-Winding," and pistols were popping everywhere, shooting off the red, green, and white "star shells" used by the Army as signal flares. And high on the bluff, overlooking the valley, were a dozen idiots dancing and singing along with the troops below, drunk with caffeine and joy.

Now, the war was officially over.

After the Armistice, the beautiful autumn faded into the French winter, which to Cain "always looked like eight o'clock in the morning or four in the afternoon." Soon the year would be over—and another Christmas away from home would be on them. The company mess sergeant spread the word that the mess fund "is over $3,000—so there'll be plenty to give the boys at Christmas," but one of the captains was enraged when he heard this because the "boys who died at Montfaucon" had not had the benefit of this money. So, again, it was to be "scum," as Cain called it, for Christmas. The day came, and Cain was sitting on a wall of the bridge at Dugny, eating, when a soldier carrying his mess kit with his Christmas dinner came up to him. It was Bryan, who had bet him 10 francs that the war would not be over by December 1. He said glumly: "Hello, Cain. I wondered if you'd be here. I've made you goddamn famous."

"Yeah," said Cain. "If you have, how?"

"You know how. Spreading it, what you said—the bet we made that day. I've been telling the guys in the hospital. They all know who you are."

"What hospital they have you in?" Cain asked.

"Would I know? Does it make any difference which one? Some god-damn place—Souilly, I guess it was. For six weeks I couldn't see. Today they sent me back. I think they're shipping me out."

"Some people are born lucky," said Cain.

"Listen, Cain, is it true?" Bryan asked.

"Is what true?"

"Is the war over or not?"

"Don't tell me you didn't hear," said Cain.

"If I did, would I be asking? In the hospital with your eyes bandaged up, you don't see nothing, and they got no time to tell you. They put your plate on your belly and run, and sometimes they empty your pot. And that's all. I asked you . . ."

"Yes, of course, it's over," said Cain.

But that was not enough for Bryan. He wanted to know how it happened, and what the fellows did after the Armistice, and every last detail about the end of the war. Cain told him—especially about that night overlooking the Moselle valley when they shot off the star shells and all the bands were play-ing and the troops were singing.

"What songs they play?" asked Bryan.

"Oh, you know, 'Over There,' 'K-K-K-Katy,' 'I'm All Bound Round,' same old ones. On 'Long, Long Trail' the guys all joined in."

"I would have," said Bryan. "I love that song. Cain—you know 'Land of My Dreams'? I know that one by heart. So they played that stuff. What did they do then?"

"They blew taps."

"Yeah, they would."

Bryan closed his mess kit, stood up ready to go, and then said: "I got to see him before he goes back."

Cain did not know what Bryan was talking about and looked blank. "That driver," Bryan explained, "so he can tell them, when he goes back, them other guys in the hospital, what you just told me—they'll know if you said it's so. I told you you're famous down there. I'll give you the ten francs if my pay ever catches up—it's been chasing me around. And thanks, Cain—you've made my Christmas."

Cain never saw Bryan again.

After orders for the 79th to take part in the occupation of Germany were countermanded, the troop set up headquarters in Souilly. And the rumors began: The 79th would be in France a year; it would return "next month"; it was nineteenth on the list to go home; then it moved up nine slots, or back seven. Boredom was now the enemy, and guard duty—two hours on and six off—began to frazzle Cain's nerves because he could never get a full eight hours sleep. "By New Year's I was in a psychosis, where things would get big and get small and I would imagine them burning down." Arrowsmith, in the novel by Sinclair Lewis, had this same problem, and later, in the 1920s, Lewis was fascinated when Cain told him of his own feeling.

Early in 1919, the Division heard it would be in France until June, although this was eventually changed to May. Now the problem was what to do for six months. Athletics were encouraged; entertainment groups were brought in; soldiers were given passes to visit the larger cities. Plays were staged, motion pictures shown, and the Division Headquarters troop started a newspaper called *The Lorraine Cross*, edited by Sergeant Harry F. Hossack and Private Gilbert Malcolm. The first issue came out February 6, 1919.

For Cain and most of the troops, the real challenge was to dream up jobs that would relieve one of guard duty. Around mid-January 1919, Cain had himself assigned as an assistant to the Division historian, and that worked fine for a couple of weeks until the historian was transferred to Germany. Then Cain was back in the ranks. He committed some offense, the details of which are lost to posterity, which put him on K.P. One morning after he had been peeling potatoes for a few days, the orderly assigned to waking him up before the other troops gave his shoulder a shake and said: "You don't have to get up, if you don't want to. You've been put on special duty. You're editor of the paper now. You and Malcolm are posted. It's up on the board already."

So Cain slept until 9:00 A.M., when he was summoned by Captain Madeira and given the details of his new assignment. Cain blandly told the captain: "I can't do it. I'm on K.P."

"It will keep," said Madeira.

"I'm sure it will," said Cain, saluting and leaving the room.

Checking the bulletin board, Cain found that his title on the paper was Editor in Chief; Malcolm was Sporting Editor.

The first few issues of *The Lorraine Cross* had been put out by Sergeant Hossack on a foot press. Measuring 6 by 9, it was an unattractive little sheet that embarrassed the Headquarters brass. They wanted something better— an order which was passed on to Colonel James Steinman, officer in charge of troop morale. In civilian life Steinman owned the *Lancaster* (Pennsylvania) *Intelligencer* and had heard of Cain and his experience on the *Sun*. He thought he might be just the man to put some life into the *Cross*.

The first thing Cain and Malcolm did was stop the foot press, tear up the next edition of the paper, and completely redesign it. They knew the troops wanted a big, snappy sheet, one that would remind them of their paper back home. And Cain understood how important the paper was to morale. "All a soldier gets out of war is glory," he said, "but he's damned particular about that . . . and a paper is the only way he can get it. When some rival outfit says they took the bridge, it's the paper which pins back their ears. When a boy wants his family to know what he did in the war, he sends home the paper with the write-up in it."

Cain and Malcolm redesigned the paper with a large format, sharp type, and a clean, attractive layout. But first there were the nitty-gritty problems of type, printing, and paper—and money. The money problem was solved on Cain's first morning as editor in chief, when a gangling, drawling boy by the name of Donald Cronin came into Cain's office. Cronin said he was tired of K.P. and infantry duty and wanted to be circulation manager on the paper. They chatted a bit, and it developed Cronin was from Baltimore and knew a little about Cain's father and that Cain had once worked on the *Baltimore Sun*. Cain asked Cronin how he would go about selling subscriptions. Cronin replied: "Cain, I don't see any trouble in getting you guys some money. I figure it's a company clerk proposition—give each clerk a free subscription and they'll do the rest for you—collect the money, distribute it and everything. So what I want to do is circulate myself around, see those boys, and try to come up with some cash."

Cain liked the idea and he liked Cronin, so he said: "O.K., you're hired. Dust off to the clerks and try to bring back some money." Cronin disappeared for three days, and when he reappeared in Cain's office he had 15,000 francs (at that time the franc was traded five to the dollar). *The Lorraine Cross* was published weekly, and its subscription price was one franc a month. But Cain and Malcolm would not accept more than three francs from any one soldier because they were not sure how long it would be before the 79th was ordered home.

With a new, interesting job and money to put out the kind of paper he wanted, things were looking up for Cain. But his excitement and enthusiasm were suddenly crushed by a telegram he received late in February.

Cain's brother Boydie was, at that time, the only member of his family he felt close to. Boydie had joined the Marines after his graduation from Washington College in 1918. He was a pilot and took his training at M.I.T. in Boston and later in Florida. Boydie and Cain had written letters to each other in the style of Ring Lardner, who by then was one of the most popular, and imitated, writers in America. Lardner was then writing his "In the Wake of the News" column for the *Chicago Tribune*, but since 1914 his short stories about a fictional baseball player named Jack Keefe had been appearing in the *Saturday Evening Post*, and they had been collected in a book, *You Know Me, Al*, published in 1916. Another collection, *Treat 'Em Rough*, about Keefe's experiences as an Army recruit at Camp Grant, Illinois, was published in 1918. Cain would write Boydie about life in the trenches in the colloquial, folksy style of Keefe, and Boydie would use the same Lardnerisms in his writing about life in the barracks. Cain later said that his letters to Boydie were the "only time I consciously ever imitated anybody," and that of all the people thought to have influenced his writing the one who probably had the greatest impact was Ring Lardner, although most of the critics persisted in naming Hemingway as Cain's stylistic mentor. Reading Cain's early contributions to the *American Mercury*, there can be little doubt he was speaking the truth.

After the war, Boydie was stationed at the Marine airfield in Miami, Florida. On February 15, the last day of his service, he went up on a needless flight and was killed when he fell out of his plane.

Cain was stunned and heartbroken when he received the news. Two men helped see him through: Gilbert Malcolm and Sergeant Troy Biddle sat with Cain for hours on a bench in front of the stove in the Quartermaster Depot, letting him talk when he wanted to talk, saying nothing when he just wanted to sit and stare and sob.

Fortunately, Cain had the paper, and there is nothing like deadlines to take one's mind off a personal tragedy. Now that they had money to operate, Malcolm suggested moving the printing operation to Bar-le-Duc. On their first expedition there, they found a good press, plenty of room, and a supply of type. But they needed printers; so after a search of division files for soldiers who had had printing or typesetting experience, Cain persuaded Colonel Steinman to transfer ten men to the paper. The enticement was special duty, which guaranteed at least one trip to Paris to bring back the cuts for the artwork, with fare paid by the paper.

Cain and Malcolm split up the operation, with Malcolm running the print shop in Bar-le-Duc and Cain the editorial office in Souilly. The paper had a few signed contributions by "outsiders," some poems, usually contributed under pseudonyms, and cartoons drawn by Lieutenant William Shuster. Cain wrote almost all the unsigned copy, and the paper's general tone was bright, sharp, and often sardonic. Its weather forecast, which did not vary for six weeks, ran: "By wireless from the Bureau of Météorologique, Paris: *Pour la semaine prochaine, il pleura*. Translation: Next week, rain."

Derision—especially of anything French—was very popular, and a favorite target were the cooties, which had almost as much space in *The Lor-*

raine Cross as news about returning to the states. The paper's poetry included an occasional Cain contribution:

L'Envoi
This talk of Mother's cooking
    Is very fine, I grant,
But there is just one other thing
    I want to have and can't.

It's Childs' golden wheat-cakes
    I long to taste anew,
Those dear old standard wheat-cakes
    All plastered up with goo.

Sergeant Alexander Woollcott, who worked for the *Stars and Stripes*, called *The Lorraine Cross* "a snappy young journal" and praised it for putting out probably the first American "Extra" ever printed in France. This was on the occasion of a move by the Division from one encampment to another, when the Division was nearly hysterical with rumors about returning to the States. *The Lorraine Cross* came out with its first and only Extra giving the latest, up-to-the-minute "when-do-we-go-home," news. It was distributed to the troops while they were on the march, a feat that impressed everyone, including Woollcott.

The printshop was running smoothly and would have been doing even better without Lieutenant Frank Gale, a G-2 officer put in charge of the paper. Cain had worked briefly for Gale as assistant historian and considered him a "complete bust," even though Gale had been a New York newspaperman. Cain felt the paper did not need Gale; rather Gale needed the paper as a pretense for having something important to do, and to get away from his infantry outfit and into Bar-le-Duc, where the printshop was located along with the bright lights, fine liquors, and women.

Not only did Gale insist on contributing a column each week under the pseudonym "Pernicious Pete," he also took to meddling with the typography. Cain and Malcolm had worked out a complex type scheme designed to produce the best-looking paper possible with the type available. Gale kept interfering with ideas of his own, wanting to mix type heads that did not work together. This infuriated Cain. But Malcolm, the calmer head, worked out his own solution. The next time Cain was in Bar-le-Duc, Malcolm took him for a walk and said: "Well, Gale at last made up his mind which type we should use for display heads. It wouldn't interchange, but it is pretty type, I admit. But as luck would have it, when we were all set to go, I happened to check the font, and what do you know? In the damned frog typecase of that style there aren't any *L*s. He was pretty upset, but I imagine that winds it up, his notions that he is going to revamp our makeup."

As they walked along to the Hotel de Metz et Commerce, where they ate lunch when Cain was in Bar-le-Duc, Malcolm casually reached in his pocket and came out with a handful of type. "Now," he asked, looking down in surprise, "where did all those *L*s come from?" Then he gave his high, cackling laugh.

But Gale continued to pester them, and finally Cain had had enough. One day he called on Colonel Steinman, and with "100 percent guile" told the colonel that he and Malcolm were concerned about the boys getting jobs when they returned to the states. Nobody was doing anything about it, said Cain, so some sort of campaign should be started in the states to wake up employers to the fact that veterans were going to need jobs. Cain recited his speech in a manner to suggest that he was pushing himself as one to go home early to start the campaign. Finally, the colonel, with just the right tilt of his eyebrow, said: "And just whom did you have in mind? Which qualified newspaperman, as you say he ought to be, should be ordered home to get this campaign started?"

With as much bland innocence as he could muster, Cain said: "We thought it should be Lieutenant Gale."

The look on the colonel's face changed abruptly. He studied Cain for a few minutes, during which time Cain was certain Steinman figured out what he was up to. Finally, he said briskly: "It—sounds like a good idea. I'll think it over and let you know."

The next day, Cain went back to Bar-le-Duc and met Malcolm running out of the printshop, very excited. "Jim, what do you think? Gale's gone. He left last night for the U.S. on some crazy job campaign they've thought up."

"Yeah?" said Cain, "Well, what do you know."

Then he told Malcolm how it had all come about, and Malcolm brimmed with admiration. Cain was delighted that he had finally shown Malcolm he could be canny, too, and was capable of something other than correcting his grammar.

Cain, in fact, was developing into an operator. To save his limited funds for more critical needs, such as buying the printers dinner when they worked overtime, he literally stole the newsprint needed for the paper. It was paper captured from the Germans, so he did not feel guilty about it. To get it he simply walked into depots where it was being stored and took it, using orders forged with the connivance of the Headquarters supply sergeant and other high-handed devices. He also had to have trucks to haul the paper, and these, too, were obtained with forged orders.

The time from February to the end of April went quickly. By early May, the 79th Division was preparing to return to the States and *The Lorraine Cross* was discontinued. Cain and Malcolm were taken off special duty and put back in the ranks, and almost immediately Cain was put on K.P., with Malcolm expected to follow soon. The primary reason for this fall from grace, Cain figured, was jealousy. Their jobs as editors of the paper had bestowed unusual power on the two enlisted men—the power to put names in the paper in dispatches sent home and to back various causes. An American Legion had been formed and it was eager for publicity. There was a continual parade of officers and other big shots to Cain's office in Souilly and Gilbert's in Bar-le-Duc, all of which did not go unnoticed by the rest of the men. As a result, the two privates had become somewhat arrogant in their new jobs. At one point, Malcolm even defied an effort by Captain Madeira to wake them at 8:00 A.M. "Oh, no, Captain, we don't get up that early," said Malcolm, and got away with it.

Still, it was conceded by everyone that they had done a remarkable job with the paper, maintaining professional editorial standards and a high degree of interest among the troops. And their work was acknowledged in a letter of commendation from headquarters.

Cain always felt the paper played an important role in his development as a writer, giving him additional exercise in the rhetoric he had studied so hard when he was teaching English at Washington College. Later, after he came home, his mother gathered up a few pages from *The Lorraine Cross* and had them framed as a Christmas present. Cain hung them on his wall with some pride, and then one day a few years later, he noticed and was taken by the syntax in one of the items written by him. It corresponded, he realized, with the literary mannerisms of H. L. Mencken, whom by then Cain admired and whose style he suspected himself of aping. But in 1919, when he was writing *The Lorraine Cross*, he had never read one word written by Mencken. He had heard of Mencken before he went overseas, of course, but had paid no attention to him, assuming he was just "a hick celebrity of the kind Baltimore produced," and had not read his column or opened his books. But this similarity he noted later in Mencken's writing convinced him that Mencken's basic thinking about language, as incorporated in his *The American Language* (first published in 1919), had been acquired from the same rhetoric books Cain had read and been influenced by. Cain later tried to force Mencken to concede the debt, but Mencken, who derided theoretical rhetoricians, refused. Whenever Cain would bring up the subject, Mencken would acknowledge a debt to Thomas Henry Huxley and one or two newspaper writers of his youth, but that was all.

With the paper discontinued, Cain peeling potatoes, and Malcolm about to, it was time for another special duty assignment, and it didn't take the canny Scot long to come up with one. Why not, suggested Malcolm, have themselves appointed Division press agents or publicity directors?

So once more, Cain reported to Colonel Steinman and outlined the suggestion. But before he was able to finish, the colonel interrupted to say that he'd had the same idea. Apparently, the colonel's own paper had sent him some clips of items Cain had sent home. The colonel had the orders drawn up, and Cain and Malcolm were put on special duty as the Division's publicity officers "until further notice"—which, Malcolm said, "is damn well going to take us onto shipboard and right to the discharge depot."

And it did. They began immediately to write a flurry of stories for the press—how the general was awarded the Legion of Honor; which awards and citations were given which infantry units and individual soldiers; human interest stories about incidents that had happened to various men in the trenches (very popular in the hometown papers). They also published a little brochure about the history of the Lorraine Cross, which was distributed to the men of the 79th going home. The brochure was written by a French scholar they found in Paris, "an incredible habitué of the libraries," Cain said, "tattered and living in such a tiny dump as had to be seen to be believed, though he had an indubitable degree from the Sorbonne." The dedicated scholar was persuaded for 1,500 francs (left over from their subscription funds) to write a monograph on the Lorraine Cross, which Cain and Malcolm translated and printed. By now the division headquarters had been established in Reze le Mante, a trip of about an hour and fifteen minutes from the embarkation center at St.-Nazaire. When the first box of brochures was ready for one of the departing troop ships, Cain and Malcolm set out to drive to St.-Nazaire, arriving just in time to deliver their Lorraine Cross brochures in a bucket up to the deck of a soon-to-depart transport.

Then came the big day: on May 15 the headquarters troop reported to St.-Nazaire for a physical examination and delousing, in preparation for sailing home, and on May 18 they boarded the S.S. *Kroonland* for an eleven-day return trip to America. Aboard the ship, Cain and Malcolm continued to grind out their publicity stories about the 79th and its exploits, but instead of sending them home by radio they devised a system of "spiking" their stories on a large spindle, where they accumulated and were picked up by reporters when they landed in Hoboken on May 29.

In the few remaining days they had in the Army, Cain and Malcolm had to account for some 300 francs ($60) left over from all the money Private

Cronin had raised in his subscription drive. To get rid of it (without having to go through the horrendous bureaucratic nightmare of trying actually to return it to the government), they suggested that it would be a good idea to take some reporters to lunch, a gesture that would help ensure the 79th of getting a good press when it returned from the war. This was agreed to. But on their last day in the Army—June 5, 1919—Cain still had $8 of the paper's money. So he and Malcolm decided to entertain one more reporter, from the *New York Times*. The lunch was successful, as they were able to set up a big story in the *Times* about the return of the 79th, a story actually written by Cain. But this one final bit of lunchtime flackery was the last straw for the men who had become jealous of Cain's and Malcolm's ability to make life a little better for themselves. When Cain and Malcolm arrived at the discharge center at ten minutes of two, they found that the discharge time had been moved up from 2:00 to 12:30 P.M. and their buddies had been waiting for more than an hour in the hot sun. None of the men could be dismissed until the entire company—including Cain and Malcolm—was present or accounted for. A half dozen of them charged up to the two publicity agents, screaming with rage, and Sergeant Elverson shook his fist under their noses.

"Go to hell," said Malcolm, with his high cackling laugh.

PART
TWO

BALTIMORE,
NEW YORK

1920 – 1931

4

"TREASON" DID NOT
A NOVEL MAKE

When Cain returned from France in June 1919, America was in a historic transition, although very few people were aware of it at the time. The post–Civil War Gilded Age of America, dominated by a coalition of industrial tycoons (soon to be labeled "robber barons"), politicians, and the Church, was rapidly coming to an end. But the new era—the roaring, booming 1920s, which would produce a revolution in manners, morals, and customs, a literary explosion, and a frenzied economic expansion—had not yet been born. The country, having dispensed with the German menace, was concerned with another enemy: the Bolsheviks. The American businessman, swaggering a little now that we had "won the war" in Europe, and impatient to get on with the business of America, unhampered by interference from either government or labor, said, in effect: "We've licked the Germans and we're going to lick these damned Bolsheviks." Licking them was one thing, finding them another.

Far more real and disruptive than the radicals was the impact of two million doughboys returning from Europe. Not only had they witnessed death and destruction, they had seen Paree, met thousands of mademoiselles from Armentières, and some, even, had learned to speak French, or at least thought they had. Cain himself had forewarned Baltimoreans of what to expect when this horde of cynical, savvy men came home. In a letter published in the *Sun*, he predicted the country would soon be inundated with "the queerest lot of stuff you ever heard, that is going to take America by the ears and become the slang of the day from its sheer expressiveness and drollery. Most of it is going to be French, the awfullest, twisted, most mispronounced and mutilated French you ever heard. . . ."

Having served with distinction in France, Cain would, on occasion, describe himself as a "combat newspaperman" who had spent time in the trenches where "the bullets were really flying." Actually, the war for Cain had not been the traumatic, disillusioning experience it was for many young men. He had had one unnerving experience during the taking of Montfaucon, but it ended in self-humiliation rather than tragedy or horror. Cain never killed a man, suffered a wound, or came into close combat with enemy troops, although he did experience heavy artillery fire and at least one gas attack. And there is no suggestion in his later writing or conversations that the war left any deep psychological scars.

Still, judging from the unsettled life he led in the postwar years, the war had its impact. And it is probably significant that, except for one article for the *American Mercury* about his experience that night in the Argonne forest, he never wrote about the war. Like many ex-soldiers, he came home a man. He was twenty-eight, tall, bearish-looking, with a rough complexion, black bushy hair, heavy eyebrows, and a mustache. And by now he had fully developed the characteristic that would mark him for the rest of his life: the habit of assuming tough, salty talk, sometimes out of the side of his mouth (despite his ability to speak perfect grammar when he was upset or wanted to impress someone, as when job hunting). Underneath this outward roughness, which most of his acquaintances saw through, was a gentle, sensitive man who loved music, wanted to write, and nursed a vague, as yet unfocused ambition for a career in the theater as either a playwright or a producer. But, for now, he took his old job back with the *Sun*, which gave the returning hero a $7 raise to $30 a week.

Cain's parents had settled in Catonsville, a suburb southwest of Baltimore, and he went to live with them. His father was doing well with U.S. Fidelity and Guaranty Company, having just been made a vice-president. His talent for convincing people, especially legislators, of the merit of his organization's point of view was serving him even better in the insurance business than it had in academia.

When Cain sailed for France in 1918, he was, in his words, "pledged" to marry Mary Clough. Now that he had a steady job and was making a respectable salary, he was in a position to honor his pledge, especially since Mary was teaching and would be able to contribute to the family income. But

Cain had changed his mind. He did not want to marry her. What caused him to back away is not clear. There is no evidence of a serious or amorous affair in France, but it can be assumed that by now he had had enough physical relationships with women to know what was missing with Mary.

Not long after his discharge, Cain wrote Mary, breaking off their engagement, and she quickly let him know he was not going to get away that easily. She came up to Baltimore from Church Hill and called him in the suburb of Catonsville where he was living with his parents. She said she wanted to talk to him. Cain stalled but agreed to come to Church Hill. When he hung up the hallway phone, he heard a noise at the top of the stairs and looked up to see his sister Virginia standing there. She had been in bed with "one of the spells she was subject to," as Cain put it, had heard the phone conversation, and obviously was upset. She knew Mary better than Cain did, having worked with her when they both taught school in Federalsburg, a little town on the Eastern Shore. Virginia respected Mary's intellect, but had some reservations about her as a sister-in-law. "Jamie," she said in a terrible voice, "you're not going! You're not going down there! Because if you go you're doomed—she'll weep and wail and take off her clothes or whatever she has to do to make you go through with what you said you would do, and— *you're not going! You're not going!*"

Cain did go, and whether Mary took off her clothes and wept or wailed is not known. But whatever she did, it was successful. Cain agreed to go through with the marriage; and on January 17, 1920, with members of both families and a few friends at the ceremony, James and Mary were married in the Church of the Ascension, in Baltimore.

After a brief honeymoon they settled into an apartment on Linden Avenue in Baltimore and a life that gave neither of them much except grief and tension. It was an "ill-starred venture," said Cain, "one that started badly and kept going downhill with no ups of any kind." But for a while neither noticed how unsuited they were, as Mary went on with her teaching and Cain became involved in his job with the *Baltimore Sun*.

His first assignment, after reporting back to work, was on the copy desk. The desk at the *Sun* consisted of six to eight copy editors who sat around a huge horseshoe-shaped table known as the "rim." In the center was the "slot man," the chief copy editor. As the stories came in off the teletype or were turned in by reporters to the slot man's basket, he would pass the copy to the men on the rim for editing. As junior man in this operation, Cain was given the "state" copy, most of which was mailed in from correspondents in Maryland, Virginia, West Virginia, and Delaware. The state news usually appeared only in the "bulldog edition," the paper that came out between 10:00 P.M. and midnight. In the morning edition, all but the most important state stories were replaced by news items from Baltimore. The majority of state stories were short, dealing with personal items—births, deaths, and marriages. The usual way of handling them was to condense them into a column called something like "Brief Jottings from Out of Town."

Cain thought this was a perfunctory way of treating out-of-town subscribers, so he began dressing up his pages by putting separate heads on the various items. He also had postcards printed, saying: "Please send us your picture, for use in connection with _____," which were sent to people due for mention in future stories. Ninety percent responded, and suddenly the state pages were being promoted by the paper in its circulation drive, with Cain receiving attention as state editor and compliments from the management.

One veteran of the *Sun* city room, John Ward, remembers Cain as a tall, rugged man, pleasant and quiet but very forceful. He was, by far, "the most intelligent man on the rim," and his superiority as an editor and talent as a writer (he would soon be writing by-line articles) were generally recognized. Others remember him as a dour young man who seemed quite bitter, tabbed as "old sourpuss" by veterans of the *Sun* newsroom.

It did not take long for Cain to realize that "correcting moth-eaten grammar" and tracking down stories in the hinterlands were not for him. One incident typified the frustrations that went with the job. A woman's body was found in a thicket out in Walbrook, a little town southwest of Baltimore. Her throat had been cut and there was no clue to her identity except a scrap of newspaper from the *Fairmont* (West Virginia) *Times* tucked in her hat lining. Cain wired the *Sun*'s Fairmont correspondent, a woman, for a dispatch covering whatever was known in West Virginia. He waited and waited, but no story from Fairmont came. Finally, he recalled, "I had to send my pages in without any Fairmont dispatch. But, next morning, the [*Baltimore*] *American* came out with a front-page story—it didn't contain any information, any identification at all, as to who the woman was, but did let us know that Fairmont was agog, for half a column or more." It seems the *Sun* correspondent had filed her story, but in the Baltimore office of the telegraph company the girl made a mistake and the dispatch meant for the *Sun* had been received by the *American*.

Cain's excuse, obviously a good one, did not pacify his boss. All he saw was that Cain had had an exclusive scored against him by the opposition. So now Cain had to do something, and the only way he could top it was to identify the woman, which he proceeded to do. He had the West Virginia correspondent who worked on the *Fairmont Times* wire him the names of subscribers living in Baltimore, whom he began to call. "I told these people I wanted to ask them one or two questions about this case we're working on, and as we heard you used to live there, and so on, very vague, very easy, very friendly—then stopping and listening for the reaction I'd get. In four or five tries I got nothing. But then, suddenly, from a man, I got guarded silence and knew I'd hit pay dirt. He admitted, when I pressed him, that from what had come out in the paper he thought he might know who the woman was, and I finally got out of him that he would be glad to go with me to the morgue and have a look at her. So I picked him up, rode him down, and brought him in to look. She wasn't pretty when the sheet was lifted by the attendant, but one look was all my man needed. He gave me her name, then, and occupation: Prostitute." Cain filed his story but received little credit for either his ingenuity or his investigative reporting.

His frustrations were not helped any when, one day late in 1920, Gilbert Malcolm, now a stockbroker in Harrisburg, Pennsylvania, showed up in Baltimore driving a Stutz Bearcat, wearing a derby, grinning, and spending money as if he had never heard of Scottish frugality. All this amused Cain's family but not Cain, who had no bankroll, no derby, no Stutz. All he had was a new suit. And at $30 a week, he could not even afford one of those hideous Model-T Fords that were becoming so popular. Malcolm was obviously selling a lot of stock.

It was hard to make this kind of money in journalism, unless you became a public relations flack for industry. And Cain had the opportunities. One man he came to know quite well was William M. Stanton, president of the Baltimore Steamship Company. Stanton was promoting Puerto Rico, which he hoped more people would visit—on his steamships. The governor of Puerto Rico, a Republican appointee named E. Mont Riley, was very critical of Stanton. Knowing Cain as a tough, describe-him-like-he-is reporter, Stanton urged Cain to go down to Puerto Rico and do some pieces about Riley. For a young writer who was making very little money, while his friends seemed to be rolling in it, the offer was tempting: a paid vacation, red-carpet treatment with the tab picked up by the steamship company. But Cain told Stanton he could not do it. "Maybe he thinks there's nothing to conceal about Puerto Rico, but when I get down there I may not see it the way he sees it at all," Cain thought to himself. "And I wouldn't be free to write what I think and, that being the case, you just can't accept it."

At the same time, Cain began to question whether he was doing the right thing trying to pursue a career in journalism, hoping it would lead to an even chancier career as a writer. He finally sought the advice of a friend, an investment banker named Jack Wilson. He told Wilson what was bothering him and asked whether maybe he, Cain, shouldn't be thinking about another career. The banker's reply surprised him: "I never heard of a man who made a success stockjobbing. It's a lousy racket. And your friend [Gilbert Malcolm] is riding for trouble, only he doesn't know it. . . . This boom, this prosperity you see all around you, is going to last until after Christmas, and then watch it all go down the drain." Then, almost as an afterthought, he added: "I'll tell you one thing. If you want to make money, go where the money is." Wilson was right. The Depression of 1920 wiped out Malcolm's firm.

Frustrated as he was, Cain decided to stay at the *Sun*. It was a steady job and afforded him a chance to continue learning the American language. But he was restless and wanted to get back on the street, so he began wrangling labor assignments. The labor movement fascinated Cain. The country was suffering a wave of postwar strikes—especially in the steel mills—and the Big Red Scare and the Bolshevik witch-hunt were dominating the headlines. The steelworkers could hardly be called radical; they were simply striking for higher wages and shorter hours (many of them worked a twelve-hour day). The steel companies, however, had managed to pin the Bolshevik label on the strikers, and the public sympathized with the mills. As for the coal miners, there was little doubt that they were Bolshies. They had already voted to nationalize the mines, and nationalization and communism were identical in the public mind.

In this climate, and with Woodrow Wilson virtually paralyzed from a stroke and totally preoccupied with seeing the treaty he had negotiated in Paris through the United States Senate, Attorney General Mitchell Palmer unleashed a hysterical counterattack to crush the strikes and flush out the Bolsheviks. Frustrated at not finding any, he broadened the search to include professed socialists and members of the labor unions. Before long, every self-styled patriotic man, woman, and organization in the country joined in. Their targets were almost anyone in the labor force, or anyone who had anything good to say or write about the laboring man. To prime himself on the subject, Cain took courses in labor problems at Johns Hopkins University, where he studied *Das Kapital* and John Commons's *History of the Labor Movement*.

At about the same time, his fascination with writing was given new stimulation by perhaps the most important event in his professional career—his discovery of H. L. Mencken. What first attracted Cain to Mencken was a column headed "The Clowns March In," written early in 1920. The "clowns" were some of the candidates for the presidential nomination—Leonard Wood, Hiram Johnson, Charles Evans Hughes, James M. Cox. Cain started to read it somewhat contemptuously, but by the time he had reached the point where Mencken called Wood "a pompous old dodo with delusions of persecution," he knew he had discovered something new and exciting. Mencken's style almost intoxicated him. He quickly went out and bought a copy of *The Smart Set*, which he knew Mencken had edited with George Jean Nathan, and a handful of Mencken's books. After reading as much of Mencken as he could lay his hands on, he knew his own writing would never be the same.

Considering Cain's rapture with the American language, it is little wonder he was stimulated by Mencken; in fact, the wonder is that it took him so long to discover the man many considered the most exciting writer in this country in the 1920s. Both men worked on the *Sun*, and Mencken had been writing columns for Baltimore papers since before Cain was in college. By 1920 he was well known not only in Baltimore but in intellectual circles everywhere. He edited *The Smart Set*, probably the most sophisticated magazine in the country at that time; and by 1920 he had written some of his classics—*In Defense of Women*, *A Book of Prefaces*, *A Book of Burlesques*. In 1919 he had demonstrated his scholarship with the publication of the first volume of *The American Language*. He had not yet become "the most powerful influence on this whole generation of educated people," as Walter Lippmann would describe him later in the 1920s, but he was on the way. His reputation as the American George Bernard Shaw—others said Voltaire, others Rabelais—was firmly established.

During the war, Mencken had drifted into an eclipse. A grandson of German immigrants, he was both pro-German and pro-Kaiser, not only in private but also in the pages of the *Sun*, which finally had to discontinue his column, "The Free Lance." His pro-German position may also have been one reason why Private First Class James M. Cain at first held him in such contempt. Cain had his own misgivings about the war, but it is difficult to admire the supporters of your enemy while you are in the trenches.

However, after America entered the war, Mencken had the good sense to keep quiet, at least in the public print, and by 1920 all was forgiven and he started writing again for the *Sun*. It was one of his first columns after he returned that attracted Cain's attention. Cain immediately wrote Mencken and began sending articles and ideas to him for *The Smart Set*. Although none were accepted, they did catch Mencken's eye, and Cain became a member of Mencken's legion of correspondents. He also became a lifelong fan of Mencken's.

Meanwhile, Cain's development as a labor reporter was temporarily disrupted in 1921 when he came down with typhoid fever. This put him in the Franklin Square Hospital in Baltimore. The illness was serious, and Cain was nearly paralyzed. He recovered, but found that when he sat for any length of time in theaters or concert halls, his legs went to sleep. This disability plagued him for the rest of his life, dampening his enthusiasm for plays and concerts, which he did not enjoy unless he had a seat on the aisle from which he could get up and take a few steps every now and then to exercise his legs.

When he left the hospital, Cain asked to be assigned to what he considered one of the most important stories since the war: the treason trial of William Blizzard, in West Virginia. Blizzard was president of UMW District No. 16 and leader of a group of coal miners who had staged an armed march against some mines in Logan and Mingo counties, where the "deputy sheriffs" were actually hired guns paid by the mine companies to keep the union out. An increasing number of people had been living in tents, unemployed and just waiting for some spark that would start trouble. "They're a-murderin' the women and children," was often heard, and although reporter Cain never saw any evidence that women and children were murdered, it was an effective rallying cry. In August 1921, open warfare between the mine operators and the union organizers erupted, and a state of martial law was proclaimed. Ten men were actually killed in a battle when the miners marched on the town of Matewan, and two union sympathizers were shot down in cold blood in the town of Welch. The miners, two thousand strong, then assembled on one side of a ridge at Blair Mountain. On the other side, the sheriff's deputies, state police, and a few patriotic citizens dug in, and Governor John J. Cornwell ordered his forces to neither advance nor retreat. The state also brought in four airplanes, armed them with makeshift bombs, and sent them up to attack the miners. Both sides held their positions and fired machine guns and rifles at each other for three days—before federal troops finally arrived and sent everyone home. It would have been a comic war right out of a Marx Brothers movie except for the fact that three men were accidentally killed.

After the dust had settled, the Logan County grand jury met in special session and, in addition to wholesale charges of murder, conspiracy, and unlawful assembly, indicted twenty-three union men—including William Blizzard and Walter Allen—for treason against the state of West Virginia. Although the *Sun* editors were more interested in the coal companies' fight with the unions, it was the charge of treason that intrigued Cain. "I simply don't believe," Cain later told his editor, "that a glorified riot that was somewhat provoked should be blown up to an act of war."

The Blizzard trial, the first of two, lasted six months. Cain had been down in Charleston only a few days when he encountered one of the most impressive men he had ever met. He was sitting in his hotel with a group of lawyers, reporters, and others interested in the trial, debating whether the unions were actually advocating communism. "As one of the seven men who actually read *Das Kapital* . . . ," Cain began, but he never made his point because a large, grave man in his fifties looked up from his paper, held out his hand, and said: "I'm one of the other six." The stranger's name was William Wiley. Cain was six feet tall and weighed over two hundred pounds, but he felt like a "squatty little Princeton quarterback" next to Wiley. He soon learned that Wiley was known as "the Colonel" because of his bearing and demeanor, not military service, and that he was the vice-president and general manager of the Boone County Coal Company, which was not located in Boone County, but at Sharples in Logan County. The Colonel had become the chief spokesman for the West Virginia mine operators, speaking at dinners, presiding at caucuses, and debating with the press the pros and cons of both sides in the dispute. But the operators were cautious in their dealings with him, because they felt he was not really one of them. As Cain put it: "He didn't believe miners were low, lazy rats, who stubbornly refused to learn how to live without food."

Colonel Wiley's main issue with the unions was their hopeless inefficiency. "To begin with," he argued, "they are opposed to the greatest means of human progress, which is invention. They resist any labor-saving device, because it throws men out of work. But *all* invention is labor-saving, and if their stand had been taken soon enough we would still lack the wheel, as the Aztecs did."

William Blizzard, the first to be tried of the twenty-three men indicted for treason in West Virginia, was widely accepted as the "generalissimo" of the miners' "army." He was twenty-eight, but had gone to work in the mines when he was ten. When he appeared in court, all scrubbed and dressed for the trial, he looked to Cain more like a college freshman. Despite obvious tension on both sides, the trial began in an atmosphere of "high spirits" and polished shoes—the latter because when a miner had nothing else to do, he would have his shoes shined by one of twenty-seven black shoeshine boys lined up in front of the courthouse. The miners' shoes all looked like "peeled onions," reported Cain.

But their shoes did not help them in the courtroom. Blizzard's lawyers lost the first round when Judge J. M. Woods refused to throw the treason charge out of court. The selection of the jury also went against Blizzard; two-thirds of the panel from which the jury was selected were farmers, who generally were known to be hostile to the miners. When the jury was finally picked, it contained nine farmers.

On the second day, John L. Lewis, with his angry face and shaggy eyebrows, appeared to sit with the defendant, emphasizing that this was primarily a case against the union, not a treason trial. And the union officials tried to play it cool, telling jokes and pretending the whole thing was a farce. The prevailing mood was characterized in a story reported by Cain: When David Fowler, an international union representative, arrived, he was solemnly met by Frank Keeney, president of District 17 and one of the twenty-three men accused of treason. "Fowler," said Keeney, "this is one of the most historic places in the United States. John Brown was tried and hanged here [sic]. They have got a wonderful old historic cemetery up on the hill. How many people do you suppose are dead up in that cemetery?"

"How should I know how many people are dead up there," snapped Fowler.

"Every damned one of them," said Keeney.

At times, the trial was conducted on about the same level. Quite a bit was made of the fact that the mine operators had imported four airplanes and loaded them with bombs, which they had then dropped on the miners, with some of the bombs landing among the women and children. Fortunately they did not explode. There was a dispute as to precisely what was in the bombs, so the adjutant general dramatically took one, sat down, placed it on his knee, and began to untwist both ends. Everyone in the courtroom, especially the jury and the press, became obviously nervous, and when the adjutant general had both ends open and dumped the contents on the floor, the jury breathed again as one man. The homemade bomb contained a collection of nuts and bolts that Cain said made ordinary shrapnel "look like a lovingly thrown kiss."

The prosecution's case had other problems. Captain John Wilson, head of an infantry regiment sent in to break up the fighting at Blair Mountain, surprised everyone in the courtroom when he said: "If you ask me, I can only say it strikes me as comic opera war: the men went up into the hills, stayed for an hour or two, then came down for a confab, or to eat, or sit around a spell, and wasted thousands of rounds of ammunition without hitting anything."

Wilson's testimony, Cain said, came like "a bolt out of the sky," and provided even more of a jolt when Wilson added that there was no talk about overthrowing the government, that the miners were just out to get the "Logan County thugs [the armed deputies] and protect the women and children."

After a few days, John W. Owens, the *Sun*'s political reporter, showed up at the trial. Then, suddenly, he was gone, and Cain was baffled at what he had been doing there. Later, back in Baltimore, Cain found out: Stanley Reynolds, his editor, called him in and said: "Jim, coal operators have been in here, trying to get you fired on the ground that your stories are biased."

Cain said he was not surprised, that to call what the miners did treason strained one's credence, and he offered to let someone else cover the trial.

Reynolds quickly said he did not want that, but he had had to send Owens down to make sure Cain was giving a fair report. Owens, it turned out, "okays your stuff completely." Then Reynolds said he did not think it was developing as much of a story, "but we can't have coal operators telling the

Sun who we fire. So to let them know where they get off, I'm afraid you're stuck with it for the duration."

Cain went back to Charleston and for six more weeks listened to both sides argue the meaning of treason. He reported that no more brilliant, exhaustive, or profound discussion of the subject had been heard in American courts. And for the rest of his life he considered himself something of an expert on treason and would take issue with anyone—including Rebecca West, the British author of *The Meaning of Treason*—on the subject when he did not think it was being discussed accurately.

By the time Blizzard took the stand, on May 25, he was obviously nervous and haggard. The judge instructed the jury that same day, explaining that under the Constitution treason shall consist solely in levying war against the United States or adhering to its enemies, giving aid and comfort; and that no person shall be convicted of treason except on the testimony of two witnesses to the same overt act. The concluding arguments by the attorneys were expected to be stem-winders, and they were. At 3:25 P.M. on May 27, the jury went out. Six hours later, it returned and rendered the verdict: Not Guilty. The cases against the other men were dropped, except for the one against a miner named Walter Allen. He was tried in September, and Cain came down to cover that trial also for the *Sun*. Allen was found guilty of treason and sentenced to ten years, but he jumped bail, so the case was never appealed.

Cain obviously sympathized with the union's position in his coverage, and this at a time when the Big Red Scare was still gripping the country and siding with the unions was almost equivalent to being a radical yourself. The head of the state police threatened to run him out of town during the trial, and after the mine owners failed in their efforts to have the *Sun* fire him, they attempted to get rid of him by having former Senator Clarence Watson accuse him of siding with the miners in his dispatches. But Cain stuck to his position, maintaining that the state and the mine operators were in collusion and that the miners were being tried, not for treason, but for their leadership in the union movement.

However, other interests were stirring in Cain. While he was in West Virginia, he said he saw a beautiful girl in his hotel lobby and, for some reason, decided instantly to shave his mustache, feeling he was virtually alone in considering it an adornment. But his trouble was deeper than that, for it involved an approaching event that filled him with depression—his thirtieth birthday. Nothing in his life seemed to have any meaning except his writing, and that was progressing very slowly. Still, it was progressing—as was his reputation. Cain's articles about the West Virginia situation—not just his reports, but also the feature columns appearing on the editorial page—were drawing attention both in Charleston and in Baltimore. People were aware that his reporting was incisive and honest, and his dispatches very well written. He began to wonder whether the time had not come to try his hand at full-time free-lance writing.

So, when he returned to Baltimore, he queried the *Saturday Evening Post, Collier's*, and a few other magazines, but none was interested in treason in West Virginia. Then he wrote Ellery Sedgwick at the *Atlantic Monthly*, and this time received a cautious green light: "The attitude of the *Baltimore Sun* regarding the West Virginia mining situation," Sedgwick wrote Cain in June 1922, "long since attracted my attention, and I consider its treatment of a difficult and dangerous situation as a public service of a high order. I am therefore very warmly disposed to say Yes to your proposal of June 5th. . . . Of your own work, except so far as I have read the columns of the *Sun*, I know nothing, and so I cannot promise you to accept what you may write, but . . . any manuscript you send will be read by all of us here with close interest and attention."

That was all Cain needed. He immediately began work on his first major magazine piece. Meanwhile, Sedgwick wrote Mencken inquiring about Cain, and Mencken replied: "I don't know Cain personally, but I am told by friends at the *Sun* office that he is a man of exceptional quality." He also told Sedgwick about Cain's standing his ground against the police and how the *Sun* had sent a reporter to check him out. Cain wrote the article and sent it to Boston, but nothing happened. Then he received a letter from Sedgwick saying he was buying the article, but that he was holding it for two or three months to give it "better display," which Cain took with a grain of salt. When the check for $125 arrived, his first sale began to seem real, but still the article did not appear. Then one day, Henry Hyde, a columnist for the *Sun*, dropped by Cain's desk and said: "I see you lead the *Atlantic* next month."

"The Battle Ground of Coal" appeared in the October 1922 issue, and Sedgwick must have been pleased with it because not only did he make it the lead article, he wrote a long item about Cain and the *Baltimore Sun* in the *Atlantic*'s "Contributors Column." Cain's article was a long, very well written account of the complex, tense, and controversial fight between the union and the mine owners in West Virginia. It traced the development of the conflict from 1898 to the trial of Walter Allen for treason, was terse and interesting, and contained some fine mood writing in the lead:

There is no soft, mellow outline about these hills. They are sharp and rugged; about their top grows a stunted, scraggly forest. Their color is raw; daring reds and yellow, hard, water-streaked grays. Here and there you see the blue-black ribbon of coal.

In this untamed section of West Virginia two tremendous forces have staked out a battleground.

After describing in detail the battle going on between the unions and the nonunionized coal mines, Cain said it might appear "that the non-union fields are more soundly organized than the union, and that the solution of the problem lies in putting the whole country on a non-union basis." Not so, said Cain: The ultimate solution "is to put the whole country on a union basis, and give all operators an equal chance at the market, and all miners an equal chance at regular work."

It was a bold stand, coming as it did when most people thought anyone who favored the unions was a Bolshevik. As a result, Cain began to develop a reputation as a controversial writer. In addition to his continuing coverage of the West Virginia situation for the *Sun*, he wrote another piece on the coal situation that appeared in the October 4, 1922, issue of *The Nation* and dealt with the case of Walter Allen. In it Cain attacked everything about the trial—its premise, the picking of the jury, and the conduct of the judge.

Back in Baltimore, Cain was something of a star now, but the sale of his article to the *Atlantic* had had a more important effect on Cain himself. He knew that to appear in a magazine of the *Atlantic*'s quality one had to be able to write and have something to say. And this gave him the courage, for the first time, to think that as a writer he would be like Mencken, a "pelagic fish," a term Cain used often to describe his developing ambition. He knew now he wanted to swim in deep water, and the *Atlantic* article gave him the confidence to think he might be ready.

Cain also knew that if a writer was going to break out of journalism, he had to write a novel, and he felt he had a novel in him. He had spent enough time in West Virginia to have become thoroughly familiar with the culture and speech of the miners and their families. In addition, he was now something of an expert on the unions and how they operated. Having absorbed dramatic material about a story of national significance, with powerful human overtones, if he was ever going to write a novel, now was the time.

In 1922, literature in America was entering a new era. The old, structured, almost formal stylized writing of the late nineteenth and early twentieth centuries, the kind of writing that appealed to Dr. Cain when he was teaching literature at St. John's, was no longer predominant. The change was symbolized, in a way, by the passing of William Dean Howells in May 1920. Although his novels, exemplified by *The Rise of Silas Lapham*, were well regarded, Howells had been born during the administration of Andrew Jackson and had survived a little too long as an arbiter of literary taste. There was new talent everywhere, and the young writers were experimenting with more realistic prose. It was just a matter of time before some young genius would appear to write *the* Great American Novel. "In those days," one commentator wrote, "people talked of the Great American Novel as ministers spoke of the Second Coming." And Franklin P. Adams, who was writing the most widely read literary column in the country (appearing in the *New York World* under the title "The Conning Tower") referred so often to the Great American Novel that he finally assigned it an acronym—G.A.N. There were some early candidates for G.A.N.—*Winesburg, Ohio*, by Sherwood Anderson, published in 1919, and *This Side of Paradise*, by F. Scott Fitzgerald, published in March 1920. But after reconsideration, the cognoscenti decided neither book quite measured up, although it was felt the handsome young Fitzgerald certainly might write a great novel someday. Then, in the fall, galleys for a new book by a young writer named Sinclair Lewis began to make the rounds of publishing, and the word was that Lewis just might have written G.A.N. It was called *Main Street*, and it took the country by storm, not only being hailed as *literature*, but rocketing Lewis into the dubious ranks of such best-selling authors as Ethel M. Dell, Zane Grey, Harold Bell Wright, Peter B. Kyne, Rex Beach, James Oliver Curwood, Kathleen Norris, and Gene Stratton Porter. *Main Street* sold 400,000 copies before it drifted off the best-seller lists. But after the first flush of excitement, the literati decided that its protagonists, Carol and Will Kennicott, were not very deep or well drawn, and that the real punch in *Main Street* was Lewis's depiction of the minor characters in the small town of Gopher Prairie. Good material, but it would take more than that to win the Great American Novel contest.

With people—including H. L. Mencken, the new arbiter of American literary taste—now saying that James M. Cain was a very promising young talent, Cain felt he ought to write a novel and, years later, possibly joking, possibly not, he conceded that he was tempted to shoot for the Great American Novel. But, whereas Lewis saw America embodied in its small towns, Cain, who had traveled southern Maryland and now West Virginia, thought he sensed America in its rural areas. So he decided that his novel would be set in mining country, and to gain an even greater understanding of his scene, he took three months off from the paper to go down to work in the mines. (Another motivation for going to West Virginia was that some of his friends among the mine operators—especially Colonel Wiley—had challenged him to work in the mines so he could see what a sap he was making of himself in his articles.)

Before going to West Virginia, Cain thought it would be a good idea to seek some advice and encouragement from Mencken. Although he had never met the great man, he had established a relationship with him through his article queries to the editors of *The Smart Set*. Mencken also knew quite a bit about Cain and obviously thought highly of him. For one thing, Cain had written a piece in the *Sun* attacking the current Gilbert and Sullivan vogue and the tendency to overpraise the British team as composers of superior opera. Cain said that not only were Gilbert and Sullivan musicals "feeble and sterile," but that the British as a people simply did not have any music in them. He also said that the current vogue for Gilbert and Sullivan was all the more amazing because if people wanted to hear some really good, exciting music, "we have it right here in this country—jazz," which he called "a pulsing, lilting, irresistible thing."

Considering Mencken's dislike of anything British coupled with his interest in music, this article no doubt appealed to him. So one day in the fall of 1922, when Cain requested a meeting, Mencken came down to Cain's desk in the city room and talked for about ten minutes.

H. L. Mencken was one of the most unusual characters in American literature. He was about five feet ten inches, a little stocky and stodgy in appearance. At that time, in the early 1920s, he always wore single-breasted blue serge suits with stubby, well-polished black shoes, and his hair was parted in the middle. It was sandy, or perhaps reddish, straight, and not very thick. His face was clear and pink, and his whole appearance was "well-scrubbed," as Cain put it. His eyes were blue, rather large, and wide open, especially when he talked, which was most of the time; they had a sort of surprised look, as though the whole human race constantly astonished him. "But when he laughed," said Cain, "they crinkled up in a strangely Mephistophelian way—but not Satanic." His speech both enthralled and baffled Cain, because he could not quite place its origin. He finally decided it was pure Baltimorese, but as spoken by a Baltimorean who used perfect grammar and pronounced every word clearly and without slur. It was a rich voice, overlaid with a city editor's bark, "a bit facetious, terse, and syntactically complete. It is pitched a bit high, as though talking to someone upstairs. It has a slight fade-away drop at sentence end, as though giving you a chance to cut in if you want to, and there is a bit of truculence in it, an amiably humorous kind."

Cain's first meeting with the man who would probably have more of an impact on his life than anyone else was a disappointment. Cain was twelve years younger than Mencken, and from the first was acutely aware of being in the presence of genius, making it difficult for him to establish a normal relationship. Although Cain and Mencken did eventually become professional friends, Cain knew he had not impressed Mencken on their first meeting, had indeed been given the brush-off with what Cain called "No. 5 of his acts for young writers." Cain said later that the conversation was useless and that Mencken had no idea how to write a novel. "Two years out of a man's life—that's a novel," was the gist of Mencken's counsel.

But Cain was not discouraged, and soon he was on the train to West Virginia. Mary, who was teaching at a junior high school in Baltimore, did not go with him. During his brief previous time in West Virginia, Cain had become fond of the mountain people, who, he decided, were descended from the losers and failures in the westward migration, the pioneers who had tired while their more energetic comrades had moved on in the historic expansion of America. But it should not be forgotten, Cain said, that "they brought from the plantations of tidewater Virginia, from the fair estates of Maryland, from the free well-tended lands of Pennsylvania, a habit of life that was anything but cheap." They lived in log cabins, and their food and clothes inspired compassion, though they had a quality about them that showed they were not clods.

In November 1922, Cain went to work at the Kelly's Creek Coal Corporation in Ward, West Virginia, and became a card-carrying member of the United Mine Workers. It was an affiliation that he would view with considerable pride until twenty-two years later, when he learned from John L. Lewis, much to his surprise, that he had been dropped from membership for having stopped paying his dues.

Cain worked underground for several weeks, and at one time was saved from being maimed for life by a young miner who grabbed his hand, which was gripping the side of his coal car, just as another car rolled out of an entry and banged into it. Cain's experience underground convinced him that not only had he not been wrong about conditions in the mines, but he should have used stronger language to describe them. He also took time to investigate the extent to which the mines had been infiltrated by Bolsheviks. Upon interviewing several radicals who had been pointed out to him, it gradually became apparent that they were a different breed from those he had read so much about in the newspapers. "I cleverly interrogated one," he said, "without revealing my design and found out he had never heard of Russia. I found out that nobody in the whole camp had ever heard of the numerous self-anointed apostles of the labor movement who get out the magazines in New York. I questioned other certified radicals and found they had no theories concerning government whatever and didn't know what a Soviet was."

He finally went to a coal operator and asked him to define a radical. His friend replied: "Oh, that's a word we have, I don't remember just how we got to calling them that. I mean a troublemaker; a fellow that wants to run things—a bully, I guess you would call him."

Cain pressed his point: "Then you don't have in mind especially a secret agent of the Russian government or a Socialist or a Communist and a Syndicalist, or an IWW?"

"Hell, no; we don't have many of those Socialists or funny ones up here. I heard there was a pair of IWW's up here during the war; they said the Department of Justice was watching them—but I never saw them."

Cain's career as a miner did not last long. One day, shopping in the company store, he met Mr. Shure, the camp superintendent and an early acquaintance, and Shure invited him to dinner, saying Mrs. Shure had scolded him for neglecting Cain. Cain agreed and, after buying a new white shirt, verifying that the companies did exploit the miners in their stores, he went to dinner at the superintendent's house. The next morning at breakfast in the company boardinghouse, Cain suddenly discovered he had become "invisible." When he asked for the butter, the miners, who had previously been friendly, simply looked through him. He had had dinner with the super, which made him a company spy and a double-crossing rat. "I dared not go back in the mine," said Cain. "I knew that one more day there would cost me my life." So he left the mine that morning, not even picking up his pay.

To familiarize himself with the terrain of the miners' big march and their battle with the operators' men, he walked thirty miles from Ward down to Sharples. On the way he stopped to beg a meal from some people in a log cabin only a few feet from the road. "The owner, clad in denims and rough shoes, politely ignored proffers of money, took me in, sat me down, and bade me wait. His wife dressed in checked gingham presently appeared, and said it would be a few minutes yet. I didn't miss the fact that she was disturbingly good-looking in a misty-eyed mountain way and had a figure a movie producer might have pondered over." During the lunch of sowbelly, greens, and coffee, the conversation was easy, polite, and "of an aristocratic kind—that is, it was on topics of interest to pleasantly acquainted equals . . . accompanied by a proper concern for the well-being of the guest and conducted in a low, well-modulated tone of voice." The only decor was a .45 Colt revolver and a Springfield rifle on the wall "and if I had made a pass at his good-looking wife," Cain said, "this man would have shot me, from ambush and from behind, in accordance with the peculiar *cavalleria* of the region."

When Cain reached Sharples, he called on his old friend Colonel Wiley, who put him up at the directors' lodge on top of a hill above the company offices. No sooner had Cain unpacked than Wiley was at his door, dressed in a yachting cap and ready to take him on a tour of the area.

That night, Cain had dinner at the Wileys', and after the liqueur they went through the Colonel's library, pausing to examine his great collection of books, then into a music room, which was rather dimly lit. Wiley offered to play on the phonograph "anything you want," and as they had been discussing Pasquale Amato at dinner, Cain called for his record of the *I Pagliacci* Prologue. Putting it on the machine seemed to involve various preparations, and comments about the synchronization of pitch. Then the Colonel snapped the switch and the room was filled with the worst cacophony of sound Cain had ever heard in his life, "as though fiddles, basses, woodwinds, timpani, organ, and Pasquale had all been dropped in a cistern, and were in some mad screaming stampede to get out."

But the Colonel was enraptured with his performance. Cain glanced at Mrs. Wiley, who looked at him with a little smile of affection mixed with pity. Cain said he knew then he was in the presence of the loneliest man on earth, one who was trying not to lose his soul on that desolate mountain top in West Virginia, a sojourner on a desert isle, reciting Shakespeare so as not to forget how to talk. At last, with the performance mercifully over, Cain said: "Nice, but they do it better in New York."

"Or Philadelphia, for that matter. Our home office is there. I can go, if I want."

Despite his friendship with Wiley and Wiley's obvious respect, Cain did not change his mind about the unions and their role in winning decent wages and fair treatment for the miners. But it is significant that at this critical junction in his life, Cain did not do as many intellectuals did in the 1920s—he did not become caught up in the labor movement or the liberals' fight for curbing the power of industry. He had more important things to worry about—his novel.

After saying good-bye to the Wileys, Cain was off to Baltimore and two months of writing. The novel he planned evolved around a daring concept for 1922, one that was taboo in literature—incest! The book also owed, he said, something in its approach to John Dos Passos' *Three Soldiers*, which had just been published: "My man was to be a radical union organizer, in the mine fields of the 1920s, winding up as part of the march of 1921, his mind on the destruction of a system he felt was constrictive like a chain around the men. My whole novel was to highlight his compulsion to break things apart, and his final discovery that he couldn't. At that point he was to be alone in a woods above the mines, between two trees, that in futile rage he kept trying to push apart, apparently thinking they might fall, as he had seen the temple fall when the hero toppled the pillars, in the opera *Samson and Delilah*. But nothing happened—the trees just stood there."

And so did Cain's novel—it would not move. He wrote one draft, but disliked it. He wrote a second and threw it in the wastebasket. Then he wrote a third, but decided that it was still bad and threw it too in the wastebasket. "That last one," he said, "I wouldn't have written at all if I hadn't squirmed at the idea of facing my reporter friends with the news that my great American novel was a pipe dream."

Discouraged, he decided he simply could not write a novel, a decision from which he did not waver for ten years. He said part of the problem was his reporter approach: "I was so preoccupied with background, authenticity, and verisimilitude that I had time for little else!" As for the writing, he said: "I didn't seem to have the least idea where I was going with it, or even which paragraph should follow which." His people "faltered and stumbled." They were also "homely characters, and spoke a gnarled and grotesque jargon that didn't seem quite adapted to long fiction; it seemed to me that after fifty pages of ain'ts, brungs, and fittens, the reader would want to throw the book at me." He also decided that the labor theme was not a good one, that although "it constantly attracts a certain type of intellectual, [it] is really dead seed for a novelist."

Cain had discovered the hard way what thousands of journalists have learned, and what Mencken did not tell him—that an ability to write good newspaper stories or magazine articles does not necessarily make one a novelist; a novel looks so simple to write when you are reading it, but it is not an easy thing to do, even for a professional writer. But Cain's West Virginia experience was not wasted. "The rocky, wooded countryside . . . together with the clear, cool creeks that purl through it, and its gentle, charming inhabitants, whose little hamlets quite often look as they must have looked in the time of Daniel Boone" had had their impact. He would later use his mining experience in *Past All Dishonor*, and his knowledge of mountaineers as well as the mines in *The Butterfly*. And the influence of rural people and their language is obvious in much of his writing.

But in 1922, Cain, now thirty years old, had "to go slinking back to work," admitting that the Great American Novel had still not been written.

DEEP WATER AT LAST

Although Cain had failed to write the Great American Novel, he was still buoyed with confidence by his *Atlantic* article, convinced that anyone who could write for a magazine of its quality was meant for something better than swimming in the small pond of Baltimore. Also, he knew his work was improving all the time. He was writing more and more feature material for the *Sun*, including music reviews and columns demonstrating a fine sardonic touch on such subjects as "Hunting the Radical" down in West Virginia, the UMW's ill-advised attempt to install the check-off system in the West Virginia coal fields, and the absurdity of the "living wage" proclaimed by the Railroad Labor Board. He also wrote an article for *The Nation* entitled "West Virginia: A Mine-field Melodrama," and the lead gives us a good idea of how James M. Cain the writer was developing in 1923:

Rough mountains rise all about, beautiful in their bleak ugliness. They are hard and barren, save for a scrubby, whiskery growth of trees that only half conceals the hard rock beneath. Yet they have their moods. On gray days they lie heavy and sullen, but on sunny mornings they are dizzy with color: flat canvases painted in gaudy hues; here and there tiny soft black pines showing against a cool, blue sky. At night, if the moon shines through a haze, they hang far above you, dim outlines of smoke; you could throw a stone right through them. They are gashed everywhere with water courses, roaring rivers, and bubbling creeks. Along these you plod, a crawling midge, while ever the towering mountains shut you in. Now and then you top a ridge and look about. Miles and miles of billowing peaks, miles and miles of color softly melting into color. Bright yellows and reds give way to greens and misty grays, until they all fade into faint lavender and horizon blue. . . . A setting for a Nibelungen epic, revealing instead a sordid melodrama.

Cain's article went on to describe that melodrama unfolding in West Virginia, in a sardonic tone that made both management and the miners look silly. It concluded by pointing out that the state was still quite young: "It may have a touch of industrial indigestion, or its malady may be more grave. Give it a century or so. Then possibly it will shoot the pianist and call for a new score."

Cain was confident now that he was a pelagic writer, which may have fostered his increasing awareness that he was not really happy as a reporter. In fact, he considered himself a second-rate newspaperman: "I could never quite believe," he said, "that it mattered a damn whether the public learned the full name and address of the fireman injured at the blaze." He also felt that the *Sun* treated him like "a worm," and in turn he thought the *Sun* was run by "blood relatives of Simon Legree." The only redeeming factor in working for the paper was a handful of good people, some of whom would remain friends for years: Hamilton Owens, Clarke Fitzpatrick, Joe Lalley, Frank Kent, Gerald W. Johnson, Mark Watson, and Paul Patterson.

So, by the summer of 1923, Cain was ready to leave the Baltimore pond and head for deeper waters. He did not really know what he wanted to do next, but an opportunity suddenly developed on one of his visits to his parents' home in Roland Park, a wealthy suburb of Baltimore, where the Cains had moved from Catonsville. Dr. Cain not only was doing very well at U.S. Guaranty, he was maintaining his connections in the academic world and had just been made a member of the Board of Governors of St. John's College. After the resignation of Dr. Thomas Fell, Dr. Cain began pushing as his candidate for president a former West Point football star, Major Enoch Garey, who had made considerable money as the author of a training brochure called *The Plattsburgh Manual*. Cain met Major Garey at his father's house on several occasions, and Garey astonished Cain by telling his father that he would go down to St. John's if his son would go with him. Cain was reluctant, but Garey persisted, offering him the job of teaching two courses in journalism and one in English. He said he also needed somebody to sit by his side, someone he could talk to, who knew colleges, how the students felt about things, and how to deal with a board of governors. Cain said he thought what Garey really wanted was a press agent, and he could not consent to that. Garey was appalled at the accusation and reassured him that he wanted a strong right arm and, anyway, Cain would be so busy teaching his three courses he would not have time for press agentry.

Cain considered the job offer for a month, and finally agreed. He figured he would still have plenty of time at St. John's to write, probably more than he did as a reporter. Also, Garey was offering $3,500 a year, close to double his salary at the *Sun*. So he and Mary moved down to Annapolis, and as he said later, the year he spent teaching at the small college was one of the "pleasantest interludes" he ever had in his life.

This was not because of his home life. It was obvious by now that he and Mary had made a mistake, although there is little evidence today to document what went wrong. Those friends who are alive and knew them together have only a sketchy idea of what happened, because neither Cain nor Mary talked about their marriage. Cain said Mary flouted the basic principle "that marriages are made in bed." She apparently was a reluctant partner, which was dramatically brought home to Cain while they were on a little vacation at Mary's mother's house in Church Hill in 1922 or 1923. "Our first night there," Cain wrote in his memoirs, "I made romantic overtures, only to get a brush. A bit baffled, I persisted, and, at last, quite peevishly, she told me that she had assumed if it was my vacation, it was her vacation." Vacation from what? Cain asked himself. From the one thing that was supposed to make a marriage work?

Mary's friends were always amazed that she saw anything in Cain anyway, and although they conceded she was an intellectual rather than an emotional woman, they recalled her as beautiful, cultured, and charming. By contrast, Cain was seen as an ugly, hard-drinking, uncouth newspaperman. He still had his terrible acne problem, and his thick black hair was always disheveled. And although his city-room manner of speech, talking out of the side of his mouth, was obviously an affectation, it annoyed Mary. Cain himself was aware of his mannerism—"the city room bark," as he called it—and said it came from "too many hours on the telephone, crowbarring stuff out of sheriffs, corporation presidents, and bankrupts, who don't want to talk but have to be made to." He was also sloppy-looking in appearance, being ever indifferent to clothes. In addition, there was his drinking, a little more, perhaps, than he might otherwise do because Mary, "a born prohibitionist," was always urging him to stop, which annoyed him.

Mary and Cain were married at the beginning of Scott Fitzgerald's "Jazz

Age," when the youth of the country revolted against the manners and morals of the still-lingering Victorian era. Virginia Shaffer, a close friend of Mary's, concedes that the spirit of the times played a part in the breakup of the Cain marriage and that the break must be "considered in the light of the young writer in the twenties." There was also the influence of H. L. Mencken, with whom Cain would soon be developing a much closer relationship, and Mencken openly and loudly denounced marriage as an institution. By the time Cain was teaching in Annapolis, the marriage had reached a point where, as Virginia Shaffer recalled, Cain would sit at the dinner table with her and Mary openly talking of his affairs with other women, including one who was doing his typing. Cain had also become friends with a reporter on the *Sun* named Leonard Cline, a man who had put his wife and children in a boardingroom and gone to New York to live the bohemian life, an act that Cain continually defended in arguments with Mary. She found the whole idea disgusting.

Cain also had a female friend from Baltimore living in New York whom he was "seeing in a wholly platonic way." Her name was Juliet Branham. One evening Cain took the subway to her apartment in the East Fifties intending to invite her to the Dempsey-Firpo fight that night—September 14, 1923. Juliet said she would like to see the fight, but was expecting a guest, a Finnish girl. She invited Cain to stay awhile, which he did, and soon the guest arrived. Elina Tyszecka utterly enchanted Cain, who described her as "small, with the round Mongol face so many Finns have, a warm smile, and occasional flashes, such as drawing the cork on her hostess's bottle of wine, of great physical strength."

Elina was born in Turku, Finland, and studied to be a registered nurse. But before completing her course, she fell in love with and married Victor Tyszecki, a Polish captain in the Black Sea Fleet of the Imperial Russian Navy. They were in the Crimea when the Russian Revolution broke out, and had to flee to St. Petersburg with their three-month-old son, Leo, who made the two-week trip in a hatbox. From there they escaped into Finland. They had another child, Henrietta, while living with Elina's mother, a successful hotel proprietor in Helsinki. After the war both the hotel and Elina's marriage failed, and she, her two children, and her mother came to New York, where she found a job as a chambermaid. She met Cain's friend, Juliet Branham, when she delivered a message to her from a friend in Finland.

Elina could not speak English and Cain could not speak Finnish, so they sat smiling at each other for a while. "At length," Cain said, "seeing how well we hit it off, my hostess retired to the other room and went to bed, while we still sat and looked at each other."

Cain described the rest of that night as a curious illustration of how little talk has to do with a relationship between the sexes. "We couldn't say a word, and yet we got along fine, in the morning being pledged for the rest of our lives—not by things spoken, but by things profoundly felt." That was the beginning of what Cain called "the great love affair of my life."

Meanwhile, Cain and Mary moved to Annapolis, where they took a faculty apartment in Humphrey's Hall on the St. John's campus. Mary did not teach in Annapolis, and Cain settled down to his classes and, when he had time, pursued his writing career, which had suddenly taken a very promising turn. He had not seen Mencken since that day in the city room when the genius brushed him off with what Cain was convinced was his standard lecture for would-be novelists. But apparently Mencken had been following Cain's work and was impressed, especially with some of his music reviews. Mencken was as much a music buff as Cain, and anyone who appreciated good music in Baltimore in the early 1920s stood out in Mencken's mind as a cultured man. The week before Cain was to start teaching at St. John's, he received a letter from Mencken inviting him to have lunch at Marconi's restaurant on Saratoga Street in Baltimore, one of Mencken's favorite hangouts (the other being Schellhase's on Howard Street, where Mencken's Saturday Night Club met to eat, drink beer, and make music).

Cain appeared promptly at twelve-thirty and was seated by Mr. Brookes at the table in back (where Cain continued to sit whenever he was in Marconi's). Mencken arrived, and it soon developed that in inviting Cain to lunch, he was doing what any editor of a new magazine does—trying to persuade a talented writer to write articles for him. Mencken, George Jean Nathan, and a young New York publisher named Alfred A. Knopf were planning to launch a new magazine in January 1924. It would be called the *American Mercury*—a title Cain did not think much of because it reminded him of the *London Mercury*. But Mencken, who agreed, did not ask his opinion. What he wanted to know was whether Cain had any article ideas for the first issue. Cain was flattered, and it did not take him long to come up with the concept of a portrait of a union labor leader, based on the material he had amassed on his trips to West Virginia. Mencken liked the idea, and it was agreed Cain would do the piece.

With that business out of the way, Cain and Mencken settled into a long conversation as Mr. Brookes brought coffee, more coffee, and more coffee. They talked about books and music and authors and ideas, with Mencken offering his usual Olympian comments. In discussing the book on which Cain had patterned his own novel attempt—*Three Soldiers*, by Dos Passos—Mencken said: "He's a one-book man—you'll not hear from him again." When Cain asked what his opinion was based on, Mencken replied: "Well, he's had another book out since that one—did you ever hear of it?"

Mencken had a point because the book he referred to was *Streets of Night*. (Still to come, of course, were *Manhattan Transfer* and the trilogy, *U.S.A.*) Cain was startled by Mencken's sweeping judgment, but would soon learn that such apocalyptic pronouncements were quite common in literary circles and not confined to Mencken.

The lunch lasted until four-thirty or five in the afternoon, well beyond Mencken's allotted time for a business lunch and Cain was naturally flattered that the great man had spent so much time with him. Mencken sat with his chair tilted back against the wall and talked continuously, and Cain was enchanted. "I felt exactly like a boy who had had his baseball autographed by Babe Ruth. Babe Ruth could inspire the small boy to be a lot better ball player than he might have been without that autographed ball to reassure him, and that's how it was in some part with Mencken. His effect on you sitting there in Marconi's was impossible to comprehend."

American literature at that time was still under the stifling cloak of the puritan critics, who censored anything that might appear slightly offensive to children and women. Mencken called the critics "the comstocks," in honor of Anthony Comstock, head of the New York Society for the Suppression of Vice. The comstocks enraged Mencken; he considered them "the enemy of literature and mankind." Mencken's enthusiasm and ideas elevated Cain's spirit, and after their luncheon he rushed home, exhilarated and ready to start work immediately on his article. As he said many times in later years, Mencken "liberated me from the village pump."

Cain had hardly been at St. John's for more than a week before he had misgivings about Major Garey as the right choice for the presidency. What caused his concern was the inaugural address Garey planned to give before an audience that included representatives from colleges all over the East. When Cain read it, he was utterly appalled.

There was page after page about plans for repairing the buildings, putting in new sidewalks, and fixing the library shelves, but not one word about the kind of college he wanted to have or anything educational.

Despite his misgivings, Cain got along with Garey for a while and his life settled into a pleasant routine. Cain taught three courses at St. John's: a lecture course in journalism which attracted nearly a hundred students; English A, a big class of fifty or sixty, in which theme-writing was the principal activity; a class in the technique of journalism that involved relaxed, easy, feet-on-the-table discussion (Cain would bring in a stack of ashtrays and proclaim smoking permissible).

Students who took Cain's courses at St. John's recall him as an excellent teacher. Bernard Gessner remembers him as "the fastest speed-reader I've ever seen." In class he was a hard taskmaster and became annoyed when students could not learn punctuation. He continually stressed brevity and conciseness and, according to Gessner, would say of almost every paper a student turned in, "Boil it down." Two of Cain's favorite pieces of writing were the Lord's Prayer and the Sermon on the Mount, which he read often to his classes to demonstrate terse writing that expressed so much.

He also stressed Dr. Johnson's famous dictum that "no one but a blockhead ever wrote except for money." Cain knew something of the markets and what would sell to editors. A friend of Gessner's worked in a drugstore in Annapolis and once was unable to do his composition. So he copied a story from *Youth's Companion*, a popular magazine of that time, and turned it in. Cain read it, then yelled out the boy's name. The boy was afraid he was going to catch hell, but, instead, Cain held up the boy's paper and said: "Send this to *Youth's Companion*, they'll buy it."

Cain was known by St. John's students as "Cinderneck" because of the heavy acne that pockmarked the back of his neck. But he was respected and well liked and the subject of many campus bull sessions because of the unorthodox manner in which he taught his classes. Felix Morley, who was also teaching at St. John's while Cain was there, remembers him as a big burly fellow, not good-looking but with a strong appeal for women. He was iconoclastic, abrasive, and somewhat tough and cynical—especially about the *Sun*. "He had a great deal of pride and expected to be treated right. But I had a feeling he was putting on a bit of an act. He had a lot of ability, no question about that, but he had not found the right channel." Morley remembers one argument about the literary future of the country, in which Cain said our literature had been mostly regional but there was room for a great national novel and the scene ought to be laid in California. "It is the real melting pot," Cain said. "People go there from Maryland, Maine, Vermont, and they all adapt."

Meanwhile, Cain finished his article for Mencken, who liked it and paid him $60. Cain was proud to be in the first issue of what he was sure would be an important magazine. He was also enjoying his developing friendship with Mencken, which, along with the writing, gave him considerable status on campus. After he had finished the labor leader article, Mencken invited Cain up to 1524 Hollins Street to discuss what he might write next for the magazine.

Mencken answered the door, mixing a dry martini, his "cocktail shaker" welcome, Cain said. Mencken praised Cain for his article on the labor leader and they decided on another American "type" to attack—the editorial writer. The uninspired, pro-Establishment prose appearing on most of the country's editorial pages was one of Mencken's favorite targets. Cain shared his appraisal, and although it is not known which man suggested the subject, Cain left Baltimore with another assignment, buoyed by Mencken's interest in him. But as the weeks slipped by, he became concerned that he had not received an advance copy of the inaugural issue of the *Mercury* with his labor leader profile. When the first issue of the *American Mercury* came out in January 1924, amid much fanfare and acclaim, Cain rushed down to the newsstand to buy it only to find "one of the greatest disappointments of my life." His article was not in it! He knew Mencken had liked the article and that it had been scheduled for that issue, and his disappointment was not relieved by Mencken's subsequent explanation. It seems the union printers at the press Knopf had picked to print the magazine had refused to set Cain's article in type because its portrait of a labor leader was not 100 percent flattering, although Cain steadfastly supported the union cause. Mencken, Nathan, and Knopf at once decided to find another printer, "as we couldn't have them dictating to us what we would publish," Mencken explained. "But in case we had to sue them, we had to show some tangible injury the brawl had caused us and so we held the article out. It'll appear next month." But Cain knew that the first issue of any magazine was the one everybody saved.

Although today any one of the early green-covered issues of the *American Mercury* is a collector's item, Cain was right about the first issue—not only was it the one most people saved, but it hit the country's newsstands like a string of exploding firecrackers. The world suffered from at least a score of painful diseases, Mencken and Nathan proclaimed, "all of them chronic and incurable." And it was evident that the magazine was not going to confine itself simply to pointing out the ills of the worlds of literature and theater. Mencken, at least, had broadened his range of interests and was now ready to attack any American institution he thought needed reforming. He looked on the new magazine as a conduit for his ideas in all areas of human endeavor. The Enemies included: the Ku Klux Klan, the Anti-Saloon League, William Jennings Bryan, Billy Sunday, lodge joiners, Methodists, Socialists, censors, capitalists, Greenwich Village, pedants, Prohibition, and the South, particularly southern cooking. That would do for a start.

The first issue contained a gentle debunking of Abraham Lincoln, a critical article on Senator Hiram Johnson of California, an exposé of the teaching of American history, essays by Mencken and Nathan, and a regular feature called "Americana," in which the magazine reported on ludicrous events and items from around the forty-eight states. Cain's labor leader article would have blended perfectly into the issue, which also featured an incendiary article by Ernest Boyd (then a reader at Alfred A. Knopf) entitled "Aesthete: Model 1924."

Cain's article, as Mencken promised, was in the second issue, and he was traveling in good company. Nathan brought in a play by Eugene O'Neill

("All God's Chillun Got Wings") and a short story by Sherwood Anderson ("Caught"). In addition, there were articles by Morris Fishbein, Gerald W. Johnson, Carleton Beals, and Carl Van Doren, most of them in the debunking spirit Mencken preferred. And at least one of Mencken's literary entourage, disappointed in the January issue, had nothing but praise for Cain's February contribution. Sinclair Lewis, in London revising his manuscript of *Arrowsmith*, read Cain's portrait of the labor leader and wrote Mencken: "Christ, that was a lovely article by Mr. James Cain."

Cain's association with the *Mercury* was a dramatic and major leap forward in his writing career, the beginning of his reputation as a major magazine writer. His portrait of the typical labor leader is etched in the tough language of the mines and is dominated by a cynical mocking tone. And it is easy to see why the union printers refused to set it: "He is recruited from the people of the sort that nice ladies call common," is Cain's lead. "Such people are mostly out of sight in the cities. . . . In the small towns they are more openly in view, to the horror of the old families. . . . They are the sort that mop up their plate with bread." Cain points out how the union leaders fight their way into leadership, serve their unions ably, and then gradually change with power. "But sooner or later, someone with a louder voice will push him out," Cain concludes, and said that he once asked a union leader, "What will you do then?"

"Who, me?" he replied. "Why, man, I can go back to the mines any time. I haven't forgotten my trade."

The speech was easy, natural, and authentic. And it was in this article that Cain was first noticed as a master of dialogue, long before John O'Hara. Two examples illustrate the kind of writing New York intellectuals would soon be talking about: Comparing the labor leader with the businessman, Cain said that just as the businessman had come to the point where everything was "a proposition," the labor leader had reached the point where everything was "a matter."

"This Matter you speak of, now, I don't want to be quoted in it, see? but if there's anything going in I want it to go in like it is, the truth about it, I mean, and not no pack of dam lies like the papers generally prints. What I say, now, don't put it in like it come from me, because I don't know nothing about it, except what I read in the papers, not being notified in no official way, see? Besides, it's a matter which you might say is going to have a question of jurisdiction to it, and I don't want to have nobody make no charges against me for interference in no matter which it ain't strickly a point where I got authority. But I can give you a idea about it and you can fix it up so's them that reads the paper can figger out their own conclusion on how we stand in the matter."

And describing other matters that took place at typical conventions:

"Say, you look like you know how to keep something to yourself: tell you something funny happened up to our last convention. Them guys had money every color there was, and all on the table, too. I seen $3,000 in one pot in one game there. . . . Well, anyhow, was a feller there from Indianapolis had his wife with him. Said it was his wife. I don't know, I reckon it was. Anyhow she was some cute baby. I seen her in the lobby one night and she give me a smile, so I says to myself, 'Me for you, kid.' So I gets the guy and takes him to a near-beer s'loon and we gets soused, see? Anyhow, he gets soused and I takes ginger ale. Then they give him the bum's rush and I has to take him back up to his room at the hotel. She is there waiting for him, like I figgered, and her and me puts him to bed and he passes out. Then her and me goes down and has some real likker. . . . Some baby, believe me!"

Cain's development as a writer in Annapolis was done under the most trying of circumstances—a deteriorating marriage. He and Mary were slowly drifting apart, and the tension at home was becoming unbearable for both of them. In his reaction to Mary's rejection, Cain continued to drink too much, which made Mary worse, which, in turn, made him even more surly. Mary's mother said that when she visited them in Annapolis, Cain "was exceedingly cool, and he was constantly reminding [Mary] that nothing about her satisfied him . . . and you could have inferred . . . that he had a heavy burden on his hands that he wanted to throw off."

Cain also continued to defend his friend who had left his wife and two children and gone to New York in search of a new life and new women. Cain said he frankly did not enjoy domesticity, did not believe in monogamy, and was in favor of promiscuity. He criticized Mary's friends who came to their apartment, constantly found fault with her, and complained that the marriage interfered with his personal life; some of the women he was interested in would not respond to him because he was married.

A showdown was approaching. It came one evening in the middle of February 1924, when Cain announced abruptly to Mary that their marriage was over. Although she knew things were not working out, Mary was stunned and argued against the break. She asked Cain if he had thought about the consequences of separation and divorce. He said he had and that no matter what the consequences, he wanted her to leave or he would go immediately. But he also said he thought it best that Mary go home to her mother, because she was not teaching in Annapolis and the apartment they were living in belonged to the college—so she could hardly remain if he left for other quarters.

Still resisting the break, Mary called Dr. Cain in Baltimore and asked him to come to Annapolis, not telling him what was wrong. Dr. Cain drove down immediately. When he arrived, Mary asked Cain to repeat everything he had told her in front of his father—which he did. Dr. Cain tried to reason with his son for about an hour, but realized that his mind was made up and nothing would change it. Then he advised Mary that, under the circumstances, her going home to her mother would offer the least unpleasant notoriety. So it was settled, Mary agreed to leave within a few days, and Cain moved out temporarily.

The next day, Mary's mother came over from Church Hill and took her daughter home. In a week or so, Mary wrote Cain asking him to consider changing his mind. He did not reply for some time, but when he did, he said he had thought the matter through again, at greater length, and still was convinced this was the best thing.

There is no reliable information about precisely what went wrong in their marriage, except the implications of physical incompatibility in Cain's writings. They parted on February 18, 1924, and were never reconciled. Mary suffered greatly after the breakup, and it was a painful experience for Cain, too. "There's no such thing as an amicable end to a marriage. It's an ugly, wracking thing, and though later a new relationship may come, at the time it is war, and pure hell."

At about the same time, Cain's gradually deteriorating relations with Major Garey also reached a crisis, brought to a head by a trivial incident. One morning, the major was due to leave for New York to meet with some men he was courting for money. As he walked from his office in McDowell Hall to his home following a brief conference with Dean Edward Sirich, he passed Pinkney Hall and heard a voice bellow out from a third floor window: "Hey, Garey! Hey, Goofer Garey!"

The major turned around, marched back to the office, and told Sirich to fire four hired football players, who he was sure had yelled at him, for yelling at him. Then he walked over to the Short Line Station, across from the other end of the campus, and took the train to New York. Sirich, greatly upset, called the four boys in and carried out the major's orders.

About this time, Cain walked into the office and Sirich told him what had happened. Cain was appalled. He paced around for a while, and finally said: "Well, Si, he may be president of the college, and he may be able to tell, just by the sound of one voice, without seeing anything, who yelled 'Goofer Garey' at him—but I'm a member of the faculty, and the charter of the college says he runs it with the faculty's assistance. I don't stand for it."

Garey returned that night and the Executive Committee on which Cain served met to discuss the firing of the four students. Cain argued that the college had a commitment, and when Garey stood firm on his decision, Cain resigned effective at the end of the semester. The next day, through pressure Cain brought to bear on the bank that did business with the college, Garey backed down and reinstated the four football players.

But Cain's resignation stood, and with unemployment only weeks away, he turned to his typewriter and spent all his free time writing furiously for Mencken. He had already finished his piece "The Editorial Writer," which appeared in the April 1924 *Mercury*. It was a curious, witty portrayal of the typical cynical newspaper reporter's transformation into a patriotic, dull, un-inspired editorial writer, a piece growing no doubt out of his observations while on the *Sun*. "The man is a Priest," Cain describes him. "He is Keeper of the Soul of the American People. He sits alone in his office, high above the madding crowd, and as he sits, soft voices rise from below. When he hears them, he passes into a long, long dream, and as he dreams, his hand (which holds a pencil) begins to write and write and write. . . . The voices are so soft that few could hear them at all, but the man hears them because hearing them is his trade. They are the Voices of the People, the Voice of God."

The article was modeled on Ernest Boyd's attack on aesthetes in the first issue of the *Mercury*, and Cain quickly followed this biting portrait with an even more acerbic attack on college professors, "Pedagogue: Old Style." Again, he was shooting at one of Mencken's favorite targets, the arrogant, see-both-sides-of-the-question intellectual, who Mencken felt dominated academia. Cain had met several of these pedants in his father's world and his own teaching years; in fact, he had written Mencken from St. John's that "there is a bird here who is the perfect type." Cain's concluding sketch ex-plains perhaps why Cain has never been very popular with academic critics, readers of old magazines that they are:

But there the gentleman is, in any college, or university, of the land. Having, by four years of servitude, come into possession of his Ph.D., he sits back and allows nature to take its course, his face growing pinker and fresher, his hair grayer and grayer and whiter and whiter, and his commencement robes more gorgeous as D.C.L.'s and Litt. D.'s and LL.D.'s descend gently upon him like manna from Heaven. Some-times he writes a book whereof the opening sentence is: "Literature is self-expression through words." And as he lectures and smiles and rebukes contumely and memorizes bright quips out of Latin grammars and the Gospel of St. Mark, so his eyes glow brighter and brighter at the thought of what a wise man goes there, and that after all, it *is* worth while.

Cain's friendship with Mencken had now progressed to the point that he was initiated into the Sunday Night Club, a beer-drinking, musicmaking group similar to Mencken's other famous sodality, the Saturday Night Club. And his growing confidence in the relationship with Mencken can be seen in an incident that happened in May 1924. For clubbers who imbibed too many spirits in the drinking sessions after the musicmaking, Mencken had prescribed his own remedy, a certain amount of Epsom salt, which Mencken claimed had been recommended by a highly esteemed physician. One morning, suffering from an especially bad hangover, Cain took the remedy with apparently the wrong proportion of Epsom salt and immediately became quite ill. When he recovered, he prepared an affidavit denouncing Mencken as "dishonest, false, fraudulent, and a common nuisance" and stating that his therapeutic remedy was null and void. He sent it to the Club and it eventually found its way to Alfred A. Knopf's office, where it hung for years.

Cain's writing was also progressing and his reputation growing, but at $60 an article he had to think seriously about what he would do next. He actually did not mind the prospect of leaving St. John's, because after a year of teaching again he was more than ever convinced one could not teach a person to write, and now he was not even sure one could teach punctuation. But the affair with Garey was unsettling. He began to wonder if maybe he was responsible for the upheaval at St. John's, and this led to the first real misgivings about himself (which he would have many times in the future), that maybe he was something of a stormy petrel, with the capacity to stir up much more controversy than his convictions were worth.

With the semester almost over, the situation was looking bleak for Cain, and by way of confirming the adage that when things are going bad, everything goes wrong, he began to have coughing spells and chest pains. A Baltimore doctor confirmed his suspicions that he had tuberculosis. "You've got it all right," said the doctor, "now let's let an X ray tell us how much."

The X ray told them that Cain had a spot about the size of a quarter in the apex of his right lung. It was an active lesion, and soon he began to have all the symptoms—loss of weight and appetite, fever, and a cough. He moved in with the Siriches, and Marjorie Sirich took care of him, enabling him to stagger through the rest of the term.

At the end of the semester, Cain packed up and went off to the state tuberculosis sanitarium in Sabillasville, "chasing the cure," as confinement in a TB ward was called in those days. Considering everything that had happened to him, Cain was curiously not downcast, at least when he first entered the sanitarium. Because of a "dim-witted, irrational, groundless optimism that seemed part of my nature," he was actually feeling optimistic. One reason was that he was receiving more money than he had ever made in his life—thanks in part to his doctor's conviction that his lung condition was aggravated by his World War I exposure to mustard gas, a disability which now brought him a $190-a-month pension. That money was in addition to the $300 or so a month the college was still paying him. On top of that, he was selling magazine articles to Mencken. Two pieces—which appeared later in the November and December 1924 issues of *Mercury*—were written at Sabillasville. The first, "Politician: Female," explored the question of the female politician, revealing Cain's constant love for women as women, but showing considerably less admiration for women when they try to become involved in the man's world of politics. Long thought and observation led Cain to the conclusion "that there is only one situation in which a woman can be completely ridiculous; that one in which her husband and her lover shake hands, fill glasses and pledge each other's health." But now he had concluded that there were many situations where women "in the mass," as opposed to woman the individual, can be ridiculous. "Woman, like a harmonica, shines best as a solo instrument. When she attempts to play *ensemble* the result is often disastrous"—and in the role of politician, women were acting *ensemble*.

In the other article, "High Dignitaries of State," Cain turned his attention to American male political leaders and produced a scathing evaluation. He was not concerned with their "usefulness," but with "the cut of their jibs, the way they look and sound, their effectiveness as dramatic figures. It may be that to the student of government they are models, and offer material for thick books, but to the connoisseur of show, there is undoubtedly something lacking in them." Contrasting Washington, Jefferson, Lincoln, Lee, and Wilson with Alexander, Caesar, Constantine, Charlemagne, William, Cromwell, Louis, Peter, Frederick, Napoleon, and Bismarck, he found American statesmen wanting. One reason was that "the source of all dramatic appeal in public men is power," and in America, naked, open power was denied the statesman. He had to pretend he did not have the power he actually possessed. True power in America lay with the political boss—Tweed, Crocker, Hanna, Gorman, Murphy, Penrose—names that "stir the imagination," but the bosses were sleeping under the hill. "And Harding has a Memorial."

Both pieces were good, vintage, 1920s idol-busting, but Cain probably had these two articles, as well as his earlier ones, in mind when he said in later years that he was not proud of some of his *American Mercury* articles, that he had fallen too much under the spell of Mencken and his iconoclasm.

Expenses at Sabillasville were only $17 a week, and even that modest sum permitted him to stay in the "Gentleman's Club," a pavilion with rooms shared by two patients. When Cain moved into the Club, he was put in with a hunchback who had tuberculosis of the spine, and on the first day, as they were putting on their pajamas for the regular afternoon nap, his roommate asked almost casually: "What do you suppose would have happened if Bessie Tate had caught up with that guy?" "I don't know," Cain replied. "I've often wondered, though." The man was referring to a scene from Cain's childhood when his sixth grade teacher, Miss Bessie Tate, had gotten angry and chased a boy around the room with a ruler. Then suddenly Cain woke up. "Bessie Tate?" he snapped. "Hey, who are you? Who the *hell* are you?" The hunchback grinned with utmost delight. "Jamie," he said, "I'm Bill Burke." Cain stared, and then at last remembered him—an old friend from grade school. They shook hands, then talked about Bessie Tate until they went to sleep.

Despite his optimism, it is hard to imagine Cain not being downcast—in fact, on one occasion, he said that in Sabillasville he was "at the end of the plank," and probably he was indeed further out on the plank than at any other time in his life: thirty-two years old, out of a job, no prospects for the future, drinking too much for his own good, ill of a debilitating disease that would probably never be completely cured, separated from his wife, his girl friend in New York, and incarcerated in a dreary little town in northern Maryland.

There was no such thing as a complete cure for tuberculosis in 1924. But if caught in time, the disease could be arrested, perhaps for life. Cain did manage to arrest his, primarily by being very realistic about how sick he was and not putting off his trip to the sanitarium, as some people did, kidding themselves that it would take care of itself. At least that was his explanation for his recovery. By September, Dr. Victor E. Cullen, the superintendent at Sabillasville, gave him a favorable report and said he could return to a reasonable normal life.

What now? A normal life for a "lunger," as Cain called himself, meant rest in the afternoon and no exertion. This would seem to suggest finding another job as a teacher. But Cain had lost interest in teaching—even as a way to bring in money while he sought a career as a writer—and in any case he probably would have had difficulty finding a college teaching job after resigning from St. John's in a cloud of controversy. This left journalism.

Cain had had time to do a lot of thinking about his future at Sabillasville. One thing he'd decided was that he no longer had to "be somebody" to make his father happy, because everyone knew a "lunger" could have only limited ambitions. For a while, at the *Sun* and at St.John's, he had soured on the literary life, primarily because of his inability to write a novel; he was, in fact, even "meditating a high pressure career of some other kind, not clearly envisioned." Now, however, he was convinced he still wanted to write. As he left the sanitarium, his pockets were literally bulging with checks and money he had accumulated from his college salary, Uncle Sam, free-lance writing, and winnings at poker. It was a nice feeling, and he wanted to keep his pockets full, agreeing more than ever now with Dr. Johnson. And he thought of his friend Jack Wilson's remark that "if you want to make money, go where the money is." He translated that to mean that if you wanted to swim in deep water, you had to go where the deep water was, which, in journalism, meant New York.

In New York there was also Elina, settled with her mother and two children and eking out a living by running a home for registered nurses. Now that Cain was separated from Mary, Elina would not resist him on the grounds that he was a married man; he would be free to court her.

Although Cain was apprehensive about his chances in the big time, he was not without credentials, having had five major articles in the *Atlantic*, *The Nation*, and *American Mercury*, three of the most important intellectual magazines of the day. He also had a solid reputation as a reporter for a prominent eastern newspaper. And before leaving the sanitarium, Cain had persuaded Mencken to write him a letter of introduction to someone in authority on the *New York World*. Mencken responded with a note to Arthur Krock, a young newspaperman who had recently come up from the *Louisville Courier-Journal* to work for the *World* as a special assistant to its publisher, Ralph Pulitzer. The letter was glowing in its praise of Cain—as Krock said, "one of Henry's rare understatements."

Cain had the letter with him when he took the train to New York. He had decided that you never apply for "a job" or a "place on your staff." What you did was assess an organization in advance, find out what kind of work you could do, and apply for a specific job—preferably with suggestions for improving on what was being done when you knocked on the door. The job Cain had picked for himself was in the *World* editorial section, though not as an editorial writer. As his *Mercury* article suggested, he did not think much of editorial writers.

Cain had been to New York often enough, visiting his friend Leonard Cline and seeing Elina, to be familiar with the *World*'s editorial page. He was impressed by the cartoons of Rollin Kirby and the columns, but he thought the rest of the section was weak and was surprised it carried virtually no articles. Maybe he could correct that. He conceived of himself as an articles-chaser, or what is called today the op-ed (opposite-editorial) page editor. It was a full-time job, Cain knew, but more important, it was a sitting-down job, which Dr. Cullen at the sanitarium had advised him to seek.

His first stop in New York was an apartment in Greenwich Village, where Leonard Cline had invited him to stay. But when he rang the bell, he was greeted by a strange face, belonging to a young man named Malcolm Ross. Cline, it seemed, had departed for St. Louis, leaving his contribution to the rent for the apartment somewhat in arrears. Cain said he would pay Cline's debt and his own share if he could move in, and this was agreeable to Ross.

By 1924, the legendary gold-domed *World* building, at the north corner of Park Row, had passed its prime. When it was dedicated in 1890—sixteen stories, towering 310 feet—it was the tallest building in the city, and incredulous visitors from the hinterlands (as well as sophisticated New Yorkers) paid to visit its domed top, from where the view was spectacular and the climate—intellectual as well as atmospheric—heady. But now the building had deteriorated. For one thing it was drafty, and when a *World* reporter died of influenza in 1922, the paper's flamboyant editor, Herbert Bayard Swope, complained to owner Ralph Pulitzer that he was probably done in by the foul atmosphere on the twelfth floor.

Swope's office, known as the "lion's den," or, as Lincoln Schuster called it, the "swope-filled room," was also on the twelfth floor, as were the offices of the *Evening World*. One floor below was the Sunday department, and one floor above, the restaurant. The condition of the restaurant had reached the point where it was said that the only good thing ever to come out of it was *What Price Glory?*, the new Broadway smash *World* writers Maxwell Anderson and Laurence Stallings had conceived over lunch in its seedy confines.

At the top of the building, in the rarefied atmosphere of the fourteenth floor, was the talented corps of editorial writers who worked for the recently hired Walter Lippmann—Anderson, Charles Merz, Allan Nevins, John Heaton, and W. O. Scroggs. Between assignments, as Pulitzer's right-hand man, Arthur Krock also contributed an occasional editorial.

Cain arrived at a critical time in the declining days of the *World*. Its rise to journalistic glory had begun in 1883, when Joseph Pulitzer, the publishing genius who had built the *St. Louis Post-Dispatch*, purchased the paper from New York financier Jay Gould. Within two weeks, the front page had been transformed from the sedate print-dominated format of the traditional nineteenth-century newspaper to an attractive, lively page featuring a large photograph, engaging headlines, and well-written news stories. The *World* had begun its crusade to lead the American press into a new era of journalism. Unlike most papers of its time, it supported the Democratic party and the workingman against the entrenched Establishment and prided itself on hard-hitting stories exposing political and economic corruption.

Since 1920, the paper had been under Swope's direction as executive editor. This dynamic journalist had been one of the *World*'s star crime reporters in the early years, then its war correspondent in France. But despite his energetic leadership, the *World*'s distinctive reporting began to decline after World War I. "By 1923," Morris Markey later wrote, "the reaching out, the sharp and arresting miracle of zeal" was gone. "Somewhere in those years, so subtly that a moment cannot be fixed with any certainty at all, the rude vigor, the yowling boisterous assurance of the Pulitzer tradition died. The times were changing. The *World* was changing. With every politician a grafter, why bellow at one? With an aura of sad futility drooping over the earth's evils, why explode to the echo of a single evil? Why snarl at a President of the United States?"

If the *World*'s reporting had declined, however, the editorial section had gradually emerged as the paper's most distinctive feature. It was intelligent and well written, and its lead items were sometimes brilliant. Although the op-ed page did not have articles by outsiders, it did have columns, including the already famous "Conning Tower" by Franklin P. Adams, Heywood Broun's "It Seems to Me," Laurence Stallings's book review, "The First Reader," and a regular column from Washington by Charley Michelson (who would one day be President Franklin D. Roosevelt's press secretary). The Sunday "Metropolitan Section" also ran a regular feature by Will Rogers. It was the quality of these sections that prompted *The New Yorker*, soon after its birth in 1925, to proclaim it intended to be a weekly comparable in intelligence, good taste, honesty, courage, news sense, and interest to the *New York World*. And "the Page Opposite Editorial, rather than the front page," wrote Markey, "became the goal of every dreamy cub in the land."

At thirty-two, James M. Cain was hardly a cub, but it was the *World*'s Page Opposite that lured him that day late in September 1924 when he sought out Arthur Krock in the upper reaches of the Pulitzer Building. And what Cain did not know was that one of the editorials that day, headed "The Insatiable Telegraph," was to be the last editorial written for the *World* by Maxwell Anderson. The blossoming playwright had specialized in what editors call human-interest editorials, little essays, sometimes light and breezy, on subjects of interest to everyone—food, transportation, human relations, animals, holidays, sports, music, etc. But now, after the success of

What Price Glory?, Anderson was ready to devote full time to writing plays, and Lippmann desperately needed a human-interest editorial writer to replace him.

Cain found his way to Krock's office on the fourteenth floor, and Krock immediately suggested they go over to see Walter Lippmann. Cain knew of Lippmann, of course; he had also read his book *Public Opinion*, which had not especially impressed him. He thought Lippmann was "intellectualizing a subject not really intellectual." But when Krock brought him into Lippmann's office, Cain was suddenly face to face with a man who did not look at all like the person he imagined from reading his books. He was nearly six feet tall with a blocky build, thick strong hands, handsome and poised and in complete possession of himself. After the introductions, Krock left, and Cain and Lippmann began to talk. Cain was somewhat surly and truculent because he was certain Krock's passing him on to Lippmann was really the brush-off. Dropping his usual tough-guy talk, he began criticizing the editorial section for its lack of articles, suggesting that he would like to develop them in such a way as to "orchestrate your themes," as he put it to Lippmann.

Cain soon realized he was not impressing the editor with his monologue on articles, but at the same time, as Lippmann stared at him with his big brown eyes, Cain knew he was listening carefully to every word he said. Suddenly, Lippmann surprised Cain by asking him if he had any samples of his writing. Cain did not know quite what to make of this because he was not applying for a writing job. He said he did not have any with him, but he could have his mother send up some from Baltimore. Lippmann said that would be fine, so Cain left and called his mother and asked her to rush to Lippman a packet of his pieces from the *Atlantic*, *Mercury*, and *Nation*.

Still, Cain was not very hopeful. He began studying other New York newspapers, trying to come up with ideas that might lead to a job. But then, only a day or two after his visit to the *World*, he received a wire from Lippmann (the apartment did not have a phone) asking him to come by his office and talk about a job. Lippmann later explained to Cain that when he heard him talk during their first interview he noted that his participles did not dangle, his infinitives were tightly knit, and his pronouns had antecedents. It was one of those rare occasions when Cain spoke the perfect English he was capable of, and Lippmann felt that anyone who talked as well as Cain must possess the gift for writing the kind of editorials he wanted. In short, Cain's lifelong obsession with grammar and the English language had opened the door to one of the most coveted jobs in journalism—editorial writer for the *New York World*. However, he did not quite have the job yet.

When Cain reported to the *World* for the second time, Lippmann said that if he was interested in writing editorials, he would give him a trial. Cain said he was; Lippmann handed him a bundle that contained all the New York newspapers for that day, said he could use an office and a typewriter upstairs, and asked him to write some "leaders," as Lippmann, in the British tradition, called editorials, on any subject he wanted. Then they would see. If Lippmann liked them, he would guarantee to buy at least two a day for $10 apiece, and if they continued to be satisfactory he would make a more permanent arrangement.

Cain could not believe it. For one thing, he did not want to be an editorial writer. And although he showed considerable knowledge about how editorials were written, he later maintained that when Lippmann suggested he write some sample editorials that day he had no idea how it was done. At the *Sun*, they had called them "idiotorials," and "to a working stiff in the news departments, they are think pieces, not respected at all, done by trained seals with green eye-shades, most of them very elderly. Their only qualification was that they be in favor of motherhood and against the man-eating shark."

Cain went upstairs to the office, a little cubicle under the golden dome, overlooking the Brooklyn Bridge. The room had a rolltop desk and a typewriter—an Underwood, his favorite model. He sat down and opened the bundle of papers to peep at the editorial pages; he hoped they would give him some idea what to write about. They were all deep pieces—on the Ruhr, the tariff, the coming presidential election, Calvin Coolidge, and the Teapot Dome scandals. He scanned the rest of the news but found nothing to spark him. Mr. Highland, a kindly gentleman from the typesetting room, said the Ruhr was a good subject to write about, and Cain said, sure, he could write about it "as soon as I find out where it is."

After an hour of trying to decide what to write about, Cain found himself coming back to the man-eating shark. He thought: Well, everyone's in favor of motherhood, but what about this fish? Why should one oppose it? "Leave us never forget," he said to himself, "the man-eating shark is viviparous—it brings forth its young alive. It's kind to its young and it's been doing this over ten million years before the human race was ever heard of. The man-eating shark was the first mother, and in a very real sense the man-eating shark is motherhood." That, Cain decided, was his editorial, and he wrote it. Then he wrote another in somewhat the same vein, about a Congressman who purposely had himself indicted for making home beer.

But then he decided this was enough. He did not have a prayer in the world of becoming an editorial writer. He dropped his impish efforts on the desk of Lippmann's secretary and "slunk down the circular stairs and out of Lippmann's life."

He was not sure what to do now. His big plan for working on the *World* had blown up in his face, so he walked around Greenwich Village for a while, pondering his next move. He finally decided to have dinner and get drunk. He ended up at a speakeasy on Grove Street, where he was supposed to meet Malcolm Ross. Around 11:00 P.M., Mike arrived with two bulldog editions of the *World*. Cain did not open his paper but continued drinking his scotch. After Mike ordered his drink, he began reading the paper, and then he began to laugh. "Pretty funny! Did you write this?"

Cain looked at the page a minute and said, "Yeah, I wrote it." He could not believe his eyes. Lippmann had used one of his editorials, the one about the Congressman. It was not exactly hilarious, but after all Cain was writing for Walter Lippmann, not Harold Ross.

Still skeptical, Cain went to the *World* office the next morning and found everybody friendly with "hellos," especially Lippmann, who asked if he had any leader ideas for today. Cain said no, "but I'll think of something." "Well, do it," said Lippmann. "Those are very funny pieces. I was very glad to get them. I didn't use that piece about the shark—a very funny piece, but I don't like pieces about the newspaper business itself." "Oh, inbreeding," Cain said. "That's the idea," Lippmann replied. "All right. I'll remember that."

Cain now had a job—at a minimum of $20 a day. A few days later, he had two editorials in the paper, including one on baseball, which would soon become one of his favorite subjects. The Washington Senators, with their great fast-balling pitcher, Walter Johnson, and boy-wonder manager, Bucky Harris, had just won the American League pennant, and Cain wrote a nice, lighthearted piece hailing the conquering heroes. Ten days later, Washington won the World Series, the victory coming over the New York Giants in the bottom of the twelfth inning of the seventh game on a now-famous grounder hit down the left side of the infield. When the ball struck a pebble and bounced over third baseman Freddie Lindstrom's head, the Senators had their first (and only) World Series title. Cain joined the hysteria: "It is given to some cities to be Carthage and rule the seas. It is given to some to be Rome and rule the world. It is given to others to win the World Series. The greatest of these is Washington."

Everything went along fine for weeks, with Cain writing his little "japes," as he called them, and Lippmann seemingly very pleased. Cain was soon averaging seven to ten edits a week (including Saturday), although on October 31, 1924, and again on November 11, he had four in one day. His edits were usually light and on subjects of interest to the average man and woman: sunken treasure; a bishop encouraging jazz in church while another bishop bans dancing in church; federal regulation of baseball (horrors!); four men disappearing in the Arctic; a woman matador (why not?); invention of a truth serum (what happens when politicians have to use it!); the trouble with American opera (it's not American).

Cain had been on the *World* less than six months when he had a minor confrontation with editorial page policy. In 1924, the *World* had led the attack against those critics who tried to suppress *What Price Glory?* But early in 1925, Lippmann decided "the line must be drawn somewhere," i.e., certain plays should not be performed. What prompted the turnabout was a play entitled *A Good Bad Woman*. The *World*, in an editorial written by Lippmann, said it pandered to a low public taste and that it was the producer's responsibility "to protect the stage against corruption from the inside, which can lead only to censorship from the outside."

Cain, who by now had become a dedicated foe of censorship in any form—a lifelong preoccupation—responded to Lippmann's proposal for what he called a "play jury" by counterattacking in *The Nation*, arguing that "one man's art was another man's poison" and pointing out that although the *World* had thought *What Price Glory?* was Art, the average Army officer would not consider it Art and might find it as objectionable as any play the *World* might consider offensive. He also said he had turned to the comic strip "Mutt and Jeff" in the *World* and been shocked by some of the things that were in there. Applying the *World*'s logic to Mutt and Jeff, he asked: Is it Art? Does the *World* think it's Art? Does it pander to low public taste? Why is it published? He concluded that it was published because it sold papers, and there was an "uncomfortably close analogy between the theatrical business and the newspaper business." He also pointed out that the average burlesque show was pretty vulgar, but if it amused sailors, soldiers, and taxicab drivers, then these citizens of the United States were entitled to their amusement.

The *World* eventually backed away from its "play jury," and Cain still had his job. In fact, Lippmann never gave any indication of having been annoyed at Cain's independent, public stand on the issue.

But Lippmann was annoyed at something else—as Cain began to notice through a change in his attitude. Without being aware of it, Cain had succumbed to the curse of all editorial writers: the compulsion to shoulder the burdens of the world and lecture his readers. He had, in short, turned serious, and it bothered Lippmann. Cain's little "japes" on baseball, music, and the human comedy had now become studious and too long treatises on such things as the Woodrow Wilson Foundation "Peace Award," the proposal for a new Department of Air, rewriting the King James Version of the Bible, and the situation in the West Virginia coal mines. He also dabbled in world affairs, which probably annoyed Lippmann even more because he considered himself the resident international expert.

It was Krock who finally set Cain straight on what was happening. One day, the two men were having lunch in the *World* dining room. Krock greeted Cain amiably and asked how things were going, to which Cain mumbled some evasive reply. Krock asked what was wrong and Cain said: "Oh, I guess things are all right, but I don't know who I'm kidding. For Christ sake, I can't write editorials."

"Nonsense," Krock said. "You're doing fine. Lippmann is pleased. But you have to stop getting serious. Keep on writing those funny pieces you started with." Then Krock cited Maxwell Anderson's experience. "He'd been doing the light editorials for Walter," Krock explained, "but instead of sticking to what he did well—the human, sentimental kind of pieces—he was getting serious, and Lippmann was relieved when Anderson quit. Now you're doing the same thing." Krock pointed out that Lippmann had Allan Nevins on history, Charles Merz on politics, W. O. Scroggs on economics, John Heaton on state politics, and Lippmann himself on international affairs. "But pleasant, light pieces, with enough intellect in them to spike up the letter column and be worth publishing, are tough to get. That's what he wants from you." "You mean this nonsense I write is worth something?" Cain asked. "They pay you for stuff like that? They actually pay you?"

Cain still could not believe that his lighthearted japes were what Lippmann wanted. But he was getting the message. He went back to his office and wrote that a man convicted of the unlawful practice of medicine handed out cards on which were printed "B.T.H.M.P.S.D.C." Asked by the judge what the initials meant, the man replied, "Baptist, Truth, Heaven, Master of Political Science, and Doctor of Chiropractic." Cain thought this was a fine idea and suggested similar sheepskins for bootleggers, brokers, and bandits, with the credentials for the last one reading: "B.S.U.Y.H.Q.O.I.B.Y.O.— Bandit, Stick Up Your Hands Quick Or I'll Bump You Off."

Lippmann was happy again, and Cain was given a three-year contract for $125 a week. Now he could go down to Baltimore and tell his mother: "You've been proclaiming for years that I don't have good sense, and events have proved you're right—but in New York they pay you for it."

Cain's admiration of Walter Lippmann as a man, a writer, and, most important to him, a literary stylist at times bordered on hero worship, and he lists Lippmann, along with Mencken, producer Philip Goodman, and screenwriter Vincent Lawrence, as the men who had the greatest influence on his life. Cain's and Lippmann's mutual love affair with the English language helped bring them together, both professionally and as friends. In fact, Cain thought their real friendship began one day when they were lunching at the Hardware Club in the Woolworth Building, and he told Lippmann about his father drilling proper speech into him as a child, the fact that he had taught English in two colleges, and that he had spent months studying rhetoric. Later, Lippmann explained his respect for Cain when he remarked: "You get more stuff in this paper than your God-given talent entitles you to. I suppose you know that." "Well, I don't," Cain replied. "If so, why?" "Because you know once I've read it for sense, that I can pitch it in that basket without having to spend the next hour translating flat-wheeled sentences into English."

Lippmann's complexion in the twenties was what Cain called "the pale color of health," and he not only gave the impression of great strength, he was indeed surprisingly strong. Once, on their way to lunch, Lippmann stopped as he and Cain reached the curb on the sidewalk in front of the Pulitzer Building and said: "Jim, I think it's up to the few to keep civilization from being pulled down by the many—don't you?" Cain was so startled at this idea that his head snapped around as he stepped off the curb, only to have an iron grip crush his arm as he was *lifted* back from the path of a taxi, which Cain felt certain would have killed him except for Lippmann.

But the thing Cain liked most about Lippmann was his gentle manner. "In my work," said Cain, "he was courtesy itself, and he never once raised the question of who was boss and who was employee. He seemed to understand instinctively that at this kind of work, writing editorials for a newspaper, opinions can't be commanded; that those which can be aren't worth very much. He didn't want men around him who could be commanded to think in a certain way." But most important, Lippmann never disparaged Cain or looked down on him for rewriting his editorials—sometimes a half-dozen times—until he felt they were right. It was for this reason that Cain said he owed Lippmann a deep, personal debt—that is, for making it possible for him to work in the newspaper business and at the same time develop as a writer.

There were many other men at the *World* in the twenties who would play an important part in Cain's life and become lasting friends. In fact, there may have never been such a glittering assemblage of journalistic and literary talent under one dome as the men and women who worked in the Pulitzer Building in 1924. James M. Cain had finally reached deep water.

BOMBING OUT IN
STAMFORD AND
WORCESTER

One morning early in January 1925, a piece enti-
tled "How the Finns Keep Fit" appeared on the op-ed page of the *World*.
Although the article was by-lined Elina Sjosted Tyszecka, it was written by
James M. Cain, who was seeing Elina regularly now that he was permanently
separated from Mary. Elina was still working as a governess, living with her
family, and operating a home for nurses, but she and Cain were meeting so
often they needed a place of their own. So Cain left the apartment he shared
with Malcolm Ross and moved to a three-room apartment on Van Nest Place
just off Seventh Avenue in the Village. There Cain and Elina would meet,
"insanely happy," Cain said, "though still unable to talk." However, Elina
did speak German a bit, and "it was, no doubt, a step toward greater intimacy. And yet I have often thought we were on better terms, with only pats and
looks and kisses, than we were when speech was added." In fact, they were
so happy patting and kissing that Cain later speculated on a novel about two
people who managed love, marriage, and children without being able to
speak to each other. He thought his relationship with Elina was ideal, and
Felix Morley remembers seeing them when they were living together and says
Cain "was almost aggressive about wanting you to know he was 'living in
sin.' "

The idyllic affair came to a temporary end when Elina had to return to Finland. Her mother needed to settle her bankruptcy proceedings and the children had passport problems. So around the end of 1925, Elina and Cain had one last idyll in the Willard Hotel in Washington, before he put her on the boat for Helsinki. She was to be gone eighteen months.

Cain was now a bachelor—separated from his wife but pledged to another woman who was still married. During the day, he was completely absorbed in his job and Elina's absence presented no problem. The evenings, however, were different. "I took to eating dinner in Lee Chumley's restaurant around the corner and he would sit down for a chat—but chats with a restaurant keeper wind up the same way: A waitress appears with an unhappy look on her face and he excuses himself and goes. You start calling up guys you know. Some of them are in the same boat as you are, but around 10:00 begin looking at their watches. That means they're due at the stage door of a theater, where a good-looking girl is playing, and at 10:25 they shake hands and take themselves off."

Then, of course, it happened. "One night, quite by accident, I ran into a girl I knew out on the sidewalk in front of the Pulitzer Building . . ." and as he describes the ensuing affair for several pages in his memoirs, it reads like a James M. Cain short story. It was the beginning of what Cain called one of the strangest relationships in his life. The girl worked in the editorial department and knew about Elina, occasionally asking when she was returning but without showing a hint of jealousy. It was a purely physical relationship, with her taking as little interest in Cain, except for what they did in bed, as Cain did in her. Eventually they separated. "And yet, if I met her on the street," Cain said years later, "I think the old excitement would stir—in her as well as in me."

Considering how much outside writing Cain did after he went to work for the *World*, it is a wonder he had any time for romantic affairs. But for a writer in New York in the 1920s, books, plays, and magazines were almost as exciting as women—and maybe even as intoxicating as gin and whiskey. Nineteen twenty-five was the first year in at least a decade in which there was no war, no postwar hysteria, no national election, and no change of administration. President Calvin Coolidge, who had come into the presidency after the strange death of Warren G. Harding, was reelected in 1924, and the nation settled down to perhaps the longest and gaudiest pleasure-seeking binge in its history. Leading the way in this endless party was New York City, where the pace was set by the writers, editors, journalists, and publishers whose *bons mots* were quoted around the nation: There was the *World* crowd, the *New Yorker* crowd, the "21" crowd, the entire membership of the Algonquin Round Table (also known as the Vicious Circle), and the Thanatopsis Literary and Inside Straight Club. Their members were interchangeable, belonging to more than one group, and most are now part of our literary lore—Alexander Woollcott, Franklin P. Adams, Heywood Broun, Laurence Stallings, Herbert Bayard Swope, Harold Ross, Robert Sherwood, Robert Benchley, Dorothy Parker, Marc Connelly, George S. Kaufman, Jane Grant, Ruth Hale, Edna Ferber, Margaret Leech, and a galaxy of part-time members from the literary, journalistic, and theater worlds. They were known for their verbal thrusts and counterthrusts, if not the quality or volume of their literary work. As Broun said, "The brilliance of the literary decade was in part reflected in its talkers."

There was also Burton Rascoe, a brilliant young literary critic for the *New York Tribune*, who attacked the incestuous book reviewing of Broun, Adams, and Woollcott only to find himself out of a job when the *Herald* and *Tribune* merged to form one of the city's brightest literary papers. And then there were the publishers: young Alfred A. Knopf, who impressed the literary community with the quality of his Borzoi editions, making most writers aspire to become Knopf authors or at least try to persuade their own publishers at lunch to improve the physical quality of their books; and Horace Liveright, co-owner of Boni and Liveright, whose advertising trade symbol was a cloistered monk, which his biographer called "the most misleading trademark that ever existed in the book trade." Liveright was renowned primarily for his sexual exploits and literary parties—or orgies, as some preferred to call them.

A great many writers, of course, fled this dreadful scene to become expatriates and live on the Left Bank in Paris. But there were still enough left to keep the gossip columnists and speakeasies busy. Not that the literary lights of the 1920s did nothing but attend parties, pursue women, make wisecracks, and drink. The books published by Boni and Liveright in 1925 have been called the most notable list ever released by a publishing house. They included Dreiser's *American Tragedy*; Sherwood Anderson's *Dark Laughter*; Ernest Hemingway's *In Our Time*; *Soldier's Pay*, by William Faulkner; Gertrude Atherton's *Crystal Cup*; novels by Heywood Broun, Paul Morand, and Konrad Bercovici, as well as Anita Loos's *Gentlemen Prefer Blondes* and the first American publication of Scott-Moncrieff's translation of Stendhal. Nonfiction included books by Hendrik van Loon, Dr. Morris Fishbein, Judge Ben Lindsey, Lewis Mumford, and Sigmund Spaeth. There were also poetry collections by T. S. Eliot, Edgar Lee Masters, Ezra Pound, and the first major publication by a poet named Robinson Jeffers.

And this was just the Liveright list. When you add the books by other publishers, it is apparent why most literary historians consider 1925 the most extraordinary year in the history of publishing: Fitzgerald's *The Great Gatsby*; *Arrowsmith*, by Sinclair Lewis; *Barren Ground*, by Ellen Glasgow; *The Professor's House*, by Willa Cather; *Death in Venice*, by Thomas Mann; *Manhattan Transfer*, by John Dos Passos; *Those Barren Leaves*, by Aldous Huxley; *Possession*, by Louis Bromfield; *Mrs. Dalloway*, by Virginia Woolf; *Thunder on the Left*, by Christopher Morley; as well as books by Elinor Wylie, Van Wyck Brooks, Amy Lowell, and many others still considered significant contributions to our literature.

In this atmosphere it is little wonder that Cain continued his interest in a serious writing career, although he was never attracted to the glittering social life in New York. He knew many of the wits and critics who made up this world, but he was not a member of the Round Table or the Thanatopsis Club. He was, in fact, not much of a socializer. He considered the "Interesting Conversationalist" one of God's most banal creatures, was not adept at bright quips and *bons mots*, and did not especially like the people who were. He preferred more serious intellectual conversation with like-minded friends, and those who knew him considered him "the angry man who wrote better than other people"—not a clever wit. He was more at home in a Village speakeasy than at the Algonquin or "21," and the parties he attended and gave were not like Horace Liveright's but rather, in his early days, typical Village affairs with often no chairs, cushions, or even mats for the guests to sit on.

The novel remained the most coveted and popular literary form, but Cain was still not convinced he would write one. What intrigued him now was the stage; along with others, he felt James M. Cain was developing as a talented natural writer of dialogue. In his time away from the office he was still writing primarily for Mencken, continuing his attacks on American types and institutions. In 1925, he singled out four—the pastor, county officials, and town commissioners, and the whole concept of do-gooding service—to be dissected for Mencken's *American Mercury*.

In "The Pastor," appearing in the May issue, Cain began by acknowledging that historically there was something genuine about the holy man, which made it all the more surprising, he wrote, that "the typical American man of God in these our days is so loathsome, such a low, greasy buffo, so utterly beneath ridicule, so fit only for contempt."

From that modest little lead, Cain went on to rip the pastor into shreds, referring to "the evangelical brother" as the only authentic American product and mercifully exempting all the other "priests and friars among us."

One man who was impressed by "The Pastor" was "the Sage of Potato Hill," E. W. Howe. In his widely quoted *Monthly*, published in Atkinson,

Kansas, Howe commented that "in a literary style not excelled by the best magazines at home or abroad, Mr. Cain calmly says pastors are not only useless, but a nuisance." Howe said he did not think such a statement was possible in the United States and that he was not accepting Mr. Cain's opinion—"only wondering at his boldness."

Two years before *Elmer Gantry*, this *was* bold stuff. And there can be little doubt that Cain's essay also had an impact on Sinclair Lewis, who read the *Mercury* and was by now a good friend of Mencken: through Mencken, these two exposers of religious charlatans would soon meet, and in all the debunking that went on in the Mencken crowd, it is hard to imagine Cain's article about the pastor not being discussed many times.

In another 1925 essay, "The Pathology of Service," Cain attempted to "isolate the bacillus of Service, the itch to make the world better." In this one Cain took a pseudoscholarly approach, lacing the article with impressive footnote references to quotations from Herbert Spencer's *Principles of Sociology* and *Data of Ethics*; Leslie Stephen's *Science of Ethics*; *Evolution and Ethics* by Thomas Huxley; and many more. Cain argued that the urge to public service derived from the idea of Progress as conceived by Herbert Spencer, although he absolved Spencer of all responsibility for what his theory had wrought in America. After pointing out that Spencer's thesis suggests there is no absolute standard of human conduct, he said that what is right in one society is wrong in another and what seems so conclusively in accordance with the Will of God is usually quite illusory. He concluded with a fine bit of Cainsian prose, saying all this "was equivalent to giving the Summum Bonum a kiss on the head with a potato masher, and indeed it has never been the same Summum Bonum since."

Cain found confirmation for his theory in the type of people who were attracted to Service as well as the types who were not. Those attracted were people who led insufferably dull lives; those not, according to their own notion, led a heroic existence. He listed several examples in both categories, exemplified by shoe store proprietors as likely to be attracted to Service, and actors who would not. He also maintained that if his theory was correct, it would seem that a person dedicated to Service who was suddenly thrust into a "heroic" job might lose his dedication, and that, conversely, a person quitting what he conceived as a heroic job would be extremely susceptible to the disease. As examples of backsliding Servists, he singled out members of Congress, most of whom were once upstanding Methodists, but who after serving in Washington awhile forsook the good and the true and became addicted to licentious practices. On the other hand, there were such men as John L. Sullivan, the Reverend William Sunday, and Benny Leonard, all of whom quit their original calling and went into Service. "Benny Leonard," for example, "after taking leave of the ring with an elegant valedictory, conceived the ambition of making the world healthy and sent Heywood Broun an exerciser."

What was the solution? "Progress be damned."

Cain's third and fourth targets in 1925—the county and town commissioners—were attacked in two *Mercury* contributions appearing in April and September. They were landmark pieces for the developing writer because in them he softened his iconoclasm by approaching the subject through fictional dialogues, as he called them, rather than with a biting essay. They also led to his first attempt at writing a play, and his first published book.

The April dialogue, "Servants of the People," concerned an incident that actually happened in southern Maryland. Some people who had died in a county almshouse were cremated in a rather primitive fashion, without a Christian ceremony and in many cases without the relatives' knowledge. In Cain's piece, the situation presents certain problems—as, for example, for Seventh-Day Adventists. Relatives show up protesting that the deceased would have objected to being cremated because it would make it difficult for them to rise up from the dead on that Day. The crisis is resolved, and the Seventh-Day Adventist votes saved, when it is agreed that if the county will pay for the cost, the almshouse will give the Seventh-Day Adventists a Christian burial.

"The Hero," lampooning town commissioners, concerns a petition to grant one Scotty Akers, a local fireman, a pension after he has been killed by a piece of falling timber while trying to prevent a family's home from burning down. The problem is that Scotty is not actually killed while putting out the blaze. His fire company, known as the Semper Fidelises, has arrived late at the fire only to find a rival company, the Water Witches, already fighting the blaze. Scotty, who is driving the Semper Fidelises' truck, yells: "Hell, ain't you got the fire out yet? Get out of the way and let some firemen get to it." This leads to a fire hose battle between the Witches and the Sempers, while the house burns down. Scotty is killed by the falling timber when his hose is trained on the rival fire company.

By late 1925, Cain had written nine major articles for the *Mercury*. Mencken considered him one of the magazine's star contributors, and after moving to New York Cain drew personally close to Mencken. Their friendship really blossomed, Cain thought, in 1925, when Cain developed a cough and thought he was having a recurrence of tuberculosis. He checked into a hospital in Blue Ridge Summit, Pennsylvania, and it turned out that all he had was a bad cold. With much relief he reported to Lippmann that it was not

TB, "so I guess you can expect to resume wrestling with my perverse imbecilities week after next—September 20." And he added: "Contrary to expectations, I am having a good time. She is about 50, with beautiful gray hair."

While he was in the hospital, Cain mentioned to a doctor his theory of voice—that it depends actually on the mass of bone in the skull rather than in the chest. "I often thought," he said, "if I ever had the chance, I'd like to weigh up some skulls and check them by means of a tuning fork against their actual resonance."

"Well, that's easy to fix," said the doctor, and soon appeared with a gunnysack full of skulls. Cain had his mother bring him a tuning fork and thereupon went to work testing his theory with a set of scales the doctor lent him, the tuning fork, and the skulls—at which moment, Mencken arrived with a bottle of red Spanish wine under his arm. When Cain explained what he was doing—and furthermore demonstrated that his theory was valid—Mencken's face lit up with astonishment. "I couldn't have invented something that would have raised me higher in his estimation," said Cain. Mencken was intensely interested, especially in the variation in the sizes of the skulls, and Cain explained that two or three were women's skulls. How did he know? Mencken asked. Because they had no frontal sinuses. Mencken was fascinated and glowed with admiration for Cain.

Twice a month, Mencken would go up to New York to work a few days on the *Mercury*, and while he was there he would stay at the Algonquin Hotel, although he was never part of the Round Table or the Thanatopsis Literary and Inside Straight Club. Like Cain, he did not enjoy the fast, precious insiders' patter of the Round Tablers. Mencken would always have plenty of liquor with him in his suitcase when he came to New York, and he usually entertained in his room, where the talk would be about magazine articles, books, and what was wrong with American society. On the weekends, especially during the periods when Elina was in Europe, Cain would go down to Baltimore to visit his folks and return on Sunday mornings, usually with Mencken going up to New York for his *Mercury* stint. They would get together and leave Baltimore on the 9:14 A.M. train. "He would jerk his thumb toward the diner," Cain said, "and that was where we would meet, though each of us had a chair in the Pullman. And so, for three hours, I would have him to myself as we ate breakfast, and listen to this incomparable monologue, with its verbal richness, endless high humor, and vast erudition."

Cain was also now the only out-of-town member of Mencken's Baltimore Saturday Night Club, which met at a member's house or Schellhase's restaurant. In these sessions, Mencken's "stooges," as Cain called them, gathered to listen to Mencken revere Bach and play Strauss. Mencken was a difficult man to be friends with, Cain said, because you never knew when he might turn on you, as he did at one time or another on several members of the Saturday Night Club. But Mencken never turned against Cain, so far as can be determined. He was continually trying to push Cain's career, as he did with many writers—Dreiser, Lewis, Willa Cather, to mention a few. In the summer of 1925, he wrote Blanche Knopf, wife of the publisher, that "Cain will be at my house on Sunday. He has ideas for several books."

On one of their train trips in 1925, Mencken said he wanted Cain to meet his friend Philip Goodman. And when Cain went over to 1524 Hollins Street, Mencken escorted him into the house. With all the doors open, they could see through the hallway to the backyard, and there, past the parlor, with a seidel of beer in his hand, back to the wall, and a huge paunch making an arc, was a man. "Isn't that a silhouette for you?" said Mencken.

"Who is he?" asked Cain.

"That's Goodman, the man I wanted you to meet."

Philip Goodman was probably the first of the modern advertising men. He was born in Philadelphia in 1885, where his father was a publisher, producing books such as *A Directory of Directories*. In the early part of the century, Goodman married and moved to New York, where his first job was working for Theodore Dreiser. The future author was then editor of the *Delineator*, a magazine published by the Butterick Company as an outlet for its dress patterns. Goodman sold advertising for the *Delineator*, then eventually started his own advertising company and was immediately successful. But Goodman's real interests were other than advertising. His early love of publishing took him briefly into the book business—first as publisher of *Bottoms Up*, by George Jean Nathan. Through Nathan, he met H. L. Mencken and published *In Defense of Women*. It was a Goodman stroke of genius, Cain said, to *defend* women rather than indict them, although the book can hardly be called a defense.

After book publishing Goodman turned to his greatest love—the theater. Through his membership in The Players club, he became good friends with a columnist for the *New York Tribune* named Don Marquis. They spent afternoons at the club drinking and talking, and Goodman would bring Marquis home to his apartment at 1000 Park Avenue, where his daughter Ruth remembers them discussing an idea for a play Goodman wanted Marquis to write. Eventually Marquis did—in three days, according to his biographer. Goodman found a co-producer, Arthur J. Hopkins, who put up half the money to produce *The Old Soak*, which opened in 1922 on Broadway and ran 425 performances, a record for the time. Not long after that, Goodman convinced a young pantomimist and juggler named W. C. Fields that he could act (before that, Fields had never spoken a word on stage) and the result was *Poppy*—another smash Goodman hit. Then there were several more hits, before Goodman went broke with one glorious flop—a musical called *Rainbow*.

After their introduction at Mencken's house in Baltimore, everyone drove out to the meeting of the Saturday Night Club, which was being held at the home of Willie Woollcott, Alexander's brother. Cain and Goodman eventually found themselves out in the yard under the trees, and Goodman began questioning him about his background. It soon became apparent that he wanted to persuade Cain to write a play. Goodman had been reading Cain in the *Mercury* and was particularly impressed by his dialogues. Cain told him about his West Virginia experience and the problem he had working the material into a novel. But Goodman was fascinated with the stories about the mines and kept coming back to something Cain mentioned—the widespread belief among the miners in the Second Coming of Christ. "It's the measure of their despair," Cain explained. "I often heard them say: 'Things can't go on like they are—they just can't, that's all!' "

Suddenly Goodman interrupted: "There's your play, Mr. Cain."

"Jim," said Cain.

"O.K., Jim, but . . . that belief shakes me up. It's for real; nothing theatrical about it."

The two men agreed there was a play in this idea, and Cain went back to New York eager to work immediately on the script. It was the beginning of a lifelong relationship with Goodman, who was "by far the closest friend I ever had," Cain said.

Working nights and weekends, Cain finished the play, which Goodman first called *Crashing the Pearly Gates*, then shortened to *Crashing the Gates*. Cain hated both titles. The story evolves around Linda Hicks, a superstitious, hysterical religious fanatic married to Buzz Hicks, a pathetic, miserable coal miner. They have a son, Oakey, who has been crippled in a mine accident, and an adopted daughter named Sally Jewell. Linda is so convinced that the Second Coming of Jesus is imminent that she sits for hours gazing out the window hoping to be the first to see Him. Down the road, instead, comes Syd Gody, a fast-talking, charismatic, confident miner-preacher, who does not hesitate to let Linda believe anything she wants about him as long as she is willing to be unfaithful to her husband. Convinced that Gody is the Saviour, she submits to him, but in the process pulls him under her mystical spell, until he half-believes he might be the Messiah returned. The plot thickens when Linda says if Gody can produce a victory for the miners in their strike against the coal operators and a miracle that will make her son well, that will prove he is the Messiah. Gody tries but fails to heal the son, who finally figures out what is going on. He tells Gody off in very strong language—perhaps the strongest language ever heard on the stage until that time—which completely breaks down Gody's confidence. He confesses his duplicity and gives Oakey a gun, inviting him to shoot him. Instead, Oakey has an accident with the gun and shoots himself. The miners arrive and, thinking Gody has murdered Oakey, tell him to stay where he is and wait for the sheriff, and that he will be shot if he tries to leave the tent. Gody waits for the sheriff, but Sally Jewell, the Hickses' adopted daughter, arrives on the scene, becomes hysterical, and flees from the tent. Outside Buzz Hicks is drunk and standing guard with a gun, making sure Gody does not try to get away. He shoots Sally when she leaves. The miners win their strike, but Gody does not take credit for it. Instead, he forsakes any resemblance to Jesus, and as the curtain goes down he is preparing to work in the mines. Linda clings not only to her faith but to the mortal Gody, whom she finds much more satisfying than her husband.

It was a powerful theme—especially for 1926, still a year before Sinclair Lewis's indictment of the pseudoclergy in *Elmer Gantry*. Cain and Goodman both thought the play had quality, and Goodman invested nearly $8,000 to produce it. One man who liked the dress rehearsal was George S. Kaufman. "You've got a show," he told Cain. "The next question is: Do they like it?"

Crashing the Gates opened in Stamford, Connecticut, in February 1926, then moved on to Worcester, Massachusetts. Its stars were Charles Bickford (fresh from his first Broadway success as Big Red in Maxwell Anderson's *Outside Looking In*), Helen Freeman (a Theatre Guild actress), and Elizabeth Allen (who later married Robert Montgomery). However, the most interesting story about the cast concerned a kid barely in his twenties whom Bickford kept insisting they had to hire. Cornering Goodman and Cain in Goodman's office one day, he yelled at them: "Listen, I hope I'm getting through to you, this guy can play any part in your play better than any actor you've signed to play it, including my part! I said, *including my part!* He's twenty times the actor I'll ever hope to be. This is not a good actor, it's a great actor!"

Unfortunately, Goodman was satisfied with his cast and did not want to fire anyone. But Bickford's appraisal was extremely perceptive. The kid's name was James Cagney.

Maybe Cagney could have saved *Crashing the Gates*, not that Charles Bickford was unconvincing as Syd Gody. But the theme and especially some of the language in the play were too much for audiences in Stamford and Worcester. They were outraged. In Stamford, ten minutes of the second act were played to the accompaniment of angry foot stomping and hissing, after which about thirty customers stalked out. The profanity that triggered the exodus was taken out of the script that night. But in Worcester the reaction was about the same—some members of the audience walked out. Those who remained, however, were held by a sense of the ridiculous. "The stylish thing to do after the final curtain and during the entire journey home," said the *Worcester Telegram* reviewer, "was to condemn it with self-conscious virtue that was still inwardly pleased with the shock."

Generally, the play itself, as opposed to the theme, was given favorable notice—except for the last act, which *Variety* called "little short of a mess." Cain and Goodman were aware of the problems but did not know how to resolve them. The main weakness was the scene in which Syd Gody tried to call people from their graves but could not do it. It was in a graveyard, which Goodman suddenly decided you could not have on the stage. So before the play had even gone into rehearsal, Cain spent several nights in his *World* office trying to write a new last act. Several versions were tried, but none of them made sense, and finally Ramond Sovey, who did the sets, sat down with Cain and said: "Jim, if you ask me, your original last act was right, the set is all built, it won't cost Goodman a dime to go back to it, and the cast knows it—they rehearsed it before all this nonsense started."

The last act of *Crashing the Gates* was not changed, and the review in the *Worcester Telegram* called the play "truly heroic in its treatment of a startling theme" and "brilliantly written." It also applauded the acting and the production and predicted the play would flourish in an atmosphere less stultifying and provincial than Worcester's. But it never had the chance. *Crashing the Gates* closed in two weeks, and the experience was as crushing to Cain as had been his failure to write his novel about the coal miners. It also taught him something that would be extremely important in his later work: "You should never jeopardize a big design by insistence on small imperfections." He realized it had been a mistake to include the profanity scene in which Oakey denounced Gody and his mother. Cain used profanity only to the extent that men used it in their speech, and it never occurred to him or Goodman that in a play about the coal mines of West Virginia, people would be disturbed by a little profanity. And the worst thing, Cain said, was that "it wasn't important. Except as a matter of cadence, it really meant nothing at all." From then on, Cain never used profanity in his writing, except for an occasional line that could not be avoided. And three years later, in an editorial for the *World*, he had more to say on the subject: The trouble with trying to combat the pruderies of the Victorian age and enhance the reality of life by including profanity on the stage was that

it does not bring about the result that was anticipated. . . . There is such a thing as profanity that seems to belong but that yet manages not to obtrude. And even with that kind of profanity, a little of it goes a long way. There is also such a thing as authentic talk that carries all the tang of profane talk but actually contains no profanity at all. It is, of course, hard to write. It is so easy to put down "The hell you say!" and rely on it for a laugh. It is not so easy to find a magical yet unprofane phrase like "Is that so?" Perhaps, just for practice, our playwrights might try the godly path for a while.

Cain and Goodman still had faith in the play, but Goodman was now involved with a production of *Love Among the Married*, by Vincent Lawrence. So Cain set to work trying to revive his play—which he now called *Jubilee*. Then, a friendship developed between Goodman and Lawrence, a tall, cadaverous, tough-talking playwright, whom George Jean Nathan called "the greatest light comedy writer in the United States." And Goodman brought Lawrence in to work with Cain on the rewrite. It was Cain's first meeting with Lawrence, who would become one of the most important men in his career, along with Lippmann, Mencken, and Goodman.

Vincent Lawrence eventually became a Hollywood legend, and although he was virtually unknown outside the movie studios, he helped shape the mind and taste of a nation during most of the 1930s and 1940s. He was one of those uneducated, uncultured naturals perfectly in tune with the mass mind, who knew precisely what made the average man laugh, cry, applaud— and buy theater tickets. As Cain said, if you asked Lawrence something like when was the Battle of Balaklava and what was its significance, "it would be most surprising if he placed it on the right continent and in the right century." On the other hand, "at all things not worth knowing, such as the number of times Cobb went from first to third on a bunt, how many times Dempsey floored Willard at Toledo, how many points Alabama scored in the Rose Bowl Game in 1926, he was encyclopedic, and his testimony needed no further checking." Lawrence was a genius at diagnosing what was wrong with a play or movie script, propounding the famous "Lawrence 1, 2, and 3 rules." But when his friend William Harris, Jr., said that these were nothing but Aristotle's Beginning, Middle, and End, Lawrence replied: "Well, General, who the hell was Aristotle and who did he lick?"

Lawrence, sort of evangelical himself, became fascinated with *Crashing the Gates* and worked with Cain on it for six months. Then one night, in Cain's apartment in the Village, Lawrence threw open the window and exclaimed: "Christ Almighty, Cain, let's let some of this goddamn smoke out of here. It's thicker than fog, and so are we, what we have been saying about this damnable play of yours. Listen, Cain, if that guy starts out to be Jesus Christ, he's got to be Jesus Christ. I'm not paying any $5.50 to see a guy that tried to be Jesus Christ and couldn't be. I'm capable of that, myself."

That was all. He walked out of the apartment, and although the two men remained good friends, Lawrence never again brought up the subject of Cain's play. Cain continued to work on it but could not make Gody's dream of being a real Messiah come to life. He finally produced a script in which Gody convinces the other miners he is Jesus—or at least they are afraid he might be—and it satisfied Goodman. So they announced it again with its new title, *Jubilee*, starring Louis Wolheim, a German-born actor who played in *All Quiet on the Western Front*. But then Wolheim accepted a conflicting Hollywood offer, and a few years later he died. *Crashing the Gates* was finally laid to rest for good.

Cain was discouraged but not yet convinced he could not write plays; in fact, it would be nearly fifty years before he was convinced, and then only after untold man-hours of work and many failures. But he did decide Lawrence was right about his first play, and the point Lawrence made became one of Cain's basic principles of narrative construction: Once you introduce a concept as powerful as a dream of being Jesus Christ, you have to go through with it or you have no story. And this was an underlying theme in most of his later books, "the dream that comes true," which for Cain was "a terrifying concept."

Before Cain finally abandoned *Crashing the Gates*, he had turned again to free-lance writing and, in 1927, produced two more dialogues for the *Mercury* and two articles for the *Saturday Evening Post*. The first dialogue, "Hemp," appearing in the April *Mercury*, takes place on the Eastern Shore, and its opening line, spoken by the sheriff, is: "I mean, I'll be glad when we get this nigger hung." The sketch revolves around two "niggers" put in jail for "carving up a bohunk." One of them has already been hung and has come back to haunt the jail, which convinces the worried sheriff that maybe they were both innocent, which they were. The unhung prisoner is finally transferred to the state penitentiary.

"Red White and Blue" describes a meeting in the Towanda, Ohio, Chamber of Commerce in which officials are discussing the recent visit by President Coolidge. They have a copy of his speech and are impressed by the fact that he seems to know more about their county than they do. This prompts them to look up something in the encyclopedia, where they find, to their dismay, that whole chunks of the speech were copied verbatim.*

*This sketch was based on an editorial Cain wrote for the *World* when he and Charles Merz actually caught Coolidge copying out of an encyclopedia for one of his speeches. Instead of scolding Coolidge in the editorial, Cain wrote a tongue-in-cheek defense, saying the President was very busy and did not have time to write his own speeches. The editorial was widely reprinted—more so, Cain thought, than if he had criticized Coolidge.

The first of Cain's two *Saturday Evening Post* articles—"The Man Merriwell"—was a profile of William Gilbert Patten, who created the Frank Merriwell series under the pseudonym Burt L. Standish. The piece is beautifully written and is not only a revealing look at one of the nation's most prolific writers of pulp fiction, but a well-researched history of the dime novel. Cain must have been drawn to Patten, whom he interviewed for the piece, because like Cain he had started out early in life trying to sell stories to magazines, except that Patten had been successful. But perhaps the most significant aspect of the meeting was a story Patten told Cain to illustrate some friend's fiendish sense of humor. The story concerned two western roughnecks who had cut off the head of an old man they had murdered, but were upset at the way it rolled around in their wagon. To Patten's horror, Cain thought the story hilarious and asked if he could use it. Patten said yes, and Cain began mulling over an approach to what would eventually be his first short story.

The second *Post* article was titled "Are Editorials Worth Reading?" and is discussed in the next chapter.

By now Cain was leading a very enjoyable social life, centering in a few close friends on the *World* and Mencken's crowd. Curiously enough, the two groups did not mix. Cain saw quite a bit of Lippmann socially, but Mencken did not like Lippmann—he considered him a snob and on the make socially—and the three seldom got together. One man on the *World* with whom Cain was especially close was Arthur Krock. The two were constant luncheon companions in the *World* dining room and remained close friends until Krock's death in 1974. What Cain liked about Krock was his substance. "I've had many conversations with many men in my time," Cain said, "but have no recollection of what most of them said to me. But I can remember whole hunks of Arthur's talks. His stories, his anecdotes about people, his observations on life, stuck with me more than anyone's I ever talked to."

It is significant that, with all the literary men around the *World*, Cain should have become so attracted to Krock, who was essentially a newspaperman. But one story Cain told reveals the turn of Krock's mind that appealed to him. They had gone to a polo game on Long Island on a Sunday afternoon sometime in 1926 and were standing on the sidelines near a "ratty-looking girl in blouse and dungarees," as Cain described her. Suddenly, one of the players rode up, dismounted, tossed the reins to the groom, and asked the girl: "He yours?"

"Yes, sir," the girl said.

"Nice horse." Then the player picked another mount and returned to the game.

"He means," Krock said to Cain, "he's a very fine mount, I'm grateful to you for letting me use him today, and hello. But all he says is 'Nice horse.' It just goes to show the difference between two different worlds. In the horse world everything is brief, laconic, and low-key. In the theatrical world, just the opposite. Did you ever see an audience rolling around in the aisles holding on to its stomach . . . at the jokes of the comedians?"

"No," said Cain.

"I never did either," Krock continued. "Nobody ever did. And yet it's a standard belief in the theatrical world. They are the clichés of the business. Exaggeration, childish fictions are what it lives on. But in the horse world, everything is terse, quiet, understated"—the way, Cain thought, Krock wrote.

It was at another *World* lunch that a much-quoted incident occurred involving Krock, Cain, and two other *World* writers on their way to illustrious careers—Laurence Stallings and Morris Markey, both of whom worked for a while in Hollywood when Cain was there and who continued as lifelong friends. Stallings, who was from a fine old Georgia family and had a deep southern accent, made a remark, based on something Cain had written, that Cain was "a phony tough guy." Cain immediately responded: "So's your goddamn accent! No real Georgia accent could be that thick." Then at lunch one day, the group was joined by Morris Markey, a Virginian Krock had hired after a recommendation from Stallings. After listening to Markey for a while, Cain concluded that Markey's accent seemed to stem from his idolatry of Stallings. So he rose from the table and, before stalking out of the room, announced: "I have to listen to Stallings, but not his stand-in on a road show."

Stallings was a tall, husky, embittered veteran of World War I, in which he had lost a leg; he possessed a powerful intellect and a graceful writing style. In 1924, the year Cain arrived at the *World*, Stallings had catapulted from a modest reputation as the author of a book review column, "First Reader," to one of the literary stars of New York with the simultaneous production of the play, *What Price Glory?*, coauthored with Maxwell Anderson, and a novel, *Plumes*, about several generations of a Georgia family culminating in World War I. Both dealt with the disillusionment of the war. *What Price Glory?* was a tremendous hit on Broadway, but *Plumes*, although well reviewed, was ahead of its time. Eventually it was said, however, to have had a significant impact on William Faulkner, who also wrote about several generations of a southern family. Krock thought Stallings was "a genius," but Cain had a more realistic view. He thought he was eminently suited for reviewing books

Cain's first wife, Mary Clough.
From the 1910 Pegasus.

James M. Cain—Professor
of Journalism, from the 1924
St. John's catalog.

*Cain's second wife,
Elina Tyszecka.*
Courtesy of Leo
Tyszecki

*Cain's stepchildren,
Leo Tyszecki (left)
and Henrietta
Tyszecka (right).*

James M. Cain in the late 1920s.

H. L. Mencken in Hollywood in the 1920s. On his right is Aileen Pringle, whom Cain would meet and marry in the 1940s, on his left is Norma Shearer.

*Sketch of Cain by
Dorothea C. Parrot
used in connection
with the publication of
his first book,* Our
Government.

*Cain in the late
1920s.*

The Editorial Page staff of the New York World, *mid-1920s: seated (left to right), Charles Merz, Walter Lippmann, John L. Heaton; standing (left to right), William O. Scroggs, James M. Cain, Allan Nevins, Rollin Kirby, L. R. E. Paulin.* Yale University Library

This photo was taken in 1931, when Cain and his stepdaughter Henrietta (seated on Cain's lap) made a special trip to Baltimore to visit Mencken, just before Cain left for Hollywood. Behind Cain are two of his sisters, Virginia (left) and Genevieve (right), both of whom were born in Annapolis and lived most of their lives in the Baltimore area. Courtesy Henrietta Holmes

Cain's mentors: (top left) H. L. Mencken (holding first issue of The American Mercury), *Vincent Lawrence (middle left), Walter Lippmann (bottom left), and Phil Goodman (right).*

Cain's friends from his New York days. Opposite page: top, Arthur Krock (Courtesy of Mrs. Arthur Krock); bottom left, Morris Markey (George Harmon Coxe), bottom right, Laurence Stallings. Above right, Blanche Knopf (Alfred A. Knopf); below right, Alfred A. Knopf (Carl Van Vechten).

Publicity photo used for the publication of The
Postman Always Rings Twice.

while getting out a novel now and then, a genuine intellectual who would have been a successful "practicing literary man." But *What Price Glory?*, Cain was convinced, gave him the false hope that he was a playwright and embarked him "on a prodigious career of self-delusion."

Stallings and Cain were immediately attracted to each other, enjoying the kind of caustic, outspoken relationship you would expect from two some-what cynical ex-doughboys in the newspaper business. A story Cain told is typical of their relationship. Cain had gone over to meet Stallings at his house next to a church in Greenwich Village, and from there they were to drive up to Arthur Krock's apartment on Central Park South. After Stallings fixed an Alexander, Cain's first encounter with the drink, they left in Stal-lings's car. "It was a Sunday, and on Seventh Avenue, around Thirtieth Street, completely deserted at the time, we ran fresh out of gas. . . . He had to buy a gallon of gas in some kind of can, put up a dollar deposit for the can, and start down on foot to the car. But 'on foot,' with him, meant stumping along on that leg, and for several blocks it could have been serious in its consequences. So of course I grabbed up the can, but he insisted on taking it. 'You have that lung to think of,' he said, 'and it could cost you your life, starting that lesion up again.' I was fresh out of the lunghouse and, as he knew, carrying, with a lunger, is strictly forbidden, and as he yanked the can and got it, he said: 'You're just a goddamn war cripple, that's all'—and cut loose with his sardonic laugh."

Morris Markey had worked on the *Atlanta Journal*, *Newark Ledger*, and New York *Daily News* before coming to the *World*. Despite Cain's reaction to his southern accent on their first meeting, the two men became fast friends. Cain greatly admired Markey for what he called his "exquisite, precisionist style, so different from the newspaper world's idea of writing." He felt it to be most pronounced in Markey's attempt to show surfaces, the things that would meet the eye of a good observer, things Markey felt were far more important than the "inside story," which bored him. Markey's ideas about reporting also appealed to Harold Ross, who finally managed to lure him away from the *World*. Between the two of them, they worked out the distinctive reporting style for the early *New Yorker*, where Markey became the first "Reporter at Large." His pieces were factual, but often written in a short-story style. "The basic idea," Markey said, "is to convey a sense of interest, of enthusiasm for the moment. I try to give the pieces immediacy without urgency, something that is happening now but not too overwhelming a thing." Cain and Markey would spend hours discussing words, phrases, and writing, but Cain always thought he was drawn to Markey for even more personal reasons—as a re-placement for his dead brother, Boydie.

Cain's friendships with Mencken and Goodman were based almost entirely on the two men's respect for Cain's writing. They were both fast-talking, gregarious characters who loved jokes and laughter. Cain, on the other hand, was shy, awkward, and almost timid socially. Goodman's daughter, Ruth, was a young girl when Cain first began coming around to Goodman's "salon" at Park Avenue, and she remembers him as a "very dear, very sweet," quiet young man and very ugly because of his horrible acne. "The first time I remember hearing anything out of him," Ruth recalls, "was when my mother was playing the piano, some Debussy, and from the other side of the room came a voice singing. My father, astonished, said, 'Jim, you sing?' and he said, 'Yes.' My mother said, 'Can I play something you'd like to sing?' and he said, 'You got any Sibelius?' My mother said, 'No' but father asked, 'If we get some Sibelius will you sing?' He said, 'Yes,' and from then on, whenever he came to the house he would sing. He had a quite lovely voice and it was obvious he had had some training."

Through Goodman and Mencken, Cain met another writer similar in talent, but as different in personality as any man could be—Sinclair Lewis. As with Cain, Mencken's attraction to Lewis grew primarily out of his great respect for his writing. He and Nathan had first been introduced to Lewis at the home of T. R. Lewis, an editor at Boni and Liveright. Despite the fact that Sinclair Lewis had published several novels and contributed to *The Smart Set*, Mencken and Nathan were not familiar with his work. On being introduced, this "tall, skinny, paprika-haired figure," as Nathan described Lewis, put his arms around the necks of Mencken and Nathan and started haranguing them in mock German dialect: "So you guys are the critics are you? Well, let me tell you something. I'm the best writer in this here gottdamn country and if you, Georgie, and you, Hank, don't know it now, you'll know it gottdamn soon. . . ."

Lewis went on like that and then let go of the two editors, who fled from the apartment as soon as they could. Out on the street, Mencken said: "Of all the idiots I've ever laid eyes on, that fellow is the worst."

But a few days later, after Mencken had read *Main Street*, he wrote Nathan: "Grab hold of the bar-rail, steady yourself and prepare yourself for a terrible shock. I've just read the book of the Lump we met . . . and by God, he has done the job! . . ."

Between 1925 and 1928, Cain saw quite a lot of Red Lewis, mostly on drinking evenings with Goodman and Mencken. The four chauvinists must have been a colorful group—Mencken, his sandy hair parted in the middle the way they did it in the 1880s when he was growing up, the round, ruddy face, the blue-serge suit, black polished shoes, the cigar, Mephistophelian grin, and steady stream of brilliant talk in either perfect English or mock German dialect; Goodman, a big 210-pound Spanish Jew with clear, olive skin, drooping eyes, Brooks Brothers raincoat, derby tilted on one side, and quick Broadway walk, which Mencken liked to copy; Lewis, tall, a pock-marked face, reddish hair slicked down to the side, a born mimic, and "as badly dressed as only the wearer of standardized fashion for men can be," in Ernest Boyd's description; and Cain, the youngest of the group and by now more sophisticated in his dress and appearance, but his face still pock-marked, dour, quiet, and cynical, an amusing storyteller, a walking encyclo-pedia of literature and music, and a responsive audience. Great wits have to have someone to laugh at them, and Cain thought Mencken was always amusing and agreed with Lewis that Goodman was one of the wittiest men they had ever heard. The talk was always literary, and against most every aspect of American society in the 1920s—Lewis especially against small-town boosters and the ministry; Cain especially hostile to rubes, academics, and politicians; Goodman, a worldly sophisticate who looked down on the human race with humor and pity; and anything these three might toler-ate, Mencken, who was acknowledged to be "ag'in everything," was sure to criticize.

In New York, they would meet most often at Goodman's apartment. But Mencken preferred restaurants and speakeasies, and frequently they would go over to Union Hill, New Jersey, for beer drinking at the Alt Heidelberg, which was an easy walk from the ferry. Mencken said the beer was great: "This fellow really believes in putting hops in his beer." Cain recalled that it was, in fact, a "green swill" certain to cause trouble the next morning, but that Mencken always established his savvy by pronouncing all beer great. Goodman, by contrast, established his by pronouncing everything lousy. Lewis had no interest in beer and usually drank hard liquor when he could get it. The group that went roistering in Union Hill also included Raymond Pearl, the biologist and author, and Dr. George A. Dorsey, the anthropolo-gist and author of *Why We Behave Like Human Beings.*

Cain liked Lewis and considered him "a gay companion drunk and an interesting one sober," although most of the times Cain saw him Lewis had had plenty to drink. He recalled that Lewis first took an interest in him one night when he, Goodman, Lewis, Mencken, Pearl, and Dorsey were all at Union Hill. It was around 1926, when Lewis still was concerned with the medical world of *Arrowsmith,* and a time when doctors were becoming in-volved in Florida real estate schemes. The proprietor of Union Hill was a man named Tommy, and when Lewis introduced Tommy to Mencken and the others he said they were all doctors who had formed their own real estate company, "Doctors, Inc." Lewis invented fine biographies for each of his guests, especially "Dr. Goodman," whom he introduced as an "outstanding gynecologist." And then he said, "This is Dr. Cain, our dentist. Of course, in a development as extensive as ours, we have to consider our prospects' teeth, and I'm glad to say that Dr. Cain has just about as advanced ideas in that line as any dentist you're likely to find."

Tommy gave the group a skeptical glare, then suddenly whipped out his uppers and handed them to Lewis: "If he's all that good, maybe the doc'll be kind enough to say what they cost me."

"What do you think, Doctor?" said Lewis, passing the dentures to Cain.

"This denture," Cain said, "you didn't get for one cent less than fifteen hundred dollars."

"Three thousand smackers they cost me," said Tommy, with the air of one who had unmasked a fraud.

"Upper and lower," Cain said.

"Why, sure," said Tommy, a bit deflated.

"Well, goddamn it, you give me the upper," Cain said. "One thing at a time, and kindly say what you mean."

Cain's quick recovery not only silenced Tommy, but impressed Lewis.

Another night at Union Hill, Lewis began an interminable story about a man on a Pullman car telling the boys in the smoking room about his friend Calvin Coolidge. It went on forever, Cain said, with Mencken roaring and egging Lewis on. Some nights later, Goodman told Cain that Mencken had persuaded Lewis to do a *Mercury* piece about the man who knew Coolidge and expand it into a book. Cain was silent for a few minutes, then said: "Phil, the thing is no good."

"It's no good, and Henry should know it's no good," said Goodman, "but—anything at the expense of Coolidge of course is the funniest thing on earth." Then, as they talked along about Lewis, it was apparent that Goodman had an uneasy concern about his drinking, his inability to distinguish between passion and indignation, between comedy and corny gags. "It's depressed me, Jim, and I regard it with real foreboding," said Goodman. "But the son of a bitch comes from Sauk Centre and you can't get it out of him, I don't care how hard you try." The idea, of course, led to *The Man Who Knew Coolidge*, and the critics agreed with Goodman and Cain.

On another occasion, Lewis related, at some length, an idea for a short story. As Cain recalled it: "A boy, the son of the village atheist, would be raised to believe a Christian was the most horrendous of men. One night when Father and Mother had to go out, he was given 50 cents to buy dinner, and walking around, trying to decide where to spend such wealth, he came to a church sign, which said: 'Strawberry Festival Tonight.' Overcome by curiosity as to what a strawberry festival was, he disregarded his careful upbringing and went inside. He had a grand time, eating strawberries and listening to the parson's jokes, which were different from any he knew. He had such a fine time that he began sneaking back and he became a 'Secret Christian,' Lewis's words."

Cain interpreted this story idea to suggest that the author of *Elmer Gantry* was really leaving a bouquet at religion's back door. "If his head had rejected it, his heart nevertheless was friendly." And he felt it showed a pattern in Lewis's thinking and explained "how he could in the end . . . write such a God-awful book as *The Godseeker*."

Occasionally, going to New Jersey, they would drive over in Goodman's big Lincoln. As they progressed downtown, it was, said Cain, like riding "in a Roman war chariot, with cops saluting Goodman." One time, Lewis insisted they stop at a bookstore, where he had some mysterious errand. Goodman was grumpy about having to park, but Lewis was insistent, so Goodman parked, and as Lewis got out, he urged Cain to come with him. As Lewis browsed, the girl who ran the store disappeared in the back room and returned with several people, who stood around and gawked at Lewis. Soon Lewis took down a book from the rack and presented it to the girl. "I'm Sinclair Lewis," he said. "I'm taking this—don't have it wrapped, no need for it."

Lewis then turned to Cain and offered the book, saying: "Jim, I've decided it's time you got educated. It's for you, with my compliments, and I hope you enjoy it, I do, I do, I do, I really do." He gave it a singsong, Cain said, that was becoming natural with him, and though his manner was completely jocular, and perhaps by that time a little alcoholic, Cain felt uncomfortable with it.

"Goddamn it, I've got a book," Cain said.

"But you should be educated," he said. "Jim, I insist. It's about time, it's high time."

"Maybe, but it's too late now," Cain said, still declining the book.

Cain was convinced that the whole incident grew out of Lewis's need for attention and his urge to impress people, the kick he got out of saying "I'm Sinclair Lewis" to the salesgirl.

Later, Goodman found the book in his car. It was *The Growth of the Soil*, by Knut Hamsun, a Norwegian author who was a great admirer of Lewis. Cain said he could keep the book, but Goodman said he could never read anything "by a man named K-nut," which he rhymed with "but." But two days later, he called Cain and said: "Jim, I read that book. God, what a book. I never read anything like it. I've ordered the man's whole list." Cain still declined to show interest—but just maybe Lewis was not showing off; maybe he really wanted Cain to read the book, which helped Hamsun win the Nobel Prize for Literature in 1920.

Whatever his personal feelings, Cain always sensed Lewis's genius and, like Goodman and Mencken, was willing to overlook eccentric traits in talented writers. Once, at Goodman's apartment, Lewis was there "sober, the first time I had ever seen him that way," said Cain. He seemed preoccupied, but Goodman talked on and then, suddenly, asked Lewis: "Red, how much money did *Babbitt* make?"

"Oh, I think I figured him up one time at a little less than ten thousand a year," said Lewis, but not really in a communicative way.

"Oh, more than that!" said Goodman.

"No—you see," said Lewis, "George never got taken in on a deal really big. He had a weakness. He couldn't keep his mouth shut."

He smiled, a shy little smile, that somehow reminded Cain of Gilbert Patten (Burt L. Standish), whom he had just profiled for the *Saturday Evening Post*. "You see," Patten had once said to Cain, "Frank Merriwell had a weakness—he loved to gamble." It flashed through Cain's mind that perhaps, to a novelist, the discovery of a good big weakness in a character was like money in the bank.

Goodman pressed for more information about *Babbitt*, particularly the legend that Lewis had drawn plans of Zenith, with everything labeled and located, which Lewis corroborated. But the more Goodman asked, the more evasive Lewis became.

In this evasiveness, Cain saw an implication of aesthetic ideals, as they went into the creation of a novel. "This was the one time," said Cain, "in all my acquaintanceship with Lewis, that I saw some shadowy glimpse of literary greatness—in this strange withdrawn evasiveness. I never forgot it. In the man, as well as in the books, the greatness was really there."

The rollicking nights out with the boys involved pranks, good talk, and beer, liquor, and food in about equal proportions. Mencken loved German food and great quantities of beer, although Cain never remembered seeing Mencken drunk. Goodman was the most capricious eater Cain ever saw. "He couldn't eat a meal without in the middle of it having something pop into his mind, like truffles, and order it at once, whether it blended in or not." Cain, on the other hand, had increasing difficulty on these outings enjoying the epicurean side of the evenings. The doctors diagnosed his problem as liver trouble, and around 1927 he had to begin watching his diet and drink nothing stronger than table wine. Years later when the problem became more serious, the doctors diagnosed it as a developing ulcer compounded by an infection.

The condition could easily have grown out of the stress in his personal life, which was approaching a climax. In 1927, Elina wrote him she was returning to New York, that she was divorced and free to marry. The message was clear: If he wanted to see her again, he had best do something about his situation with Mary. But Mary still was reluctant to grant Cain his freedom and tried to persuade him to consider a reconciliation. She finally accepted the inevitable, however, in May 1927. She filed for divorce, and it was granted in the historic little Centreville, Maryland, courthouse. She never remarried, and as far as can be determined she and Cain did not see each other for the rest of their lives. "While she was an intellectual," Cain once said, trying to sum up what went wrong, "she was also of the Eastern Shore squirearchy in other personal ways, and had little use for my attitude toward life, letters, and love." After the divorce, Mary moved to New York and in 1942 earned a Ph.D. in education from Columbia, doing her thesis on "The Historical Development of State Normal Schools for White Teachers in Maryland." She spent the rest of her life teaching in New York public schools, and some indication of how she felt about the marriage can be seen in a note she wrote Washington College at the time the *Alumni Review* was preparing to review her Ph.D. thesis: "I am sure you would delete any reference to the family of James W. or James M. Cain." Her friends said she was very bitter about the marriage and never talked about it with anyone, even her closest friends. She died in 1951 in New York, a year before she planned to retire.

Mary's bitterness about the marriage can also be seen perhaps in her attitude toward the settlement. As Cain put it: "Don't think that Mary was a friendly, forgiving girl, who would realize she had not been too loving a wife, and for that reason would let me up easy. She had me over a barrel and let her lawyer hold me up for all the traffic would bear."

What the judge figured the traffic would bear was $150 a month for life, or until Mary remarried. At that time, Cain was making $125 a week, plus what additional money he could bring in from his magazine articles.

With one of the most unpleasant experiences in his life over, Cain was now ready to face Elina's return. He and his interim lover spent one last night together and kissed good-bye in the morning. If Elina had any suspicion about Cain's other woman she never mentioned it. "But a woman is hard to fool," said Cain, "especially that woman, and I've never been able to convince myself she didn't guess." (In fact, Leo Tyszecki, Elina's son, says Elina not only knew about the woman but knew who she was.) Cain also suspected that one reason she never accused him was because of an involvement she had had in Belgium, where she spent the last few months of her stay in Europe. Although Cain did not think her dalliance had gone as far as his, he said it did seem "to occasion all sorts of talk."

But Cain was insanely in love with Elina—at least he was before she went away—and now he made plans to marry her, which upset Phil Goodman. Ruth Goodman remembers her first meeting with Elina—"a very timid, slim little woman. She looked like a waif. She seemed very modest and a humble little creature. Never said a word" . . . hardly surprising, since she still did not speak English, communicating with Cain only in German. Eventually, Elina learned to speak English, but with an accent and strange syntax that continually delighted Cain, who said he never heard Zsa Zsa Gabor on TV without being reminded of Elina.

More important about her, said Cain, "She had a beautiful mind, particularly for one writing the things I write—sardonic, ironic, sometimes almost savage in its comprehensions of basic things. There was always her amusing point of view, expressed with this preposterous accent, so fresh, so delightful, that I have seen saleswomen in department stores gather around her, to listen a few minutes and be entertained by her."

But she did not entertain Phil Goodman, and Ruth remembers one night at the dinner table when her husband said, "You know, Cain is actually thinking of marrying that girl."

Mrs. Goodman said: "Is he?"

"Yes, he's crazy," said Goodman.

But Mrs. Goodman said: "You don't know that girl. She seems all right."

"Well, I told him what I thought of her. I thought she was a nitwit."

"Was that wise?" asked Mrs. Goodman.

"A man asks you whether he ought to marry a woman or not, you have to tell him what you really think," Goodman replied.

Cain did not follow Goodman's advice, and a few weeks later, on July 2, 1927, he and Elina were married at City Hall in New York. Elina's children were still in Finland, and the Cains moved into an apartment on 19th Street at Second Avenue. The marriage started out well enough, but something was different. The time they had spent apart had changed them. "It wasn't long before both of us knew it was gone, the old black magic we had had," said Cain. "And we spent the next twenty years trying to get it back, unsuccessfully."

7

THE CORPORATE
AWFULNESS

"Many years ago, Jim Cain was nothing but a newspaper editorial writer. They didn't even assign him to any of the serious subjects. He wrote the short light pieces on Santa Claus and southern cooking and the New Haven Railroad. Two hundred words was the most he was permitted to do at one sitting."

This little dash of vitriol was included in a 1937 review of Cain's novel *Serenade* by Heywood Broun, one of the aging heroes of the Algonquin Round Table. The only explanation for its inaccuracy and peevish tone must be the contempt the *World's* egotistical by-line writers, of which Broun was one, had for the anonymous editorial hands, particularly Cain. Most of the by-liners probably agreed with F.P.A. (Franklin P. Adams), who thought Cain was a Mencken sycophant trying too hard to imitate the master. In the case of Broun, there was probably also a grudge against Cain going back to their differences over the proper editorial approach to the Sacco-Vanzetti case.

The fact is, Cain was encouraged to write his little lighthearted pieces. But he could also write long, serious editorials, as he demonstrated many times. Nor was he ever discouraged from writing more than 200 words at one sitting. His total output on the *World* and *Evening World* editorial pages and in his signed column in the Sunday Metropolitan Section, which he started in 1928, was staggering. By rough estimate, from September 1924 to February 1931, he wrote at least 1,300 editorials, varying in length from 15 to 1,000 words. He also wrote at least 90 by-lined pieces in his columns, beginning in September 1928. Cain was, in fact, one of the most prolific and respected editorial hands that ever worked for the *World*. John Lee Mahin, a scriptwriter who later met Cain in Hollywood, recalls that when he was on the *New York Sun* in the twenties and became interested in editorial writing, someone told him, "If you want to learn about editorials, there's a guy over on the *World* who writes them." He was referring to Cain, so Mahin began reading some of his editorials, "and they were masterpieces."

Indeed most of the *World* editorials in the years 1925 through 1931 on subjects other than economics, politics, or national and international affairs were written by James M. Cain. Their kaleidoscope of subjects included: religion, music, literature, sports, food, movies, civil liberties, art, censorship, animals, all forms of transportation, the younger generation, the human side of the presidency, feats of derring-do (Lindbergh flying across the ocean, etc.), holidays, the weather, and the eternal love and war between man and woman.

Cain was well aware of the limitations of the editorial page as an outlet for good creative writing, but "the undertaker clothes are, to some extent, obligatory," he said. "The corporate awfulness of the newspaper speaks here, remember, and any undue frivolity in attire would not be seemly."

The truth is, said Cain, the editor is usually just as bored by what he has to write as anyone else, but the paper must comment on national, international, and civic issues to maintain its "contact with everyday life which is the heart of every newspaper." Cain argued that the editorial writer has a tough time making these subjects interesting. Political editorials are hollow, for "they assume something that is palpably not true, that a Democrat is better than a Republican, or vice versa." Civic editorials are flat because it is hard to take a lofty position on "the question of whether Main Street should have two traffic lights, red and green, or three traffic lights, red, green, and yellow." Policy editorials are repetitious because "after a newspaper has said for the thousandth time that there should be a seat for every child in the public schools it has said it." But the worst of the lot are the Big News Editorials. "When the Coast Guard cutter *Seminole* makes a great rescue at sea, taking 22 Lascars from the sinking tanker by skillful use of the breeches buoy, you may think it is a simple matter to turn out two graceful paragraphs of tribute." But try it, said Cain, and you will be amazed to learn "how many banal phrases your brain can hatch in an hour."

There were, however, some interesting types of editorials, and at the head of the list was "discussions of national affairs" when they concerned more than party wrangles. Next came "obituary editorials"—especially if the deceased was a significant person and someone the editorial writer was really interested in. "I doubt," said Cain in 1927, "if any finer writing ever appeared in American newspapers than that which followed the death of William Jennings Bryan."

Then, comments on the fine arts. "It is not commonly realized that some of the best criticism of literature, drama and music . . . printed in American newspapers appears in the editorial columns rather than in the columns regularly devoted to them." A book or a play, for example, had to be truly important to rate discussion on the editorial page, and an editorial on the arts was usually much better written than a review because the writer was trained at analysis. Also, because the page was addressed to the general public, the editorial writer had to use plain words, and in doing so, he avoided the "gibbering nonsense" most critics wrote.

Next Cain nominated "tongue-in-cheek editorials" in which the writer spoofed his readers—done primarily "to start something that will lead to an amusing flurry in the letters column." Finally, came "editorials born of the writer's hobby." Every editor had "some pet subject that he would rather write on than anything else and, as a result, he usually turns out, during the course of a year, two or three editorials that are out of the ordinary and worth reading."

James M. Cain, the editorial writer, was not really interested in day-to-day events unless they concerned Man, "the subject of subjects." As for political issues: "One feels that if a cigarette were held against them they would go *pop* like a toy balloon. We should then be as well off as before . . . it would take a wise man to say what difference it makes who gets elected, and on what issue."

In a self-appraisal made in the early days of World War II, Cain concluded that he had "a mind of appalling usualness . . . full of special abilities and lack of abilities as it grapples with daily problems, but ideationally speaking, filled with trade goods right off the national stockpile." In attempting to arrive at an understanding of what we were fighting about in World War II, Cain said that most of the American people, himself included, were guilty of "a lack of interest in politics, an amused indifference to the whole tiresome subject. *While Rome Burns*, the title of Mr. [Alexander] Woollcott's book, is more than a light wheeze. It is the expression of a viewpoint that was fashionable a few years ago. We are in the position of a man who preferred the bar next door during Acts I and II and now hurries into the theatre to join his wife, and desperately whispers to everybody in his row to find out what the play is about."

In this analogy, the play was about the events leading up to World War II, and Acts I and II were the 1920s and 1930s. Cain was definitely in the bar next door in Act I, interested primarily in music, sports, the theater, literature, and food, as they involved the "subject of subjects."

Every editorial page of a large newspaper has a human interest writer, and Cain fulfilled that function on the *World*. It was an educational experience. Gradually, as he produced his little pieces and saw which subjects brought reactions from his readers, he learned what really interested the American people. His first big hit came in July 1925, when he commented on "a neglected public issue—the deterioration of huckleberry pie." As originally intended, wrote Cain, this special American pie was "poetical" and contained a "lyric quality." He described how it *should* be made, then how it *was* made now that huckleberries had "come under the pie-baking trust." Cain issued a call to arms, insisting that free men demand their rights! The response was incredible. Letters poured in, most of them agreeing with Cain. The Rotary Club debated the matter at its weekly luncheon, and other organizations took up the cause. The president of Schrafft's sent over two huckleberry pies to the *World*'s "pie editor" as proof that his company made its pies with free-running juice.

Then there was the time Cain emerged as "the frogs editor." He was having dinner one Saturday night at the Divan Parisienne on East 45th Street with a woman reporter introduced to him by Mencken, who had told her: "If he makes any passes, call Arthur Krock, and if Krock does, call the police." She opened the conversation by saying: "You caused me the worst five minutes of my life today." Cain reminded her that they had not seen each other that day, and she said: "No, but you were the cause just the same. I was sitting there in the *World* city room, at my typewriter, meditating on my misspent life. O.K., I was slightly hungover, if you have to know, and was trying to make up my mind whether to go off the stuff altogether or find a better speako. Anyways, as I sat there, bang, just like that, there appeared on my typewriter this THING. It was green, and shiny, and shaped like a frog, but bigger than any frog I had ever heard of. It was the size of a chicken, and as it sat there looking at me, I thought: 'Lady, it's later than you think.'"

Cain interrupted. "Wait a minute, something comes back to me. I wrote an editorial a couple of weeks ago complaining that New York frog legs were O.K. but much too small. In West Virginia, I said, two were considered a portion, and they were so big they stuck out from both sides of the plate. But a fellow wrote in from Richmond to say I didn't know what I was talking about, that Old Dominion frogs were much bigger than West Virginia frogs, as he would prove to us, all in due time. Don't tell me—?"

"Yes," she said, and explained how the box was delivered to the "frogs editor," and when Jim Barrett, the city editor, opened it, there were frogs all over the place.

There was also James M. Cain "the hog editor." Hearing about a hog-calling contest at the state fair in Omaha, Cain wrote a piece in which he said: "Most bucolic contests, such as the three-legged race, the potato race, the calf-roping contest, and steer-riding, bear some relation, even though fanciful, to life as it's lived on the farm. But for what conceivable reason would anyone ever call hogs?"

The reaction was even more explosive than the response to his comments on huckleberry pie. Every editorial writer on a nonmetropolitan paper took it on himself to set the ignorant, citified fellow at the *World* straight, many of them calling him by name, since by now he had acquired something of a reputation for poking fun at Americana. They let him know that you call a hog to feed it, and what you call, or at least what some called, was "Soo Pig, Soo Pig." The *Literary Digest* considered the controversy of such import that it devoted two pages to it, and one of its contributors came up with a musical score to accompany the calls.

Cain had the last laugh, however, because when all his critics rushed into print with their hog calls, it developed that virtually no two calls were alike. So Cain ran an anthology of hog calls and said if the experts themselves could not agree on what a hog call sounded like, it was presumptuous for a New York City fellow to even have an opinion. Finally, one day, Lippmann came striding into his office. "I'm sick of those goddamned hogs," he announced to Cain. So the hog calling was over—but not before NBC put the Omaha hog-calling contest on national radio.

Another editorial of Cain's that had an extraordinary reaction is reprinted in its entirety below:

QUERY

A propos nothing whatever, what *does* one do on meeting a man-eating tiger?

This caught the eye of the American representative of the Indian National Railways, who lived in New York. He wrote a 1,200-word letter stating in detail what one actually does do on meeting a man-eating tiger. It was reprinted in papers all over the world, and thirty years later, Cain would write a short story about a suburbanite who suddenly meets a tiger.

Among Cain's favorite subjects, of course, was music. He especially impressed Lippmann with his many editorials about "The Star-Spangled Banner," which he said was outstanding among national anthems in part because it was unsingable, thus had always to be played smartly by a band or orchestra. In fact, he did so well writing music edits that in 1925, when the regular music critic, Deems Taylor, left to devote more time to his own music, Krock persuaded Swope to try Cain as the music critic. "But at the very first concert I attended," Cain recalled, "I had a queasy realization I no longer cared a great deal that the woodwinds were slightly ragged, and no longer sure that I knew. It was, I knew, a fatal disqualification, for the basic qualification of a critic is the illusion of infallibility." He also said later that he was trying to cure himself of an addiction to music. Arthur Krock, however, remembers it differently. He said that Cain's critiques were so good that readers were soon comparing him with the legendary James Huneker, who had reviewed music in the glory days of Joseph Pulitzer. But then, according to Krock, when one of Cain's critiques "included a passing judgment that Beethoven was the most overrated of composers, the reader protests poured in in such volume that other assignments for Cain seemed the judicious course to pursue." The Beethoven debunker went back to writing his little human-interest pieces—and Lippmann was glad to see him back.

The *World*, like every other paper in the country, went overboard covering the Scopes trial in 1925. The press descended on the little town of Dayton, Tennessee, that July like a swarm of excited bees, and the intellectual community, led by Walter Lippmann and H. L. Mencken, rushed to the defense of Scopes. Lippmann wrote editorial after editorial about what Cain considered essentially "a clown's show."

Despite his contempt for what was going on in Tennessee, Cain took one crack at the Scopes trial in a 900-word lead editorial in which he came out on the same platform with his boss, although in somewhat harder-hitting language. He conceded that "beneath the uproarious comedy" there is a serious issue at stake—religious freedom. He reminded his readers of the Ku Klux Klan, "the 100 Per Cent American" doctrine, and Prohibition, and he pointed to recent actions of Congress which suggested that the government might soon be regulating our religious beliefs. It was a strong statement in the best tradition of American editorial writing, and it demonstrated that whenever he was called upon or aroused, Cain could be the biting enemy of cant and oppression—as in his scathing attacks on puritanism and conformity for the *American Mercury*.

Not long after the Scopes trial, a huge brute of a fighter named "Battling Siki" was murdered, and Cain's special interest in boxers and boxing led him to write an editorial that was reprinted by *The New Yorker*, giving Cain what he called "the greatest moment" of his life up to then and inspiring rumors, according to Cain, that the editorial "almost got the Pulitzer Prize for the year 1925."

In the spring of 1926, Cain was spending an evening with Phil Goodman when the theatrical producer suddenly made a remark startling at the time. "The *World* is for sale," said Goodman.

"Interesting, if true," Cain replied.

"I know the will prohibits it," Goodman said, referring to a provision in Joseph Pulitzer's will, "but it's for sale."

"All right, go ahead and buy it," Cain said.

To Cain's surprise, Goodman did try to buy it, with money raised from one of Goodman's rich friends. Cain arranged for Arthur Krock to act as the go-between, and negotiations were initiated, with Cain present at Krock's apartment at one negotiating session when a price of $18 million was discussed. "But," Krock said to Goodman, "this is only a hypothetical figure, mentioned chiefly to give an idea of the size of the project you have in mind. As a matter of fact, the *World* is not for sale. Mr. Pulitzer reminds you that disposition of the property is forbidden by his father's will. Lawyers, of course, might find a way to get around that. However, he directs me to inform you that there is no desire to get around it. He is deeply interested in the *World*." Shortly thereafter, Goodman's backer lost a lot of money and then died, so the negotiations ended. But Goodman continued to insist that the *World* was for sale.

In fact, troubles were beginning to develop under the brass dome, and one of them was the growing tension between Lippmann and Herbert Bayard Swope.

Swope was an impressive man, over six feet tall, ramrod straight and topped with a thick layer of bright red hair. He was always dressed in the latest fashion, moved and talked in rapid cadence, and, according to some, spent at least half of his life on the telephone. Cain always liked Swope and regarded him with affection—mixed with pity. When Cain later began writing a column for the Sunday *World*, he would stay at the office once a week until around 11:00 P.M. By that time Swope would be in the city room barking orders and striding around, "his pink hair streaming behind him." Cain was fascinated by the show Swope put on. "The place would be in a turmoil, with reporters and especially copy readers trotting around, their eye shades askew, their pencils crosswise in their mouth. . . . And I would wonder to myself why it hit me not as dramatic but as funny. Try as I would, I couldn't take it seriously. . . . It dawned on me one night that he barked but had no bite. He was gruff, often impatient, sometimes sharp—but never really mean. In other words, at the inner core of his being he was phony—he was giving an imitation of a tough executive, having no capacity to be one. . . .

For him life was a grand posture, the world a stage to perform on. And the only one he really deceived was Herbert Swope himself. . . . After subtracting the noise, the manner, the stride, the show, and the rest of these external items, you would be hard put to find anything else."

By 1927, the tension and competition between Swope, Lippmann, and others had reached the point where Pulitzer felt it might be a good idea to have Arthur Krock "ride herd" on Swope. This put Krock in a delicate position, which became more and more difficult as Swope complained to Pulitzer about Krock's interference. Krock also had a dispute with Walter Lippmann concerning an editorial criticizing aspects of a deal about to be negotiated by Dillon, Read and Company, on which Pulitzer sided with Lippmann. Finally, Pulitzer decided to relieve Krock from having to ride herd on the brass. He demoted him to a minor executive position and, worse, banished him to an office several floors below the golden dome. This was enough for Krock, who left for the *New York Times* in May 1927. The tension between Krock and Lippmann was particularly trying for Cain, who liked and admired them both.

The year 1927 also produced one of the most celebrated flaps in New York journalistic history—the feud between the *World* and Heywood Broun, triggered by the Sacco-Vanzetti case, in which Cain was very much involved.

In 1927, after several years of attempts to have the case retried, Judge Webster Thayer in Boston suddenly denied the last appeal and ordered the two men executed. But public opinion forced the governor to appoint a committee to study the case, made up of Presidents Abbott Lowell and Samuel Stratton of Harvard and M.I.T. and Judge Robert Grant. The committee made its review and decided Sacco and Vanzetti were guilty and should be executed. Lippmann, of course, sided with the liberal position on the issue, which was that the two men were innocent, but many *World* staffers, including Cain, did not feel he argued the case strongly enough on the editorial page. Lippmann was apparently unable, said Cain, "to get through his head that two human lives were at stake." Lippmann urged a commutation of the death sentence, but praised the governor and the committee, saying that the governor "sought with every conscious effort to learn the truth" and warning that against the committee's verdict "there would conceivably be other appeals at law. But there can be no appeal outside the law." Lippmann, himself a Harvard graduate, accepted the committee's verdict, and Cain concluded, unhappily, that "it was hard to escape the suspicion that the Old School had figured in his approach."

If Cain was unhappy, Heywood Broun was enraged. He did not accept the Lowell committee's report and repeatedly attacked it in his *World* column, charging that Harvard would become known as "Hangman's House."

The *New York Times*, in turn, attacked Broun's column, as well as the *World* for permitting it to appear. This was enough for Ralph Pulitzer. He let Broun have two columns to present his position, then refused to let Broun write any more on the case. So Broun resigned. His contract said that when he left the *World* he could not write for another newspaper for three years. He got around this by transferring his column to *The Nation*, where Dorothy Parker warned he would have a hard time working because of the "clanking of the Phi Beta Kappa keys."

Meanwhile, Felix Frankfurter, then on Harvard's faculty, arrived at the *World* editorial offices with one of three copies of the Lowell report, which showed conclusively that the committee had not read the testimony at the trial and that its findings were perfunctory. Working with Frankfurter—who Cain said was "the most offensive, disagreeable human being I ever had contact with"—Cain wrote a long editorial saying that Massachusetts could not go through with the execution of Sacco and Vanzetti, that it would be a travesty on justice. But still, in Cain's opinion, Lippmann was not as aroused as he should be. When Cain called his boss to tell him that his portion of the editorial was ready, Lippmann said there was no hurry, that the editorial was so long it would have to run in two parts.

Cain was appalled! He knew one blockbuster of an editorial was more effective than two short pieces, so he charged down to Lippmann's office to find out why his boss was reluctant to fire both barrels. To Cain's disbelief, Lippmann said the editorial could not possibly be set in time to run in one piece, so why the hurry? Then Cain realized that the problem was primarily Lippmann's ignorance of the typesetting and printing process. He did not know that the composing room chopped copy into "takes" and that several men could set type at the same time on the same article. "Walter," Cain yelled, "will you for Christ's sake wake up? Don't break this thing apart—run it all in one piece so it scores, if scoring is possible now. Give it to me when it's finished and let me take charge downstairs."

Lippmann reversed his decision and Cain saw his editorial through to completion in the composing room. It analyzed the Lowell report, pointed out its deficiencies, and said the *World* could not endorse it. The next morning, on the subway, Cain was sitting beside a woman who was reading the *World* editorial page. Suddenly, on one of the editorials, three round, gray spots appeared—caused by spit. When he reached the office and examined the paper to see what the woman had spit on, he found it was an editorial Lippmann had written without telling anyone else on the staff. It said that those associated with the case were all honorable men and had done what they thought was right, and that the important thing now was to get on with living and forget about this case. Cain was thunderstruck. Lippmann still did not understand that two innocent men were being executed. Fifty years later, in what was an otherwise warm and touching remembrance of Walter Lippmann, Cain wrote: "I don't forget this case, even now. To him first, last, and all the time, it was an intellectual exercise, nothing more."

Broun's fight with the *World* was quickly forgotten, primarily at the insistence of Swope, who was well aware of Broun's value to the paper. Within four months after his break with the *World*, Broun was back in his old familiar op-ed spot. And, curiously enough, the *World* permitted him to continue to write for *The Nation*. This lasted for four months, until one day in May 1928, Broun wrote a *Nation* column assessing the state of the city's press and stating that what it really needed was a courageous liberal newspaper. He thought the *World* was the closest thing the city had to one, but it could not be counted on to maintain its position. "So constant were the shifts during the Sacco-Vanzetti case," Broun charged, "that the paper seemed like an old car going uphill."

What had sparked Broun's assault on the *World* was an editorial written by Cain in which the paper defended a decision by the city not to permit a birth control exhibit in Grand Central Palace. Cain, at Lippmann's insistence, had gone to the Palace and studied the exhibit carefully, then concluded "it is quite obvious that a building swarming with children is no place for a birth control exhibit."

Broun thought just the contrary: It was the perfect place for a birth control exhibit. And he concluded that "in the mind of the *World*, there is something dirty about birth control."

Broun's attack, plus his reopening of the old Sacco-Vanzetti wound, was enough for Ralph Pulitzer. On May 3, 1928, in place of Broun's column in the *World* was a notice that the paper had found it necessary to dispense with Mr. Broun's services. The reason: disloyalty. Meanwhile, Cain drafted a letter to *The Nation* setting forth precisely what he thought of Broun and especially the columnist's conduct during the Sacco-Vanzetti case. He described it as "inept, stupid, and not remotely to be associated with courage." He said Broun was just throwing spitballs and monkey wrenches while the editorial page of the *World* went to the aid of two men sentenced to death "with every bit of intelligence and persuasiveness we could muster. But we tried to do our job like men and not like schoolboys." Similarly, he said he stood by his editorial on birth control and did not particularly care what the liberals thought. "We are not trying to live up to the ritual of liberalism. We are trying to get out a newspaper . . . frequently we reverse ourselves. Frequently we think differently today from what we thought yesterday. Frequently we learn something today that we didn't know yesterday."

Cain concluded by saying he was weary of this talk of courage and that maybe "if we hear much more of it, we may have to have a showdown. Most of us are young and are in the heavyweight division."

The letter was addressed to the editor of *The Nation* and is significant in that it reveals the kind of journalist Cain was. He had demonstrated his independence when he rebelled against Lippmann's "play jury" and openly criticized the idea in a *Nation* article. But he had not attacked the paper, and certainly the issue was not as inflammatory as the Sacco-Vanzetti case. When Broun attacked the *World*'s position on the birth control exhibit in *The Nation*, he also attacked the *World*. And he continued to write inflammatory columns in the *World* about the Sacco-Vanzetti case at a time when public opinion was so aroused over it there were bombings in the subway. Cain said he did not disagree with Broun's position on the issue, just his tactics. And Cain felt loyalty to the paper. It took precedence over his own independent statement because the paper had a better chance of saving the two men's lives and could serve as a restraining influence in an explosive situation. Thus Cain demonstrated a perceptive understanding of the role of a newspaper—that it must be rational and responsible in debating public issues or it lost its effectiveness.

Through all the tension and feuding aroused by the Sacco-Vanzetti case, Cain continued his running commentary on American culture. The American composer George Antheil was a modernist who, among other things, had composed the controversial *Ballet Méchanique* for ten pianos, one mechanical pianola, six xylophones, two bass drums, and a variety of mechanical effects, including the climactic sounding of a fire siren. It was creating a sensation in Europe, where music lovers in Paris literally rioted when it was performed. Cain wrote an editorial saying that modern music was cacophony, that Antheil was incapable of composing a melody one could enjoy or whistle, and that *Ballet Méchanique* was a stunt. Unfortunately, the ballet had never been performed in America, and Cain wrote his anti-Antheil edit without ever having heard the composition; nor had he heard Antheil play.

When Donald Friede, a publisher who was promoting the American debut of the ballet, read the editorial, he called Lippmann and asked who wrote it. Lippmann told him it was Cain. So Friede said Cain should at least hear Antheil play and invited him over to his apartment where Antheil was staying. Lippmann called Cain in and said: "You're on the hook. It's a point I can't argue with. Secretly I agree with you, and I ran your editorial, but it crossed my mind that you were in a very shaky position since you hadn't heard the thing and it hadn't been played in this country. I think you've got to go up there this afternoon and meet him and listen."

Friede, recounting the story in his autobiography, said: "To my surprise he came. He listened to Antheil playing for almost an hour, went back to the *World* and wrote another editorial, taking back everything he said the previous day. As far as I know, this is unique as a newspaper reversal."

Cain's version of the story is slightly different. When he arrived at Friede's apartment, he was greeted by "a very good-looking number," Friede's wife Evelyn, whom Cain had known before she married Friede. She and Cain spent the whole time talking. "I paid almost no attention to this tiny guy, Antheil," who, playing with a Mexican cartoonist named Covarrubias, "mumbled and groaned and hollered" at the piano. Cain then went back and wrote an editorial retracting some of what he had said: "I ratted on account of her. I was kind of stuck on her." In the editorial, he said that Antheil had played some tunes that were melodic and even beautiful, but concluded that "we cannot yield this music unqualified admiration. There is something fragmentary about it; it suffers from the same lack of completeness that you feel in 'modern' painting and 'modern' drama. For a moment you are under a spell and then nothing happens: the music is off on some wild tangent that seems to have nothing to do with what went before."

In May 1927, when Charles Lindbergh flew the Atlantic alone, Cain went mad with the rest of New York and wrote a tingling lead editorial, which was reprinted years later in James Boylan's *The World of the 20s*. It called Lindbergh the ultimate sports hero, the boy who scored the greatest winning touchdown of them all, a Casey at the bat who did not strike out. Later, when Lindy returned and New York went hysterical during the big parade, Cain went down into the streets and marveled at the blizzard of confetti falling from the high buildings. Then he wrote a long lead edit which captured the moment, in part by repeating snatches of conversations heard along the parade route. Later in the year, when transoceanic flights became something of a mania, Cain, in another long edit, denounced them as purposeless stunts.

In another piece, "The Wages of Swat," Cain responded to the criticism that Babe Ruth had signed a contract which paid him the unheard-of sum of $70,000 a year to hit home runs by pointing out that the reason Enrico Caruso was paid $2,500 an appearance to sing *La Bohème* was simple—when Caruso sang *La Bohème*, the opera house receipts were $11,000; when he did not sing, the receipts were $3,000.

In still another, he said that opposition to the concept of evolution would disappear overnight in this country if it were discovered that man was descended not from the ape but from the eagle. "Breathes there the man with soul so dead that he would not be proud to be descended from the American Eagle?"

Finally, Cain closed out the year with another long editorial (also reprinted in *The World of the 20s*) on "The New Flivver." Henry Ford usually was given rough treatment on the editorial pages of the *World* for his bigotry and ignorance, but with the introduction of the Model A Ford, replacing the Model T, the *World* applauded the pioneer in mass automobile construction.

By 1928, Cain was well established as one of the city's most respected editorial writers. Lippmann, perhaps more than anyone on the paper, appreciated his talent, and when contract time came around again Cain was given a $1,000 bonus and a three-year renewal at $125 a week. However, now that he was married and had to pay $150 a month alimony, $125 a week did not go very far, especially in New York. So Lippmann arranged to have him contribute to the Sunday section (at $25 a week) and the *Evening World* editorial page (at $50 a week), bringing his weekly income to $200. With additional magazine articles, Cain's income for 1927 was between $13,000 and $14,000.

His contributions to the *Evening World* consisted of one editorial a day in addition to what he called "five comic paragraphs." Cain's only editorial achievement of note on the *Evening World* was his campaign against the Third Avenue Elevated Railway. Urged on by the "young Master," as Cain called Herbert Pulitzer, the man in charge of the *World* during much of its last years, Cain announced that the El ought to be torn down, as "we are sick of looking at it." In follow-up edits, he analyzed the numbers and types of people it served and showed how they could use the subway just as well. The response was astonishing. Letters flooded in and the city was on the verge of ordering the El's demolition when a delegation of concerned citizens and merchants called on Pulitzer. This produced a phone call to *Evening World* editor Harry Pollard saying there would be no more edits on the El. Pollard went to Cain's office, sick at heart. "We had it," he exclaimed. "It was in our hands, all ready for us to win and claim for our own—and now what?" Voicing his opinion of young Pulitzer, Pollard added: "It just goes to show, you can call a jay bird a hawk, but it doesn't make him one."

The year 1928 was something of a letdown. There were no major news stories or controversies to write about, and Cain had to fall back on his old reliables—food, music, and sports. It was another big year for the Yankees, but the question was not whether they would win the pennant or the World

Series, but who would hit the most home runs—Babe Ruth or Lou Gehrig. Cain had quite a bit to say about the contest, in addition to which he felt that in all likelihood the 1928 Yankees were "the greatest team that ever trotted on a diamond."

Easily the most talked-about event on the *World* in 1928 was the sudden and dramatic departure of Herbert Bayard Swope that October. It was inconceivable to most people that Swope would ever leave the paper. But according to his biographer E. J. Kahn, Swope was walking down Fifth Avenue one day when he suddenly decided: "I don't want to be a hired boy any longer." One of the problems was Herbert Pulitzer, youngest of the three brothers who shared in Joseph Pulitzer's will. Just a boy when the elder Pulitzer died, Herbert had graduated from Harvard, where he was best known for his Rolls-Royce, then had spent some time in France, where he exchanged his Rolls for a polo pony. Ralph Pulitzer, although hardly a great newspaperman, was at least dedicated; Herbert was a dilettante. Ralph was able to take charge of his paper and give Lippmann, Swope, and the business manager, Florence White, some guidance and, more important, maximum authority in running their departments; Herbert was aloof, more inclined to try to run things himself, and essentially lacked interest in the newspaper business. He also used perfume.

Inevitably, Swope decided to move on, and many, including Cain, thought it was a good thing. In the last few months of his tenure, Swope hardly showed up at the office at all, and when he did the result was primarily confusion. "By funny coincidence," Cain wrote Kahn, "during this time the paper had entered a spin, and whether its downward plunge was caused by this state of turmoil nobody really knew, but few would argue that the turmoil helped it any."

The day Swope left, the front page of the *World* carried the words "Swope Quits" in thirty-six different type sizes, and the staff gave him a farewell dinner. One of the speakers was Walter Lippmann, who called Swope "a lucky, fascinating devil" and paid him the customary tributes. But another speaker, Alexander Woollcott, who had known Swope in World War I, took a less flattering approach, telling uncomplimentary stories about Swope's early career and sketching his rise to eminence in less than flattering terms. Cain was also at the dinner, and vividly recalled the moment. His account was used by Kahn in his biography of Swope: "What fascinated me was Swope and how he took it. He sat there, to all outward appearance overcome with delight. If there was any resentment whatever at this waspish, malevolent recital, no hint of it showed on his face. And when at last it was his turn to speak, he did so with the utmost good humor, and to terrific applause."

Cain's relationship with his fellow editorial writers was friendly, but less close than with Lippmann, Krock, Stallings, and Markey. John Heaton was an elderly gentleman, much older than Cain, and W. O. Scroggs was, as many economists are, somewhat withdrawn from the caustic, in-the-know cynicism of the intellectual journalists. A better acquaintance was Charles Merz, Lippmann's second in command. A tall, friendly man a year or two younger than Cain, Merz was exact, quiet, and efficient, with his own neat clipping file. Cain remembered him as addicted to "summaries," rather than pieces that took all-out positions. Merz preferred to state the facts and let them speak for themselves, and when he set them up (a), (b), (c), he proved that facts could speak much louder than opinion. From Merz, Cain learned another thing that would influence his writing: Attitude and conviction are important, but information, if you have enough of it, will speak for itself. Thus Cain's almost fanatic obsession in his writings, including his novels, with reporting and accuracy.

Cain considered Allan Nevins one of the most baffling human beings he ever knew. Nevins wrote and researched editorials involving history, and he was encyclopedic in this field. He also wrote beautifully. And whenever he came downstairs from his fourteenth-floor office, chatting before going in to see Lippmann, he was invariably friendly, courteous, and talkative. Cain saw Nevins almost every day and thought of him as a friend. But somewhere along the line, he finally decided he did not know him at all. In fact, he realized there was no one, on or off the *World*, who really knew Nevins or was on more than casual terms with him. Nevins never ate with the staff, and the question of where and what he ate became a subject of such speculation that one day when a copy boy came upstairs to announce that "Mr. Nevins is sitting on a bench down in City Hall Park eating peanuts," it was considered a major news item. But despite Nevins's eccentricity and withdrawn nature, Cain revered and envied the man. "If I had that much character . . . I would be a success in life."

By contrast, Cain thought Charley Michelson, the Washington columnist, had "the mind of a Hearst feature writer." One of Cain's assignments every Friday was to translate Michelson's column, "Political Undertow," into English for the Sunday paper. He considered this "a filthy chore" and wondered "how the mind which produced such slip-shod, unparsable sentences, such dull wheezes, such obvious banalities, could be capable of the Machiavellian subtleties ascribed to it later."

The years of writing editorials on the *World* were critical to Cain's development as a writer. Through that basic education, he learned about those aspects of life with which the tabloids are preoccupied—violence and the average person's fundamental concern with sex, shelter, and food. And as the "pepper upper," as he called it, of the letters column, he quickly learned that "the perennial, never-fail, always good for a ha-ha subject of subjects" was food. He became convinced it was a major concern in people's lives, as was reflected in several of his later books—*Serenade*, *Mildred Pierce*, *Galatea*, and *The Magician's Wife*.

More important was Cain's continuing preoccupation with his style, an obsession that intrigued Lippmann, who once asked Cain if he realized that 40 percent of the allusions in his editorial were to *Alice in Wonderland*. Although Cain still did not consider the newspaper business "a high human enterprise," he did feel the editorial page of a paper was an excellent place to learn how to write, especially if you were lucky enough to work for someone like Lippmann, who was as finicky a perfectionist as Cain. Their relationship encouraged Cain to feel that his own obsession with style was justified. "He didn't laugh at me, or sneer at me, or look down on me for rewriting my editorials. He knew, of course, he had to know, that some of them went through the chopper a dozen times—something the newspaper business scorns, in spite of its supposed dedication to 'good writing.' And he didn't mind that I polished and repolished and polished six times more, as though it was a Wilkinson Sword Blade."

Lippmann's attitude toward writing, said Cain, "as compared with the attitude of the average city editor I was accustomed to, who thought it all right to assign some copy boy to yank pages out of your typewriter before you had even read them over, was so startling to me I could hardly believe it." Lippmann lost his temper with Cain only once—and it concerned a matter of style. As Cain described the incident, he, a few of the women who worked in the office, cartoonist Rollin Kirby, and editorial writer John Heaton were standing in the hall chatting after lunch when, suddenly, Lippmann emerged from the elevator. "Instead of the suave, friendly, and elegant chief we were accustomed to, a stranger stood before us, savage with rage." When Lippmann's eye fell on Cain, he snarled: "You, it would be you!"

"Well," Cain replied. "Obviously, I'm charged and I plead guilty at once, but just for laughs, I would like to know what I've done."

Lippmann had in his hand an editorial that had been written by Cain while Lippmann was away. It was on writing—and the last sentence read: "Writing, apparently, is not as easy as it looks." Lippmann kept reading it aloud, but Cain was still not quite sure what made him so angry. Finally, Lippmann bellowed: "Don't you know that after the negative the word is 'so'?"

"Oh, so it is, so it is," Cain replied. "I forgot for the moment. I'm sorry."

Lippmann stomped off, and Cain returned to his cubicle and wrote the following editorial for the next day:

MISTAKE IN AN UNFORTUNATE PLACE

Excerpt from our remarks yesterday on the subject of quotation marks:

"But writing, alas, is like billiard playing. It is not as easy as it looks."

In a constructive spirit, an old subscriber calls up to point out the fact that, in view of the negative, the correct form should be: "It is not so easy as it looks." So, apparently, alas, it isn't.

Although he had been embarrassed in front of his friends, when Cain thought about it he was rather pleased at Lippmann's outburst. "I was working for the one man in the newspaper business to whom such things mattered." What probably annoyed Cain most, on this particular occasion, was his conviction that Lippmann was not 100 percent correct in his grammar. "So," after a negative, "is mainly to the ear," he felt. "As" parses just as well, and it should be noted, Cain said, "that one man's euphony is another man's pain in the neck." Cain considered Lippmann to be the finest stylist writing in the twentieth century; "the truth is, he writes better than Churchill." Not only did he have a natural gift for writing, but he had also made an exhaustive study of rhetoric. He was "a nut, slightly unbalanced," according to Cain, on the subject of the English language.

Lippmann gave Cain something else indispensable to the development of a writer: freedom to write about the things that concerned him and to say what he wanted to say. "He never tried to dictate what I should write," Cain recalled. "Just once he suggested an editorial, and I said, 'Well, I don't know,' and he said: 'Forget it.' " Lippmann also backed Cain up; in Lippmann's files was a memo he had prepared in defense of Cain, and although the issue that provoked it is forgotten, there is little doubt how Lippmann felt about him: "Needless to say, Mr. Cain is not our expert on government. He is, however, our expert on stuffed shirts and clay feet and this brief treatise [by Cain] contains a staggering amount of the most horrible truth."

Lippmann was accused by many of being weak and vacillating, and a spokesman for the vested interests. Cain felt that such criticism was unjustified, but he had his own, rather unique appraisal of Lippmann as thinker and editor. "He was a realist," Cain concluded, "and adjusted to realities of the situation, whatever it happened to be. But the adjustments, always, were on marginal matters, not involving his inner convictions." And this inner conviction was a planned effort *not to have any inner conviction!* "I think in the morning, when he started to work," Cain said, "he tried to fashion his mind into what Scholasticism called *tabula rasa*, a wiped clean slate, with no preconceptions, no party affiliations, no bias of any kind, so he could tackle each thing as it came up, strictly on its own merits, and not on any other." He was never a Socialist or a Liberal or a Democrat or a Republican. This enabled him to elucidate, "with a beautiful absence of prejudice, and gained him a position in the newspaper world that was unique."

Lippmann's journalism was "personal," and his most important contribution was "to explore new lines of thought rather than take solid positions of value to his paper." He was indifferent to what might be good for his paper, not from temperamental unreasonableness but from an inability to gear his mind to such special considerations. As a result, he was often not interested in what the front office was thinking about or what the American people were worrying about. "And yet, when most of us were worrying about cars, or something of that sort, he was proclaiming the impending collapse of Europe. You can't exactly say he was out of step with reality on that."

It was Lippmann's unwillingness to maintain a conventional liberal, conservative, Republican, or Democratic position on the issues that got him into trouble on the *World*—that, and his tendency to take some issues too seriously. Cain's favorite example was the Scopes trial. One day at lunch, Cain tried to explain to Lippmann why he had made a mistake in going overboard in 1925. "You rode a hobby horse without any regard to whether it was worth all you were writing about it, and you were also guilty of trying to make an editorial more than it can be, and usually achieving something less than it ought to be."

"I don't know what you mean," Lippmann replied.

"Well, if you ask me," Cain said, "the most that any newspaper should try to do is choose sides in a fight, and then fight as hard as it can, even when it secretly wishes the fight were going a little differently. But you are always trying to dredge up basic principles. In a newspaper it won't work. For example, turn to music. A piano has eight octaves, a violin three, a cornet two, and a bugle has only four notes. Now, if what you've got to blow is a bugle, there isn't any sense in camping yourself down in front of piano music."

"You may be right," Lippmann said. "But goddamn it, I'm not going to spend my life writing bugle calls."

This, Cain thought, was the essence of Walter Lippmann. "He never felt that while a bugle call may be the most utter banality as absolute music, it may be the most glorious thing in the world when the battle is going hard. Partly as a matter of intellectual pride, partly just because he was really a poet, and jarred by all banalities, he never let himself lose his perspective through the emotions of combat. Indeed, when he was aware of the combat, he was always trying to bring it to a gentlemanly level; he seemed to regard it as a sort of amateur tennis tournament, as indicated by his inevitable desire to shake hands afterward. But Cain did not consider that a serious criticism of Lippmann—the man or the journalist. And Cain paid him the ultimate compliment: "He cannot be frightened and he cannot be bought."

There was one more thing Cain learned writing editorials for the *World*, a self-realization more important than anything Lippmann or preoccupation with the passing parade taught him: *He could not write unless he pretended to be someone else!* "I have no capacity to be Cain. I can't be Cain. I can be anybody except Cain," he said. On the *World*, he learned to be "the corporate awfulness" of the paper, as he called it. "This newspaper job," he said, "as the whole of the paper talking through a solemn editorial 'we,' was, in its way, a portent, a sign of my latent strength . . . and of my very real limitations."

Having learned what he could do when pretending to be someone else, the problem now was how to translate this ability into writing about the people in whom he was most interested—the average men and women one read about in the tabloids, the people who committed the crimes of passion, who were victimized by the system, and who lived their lives unconcerned with what was going on in Washington or the board rooms or on Wall Street. To write a novel—still his secret desire, despite his earlier failure—he had to pretend not only to be someone else, but someone not in his walk of life. For some reason, James M. Cain was too sensitive and, perhaps, too much of an Eastern Shore gentleman to write about himself, or about his friends and the people he knew best.

THE LITERARY LIFE

Pretending to be "the corporate awfulness" helped James M. Cain learn how to write, but he knew very few writers who had made their fame and fortune writing anonymous editorials. He was, however, finding another way to solve his stylistic limitation—in the dialogues and one-act plays for Mencken and the *American Mercury*. In these, he not only could pretend to be someone else, but he could write in the "low speech" of rural America, which had fascinated him ever since his childhood conversations with bricklayer Ike Newton. By the end of 1927, Cain had written four dialogues for the *Mercury*, and they were attracting so much attention he began to talk with Mencken about the possibility of a book of them. But it was agreed he needed a common theme and several more sketches; Mencken suggested about a dozen. So, in his spare time, Cain continued working on them, and by 1928 two more were ready for publication. The first one, "Trial by Jury," centered on twelve jurors debating the fate of a man charged with murder. A group of Ku Klux Klansmen had gone out in white sheets one night, around 3:00 A.M., to sing hymns on the porch of the defendant, Mr. Summers. One of the Klansmen just happened to have a thick leather strap with him suitable for beating someone. Mr. Summers's offense, in the eyes of the Klan, was that he had bought a disk harrow from a mail order house rather than from a local store. Apparently he had also bought a 12-gauge shot-gun, with which he let the Klansman carrying the thick strap have two rounds at close range through the front door, killing him. The jury was obviously moving toward acquittal until it developed that one jury member had connections with the Klan. This changed the mood in the jury room immediately. So amid many statements that "we hadn't ought to forget, Ku Klux is a fine order," the jury handed down a verdict of manslaughter.

The second, "Theological Interlude," took place on the front porch of a boardinghouse at a summer resort on the coast of Delaware. The conversation was between Mr. and Mrs. Nation, who live there, and Mr. Barlow, Mrs. Nation's brother, who had been asked to come for a visit because something was worrying the couple. The trouble was that the Nations' daughter, Laura, had died—was actually pronounced dead by the doctor. Then a young medical school graduate, staying in the boardinghouse, happened to come in the room. When he saw Laura, he went into action, and with the aid of a pulmotor managed to revive her. A few days later, Laura decided she had been to heaven during the time she had been pronounced dead, and soon, accompanying herself on her "banjer," she began telling everybody who came to the boardinghouse about what heaven was like. Before long the Reverend Day, who was holding a revival over in Greenwood, heard her and insisted that she come up there. This was all right with Mr. and Mrs. Nation, except now Laura had moved in with the Reverend and they were not sure this was proper, especially in that they figured Reverend Day was married. But Barlow assured them he was not, so they all agreed if they could get Laura married to the Reverend everything would be all right, because they had heard "there ain't a word in the Bible agin a little cutting up" before you were married.

One person who was particularly impressed with Cain's dialogues was Alfred A. Knopf. He had discussed them with Mencken, and when Mencken told him Cain was thinking about making a book of them as soon as he had enough, Knopf wrote in late July 1928, saying he was very interested in the project and hoped Cain had not made arrangements elsewhere. Cain did not reply for several months.

Cain had also been thinking about the story given to him by William Gilbert Patten, of the two westerners who had cut off a man's head and didn't know what to do when it started rolling around in their wagon. He shifted the locale east, added some characters of his own, and put the story in the mouth of an eastern roughneck. The result was his first short story, called "Pastorale," a deceptively bucolic title for the black humor it contained. Mencken liked it and ran it in the March 1928 *Mercury*. Since then it has been reprinted many times, and David Madden, in his study of Cain, calls it his best short story.

"Pastorale" concerns a young man named Burbie who comes back to his hometown on the Eastern Shore to find that his childhood girl friend, Lida, has married an old man because he bought her the clothes she liked. Burbie and Lida immediately begin seeing each other again and soon decide to kill the old man. Burbie arranges for Lida to go away for an evening and persuades his friend Hutch, who has served time in prison, to go with him to rob and kill the old man, who supposedly has a pot of money hidden in the fireplace. So they kill him, only to find there isn't even $20 in the pot. This starts an argument between Burbie and Hutch that continues as they carry the old man down the road and bury him in a shallow grave. On the way back to town, Hutch starts drinking corn liquor and knocks Burbie down in the wagon for lying to him about the money. Burbie finally tells Hutch about Lida, so Hutch decides the only thing to do is to go back to the grave, cut off the old man's head, and give it as a present to Lida. After Hutch has cut off the old man's head with a shovel, they start a wild ride back to town, with Hutch yelling and screaming, and the head rolling around in the back of the wagon. But the horse gets tired as they reach the creek, which has a slight crust of ice on it. Burbie takes the opportunity to throw the head out of the wagon, but when Hutch sees the head sliding along the ice in the moonlight, he becomes enraged and threatens to kill Burbie, who leaps out of the wagon and runs away. Then Hutch hears a loud crack, like a pistol shot. It is the ice breaking—and the wagon settles into the creek. The next morning the sheriff and his men find the old man's head and Hutch drowned in the creek. They figure Hutch robbed the old man and killed him. But one night, in the pool hall, some time later, Burbie admits killing the old man, saying it was women who had ruined him and he was happy now that he told everybody. "So, Burbie, he's going to get hung sure as hell," Cain's narrator says, "and if he hadn't felt so smart, he would of been a free man yet. Only I reckon he done been holding it all so long, he just had to spill it."

It was a fine story, well told in the Ring Lardner style and extremely important in Cain's development. In the first place, he had now found that he could tell a story in some other manner than a dialogue or one-act play—by writing in the first person, preferably in the voice of some "low-life" character, as his mother called the type. "The only way I can keep on the track at all," he said, trying to explain his difficulty writing fiction, "is to pretend to be somebody else—to put it in dialect and thus get it told. If I try to do it in my own language I find that I have none. A style that seems to be personal enough for ordinary gassing refuses to get going for an imaginary narrative. So long as I merely report what people might have said under certain circumstances, I am all right; but the moment I have to step in myself, and try to create the impression that what happened to those people really matters, then I am sunk. I flounder about, not knowing whether I skip to the scene at the church or pile in a little more of the talk at the post office. The reason is . . . I don't care what happened."

In "Pastorale," Cain not only managed to make his narrator care what happened, enabling the story to move, he also found his favorite theme: Although one might get away with committing a crime, one can't live with it. In fact, five years after "Pastorale," Cain would again try to write a novel and its plot would be very similar to that of his first short story.

In future years, Cain was able to demonstrate with "Pastorale" that his style was in no way influenced by or copied from Ernest Hemingway, as some critics charged. It was written in late 1927, and by then Cain's narrative technique and ear for dialogue—which in a few years would constitute one of the most widely discussed and imitated literary styles in the country—were clearly established. His use of realistic, colloquial speech had gradually emerged from the pieces he had been writing for Mencken since 1924, and the technique he used in most of his novels, writing in the first person, originated more or less with "Pastorale."

Although Cain did not read Hemingway's short story "Fifty Grand" when it was published in the *Atlantic Monthly* in 1926, he remembered all the excitement it caused, with everyone at the *World* agreeing a new voice had been heard. He said—and there is no reason not to believe him—that he did not read Hemingway until *Men Without Women* appeared in 1928, and he was tremendously impressed. But what surprised him "was an echo I found in it, of something I couldn't place." Then he remembered the voice: It was that of Roxy Stimson, the divorced wife of Jess Smith, a lackey of Attorney General Harry Daugherty, one of the key figures in the Teapot Dome scandal. In 1924, Roxy testified at the Senate Hearings on Teapot Dome, and her manner of speech, as Cain recalled, "burst on the country like a July 4th rocket." Her tale, describing Smith's slow deterioration as he was caught up in the scandal and his own foolish speculations in the stock market, electrified the country, especially the literary world, for which Roxy briefly became a cult figure. "She could come popping out with some bromide," Cain said, "a cornball expression that should have been pure hush puppy, and somehow transform it, the way Dvorak transformed folk music, so it stayed in your ear a classic."

Roxy's testimony was carried in full in the *Times* and, Cain assumed, in the English-language paper in Paris, where he was certain Hemingway had absorbed it. He was even more convinced of his theory when he finally read "Fifty Grand" and noted the similarity in its plot and an incident described by Roxy Stimson, prior to Jess Smith's suicide. Cain had no objection to Hemingway's using the idea for a story; he himself had done the same thing with items he read in the newspapers. But considering the number of people to whom Cain expressed his theory—including Hemingway's biographer Carlos Baker—it is obvious he devoutly believed it. As for Roxy's influence on Cain's style: "She taught me respect for the cliché. I'd say she influenced me plenty." Cain never met Hemingway; in fact he shied away from a meeting "for fear he wouldn't like it when I didn't call him Papa"—a nickname which Cain considered too cute to acknowledge.

While writing his dialogues for Mencken and his "solemncholy," as his father called it, for the corporate awfulness, Cain found still another medium for his developing style. In September 1928, in part to help earn extra money for the alimony payments to Mary, Cain started writing a by-lined column for the Metropolitan section of the Sunday *World*. It had no running title and consisted, in the first year at least, of dialogues similar to the ones he was writing for the *Mercury*, although shorter and less shocking. He could not, after all, write about "niggers" and murderers and burning "stiffs" in a county almshouse for a family newspaper. For his *World* sketches, he wrote about more conventional family life, and over its first year his column was devoted entirely to a neighborhood revolving around Bender Street in a city, obviously New York.

It is hard to imagine these sketches being written by the author of "Pastorale," but the voices are authentic, the dialogue excellent, and each one holds your interest once you get into it. But Cain must have taken a verbal shellacking from sophisticates such as F.P.A., Broun, and Woollcott for writing what to them must have been pure, unadulterated corn. Cain himself grew unhappy with these attempts at urban dialect and said that some mornings he dreaded opening up the paper and reading his column.

After a year, Cain, or someone else on the *World*, tired of the Bender Street gang and Cain shifted to other locales and characters. He also changed his style, no longer writing dialogue in play form, but now using the conventional short story form. He also returned to his favorite type of character, the Eastern Shore roughneck. Many of these *World* sketches begin: "Down in the country one time. . . ." They were important in his development, for not only did they give him still another outlet, but in them he had even greater freedom to pick his subjects than he did on the editorial page. He also learned from them that there were a number of different ways to tell the same story.

The sketches were widely read and drew attention to Cain, still a relatively unknown writer. One day Claude Bowers, a *World* writer and historian, brought Robert N. Linscott, an editor from Houghton Mifflin, in to see him. Linscott had read the sketches and wanted Cain to try a novel. Cain told Linscott of his unsuccessful attempt to write long fiction and claimed he was not capable of it. But Linscott said he did not agree and predicted that some-day Cain would write a novel—and he hoped Houghton Mifflin would be its publisher.

While finding that he was more comfortable pretending to be someone else in his writing, Cain also was continuing to prove that he could write remarkably good and enduring essays under his own by-line. In 1928, one of his finest articles, "The Solid South," appeared in the November issue of *The Bookman*. In it Cain attempted to explain why the South was expected to vote for the Democratic candidate for President, Al Smith. All the more remark-able, coming from a close friend of H. L. Mencken, who had long ago given up on the South as a culturally barren land of religious zealots and fascists in white sheets, the article comprises one of the best brief defenses of southern society and culture of the 1920s ever written.

Cain, meanwhile, had not forgotten Knopf's interest in doing a book made up of his *World* sketches, and late in 1928 he responded to the pub-lisher's midsummer letter, saying that he had written several additional sketches, many of which had not appeared in the *Mercury* (although three of them would be published in the magazine the following year) and that his book was almost complete. His plan for the collection was "to give it some solemncholy title such as: 'GOVERNMENT: An Absolutely Impartial Analy-sis.' " Then he would write a very intellectual preface saying, tongue in cheek, that the book was an effort to examine government as it is, by the case system. Cain promised copy within a month, if Knopf was interested, and estimated that the book would total 30,000 words.

The response came from Blanche Knopf, who wrote that they were inter-ested. But then the Knopfs did not hear from Cain again for two months, so in early March 1929, Alfred Knopf wrote saying he had just read the advance proofs of Cain's next *Mercury* dialogue, which he thought "a perfect scream," and had been reminded of the book they had been discussing. Cain respond-ed immediately, saying the book was "10/12ths" done and should be finished at the end of the month. "What takes me so long with these pieces is that they have a tantalizing way of not coming off, and then there is nothing to do but work them over." A month later, he was able to write: "The book I have been corresponding with you about for the last seven years is now done." Knopf replied with enthusiasm, saying he had read another *Mercury* piece in galleys and it was "perfectly scrumptuous." When he finally received the manu-script of the book, which they had now decided to call *Our Government*, he was delighted and invited Cain to lunch.

The first piece Knopf had read in galleys, "Will of the People," ap-peared in the April 1929 *Mercury*; it concerns three members of the Committee on Education in a state legislature, who, while considering legislation, come to "this here Evolution Bill" prohibiting the teaching of certain doctrines in educational institutions supported in whole or in part by public funds. This presents a problem for the legislators, not that anyone is *for* the bill. But it turns out that one member of the committee not only has not read the bill, but simply cannot read. Furthermore, he is not interested in evolution, but solely with the question of a bill to give Flint Neck a schoolhouse, which he was elected to vote for. The ensuing "debate" creates a hilarious picture of the ignorance prevalent in some rural state legislatures of the 1920s.

But compared to Cain's vision of what went on in the governor's office, the legislators looked like graduates of the Harvard School of Government. "Citizenship," the second piece Knopf read in galleys (and which appeared in the December *Mercury*), concerns a coal country citizen who has become involved in an armed march by the miners and is given ten years in jail. He has served three years of his sentence and is now petitioning the governor for a pardon. The governor, portrayed by Cain as an ignorant, drunken oaf, is completely confused. He thinks he has been asked to grant a stay of execution. So he commutes the petitioner's sentence to life in prison. Then the prosecutor brings out the fact that the petitioner's citizenship is questionable because he was discovered in a sewer by a Coal City Fire Department horse. The governor mistakenly thinks the petitioner is a member of "The ol' Coal City Vol'teer Fi' D'pa'ment" and sets him free. Although the governor's dialect is so thick it is almost impossible to follow, it is one of Cain's best sketches and has been reprinted in many anthologies, including Katharine and E. B. White's *Subtreasury of American Humor*.

Cain also wrote a third *Mercury* piece in 1929—"The Taking of Montfaucon," which appeared in the June issue. In this one, Cain describes his experience in France the night of September 26, 1918, at the beginning of the Meuse-Argonne offensive. It is a first-person factual account of what happened, except that again Cain tells the story in the dialect of a country yokel, thereby making it identifiable to the average man in the trench. "The Taking of Montfaucon" was reprinted in 1929 and 1942 in *Infantry Journal*, which said the story "has never been excelled as an accurate description of conditions in the war, and few stories of any aspect of war will stand beside it."

Our Government, James M. Cain's first book, ended up just about the way Cain had described it to Knopf, with two important differences: Instead of writing an original satire on the Congress, he decided Congress did a good job of satirizing itself in the *Congressional Record*, so he picked a few pages from the *Record* for April 1928 and included them verbatim as the chapter on "Congress." Cain also decided not to include "Theological Interlude" as the last chapter. Instead, still thinking the book needed a change of pace for the ending, he put in "The Taking of Montfaucon," calling it "The Military Forces."*

The preface to the book was developed precisely as Cain had proposed—as a mock-intellectual introduction written in "solemncholy" and laced with academic words and phrases, such as the "syllogistic process" and "*cogito, ergo sum.*" "There is no book, so far as I know," Cain wrote, "which sets out to paint a portrait of our government; to depict, without bias or comment, the machine which passes our laws, educates our children, and polices our streets, to show the kind of men who man it, the matters that occupy them, and the nature of their deliberations." He also tendered thanks to Charles Merz, Arthur Krock, Hamilton Owens, Herbert Bayard Swope, Walter Lippmann, Morris Markey, Philip Goodman, Gilbert Malcolm, and especially H. L. Mencken, "who gave me many inspirational talks when my interest flagged," and his father, "whose manipulation of legislators for college appropriations forms the foundation of my political education."

Cain's first meeting with Alfred A. Knopf—at lunch on August 25, 1929—went well enough, although Cain apparently did not try to impress Knopf as much as he had Lippmann. Knopf, to this day, remembers Cain as "a real roughneck—sort of gruff," although he eventually came to consider him a friend.

The reviews of the book were enough to warm the heart of any author. Louis Sherwin, in the *New York Post*, called it "a brutal photograph, an objective work of almost sadistic skill." Although the book was anything but objective, Sherwin did manage to convey that it was essentially a satire. Harry Hansen, writing in Cain's paper, the *World*, said that the process of government, to Cain, masked a huge joke, but he missed what Cain was trying to achieve in the preface. "The serious framework affects the forcefulness of the book. Presented purely as fiction it would have been much more effective than as a tract." Cain's friend Hamilton Owens, on the *Baltimore Sun*, appreciated the sardonic thrust of the book and said that although some of the tales seemed incredible, most of them had a basis in fact. He also said the book showed Cain as a master of rural dialogue. John Carter in *Outlook* called it an accurate picture of American politics and said it had "just that touch of Aristophanes which is necessary to act as a preservative and make it as readable and comprehensible five centuries hence as now." The *New York Times* was less enthusiastic, saying some of the dialogues "reached the height of clever satire," but others were "mere take-offs," though all arrested the attention

*For a detailed description of *Our Government* showing which *Mercury* dialogues were used, see page 645.

because they were so "sordidly photographic." The *Times* reviewer concluded that Cain had done a good job and hoped he would go on and write a play, which would enable him to make better use of his dramatic powers. "Scenes such as he writes are meant for the stage." It was an assessment with which others were to agree, for over the years many of the dialogues from *Our Government* have been produced as one-act plays by various dramatic groups.

Despite the rave reviews, *Our Government* did not do well, which puzzled Mencken. Thirteen years later, he still could not understand why it did not "create a sensation; . . . there was capital stuff in it," he wrote Cain. Still, *Our Government* may be James M. Cain's most significant book—not for what it achieved, but for what it did not achieve. By 1930, when it appeared, its author was thirty-seven years old. He was an acknowledged literary craftsman considered in the same league with Sinclair Lewis and the emerging John O'Hara as a master of satiric dialogue. But both Lewis and O'Hara fashioned from their experiences—in, respectively, Sauk Centre, Minnesota, and Pottsville, Pennsylvania—a body of novels and short stories, many of which have become part of our permanent literature. From a comparable period in Cain's life—growing up on the Eastern Shore, spending a year and a half in France during World War I and several months in West Virginia reporting for the *Sun* and gathering material for a novel—Cain managed to produce only a dozen or so dialogues and one short story ("Pastorale"). His one attempt to develop a novel out of the West Virginia experience failed. (Eventually he would write two books out of his early experience—*The Butterfly*, a short novel about incest in the coal country, and *Galatea*, an embarrassingly poor novel about a love triangle in southern Maryland.)

Cain's inability to write fiction unless he pretended to be someone else, preferably someone not of his own social class, may well have kept him from achieving the contemporary status of a major American writer that was accorded to Lewis, and even to O'Hara, despite the fact that he was acknowledged to be their equal as a craftsman. Why Cain could not write about people in his own walk of life is a paradox yet to be resolved.

Although *Our Government* was a commercial disappointment when it was published in 1930—earning only $250 of the $500 advance—it did turn the promising *Mercury* writer and *World* editorial hand into a full-fledged author. He now had one well-received book to his credit and an option with Knopf to do two more, although he apparently had little idea what they might be.

Cain and Elina were getting along in the language of love, and speaking German when it was necessary to communicate about other things, but all was not idyllic. For one thing, she was tone deaf. "But she didn't like to be left out," Cain said, "so we would go to concerts together, and along about the second movement of the symphony, she would get itchy. By intermission time she was bored. By the second part of the program she was sniping at the conductor, in whispers, and all in all going to music with her left something to be desired. So we quit going."

Elina was also becoming extremely dominating, according to at least one person who knew the couple. Although she was barely more than five feet tall, Elina was very strong, and Ruth Goodman Goetz recalled Cain saying one night at dinner, in the late 1920s, that "whenever she gets mad, she throws me around"—probably with good reason. Cain left her alone many nights, often staying out until 3:00 or 4:00 A.M. and occasionally coming in with lipstick on his collar.

Ruth Goodman was a precocious young lady who by now worked for Alfred A. Knopf and herself aspired to a literary career. Later she would write, with her husband Augustus Goetz, several hit plays—*The Heiress, The Immoralist, The Hidden River, Sweet Love Remembered,* and *Madly in Love.* Cain spent many evenings at the Goodmans', but usually without Elina. Although she and Ruth got along all right, Elina was uncomfortable with Phil, probably because she sensed he did not like her—or perhaps Cain had told her this. Cain's friendship with the Goodmans was conducted primarily during those long periods when Elina was in Europe—from the winter of 1929 until the summer of 1930 (when Cain went abroad to meet her and returned with her on the ship), and from May until September of 1931 (during which period she went home to bring her two children to New York).

Cain loved an evening with the Goodmans, where Mencken or any number of their friends would be present. The talk would usually be about plays and the theater, which interested Goodman and Lawrence, though not Mencken; he always thought the theater was second-class art and had nothing but contempt for it.

Ruth remembers Cain at these regular dinner parties the Goodmans gave, usually sitting silently at the table. Cain was not exactly Goodman's or Mencken's type socially, but Goodman was attracted by Cain's ability as a writer. "Both Mencken and my father, you must remember," says Ruth, "had the greatest respect for writing talent. They thought it was almost something to be revered, and they were very generous men, always trying to help and encourage writers." Mencken later said he thought Cain was "the most competent writer the country ever produced." And Goodman's respect for Cain's talent verged on reverence, for which Cain was always grateful. "Belief in you by someone who means something can be so important it speaks to your soul," Cain said of Goodman.

One time, Phil Goodman invited Cain over for an evening when W. C. Fields was also going to be there. Goodman had already persuaded Fields to do *Poppy*, the play that created Eustace McGargle, the character Fields more or less played the rest of his life. Goodman and Fields had decided they wanted to do a movie, and Cain was being invited in to do the script. The basic idea centered on Fields as the proprietor of an *Uncle Tom's Cabin* company in the 1890s, and in love with the girl who played Little Eva, but who in real life would be a little older than the character Eva. Cain said this was no problem because, although Eva was a tot on the stage, in the novel she was a comely teen-ager who rode around with her boy friend in Audubon Park in New Orleans.

So Cain suggested that in Fields's script Little Eva be cast as a late-teen-ager, small enough to wear tot's clothes and go to heaven in Act III, but actually quite a sexpot. All agreed this was the way it should be written. Cain set to work on a story line evolving around Little Eva and the problems caused by the difference between her age and the age of the character Fields would play, particularly the fact that Eva was really in love with a boy her own age. But when Cain would get together in his apartment with Fields to develop the script, he could not keep Fields's mind on the plot. The comedian would invariably launch into another gag, or interrupt Cain to tell him about something that had happened that day.

This went on for two or three months, with Cain reassuring Goodman that they were making progress when actually very little was being done on the script. Finally, the project was abandoned when Fields accepted an offer from Hollywood. On his last night in the East, Fields invited Phil, Lily, and Ruth Goodman and Cain to dinner at an Italian speako in the Forties, where he was well known. It was a memorable evening for Cain. They were looking at the menus when a ten-year-old boy—the proprietor's son, "that nauseous brat," as Ruth called him—planted himself in front of Fields and said: "Hi, big nose."

"Hi," Fields replied, paying little attention to the boy.

This would have ended the incident, except that a waiter revealed it to the boy's father, who took the kid out in the back and whacked him loud enough for Fields to hear it. Fields leaned over close to Cain and said: "Jim, that is all for my benefit. What kind of imagination is it that thinks I'm going to be pleased at a boy being walloped? I do have a big nose, and I suppose to him that's a fact like the Grand Canyon or the first cataract of the St. Lawrence. He has to say something about it."

As he talked, Fields's nose was within inches of Cain's eyes, and it was the first time he had really seen it. It was not, Cain thought, so terribly big, but it had an odd, lumpy look, as though it wasn't really sound tissue. And then Cain realized it looked that way because it had once been frozen, and suddenly he was struck with compassion.

In a moment, the Italian proprietor brought the boy back, holding him by the arm, and made him apologize. "I'm sorry, Mr. Fields—I didn't mean it, honest I didn't."

Fields ignored the father and said: "Come here, son." And then for twenty minutes, as Cain tells the story, "this man, already celebrated for the line, 'The man who hates dogs and small boys can't be *all* bad,' gave a show for this small boy that, had it been put on film, would have been played over and over and over for years. In addition to being a juggler, he was also a master magician, and he made half-dollars come out of the boy's nose, letting him keep the half-dollars. He stuck toothpicks into the dinner rolls and made them dance on the table. . . . It went on and on, with the boy utterly entranced, Ruth utterly disgusted, and Lily, Phil, and I fascinated."

Despite the fact that Cain would follow him to Hollywood in a couple of years, it was the last time Cain ever saw Bill Fields.

In addition to his undying urge to write a play, Cain also had a deep-seated desire to produce one—an ambition that led to a brief involvement with another man on the way to national fame. In 1927, a piece by John O'Hara appearing in one of F.P.A.'s "Conning Tower" columns enchanted Cain. It was entitled "The Christmas Spirit—A Speech by George F. Gabbitry at a Christmas Party," delivered to an Ohio high school, and was a parody of George F. Babbitt's manner of speaking. Impressed by O'Hara's ear for dialogue, Cain reprinted it on the *World* Christmas page, which he edited at the time, and this led to his meeting O'Hara. Later, when Phil Goodman was in touch with big money, Cain asked O'Hara down to his apartment on East Nineteenth Street to urge him to write a play that Cain and Goodman would produce. Cain had the idea, but later could not recall what it was. He said O'Hara was "not the easiest person to like" and had the annoying habit of "seeming to be thinking of something else other than what we purported to be talking about." They spent two or three evenings discussing the idea, but nothing came of it. "O'Hara seemed surprised at my admiration for the [Christmas] piece, indifferent to my idea, and utterly indifferent to me."

In the course of the preparation and publication of *Our Government*, Cain had become friends with Blanche Knopf, who would invite him to dinner quite often. "I used to bounce around and make myself sort of a lackey cavalier for her." One night, asking Cain to dinner, she mentioned that she was also having Mencken and Willa Cather. Cain was delighted and anxious to participate in what he thought would be a historic literary event, inasmuch as he considered Cather Mencken's "Galatea." By now she was an established author, having arrived with *O Pioneers!* and certified her position with

My Ántonia, *A Lost Lady*, and *The Professor's House*. In Cain's eyes, however, before arriving as a novelist, she had been a not too talented serial writer for magazines, until Mencken discovered her, and "if ever a writer was created by a critic, she was by Mencken."

At the Knopfs', Cain happened to be standing at the elevator with Mencken when Miss Cather arrived. She shook hands—"Mr. Mencken"—and then went into the Knopfs' living room. Also at the dinner were the Knopfs' lawyer and Sir Thomas Beecham, the British conductor. The lawyer, as Cain recalled the evening, "kept feeding Mencken cues and talking across Miss Cather, and Mencken talked and talked and talked, and we sat there. Mencken didn't address one word to Willa Cather. She was sitting within touching distance of him. Beecham sat there looking at me as if I were some kind of snake that got in there and that somebody ought to step on the head of. . . . Alfred sat there occasionally feeding Mencken cues, and Mencken talked and talked and talked."

Cain kept thinking: Mencken, why don't you shut up? But Mencken didn't, and finally when it came time to go, Miss Cather said: "Mr. Mencken, it's so nice seeing you again."

That was the end of the historic meeting between Mencken and his Galatea. Cather made no impression on Cain, except he felt that if you poked a finger in her cheek the hole would stay there. She was pale, very soft and plump. But Cain never found out what she might have had to say.

As far as Cain was concerned, the evening at the Knopfs' was a typical Mencken performance: the never-ending monologue, with Mencken always the center of the stage. This to Cain—and others—was Mencken's essential attraction: his engaging charm and the arresting language he used that held his listeners spellbound. "The man is bigger than his ideas," Lippmann said of him, and Cain concurred, rarely agreeing with Mencken's politics or his sweeping literary judgments. His essence was verbal, said Cain, and "his ideas . . . stripped of the incomparable language he expressed them in, hardly differed from the corner bartender's." Later, he would compare Mencken's thinking to Barry Goldwater's.

Cain also saw Mencken as "God's masterpiece in the way of a neurotic." Both men were uninterested in having children or achieving immortality through offspring, but Mencken believed he would be immortal because of his achievements and, said Cain, "it was no accident that to him Beethoven was the greatest human being who ever lived. He achieved immortality on this earth, and that was Mencken's idea, his only idea, of human existence. . . . He simply could not understand any purpose in life but glory, which in his case was always related to notoriety, and his philosophy . . . was always mixed up between substance and commotion—his thinking was a stew of Darwin, Nietzsche, Huxley, Shaw, and Theodore Roosevelt, the prevailing moguls of the eighties and nineties." Cain also never recovered from the shock of learning that the most influential literary critic of the 1920s had never read his favorite book, *Alice in Wonderland.*

Mencken's shallow thinking and egocentricity contributed, in part, to Cain's ultimate criticism of the *American Mercury,* and of Mencken himself, who Cain thought, as an editor, was too prone to dictate to his authors and not inclined to let them invent or originate. You could search back over old issues of the magazine for a key to his spark, Cain said some years later, and you would not find it. Most of it was personal magnetism, which did not make for good editing. Cain thought that of all the magazines he wrote for, the editing on the *Mercury* was the worst. Much of the excessive dialect in his *Mercury* dialogues (and ultimately in *Our Government*) was the result of his not wanting to argue with Mencken about style, despite his own strong convictions on the subject. "When I would write, 'As the fellow says,' and he would change my copy to read, 'As the fella says,' I would just hate it." Cain would tell him that he wanted the copy to express what the character *thought* rather than what came out of his mouth, which is hard to believe, reading some of Cain's *Mercury* dialogues. But Cain's approach is confirmed by the fact that in his *World* sketches, often dealing with the same country bumpkins, the dialect is much less pronounced. "But you couldn't argue with Mencken," Cain said. "You had to make up your mind to take it and like it, as I decided to do, or not write for him at all."

One person who refused to keep writing for Mencken was Arthur Krock. The break developed over Mencken's inclination to give everyone who had ever received an honorary degree the title of "Dr." In an article on Woodrow Wilson, Krock had refused to refer to Wilson as "Dr.," and Mencken had changed it. At a subsequent lunch with Cain, Krock said: "Can't Henry see that this silly gag is what excludes most professional writers from his magazine and means he gets it out with an endless succession of pieces by amateurs? Because the pro is not going to submit to a rule that makes it appear to the reader . . . that he is one more guy trying to write like Mencken."

In his dialogues, Cain managed to retain his individuality despite Mencken's editing, but in his essays he sounded too much like Mencken, and this began to disturb him. "I was a big boy then, and should have stood on my own feet more." But at that time, as he conceded years later, he was under Mencken's spell as to both ideas and style.

He thought Mencken, Nathan, and Knopf had created a smashing magazine success that they had not expected and did not know how to handle, managing ultimately to turn "a potentially great . . . and financially big magazine into a sort of house organ, with Alfred Knopf adding the finishing touch by flooding it with Borzoi notices." Cain said many of his writing friends "felt Mencken had a leviathan, a mammoth, in his backyard, and persisted in treating it like a pet rabbit."

Cain eventually considered doing a book on Mencken. He thought most biographers started out with the idea that Mencken's insolence was a joke, but were shocked to learn that he was indeed the anarchist he claimed to be. "They always take him at his own evaluation," said Cain, "iconoclast, mocker, a heaver of dead cats into the sanctuary! That's the way he put it one time, and he was certainly all those things. But a man who writes novels knows that there comes a point where you have got to ask: What is this guy for, what's he in favor of? And the way he tells it is that he's in favor of liberty. And he was—a certain kind of liberty. He was in favor of literary liberty. But I don't think Mencken would have lifted a finger to defend the right of some colored man in Baltimore to get up and make a speech against the white society. To him, that would just have been funny. He was all hot for free speech and some professor at the University of Pennsylvania who lost his job for saying something or other. But a commie organizer out on the street arrested for making cracks at the flag—I don't think he would have been willing to go to bat for him at all. What I think he was for, what got a response from him at all times, was anything German. He was passionately a Germanophile."

As for Cain's personal feeling and friendship for Mencken, it was ambiguous. Cain started out approaching Mencken as a Babe Ruth who had autographed his ball, and, as he said, "the small boy is never really close friends with an idol like Ruth." Gradually, however, Cain outgrew Mencken, although he never lost his fascination for him and the respect for his genius, which, in itself, made friendship awkward. He was indebted to Mencken for encouraging him to write his *Mercury* sketches, which led to his first book and helped establish his reputation as a writer of dialogues. But he was leery of getting too close, aware of Mencken's habit of turning against his friends, as he ultimately did with Hamilton Owens, George Jean Nathan, and even Philip Goodman. Cain did not want to be included in that group. So, on those Sunday morning train trips to New York, he said, "I listened, enchanted as always with the brilliance of his talk, but when he would begin sliding toward a greater intimacy, perhaps with some anecdote about romance, of the kind that only close friends discuss with each other, I would become fascinated by the New Jersey road outside, and not quite hear what he said."

Cain felt Mencken preferred it that way, that he liked people to keep their distance. But "I often thought," said Cain, "his gay, rollicksome manner was partly a screen, we could even say a mask. Back of it was a moody, introspective nature that often felt very bitter, as his times, as one of his friends put it, 'began passing him by.' "

The times were, in fact, passing them all by. By the late 1920s America's phenomenal literary explosion was coming to an end, although few realized it then, any more than most of the financiers were aware that the economic bubble was about to burst. But at least one of Cain's friends was more sensitive to what was happening. In 1928, Sinclair Lewis, returning from Europe where he had just married Dorothy Thompson, was en route to his publisher's office when he stopped on Madison Avenue to exclaim to his new wife: "Within a year this country will have a terrible panic. I know. Can't you sense it? Can't you smell it? I can see people jumping out of windows on this very street."

Lewis's prophecy was soon borne out, and with the crash came an end to the whole gaudy, roaring life for which the 1920s have become legendary. The high-living literary stars, such as Fitzgerald and Lewis, were on their way to becoming embarrassing drunks, and as the nation failed to recover from the crash and depression slowly spread over the land, the bright witty remarks at the Algonquin began to sound a little hollow, like the music at the dances in those big southern plantations during the Civil War.

By the late 1920s, time and events were also beginning to have an impact on Cain's life. There is no evidence that he suffered especially from the stock market crash. He did not have extra money to lose in the market, and until he left New York at the end of 1931 his income remained the same— except that he was doing less writing for the *Mercury*. As the Depression set in, ikon-busting and the Mencken philosophy seemed dated. As Cain wrote one person studying the *Mercury* in later years, "it was utterly unable, once the times grew darker, to meet the new challenge, as howls of laughter don't cover much ground at the expense of the bread-line."

Mencken's jabs at Presidents Harding and Coolidge during runaway prosperity were hilarious. But his continual sniping at Roosevelt, with a nation in economic crisis, seemed more like a noncombatant criticizing the leaders in a war. "With Henry, music is the love of his life," said Cain, "and anyone that threatens it . . . is his enemy, and he will fight him to the hilt. Anything that does not threaten it, like a Depression, he is utterly indifferent to."

By 1928, Cain's drinking nights with the boys had gradually disappeared, as first Lewis married Dorothy Thompson, and then Elina returned to New York. Then Goodman went broke backing a play that, curiously enough, according to Cain, led Mencken to lose interest in Goodman, because one thing Mencken insisted on in his friends was success. It was also the beginning of the end of Cain's friendship with Goodman—but for a different reason.

The play was *Rainbow*, a musical written by Laurence Stallings and Oscar Hammerstein. Cain did not think the project made sense and told Goodman so in no uncertain terms: "I don't think an embittered Georgia intellectual [Stallings] could write a show for the Rialtos of the world; I don't think you [Goodman] have any affinity for the operetta. You're the king of Broadway comedy and you ought to stick at what you're good at. And you're telegraphing to these guys [Stallings and Hammerstein] that you want them to steal *Showboat*—and they're getting the message." Cain insisted that everything he said was true, but regretted laying it out for Goodman, who was deeply offended. The play was a complete failure, and on the day of the crash in 1929, Goodman took what little money he had left, said to his daughter, Ruth, "Let's get out of this," and together they boarded an inexpensive liner for Europe.

The following year, Mencken surprised the world by taking a wife, commenting: "Getting married, like getting hanged, is probably a great deal worse than it has been made out to be." The woman was Sara Haardt, whom Cain had dated a few times and whom he admired very much. When the marriage was announced, Cain approached Sara for a photograph to be used in the *World*, and warned her that inasmuch as she was getting the country's model husband, she should not try to break him of smoking cigars. Sara had large, bright, black eyes and an ivory pink complexion, and she "was something to look at," as Cain recalled. She also had a gift that might explain Mencken's breaking with some of his friends after he started courting her: "She could see through people," Cain said, believing that some of Mencken's roistering buddies did not survive her character analyses.

With H. L. Mencken's marriage, a way of life came to an end. In the summer of 1930, Cain went to Europe to meet Elina, who had been there since the winter of 1929, and the two of them returned to New York in the fall. By now, James M. Cain the writer had clearly emerged: He liked to shock his readers, but to write his best he had to pretend to be someone else. Yet with his limited imagination, almost everything he wrote had to be based on personal experience or things he had observed happening to others. He was essentially a journalist, but his newspaper career, like his New York literary life, seemed to be sputtering out.

END OF THE
WORLD—AND THE
TWENTY-SIXTH JESUS

By 1929, James M. Cain was writing stylistically perfect editorials, but they also seemed to have lost some of their originality; his creative energy apparently had shifted to his *Mercury* by-lined pieces. Nevertheless, he could write a brief essay on almost any subject under the sun, and the world, you might say, was his oyster—or lobster, or frog's leg, or huckleberry pie, or any food that would inspire letters to the editor. In 1929, he came out solidly in favor of the hot dog; and when a Massachusetts lobsterman caged a lobster measuring 34 inches from the tip of its claw to the end of its tail, he said that big lobsters were superior in every way to little lobsters—arousing a storm of letters. He also applauded and explained the need for the proposed bridge over the Chesapeake Bay several decades before its completion, and said that if radio did nothing else but rid the world of tenors (who sounded squeaky over the air) it had served its purpose. He continued to comment on new evidence in the Sacco-Vanzetti case; was intrigued by a new sport, the six-day bike race; applauded doctors' suggestion that we should all take winter vacations; was concerned about presidential handshakes (on one day, Hoover shook 1,757 hands; on another, 1,095). He was also worried about the country's not utilizing ex-Presidents and ex-presidential candidates; came out against another Yankee pennant; deplored

Floyd Gibbons's writing a story for *Liberty* about the Second World War, to be fought in 1933–36; supported the appointment of Robert Hutchins, at the age of thirty, to be president of the University of Chicago, pointing out that Alexander, Shakespeare, Washington, Beethoven, Jefferson, and Jackson all had important jobs or achievements by the time they were thirty; came out against roadside signs and for Mother's Day; cited a study that showed 65 percent more arithmetic is taught in schools than is required by "life situations"; wasn't sure that "Miss Universe" was the proper title for the winner of a beauty contest in Texas, but conceded, after seeing her picture, that the Republic of Mars would be hard put to beat her; and when it was reported that Yale had been forced to sink its goalposts in concrete, he said if the school wanted to win games it should be putting the concrete in the heads of its players.

The future author of *The Postman Always Rings Twice* and "Double Indemnity" was also skeptical that talking pictures would ever be any good and deplored the amount of crime in the talkies. "If you've seen one crime movie," he wrote, "you've seen them all, and you haven't seen very much at that." Responding to a *Nation* article criticizing the black and white morality in the movies, Cain explained why it was inevitable. "Nice subtle colors are the product of single minds and they will be found only in those arts produced by single minds. . . . [Movies] are a broth condemned to the talents of too many cooks, and we all know what such a broth tastes like." It was a belief Cain never lost; in fact, his years in Hollywood only confirmed it.

The most important single event in 1929, of course, was the stock market crash in October, which the *World* viewed with optimism. On October 31, W. O. Scroggs assured *World* readers that the stock market "is like a patient recovering from a painful but necessary operation. It may feel quite ill for a brief period, but the long augury carries a promise of better health." On the same day, Cain blasted Maryland's Senator Millard Tydings, a Democrat, for saying that the "stock market crash belongs to the party in power." Tydings arrived at this conclusion after noting that Republicans controlled both the presidency and the Congress. Cain said this was "nonsensical—no party has anything to do with prosperity."

And as economic conditions around the country grew worse, the situation at the *World* slowly deteriorated—a process Swope maintained he had seen coming and one of the reasons he had left in 1928. Long after Phil Goodman's effort to buy the *World* (with someone else's money) had failed, Goodman continued to argue that the paper was for sale. He based his case on an analysis of the paper as seen from an advertising man's point of view. The first problem, in Goodman's opinion, was "the man at the top"—and by early 1930, most newspapermen in New York would agree. On February 10,

Ralph Pulitzer, on his doctor's orders, had turned the paper over to his younger brother, Herbert Pulitzer, who simply was not cut out for the job. As *World* city editor James W. Barrett said, Herbert "lacked the ability to get down into the grime, the heat and toil of a great newspaper."

Another sign of the *World*'s weakness, according to Goodman, was the classified ads. "They pay well, but they cost more than they bring in because too many people buy the *World* for the want ads, just to get a tip on a job," which meant that a great many *World* readers were low-income or out-of-work people "and don't kid yourself that the advertisers in this town don't know it." Even worse, Goodman told Cain, the *World* was not read thoroughly by its more affluent readers. "You have one crowd buying it for Broun, another for Adams, another for Lippmann, another for Webster [the cartoonist], and all of them add up to quite a few thousand. But I don't believe there is a single subscriber who buys the *World* to begin on page 1 and read it through. . . . The *World* hasn't got the news."

Finally, said Goodman, nobody at the paper could describe the composite reader of the *World*, a very important figure to advertisers: "It's an agglomeration of twenty different newspapers, one or two of them good, most of them bad. And it's for sale. You wait, and you'll see."

Goodman was right, the *World* was for sale. The first discussions between the Pulitzers and Roy Howard, president of Scripps-Howard, took place in April 1930 and dragged on through the remainder of a horrible year for the *World*'s staff. Rumors were as persistent as if they were in combat, and no one knew from day to day whether the issue they were getting out would be their last. The paper had skipped its Christmas bonus in 1928 and again in 1929. Everyone was tense and edgy. Herbert cut a half inch off the width of the paper, which he said saved a million dollars a year. But it made the paper look skimpy, the columns narrow, the makeup constricted, and the ads queer. "Nothing the young master did," said Cain, "seemed to hit anyone right, and the narrowness of the paper, which sliced at our eyes every day, kept reminding us how we felt."

One time Cain went into Lippmann's office and, sniffing the odor of perfume, said: "Ah, the young master's been here."

"How'd you like to go to hell?" snapped Lippmann, usually the most courteous of men. Then, shaking his head: "I'm sorry, Jim—yes, the young master was in, and it was all I could do to keep myself from taking him by the back of the neck and the seat of those silly pants he wears, and throwing him out on his face. But I beg of you, don't joke about it."

Around this time Cain tried to persuade Lippmann to revamp the *World*'s editorial page, which he thought was archaic. He finally persuaded Lippmann to let him work up some dummy pages, and one day, with editorial writer John Heaton sitting in, he showed Lippmann what he would like to do. But Lippmann was not in the mood for cosmetics. "I knew by the look on Lippmann's face," said Cain, "he . . . was just going through the motions to humor me."

By March 1930, Cain was so concerned about his job that he permitted Goodman to investigate a column-writing assignment from either *The Nation* or the *New Republic*. But then he told Goodman to forget it. "I don't see what help anybody could be to me," he wrote Mencken, "until I figure out what I am going to do about it. I can probably make a living easily enough, and my problem, if I have one, is not so much to find a job as to find something that will be more interesting to me than writing newspaper editorials or adding them up and calling them a column. So far, I haven't found it."

And he did not have much time. By December 1930, the end of the *World* was near. The staff got roaringly drunk at the Christmas party, which, everyone agreed, would be their last. They were right. By mid-February 1931, the sale to Scripps-Howard was almost completed. Morale on the staff was reflected in a Sunday column by Cain, which was to be his last. It began: "This piece, I am afraid, is going to be like Mr. Charles Winninger's scene in 'Show Boat' when he told what the show would have been like if there had been one."

The spirit of most of the *World* staffers, Cain among them, was broken, but they still had enough left to make one last frantic effort to buy the paper themselves. Under the direction of city editor Barrett—and with Swope saying he had $20 million pledged, and Barrett certain the staff had raised nearly $1 million cash for the down payment—they held a mass meeting in the ballroom of the Waldorf and formed the Joseph Pulitzer Employment Association to buy the paper. Curiously enough, Cain cast the one dissenting vote. "Otherwise it would have looked too much like a steamroller," he later told Barrett. But he was with them and was impressed by their leader. "When Barrett stood up in front of the meeting at the Waldorf," he said, "and stuck out his jaw, it was the most inspiring sight I think I ever saw while I was on the *World*. I felt that what he was attempting could not be done, and yet he tried to do it."

But it was not enough. On February 27, the last issue of the *World* carried the headline: SCRIPPS-HOWARD BUYS WORLD AS COURT PERMITS SALE AND PULITZERS FULFILL CONTRACT. The price was $5 million. Howard planned to combine the paper with the *New York Telegram*, and those on the *World* who were chosen to be transferred to the new operation were quietly asked if they wanted to go. Cain was not one of them, and within two weeks he would be off the payroll. For the last editorial page, he made two contributions: one, a comment on Bertram Thomas's trek across southern Arabia, a part of the world generally unknown to Western man; the other, a lament that Franz Lehár was preparing to rewrite his music to bring it up to date.

After the sale of the *World*, many of the ex-staffers wrote obituary articles on the paper for various magazines, and Cain made his contribution to *The New Freeman*; the *New York Herald Tribune* said it was the "sharpest and most original" of all the articles about the end of the *World*. On the publishing side, Cain quoted Goodman and said he agreed with his assessment of the people who read the *World*; on the editorial side, he said the main problem was that the paper had been run by gentlemen—specifically, Ralph Pulitzer and Walter Lippmann. He expressed the highest respect for the two men, but said that their gentlemanly manners prevented them from running a good newspaper. Pulitzer's problem was that not only was he too much of a gentleman, but when the older hands at the *World* who had given the paper its reputation died or retired, he hired gentlemen to replace them. Lippmann he called a "poet of ideas" who was "always trying to get away from the plain headlines of polemic and find the grain of ultimate truth, the aspect of the discussion which might conceivably be valid ten years from now." Lippmann's willingness to shake hands after a fight, as if it were a tennis match, was a "public proclamation of the fact that it really didn't matter. But the sole excuse for a newspaper's activity is that it *does* matter." Cain said he esteemed a certain "churliness" in a newspaper but that Lippmann was too much of a gentleman to accept this. "You have to admire it, but at the same time you have to query his qualification for an editor."

Although Cain did not realize it at the time, his newspaper days were over. He did write a column for Hearst for a while in California, but he never felt it was real newspaper work. He always listed himself in *Who's Who* as "a newspaper man" and, in that he did not consider himself a good reporter, this meant he identified himself primarily as a *World* editorial writer. He liked being the "corporate awfulness" of a newspaper; and he liked writing editorials and was good at it. Years later, he said he regretted not returning to editorial writing instead of hanging on with the studios in Hollywood. Even then—in his seventies—he would have returned to an editorial page if anyone would have had him. Sadly, no one would.

Cain was not out of a job long. His good friend Morris Markey had left the *World* in 1925 to work on the fledgling *New Yorker* and seemed to be enjoying it, despite the fact that like almost everyone on the magazine he had trouble getting along with its eccentric editor, Harold Ross. Markey had been lured away from the *World* by Ross, who told him that what he wanted most on the magazine was "honesty" and "you can write exactly what you see, exactly the way you feel." This was a novel idea to Markey, who had been chafing at the restrictions of newspaper writing. He also said that "the only thing I had talent for was looking at a thing and trying to tell people exactly what I saw," and if that was what *The New Yorker* wanted, it seemed the place for him.

His first regular feature was titled "In the News," patterned after Ring Lardner's old column "In the Wake of the News" for the *Chicago Tribune*. Then Markey started writing an occasional piece on New York newspapers called "The Current Press" (which eventually grew into "The Wayward Press"). His "News" column soon evolved into "A Reporter at Large," and it was Markey who is given credit for pioneering the early text pieces of the magazine and creating what came to be known as "*The New Yorker* style."

By 1931, Markey was a mainstay of *The New Yorker* staff, and any recommendations he made to Ross were taken seriously. As usual, Ross was looking for someone to be the "hub" of his magazine. On most journals such a position is called managing editor, but at *The New Yorker* it was referred to as "genius," later corrupted to "Jesus," because it was generally agreed that the only thing that would satisfy Ross in the hub was a miracle man.

According to Ross's biographer, Dale Kramer, the first man to hold the job was Joseph March, a twenty-five-year-old nephew of Alden March, an editor at the *Times*. Young March had tried unsuccessfully to sell art to the magazine; his only publishing experience had been with the New York Telephone Company house organ. Another early "Jesus" was Ralph McAllister Ingersoll, a former *New York American* reporter who was related to Ward McAllister (originator of the idea of a New York Social Register of four hundred top families). The first staffer to be called "Jesus" was a young man named Oliver Claxton, a Philadelphia bond salesman who took the job on *The New Yorker* because he thought it would enhance his social status. Claxton was soon transferred to movie criticism, and the parade of "Jesuses" who had tried to translate Ross's incoherence into reality became legend. James Thurber once held the job, as did Wolcott Gibbs.

In early 1931, everyone on the magazine was painfully aware that the twenty-fifth "hub"—currently a charming young fellow named Ogden Nash—was not working. Markey knew that his friend Jim Cain was unemployed, and not only was he a good copy editor and a great literary stylist, he was an organized, no-nonsense guy who should be able to control the bedlam at 25 West 43rd Street. He persuaded Ross to interview Cain for Nash's job, and so one morning Cain was escorted into Ross's office by Markey. As he passed a door where Markey told him Ogden Nash would be sitting, he glanced in and there was a young man who looked away quickly "with a little smile of relief," Cain thought, "and a little pity, all of which told me a lot of what might be in store."

Ross, an old *Stars and Stripes* editor, had probably heard of Cain as the editor of *The Lorraine Cross*. Cain also had one book to his credit, a reputation as a contributor to the *Mercury*, and one recent contribution to *The New Yorker*—the poem "Auld Lang Syne," in which he recalled the pledge of his 1910 college classmates to hold a reunion in twenty years (see page 28). Cain had never met Ross, but he did remember meeting Raoul Fleischmann, *The New Yorker's* publisher, in 1926, at Arthur Krock's house. On that occasion Fleischmann had asked Cain what he thought of the new magazine. With what he called his usual tactless candor, Cain had replied: "Well, I read your ads in the *Times* and I feel I want to like the magazine. But when I buy it and snicker at its drawings, I then find nothing to stick to my ribs—it's fluff." Fleischmann smiled. Cain thought he had filed the remark away for whatever it might be worth.

There is no record of how Cain's interview with Ross went. However, Cain did recall being impressed with the fact that the man who was already a legend as the editor of a very sophisticated little magazine was so rawboned as to suggest "wide-open spaces, pack-mules, and rocks." His features were stubby, but attractive in a homely way. His bushy hair stood almost straight up (from the fear—said Ross, who came from Colorado—felt in a childhood stagecoach accident), and his grin was wide and gummy. Unlike Caruso, Ross made no attempt to hide the fact that his front teeth were at least a quarter of an inch apart. "And on top of the rawboned look," recalled Cain, "the somewhat homely face, and the grin, was his mode of speech, which was so Western, so twangy, so devoid of distinguished overtones, you found it almost impossible, at first, to connect the man with his accomplishments."

First meetings with Ross were often memorable. Charles Morton, who later went on to become an associate editor of the *Atlantic*, recalled a job interview with Ross a couple of years after Cain's—probably for the same job. Morton said that when he tried to tell about his qualifications, Ross yelled: "Goddamn it, let *me* talk," and persisted in telling Morton about all the troubles he had getting out the magazine and how many jobs he held when he was a young man. "If I stayed anywhere more than two weeks, I thought I was in a rut." The interview finally concluded with a job offer—"at $150 a week." But as Morton was retreating, Ross yelled: "Goddamn it, Morton, I don't want a hundred-and-fifty-dollar-a-week man, I want a three-hundred-dollar-a-week man." Morton, young and naïve as he was, considered this encouraging.

Cain's first meeting with Ross ended with a job offer to be the twenty-sixth "Jesus"—at $200 a week. Cain accepted the job and began "the most compromising, to self-respect, of any period of my life." He was never sure why he felt this way. He recognized Ross's brilliance and his ability to inspire talent, but said "he wasn't for me." The feeling was mutual. James Thurber reported in his *Years with Ross* that Cain was a puzzle to Ross. For one thing, Cain was a big man, one of only two big men, according to Thurber, ever hired as "Jesus" (the other was Ralph Ingersoll)—and "Ross was always a little wary of big men." Cain's nine months at *The New Yorker* were stormy ones. Nearly thirty years later, Thurber wrote that the "memory of him has not dwindled."

When Cain arrived at *The New Yorker*, its essential character and quality were well established, due, it was generally agreed, to the genius and talent of five editors—Ross, James Thurber, Katharine and E. B. White, and Wolcott Gibbs. Thurber and White wrote "Comment" and "Talk of the Town" as well as by-lined "casuals." They also performed a variety of chores, such as writing captions for cartoons and those little bright one-liners commenting on some absurd, pretentious, or asinine item culled from the world's press, or sent in by a contributor, and reprinted at the bottom of a page. Katharine White handled the literary talent and developed the short fiction, which was gradually becoming a required element in *The New Yorker* format. Wolcott Gibbs could handle almost any editorial assignment and was probably the best parodist the country ever produced.

In addition to the regulars, the magazine also had a galaxy of contributors that reads today like a *Who's Who* in American letters. During the nine months Cain was on the staff, *The New Yorker* carried pieces or poems by: Elmer Davis, S. J. Perelman, Dorothy Parker, Robert Benchley (who also wrote "The Wayward Press" under Guy Fawkes), John O'Hara, Frank Sullivan, Wyndham Lewis, Robert Nathan, Henry F. Pringle, Janet Flanner (who wrote from Paris under the name "Genet"), Joel Syre, Gilbert Seldes, Morley Callaghan, Ford Madox Ford, James Reid Parker, Alva Johnson, Price Day, Will Cuppy, Kay Boyle, Elmer Rice, and Sally Benson, one of Cain's favorites. "Of all the idiots who submitted little comical pieces while I was on *The New Yorker*," Cain once wrote Mencken's replacement on the *Mercury*, Charles Angoff, "she was the only one that attracted my attention."

Cain, himself, wrote very little for the magazine while he was there. His two contributions consisted of a short, amusing little piece called "Sealing Wax" (about trying to mail a registered letter and learning that the post office no longer provided the sealing wax) and a poem, "Gridiron Soliloquies."

It did not take Cain long to find out that Ross was going to be a peculiar boss. "As he passed by my desk," Cain said of the first day, "I looked up to say hello, but he went by without seeming to see me, apparently preoccupied with whatever was on his mind. However, almost at once, within a minute or two, he was there by my desk again, a grin on his face, to tell me something funny Benchley or somebody had said the night before—but with no 'good morning,' 'hello,' 'hi ya,' or anything of that kind. . . . When this entrance of his was repeated day after day, with his invariable reappearance, affable but always without any greeting, I began to realize that in this otherwise courteous man, so easy in conversation, there lurked something peculiar, a streak of self-consciousness, or shyness, or social kinkiness, that was anything but easy, and was in fact downright wacky."

Ross was quick to let Cain know what was expected of him. Over and over again, drawling like a Colorado hillbilly, he would tell Cain: "We gotta get this place awganized." At first, Cain did not know what he meant or what he, Cain, should do about it. But then he began to diagnose the problem, which first appeared in the form of his own secretary. He had inherited from Ogden Nash a girl he considered completely incompetent and soon found he was spending most of his day not only doing his work, but telling her how to do hers. She was making $22 a week, but when he called the employment agency he found that to hire a good secretary would cost at least $35 a week. It took a little adjusting in the budget before he hired a new girl named Eileen Collins. His secretarial problems were over. But when he told Ross, Cain realized his boss was not even listening; he was just sitting and staring, utterly stunned. "Did you say thirty-five dollars a week?" Ross asked.

"That's right," Cain answered, annoyed. Then he said: "Listen, I have to have a girl that's working for me, not a stumblebum that I work for and takes up more of my time than you do." Ross was still in a sulk when Cain left him.

By the end of his first month there, Cain concluded that what ailed his own operation ailed the whole magazine. "The main reason," he said, "the place seemed to be in a chronic state of paralysis was not anything big, but something so easily fixed I couldn't understand why it hadn't been fixed long before. It was incompetent secretaries, girls with poor gifts to start with, little training and less experience, whom *The New Yorker* had loaded up with by a policy of paying too little."

So when Ross hit him again with "We gotta get awganized," Cain suggested hiring competent girls. "If I'd told him I had leprosy I couldn't have got a more hostile reaction," said Cain. Ross, it appeared, regarded secretaries and all other nontalent employees as virtual thieves and begrudged them every dime they made. "Plugs, Cain, plugs," he said. "I can't get a writer except by watching everywhere and grabbing him off. But I can get a line around the block of these secretaries just by putting an ad in the paper. They're all plugs." (Ciphers, he meant.)

"Look," Cain said, "to me they're human beings and there's no such thing as a plug. But for the sake of argument, let's call them plugs. There's good plugs and there's bad plugs. By getting competent secretaries and paying them enough that they can do their work, you can save money because you won't need as many editors." This was, Cain said, because they had three highly paid editors sitting around waiting for one incompetent secretary to do her work. "If you'd hire one more secretary, two of those editors would save so much time that you could fire the other one and save a lot of money."

Ross fired one of the editors, but never did agree *The New Yorker* needed better secretaries.

Another thing that annoyed Cain was *The New Yorker*'s system of drawing accounts. He was opposed to it in general and insisted that if he was to do his job properly, he had to be informed about each advance to a writer or artist and the exact amount. But Ross was devious about this. He would put through an advance without telling Cain, and when Cain confronted him he would have some excuse like: "I didn't want to tell you till the money was actually paid," always adding: "I know your hostility to the whole idea of advances." Cain would explain that he was not against an advance, just the left-handed way the magazine had of getting them paid back—or not paid back, as the case might be. They also haggled over the rates paid to "Talk of the Town" and "Comment" writers—especially Thurber and White. Cain recalled that, at the time, White was getting 19 cents a word for his contributions and Thurber 17 cents. The difference upset him because he felt that after *Is Sex Necessary?* (written by Thurber and White) was published in 1929, they were equally well known. He also felt that if Thurber ever found out he was getting less than White, he might get angry and leave. But Ross insisted that in subtle little ways White was better, which finally Cain admitted, but in a peevish way: "Could it be," he asked Ross, "that White's superiority is due to having a wife on this magazine, in charge of fiction pieces, who wouldn't like it at all if Thurber were held to be equal to the man of her dreams?"

Ross made no answer, but it was obvious he didn't like the inference. Cain realized he was skating on thin ice, but he also was beginning to feel that he did not much care. He was slowly coming to accept the fact that *The New Yorker* was no place for him. Furthermore, his reputation as a writer of dialogue had now become a salable commodity in Hollywood, and his agent, Jim Geller, was tempting him with offers from the studios.

New Yorker alumni of the early 1930s remember Cain as a personable, likable staffer. "He got along well with everyone at *The New Yorker* except Ross," said B. A. Bergman, "but who did?" Bergman said he especially enjoyed talking with Cain, who "was a rare conversationalist."

From his side, Cain thought Alexander Woollcott was "cold, androgynous, fat, gabby, brilliant, but not really likable." On the other hand, he liked Dorothy Parker immensely, recalling that "she had the most beautiful manners, along with those luminous dark eyes. . . . Sure she could destroy you, but you had probably put her in pain first by boring her." And Cain was there when Ross came grinning out to his desk and told him about calling to ask Dorothy why she had not submitted a book review and she said: "Aw, Harold, I've been too fucking busy. Or vice versa, if you prefer."

E. B. White remembers Cain as "a compulsively neat man, an ashtray mustn't have any stale ashes in it." The Whites both felt friendly toward Cain—they continued a correspondence over the years—but there was no close relationship. "I remember his entertaining us one Thanksgiving Day at his apartment with a turkey dinner. . . . The turkey was bigger than the platter, and Jim delivered a monologue as he carved, while the slices of meat slipped quietly to the floor." White was always impressed by Cain's ability to ignore the disappearing meat—"an exercise in imperturbability."

Cain was a family man now, although with Elina being gone so much to Europe, he learned to live without her, and he was struck by the curious realization that "when you find you can live apart, you must live apart." On one of her trips, Elina had learned English, in his honor, so they were communicating much better. But Cain confessed that when Elina went back to Finland in 1931 to bring her two children to America, he resumed his friendship with his "little interim sweetie," as he called the girl he had had an affair with when Elina had gone to Europe in 1926 and 1927.

Then Elina came back, bringing her children—Leo, then a boy of fourteen, and Henrietta, a hauntingly beautiful subflapper of twelve. Cain took to them both, especially Henrietta, whom he played with as though she were some kind of live doll. They all went down to Baltimore to visit Cain's parents, and Henrietta especially charmed not only his father and mother but all three of his sisters. They also took Henrietta over to see the Menckens, who were equally enchanted with her.

Despite his distress at the office, this was a very happy period for Cain at home and leads to speculation that his life might have been changed if he had had children of his own. His attitude toward children was curious: although love, to Cain, was "a colossal experience, poetic, shaking, memorable," never once did he associate children with marriage and love. The reason Cain himself never had children is unclear. In his correspondence, he suggests the mumps he had as a child might have sterilized him. But a friend says that he told her he was made sterile by the typhoid fever he had in 1921. Leo, however, says his mother told him that Jamie had had a serious accident as a boy, which injured one of his testicles. It did not prevent him from having a normal relationship with a woman, but it did prevent his ever having children. There is, however, no hint of a boyhood accident in any of the thousands of Cain letters I have read.

The real reason for Cain's childless marriages will probably never be known. He thought the absence of children in his life and writings "may account for the effect I seem to have, particularly on critics, as standing for something unwholesome, impious, even in defiance of God." He did not know what he could do about it, and was quite frank in stating that "the idea of causing the creation of another human being utterly horrifies me."

On the other hand, the love and affection Cain showed for Leo and Henrietta, plus his treatment of the many children he had as neighbors, especially in his later years, demonstrated that he was not an ogre in his attitude toward kids. Leo also says that Cain was a very good father, although Leo was curious for years why Cain never legally adopted him and Henrietta—a matter that Cain eventually explained. When they were married, Cain told Elina: "It would be pleasant to make them my own children, and I certainly feel that way about them. But I suspect, as they get older, they'll want to be who they really are, especially considering their distinguished lineage, and any move on my part that robbed them of that lineage, that name, would be resented by them later on."

James Thurber said that some of the staffers at *The New Yorker* were baffled by Cain, who liked to work on the floor of his office when putting together the "Talk" department. They called him "Dizzy Jim," as opposed to Thurber, whom they called "Daffy Jim." Cain found Daffy "damned hard to like," but said Thurber "cared not a hoot whether you liked him or not." Thurber's manner of speech was also hard to endure. He had the habit of "always talking as though one side of his face had been shot with Novocain."

Thurber recalled that it was Cain whom Ross sent to try to persuade him not to buy a house in Sandy Hook, Connecticut, because Ross felt commuting discouraged literary production. Cain conceded that he talked to Thurber about buying a house and that he probably cleared it with Ross. But the idea, he insisted, was his. Thurber was borrowing money to buy the house from his drawing account, which Cain did not approve. "Having myself," Cain said, "directly and bitterly found out what it means to be due with a check on the first of each month for a dead horse [meaning, in this case, his alimony payment], I went to him in a somewhat avuncular frame of mind, as an older man to a younger, to plead with him not to get himself handcuffed to something that could be an old-man-and-the-sea around his neck. The interview was a bit gritty and in fact he didn't even sit down. He was standing up when I entered his cubicle, shuffling some papers, and we barely got started before I detected his hostility, not only to giving up his project, but even to hearing me out."

Cain asked Thurber: "How old are you?"

"Thirty-seven," Thurber replied, in his surly what's-it-to-you tone of voice.

Cain had expected twenty-eight, or some such answer, and thirty-seven surprised him. He was only two years older than Thurber, which "left me with all the wind taken out of my sails and feeling, to tell the truth, a bit like a fool." So Cain retreated, saying to Thurber: "This is none of my business, or Ross's either. I'm sorry I mentioned it. Live where you want and the way you want to."

Ross, as most people who have written about him concur, was deathly afraid of lawsuits. One question of libel came up during Cain's tour of duty on the magazine, and Cain was rather proud of the part he played in resolving it. It concerned a three-part Markey "Reporter at Large" piece about a Negro aviator named Colonel Hubert Julian, something of a legend among white pilots. Ross decided it was libelous and submitted it to the magazine's lawyer. He then asked Cain what they ought to do about it and Cain said he had not seen the piece yet. But when he took the galleys to his desk, he could hardly read them, they were so covered with queries and corrections. When he looked up from his desk he saw Rogers Whitaker, head of the proofreading department, standing at his side. "As well as we can make out," Whitaker said grimly, "there is a guy named Julian, who's colored and who flies. Beyond that we can't find one goddamn thing in any of these three installments that bears any relation to fact."

Cain told Ross that the first thing they had to do was talk with Markey and find out more about how he had done the article. Markey admitted, somewhat truculently, that he had written of the legend more than the man, but he also said, to Cain's astonishment, that he had not bothered to see Julian—it would not have been any use "as he doesn't see anyone, and I didn't want to get the magazine into the position of getting the back of his hand."

Cain looked Julian up in the phone book, called him, and asked him to drop in. Within the hour he was there, and after calling Markey, Cain arranged for the two of them to talk things over the next day. They did, and Markey made some changes in the piece. Whitaker's revised proofs had almost as many queries on them as the originals, but this time when Ross asked Cain what he should do, Cain said: "Run it."

"Why?" Ross replied.

"Because," Cain said, "a magazine comes to a point now and then where it has to prove it's a magazine and not a souvenir program. I've kept asking myself one basic question: Does this piece do Julian any substantial harm? The only answer can be, It does not. Now, he's an obscure colored flyer no one has heard of except the white flyers, who've made him the subject of stories. When these three pieces run he'll be an international celebrity—because, leave us face it, Markey has outdone himself on this man—simply as reading matter, the thing is a masterpiece."

Cain's arguments, especially the crack about not being a souvenir program, persuaded Ross, and he ordered the series run. The first installment came out, and that afternoon Eileen Collins came in to tell Cain that Colonel Julian was in the waiting room and wanted to see him. Cain went out expecting a smiling guest, ready to thank them for the fame they were giving him. Instead he found a grim visitor. After they shook hands, the colonel said that he did not like the kind of fame the magazine had given him. "Mr. Markey meant to ridicule me."

Cain protested that Markey meant no such thing, that he knew only admiration and felt "real affection for you." Julian heard Cain out, then repeated his original statement, and concluded by saying he had not yet decided what he would do, but he had talked to his lawyers on the basis of stopping publication of the other two installments.

Cain reported this to Ross, who asked: "What are you going to do?"

"Talk," Cain said.

He talked with Julian for the next two days, stressing the difficulty he would have in convincing a court that Markey intended to ridicule him. Cain was sincere in his argument because he knew Markey took real delight in what he had written and thought he was flattering Julian. But he was getting nowhere until it came to light, from the magazine lawyer's report, that Julian could not prevent publication without putting up a bond covering the total overall income from the issues involved—an amount which hardly anyone could afford to pay. Julian agreed, but he still had the option of suing for libel any time later.

The second installment came out and Julian continued to talk with Cain. Then one day the magazine received a communication in Julian's lawyer's envelope, which Cain fingered a long time before opening. When he did he found a letter from Julian in which he absolved the magazine of all malice, all intent to misrepresent him, everything he had been arguing with Cain about for a week. Cain took it in to Ross, who was very happy about the outcome. Then, that same afternoon, Eileen Collins whispered to Cain: "Colonel Julian is in the waiting room and wants to see you."

"Has he got a gun?" Cain asked.

"I didn't see any," she answered.

Cain went out and, playing it friendly, said he had received Julian's letter. He added: "And I'd like to say I think you did the right thing—even looking at it from your point of view. Lawsuits are tricky, and horribly expensive—and a court might feel, as I do, that you grossly misread Mr. Markey's intentions in writing that piece about you."

Julian heard Cain through and quietly began his speech, and what he had to say Cain never forgot.

"Mr. Cain," Julian said, "I hear what you say, but know in my heart Mr. Markey meant to ridicule me. However, when I came in here that first day, and you came out to shake hands, you didn't treat me as a black man and didn't treat me as a white man—you treated me as a *man*, and you're the first one, and the only one, in this country, who ever did." He alluded briefly to the fact that he was a West Indian, then went on: "Mr. Cain, I couldn't sue the magazine whose editor made me feel as you made me feel that day. It's what I came in to tell you."

"Well," Cain replied, "you quite overwhelm me, but not to sail under false colors, I must tell you I have no consciousness that I treated you at all differently from the way I'd treat anyone else."

"*It's what I'm talking about!*" Julian whispered, so passionately that Cain confessed he was shaken.

Cain was not only proud of what Julian said, but peeved at Ross for never bringing the subject up again or ever, in any way, acknowledging his role in getting Julian to accept the piece. The incident also strained his relations with Markey. As a result of the Julian story, and probably some others, Cain remarked to Thurber that "Markey would sacrifice a fact for phrase any time"—and Thurber repeated it for years. Markey denied it vehemently, but Thurber would always bring it up, especially when drunk, when also, according to Markey, he would launch into a passionate denial that he had stolen Markey's ideas. Markey thought this was an expression of Thurber's guilt because, as he wrote Cain: "He has stolen my ideas and knows it—but I never even hinted that I was aware of it. His famous Mitty story—pukkyty-pukkyty—was straight from my *Harper's* story called 'The Strange Noise of Dr. Beldoon.' "

Cain was also proud of the part he played in bringing a regular Ring Lardner column to *The New Yorker*. Ross had asked Cain whether he thought they could afford to pay Lardner $400 a week for a column, and Cain replied, "We're not able, but I'll make us able, by cutting down on something else, and I think we're warranted in doing it. I think Lardner is the kind of writer we ought to have, and that one of him is worth twenty of these who-are-they's that are doing our profiles and journalistic pieces. If it costs four hundred dollars, then O.K. We ought to be paying more than we do pay, and this is a good place to begin."

So Lardner's radio column—"Nowheres, California"—began in *The New Yorker*, and Cain said he never could shake off the idea that one reason Ross took it on was that Lardner was confined to his bed and Ross thought he needed the money. Lardner died two years later, leaving, Cain heard, $400,000, and he often wondered what Ross thought.

Ross was conducting a continuing war with Fleischmann and the publishing department, with the publisher at a distinct disadvantage. Fleischmann, Cain recalled, had a respect verging on reverence for anybody who had the slighest trace of the talent he wished he had. But Ross had only contempt, verging on nausea, for anything resembling a businessman. He thought businessmen were fakes and once said to Cain: "If the magazine is right, anybody can sell advertising in it; if it's not, nobody can."

Every now and then Lois Long, one of the "Avenue" writers, would mention in her column that she found it at Macy's and "all hell breaks loose," Cain recalled. "Russeks and Lord and Taylor and the Cuti-Pie Shoppey all call up, and the smell of ozone is in the corridors and the copy boy is running memos and then at last there is a CONFERENCE. It is attended by Ross, Fleischmann, Jesus, the Front Office Contingent, and perhaps a secretary or two, to get it all in writing. Fleischmann, affably, opens it and we're off to a pleasant start. Then the front office boys explain what has to be done in words of one syllable, so Ross can get it through a head not born for the intricacies and subtleties of business. To all this, Ross listens with obvious pain, but with some sick imitation of a smile pasted on his face. Then one of them pats the arms of his chair, with a that's-that air, as though we could all now go home. It has been sensible, friendly, and constructive, and Fleischmann, a born optimist, looks quite hopeful. Then nothing happens for perhaps five minutes. It becomes obvious that back of the pasted smile, the conscientious efforts at courtesy, Ross hasn't been listening at all. Then slowly, haltingly, he begins to talk. He announces, not in the I-want-to-speak-on-the-motion way the others have done, but in a flat, definitive tone, like a rector beginning 'I am the Resurrection and the Life.' Presently, he says: 'So this is the way we're going to do it.' He explains the way. He explains the reasons. They're solid, cogent reasons that take account of pesky business angles the businessmen don't appear to have thought of. It's wholly different from their way, but before he gets through all of them know it's the right way and the only way.

"As he talks he gesticulates with his hands. They droop off his wrists like dead things, all the fingers hanging separately, and seeming to have grown twice as long. He finishes, then gets up and goes out, with no farewell of any kind: too preoccupied. All sit looking at each other, then somebody looks at his watch. Fleischmann looks relieved, as though at last it's settled with less fuss than might have been expected, considering Ross."

For all the difficulty Cain had with Ross at the office, he remembered their few social meetings as very pleasant. "After hours, he was utterly delightful, congenial, likable and worth listening to." Once, Ross stopped by Cain's desk about closing time and invited him to have dinner with him at "21." When they arrived, Cain recalled, "it was as if the King of England had come," the way the staff as well as the customers treated Ross. Glasses were raised in his honor, people dropped by to talk—Ross would motion the waiter to bring another chair and the person would sit down and talk and the conversation was scintillating. Soon Robert Benchley, Alfred A. Knopf, Paul Palmer (a *Mercury* editor), and others were all gathered around. "They brought their little items, as a contribution they'd make, in return for the infectious grin, the appreciative reaction, the shrewd comment." Ross was not like Mencken, who talked a steady monologue, but was genial and friendly, carrying on a normal but witty conversation.

One incident that night he had dinner with Ross suggests the difference between Cain and the New York sophisticates and why he did not really belong in the Round Table life. Benchley had remembered a phrase Cain had used in the *Mercury* to describe a certain woman: "She would have been as safe as Mary Pickford at an Old Soldiers' Home." As his little contribution to the insiders' talk, Cain remarked that when he sent the article in to Mencken and Nathan, the phrase originally read "as safe as Lillian Gish in an Old Soldiers' Home."

"But at that time," said Cain, "I knew nothing at all of George Nathan's constant seeing of Lillian Gish." The phrase was changed, Cain said, because it was assumed that Nathan was sleeping with her. "Benchley jumped on this like a cat on a mouse. To him it was an exciting piece of news. It suddenly crossed my mind that it was more exciting to him than it should be. But he sort of regarded this as something to be memorized and passed on to Dorothy Parker. . . . Ross [also] took far more interest in it than I thought he had to."

This was the kind of gossip the Round Tablers thrived on, but to Cain it did not seem important. However, he did recall the dinner fondly and years later said that despite all the headaches Ross gave him, "the sparkle he lent that evening is what I remember now."

Cain's appraisal of Ross as an editor is somewhat ambivalent. For example, he told one former *New Yorker* hand that he thought that, beginning with Ingersoll, the "Jesuses" really ran the magazine and that Ross was just "a problem child in the office perpetually creating the chaos he wanted to cure." He also thought not enough credit was given to Fleischmann and Katharine White for their contributions to building *The New Yorker*. He felt that Ross did not discover talent, that he, in fact, discouraged talent and was responsible for losing more good writers than he kept. And he noted that when Ross died *The New Yorker* went right on running, as the *Saturday Evening Post* did not after George Horace Lorimer's death. In other words, *The New Yorker* succeeded in spite of Ross.

On the other hand, Cain said, "I have a prodigious admiration for Ross." He gave him credit for discovering a great many writers who went on to become famous, or at least giving them their first real show window. "He illustrated the principle that an editor must spark contributors. He was marvelous to talk to, and the effect he had on writers, artists, and such people was electrical. He had an original mind, with enough naïveté about it to go questing for fundamentals, sometimes the fundamental everyone takes for granted."

As for Ross's presumed wackiness, like not running a piece after he had paid for it, and his inability to articulate what was wrong with it, Cain said he had all the more respect for his decisions because of that. "Whether in magazine editing, playwriting, or whatever, the creative process in most of its stages is intuitive, with explanations thought up after the fact, not considered in advance of it. The article [Ross rejected], you would usually find, had its own adequate disqualifications, even if Ross would be somewhat inarticulate as to what they were. . . . I think most who knew him well would say there was a bit of a gap between what went on in his mind and what came out of his mouth."

Cain maintained that he had known two "great editors"—Mencken and Ross. "And they could be wrong so often it made you dizzy, but I never heard a dull word out of either of them." And, with all his complaints about Ross, Cain said he "never took a peeve home and nursed it . . . for his main qualities simply could not be laughed off, and they made up for the minor aspects that were in part an outgrowth of his virtues."

As for his own virtues as a *New Yorker* editor, Cain felt he had few. He found it impossible to think up ideas in July suitable for November. His mind was geared to a newspaper deadline, not magazine publication. He also could not get used to the idea that the magazine was conceived as entertainment rather than news. Cain continually came up with ideas that would have been good on a newspaper—and Ross would respond: "Cain, let's let the other magazines be important. We're just a little package of entertainment that sells for fifteen cents—we don't have our mind on big things."

Although he always felt Ross was disappointed in him because he did not turn into another Ingersoll with Park Avenue connections, he also felt

Ross thought he was doing his job—at least he kept piling more and more work on him, which Cain could not have handled except for "that marvelous girl," Eileen Collins. He had few memories of his work on *The New Yorker*, but he did learn that you could not write free-lance contributors congratulating them on their work, as he did for a while, much to Ross's amusement. "At the end of a week," he recalled, "I had the whole profession, to the number of 350 a day, out there in the waiting room on hand to 'meet me,' to 'thank me for my interest' and to 'see how this idea hits you.' "

He also remembered going out to Greenwich, Connecticut, every Sunday to put the magazine to bed. There, one time, he read a little bit of Dashiell Hammett, who was said by some to have influenced Cain, and which Cain denies vehemently. Lying around the printshop in Greenwich, Cain said, was *The Glass Key*. "I would pick this thing up and try to read it and, at the end of four or five Sundays, when I'd read only about twenty pages, I said forget this goddamn book. And that's my total knowledge of Hammett." And he remembered one article in which Benchley had mentioned seeing an obelisk on the Place de la Concorde from the window of a hotel. Rogers Whitaker checked it out and decided it was impossible. Forty years later, when a *New Yorker* review had three minor, but easily checkable mistakes in a derogatory review of one of Cain's books, he wondered whatever had happened to their passion for accuracy. He also used to be "appalled" at Katharine White's method of returning a profile with fifty-eight numbered objections. "This is a most discouraging way to deal with a writer," Cain thought.

Within a few months after becoming Ross's "Jesus," Cain "was about as miserable a human being as I have ever encountered," said his successor, B. A. Bergman. And Cain confessed that "I was so little qualified for my job on *The New Yorker*, and detested it so, my mind began to play me tricks. I would talk to someone in the waiting room, then next morning have no recollection whatever that any such meeting took place."

This amused his secretary at first, but then it began to worry her. Cain appeared to be "a nervous wreck," and he admitted to E. B. White that on "my last days on *The New Yorker* I was going somewhat mental," which made it even more irritating when Ross would do something like fire a boy Cain had promoted without telling him about it. But the incident that finally triggered Cain's break with Ross concerned John O'Hara, who was now writing regularly for the magazine. Ross promised O'Hara an advance of $1,000 without telling Cain about it, and this was the last straw. He said to Ross: "I'll be goddamned if I'll sign this thing since you didn't clear it with me." But when he went home that night, he was furious with himself and thought: "What in the hell are you making an issue of these things? Here is a man, O'Hara, who's personally cold but who is a very gifted writer. He ought to be in this magazine; you're making an issue of the thing! What in the hell are you doing this goddamn job for anyway?"

So the next day, early in November 1931, he had lunch with his agent, James Geller, and told him: "You've been making noises about sending me out to Hollywood. O.K. If you can get me an offer, I'll take it.

By three o'clock that afternoon Geller had the offer firm—$400 a week at Paramount. Cain accepted, and by five-thirty he was through at *The New Yorker*. As a parting gesture, he framed in leather one of Ross's memos—preserving the misspelling—that Ross had sent him with a rejected manuscript:

WHAT IS THE SIGNIGIFANCE OF IT ALL?

He presented it to his successor, B. A. Bergman, who still had it when he died in 1980.

Years after Cain's departure, on the occasion of Ross's death, Fleischmann wrote Cain that he remembered him as "probably the only 'Jesus' who was smart enough to know that he couldn't live forever in the unbelievable atmosphere of topsy-turvy-dom in which the magazine was functioning in those days and departed under his own will without any pressure from behind."

Cain's feeling about the magazine, at least immediately after leaving it, can be seen in a note of advice he wrote Sally Benson in 1934: "For God's sake, can those little *New Yorker* pieces and spread out. That magazine, excellent as it is, is dedicated to precociousness, which means it is got out by a lot of precious amateurs, who are not the less amateurs because they are very gifted."

After *The Postman Always Rings Twice* was published and Cain was a nationally celebrated author, Wolcott Gibbs wrote Cain asking him to consider writing something for the magazine. It is unlikely that any *New Yorker* editor ever received such an emphatic rejection: "On the whole, I would rather be dead," replied Cain. "You see, by the time I thought up a list of ideas and submitted them and found out the one I liked Ross didn't like, and then wrote one up and sent it on and then got it back again with 32 numbered objections from Mrs. White, and then rewrote it and sent it back, then considered the proposal to buy the facts from me for $50 and have Andy White rewrite it, and finally it came out as a 'Reporter' piece by Markey—I would probably be dead anyway."

PART THREE

HOLLYWOOD

1932 – 1948

10

MURDER ON THE
LOVE RACK

Leaving New York was a terrible wrench for Cain, but he knew it was time for a change professionally; in fact, he had the feeling that he was a failure as a writer in New York. "I'd been gradually coming to the conclusion that if I was to write anything of the kind I'd been dreaming about for so long it could not be based in New York. . . . Those killingly funny drivers of New York cabs, secretaries, bellhops, and clerks behind the counters were completely sterile soil. I drew nothing from them, and when I tried to, as in my Sunday column in the *World*, the results were so bad I hated to open the paper and see what I had written." But the dialogues he had done for the *Mercury* were different. He took pride in them. They were in the colloquial, "down home idiom of Anywhere, USA—Anywhere but New York." Writing, he knew, had to have its roots—"it can't wriggle down from the sky, as Alice did, in Wonderland"—and he felt, just maybe, he would find his in the West. His instincts were right, of course, and moving to California in 1931 would prove the wisest decision James M. Cain ever made.

The idea of the move was greeted with "near-delirium" in the Cain household. Elina, having lived in Finland most of her life, could hardly wait to experience the fabled Southern California climate, and the children were so ecstatic they jumped up and down when they heard the news. Leo, a rabid sports fan, was jubilant at the idea of being in Los Angeles, site of the 1932 Olympics. And Henrietta had no doubt she would be a motion picture star. "She was the one factor," Cain said years later, "that really gave me a pause. For while she was pretty enough to be a star, I had every doubt she could act . . . and it concerned me that her hopes should soar so high and perhaps in the end be dashed." But that was in the future. For now, everyone was caught up in the excitement of the moment.

It was decided that Cain would go ahead by train and the family would follow by boat, through the Panama Canal, once he was settled and the children had finished their semester in school. But before leaving for Hollywood, Cain wanted to check in with D. A. Doran, head of Paramount's New York office. His conversation with Doran was a strange one, not so much directed at what Paramount expected of him as at what Cain should do to "win" out there in Hollywood. "You don't have to take every assignment," Doran told Cain. "They won't expect you to, and in fact will respect you more for not accepting an assignment unless it really appeals to you. . . . Jim, I plead with you to get the studio history of whatever they offer you, whether you like it or not, before you make the commitment. Because if that script has been worked on by twenty writers already, there's something funny about it, some angle that can't be licked, and you'd be nuts to be tangling with it." It was good advice, to which Cain paid little attention.

Cain left for Hollywood on Armistice Day, 1931, and he had his first glimpse of the attention given anyone associated with the movie industry when the president of the Western Division of the Union Pacific, who boarded the train at Salt Lake City, dropped by his Paramount drawing room for a chat, just to make certain everything was "all right." Cain was impressed. He was met in Los Angeles by Fred Kolmar, then in the Hollywood office of the William Morris Agency and on his way to eventually becoming a movie producer. In a violent rainstorm they drove to the Knickerbocker Hotel, where Cain planned to stay until he could find an apartment. It was Sunday, and everything seemed frighteningly deserted. But then, when it stopped raining and he went for a walk on Hollywood Boulevard, he noticed other things: "I didn't see one dead dog, banana peel, coat hanger, old shoe, basket of rotten fruit, or any of the things that would have been commonplace in New York. I began noticing the wide, beautifully paved streets, the parking lots, many more than eastern cities would have, and the movie theaters." But when he came to a corner where he could see down some street, with an unobstructed view, he was struck by a sense of vast stretches reaching for miles, of structures of one kind and another and yet of an incredible monotony: "Eighty square miles of nothing whatever," as Veda would say in *Mildred Pierce.*

In the lobby of one of the movie houses was a big picture of Charlie Bickford, bashing an alligator over the head with a club. When Cain returned to the hotel he called the actor. Bickford wasn't in, but Mrs. Bickford was, and remembered Cain. They chatted a few moments, and then he asked if that was a real alligator Charlie was swinging at in the picture. "Well, he certainly was real," she answered, "and he wasn't supposed to be there at all. When he climbed out of that crate, Charlie didn't know what to do as they had three cameras on it and he hated to mess things up, so they had to start all over. So he banged at him with that club he had in his hand and he went away, but my how Charlie was scared."

It was his first real taste of Hollywood, where everyone lived, breathed, and talked pictures.

The next day Kolmar took him around to the Paramount "lot" on Marathon Street off Melrose: "An austere, dignified place on the outside," Cain recalled, "with a pink wall around it interrupted by various buildings, all in a vaguely Spanish style. On the inside grass, sound stages and sets, Greek temples, German Bierstuben, western storefronts, New Orleans street corners, all standing side by side, massively real in front and canvas-stretched tight behind." Cain was starting to work in the Hollywood that would soon become legend, although he would hardly suspect then that Paramount was heading into its golden years. When Cain arrived, it was the last year of B. P. Schulberg's reign, and the studio was on the verge of bankruptcy. Still in its future were the big pictures starring John Wayne, Bing Crosby, Bob Hope, Dorothy Lamour, and Barbara Stanwyck.

Cain was prepared not to like working at a studio, and nothing he saw on that first day changed his mind. Kolmar helped him find his cubicle at Paramount and said he would probably not be called to work on a script for a few days. When he was summoned he should report as directed, without Kolmar, but should keep him informed as to what they wanted him to do and what he told them. Strange way to run a writing operation, Cain thought.

But he did like the friendly atmosphere and the people. The girl at the switchboard called him "Jim," as did the two or three writers he met, none of whom seemed busy and all of whom said "welcome to Hollywood." He sat around his cubicle for a while, twiddling his thumbs, then decided to see if he could find Herman Mankiewicz, also working for Paramount. He had met Mankiewicz back in Asbury Park, New Jersey, when Phil Goodman was producing his play *The Wild Man from Borneo*. Cain had made a few suggestions on revising the play for Broadway, which Mankiewicz accepted, and they had become friends. He found Mankiewicz in his office, but he was busy and said he would meet Cain at the commissary for lunch.

The commissary also intrigued Cain. Everything on a studio lot, he noted, was designed for possible use in a picture, and the lunchroom was a replica of a Paris restaurant, even to the waitresses' uniforms. When Mankiewicz arrived, they picked up on their friendship immediately, with Mankiewicz giving Cain a brief account of his play, how it had done on Broadway, and thanking Cain for his contribution. They talked about old *New Yorker* friends and Harold Ross, and then Mankiewicz asked: "Do you ever see anything of old Massa Stallings?" (who had preceded Cain to Hollywood).

"Oh, yes," Cain answered. "He said you stole fifteen thousand dollars off him, but there's no hard feelings, and tell you hello anyhow."

"He said *what?*"

"I doubt if he meant it seriously," Cain replied, "but—it's what he said—you stole fifteen thousand dollars off him, but there's no hard feelings and tell you hello anyway." With a yelp that could have been heard in Pasadena, Mankiewicz bellowed: "I stole fifteen thousand dollars off him! Jim, the guy doesn't know the meaning of truth! *Fifteen thousand dollars!* He knows goddamn well it was only ten!"

From then on, Cain said, he had a genuine Hollywood story. One night, he told it to director Lewis Milestone (*All Quiet on the Western Front, The Front Page, Rain*) who said, "That's a funny story and I will now relate the circumstances under which Mank came to owe Stallings ten thousand dollars." Milestone went on to tell how a bunch of Hollywood writers and directors, including Milestone, Mankiewicz, and Stallings, were gathered on the lot when one of them repeated a remark made by producer Wilson Mizener at the Palmer House bar in Chicago after hearing that another producer named Ketchel had been shot. Mizener dropped his martini, and as he stared at the broken glass he said, "Count ten over the son of a bitch, he'll get up." Milestone then said: "Boys, this is a remark that deserves to ring around the world. It's a picture if I ever heard one." The boys thought so, too, and by the time they had coffee, Milestone said, "they had a story all lined up, even to the point of quarreling over the rights. Stallings, vain, literary, thinking only of fame, wanted the dramatic rights. Mank, practical and fond of money, wanted picture rights. So they split it up that way. Whereupon, Mank walked over to B. P. Schulberg's office and sold the picture rights for ten thousand bucks."

Later, Cain told his long version of the story to another director, Richard Wallace (*The Little Minister, The Young in Heart*), who said: "Milestone left out something—possibly he didn't know it. On that particular afternoon, Mank owed Schulberg ten thousand dollars from a poker hand the night before."

After a few more days of thumb twiddling (at $400 a week), Cain finally had a call from Percy Heath, the Paramount story editor. He had an assignment. To the end of his days, Cain wondered how Heath, after talking to him and reading some of his writings, could ever have decided to assign him to rewrite the script of Cecil B. De Mille's *The Ten Commandments*, first produced in 1923. Everyone said it was "one of the big hits of all time," and that's all you needed to know about it. "That it stank, that it was a glaring, monstrous piece of slimy, phony hokum," said Cain, "seemed to make no difference," and he wondered whether anyone in the studio was even capable of appraising it.

He finally realized that Heath had never read one line Cain had written. But this, he decided, was just part of Hollywood's lunatic approach to everything, especially scriptwriting. "At the time," Cain said in an indictment of Hollywood, based on his first days at Paramount, "the picture business regarded the script as an inescapable, but loathsome evil, and approached it accordingly. The director still was King, though if the actors were going to speak they had to know what to say. This King still regarded himself as the creative one, who would decide on what story to tell. So, as a preliminary nuisance, this overworked story editor would work with the writers on all scripts, believe it or not, and then when their work was done, turn their product over to the director. The system worked very badly because, in addition to driving the story editor very close to insanity, it resulted in all scripts being alike. But that didn't bother the executives, who still had an obsessive idea that 'action' was the essence and pith of pictures, the sound track, including the dialogue, being incidental. And indeed it was said so often it became cliché, 'we're talking 'em to death.' "

Taking Doran's advice at least to the extent of seeing what had been done earlier on the Cecil B. De Mille script, Cain found that no one had worked on the remake. He would be the first writer—he and Sam Mintz, another Paramount hand assigned to work on it with him. For days Cain and Mintz sat around talking about it, both aware they had no idea what they were doing.

Finally, in about a week, Heath's secretary called to set up a story conference, and Cain and Mintz trudged over to Heath's office. Sam was obviously distressed because he knew they had nothing to tell Heath. The secretary ushered them into Heath's inner office. "Well, boys, what have you got?" Heath asked, looking mainly at Mintz. After an uncomfortable moment, Sam answered: "Percy, I'm not ready to talk. I might just as well tell the truth, I'm not clear in my mind on this thing, and have to pass."

"Jim?" Heath said, looking hopefully at Cain.

"Well, Mr. Heath—"

"Percy."

"Well, Percy, I'm not really quite ready either, and perhaps should do like Sam, beg off till I have more. But we do have a little, and if you want to hear what it is—?"

Then, after the chorus of encouragement, Cain launched on a plan for the picture that had them, he recalled, hanging on the edge of their seats. He told them what was wrong with the De Mille script. He was so emphatic that at one point one of the producers present interrupted him and said, "Jim, do you really like this story?"

"Yeah," Cain replied. "I liked the book. But what you want to hear from me is what's wrong with it." He continued for a few moments, then, abruptly, shut up, apologizing and saying they really didn't have much yet on the actual script. They all agreed that what Cain had said was fine—and told him to keep up the good work. And as he and Mintz walked back to their offices, Sam exclaimed: "Boy, oh boy, oh boy, Jim: the way you told it, we're in. But I had no idea we were anywhere with the damned thing. My hat's off to you, pal."

"How did I tell it?" Cain asked.

"Well—how did you?"

"I don't know."

"What did you say, Jim?"

"I have no more idea than the man in the moon. I let my mouth take over and it did us proud, apparently. Anyway, we got away with it. But as to what I said, I have no more idea than you have."

"And where does that put us?"

"Nowheres, California, as Ring Lardner calls it."

Sam could see they were headed for disaster, so the following day he asked to be relieved of the assignment. The next month, Cain was also relieved. He had hurt himself seriously at the studio and he knew it. He also wondered why he had not followed Doran's advice to turn down any assignment that didn't really appeal to him. Trying to explain his stubbornness, he finally decided that the Doran suggestion had conflicted with his belief, reinforced by the old newspaper tradition, that the tougher the job, the harder you try. Much deeper, though, was his basic dislike of the movies. He knew "there was no such thing as a picture I'd like. Some might be worse than others, but there was no such thing as a good one. That being the case, why try to cut it too thin? Maybe *The Ten Commandments* was a pretty god awful assignment, but if no assignment was going to be any better, it might as well be that as any. . . ."

There was a humiliation and embarrassment to working in Hollywood then. In the 1930s, writers who went out to California to work in pictures were looked on with scorn and contempt, and the better the writer the greater the contempt. Authors such as William Faulkner, F. Scott Fitzgerald, John O'Hara, Aldous Huxley, and others who worked in Hollywood studios— "some time in the sun" as the phrase went—were accused of having "sold out." It was hack work to write for the studios, and Cain could not help but feel some of this scorn, although at the time he had no literary reputation, except among a few East Coast intellectuals.

Dropped from *The Ten Commandments*, he sat around his cubicle for weeks doing nothing—and no doubt thinking of one of Mankiewicz's stories, about a Metro executive named Maurice Revnes who had an office on the fourth floor of the writers' building—"The Iron Lung"—where he would have an unobstructed view in all directions. According to Mankiewicz: "His job, in the event he sees a glacier moving down Washington Boulevard, is to apprize Louis B. Mayer of the fact with all possible speed." After a while, Cain would come into the office, leave his name with the switchboard girl, then go out for a drive most of the day, returning at closing time to see if there had been any calls. After about three months of this, he was assigned to work on a script, *Hot Saturdays*, based on a novel by Harvey Ferguson, whom Cain knew and admired. But that did not go well, either, and after two months his contract expired and was not renewed. He had flopped in his first attempt at screenwriting—"hit the deck like a watermelon that has rolled off the stevedore's truck," he said.

Despite his apparent distaste for screenwriting, the failure hit him hard. The successful journalist who had "usually been the white-haired boy of editors," as he put it, "found there was one kind of writing I was no good at; I couldn't write pictures." And his situation looked bleak. It was 1932—the middle of the Depression—and he was broke, forty years old, out of a job, with his professional contacts and reputation 3,000 miles away. By now, Elina and the children had arrived in Hollywood, and they were all living in two apartments at the Montecito Hotel, a block from the Knickerbocker, at Franklin Avenue. It was costing Cain over $300 a month. In addition, his health was not good; his stomach problem, diagnosed as liver trouble, was getting worse, and Leo recalls that on their automobile trips around California, Cain would often have to stop the car, and go over to the side of the road and vomit.

He had no idea what to do. "It is obvious," he wrote Mencken, "that I have come to some sort of point, for one thing, the arrival at forty, for another the discovery that I am washed up in the newspaper business. I don't know why! Probably never liked it much anyhow. . . . I don't want to go back East; the thought of New York sickens me, and I have always disliked Baltimore. . . . It has taken me several months to get used to the idea that I now have time to do some decent writing; it may turn out that I haven't any in me, I don't know."

Elina settled the matter by saying flatly that they were staying in California. Having lived through the Russian Revolution, she could not see their present situation as all that bad. The children were doing well and going to a good school, and he should stay in California and start writing again.

So Cain became what all unemployed writers become: a free lance. Of course, they could not continue to live in the Montecito, so they drove around the Hollywood suburbs looking for a less expensive place and eventually found a small one-story white frame house in Burbank—then a pleasant little town of about 15,000 people. The house was on 616 East Tenth Street (now Bel Air Road) and cost $45 a month.

As soon as Cain settled down to conceiving articles, he became depressed. He could not adjust mentally to being in the West. He felt he was 3,000 miles away from his usual coordinates, ideas, and sources of information. But then he began to think. "Unconsciously," he said, "I had assumed that the East was the only good seat for the show that started in 1492, and the white man began his reduction of the continent. But actually, if the Atlantic was the starting line of the great trek, the Pacific was the goal, and just as valid a place to study it from as the other side of the country."

So he began to study the West, especially California, and decided he had been making false assumptions. "I had supposed the West to be a bit naïve, a bit recent, a bit wild, woolly, and absurd. When I examined these facts, however, I found them rather different. Actually, the country is the heir to a prodigious, rich, colorful civilization that sprang into being with the first gold strike on the American River in 1848 and, indeed, went back years before that, for the life that was led by the Spanish ranchers, to say nothing of the contribution of the Russians, was wholly charming."

Gradually, as he continued his research, he gained a respect for the West, which would soon work its way into magazine articles. But first, he wanted to try fiction again, having been encouraged by the response to his 1928 *Mercury* short story, "Pastorale."

Even in 1932, one of the principal forms of recreation in California was driving an automobile—through the canyons or out into the valleys or down to the beaches. Cain loved to drive and took hundreds of such excursions alone or with friends, or with Elina and the kids. And as he drove around in his 1932 Ford roadster with a rumble seat in the back, he began to feel more and more that California and its people provided him with a natural milieu for his writing. While still at Paramount, in fact, he had started thinking about a novel suggested by something that happened at a filling station at which he regularly stopped. "Always this bosomy-looking thing comes out—commonplace, but sexy, the kind you have ideas about. We always talked while she filled up my tank. One day I read in the paper where a woman who runs a filling station knocks off her husband. Can it be this bosomy thing? I go by and sure enough, the place is closed. I inquire. Yes, she's the one—this appetizing but utterly commonplace woman."

What about a novel in which a woman and a typical California automobile tramp kill the woman's husband to get the gas station and the car? He and Elina talked about this for months, but Cain was not quite ready to write a long story. He still only felt comfortable writing fiction in the first-person style of Ring Lardner, in the speech of a rural roughneck of the Eastern Shore. And he had learned from his first attempt at writing a novel ten years earlier that too many "ain'ts, brungs, and fittens" would drive the reader crazy. They were all right in short stories, but not novels. So he put the idea in the back of his mind and decided maybe the best thing would be another short story.

One place Cain and Elina liked to visit on their automobile tours was the Goebels Lion Farm, on the road to Ventura. He always enjoyed smoking a cigarette with the chief attendant, with whom he eventually became good friends. And it was at the Lion Farm that Cain got the idea for his first California story. It would be about a couple who run a gas station and lunch house on the road to Ventura. But the husband, Duke, decides to add some cats—first mountain lions, then a tiger—to interest children and draw more customers. Eventually, his wife, Lura, becomes pregnant, and Duke is convinced the father is a phony traveling doctor, known as Wild Bill Smith, the "Texas Tornado." The baby is born, the Texas Tornado disappears, but Duke is still convinced he has been double-crossed and the baby is not his. So he arranges to let a 500-pound tiger loose in the house when Lura and the baby are there. What he does not know is that Lura can handle the cat. While keeping the animal at bay, she wraps the baby in a blanket, puts him in a disconnected refrigerator, and leaves the tiger in the house. Duke shoots Lura on her way out, wounding her, and having forgotten about the tiger goes into the house to call the police, leaving his gun in Lura's hand to make it look like suicide. The tiger turns on Duke and kills him, and is in turn killed when the house catches on fire. The baby survives in the refrigerator, and Lura eventually recovers and goes off with the Texas Tornado.

Cain called the story "The Baby in the Icebox" and sold it for $250 to Mencken, who thought it one of the best things Cain had ever done. It appeared in the January 1933 *Mercury* and caused much excitement. The story was reprinted many times over the years, in Europe as well as America, but more important, it played an immediately significant role in advancing

Cain's strange Hollywood career. The Morris Agency sold it for $1,000 to Paramount, which then declined to rehire Cain to do the script, turning instead to screenwriters Casey Robinson and Frank Adams. The movie was to be called *She Made Her Bed* and would star Richard Arlen, Sally Ellers, and Robert Armstrong. Paramount had wanted to cast Baby LeRoy as Lura's son, but by the time they were ready to film he had outgrown the part. Instead, they hired Richard Arlen, Jr.

After "The Baby in the Icebox," Cain had an idea for a short piece dealing with the government's decision to go after Al Capone for income tax evasion, rather than bootlegging beer. California was already releasing men who had been sent to jail for violating the prohibition laws, and Cain's point was that if the government tried Capone for bootlegging, he would all too soon be out of prison—whereas trying him for tax evasion would put him in jail until the unlikely day they eliminated the income tax. He put his story in the form of a dialogue between two Babbitts and a Justice Department lawyer on the 20th Century Limited as it approached Chicago. He eventually sold it to *Vanity Fair.*

Next came a long article about California. He called it "Paradise" and sent it off to Mencken, who thought it was "the first really good article on California that has ever been done" and printed it in the March 1933 *Mercury.* It is probably one of the best descriptions of California in the 1930s ever written, as well as being—in my opinion, and, incidentally, Cain's too—the best article he ever wrote. And it had other admirers: Ralph Thompson, who by 1937 would be writing "Books of the Times" for the *New York Times*, recalled running across "Paradise" in a university library and thinking it was "a positively vicious masterpiece. Who was this James M. Cain?"

"Paradise" is not so much vicious as ruthlessly honest in its evaluation of the pros and cons of living in California. Cain concluded that although its present might be depressing, it had a promising future—primarily because the place had been populated by a selective process that had occurred in no other state. Most sections of the country, Cain felt, had been populated by "failures." Although they had subsequently been romanticized as "pioneers," most of them had pulled up stakes because they were not doing very well where they were. But the California migration brought people who were attracted by the climate and the geography after they had achieved a certain measure of success at home. What impressed Cain was that almost everyone in California felt "some sort of destiny awaits this place," and it was going to be fascinating to see what would happen. As for himself, "I stay, the climate suits me fine." James M. Cain had apparently found a home—and the perfect setting for his lean, matter-of-fact prose.

Cain's decision was also influenced by the fact that he was gradually getting to know some people and was even beginning to like the Hollywood social life. His closest friend in that set was Vince Lawrence, the playwright Phil Goodman had called in to help salvage *Crashing the Gates*. As for Goodman himself, something had happened to their friendship that neither Goodman's daughter, Ruth, nor Cain's stepson, Leo, fully understand to this day. The break came around the time Goodman was, in Cain's description, "a broken, beaten, thoroughly demoralized guy"—because of the failure of his play *The Rainbow* and the effects of the Depression. Vince Lawrence, on his way to becoming an established screenwriter, invited Goodman to Hollywood, hoping to find him a job with one of the studios. Goodman came, but no job materialized, although Benn Levy, another successful playwright and friend of Lawrence, also tried to help. Ruth thought that during this discouraging period in her father's life, it was likely that he "turned Jim off with a kind of self-destructive pride," rather than that Cain did anything to her father. Cain thought his negative attitude about *Rainbow* was at the core of the break, though allowed that during this period of despair Goodman "took it out on feuds that made no sense, against everybody." Whatever it was, Leo recalls that when he and his mother ran into Goodman on Hollywood Boulevard shortly after they arrived, the talk was "very guarded about Jamie. And after that Jamie and mother just said that some dirty tricks were played and Jamie would never see Phil Goodman again." But Cain did not lose his great affection for his old friend, and Ruth recalls that when she saw Cain in Hollywood in the 1940s, he showed her her father's photograph, which he still carried in his wallet.

The Cains did continue to see Lawrence in Hollywood, and although Cain found Lawrence's boozing "very hard to take," he revered his story sense and knowledge of playwriting and screenwriting. Through Lawrence, Cain began to meet a few Hollywood writers and actors, and found that he liked being around the movie lots, watching the stars and meeting them occasionally in the evenings. However, the Cains were never Hollywood partygoers, as might be assumed from Cain's classic description of a typical Malibu bash in the early thirties. On arrival, you had a brace of cocktails, then surveyed the scene. And this is what you were likely to see: "Three extra girls in evening dress, grateful for having been invited; four actresses in blue pajamas; one actress in a bathing suit; one actress in ceremonial Chinese robe, weighing ten pounds: cost, $2,300; one man from New York in dinner coat; four men in sweaters and knickers; four supervisors in middle of floor, shooting dice. This is the party, except for the host and hostess who have not arrived, having forgotten about it. There is no dancing, no necking, and no light infectious gaiety, with merry madcaps deciding to jump in the ocean at 1 A.M." There would be nothing but dice, drinks, and conversation, which, according to Cain, went like this: "Well, he's got a hit." "And who wouldn't? They buy him *Dinner at Eight*, paid a hundred and ten thousand dollars for it. Louis B. Mayer told me so himself and showed me the check, paid a hundred and ten grand for it. Then they give him Dressler, Beery, Harlow, Tracy, Evans, Hersholt, Morley, Tone, Cukor, and both Barrymores." "And Robson [Dame Flora]." "She was going to be in it but they yanked her. He told me so himself and Christ he ought to know oughtn't he?" "Robson's in it." "That's right, they got to sell it to Siam, Iceland, and the Sailor's Snug Harbor to work off that nut." "That picture was sunk before it started." "All right maybe it don't make money but it makes him don't it?"

Cain and Elina preferred small spontaneous private parties, where he and Lawrence and other writers could talk about stories and technique. Through these affairs, he gradually met a few movie people—Harold Lloyd, for example, when Lawrence persuaded him to invite Cain and another screenwriter, Samson Raphaelson, over for a screening of *Movie Crazy*, which starred Lloyd and for which Lawrence had written the script. Cain particularly liked Raphaelson (whom he had envied from afar at Lee Chumley's in the Village, when Raphaelson's play *Young Love* was running on Broadway) and his wife, "Dorshka," the former Dorothy Wegman, a Ziegfeld Follies girl.

And it was at Raphaelson's that Cain first met Charles Laughton, with whom he had a brief and rather strange friendship. Laughton took no notice of Cain on their first meeting, but a little later, when Laughton's *The Sign of the Cross* was released, Cain went to see it. Laughton played Nero—"a thoroughly effeminate Nero, with curled hair, a leer, and all the other trimmings." But something bothered Cain about the portrait, although he conceded it was damning and unforgettable. He saw it again, then read the script, and he knew what it was. The next time he met Laughton at the Raphaelsons', he went up to him and said: "I checked on that picture of yours, that portrait you gave of Nero as a practicing homo, and there's nothing in the script that accounts for the way you played that part. You never heard of me, but I'm a writer, specializing in dialogue, and I know what I'm talking about. Nero, in the script, was a straight Cecil B. De Mille heavy, who corresponds to Gibbon's account in *The Decline and Fall*. Where did that fag come from?"

Laughton's face lit up, and immediately, Cain felt, they were friends. Laughton was delighted that someone had finally detected that this Nero was his own invention. He told Cain he was in utter horror when he first read De Mille's script and began groping for something he might do to make Nero interesting. He said the opening shot, having his toes pedicured, was his idea, and that "Freddie March warned: 'You'll never get away with it, you'll see.' " But he said that when he looked up, as the scene was being shot, De Mille was there staring at the scene, then turned away without saying anything. "That's the reward I got for doing, if I say so myself, a pretty good job." Laughton said he appreciated the fact that Cain had noticed his contribution, even if it did conflict with Gibbon's portrait of Nero. The Cains soon were good friends of the Laughtons and had them to their house for dinner. Elsa Lanchester they especially liked, finding her a very amusing lady.

Cain's burgeoning attraction to California was also influenced by the fact that all the clamor over his California short story, "The Baby in the Icebox," had given his sputtering literary career something of a charge. In the first place, Alfred A. Knopf, who still had an option on his next two books, wrote him in November 1932, saying Mencken had let him look at the story before it went to press and that he thought "it is a whopper—one of the best I have read—and it encourages me to believe that one of these days you may try your hand at a novel."

Cain wrote back that he had started a novel about a month before, but his fixation that he could not write a novel was so great he did not have the heart to go on. "Your note may turn out to be the push I needed." Then he outlined his story, and it is apparent he had given a lot of thought to the girl in the gas station. He called it more of a novelette: "A simple story, laid in California, about a youth who commits the perfect murder with a girl, then has fortune kiss him on the brow, then gets so bored with her as she murders her former husband every night for the kick it injects into their carnal relations, that he is sunk. That is, he finds that the bond which put such a tingle in their doings in the beginning can also be a chain that he doesn't dare break. An accident saves him the trouble but he is hung for this one anyway. Sounds dull, I suppose, but I might pull it off."

Knopf showed Cain's letter to Mencken, who wrote Knopf he thought the idea "somewhat meshugga [Yiddish for 'crazy']," adding "Cain, in fact, not infrequently wanders across the boundary line of sense. However, it is conceivable that he may make a good novel of the idea. Certainly it is worth while to be polite to him." The day he received Mencken's note, Knopf wrote Cain a letter of encouragement and said he was anxious to see the novel.

Despite Knopf's interest, Cain was getting nowhere with the novel, in part because he began it in the third person, still feeling that the rube language in which he had written "Pastorale" would pall after fifty pages of a novel in the first person. He was also deterred by the fact that the Morris Agency, on the strength of the talk about "The Baby in the Icebox" having finally reached Hollywood, suddenly had Cain a new studio job—this one for $200 a week with Columbia Studios. Cain jumped at the offer, hoping still "to get a toehold in pictures."

In 1933, Columbia was just emerging from "Poverty Row" (a group of B-picture studios down on Grover Street) and was ready to challenge the Big Five: MGM, Fox, RKO, Warner, and Paramount. Columbia was under the direction of the legendary Harry Cohn, who apparently did not intimidate Cain, as he did others, "He has another side," Cain said, "that I saw a number of times when I'd be with Elina, whom he treated not only with courtesy, but courtly consideration, seeming to like her—or possibly sensing that a Finn was not one to monkey with. He could be the most elegant, gracious guy you could imagine. He could also be a rotten, dirty s.o.b. and he often was. But he seemed to be putting on an act."

Maurice Zolotow, in his biography *Billy Wilder*, said that it was Cain— "a stocky gentleman with hornrimmed glasses, who talked out of the side of his mouth like a stevedore and knew more about grand opera than any Viennese"—who told a new writer, Billy Wilder, that he could take it easy until 11:45 A.M., because Cohn never got to his office until noon. But once Cohn arrived at his office around ten, the story goes, and as he walked through the courtyard to his office, he noted that he did not hear the rat-a-tat of a single typewriter. So he started screaming: "What the hell is going on around here? I pay you fuckin' writers a fortune to write and nobody is writing." Soon, the sound of typewriters came from every window—and Cohn waved his fists at them, yelling: "Liars! Liars! Liars!"

Cain did not do any better at Columbia than he had at Paramount. He and screenwriter James Kelvin McGuinness (whom he had known at *The New Yorker*) were supposed to write a film about Samuel Insull. McGuinness and Cain tried to work out a story idea, but nothing came of it, except that they developed a close friendship based (as with so many of Cain's friendships) on a mutual interest in writing and stories. In one of their luncheon conversations, McGuinness made a remark that would keep buzzing around in the back of Cain's mind for years: "Of course, Jim, there's one story line that's never failed yet, and that's the story of a woman who uses a man to gain her ends."

Cain was soon let go by Columbia, but despite his failure he had managed to impress Cohn personally. Baffled by Cain and wanting to know what made him tick, Cohn asked one of his writers, Robert Riskin, to have a talk with him. Riskin had written a lot of the Frank Capra hits and was just finishing *It Happened One Night*.

After Riskin explained to Cain why he had wanted to talk with him and put him through a couple of hours of grilling about his approach to writing, he finally said: "I don't think I ever met anyone with quite the slant that you have on a story, and on story-writing in general. You seem to regard any story as a sort of algebraic equation, to be transformed and worked out until it yields the inevitable story that lurks in the idea somewhere in the theme, or whatever we're minded to call it. But it's not like that at all. A story has to be *your* story even if you're working for a picture company. There's no ultimate, inevitable, perfect 'move' that's going to give you an outline, determine your situation. It's not mathematics. It's a living thing. It's *you*."

Cain laughed. He knew Riskin was right in his diagnosis of his approach to storytelling, although he did not think it was necessarily a fault. In fact, the approach might well be one of his strong points, he thought. But the talk had an impact on him; he knew he had been told things worth thinking about—especially that you had to tell *your* story.

So, finding himself again out of a job, Cain made the decision to tell *his* story. This was in February 1933. First he would drive down to Agua Caliente for a few days. But the bank holiday closed the town down, so he returned to Burbank and with continual prompting from Elina sat down at the typewriter. By now he had made a critical determination about his fiction: instead of lapsing into the rural language of the eastern roughneck, which he preferred when writing in the first person, he would try, as he had in "The Baby in the Icebox," to use the language of the western roughneck, "the boy who is just as elemental inside as his eastern colleague, but who has been to high school, completes his sentences, and uses reasonably good grammar." Cain's ear "had put this on wax"; he thought he had it. He could now tell a longer story in the first person.

Equally important in the evolution of Cain's first novel was the role played by screenwriter Vincent Lawrence. Lawrence was probably the prototype of the Hollywood writer of the 1930s, the kind of guy who called everybody "pal" and "laddie" and "lassie." He would go into a bar, says Raphaelson, "and there would be a couple and he would look at them fondly and say: 'You've got the moon, ain't you pal?' When you'd offer him a drink, he'd say: 'Tell me this, pal, why isn't everybody sitting on a fence in the moonlight playing a banjo? That's all I want to know.' That was as close as he got to philosophy. He had a very special gift, writing that kind of romantic urge in masculine dialogue. If you wanted Gable to be in love and not sound like a fool, Vinnie would write the words . . . that was his function in Hollywood." Lawrence was tall and slim with curly brown hair, and Leo remembers him as "the most charming man I ever met." He was also something of a legend in Hollywood, having laid down certain principles of story development that had become law in many of the studios. He wore $45 suits, although he was making enough money to have "learned the difficult art," as Cain said, "of giving $20 tips without being sent to psychopathic." Cain would spend an evening with him at his apartment at the Château Elysée on Franklin Street, or Lawrence would drive over to Burbank in his big Packard convertible with its separate windshield for the back seat. And they would talk story construction for hours.

Lawrence's effect on a writer he liked "was a magical thing," said Raphaelson. "It was like when John Barrymore was drunk and liked you. They resembled each other in that sense. There was such a great, fantastic appreciation of you that would emanate from Vinnie. You were the greatest guy in the world. You felt it. I felt it." And Cain felt it too.

Cain always thought the most important element in a story was that it correspond to life and give a picture that revealed the *truth*. Lawrence said that was O.K., but the truth was not all, otherwise you would be competing with a $3 camera and you might as well write a case history. He pointed out that Dreiser's play *The Hand of the Potter* was truthful enough, but utterly pointless because it made a plea for a degenerate without ever getting you interested in that degenerate. Writing any kind of narrative, Lawrence argued, you had to make the reader or audience *care* about the people, which inevitably led into a love story. Then Lawrence would expand his principle of "the love rack," which Cain never completely understood, except that it was the poetic moment in any story when the lovers fell in love. "Before Lawrence got to Hollywood," Cain said, "they had what was called the mixmaster system. You know, the hero would look at the heroine through the forest window, looking over the lilies, and then they'd go down to the amusement park together and go through the tunnel of love, and all the rest of it. And at the end of the montage they're supposed to be in love. Lawrence just wouldn't have this. He said this love rack had to be honest, it had to be real poetry."

Raphaelson had a slightly different concept of Lawrence's "rack." It was "where the lover hangs his hat." Who and what is he? What, besides the fact that he is in love, makes me want to give a damn about him? Lawrence would say: "Who's your losing lover, pal?" One of the lovers had to be a losing lover.

So Cain and Lawrence would talk story construction into the night, with Cain all the time thinking about that girl at the gas station who had apparently killed her husband. And then, one time when Lawrence was talking about his love rack, Cain asked: "Why couldn't *the whole thing* be a love rack; why such attention to the one episode where they fall in love?" Cain asked why every episode in the story could not be written with a view of its effect on the love story? Lawrence thought this had possibilities, and then, in a later conversation, he provided the catalyst Cain needed.

They were talking about the Ruth Snyder–Judd Gray murder case, which had dominated the newspapers in 1927. Albert Snyder was a mild little Long Islander and art editor of *Motor Boating* magazine. His wife Ruth and her lover, Judd Gray, a corset salesman, conspired to murder Snyder, then turned on each other after the murder. Lawrence said, "I heard that when Ruth Snyder packed Gray off to Syracuse where he was to stay the night she murdered her husband, she gave him a bottle of wine, which he desperately wanted on the train. But he had no corkscrew with him and dared not ask the porter for one, for fear it would be the one thing they'd remember him by. When the police lab analyzed it, they found enough arsenic to kill a regiment of men. Did you ever hear that, Cain?"

Cain had not, but then said to Lawrence: "That jells the idea I've had for just such a story; a couple of jerks who discover that a murder, though dreadful enough morally, can be a love story too, but then wake up to discover that once they've pulled the thing off, no two people can share this terrible secret and live on the same earth. They turn against each other, as Judd and Ruth did."

Lawrence was a little startled at the idea, but thought it might work. So Cain started the novel with an opening sentence that would eventually be quoted repeatedly in university writing courses: "They threw me off the hay truck about noon."

The young California drifter thrown off the truck is named Frank Chambers. He soon arrives at the tavern out in the Thousand Oaks section of the San Fernando Valley—a gas station and lunchroom run by a middle-aged Greek, Nick Papadakis, and his wife, Cora. Frank, after seeing Cora, agrees to work for Nick, and he and Cora quickly develop a passion for each other. Then they begin plotting to kill Nick, which will give Cora the gas station and lunchroom. They manage to murder him after one unsuccessful attempt, and then stage an automobile wreck to make it look like an accident. And they get away with it. But the murder eventually becomes their love rack, as they are brought to justice when Cora is killed in an automobile accident and Frank is wrongly found guilty of her murder. The story is told in the first person by Frank, as presented to a Catholic priest while Frank awaits the electric chair.

Despite the fact that everything had fallen into place now, Cain still had trouble writing the novel. In the first version, he had Cora go through a lengthy trial, all the while in jail, before finally getting off by telling a desperate lie. But the love story stood still, and Lawrence, after reading the draft, said, "Get her out of there, Cain. I don't care how you get her out—but your story doesn't move until she's free and they start up their lives again."

Cain struggled with this until he invented a crafty lawyer who comes up with a ploy that catches the prosecutor in a squeeze between three insurance companies, two of which stand to lose more if Cora is found guilty. They finally agree to chip in and pay off the company that will lose the lesser amount ($10,000) if she is found innocent. Of course Cain, the inveterate reporter and researcher, had to make certain this was plausible, so he outlined his scheme to a Mr. Harrington of the AAA insurance division, who said: "Hell, it not only can happen, it has happened to me. And believe me, there's many a district attorney that's been left holding the bag just the way the guy did." Later he sent Cain a marked copy of the Motor Vehicle Act, with some information "that'll make it better." When Lawrence read the revised section, which cut 80,000 words from the novel, he was satisfied: "Christ, we didn't only get away with it, we got ten thousand dollars for doing it!"

Another device Cain developed for moving his story was even more fundamental. Not only did it play a significant part in establishing Cain's reputation as a stylist, it ultimately would have a considerable impact on American literature. When telling his story in the first person, Cain found that in writing dialogue for his automobile tramp he could only lead into a quote or close it with "I said," or "he says," without stylistic or literary embellishment. This was almost as monotonous as the "fittens" and "brungs." "Why all this saying?" he finally asked himself. He could think of no real answer, and decided it would not only read a lot better but speed up the story if he just eliminated the identification, writing long patches of dialogue without indicating who said what, leaving the reader to figure it out from the content of the conversation.

"While this may seem abrupt for a few pages until you get used to it," he was to write his publisher, "it does get around the monotony that commonly goes with the naïve narrator." And when the book came out, no reviewer jumped on him for it; in fact, many applauded it as an innovation in literary technique. So Cain decided he had hit on something, and eventually, in one of his later prefaces, he would plead with his fellow writers to follow his lead. "If Jake is to warn Harold, 'an ominous glint appearing in his eyes,' it would be a great deal smoother and more entertaining to the reader, though I grant you nothing like so easy, to slip a little, not too much, of course, but just the right subtle amount of ominous glint in the speech."

Cain worked on his story steadily for nearly six months, and by June 1933 he had his first novel. He titled it *Bar-B-Que*—and sent it off to Knopf, concerned that his efforts to economize with words and tell the story at breakneck speed had produced something less than a novel. He also made extra copies of the 159-page manuscript because Elina kept reminding him "you promised to send it to Voltaire," as she always called Walter Lippmann, who was now writing a column for the *New York Herald Tribune*.

Lippmann was also writing books, which he would send to Cain, who, in turn, would comment on them with long, thoughtful letters. In late 1932, when he had received Lippmann's *The U.S. in World Affairs*, the second of three yearbooks he edited with his old *World* colleague W. O. Scroggs, Cain had written his former boss that he liked his articles on things and people much better than his essays on international relations. "You have a curious gift of handling personalities without malice, which permits you to assume a directness and realism that the average writer is quite incapable of." He also advised Lippmann he was working on a novel, and Lippmann told him to be sure to send it to him in New York and he would help find a publisher. But Cain did not send it at first because he had seen on the dateline for one of Lippmann's columns that he was in London.

Considering the impact Cain's first novel was to have on the American public and literary world, the strange story of its life from the time Cain sent it to Knopf to its eventual publication in the winter of 1934 is of more than passing interest. After gnawing his fingernails and trying to work on some articles about Malibu for *Vanity Fair*, Cain finally decided to send that copy to Lippmann, telling him that he wasn't sure he would take him up on his offer to help him get it published and certainly would not expect him to do anything unless he liked it. Also, even if he did, he should leave the details of the negotiations to his agent, Jim Geller.

A few days after writing to Lippmann, Cain heard from Knopf, and he was crushed. Although Knopf started out by saying he liked *Bar-B-Que* "immensely," there were a few problems: First, Knopf thought it needed "a certain amount of tinkering," particularly concerning the insurance deal, which enabled the lovers to get off from what he called "their first attempted murder" (which was foiled when a cat put a paw in a fuse box). Knopf also thought the last pages were "soppy" and the manuscript was too short to qualify as a novel (*Bar-B-Que* was only 35,000 words, and the Knopf option called for Cain's next book to be at least 40,000 words), therefore it did not come under the option clause of the contract for *Our Government*. So he could not offer Cain a $500 advance for *Bar-B-Que* (a title which Knopf did not like), and he reminded Cain that he had been against paying a $500 advance for *Our Government*, a book that earned only $250. He also said the company was now paying 15 percent royalties on the *wholesale* price of the book and he would pay that, up to the first 5,000 copies, then go to 17 percent, then 20 percent. But the last paragraph, containing some faint praise, must have been the most crushing to Cain. "You have done some superb things for Henry Mencken," Knopf concluded, "and I think it is only a matter of time before you reach out into more sustained efforts that will be capable of making some real money as books."

Cain was hurt and mad, and for years, according to his correspondence, he questioned Knopf's judgment. However, a few days after receiving

Knopf's letter he had a wire from Lippmann, which buoyed his spirits: IN-TENSELY INTERESTED THINK IT SURE FIRE STOP WISH YOU WOULD WIRE ME FULL AUTHORITY TO DEAL WITH MACMILLANS.

Cain wired back immediately: OK GO AHEAD STOP DELIGHTED YOU LIKE IT STOP KNOPF WANTS IT BUT HAS PLAYED SMOOTH TRICK THAT RE-LEASES IT.

Cain wrote Knopf the same day, and the tone of his letter reveals his mood: "I don't know what to say to your letter, as I can't make out what it is that you think should be changed. You speak of the 'first attempted murder,' which sounds like the bathtub incident, but then you speak of the 'legal points' involved, which sounds like the insurance deal, as I can't think of any legal point involved by a cat's stepping on a fuse box. Both these incidents, however, were the result of endless revision, which involved the heart of the story, and both were submitted to experts. The insurance people read the book before I sent it to you, and gave it a complete O.K., telling me that such things happen all the time, so I don't worry about it on the score of plausibili-ty. As for the end, you say it is soppy, and that it should be cut, but as there are only four pages of it, I don't know where to cut, as it seems to me that the book must taper off to a close, and if it is soppy, a man in the deathhouse is generally a little soppy. In short, I don't see how I can revise, and I think I had better offer it somewhere else."

Next he wrote Lippmann a long letter, enclosing Knopf's note, which he said was primarily a putdown designed to get the book for nothing. Although still obligated to submit Knopf his next two books, Cain would not sit still for this ploy, and he told Lippmann: "I will be greatly relieved if Macmillan takes it, and I will accept any arrangement you can make." He said he was upset at the thought of revision because the changes Knopf wanted would take him back to the first draft, which "led me into all sorts of trouble" (meaning the 80,000 words of Cora's trial). "Superficially, this is a murder story, but basically it is a romantic love story, and if this love story doesn't move, everything goes to pieces."

Meanwhile, things were happening in New York: Mencken had read the novel and told Knopf he was enthusiastic about it. Macmillan, on the other hand, was cautious. Then Blanche Knopf expressed her enthusiasm. As Al-fred Knopf recalls it: "I was playing golf when Mrs. Knopf called and said 'We'd better buy that book.'" So within a week after Cain's letter to Lipp-mann, the columnist wired back: MACMILLAN SQUEAMISH STOP KNOPF REALLY EAGER TO HAVE BOOK WITHOUT REVISION WHICH LEAVES OPEN QUESTION OF TERMS. And he recommended Cain accept Knopf's terms if they proved satisfactory.

At almost the same time, Cain received a wire from Knopf: DELIGHTED ACCEPT MANUSCRIPT AS IS STOP WRITING REVISED TERMS. Cain wired Lippmann: YOU ARE WASTING YOUR TIME WRITING YOU OUGHT TO BE AN AGENT STOP I LIKE KNOPF ALL RIGHT STOP HE WIRED ME BUT DIDN'T STATE TERMS STOP ANY ARRANGEMENTS YOU MAKE ALL RIGHT BUT I COULD USE A LITTLE MONEY.

Soon Cain received a phone call from Lippmann, who explained how Knopf actually felt: "Jim, he really doesn't like the book—its rough, impromptu style I think is what repels him, but he'll put it out, just the same. I think mainly for a personal regard for you, and my suggestion would be to take his deal, get the book in the show window, and then we'll see what we see."

The deal Knopf offered was: $500 advance, half on signing contract, half on publication date; royalties would be on the retail sales—10 percent up to 2,500 copies; 12 percent up to 5,000, 15 percent thereafter. But Knopf would still have an option for Cain's next two books.

Cain accepted, and by the time Knopf sent him the contract and Cain signed it and sent it back, he was much more relaxed and conciliatory: "I am very glad you have finally decided to take this book, as I felt from the beginning that you were the publisher for it, and sent it on, although I knew that it did not come under the contract I had with you. I wish I could have waived the matter of an advance and hope by the time the next one is done I can; [but] I had spent most of my money writing it, and badly needed a small amount to tide me over until I can cash in on some things [magazine articles] done since I finished it. When you are camped out here, 3,000 miles from the center of things, such matters involve a great deal of time."

The next day, Cain wrote Knopf again, saying he had forgotten to include the dedication: "To Vincent Lawrence."

It looked like clear sailing now, but there was still one problem—and once again it was Lawrence who provided the solution. Within a few days, Cain received a letter from Knopf reminding him that he did not think *Bar-B-Que* was such a good title. Cain said he was also unhappy about it and suggested some others, including *Black Puma* and *The Devil's Checkbook*. Knopf did not like these either and asked for more suggestions, saying he would also try to come up with a suitable title. Around this time, Cain and Lawrence were musing on the agony of sweating out the publication of a first novel, and Lawrence told him about sending his first play to a New York producer. Lawrence was living in Boston at the time, and every day he went to the window to watch for the postman; then, when he could not stand it, he would go into the backyard, but always listening for the ring. "And no fooling about that ring. The son of a bitch always rang twice, so you'd know it was the postman."

By now Cain wasn't listening. "Stirring in me," he recalled later, "was a dim recollection of the English tradition, and particularly the Irish tradition, that the postman must ring twice, and in olden times, knock twice." He said. "Vincent, I think I've got my title."

"What title?"

"*The Postman Always Rings Twice.*"

Lawrence thought for a minute, then said, "Hey, that is a title, he sure did ring twice for Chambers, didn't he?"

"That's the idea," said Cain.

Meanwhile, Knopf had decided on a title himself—*For Love or Money*—and wrote Cain suggesting it. When he received Cain's idea, he wrote back that he still preferred *For Love or Money*. The response bothered Cain, who thought that novel titles were very important and held some strong views on the subject. "There is only one rule I know on a title. It must sound like the author and not like some sure-fire product of the title factory. *The Rivet in Grandfather's Neck*, to my taste, is a lousy title, but as it sounds like [James Branch] Cabell, it is perfect for him." So he wrote Knopf that *For Love or Money* was one of those titles that would sound all right for a musical comedy, a movie, or almost anything; one of those roving titles like *Hold Everything* or *Hell and High Water*. Then Cain offered a few other suggestions, including *Western Story, Malice A Forethought* and *The Quean Commands*, which intrigued him because of its play on words. But he still preferred *The Postman Always Rings Twice*. Knopf replied that turnabout was fair play; Cain had dropped *Bar-B-Que*, he would drop *For Love or Money* and settle on *The Postman Always Rings Twice*. And just as well, because many critics and booksellers agreed that this title, even though few people were sure of its meaning, was an important factor in making the novel one of the most talked-about books of the 1930s.

Cain was in a critical financial position when he finished *Postman*, although Leo recalls that there was no particular panic in the Cain family. In California in 1933, people did not worry too much about money. The whole country may have been in a financial mess, but the Cains were in Paradise, where the living was easy and relatively inexpensive. Still, Cain now owed Vincent Lawrence $1,000, borrowed while he wrote *Postman*, and he had his rent and alimony to pay. He felt there was little hope of finding another studio job unless *Postman* hit big—he knew the studios hired more on reputation than ability, and he still had no reputation as far as Hollywood was concerned. In those anxious months between acceptance of his book and publication, he did not kid himself about the chances of a first novel solving his financial problems. "More than five hundred novels," he told Elina, "come out every year in this country, and not many attract attention. If I sell a couple of thousand copies, get my name in the papers, and pick up a little money, we'll be all to the good and I'll try to think of another one. We're not starving to death, so if we keep our fingers crossed we may run into some luck."

With the novel done, Cain turned once again to magazine articles. His first effort, a little gem for *Vanity Fair*, described the history of Malibu Beach and life in the movie colony. It was a fine piece of reporting, often amusing. As Cain concluded about the Malibu sands, "it is the most deserted beach this side of Paradise." The movie people, he found, did little else at Malibu except give or attend parties. When Cain sent the manuscript to *Vanity Fair*, he addressed the editor as "Dear Mr. Brokaw," not realizing the editor was Clare Boothe Brokaw, soon to become Clare Boothe Luce. This little blooper would bother him for years.

His next piece, a thoughtful attempt to analyze just what it was about writing for pictures that made writers so unhappy, went to the *Mercury*. "I know fifty," Cain said, "and I don't know one who doesn't dislike movie work and wish he could afford to quit." This piece is probably the best summary extant of Cain's early attitude on working in Hollywood—and explains how he was able to write for the studios for sixteen years without agonizing about his situation. But as he still maintained, a prostitute had to like her work, and he did not, even though he understood what he was doing and the nature of the job. He simply could not do it successfully, although eventually he came to think he could.

But Cain was careful not to bite the hand he hoped would soon be feeding him. "You have heard, no doubt," he wrote in his *Mercury* article,

> that moving picture studios are dreadful places, run by barbarians with no ideas of manners, and callous to the finer ideals that are supposed to animate a writer. This doesn't happen to be true. I have worked in a number of places in my time and I have never worked any place where courtesy was more in evidence than on a movie lot, or where daily contacts were more pleasant. . . . If you are bothered by street noises, they will whisk you to a place where you can hear nothing but birds; if you dislike to talk over the telephone, a girl at the board will tell your lies for you; if you like tea at 4:30, it will arrive at 4:30 sharp.

He also liked the camaraderie among the writers and concluded that "a movie lot . . . is more like a big club than a place of employment." And he had some kind words for the men who did the hiring and firing—the movie executives. It was probably a genuine sentiment, because he considered them self-made men, a type he usually admired. But they did have one fault: "They are prone to condone bad work if the picture makes money and overlook good work if the picture flops." Still, he acknowledged the pressure to produce profits and said they had found that "good work is usually profitable and bad work is not," a viewpoint he also held regarding novels.

With his Hollywood article on its way to the *Mercury*, Cain immediately went to work on another piece for the magazine recounting the gridiron exploits of James Garfield Moore while Cain was a student at Washington College. When it appeared, the article was well received most everywhere—except in Chestertown, where Moore never did acknowledge it, leaving Cain assuming he did not like it. In the piece, Cain, probably still smarting from his father's having been fired in 1918, said some rather unkind things about the college, and the local press countered with some equally unkind remarks about Cain's ineptitude on the football field. When running, it was recalled, Jamie resembled "nothing so much as the slow motion antics of Carrie the Cow in Walt Disney's screen cartoons."

Cain was paid $250 each for his *Mercury* pieces, but the money may have strained the magazine's bank account. By the end of 1933, the *Mercury* was having financial problems, compounded by the fact that the tension between Knopf and Mencken had reached the breaking point. Knopf felt the magazine should be devoting more attention to the developing crisis in Europe; Mencken still seemed more concerned with the follies of "the Rotarians, Babbitts and lower inhabitants of the Bible belt" (Knopf's phrase). The impasse came to a head when Mencken wrote a long article about Hitler and *Mein Kampf* in the December 1933 *Mercury*, which Mencken thought was balanced but Knopf felt was too gentle. Finally, both agreed a new editor was needed, and Henry Hazlitt, a conservative literary critic, took Mencken's place. Cain was upset about Mencken's leaving; it "knocked me for a loop," he wrote him. He also said the *Mercury* was "the only place I ever got that curious excitement that one ought to get when he has something in print." But he also told his old friend that he should have left long ago—to devote more time to his own writing.

Mencken wrote back, agreeing it was time to move on and congratulating Cain on his contributions to the magazine. "I tell you the literal fact when I say that they were among the best things I printed, if not actually better than any other."

Cain did, however, think Mencken's valedictory in the December issue was perfunctory and said "it left me with the irritated feeling that I thought more of the magazine than he did."

Cain did not think much of Hazlitt, and as for the articles he was running, Cain said, "Henry [Mencken] in his laziest summers never put in such tripe as that. It is a combination of *The New Yorker, The Nation, Liberty*, and *Esquire*, offering all the worst features of each. But I never saw anything in Hazlitt but a dull guy, in person or on paper. How he could edit a magazine is beyond comprehension."

Knopf apparently agreed, and within a few months Hazlitt was replaced by Mencken's editorial assistant, Charles Angoff, who in turn was succeeded by Paul Palmer. Cain got along fine with Palmer, although after "Tribute to a Hero," his piece about Moore, he would write only one more story for the *Mercury*.

One reason Cain wrote less for the magazine was that by the end of 1933 he had found a new outlet for his journalism. B. A. Bergman, who had succeeded Cain as the twenty-seventh "Jesus" on *The New Yorker*, was now editorial page editor of Hearst's *New York American*. He wrote Cain to see if he might be interested in doing a three-times-a-week column, which would also be syndicated in the other Hearst papers. Cain accepted immediately, despite his acknowledged weakness at writing signed columns. But he needed the $85 a week Bergman said the syndicate would pay, and he would be free to write about anything that interested him—except politics, a restriction that did not bother Cain, who considered politics the least interesting subject on earth.

Cain would be traveling in good company on Bergman's op-ed pages: other columnists included Aldous Huxley, Emil Ludwig, Frank Sullivan, and G. K. Chesterton. He started out well enough; his first column, which appeared November 11, 1933, may have been the most substantial of his year and a half of column-writing for Hearst. It began by commenting on the flood of cheap books that told the story of the West, particularly the publications of Erasmus Beadle, who founded the Beadle and Adams dime library in 1860. These books, Cain said, marked the departure from the "polite writers" of the early nineteenth century—Hawthorne, Poe, Longfellow, and Irving, etc. The western novels were "literature of the people," and out of them grew literature of the nation: "Mark Twain, who wrote for Beadle, Bret Harte, Ambrose Bierce, Jack London, Frank Norris, O. Henry, Willa Cather, and a host of others. The great works of these writers were all on one thing: The West." And they told a story, preferably "one that fires writers and sets readers atingle, one that transcends plot, characters, and writing as writing." Cain said he was reminded of all this by seeing in a bookstore several current books: *A Farewell to Arms*; *Sanctuary*; *Miss Lonelyhearts*; *Ann Vickers*; *Anthony Adverse*. "I can't read these stories," he said, and thought the reason was "they bear no relation, except in a purely journalistic sense, to the times in which I live. I yearn in these directionless days for another western story. I want something that knows what we are headed for."

Could anyone write it? "I don't know," Cain concluded. "Before they can, I guess it is essential that we be headed somewhere."

Over the next month he had further thoughts on the plight of the modern novel, noting that too many novelists were retreating into historical fantasy, had "gone Thornton Wilder," as he put it. "It has become quite hard to write about the present," he conceded. "For if you imply, by a happy ending, that everything is swell, then people wonder if you are quite bright; and if you imply by a sour finish or otherwise that everything is terrible, then they wonder where you got the idea *that* was news." But he added: "Terrible or not, these times are going to bulk larger in history than most other times, and it is important, for historical reasons, if for no other, that they be recorded, vividly and imaginatively, as only the novelists can do it, before their flavor is lost forever. These are important times, and it is up to the literary boys to quit fooling around and get to work."

Whether *Postman* told us where we were going is a matter of debate. But it is a western story and vividly records aspects of the new society that resulted when the people who went farthest in the great western trek reached the Pacific, found they could go no farther, and settled down to enjoy the good life.

Cain quickly let it be known that he was not writing a literary column, as he picked up on such subjects as formal parties for teen-agers (invented by girls, just as sports were invented by boys); the next war (inevitable); catfish sandwiches (ate five and loved them); nostalgic recall of reflections in his World War I observation post; textbooks (they were terrible); homework (he was against it); telephone calls (far too many, especially by teen-age children; recommended installing pay phone in house); tipping (nonexistent in the West, which he applauded); and so on. Cain was a human-interest writer in his column, just as he had been on the *World* editorial page. But soon he began to detect the same problem he had had writing signed columns for the Sunday *World*. When writing as "the corporate awfulness" of the paper, his editorials had had point, definite style, and they had moved. Writing under his own name he bogged down in awkward self-consciousness. But he did not hear any complaints from Bergman or Hearst—at least not for a while. So he continued writing his column, while nervously awaiting the publication date for *Postman*.

By the end of the year, galleys were available and some interest was being shown by the movies. Jim Geller, Cain's New York agent, now working in the Morris Agency office in Hollywood, reported optimistically to Knopf, although there were problems in its present form. But with "certain drastic changes" it might "get by." Knopf questioned whether Geller was the right agent for Cain, but Cain said he would stick with Geller because he was honest, devoted, doggedly persistent in his sale efforts, and not a "fair-weather friend."

Meanwhile, Cain was seriously contemplating a book growing out of his researches about the West. He summed it up to Knopf as "a new history of the United States," but written "not in terms of government, but in terms of, let us say, conquest. It would trace the movement (across the continent) in terms of great staples, tobacco, cotton, lumber, fur, gold, corn, cocoa, and wheat, and show what happens when these big lodes of export staples begin to run out." He hoped to write it in a year and thought his Hearst job would support him. "As a publishing venture," he said, "it will be worth a dozen novels," and added that this project gave him "the first real feeling I have had, of being headed somewhere, since I came here." Knopf liked the idea and gave it his encouragement. But nothing ever came of the project.

The first sign that *Postman* might be something big came when the bulletin put out by the American News Company, which distributed books, gave the book a four-star rating, commenting: "If this one doesn't smash, we're going to look for another job." Then Cain received a telephone call one morning from Louis Weitzenkorn, author of *Five Star Final* and other hit movies, to whom Cain had given a carbon. "Jim," he said, "I called up about that book. I make a confession to you. When I went to bed last night, I took it with me, expecting to read twenty pages to know what it's about in case I ran into you—and perhaps finish it some other time. I put that book down at three o'clock in the morning, having read every last page. And what I called to say is: I think when that book comes out you're going to wake up famous."

THE "UNLAYDOWNABLE"
BOOK LAUNCHES
A STRANGE CAREER

The furor caused by *The Postman Always Rings Twice* is difficult to comprehend today when so many big novels make news with a six- or seven-figure sale to paperbacks and a rich contract for TV or movie rights, followed by a deafening hype when the movie appears. In 1934, that kind of success for a book was unknown. In fact, *Postman* was probably the first of the big commercial books in American publishing, the first novel to hit for what might be called the grand slam of the book trade: a hard-cover best seller, paperback best seller, syndication, play, *and* movie. It scored more than once in most of these mediums and still sells on and on, even today.

Perhaps the most important review for any book is the one in the Sunday *New York Times Book Review*, and *Postman* did well there for a first novel. Headed "Six Minute Egg," the review appeared on page eight. Harold Strauss, the reviewer, was impressed by the book's realism and said Cain had developed the hard-boiled manner as a perfect instrument of narration. He commented on Cain's opening sentence and its "tremendous impact." Then, after summarizing the story, he concluded: "Cain is an old newspaperman who learned his reporting so well that he makes Hemingway look like a lexicographer. . . . He can get down to the primary impulses of greed and sex in fewer words than any writer we know of. We want to see more of his work and defy anyone who has broached that remarkable first sentence to put his book down."

However, if there was any single review that started *Postman* on the way to its dizzying success, it was Franklin P. Adams's in the *New York Herald Tribune*. F.P.A. was positively ecstatic in his praise, which could not be attributed simply to the fact that he and Cain were old colleagues on the *World*. Adams was part of the clique of columnists who considered the paper's faceless editorial hands somewhat beneath them. Furthermore, as F.P.A. said in his review, when Cain came up to New York from the *Baltimore Sun*, "he wrote with no thought in his mind but what Henry Mencken would think."

But now Cain was liberated. *Postman*, said F.P.A., was not written with Mencken in mind, not unless Cain said: "I'll show Mencken I can write first-rate fiction." F.P.A.'s rapturous review went on with a statement that followed Cain from dust jacket to dust jacket through most of his literary career: "Mr. Cain has written the most engrossing, unlaydownable book that I have any memory of." And that was just a starter. Whereas the *Times* review (like many to follow) quoted the first sentence of *Postman*, F. P. A. said, "I once thought the first chapter of Hardy's *The Mayor of Casterbridge* was the greatest first chapter in English fiction," and went on to assert that *Postman*'s first chapter might be even greater. In fact, he was so carried away he reprinted that chapter *in its entirety* as part of his review. He also said: "Cain's style, which some will compare to Hemingway's, is better than most of Hemingway's and as good as the Hemingway of the 'Twenty Grand' [meaning "Fifty Grand"]. It is as tightly written and as vernacularly dictaphonic as Lardner. . . . I can't detect a stylistic flaw in it."

Just about every book review publication in the country reviewed *Postman*, and most of the reviews were raves. Even the adverse reactions had to acknowledge the book's power. There was Lewis Gannett, for example, who did the "Books and Things" column for the *New York Herald Tribune*. As soon as he recovered from the shock, Gannett wrote: "I hate the book! Ever since I read it two weeks ago, it has been sticking in the back of my mind and I can't stop talking about it." In fact, Gannett never could stop talking about Cain in his column.

Another critic, the novelist Gertrude Atherton, was just as shocked as Gannett, but even more awed. "There are several disgusting scenes and the characters are scum," she wrote, "but that book is a work of art. So beautifully is it built, so superb is its economy of word and incident, so authentic its characters and so exquisite the irony of its finish, it is a joy to any writer who respects his art."

Across the seas, the British were stunned by the book. "Brutal and shocking," said the *Sunday Times*. And James Agate wrote in the *London Daily Express*: "One day last week the postman slipped into my letter box a slim package containing a little volume of fewer than 200 pages. This opuscule . . . is a major work. Unheralded, it takes the reviewer's breath away, at the same time it takes the wind out of its swollen rivals, so that in comparison they seem puerile and as empty as hot water bottles. . . . The book shakes the mind a little, as the mind is shaken by *Macbeth*." The *Birmingham Post* said the book affected the mind—"with nausea"—and James Hilton in the *London Telegraph* called it a "nearly perfect American conte, bare of every ornament and as ruthless as the kind of life it portrays."

Reader reaction to the novel flooded in, most of it enthusiastic, although some was negative. Cain's mother and father wondered where he had ever learned such language (which puzzled Cain because there was no indecent language in the book), but Clarke Fitzpatrick, his old editor at the *Sun*, reported seeing "pride of ownership" written all over the elder Cain's face. Fan letters were divided in sentiment between the woman who said the book was a "masterpiece" that was going alongside her Chaucer, *Huckleberry Finn*, and the *Autobiography of Benjamin Franklin*, and another who thought it was "shocking, disgusting and would corrupt people's morals." To the latter correspondent Cain replied: "If you read the book without having your morals corrupted, why do you assume that others will be less fortunate than you?" The Baltimore Library had a waiting list of more than forty people and could not order enough copies. The librarian at Cain's alma mater, Washington College, refused to put the book in the library.*

Most of Cain's personal friends and associates joined the public acclaim: Arthur Krock, in a blurb written for Knopf, compared Cain to Zola and Tolstoy and said "he has the most accurate ear for the speech of common Americans of anyone I know." The *Mercury* review, by Charles Angoff, said "he makes the art of Hemingway look like the befuddled and stuttering thing it is." Samson and Dorshka Raphaelson were wild about the book, and Raphaelson sent a copy to director Lewis Milestone, who replied with flowers and a telegram thanking him for introducing him to "the American Dostoyevsky." Vincent Lawrence was a little disappointed, thinking Cain had not handled the love rack properly. But another friend thought he had. One night at dinner at the Cains', Dorothy Parker said: "Well, there's all sorts of stuff being written about what kind of novel it is—it seems to baffle these critics as they keep trying to label it. But to me it's a love story and that's all

*Today Washington College has most of Cain's books, in addition to his personally donated collection of foreign editions.

it is." And Cain's old friend Morris Markey wired: STALLINGS OVER YESTER-
DAY WITH BOOK AND WAS VIOLENTLY ENTHUSIASTIC I READ IT AND HAVE
BEEN HAUNTED BY THOSE MARVELOUS PEOPLE MY FEELING IS NOW SIM-
PLY ONE OF PRIDE IN SUCH AN ACHIEVEMENT BY A FRIEND OF MINE AND IF
YOU AIN'T IN THE MONEY NOW I AM JUST PLAIN CRAZY.

Cain was in the money. Within a month after publication Geller was
closing a deal for *Postman* with MGM, which had offered $5,000. But Elina
"hit the ceiling," according to her son. " 'Nothing less than $25,000,' she
said, and Jamie was shaking. He was such a lousy businessman," says Leo.
They agreed to hold out for $25,000, and at that point Columbia entered the
bidding. But then Columbia retreated, apparently out of fear that the movie
would never clear the censors, a consideration that was also discouraging
other companies. Geller, detecting that MGM did not know Columbia had
withdrawn, pushed for a deal with MGM before it discovered it was the only
studio bidding, and MGM agreed to $25,000. As they were preparing to sign
the contract, Sam Marx, an MGM executive, said: "That's all rights, isn't it?"
Geller hesitated, but fearing that if he haggled MGM would find out about
Columbia's withdrawal and want to start over again at a lower level, he finally
said: "O.K., why not." It was a decision Cain would regret the rest of his life.

As the reviews poured in from the clipping services and the book began
to creep up the best-seller list (*Redbook* said *Postman* had restored booksellers' faith in Santa Claus), Cain knew he had finally achieved the goal of every
professional writer: a commercial success that was also praised as a literary
achievement.

The book also established his by-line and enabled him not only to sell
his stories, articles, and books, but find studio jobs with relative ease—at
least for a while. And the novel had critics talking about his style, as they
would for years. Today Cain's stories are used in writing classes all over the
world as examples of a literary style that can say more in fewer words than
perhaps any writer ever achieved. One writing teacher even set a page of the
novel up in a poetic form to demonstrate that Cain's language, when it appeared on the printed page as poetry, was "unmistakable verse."

Still, the furor took Cain by surprise. And even in the warm glow of
those first few weeks of rave reviews and acclaim from his friends and fellow
writers, he could not have foreseen that *Postman* was on its way to becoming
part of the culture. H. L. Mencken pointed out in his *American Language*
that the use of "postman" over "letter carrier" in our culture was primarily
due to Cain's book. The novel would also inspire a popular song ("The Postman Always Rings Twice, the Iceman Walks Right In") and in *The New
Yorker*, James Thurber did a parody on it ("Hell Only Breaks Loose Once").
By mid-1934 the whole country was talking about the book, which was well

on its way to becoming one of the most phenomenal successes in publishing history. In 1936, it was brought out in a paperback edition published by the *American Mercury*, then it was picked up by Pocket Books and Cain was eventually awarded a "Gertrude" (a silver replica of their kangaroo insignia) when the book passed the one million copies sales figure. It was also reprinted by Penguin books and in at least seventeen languages abroad, where it is still being sold. The book was serialized after publication by the *New York Mirror*, the *Boston Daily Record*, and the *London Daily Express*. And in 1936, Cain wrote a stage version that starred Richard Barthelmess and Mary Philips. The play was done again in 1953 by a road company, starring Barbara Payton and Tom Neal. It took MGM ten years before it could develop a *Postman* script acceptable to the Hays office, which had to approve all scripts, but when it did the result was one of its biggest box office hits, starring Lana Turner and John Garfield. In Italy, Luchino Visconti plagiarized *Postman* for a movie he called *Ossessione*, and the French made their own unauthorized version called *Le Dernier Tournant*. MGM was unable to prevent these films but did successfully ban them from the U.S.—until it finally permitted a showing of *Ossessione* at the 1976 New York Film Festival. In 1978, Vintage Books brought out a new reprint (along with three other Cain novels), and in 1981 there was the new Lorimar movie version of *Postman* starring Jack Nicholson and Jessica Lange.

Although his stepson and friends recall that the phenomenal success of *Postman* did not affect Cain personally, he knew he was now "an item for the columns." In the spring of 1934, the movie *She Made Her Bed*, based on the Cain short story "The Baby in the Icebox," was released, and by then Cain was so well known that the lead for most of the reviews of the film referred to him or "the short story by James M. Cain," rather than the name of the movie. Although the movie was panned, Cain's stature as a novelist and short story writer was now such that the reviewers did not find Cain at fault for a very improbable tale. As the *New York Times*'s Bosley Crowther put it: "Though it is fastened upon a story by James M. Cain, the blame for this picture is too large, too richly complicated, to be attached to one person." And the *Bradenton Herald* called it an excellent short story, praising Cain as a novelist while criticizing the movie.

Suddenly, the struggling free-lance writer who made $3,000 in 1933 was in demand everywhere. Three book houses—Houghton Mifflin, Farrar & Rinehart, and Smith and Haas—approached Cain saying they had heard rumors that he and Knopf were not getting along, and each let him know they would be delighted to publish his next book. Cain told them he was committed to Knopf for two more books, but kept the doors open. The shortness of *Postman* and its regular climaxes also suggested to periodicals that Cain would be an ideal installment writer, and soon he had requests from the *New York Herald Tribune* and *American Magazine* for serials. *Liberty* wanted short stories, as did *Redbook* and *The New Yorker*. And his new New York agent, Edith Haggard, was pleading with him: "Please don't go in for articles at this point. Editors are crying for short stories by you and the field is wide open." Cain, however, was more interested now in breaking into the movies; he felt he needed the money. One of the first things he did after the sale of *Postman* to MGM was send a large check to his sister Rosalie, now divorced and with a young son to support. He thought it might help her buy a house. In addition, he and Elina had decided to take what money they had left and pay Mary her alimony in a lump sum—if she was agreeable.

Cain was having lunch regularly with Geller, and there he would bombard his agent with movie ideas. One day Geller finally said: "Cain [they called each other by their last names because they had the same first names], I can't sell ideas, I need scripts." So they agreed on a couple of ideas and Cain went to work. One, to be called *The Traitor*, was about Benedict Arnold and his treason during the Revolutionary War. Cain's story would focus on a love affair between Arnold's wife and Major John André, the Englishman who was hanged for his part in the conspiracy. The other script was to be for Mae West and was called *Aida*. Cain wrote *The Traitor*, but it never sold. And there is nothing to suggest that he ever finished the *Aida* script, though he did have a meeting with Mae West, whom he thought "preposterous and for some reason rather appallingly decent."

He was getting absolutely nowhere with his free-lance scriptwriting, when suddenly he had a studio job offer—from MGM to work on a movie called *Duchess of Delmonico*, to be produced by Walter Wanger and starring Clark Gable and Jeanette MacDonald. Now he was really heading for the big money. Geller insisted that Cain would not do the script for less than $10,000, telling Wanger that he was "a goddamn nut. This guy reads history, believe it or not." So Wanger said: "Well, in that case, there's nothing to do but pay him." It was agreed Cain would get $10,000: one-third down, one-third when the script was submitted, and one-third after he made any changes the studio requested. Wanger was not long finding out that Geller was right, he really did have a nut on his hands. One of the first things Cain did at MGM was get in an argument about the traditional sock in the jaw Gable had to administer in his pictures. "It doesn't make him look like a he-man with hair on his chest," Cain argued. "It makes him look like a psychiatric zany and you ought to stop having him do it." MGM ignored his advice.

The story was to be set in Goldfield, Nevada, site of a famous gold strike, and Cain went out there for a few days to absorb some background and do research. One thing he had to find out was whether there had been an interlude during which nobody really knew if the Goldfield mine would come in big or not. He put this question to an old miner who said: "Oh, yes, it was quite a while between the time when that Indian found the first nugget and the time when the miner really began to get it out . . . there wasn't hardly any surface gold around Goldfield. It was all deep, below the three-hundred-foot level. . . . And when it did come in, they had to revise their ideas about it. . . . It's a funny metal. It taught them what they had all forgot. . . . Gold is where you find it."

Struck by the phrase, Cain decided it would make a great title for one of the songs that the movie would naturally include for Jeanette MacDonald. He wrote Wanger, telling him about his conversation with the old miner and suggesting a scene that would produce such a song: "Gable is a prospector and all in, and she pulls him off the desert, and an Indian, right where he had been lying, finds a nugget of gold. And that night, right after his first real love scene with MacDonald, Gable finds out that after all his mining, college training, and ten years of prospecting, without any luck, an Indian has to steal his first strike away from him. It is there that I want MacDonald to sing him the number, buck up his courage, and get him to make another try." He said he wanted Herb Brown and Arthur Freed, the songwriters assigned to the story, to work up a tune. He also said he had about "twenty pages on paper, and will have forty more by the end of the week."

Cain seemed to be off to a roaring start on his first post-*Postman* movie, but then, abruptly, he lost interest. For some reason, he decided while still in Goldfield that this was not a script for him. So he went back to Hollywood and stunned everyone, from the Brown Derby to the Iron Lung, by letting it be known that he was returning the $3,333 advance he had been paid. "You're crazy," said one of his writer friends at the studio. "Don't you know this is a corporation? It isn't as if you're holding back on an individual. They'll appreciate your honesty in quitting now instead of holding them to the rest of the contract." But Cain's stubborn integrity persisted, and he returned the money by personal check. Suddenly he was a cause célèbre and in all the columns, with people taking sides as to whether he should or should not have done it. The refund had also thrown MGM's accounting department into a tizzy, and it was six months before his check was cashed. Each week when he would draw a check at the Bank of America, Hollywood Branch, the manager, one of those opposed to his action, would drop by and whisper: "That check hasn't come through; you can still stop payment on it."

MGM never did make *Duchess of Delmonico*, and Gable and MacDonald were soon working on *San Francisco*. But fourteen years later, MGM came out with a flop starring Frank Sinatra and Kathryn Grayson, the high point of which was a little song titled "Love Is Where You Find It."

The failure at MGM was especially disappointing because he had planned, after finishing the movie, to head East to settle Mary's alimony, for which he needed all the money he could raise. In May, he went East anyway to negotiate with Mary's lawyer—William Pepper Constable—in Centreville, Maryland. The trip also gave him material for several columns, including one on that perennial favorite of columnists, spring. He took a southern route across the country and noted the progress of spring as it crept north, but his reaction was not as rhapsodic as it is with most pundits. Spring, for Cain, was too contented. "It makes me feel as church bells do when they ring on Sunday evening; that peaceful pastoral ding-dong to me is the most dismal sound in the world."

This first trip East in three years was not exactly an emotional excursion down memory lane. He did see Mencken again, but abruptly "shoved off in my usual Arab fashion," as he wrote his old friend later, "which is the only humane way to do it." Baltimore he found depressing. "I don't know exactly why," he wrote another friend, "except that everything in the East seemed dull, and dead and hopeless. . . ."

In New York, it was the same thing. "Quite a few people seemed to remember me, even the headwaiters came running over to shake hands. But we didn't seem to have much to say, after giving each other the Masonic grip." In several Hearst columns, he confessed that the trip back to "Baghdad" served to remind him just how much he disliked New Yorkers, although he respected their drive and energy. And he confessed that his distaste for New Yorker speech had affected his career as a journalist. "When I wrote it, I was a phony and knew it." Nothing was right about New York: the traffic was handled wrong; the filling stations didn't give service; the hills were too small; the air was too hot; the rains came too often and then only half rained. Even the food tasted bad, which he thought was odd, because that was the one thing about the East, besides Annapolis, that he remembered with pleasure.

The trip to Centreville, however, was successful, although he ended up needing help. After one session with Mr. Constable, he realized that the only person in the Cain family who was good at business matters was 3,000 miles away. So he called Elina and asked her to come East immediately. She met with Constable without Cain present. That Cain had received $25,000 for *Postman* had been in all the papers, so the problem was how to convince Constable that the Cains were, in fact, offering all they could afford. This difficulty was resolved by Elina, who slammed her checkbook on the table in front of Mr. Constable and yelled: "Look. Look for yourself. You shall see." He did, and noted a balance of $13,000. He finally settled the divorce for $12,750, leaving them $250—enough to get home. But when they arrived home, they discovered Elina had made a mistake in entering a deposit and they had $800 more than they thought.

The trip proved a milestone for Cain, and not just because of the settlement with Mary. For the first time since leaving Annapolis in 1924, he began to realize he had found a place where he wanted to live. "The Western virus" had reached him, as it had thousands of Americans. The first symptoms he noticed were the dissatisfactions with everything Eastern, which could have been written off as the usual difficulty the immigrant had returning to the old country. "But really it was much more than that," he wrote in one of his columns. "I was full of this Western thing. . . . It involves, somehow, a belief that the West affords a better, richer way of life, that it offers something to the soul as well as to the body; it is esoteric as well as material. . . . The truth is, there is something mystical in it . . . you feel it, yet you can't lay your finger on it. . . . But this much you know: Once it gets you, you are no good for anything else."

Cain returned to California ahead of Elina, who stayed on to negotiate details with Constable. While Elina preferred to fly, Cain chose to go by train, and it was on the train as he approached the Mohave desert that he really became aware of this spell the West could cast on a person. "It was so hot you didn't dare move. The club car was gray with dust that not even the tightest doors and windows could keep out. All you could see was sand that drifted like snow, and bleak, brown hills in the distance. It would be hard to imagine a more horrible place, and yet as I looked out on those stunted desert bushes, all warped and twisted by the wind that never stops blowing . . . it was a grim, desperate struggle for existence, and all of a sudden I was stirred by it, excited by its drama, lifted by its stark, lethal beauty. They say the desert gets to you, after a while, that once you begin to feel it, no other place seems like home. I suppose so. I have been in the Southwest now for three years, and like all the rest, have begun chasing mirages."

Cain was glad to return home. "Hollywood looks exactly the same only more so," he wrote Edith Haggard as soon as he got back. "I took the kids to the Brown Derby last night, and nobody even knew I had been away. Noah Beery was still sitting in the same old place and they had the same live lobster, named Gus." Cain felt refreshed and ready to go to work—and a good thing because he needed money, and quickly. He did not have any idea for a novel, and besides a novel would take too long and not bring in the cash fast enough. He had had a dozen ideas for stories and columns while on his trip, but they seemed to vanish when he sat down at the typewriter, a realization he found interesting. "I wanted to write about the food in New Orleans," he said in one of his columns, "the gigantic black and dignified negroes in San

Antonio. I wanted to write about the architecture of Annapolis, I wanted to write it while it was hot. That is the only way it ever gets down on paper."

Fortunately, with all the ideas from his trip fading into the California sunset, something else developed: MGM was having trouble writing a script for *Postman* that might be acceptable to the Hays Office. (In fact one "treatment" still in the MGM files eliminates Nick's murder and has him die in an automobile accident brought on by drunken driving. Cora and Frank are tried, accused of staging the accident, but are then found innocent. Later, after they are married and Cora is pregnant, Cora is killed accidentally and Frank is found guilty of a murder he did not commit and is executed.) The studio had another idea: It owned dramatic rights to *Postman*, so why not do a stage version? After a Broadway success and recognition, the Hays Office would be more amenable. This strategy was approved, and MGM assigned a writer to the play. But when Geller heard of this he urged Cain himself to write the play.

At first, Cain did not want to become involved. He knew it would take a lot of work, and if it flopped there would be no financial return. But then that old urge to write a play began to stir, compounded by Cain's pride of authorship and horror at the idea of somebody else doing a play based on his book. So he agreed to do it and spent the summer working on a script. His financial problems were eased slightly by the sale of second serial rights for *Postman* to the *New York Daily Mirror* and *Boston Daily Record*, but as the summer wore on he began to feel the pressure again. He finally finished the script, a two-acter that he thought was solid enough until the middle of Act II. He was particularly fond of the third scene in Act I, in which Cora sells Frank on the idea of murdering Nick, and he felt the whole play achieved the impressionistic style of *Waiting for Lefty*—Clifford Odets's widely acclaimed play. But his enthusiasm was crushed when he learned that his contract with MGM gave the studio a one-third cut on all stage royalties—and then he found that his Knopf contract cut that company in for one-fourth.

Cain sent the play off to the Theatre Guild. The reaction there was favorable, but there was mention of revisions, and while he was waiting to hear something concrete he started writing for the magazines again at a furious pace.

He was also still doing his newspaper column, although he had heard that "the old man" (Hearst) did not like it, and that Bergman had persuaded the old man to keep him only because "Cain is hot." Occasionally, he would produce a little gem, such as his essay "The Influence of Stenography on Literature," inspired by Herbert Hoover's book of memoirs, *The Challenge of Liberty*. "If stenography was abolished and big shots compelled to hitch up to their typewriters, as lesser hacks do, the quality of their prose might be distinctly improved or, more likely, they would decide not to write the book at all." But the truth was, the columns were beginning to read more and more like the work of a hack writer, hitched to his typewriter. Gradually, during 1934, Cain's contributions deteriorated, and Bergman's copy desk was evidently aware of it because the columns were appearing shorter and shorter on the page. Cain was spreading himself too thin, "working like a wildman," as he wrote Edith Haggard. In addition to his movie scripts for Geller, his play, and his column, he was still trying to come up with some idea for a magazine serial for the big money. And then he got sidetracked on a series of articles which just about drove Edith Haggard mad.

It all started when he agreed to write a few 1,500-word "light pieces" for Jack Wheeler, who owned several western newspapers. Wheeler offered Cain $150 a piece, and since Cain was being paid only $85 for three columns a week from Hearst and knew he could do one of Wheeler's pieces in an afternoon, he agreed. The first one—about some boys hired to build a summer cottage for 50 cents an hour and the reaction of the labor unions—was rejected. But then Cain did one on making flapjacks and another on mint juleps, and Wheeler bought them, though stipulating that there be no more food articles. Cain's reaction was to write Edith Haggard in New York, enclosing the two food pieces he had done for Wheeler and outlining a series of magazine articles on such subjects as Midnight Spaghetti, Crêpes Suzette, Carving Game Duck, Carving Turkey, Christmas Eggnog, etc. Mrs. Haggard could hardly believe that the author of the most provocative novel of the year, the hottest, toughest fiction writer in the country, was now on a gourmet kick. "You have made me an old woman, my lad," she wrote Cain. "With the magazine world at your feet, with their hands raised high over their heads pleading with you for short stories, you want to write food articles."

She did concede, however, that they were good food articles and that she would do "the Haggard damnedest to sell a series. And please," she pleaded, "for the little widow, do a story. I just know the winter will be long and hard." Cain obliged with two more food pieces and started thinking about a serial, as a short story would not bring in enough money.

Cain worked in his little study at the rear of 616 East Tenth Street in Burbank, typing furiously—"the fastest two-finger typist I ever saw," says Leo. When he was chilly, instead of turning on the heat he would put on an overcoat and the same old hat he had worn for twenty years, and keep typing away, all of which amused the family. When he was restless, Elina would make him go on writing.

With all this output, he still had time to keep up with his colleagues back East, especially Walter Lippmann and H. L. Mencken—two friendships that required a lot of reading and letter-writing. After reading Lipp-mann's latest book, *The Method of Freedom*, Cain reluctantly came to the conclusion that "I don't agree with you, there is no getting around it"—and then took three pages, single spaced, to tell Lippmann why: "Freedom is a too nebulous, constantly shifting concept to serve as the steering star for any such complex governmental function as you outline. . . ." He concluded, commenting that the "charming thing about our relationship is that although we have always been as far apart as the poles on most things, we manage to discuss them amiably and get along. Well, one thing we have in common is a passion for craftsmanship, a compulsion to say it well, whether it is right or not. That much I can certainly hand your book. It packs into a few pages what you mean even if I think it is all wrong."

At that time, he was also trying to help H. L. Mencken become estab-lished in Hollywood. Unhappy and complaining loudly in his *Sun* columns about United Railways and Electric Company defaulting on his bonds, Mencken thought his financial problems might be solved in Hollywood. Cain recommended Jim Geller as his agent, and Geller finally did wrangle a job offer from one of the studios for Mencken, who turned it down and then, ac-cording to Cain, acted rather frosty about it the rest of his life.

Another thing occupying him was a little crusade to promote the literary career of a young girl who had impressed him while he was at *The New York-er*—Sally Benson. Cain wrote Knopf, Edith Haggard, and *Mercury* editor Charles Angoff, telling them they ought to encourage her to write more. So Miss Benson wrote Cain, thanking him and telling him about her meeting with Angoff, who had shouted at her and, according to Cain, "said I probably had literary asthma."

Cain wrote back to her, as exasperated as Angoff: "You more or less give me a pain in the neck, with your talk of avoiding brass tacks and not being able to think of stories. Out in this place where nobody ever thinks of anything but stories, and all the jumbled ideas finally superpose on each oth-er to make a gigantic shadow called The Story, you find out that nobody, ever, can think of stories. And when you read back over a few that were sup-posed to exude them as they sweated, the prolific boys, who wrote Literature, you find out that they had it just as tough as anybody else, and wrote just as few that were really worth anything after they were finished. *In other words, stories are tough*: they are supposed to be tough. . . . So spend your juice on story, story, and story, rather than dialogue or descriptions of the scenery. Dialogue is fine, and you write it beautifully, but what they pay their money for is yarn—excitement, the only thing that can light up your characteriza-tion so that it really glows, makes the reader feel it."

He also advised her to stop writing for *The New Yorker*, advice she ignored. But she did "get down to brass tacks" and started thinking more about stories, which eventually led to *Junior Miss* and *Meet Me in St. Louis* before her untimely death.

Cain was also writing to Alfred Knopf, about another thing on his mind: his image. "I wish you would stop advertising me as tough," he said. "I protested to the New York critics about their labeling me as hard-boiled, for being tough or hard-boiled is the last thing in the world that I think about, and it is not doing me any good to have such a thing stamped on me. Actually, I am shooting for something different, and plugging me as one of the tough young men merely muddles things up."

Knopf wrote back that he would stop the advertising but he could not do anything about the critics. "I suspect that every other review of every other hard-boiled book that may be published in the next three years will drag you and the *Postman* into it." Knopf was right. Hard as he tried to discourage it, Cain could never erase his tough-guy label.

By the summer of 1934, the Cains were becoming anxious to move back into Hollywood itself, to a home more suitable for the country's most controversial writer. They enjoyed social evenings, but their little house in Burbank was no place for entertaining; in fact, the Raphaelsons recall that the Cains, during the early days of their acquaintance, were reluctant to invite them to Burbank because of how modestly they lived there. Now that Cain was a big-name novelist, he and Elina were being invited to dinner constantly in Hollywood, although he still preferred evenings with close friends, talking about plays and stories, or just driving around Southern California with Elina and the kids or with friends. (Cain was a very slow driver, Leo says, one reason being that he liked to think about stories and plan his next day's work while he drove.)

Despite the lure of Hollywood, Cain's primary interest was still writing, and the one thing he still wanted to write more than anything else was a play. He enjoyed most the evenings he could get together with Raphaelson and Lawrence to talk plays. "Because his dialogue was so damned good in his books and stories," says Raphaelson, "it seemed to him that it ought to be a very simple matter to write a play." Once Cain and Raphaelson went to a play together in Hollywood. After walking out on the show because it was so bad, they were drinking beer in a sour mood when Raphaelson said, "A bad play is an awful thing, isn't it?"

"Yeah," said Cain.

"You know, it doesn't only bore me," Raphaelson continued. "I could stand that. I would even sit there and look at it. But it *terrifies* me. A good play is always simple. It makes you feel, why I could have written that if I'd only thought of it. And it makes you feel that writing a play is hot stuff, something worth doing. But a bad play? It makes you sick. It's always complicated and dull and flat . . . and makes you feel you ought to have stayed in the advertising business."

Cain agreed, saying it was not the purpose of a play or a book to inspire other men to write, but a good one could have that effect. Cain, Raphaelson, and Lawrence would comment freely on one another's work. "But one thing I think is important about Cain," says Raphaelson, "is that he couldn't take more than a certain amount of adverse criticism . . . it took the spirit out of him. It would kill the writing."

In 1933, Rafe, as Cain called him, had written the first draft of a tragedy about an older man who falls in love with a younger woman. But he was not happy about it. The next spring, when he was in England, he began to turn it into a comedy, which he called *Old Love*. But he still did not want to finish it, feeling it was too much like his earlier hit, *Young Love*, and so put it aside. After he returned to Hollywood, he, Cain, and Lawrence were having one of their sessions when Raphaelson told them he had an idea for a big, tragic play—about Hitler. "They trampled on it," he said. Then, just to pass the time, he told them the plot of his comedy—and they would not let him leave until he had agreed to finish writing it. One night after he had written the first act of the play, Elina and Cain came by to take the Raphaelsons to dinner at Perino's, and Cain read the script in the car on the way to dinner. He pronounced it "terrible," so Raphaelson and Cain started to examine the act, scene by scene. And every scene, Cain thought, was good. "But not the total act! And by God, he was right," says Raphaelson. "It was a series of consecutive scenes between the lovers. I needed something to open it up, to make it roll and to give background. I took a long ride in the car with my wife the next day and wrote a whole scene. In fact, it is the only thing I ever dictated in a car. A brand-new scene that went in the middle, introducing a new character. I was deeply grateful to Jamie. The play was produced. It opened in New York. And, by God, the opening night, Christmas night, I stepped out between the acts on the sidewalk and there was Jamie. He took the train all the way in from California without saying a word to me about it." The play was called *Accent on Youth* and it was a big hit.

In the fall of 1934, the Cains had found a home in Beverly Hills. Not only did it put them closer to the social center of Hollywood, with a place where they could entertain, but it also positioned Cain nearer the studios, where he still hoped to find regular work. More than that, Cain had really come to like Hollywood. "Indeed if I am honest about it, I like it better than any other place I have ever lived."

To help pay for their new home, Cain tried even harder to come up with an idea for a serial. Finally, one day, it came to him. He had recalled a conversation with Arthur Krock when they were both working in New York on the *World*. Krock was telling about what happened one night when he was working at the *Louisville Courier-Journal*. A dreadful typo appeared in an ad showing ladies' underwear. The original ad had read: IF THESE SIZES ARE TOO BIG, TAKE A TUCK IN THEM. But in the paper that hit the street, the *T* in Tuck had been changed to an *F*. Krock had the ad reset for the next edition, then called the terrified printer down for an explanation. He had none. Two days later, Krock cornered the printer and bullied the information out of him. Trembling a little, the man explained: "Mr. Krock, you do nothing your whole life but watch for something like that happening, so as to head it off, *and then*, Mr. Krock, you catch yourself watching for chances to do it."

As Cain began to think about Krock's story, it occurred to him that dynamite was lurking there in the printer's compulsion. He remembered the conversation he had had with the AAA men in Los Angeles when he was verifying the insurance details in *Postman*: "This stuff of yours in this book is right from beginning to end," one executive told him. "No insurance man will laugh at you for it, and it's so right that you ought to write more stuff along that line. Because, boy, I'm telling you they think this stuff all comes from the police. That's wrong. All the big crime mysteries in this country are locked up in insurance company files, and the writer that gets wise to that one of these days is going to make himself rich."

What if an insurance agent, Cain thought, mulling over the Krock story, spent his whole life on guard against people trying to defraud his company, then suddenly began looking for a chance himself? And what would make a man who had been honest all his life want to defraud his company? The author of "Pastorale" and *The Postman Always Rings Twice* knew the answer: a woman. Once again, murder was to be his love rack.

As for the insurance business, Cain felt he had everything he needed to know from his days selling insurance in Washington in 1914, plus the information he had picked up from talks with his father, who had been an insurance company executive since 1918. Now he had his basic plot and the background, and according to Leo, sometime before the Cains moved from Burbank in November 1934, Cain started to write his serial. It was to be about a Glendale housewife who persuades her husband's insurance agent to conspire with her to kill her husband for his insurance. And because the policy provided for double indemnity if the insuree died in a train accident, that was how they would do it. The husband would be killed falling from a train. Cain even had a model for Phyllis Nirdlinger, the character who lures the insurance agent into murder: a Glendale widow, very good-looking, the aunt of some friends of Leo and Henrietta's.

Although Cain never really liked the story, he knew it would sell and, if he ever finished it, would bring in some quick money. But there were several interruptions. For one thing, there is reference in his correspondence with Charles Angoff at the *Mercury* to "the Sinclair piece," which remains otherwise unidentified and, although apparently written, was never published. For another, Edith Haggard had finally sold a three-part series on food to *Esquire* for prices ranging from $135 to $150, and she needed another quick piece on Crêpes Suzette. And then there was the move to Hollywood itself, which always seems to throw a writer off schedule. Although the rest of the country may have been in a Depression, Cain felt he could afford to move into one of the West's most luxurious neighborhoods—despite the fact that he was flat broke. He was confident in his ability to make money in Hollywood, and was even beginning to think the Depression was showing signs of being licked. He deduced this from the length of the freight trains at the railroad crossing near the edge of Burbank, where by November he was being detained more and more; he took this to mean that car loadings were up, an encouraging economic indicator. Even more heartening was the fact that the hoboes—"the hundreds of human derelicts perched like crows on top of the cars, going nowhere and knowing they were going nowhere, silhouetted against the Verdugo Hills"—seemed to have disappeared. He was not sure what had caused their disappearance—the NRA, the CCC, the PWA, or what—but he remembered how he had agonized at the horror of all these human beings with no place to live, no place to sleep, nothing in their lives but drifting. He also knew there was a story there, but it would be several years before he could figure one out.

The Cains' new house at 2966 Belden Drive in Hollywood Hills cost $7,500 and was truly spectacular—an "upside down house," Cain called it, built on the side of a hill below the famous "Hollywood" sign pictured in so many documentaries about the film capital. From the front on Belden Drive, it looked like a modest little bungalow, but from the rear, looking up at it from Beachwood Drive, it was a "tudor castle." You entered on the top floor, which contained the maid's room, dining room, and kitchen. Below were the living room and study, and below that, on the bottom two floors, were the bedrooms. It even had a "ghost," which made loud tapping sounds up under the ceiling. Cain said in one of his columns that it was a first-class ghost in every respect, a ghost that seemed "to see everything you do, hear everything you say, and disapprove all the way down the line as a matter of principle. Indeed, it is such a fine ghost that I am sure if it haunted some castle in Scotland or an inn on the New England coast, or the old brick house I was born in in Annapolis, it would be a local celebrity." But alas, California "hasn't got the climate for ghosts. In this fragrant night, with the bright stars shining overhead, the lights of Hollywood blazing far below . . . our ghost is a flop. . . . No, in this clear-eyed place, dedicated to the fresh air and common sense, you can reflect that a metal weather vane, anchored in the wooden roof, will do some queer things when the time comes to expand."

All through the summer and fall, Cain had become increasingly pessimistic about the fate of his play based on *Postman*. He had heard nothing from the Theatre Guild and, despite the words of encouragement from Geller, assumed that once again he had flopped as a playwright. Then, suddenly in late November, he received a note from Thelma Helburn at the Guild saying it was interested in the play, but mentioning possible revisions. Cain wrote back, enthused, promising to do anything needed to put the script in the best possible shape for production; he requested suggestions from the Guild and mentioned his concern about the scene in the second act, where he felt it sagged after the hint that Frank and Cora might go free. Miss Helburn replied that they did not agree with him about that scene, but listed five places in the second act they did feel should be revised. Cain made all the revisions, except one in the courtroom scene at the end, which he decided to cut altogether. He put the revisions in the mail on December 19, just before he was to depart for a Christmas trip to Baltimore.

Elina remained behind with the children, giving Cain plenty of time for business and renewing old friendships. He saw Mencken in Baltimore, went up to New York to work out a contract with the Guild and discuss further revisions in the play, met Charles Angoff, and had lunch with Walter Lippmann. "At the end of three days, I had the most beautiful case of the flu or grippe or something of the sort that the doctor had ever seen." So he spent two weeks in bed at his parents' home in Baltimore.

When Cain returned to Hollywood, he was immediately offered another studio job—with Paramount, the scene of his first failure. He still wanted desperately to work in the studios, not only for the money, but because he seemed to enjoy the studio life—the pretty women and the endless talk about scripts, stories, and plays. He also seemed to hold scriptwriters and playwrights in awe. John Lee Mahin, who had admired Cain's editorial writing on the *World*, was now in Hollywood, having just finished the script for *Naughty Marietta*. One night at a party, says Mahin, "there was this heavy-set, kind of craggy guy talking almost purposely tough, saying such things as: 'that ain't the way I seen it.' " So Mahin asked, "Who's that guy?" and someone said James M. Cain. Mahin introduced himself and said, "I know you. You're the guy that wrote all those beautiful editorials for the *World*." Cain replied: "How the hell did you know?" From that first meeting, Mahin and Cain maintained a rather odd Hollywood friendship: "He always looked up at me in awe because of my screenwriting [Mahin eventually wrote dozens of Hollywood hits, including *Captains Courageous, Dr. Jekyll and Mr. Hyde, Trea-*

sure Island, Tortilla Flat, and *Boom Town*] and I always looked up to him in awe because of his editorial writing."

Cain was at Paramount only six weeks, and he came away still holding successful screenwriters in awe. He had been assigned to work on a story called *Doctor Socrates*, originally written by W. R. Burnett. He outlined his approach to the script to the story editor, who approved it, and was reworking the script to incorporate his suggestions, as well as some the story editor made, when suddenly the script was sold to Warner Brothers. Cain told Geller to let Warner Brothers know he was working on the script and would like to finish it, but the studio ignored his wishes.

Cain did make $5,000 on the assignment, and he even found time at night to dictate a story, which he sent Edith Haggard. It was titled "Hip, Hip, the Hippo" and was about a Hollywood bit player who tried to make a comeback riding a hippopotamus in a big movie. It was not one of his better efforts. But Edwin Balmer at *Redbook* thought it very amusing—until the end, which he asked Cain to change. Cain agreed. The reworking took longer than he'd expected—"I never had such a hell of a time with a story in my life"—and when he sent it on to Edith Haggard in late March, he said if Balmer rejected it he would personally come to New York and shoot him. *Redbook* bought it with the new ending.

By now Cain was beginning to have occasional insights into his inability to make it as a screenwriter. One came at a meeting he had with a group of screenwriters, including Sam Taylor (remembered primarily for the credit line he was given in 1928 for *The Taming of the Shrew*—"By William Shakespeare with Additional Dialogue by Sam Taylor"), Raphaelson and Lawrence, and Harold Lloyd, who would star in the film. They were trying to develop a script from the novel *The Cat's Paw*, by Clarence Budington Kelland, about the son of a missionary in China who comes home, is elected mayor, and defeats the gangsters by using Chinese methods. Lloyd was desperate to make something out of the book, needing a vehicle to revive his career and having paid a considerable sum for the rights to the novel. So naturally, he was concerned when Cain said he did not think much of it, although the other writers thought it was a honey of a story. But Sam Taylor, who said very little that night, went home and turned out a script adhering closely to the novel. Later, when Cain saw the movie, he confessed that he laughed hard. And people were standing in lines around the block to get in. Cain could not help but wonder why he had disliked the original story, and why it made such a good movie. The answer, he finally decided, was: "I couldn't believe it. And because I couldn't believe it, it carried no real terror at its core. It was merely an interlude of cock-eyed nonsense, [but] it charmed me up there on the screen." He also decided that the first test of a good movie was complete incredibility. "Who, after all, could believe 'The Champ,' or 'Lady for a Day,' or 'The Three Little Pigs'?" It was beginning to look as if scriptwriting was no place for a writer who considered himself primarily a newspaperman.

When he left Paramount, Cain went back to revising his play based on *Postman* and finally sent it off to New York. He heard nothing for a while, and then found he had another problem: his newspaper columns were showing signs of neglect. Not only were they being cut considerably, but Bergman would occasionally not use a column, which Cain took as a personal affront. He was, in fact, gaining very little satisfaction from them. In addition to his self-consciousness about by-line writing, he also felt restricted in writing about "your favorite flower," as he complained to one interviewer. Actually, he was using just about any subject that came to mind—inventors (creative like playwrights); librettos for musicals (as important as the music); skyscrapers (against); what's wrong with banquets (plenty); public statues (a waste of time, unless they are huge); and so on. Some of his columns had repercussions, such as one criticizing textbooks and another commenting on Edgar Lee Masters's call for a "spiritual history" of America. Cain suggested another book, an aesthetic history of America. "We have striven so hard for culture," he wrote, "and on the whole so unhappily, that it ought to be clear by now that there is something screwy about the whole quest; that we are not as other nations are and that our culture cannot be forced to take the form that their cultures have. . . . Our aesthetics tend to demand more and more an absolute notion of values." The study Cain proposed would result, he said, in "a much more vivid appreciation of what we do well and an end to apologizing for what we do badly." Leonard Schuster at Simon and Schuster, after reading Cain's column, was so impressed with the idea that he approached Masters to see if he might be interested in doing it. Masters replied that he did not have the time and suggested Mencken or Van Wyck Brooks, but the book was never written.

Cain's own favorite column was one in which he said that despite Bagheera in Kipling's *Jungle Books*, there was no such thing as a panther. In Asia and Africa the panther is a leopard, in South America a jaguar, and in North America a puma. "But as for a panther, there ain't no such animal." The column inspired considerable anguish among his readers and several abusive letters. But what Cain liked most was Vincent Lawrence's reaction. Lawrence was working on a script for Cecil B. De Mille, *Cleopatra*, to star Claudette Colbert. The script called for Colbert to have a black leopard as a pet, but Lawrence told Cain he was going to persuade De Mille that a black leopard was too bony and that what they really needed was a panther. Then he would convince De Mille to send Frank Buck, whom Lawrence hated, to Africa to bring a panther back alive. "Of course, Buck won't find the goddamn panther," Lawrence said. "The son of a bitch will stay out there twenty years and not find one and not know any different either, because he don't know any more about cats than this Kipling, whoever he is."

Hearst still did not like the columns (he never did invite Cain to "the ranch," as San Simeon was called by Hearst regulars), and finally he over-ruled Bergman's insistence on keeping Cain with a memo that, according to James Thurber, read: "Get rid of Cain. I thought Abel had done it. Sorry he failed."

And so, by April, Cain was writing Lippmann: "It's the same old round. I get rich and go broke so fast it is hard to keep track, but at the moment I'm broke." Which was all the more distressing because now he had another pressing need for money. He wanted to finance a trip to Guatemala and Mexico to "get some dope," as he always called it, for a novel. He had abandoned, at least for the time being, the story of the Southern California drifter working in the oil fields, and now he wrote Knopf that his current idea was "about an opera singer and a Mexican whore, although the singing part will be used as an engine for the story situation I want to develop."

The story situation had been developing for a long time—since 1915 when he discussed with Professor Townsend at Washington College the idea of a story in which a famous singer would commit a crime, get away with it, but then realize that he could not sing again without being discovered. In time, Cain decided to have someone else—probably a woman—commit the crime for the singer, who would then be unable to sing without betraying his partner. The next step in the evolution of the story occurred in the 1920s when Cain was in New York, regularly attending operas and concerts. He began to see a relationship between a singer's "sex coefficient," as he put it, and the quality of his voice. When Cain heard a man he sensed was a homosexual, he often considered the voice to be "very disagreeable and of a peculiar kind." So he began to mix these ideas up in his mind and, after moving to California, started work on a story of a male singer who had voice problems but did not know why—until someone told him. But who? A psychiatrist? "That seemed very dull," Cain thought, "and it had the smell of formaldehyde all over it. But I thought, a prostitute might know. . . . The story began to get rather vivid in my mind when I began going down to Tia Juana and Caliente. We would pass through Tia Juana, and it is a rather dismal place, and I was going to have this singer washed up as a sort of beachcomber in Tia Juana. Then I would have the singer meet a Mexican whore, be forced to spend the night with her in a church in Tia Juana because of a tremendous storm. They would make love and the singer would get his voice back and the Mexican whore would understand and explain why. Then the singer would resume his career, meet his male lover again, lose his voice, and the Mexican whore, by now his constant companion and lover, would kill her rival and the two would escape to Mexico. But he could not sing again without her being discovered."

That was the story continually playing around in the back of Cain's mind in the mid-1930s. He would tell it to playwright friends, like Raphaelson, and some, though not all, urged him to write it. But he was still concerned that the story was too pat and that medically there might be some flaws to it, and as an old reporter he did not want to write anything that was factually inaccurate. "I don't want to do a book doctors will laugh at," he often said. But then, in late 1934, a development in his social life occurred which probably had a significant bearing on the story. Cain became intensely interested in singing again and had a chance to observe singers and singing at close hand.

Despite his warm feelings for Hollywood, Cain still did not like Hollywood parties. For one thing, there was the drinking: not that he was a prude about liquor, but his stomach was getting much worse. His problem was still diagnosed as liver trouble growing out of his TB, despite the fact that as early as 1930, "Dr." Mencken thought he might have an ulcer and urged him to let Dr. Louis Hamburger in Baltimore look him over. But Cain never did, and now he could hardly touch a drop of liquor. He was also finding his inability to take a drink a social problem. Common courtesy, of course, demanded "some sort of mumbled explanation," as he lamented, "but this usually provokes a sales talk from the host. Partly he wants to be hospitable and partly he begins to be worried when he finds a teetotaler in the room, for sad experience has taught him that teetotalers make bad parties. Then comes a fuller explanation and if it comes out that I am permitted a little wine now and then, there follows the dive for the sherry bottle, and I begin to feel like a nuisance. And by that time the whole room is discussing my liver, and Uncle Charlie's liver and Grandpop's diabetes, and an exceedingly dull subject is on the agenda for at least a half hour." At dinner, it started all over again when he had to take it easy on the meat and decline the offer of an omelet because eggs were an even greater poison than meat or liquor. In short, said Cain, a man on a diet had a social problem, not a health problem.

However, when they moved to Belden Drive and had plenty of room for entertaining, a new possibility opened up that did not involve a lot of drinking and eating. One of his Hollywood friends was Henry Meyers, a playwright who worked on the scripts for *Million Dollar Legs* and *Destry Rides Again*. Like Cain, Meyers had studied music in his youth before—"to his mother's horror," as Cain put it—deciding he wanted to be a writer. But he could sight-read music and play almost anything on the piano. One night

Cain and Meyers were sitting around talking about music and deploring the fact that people didn't play instruments or sing in their homes anymore. They recalled that before radio and the phonograph, people would make music in their homes, and they decided that human nature had not changed much, that given the chance they would step forward and betray their natural exhibitionism, if nothing else. They decided they would organize musical evenings every Friday night at Cain's home.

The idea was a smashing success, with Cain "a darling host, thoughtful, amusing, interesting," Dorshka Raphaelson recalls. Leo tended bar and Elina would keep things organized and fix a big spaghetti dinner (using Cain's special recipe) to close the evening. They found that the ideal group consisted of eight singers—a double quartet—but before long they had a huge chorus. The regulars, in addition to Cain and Meyers, who played the piano, were the Raphaelsons, Dorothy Speare, a writer who had once sung opera, Gertrude Purcell, a former Ziegfeld girl, then a screenwriter who worked on *Destry Rides Again* with Meyers, Jay Gorney, the composer who wrote music for *The Wizard of Oz*, and a San Francisco Opera baritone, Mostyn Thomas. One night Franson Manson, a Columbia Studios story editor, was invited providing she brought a tenor. When a story conference prevented her from attending, she sent her tenor along with Jo Swerling, invited because his wife, Florence, was a contralto. The tenor was introduced as "Mike Swartz" by the Swerlings, who said they could not vouch for his talent. But when he opened up, Cain knew he had a tenor—and as it turned out he was right. Mike Swartz was, in reality, Michael Bartlett, recently of the Philadelphia Opera Company—in Hollywood to make *Love Me Forever* with Grace Moore. But Cain did not care. Bartlett was welcome. Anybody was welcome if he had a voice and, more important, could read music and not object to singing a part, rather than solo (although Cain himself would occasionally end the evening with a certain breezy number that began, "George Washington was the father of his country," and ended with Cain taking a handkerchief from his pocket and waving it at his audience, which more often than not would boo).

The evenings were mostly devoted to serious music, however, and it is obvious from Cain's writings and interviews that he was continuing his musical education and learning quite a bit about singers and singing. He discovered, for example, that much of Gilbert and Sullivan and grand opera simply do not stand up for singing in the home and that Arthur Sullivan was truly an overrated composer who would have gone nowhere without William Gilbert. The music that really stood up for singing was "the same music you have heard about all your life"—Mozart, Handel, Haydn, Bach, Brahms, Mendelssohn, Palestrina, the Scarlattis, and, the greatest discovery of all, Rossini. Cain also learned how good amateur musicians could be, at least in California, and found that if people had the opportunity, they were eager to participate in home singing. In fact, they were soon coming uninvited to the Cain Friday night festivals, in such numbers that the Cains finally had to ring down the curtains on the evenings. Cain and Meyers also found they were spending so much time locating scores and studying music that it was interfering with their work.

But the singing did make an important contribution to Cain's writing. During these evenings and later when he was attending local opera, he was giving more and more thought to the timbre and quality of a man's voice and what made it different. "At last, I begin to see dimly what makes a singer good," he said. He mentioned one baritone he knew who had "a superb voice, but he really isn't any good. Well, why? I'm figuring it out, little by little. . . . This much I know: This mob has better voices than the professional mobs have, and yet they don't get there. It had something to do with that mystical thing the teachers call voice line; that is, how to hit the tone quality that a scene calls for, maintain it constantly, and develop it so it rams home the intent of the music. Sounds simple, but I can see that it isn't."

And the more he thought about the human voice, the more confidence he gained in his theory that there was a relationship between homosexuality and voice. John Lee Mahin recalled Cain's remarking at concerts "that a guy sang with his balls. And sometimes, if Cain didn't like a singer, he'd say: 'He doesn't have any balls; a guy's got to have balls.' " Cain would talk with singers about this and they would understand, especially the women. One singer in particular, Mary McCormick, became very excited about the idea and told Cain she knew exactly what he was talking about—"this peculiar color of a homo's voice," as Cain called it. He also was impressed by the fact that all the really great male singers were macho, high livers—Caruso, McCormack, etc. And he had met a male singer who told him he had such feelings of guilt about liking a man that it sometimes made a difference in his singing. "Naturally, I have no means of knowing which singers are homos, but it is not too difficult to hazard a guess, from their appearance, walk, manners, etc., which might be, or at least if not outright a hundred percent, would have a leaning in that direction." With these men he thought it was easy to detect what Juanita, the Mexican whore in the novel he would write someday, would identify as an absence of "toro." And he knew he would write the novel now because not only did his associations with singers help convince him he was on to a significant fact, but one night at the Raphaelsons' he had met a prominent Los Angeles physician, Dr. Samuel Hirshfeld, to whom he told the story about the singer and the Mexican whore. Dr. Hirshfeld wanted to know why he had not written it, and Cain gave his usual reply. "Oh, I don't know—I just don't care to write a book a doctor would laugh at."

"Well, I'm not laughing," said Hirshfeld, "I'm hanging on the edge of my seat." And then for an hour he described the importance of voice in a doctor's diagnosis and how much attention a doctor pays to it. Dr. Hirshfeld's endorsement was all Cain needed. He decided it was time to write the novel. But first he needed some money and a couple of weeks away from his type-writer. He thought maybe his serial would bring in the money, but before getting back to that he had one short story idea he wanted to develop, about a girl and a boy and the boy's fear of diving off high places. He called it "The Birthday Party" and sent it off to Edith Haggard, who, once again, was flabbergasted. "It's a new writer who signs himself James M. Cain," she wrote him. She had been pleading for short stories, but a children's birthday party! However, good soldier that she was, Mrs. Haggard agreed again to do her damnedest. First she tried *This Week*, where they had been crying for something from Cain. But the assistant fiction editor was just as shocked as Mrs. Haggard. "It would be hard to imagine anything more different from *The Postman Always Rings Twice*. Although we are by no means demanding that he spend the rest of his life rewriting *Postman*, we had hoped for something as swift-moving and full of action." *This Week* rejected the story, and Mrs. Haggard pleaded with Cain again for a murder script, although she finally sold "The Birthday Party" to the *Ladies' Home Journal* for $750.

Meanwhile, Cain had the message. He realized that he was indeed re-writing *Postman* in his serial about a wife conspiring with an insurance agent to murder her husband. "I have no interest in murder stories *per se*," he wrote Mrs. Haggard, "but so long as they don't come out in book form, it doesn't count." And his outline of the story must have warmed the little widow's heart. "It would be told almost in exactly the same style as my *Postman* book and, as a murder story, have the novelty that the insurance man who solves it never relies on any clues at all, in fact never even gets a clue. His weapons are the big human factors that people always overlook when they try to pull something smart. It would, perhaps, be more of a love story than a murder story, but as jealousy is the main theme that wrecks them it would move all right on an exciting end." He said the story was in good shape and would be ready in three or four weeks—in early August. Slowing him down was still one more revision on his *Postman* play.

Mrs. Haggard said that he should keep working on the murder story "because if you don't get too rough on the lover business, I know we can sell it for at least $5,000." By the end of summer Cain had finished it. He called it "Double Indemnity," a title suggested by Jim Geller, and sent it off to Mrs.

Haggard. But then *Redbook* declined it! Cain was instantly discouraged, and when Knopf inquired how his work was coming, Cain said he had just finished a magazine serial and, while those who had read it thought it was a "swell yarn," he thought it was "a piece of tripe and will never go between covers while I live. The penalty, I suppose, for doing something like this is that you don't even sell it to magazines."

There was one bright spot on the horizon. Geller had had five copies mimeographed and sent around to the studios, and all five were showing interest! When Cain and Geller had lunch at the Vine Street Brown Derby one day to assess the situation, Geller said: "I've never had such interest in a story. But what's bugging me is I quoted them $25,000, and if one of them offers that I have to let it go for $25,000 or I'm out of business. But I'm terrified that I could have gotten $50,000. You have no idea of the interest."

There was one problem: the Hays Office report. All the studios were waiting on that before making their bids.

That afternoon, Geller called Cain at home. "The Hays Office report on that story just came in," Geller said. "It starts out: Under no circumstances, in no way shape or form . . . want to hear the rest?"

"No, I can guess," said Cain. And that was the end of that. "Double Indemnity" apparently was not going to make it anywhere. And now Cain was really down on the story. He had written it fast to make some quick money. The ending, he knew, was not done well. He felt he should have written it over twenty times, as he would later do with most of his novels. He also felt that in his haste, and at this stage of his career as a writer, he had not given enough thought to Phyllis Nirdlinger's development. "It was enough for me to indicate she was not wholly sane, but I don't think I realized at the time that exploration of these borderline insanities has been the basis for some of the great literature of the world. And I don't think I realized the reverence with which murder, as an element in a tale, should be approached by an American novelist." Murder, Cain was eventually to understand, was an epic subject, and such subjects "*always* beget a mountain of trash, as the winning of the West did, in the form of the dime novel, the nickel weekly and the cowboy western. But if the trash occasionally produces a Mark Twain, a Bret Harte or a Frank Norris, then it has justified itself. . . . What I forgot in 'Double Indemnity' is that murder is not only the starting gun for a great manhunt, with God's bloodhounds waiting, even supposing the sheriffs are outwitted. It is also a Bridge of San Luis Rey, laying a mandate on the writer to discover, if he can, what forces of destiny brought these particular people to this dreadful spot, at this particular time on this particular day."

It is quite possible that, given this attitude, he eventually would have rewritten "Double Indemnity." But suddenly Mrs. Haggard sold it to *Liberty* for $5,000, and it was scheduled to begin as an eight-part serial early in 1936. Still, he could not, as he had hoped, take the money and run off to Guatemala and Mexico to gather background for his novel. Instead he had to remain in the country because his contract with the Theatre Guild specified that he be on call for revisions on the production of *Postman*. By October, however, they were still acting in a "shilly-shally way," as Cain wrote Knopf, and he did not even know whether they were going to bring it in. Then he heard from Miss Helburn that the Guild had decided not to do it.

It was also about this time that Cain's curious friendship with Charles Laughton came to an end. Laughton and Elsa Lanchester had dinner at the Cains' home quite often, but the real basis of Cain's friendship with Laughton, according to Cain, "was this game we constantly played of my seeing things in his portrayals that everyone else missed." It went back to the incident that had first brought them together—Laughton's portrayal of Nero in *The Sign of the Cross*. There was also Laughton's Javert in *Les Misérables*, which they discussed often. Then one day, when Cain was home writing, Laughton suddenly appeared at the door. "You never saw such a sight," said Cain. "The man I had known as a sedate English actor had become the Hollywood boy, in white flannel trousers, white open-throat shirt, white shoes, and a grin." He had come to tell Cain of his triumph at the studios—avoiding the part of Micawber in *David Copperfield*. It was going instead to W. C. Fields, and knowing that Cain knew Fields, Laughton had wanted to tell him. Then, as he was leaving, he asked Cain if he would like to go with him that night to see his latest release: *Ruggles of Red Gap*.

Cain accepted, and that night he picked Laughton up at the Garden of Allah apartments and together they went to the Western Theater at Wilshire and Western Avenue. In the picture, Laughton was an English gentleman's valet who had been lost in a poker game to the owner of a ranch in Red Gap, Wyoming. Cain and Laughton sat on the aisle, and clearly Laughton was absorbed in the show, hardly noticing the parade of people who kept walking by their seats wanting to see him. The high point of the movie was Laughton's recital of the Gettysburg Address, and the audience broke into applause, knowing that Laughton was in the theater. Afterward, the two men were walking to the car still playing their game of detecting things in a film others had missed when Cain began to recite "Government of the People," beating four-four time as he went. "It's not commonly known," he said to Laughton, "that it beats in measure like blank verse."

"Yes, yes, yes, I could feel it," Laughton replied.

Then, continuing their game, Cain said: "I know why that picture delights you. It's an autobiography, isn't it?"

"Oh, you caught that, didn't you!" Laughton said. Then Laughton's demeanor changed abruptly. "This man of such eminence," Cain said, "that a theater full of people had been agog just to glimpse his face, perhaps of an eminence greater than any actor had ever enjoyed, turned into a nothing, a sniveling, stammering thing, who grasped the lapels of my coat and started to talk, to gasp, to whimper, to whine, in a way I could scarcely believe. He said I could never know what it meant to him 'to say good-bye to all that—to come to this country—to make a fresh start, to hold my head up at last, to. . . .' Then he let go and stepped away, standing for some moments, rubbing his fingers together, in a curious, fidgety way."

They drove back to the Garden of Allah, and Cain was invited in to see Laughton's Mexican paintings. It was a remarkable collection—Rivera, Orozco, Siqueiros. He had bought them recently and they were just stacked on their edges against the living room wall. And as Cain tilted the paintings back with one hand to look at them, Laughton would say: "Shettering." But Cain noticed something else. "Allowing for all vagaries in pronunciations, he sounded slightly different." And when Cain looked around at Laughton he was staring at him with "a cold little smile that wasn't a smile."

Cain had committed, he knew, the one offense friendship cannot stand: "I had let him pour out to me things he now wished he hadn't said. He never called me again and certainly I never called him."

During this period, Cain was also seeing a lot of another Hollywood star, Harold Lloyd, and it was through Lloyd that he met Constance Cummings, a young actress who had starred with Lloyd in *Movie Crazy*. Miss Cummings eventually married Benn Levy, an English playwright who was in Cain's group of screenwriters. She was also the daughter of Kate Cummings, whom Cain later met one day at the Raphaelsons'. He and Kate were to become close friends.

Meanwhile, Knopf was becoming irritated with Cain's failure to produce, and wrote him asking to see the serial. "It's important for us and important for you to get out another book." The publisher also expressed annoyance that communications between them were not better, and said he had heard that the Theatre Guild "has definitely abandoned any plan to do the play this season. In other words, they have handled your play just exactly the way they handle the great majority of the plays on which they take options. I could have told you that in the beginning but I doubt if you would have thanked me much for it." Knopf was clearly annoyed at Cain and felt he should be writing books, not plays or serials or short stories.

Cain, however, was working on another short story. In thinking about the hoboes he used to see perched on top of the freight trains that came through Burbank, he began to wonder: What would happen if one of the hoboes, perhaps unwittingly, became involved in some scrape, such as murder? As usual, Cain was more interested in the man's subjective reaction than his battle with the law. "When a murderer comes to grips with the law," Cain thought, "he has a better than even chance to win. But, because of forces inside of him, his crime eventually catches up with him." So he wrote a story which he called "Dead Man," about a hobo who accidentally kills a railroad detective in a fight and then is driven by his religious upbringing to turn himself in, even though he knows that the police regard the detective's death as accidental. It was "Pastorale" again—a young man not able to live with the knowledge of a crime for which he would probably not be arrested.

Cain sent the story to Mrs. Haggard, and she wrote back one of what Cain called "those Mama-knows-best letters," suggesting the story would have a much better chance of selling if he made the ending more pleasant. Cain must have wanted the money badly, because in uncharacteristic fashion he changed the ending to make it more commercial. But still it did not sell to a commercial magazine.

Cain also wrote an article for the *Mercury* about his musical evenings, and in another uncharacteristic act he concluded by saying that he wasn't telling the reader anything any musician could not tell him. "But this much you must admit: I tell it a lot better than they do." A strange tag for a writer who was usually very modest about his work.

Meanwhile, Cain was "driving like a wild man" on a new play—this one "about an out-of-work musician in Paris, who finds a rich sucker who makes the greatest conductor in Europe out of him." It was an improbable plot, but Cain had discussed it with Joe Pasternak (a Hollywood producer whom he had just met and whose musical knowledge and ability so impressed him that he hoped to recruit him for the musical evenings, should he and Meyers ever resume them), who said it not only could be done, but had been done. The play was never completed.

Cain had also been working on another article for the *Mercury* about college education, but it seemed never to end, and Paul Palmer kept pressing him for it. In the fall Cain wrote Palmer that it was getting better and better and would be a good fat piece. Its thesis was that "colleges are not run for the students, but for the colleges. I shall then trace out a curious process, whereby building the college becomes more important than educating the student, that stems from the theorem that all college alumni in the United States are secretly ashamed of their diplomas and are constantly trying to bolster them. . . . Stirring up a stink is the fondest thing I'm of, and the mostest I have talent at. But when you get hold of an idea that gives you a good swipe at the bell, you don't like to hit it with a tack-hammer." By the time Cain worked up his sledge hammer, however, he could hardly lift it, and the piece, obviously based to some extent on his father's experience at

Washington College and his own experience at St. John's, began to take on the weight of a book.

Then, suddenly around the end of November, he heard that Jack Curtis had bought his play on *Postman* and wanted to rush into production. It would star Richard Barthelmess (marking his return to the stage after several years in Hollywood), Mary Philips, and Joseph Greenwald as Nick. The stage set would be designed by Jo Mielziner. So Cain put aside his education study and took the train East for "a dreadful experience from beginning to end."

He must have been feeling flush with the money from *Liberty* in his checking account, because just before Christmas he went into Jaeckel's in New York to price a fur coat for Elina. He knew she liked chinchilla, which he thought might do just as well as any fur and cost less. When he asked to see a chinchilla coat, the clerk looked rather oddly at him, then said: "We don't have chinchilla in stock at the moment; you see, there is some difficulty in getting skins. But could I show you a chinchilla cape?"

Soon a model appeared wearing a beautiful, pearl-gray-white cape, and after Cain oohed at it for a moment he asked, "And how much is the cape?"

"Twelve thousand dollars," said the clerk.

A few seconds later, according to Cain, "we were all laughing merrily, ha-ha-ha, and I was saying no wonder my wife liked chinchilla, and the salesman was saying as a matter of fact, it suited them just as well to keep the cape in stock right now, and the model was saying perhaps there was something *else* I would like to look at."

Someday, James M. Cain would be able to afford the cape. But right now, all he could do was what he usually did when something interested him—write about it, in a magazine piece about chinchillas.

12

"HOW YOU WRITE 'EM
IS WRITE 'EM"

Christmas 1936 at the Cain home in Baltimore was not a very pleasant time. The elder Cain was very old and feeble, and the doctors gave him only about six months to live. Things were even worse at Mencken's. Sara had died the previous summer, and the sage was living alone at his Cathedral Street apartment, waging his one-man war against FDR. "Mencken does not seem like himself," Cain wrote Elina, "and he ought to move out . . . the ghosts stalk that dreadful apartment, and he does nothing but talk, almost mechanically, as though that were the only way to keep them from jumping out and saying boo. It depressed me."

After the holidays, Cain left for New York, and Jed Harris, the Broadway director, rode up with him on the train from Philadelphia. They naturally talked shop, Cain telling Harris about *Postman*, then outlining a new idea for a play, about the murder of a movie director. Harris thought it was a honey and wanted to talk more about it sometime. As soon as he reached New York, Cain wrote Elina that he liked Harris and was tempted to give him the new play; he was also feeling a lot better, eating three-pound lobsters, practicing for the four-pounders.

But Cain was having trouble with *Postman*. Barthelmess was sending him twenty-page letters explaining how the play should be written, and Cain wrote Elina that in some respects Barthelmess was "the most absurd product of twenty years in Hollywood that I ever saw. In addition to that, we haven't the faintest idea whether he will be any good or not, and neither has he; Jed Harris tells me he is scared to death."

Cain rewrote the play several times, without making it come to life. But then "the miracle man," as he called director Robert Sinclair, began to work with him. He thought they had a hit, although he was still concerned about the scene in the second act where the audience had its first hint that Frank and Cora would go free. "So we . . . wrote a new scene every day for two weeks," Cain said, "then, when we were getting up tight, we wrote a new scene by day and another new scene by night. What we finally handed the cast . . . was stuck together with adhesive tape, string, wire, and chewing gum."

Reporting on opening night in Philadelphia, Cain said the first two scenes went very well, and then he settled back to enjoy the third scene, which was his favorite. Suddenly, "the audience got a severe case of tickle in the throat, and when the scene finished it sounded like a Smith Brothers Convention." In the second-act scene on which they had worked so much, the audience broke out in loud applause.

Cain was puzzled. But thinking about it, he decided that the playwright becomes so preoccupied with character, situation, and structure, and so proud of how he handles it all, he is amazed when the audience does not respond to his dazzling technique. What the audience likes is "a situation with some bounce to it, writing that gets the situation into words and acting that makes the writing come to life." The underlying principle of good theater was, in Cain's view: "To make 1,000 people lean forward in their seats and catch their breath—it would seem that something very profound should be involved in that. But apparently not. What you need is good jokes and that is just about all."

Postman was hardly a barrel of laughs, but when it opened at the Lyceum Theatre on February 25 it was warmly received by the audience. When the curtain went down, Barthelmess was given a standing ovation, and there were even calls for "Author! Author!"

The reviewers, of course, were set for the play, and most of the reviews were negative. There were a few exceptions: Robert Benchley in *The New Yorker* said it was certainly no comedy, but it would be "worth your while" to see it; Percy Hammond in the *New York Herald Tribune* called it "lively and literate entertainment"; Arthur Pollack in the *Brooklyn Eagle* said it was a "workmanlike play . . . a straightforward thriller"; *Women's Wear Daily* thought it "exciting, fast-moving." But the most significant praise came from *Time*, which had ignored *Postman* when it was published. Now it called the book a "minor masterpiece" and the play an "exciting chronicle."

The unfavorable reviews placed the blame in about equal parts on the original story and the casting. Brooks Atkinson in the *Times* chilled sales when he said "these are loathsome people when their crime is offered in the realistic style of footlights display"; Richard Lockridge, the *New York Sun*, thought it suffered from not having the "almost offhand objectivity of narration" which had made the novel so impressive, and called it "subversive" because "it makes us sympathize with Cora and Frank and forget about poor Nick"; the *New York World-Telegram* thought Barthelmess and Philips were both miscast; the *New York Evening Post* thought Mary Philips as Cora was "as wrong as Florence Nightingale would have been as Cleopatra"; and *Time* thought Barthelmess "looks, talks and acts too much like Rear Admiral Richard Byrd to impersonate Frank Chambers"—which was probably why most of the cast prayed that for just one night Barthelmess would get sick, making way for his understudy, one of the policemen played by a young actor named Joseph Cotten.

Soon after the play opened, Cain and Sinclair changed the format from two acts to three acts, which the *Hollywood Reporter* said helped Barthelmess (who was used to "short takes") and "wrought wonders" in the play. But it did not help; the play closed after seventy-three performances.

The experience was one more crushing blow for Cain, who accepted the blame. "The real trouble was as Vincent diagnosed it," he wrote Ruth Goodman in a long analysis of the play's difficulties. "His point was that I should never have written the play at all. He was right. If you tell a story once you have no business rewarming it. . . . "

Cain did have one minor triumph in New York. While working on his play in his hotel room, he received a phone call from Paul Palmer, editor of the *Mercury*. Palmer was inquiring about the story "Dead Man," which Edith Haggard had submitted to him after it had been turned down by the higher-paying markets. "Jim, I like it fine," said Palmer, "and want to run it in the next issue, except that this damned Pollyanna ending doesn't sound like you. . . . Could you fix me up another?" So Cain told Palmer to send over a messenger and he would have the old ending written before the messenger arrived. The story appeared in the March 1936 *Mercury*, has been reprinted six times, and is considered one of Cain's best stories.

Back in Philadelphia, Cain also had a chance to see his buddy from the Army, Gilbert Malcolm, who came over from Carlisle, where he was working at Dickinson College. But it was a disturbing reunion. Malcolm did not seem to be doing anything with his life. "All I could see," Cain later wrote his widow, "was a man marking time with the years, and it upset me."

No doubt, Cain was beginning to feel that maybe he was marking time with his own life. The failure of his play had not only demoralized him, but the expense of three months in the East and the time taken from other writing had put him near bankruptcy again. When he returned to Hollywood, he found another brief job with a studio. Which studio and on what script he worked is not known, but the assignment did not last long, and it left him convinced that his movie career was "a complete bust," as he wrote one friend.

By mid-1936, Cain's discouragement was so deep that he was giving serious thought to moving to Mexico permanently. He had resigned himself to making a living as a magazine writer, with an occasional book and play thrown in, and he felt he could do it just as well, maybe better, in Mexico where living would be a lot cheaper.

It is understandable that Cain was beginning to view magazine writing as his only hope. While his play was fizzling on Broadway, the serialized "Double Indemnity" had been appearing in *Liberty* and was creating a national sensation. As the serial progressed week by week, people across the country were reported standing in lines at the newsstands waiting for the next issue to appear.

Of course, *Liberty* and all the magazines were pressuring Edith Haggard for another serial—or at least some short contributions by Cain. He responded with two short stories and an article,* and was also trying to write a serial that somehow would not jell.

At the same time, Knopf persisted in asking for another novel. He had been to Europe the previous year, where he discovered that American writers—espcially John O'Hara, Dorothy Parker, Thomas Wolfe, Ernest Hemingway, William Faulkner, and James M. Cain—had a tremendous following. But James M. Cain was suffering from writer's block and other miseries, which he poured out in long letters to Knopf:

> I get stuck on stories, and spend days on end lying in bed, looking at the ceiling, and at such times it seems impossible for me to go to the typewriter, or do anything except pound my problem and wonder if I am headed for the booby hatch. I wish, for a book to be published between covers, I could once get hold of an idea that wouldn't be censorable,

---

*"Brush Fire" (*Liberty*, December 5, 1936) is about a twenty-two-year-old CCC camp worker who saves a man's life in the morning during a California brush fire and then kills him in the afternoon in a fight, after the man learns the boy seduced his wife. "Coal Black" (*Liberty*, April 3, 1937) is about a nineteen-year-old boy and a sixteen-year-old girl who find a ghost, terror, and love in a mine that is about to be blown. The article "Fit for a Queen—Worth a King's Ransom" (*McCall's*, March 1937) is an amusing, interesting account of chinchilla raising in the United States, which grew out of Cain's effort to buy Elina a chinchilla coat for Christmas, 1935.

and that for this reason might be available for pictures so it might reasonably promise a return, but all my good ideas seem to be about as impossible, so far as pictures are concerned, as the *Postman* was, so I haven't much hope of relying on them for a living! God knows what twist there is in my mind that makes it run in these directions, but even when I try to write a serial, before I get done with it, it gets a very censorable cast to it, and if it doesn't, goes feeble on me. It is getting to be a rather serious problem, for I certainly don't want to go back in the newspaper business.

Knopf replied in a letter showing little patience and considerable sense:

Unfortunately I have no gift for even trying to play God to my authors, but I honestly can't see why you risked what you did for the play. You could have had from me, following the success of *The Postman*, a substantial advance—at least I think it would have been substantial enough to have enabled you to write the book you wanted to write.

You can't write fiction with one eye on the movies. If your problem weren't that of censorship, it would turn out to be something else just as hobbling. *The Postman* gave you an elegant chance, it seems to me, and you always did seem meant to become essentially a book writer. You can't live as a rule very richly on book royalties, but some people manage and you've got so much better start than the average [writer] that I don't see why you don't drop everything else and follow it up. If I am wrong, then the sooner you know it the better, but the life you describe yourself as living now is certainly not what yours ought to be.

How much money would it take to persuade you to drop everything else and do this book? How long from the time you dropped everything else would it be before we had the manuscript? I mean, forgetting serials, magazines, newspapers, movies, every single damn thing except turning out a novel by the author of *The Postman Always Rings Twice*.

But Cain still had his phobia about advances. He feared that he might accept one, fail to produce, and then be in debt to Knopf. So he declined the offer. He said he needed more money than he knew Knopf would advance, money that could come only from a killing with a magazine serial reinforced with possible sales to pictures—or a job on a movie lot. Knopf replied that there was little else he could say, but pointed out that it was *Postman* that had made him famous out West and "it will take another good book to put you in the money again."

Cain knew Knopf was right. The truth was that he was suffering something of an emotional crisis brought on by overwork and a variety of domestic and financial pressures. He had been going in too many directions at once—serials, short stories, novels, plays, scriptwriting—without focusing on any one thing. There were also the problems of trying to pursue a writing career and lead a normal domestic life. Cain, according to his friends and Leo, was a very good father. He loved Leo and Henrietta and treated them tenderly, always including them in dinner at home and at restaurants, drives to Santa Barbara or Malibu, parties at home. "We were always part of everything that was happening," says Leo. And "the nice thing about Jamie was whatever I would ask him about anything, he would take time to answer my questions. Whether it was geometry, history or sports, or anything." But it was clearly understood that there had to be absolute quiet in the house when Jamie was working.

Cain's health also was getting worse, although he thought it was on the mend after his stomach trouble was given a new diagnosis. The problem appeared to be caused by his gall bladder, and a simple operation seemed to have cured it. But he also had the undiagnosed ulcer, which, understandably, was not getting any better. And a tension was growing between him and Elina.

The Raphaelsons, who saw a lot of the Cains during this period, are divided in their recollection of the relationship then: Dorshka recalls very little tension and feels that not only were Cain and Elina right for each other, they got along well. Raphaelson, on the other hand, thought Elina treated Cain badly, spoke rudely to him, and "the general atmosphere was one in which she ran the place." But Cain and Elina still had an excellent rapport intellectually, and he relied on her judgment constantly in his writing. They would discuss his stories, and when she would make a remark that seemed to solve a story problem, his face would light up, Leo recalls, "and he would snap his fingers: 'That's right, Moussi, that's just the way we should do it.' And he'd rush down to the study and we'd hear his big Underwood start to clack." But Cain said that when Elina came back from Europe in 1931, they both knew something had gone out of their relationship, and apparently they never completely found it again. When they were still living in Burbank, they would sleep in separate bedrooms, although Leo thought this was partly due to Cain's desire not to disturb Elina with his late-night reading.

As for other women, although Cain was known as a man who always had an eye for a pretty leg, he had not, according to his friends, gone Hollywood and become a playboy. "He was not the kind of guy," says Raphaelson, "who would look at another woman or go over to a woman at a party and start anything—he didn't have that kind of slickness. If he fell in love with anyone, that wouldn't be how he'd do it. It would have to happen in a different way with a guy like that because he was such a homely fellow." And the typical Hollywood "quickie" was not for him. "Anyone who has rolled a couple of Hollywood picture actresses, who make a cult of profane love, especially with four-letter words," Cain said, "has discovered what a boring, somehow poetically stifling thing it really is."

In the fall of 1936, Cain had a brief job with one of the studios, but again there is no indication what he worked on—except that he wrote one friend saying this picture "is driving me nuts, this business of having to end every sentence with 'the woman I lav.' " You do not have to be much of a movie detective to guess that he was working with Charles Boyer.

He went East for the holidays, and it was a miserable trip: most of his family was sick, Mencken was in the hospital, and he did not get up to New York to see his publishing friends. He hit terrible weather coming back and arrived in California sick and discouraged. It had been only two and a half years since Cain had suddenly become the most talked-about novelist in the country and one of the most famous writers in Hollywood. But he had made less than $11,000 in 1936. He was forty-four years old, could not find a job in the studios, was in poor health, had the responsibility of a family in a disintegrating marriage, had no specific career, and was finding it impossible to write.

It was a gloomy January 1, 1937. Cain was sitting in his study on Belden Drive, feeling down and pondering how he could be so famous and broke and not be able to write. He kept thinking about Walter Lippmann's remark that when he reached a state when he could not write, he wrote—anything! Then Cain heard his own voice telling him: "How you write 'em is write 'em."

The next day he started writing a story intended as a magazine serial and, with luck, a sale to the movies. This one had to make quick money, so he tried to curb that twist in his mind which seemed to make all his stories come out censorable. He was still preoccupied with his musical evenings and singing, and with a theme he hoped someday to turn into a major work—the story of a woman whose husband walks out on her, leaving her to raise the children. The story began to take shape: a woman, a successful buyer in a department store, is married to one of those nice guys who cannot make a success of anything, though she loves him and is decent about his deficiencies. Then, by accident, he finds he has a voice and actually goes out and has a fling with an operatic career. Now his wife is unhappy; his failure endeared him to her, but she cannot stand his success.

Cain mulled it over and decided it did not work. So he made the woman a singer with a career thwarted by domestic considerations. But he did not like that, either. Then he thought: Why not make her a singer and a bitch? He did, and the story took off. He called it: "Two Can Sing," wrote it in twenty-eight days, and Geller sold it almost immediately to 20th Century-Fox for $8,000. But then, oddly enough, it did not sell to *Liberty*, which had been crying for anything as a follow-up to "Double Indemnity"—anything, it turned out, but a story about a marital conflict and singing.

Just before the sale to Fox, there was a curious little incident which revealed how close to the wire Cain was financially. In early February, an Internal Revenue agent called him to collect $34 he owed on his 1934 income tax. Cain could only pay half, but promised to pay the rest when the story he had just finished sold somewhere. When it did sell, he immediately wrote the IRS asking them to wait until he was actually paid, explaining that he did not want to borrow the money. "To borrow any amount," he wrote the IRS, "particularly a small one, is to betray one's financial position to all and sundry, and it is most important that a man dealing with picture companies be thought reasonably affluent. In other words, for this trifling amount, I don't want the word to get around that I am strapped; I lose at once all bargaining advantage, as I think you can readily see."

Cain had been talking with Geller for some time about the possibility of starting a syndicated newspaper column, to be called "Bright Gold." This one would be a little different. Editors would be free to use the Cain by-line, but he recommended against it. He sent several sample columns to Geller, using "the editorial we" instead of the "I cap," whenever possible. However, he was aware of the difficulty the idea presented: he would inevitably (an understatement) express *some* idea that might not coincide with those of the editorial page editor. Whether this was the problem or the editors simply did not like Cain's "Bright Gold" samples is not known, but Geller was unable to sell the feature.

With the money from "Two Can Sing," Cain could now afford the trip to Mexico and Guatemala, but there was no time for a leisurely boat trip. So on April 3, Cain and Elina boarded a Pan American flight that took them first to Mazatlán and then to Mexico City. The trip lasted only two weeks, during which they also visited Guatemala City and Tegucigalpa. In addition to his need to absorb some Mexican atmosphere, Cain was looking for something specific: he wanted to find a Mexican prostitute who might be the model for his heroine. And he found her in La Locha's whorehouse in Guatemala City, cutting up at the bar. "In size she was medium, but with a figure to write home about. She had curves, but with no suggestion of fat, an arresting face, with features a bit on the round and pudgy side. Her color was enchanting—a bit of dusty grey with a slight lemon tint. Her eyes were large, dark, and inclined to an occasional squint." Cain was with a friend, and when he asked who the girl might be, his guide said: "Well, I don't know her, but I can pretty well tell you a bit about her. She is probably the child of minor government people—the government is the sole business of Guatemala—living perhaps at Chichicastenango. The family aren't embarrassed at all at her way of earning a living—rather proud of her, that she's able to hold down a job, which enables her to help out a bit at home."

Cain bought her a can of asparagus, which he was told was the way to a girl's heart in Guatemala, but just to make sure he threw in a little cash. He wanted to talk, and he asked her her name, but suddenly she sensed there was something odd about this alleged Pan American official who had just arrived in Guatemala, who gave her money but was in no hurry about going upstairs. She stepped back from the bar and began a long speech in Spanish, apparently explaining to Cain that she preferred to remain nameless. She had lost all trace of the floozie who had first welcomed him: "In front of my eyes," said Cain, "she was transformed from a cheap tramp to a perfect dame. I suddenly knew I had my girl, dignified, correct, a perfect lady, and incomparably beautiful to look at."

Cain had decided that in his story the singer and whore would take refuge from a terrible storm in a church, where they would make love and he would regain his voice, but he was not sure they had such storms down there. So he checked with Mr. Gallo, head of the Mexican weather bureau, and Gallo said they never had storms like that in Mexico City. They did on the east coast. But Cain wanted his story to take place on the west coast. Gallo thought awhile and then said: "Ah, in Acapulco sometimes once every two or three years, we have such a storm." And he drew Cain pictures to show how the storm would go up one valley and down another "and sort of play shuttlecock with itself back and forth." With that, Cain and Elina rented a car and, on the drive over to Acapulco, he solved another problem. He had wanted the church in which his couple were to make love to be a locked church, which they would enter by battering the door down with a car the prostitute had won in a lottery. But, in Mexico, most churches sat up on a hill with no road approaching them, and Cain had to wonder how his hero would get the car up there. But driving to Acapulco, they saw a little church below the level of the road, and it dawned on Cain that it would be a simple matter to batter in the church door driving *downhill*.

On the way, he also wanted to find out what it was like inside a typical Indian hut. They saw them everywhere, but, as Cain said, "I never quite had the nerve to proposition them to let me in." Elina went in one, however, quickly gained the confidence of the Indian woman inside, and came out with a very accurate account of what went on in such a mud hut. One thing she learned was that Indians frequently put eggs on the altar of a god. And in his novel, Cain decided he would have the Mexican whore put eggs at the foot of the crucifix. "All this seemed to me to have a great deal of quality," Cain said, "and to have some bearing on the general theme of the book, which was the triumph of a primitive Mexican girl who was wise—though ignorant—over the more complicated, apparently civilized world of the other characters."

They finally reached Acapulco, which, in 1937, was nothing but "a hotel with a string of adobe cabanas up the side of a hill, a fissure in the rocks that the ocean washed against, that boys dived into, a small platform from which the spectators watched the show—and that was all." But it was all he needed. Cain not only had his characters and locale, he felt he had absorbed enough Mexican atmosphere to make the story ring true. He was also affected by Mexico, "a tragically backward country," he wrote Lippmann. "I had the most dismal feeling while I was there," which may explain why the Cains never moved to Mexico permanently, as they had been contemplating in 1936.

Returning to Hollywood, Cain was now ready to start work on what would eventually become his most controversial story. It took off with the usual Cain start: "I was in Tupinamba, having a bizcocho and coffee when this girl came in." But he began to have trouble in the early pages, especially writing about the singer. "It turns out all those exciting moments in the opera house aren't exciting on paper," he wrote one correspondent, "and how the hell you write a novel about a singer and leave most of that out, I don't know."

At the end of some days of writing, he would flop into his bed so tired he could hardly stand, and Jean, their cook, would serve his dinner in bed. As he told Mencken, "I hated it while I was writing it." His personal life was also becoming increasingly complicated by his growing friendship with Kate Cummings, perhaps the most difficult relationship in his life to understand completely, at least from a distance. Even today, Cain's stepson is very resentful toward Kate, who was older than Cain and who Leo felt had ulterior motives in her friendship. He says his mother was always pleasant to Kate and never objected when Cain would ask if she minded if he had lunch with her. But it bothered young Leo, though his mother would say: "Don't worry about it, Jamie needs to talk about things." Neither Leo nor Constance Cummings, Kate's daughter, thought Cain and Kate were having a real love affair, but Cain's later correspondence suggests otherwise. In addition to seeing her at lunch and taking her to parties, he wrote of occasionally "sneaking" off to see Kate while he was writing his novel about Mexico.

The book was finished by early July, and to add a little spice to the love scene in the church, Cain had John Sharp, the hero, make some now-famous soup consisting of iguana meat, sherry (sacramental wine from the church closet), and sliced eggs, all sprinkled with salt and pepper—essentially his old friend Henry Powell Hopkins's recipe for Maryland terrapin soup, with the iguana filling in for the terrapin.

Another much-discussed scene from the book occurs at a party in New York where Juanita, the Mexican whore, realizes that a famous conductor is her rival; while he is pretending to be a bull and Juanita is pretending to be a matador, she runs him through with her *espada*, assuming this will restore her lover's voice, which it eventually does. Then they flee to Mexico with the aid of a salty old steamer captain who had brought them to America earlier. Juanita is finally discovered and killed because Sharp, unable to stifle his powerful voice, breaks vocal silence and reveals their identities. Sharp vows never to sing again, and as Juanita's coffin is lowered into her hillside grave, "an iguana jumped out of it and went running over the rocks."

It was a powerful story, destined to arouse even more notoriety than *Postman*. At the core of the book is the conflict in Sharp between his latent homosexuality and his love for Juanita, and the impact of this struggle on his voice. Only after Cain had reassurances from both singers and doctors that there was some validity to the connection did he gain the confidence to embark on the novel. With what we know about homosexuality today, the theory is certainly questionable, but in the 1930s, Cain thought he had hit on a real discovery concerning a subject rarely discussed in public print. Furthermore, the shakiness of the premise in no way affects the story, which is very plausible as Cain tells it. Obviously he had to make Sharp's homosexuality a sometime thing, and he did this by maintaining that "every man has got five percent of that in him, if he meets the one person that'll bring it out." Still, he suspected it might be a questionable thesis, and he discussed the problem in a letter to Mencken, replying to some reservations Mencken had expressed. Cain wrote:

> The point you take exception to, I suppose is the vocal restoration through female companionship. This is an illustration of the trap a novel writer gets into every time he grazes a scientific boundary. The lamentable sounds that issue from a homo's throat when he tries to sing are a matter of personal observation, and if I could have stopped there I could have been completely persuasive, and made a point of some interest. But the theme demanded the next step, the unwarranted corollary that heavy workouts with a woman would bring out the stud horse high notes. Right there is where it goes facile and I suppose silly. Several doctors of eminence assured me that they could believe it, and pleaded with me to

write the book, as the idea interested them; all I can say is I have my serious doubts. There is something about a novel that seems to put a premium on the phony; I wish I could ring the bell at something else, but my other work seems to be competent and no more. Of course, the idiotic part is that this affront to Freud doesn't bother me much, really. What really worried the hell out of me is whether all that stuff can be played on the guitar. I checked as well as I could, but I hope to Christ no magazine asks Segovia to review it. [Note: It turned out the virtuoso guitarists all loved the book.]

Mencken replied that it was not the physiology that bothered him but the coincidences in the plot. But "the main thing is that the story tells itself magnificently. I defy any person under the rank of archbishop to read ten pages and then fail to go to the end."

When the Knopfs received the novel in July, they were ecstatic. Alfred was in Falmouth, but Blanche read it and wired Cain that it was SUPERB, and that she was taking it up with her to Falmouth. Alfred read it coming back to New York on the train and immediately wired Cain: I AM PROUD THAT MY NAME IS GOING TO BE WITH YOURS ON THIS BOOK. He also told Mencken it was a "masterpiece." Out of his enthusiasm for the book (combined with his desire to get another Cain title in the stores), Knopf decided to rush the book out by December 1, a superhuman feat for the publishing industry, even in 1937.

As usual, there were title problems. Cain's working title was *Sombra y Sol*, taken off the sides of the bullring, but this soured on him during the writing. His next choice was *Serenade*, but he thought it lacked punch. Knopf was stumped too and leaned toward *Sun and Shadow*, but they finally settled back on *Serenade*. There was no dedication. Vincent Lawrence not only had not contributed much to this one, but, as Cain said: "put on a campaign to head me off from a book about a 'goddamn fairy.' " Raphaelson, on the other hand, encouraged him all the way, and Cain acknowledged this in his inscription in Raphaelson's copy: "For Rafe: without whose belief in this I would never have written it. For things like this no thanks can be offered. I can only spread on the record the unpayable debt."

Meanwhile, Cain had become involved again with a play—the one he had discussed with Jed Harris on the train to New York, about a movie director who is murdered in a 52nd Street restaurant similar to "21." Actor-producer Anton Bundsman was interested in producing it, now called *7-11*, but he wanted Cain to make some revisions. When Cain agreed, Bundsman scheduled it for a late winter opening in New York. The gossip columnists took over the casting. The characters included a temperamental movie actress and a writer, and the word went out immediately that Lupe Velez and Robert Benchley would play the two lead roles.

Things appeared to be breaking for Cain. His serial "Two Can Sing," after bouncing around New York between magazine editors who thought it was either too strong or not strong enough, finally sold to the *American* for $5,000. And suddenly another studio job turned up—this one at MGM for $1,000 a week. Cain was assigned to producer Larry Weingarten to work on a script called *That Was No Hero*.

This time he was on the lot only four weeks—long enough, however, to be given an office in the Iron Lung with a nameplate on the door.

One morning around nine-thirty there was a knock on the door. Cain said, "Come in," the door opened, and there appeared "this collegiate-looking character, in Hollywood slacks and lounge coat."

"Mr. Cain?" said the man.

"Yes," replied Cain.

"I'm Scott Fitzgerald—just dropped in to say hello and welcome you to the lot."

"Oh, thanks."

"Well," said Fitzgerald, and backed out the door.

Then Cain got to thinking that was hardly any way to treat the great Scott Fitzgerald, so around noon he went down the hall, found Fitzgerald's name on a door, knocked, and was invited in. Fitzgerald was not doing anything; he was just walking around, no secretary with him. Cain suggested lunch, and without saying anything, Fitzgerald nodded and came out. They went to the commissary and took their seats, with Cain chatting amiably, until he realized that Fitzgerald had said nothing and was saying nothing. "He just sat staring at me."

Finally Cain said, "Well, nice seeing you," stood up, paid his check, and left. Later, someone who knew Fitzgerald—John O'Hara, Cain recalled—told Cain that Fitzgerald probably figured "you were pitying him for being a has-been and had invited him to lunch for that reason." Whatever it was, said Cain, it was the most uncomfortable hour he ever spent in his life. He never saw Fitzgerald again.

Meanwhile, *Postman* was about to make a significant contribution to the evolution of publishing. Paul Palmer at the *Mercury* press had decided to experiment with cheap paperback editions of current books to sell on the newsstands for 25 cents. This was two or three years before any of the major reprint houses tried current fiction. Cheap editions, of course, were nothing new, and Cain himself was a great admirer of the old dime novels and nickel westerns. But when Palmer wrote him that he had picked *Postman* as his first title and it was about to go on sale, Cain was irritated, not because he was opposed to cheap editions but because Knopf had not told him about the deal. He went into a sulk for a while, before Knopf convinced him that under their contract he had the authority to sell reprint rights without consulting the author. *Postman* was a big success in its first—but by no means last—paperback edition, and it encouraged Palmer to go on with additional titles.

While Cain was at MGM, there was also another new book by Lippmann, *The Good Society*—which necessitated a long analysis. And this time Cain agreed with most of what Lippmann had to say. Lippmann responded that he was pleased that Cain liked it, "For you probably will have realized that, back to our days on the *World* together, what you thought about what I did mattered very much to me. I have somehow always thought you had a subtle nose and a delicate palate."

Cain had also been keeping up his correspondence with Mencken, exchanging thoughts on food and word origins, although he had confessed to Palmer that Mencken's Red-baiting in his *Mercury* column annoyed him. He also reread *The American Language*, said he was proud to be a footnote in it, and "how a man can manage to learn so much about anything whatever is quite beyond me."

With money once again rolling in, and sensing that he had another publishing success in *Serenade*, which in turn might open up the studio doors again, Cain felt confident enough to buy a new car. He paid $1,240 for a 1937 Buick sedan, befitting transportation for a successful Hollywood writer and, maybe, Broadway playwright.

Late in the year, Cain went East to work on *7–11*. It was to be the first production of a new corporation called Almyno, backed by Richard Aldrich, Richard Meyers, and Peter Arno, and was scheduled to open on Broadway January 17, 1937. But suddenly, there were problems. Fred Keating was set as the male lead and Lupe Velez had indeed been signed to play the temperamental actress, showing her qualifications by being somewhat temperamental herself. A movie she was making in Mexico was behind schedule, and this prevented her from being in New York in December, when rehearsals for *7-11* were to begin. So there was a frantic search for a replacement, with the names of Margot Grahame and Germaine Aussey mentioned in the columns. There were also reports of "third-act trouble" created by production problems. As a result, the opening date was delayed until March, then put off until fall.

While Cain was staying at the Warwick in New York, preoccupied with his play, the reviews of *Serenade* began to appear. The new novel was creating a sensation. It stunned the reviewers, many saying it was just what you would expect from the author of *Postman*. A few thought Cain had gone too far and that the theme of the book was simply a calculated effort to shock the readers and surpass *Postman* in sensationalism. But many reviewers also praised it; for example, the mild-mannered J. Donald Adams wrote in the Sunday *New York Times* that it had substance and was "not easily set aside," although, he concluded, "I don't think Mr. Cain's tensely strung narrative method is best for a tale of substance—you can't take in the landscape at 60 miles an hour." And Lewis Gannett, in the *Herald Tribune*, still could not make up his mind about Cain. He praised the book's commentary on music, but said that although "the bare outlines of Mr. Cain's plot are consistently revolting, he manages to invest his most sordid details with glimpses of the human subconsciousness which give them much dignity."

Most reviewers had less trouble making up their minds. Despite the shocking story, sacrilegious love, and theme of male homosexuality, they agreed with the *Pittsburgh Post Gazette* that "the sensationalism of its subject matter was more than matched by the brilliance of its execution," that it was "literature of a high order." Several reviewers continued the favorable comparison with Hemingway. The *Chicago News* reviewer said *Serenade* showed that in the herd of American writers Cain was on the way up and Hemingway (after *To Have and Have Not*) was on the way down, and "the only serious competitor for the position of young bull of the herd is John Steinbeck."

Once again, James M. Cain was the center of a literary tempest. *Serenade* was one of the most widely discussed books of 1938, with people divided on whether he should have written about such a forbidden subject and on the soundness of his thesis. The medical profession did not, however, criticize it, and Cain had letters in his files from psychiatrists supporting it. And Dr. James Nielson, a Los Angeles psychiatrist, told Cain at a party one night: "You know, that story of yours, *Serenade*, is now required reading in most psychiatry courses in this country."

The book did create some personal problems. "For a while," Cain told one interviewer, "there were people who would come up to the house in pairs thinking I was a 'brother.' Well, I'm not." In fact, his own views on homosexuality were very emphatic. When one reader wrote him, implying he was behind the times in not realizing that homosexual love is as valid as any other, Cain responded flatly: "It is not. It is abnormal and the fact that the modern world refrains from persecution in no way implies that it should embrace this relationship."

The Catholic Church, not surprisingly, denounced the book. Its merits and morality were also widely debated in the literary community and gave libraries fits. One Virginia librarian says that when *Serenade* first came out she was approached by an agitated mother and father who were members of the local Baptist church. They had found the book in their daughter's room and were enraged that their money was supporting "dirty literature."

Still, the book was not selling as well as had been hoped, and Knopf wanted to launch a special advertising campaign to capitalize on the controversy it had aroused. Cain was still in New York at the time, and he vetoed the plan. "You advertise a good book—if you think it is a good book," was Cain's reply. When Knopf said of course he thought it was a good book, Cain said, "Then, to my mind that is as far as the advertising ought to go. If the controversy makes for publicity, O.K., but you do nothing to stir it up." Cain said he thought that convinced Knopf, who did go ahead with conventional advertising.

When the sales of *Serenade* suddenly tapered off at around 25,000 copies, the publisher thought the Church's indictment was primarily responsible. But Cain was more inclined to agree with a friend who speculated: "Could be that when people were reacting to the wonderful color and emotion and excitement of the first three-fourths of that story, and telling their friends about it, it went like a prairie fire. But then when they finally found out what ailed the guy, could be they froze."

"But," Cain protested, "it didn't ail him, really. Except for that one guy, the curse of his life, he was as normal as anyone else!"

"That one guy was enough."

What disturbed Cain even more was the reaction at a lunch with his scriptwriter friends, all of whom agreed that *Serenade* sagged after Juanita and Sharp escaped from New York after the murder. "So, two body blows," Cain wrote Knopf, "in vital places sank it. But that was my story and there was no way to trick it up." Knopf wrote back not to worry, that although the sales of *Serenade* had disappointed them both it was a good book and "neither of us has any right these days to feel sore about the figures it did achieve."

Serenade's falling off was all the more of a disappointment to Cain in that he had been thinking about the story for twenty years. Of course it did not sell to the movies—at least not immediately—because the studios knew there was no way to fix it up for the Hays Office. At one point, Cain and his lawyer, Martin Gang, gave serious thought to suing the movie industry on the grounds that the Hays Office ban was an infringement on the First Amendment and a violation of the antitrust laws. "I look back on this with some regret," Gang says. "But he could not afford a long litigation and the suit was abandoned." Eventually *Serenade* did sell to Warner Brothers, and Jerry Wald made a pale version of it, starring Mario Lanza.

Whatever Cain's disappointment, the book had its impact, and with all the talk in the columns about his yet-to-be-produced Broadway play, and the success of "Double Indemnity" and "Two Can Sing" in the magazines, Cain found he was again "hot." Back in New York, in fact, the Morris Agency was screaming for more Cain manuscripts. Robert Goodhue at Morris wrote him, "Your market is almost unlimited—practically every editor in the business is anxious to get you and the time is ripe to push your price up to the top." A new serial, Goodhue thought, should bring $25,000—and double for motion pictures, by the current rule of thumb. But he also pleaded for short stories.

So Cain settled down to think about more stories, but before he could finish one he was offered another scriptwriting job, with Universal Studios working on a Walter Wanger production. It was based on a successful French film entitled *Pepe le Moko*, directed by Julien Duvivier and starring Jean Gabin. Wanger intended to call it *Algiers*, and it would star Charles Boyer and a young Austrian actress working in her first American film. Her stage name was Hedy Lamarr, and Cain thought she was the most beautiful creature he had ever seen.

It looked like a sure-fire combination—except that script problems developed almost immediately. Wanger and his director, John Cromwell, wanted to follow the original French film almost shot by shot. "This was impossible," said Cain, who complained that he was unable to develop a free-flowing narrative with someone else's script. So, after four $1,000 weeks, Cain was dropped and Wanger brought in John Howard Lawson (later one of the famous "Hollywood Ten" who defied a Congressional committee investigating Communism in Hollywood). The first twenty minutes of dialogue in *Algiers* remained Cain's, however, and this gave him one of his few credits as a screenwriter. When he eventually saw *Algiers* in a theater, he noted a lot of laughter from the audience in the first twenty minutes, but none after that. He always felt Lawson's section was too heavy.

So Cain returned to his Belden Drive study to resume his magazine writing career. And despite having been fired once again from a studio, he was apparently in no way discouraged about the peripatetic life he was leading. In fact, he rather enjoyed it, as can be seen from a curious exchange of letters with Wolcott Gibbs in which he tried to persuade *The New Yorker* writer to come to Hollywood. "If you are interested," he wrote Gibbs, "this is the way things are done. The agent is Hollywood's attention-caller, and a man without an agent is a sort of outlaw asteroid drifting around in space, undiscovered, unlocated, and invisible to the strongest telescopes. Being suspected of a mercenary attitude toward your work needn't bother you: It hasn't occurred to anybody out here that there can be any other, and very possibly they are right. . . . For my own part, I manage to get along with them fairly well, although I am one of those who really wasn't intended to write pictures, and until lately, I haven't done well at it. I soak them a pretty good price, and get it because I am allegedly successful in other fields. I work a few weeks a year, and collect the main part of my living expenses, which leaves me free to do my other work without having to worry much about the rent. It works for me, I don't go nuts, and I don't have to get a headache every day over the policies of some publication that happens to have me on the payroll. In other words, for five or six years I have managed to racketeer a living without having a boss. If I could make a suggestion to you, it would be that your writing is developing to a point where you ought to consider whether you ought not do it as your main activity, in the years when you can't really turn on the juice, rather than as a sideline of a somewhat routine job, however much you may be the white-headed boy at the moment. Having said that much, I shut up."

Gibbs thanked Cain for the advice, saying he had signed a contract with Leland Howard and that he might be willing to go out that summer if Howard found him a job, but that for various reasons "I guess I'm better off right here."

Cain wrote back to Gibbs: "What to do is a riddle. There is such a thing as knowing when you are well off and there is such a thing as playing still bigger chips when your luck is running, as yours seems to be." He said he couldn't see what Gibbs had to lose and "probably the real truth is I'd like to see you out here."

Back in his study, possibly with Charles Boyer's accent and Hedy Lamarr's haunting beauty still on his mind, he was having trouble focusing on a story. He could hardly have been discouraged by a note from the *American* editor, Albert Benjamin, who deplored the news that Cain had "temporarily deserted magazine fiction" for Hollywood. He pleaded the case for his millions of readers who wanted more Cain, saying the mail inspired by "Two Can Sing" had been overwhelming and it was "the most popular short novel we have ever published."

But what to write? He queried one editor, who expressed interest in a "fluke conductor" idea, telling him he might give it a try. He also considered a newspaper story—James M. Cain style. "My objection to most newspaper stories," he wrote an editor, "is that they are always about the crooked politicians, the crusading owner, and the great story that is going to blow the ship out of the water, which is to say, about a largely imaginary state of affairs. I would like to do some stories that mirror the daily routine of a paper, the fires, accidents, and parades that really occupy the staff."

But the conductor and the newspaper stories were abandoned when Cain finally managed to focus on a story he had earlier discarded. Years ago, he recalled, he was having lunch with Kenneth Littauer, a *Collier's* editor, who had asked him: "How about a Cinderella story with a modern twist?" At the time, Cain thought, "Oh, God, what a formula!" But that was in the rarefied intellectual climate of New York. Out here in the Hollywood dream factory it seemed plausible. He began to speculate: What about a modern Cinderella? What about a waitress marrying a Harvard man?

He started to write, but before he was many pages into the story MGM suddenly wanted him to write a script. So Cain put the modern Cinderella aside and went to work at Metro, where his "hotness" was reaffirmed. "There was a man on the lot," he said, "with a face not even a mother could be sure of, who when I'd appear without hotness would pass me on the walk to the commissary with a frigid, distant bow, and say: 'Mr. . . . . Cain—?' But if perchance I was hot, this same faceless object would stop on seeing me, gurgle ecstatically, and exclaim: 'Jim! Jim! Long time no see! It's great having you back—just great having you back!' I would pass him, say 'Kid, I love you,' and continue to my office. And then I would ask myself was he there? Did he exist? Or was he something the Special Effects Department ran up, as a pleasant little feature for my first day on the lot?" But now from everybody it was "Hi, Jim, it's great to have you back." And it was great to be back, because the script was an intriguing one for Cain. It was called *Stand Up and Fight*—a Mervyn LeRoy production, directed by W. S. Van Dyke (*San Francisco, The Thin Man*) and starring Wallace Beery and Robert Taylor. Metro was trying to remake Taylor into a he-man after several pretty-boy roles, primarily by mixing Taylor up in three bruising fights—two with Beery and one classic barroom brawl.

The story was based on a novel by Forbes Parkhill and was set in the 1850s, primarily in Cumberland, Maryland (where Cain once worked for the State Roads Commission), when the Baltimore and Ohio was pushing west through the Alleghenies, challenging the stagecoach lines. Robert Taylor plays a Baltimore aristocrat who loses his estate and is forced to find a job. He ends up working for a stagecoach company owned by Florence Rice and managed by Beery, a tough ex–mule skinner also in league with a couple of heavies (Barton MacLane and Charles Bickford) who trade in stolen slaves. When Taylor learns this, he goes into action on the side of the railroad, and the story starts high-balling along to a climactic race between a locomotive and a stagecoach. MGM spared no expense to create the proper mood, reconstructing two 1850 Cumberland towns, one on MGM's "60 acres," another on location, complete with railroad tracks and Conestoga wagons. The studio also imported an 1837 Galloway locomotive from the Baltimore Museum, along with two Imlay coaches actually used to carry Abraham Lincoln from Springfield to Washington for his inaugural in 1861.

In addition to the historical lore, which appealed to Cain, his old friend from the *World*, Laurence Stallings, was now under contract to Metro and worked briefly on the script, although the three writers of credit on *Stand Up and Fight* were Cain, Jane Murfin, and Harvey Ferguson. The nine weeks (at $1,000 a week) were as educational as they were profitable and, among other things, Cain learned for the first time that pronunciation in the dialogue has to be emphasized in the script. He had dictated a scene to his secretary and was about to leave the room to give her a chance to type when she asked: "Shall I nigger it up?"

"Shall you what?" Cain responded, quite startled.

"Well, that's what we call it, niggering it up, when we leave off the *g*'s and stuff: 'You goin' home,' 'stead of 'going home.'"

Cain replied, "No, just type it straight. I never, but never indicate pronunciations. I write what the character thinks he's saying."

Later, Cain found this could create problems. Beery did not like to memorize a script, so he would have his dialogue put on a blackboard and read it while playing a scene, "the real reason," said Cain, "he'd be peering off to one side, meditating villainy, when he was actually reading his lines." When Cain finally saw *Stand Up and Fight* he was startled to hear Beery, the tough, uneducated manager of a stagecoach line, elegantly reciting Cain's perfect English as it had been copied on the blackboard—one reason, perhaps, why some of the reviewers said *Stand Up and Fight* would have been better if there was a little more "brightness in its talk." They also thought it was at least fifteen minutes too long. Otherwise, the critics thought it was a rousing, exciting spectacle—something of an Eastern Western.

Jack Rubin, then working at MGM, also played an important role in Cain's cinematic education. The two writers discussed the script in Rubin's office and Rubin would start walking around the room and say "BOOM, we're in the drawing room" and "BOOM, they're out in the moonlight" and "BOOM, we're into the chase." At first this annoyed Cain, but then one day Rubin tried to explain it to him: "Listen, Jim, I understand why you shy away from all this picture talk. But there's a reason for this 'interior' . . . 'exterior,' 'street,' 'medium,' 'shot.' Lighting for an exterior is a very different problem from an interior. The kind of shot gives the director a general idea of whether it's a two-shot, three-shot, a medium shot, a full shot or a close shot, or a moving shot or a dolly shot or a boom shot. All those different kinds of ways of using the camera you should put in there so at least they know what you have in mind. They may do it differently themselves when they begin to shoot it, but at least they know what you're trying to do. Also, day lighting and night lighting are two different concepts of lighting, and you must remember that your script is not only read by me and the director but a copy goes to the production department, a copy goes to the front office, a copy to Louis B.'s office, to wardrobe, camera, casting, so you must get accustomed to doing it that way or you'll send everyone nuts."

Cain said that after this advice from Rubin, his scriptwriting began to be more acceptable to the studios. But, curiously, Rubin's advice was at sharp variance with what scriptwriter John Lee Mahin was telling him. Mahin told Cain he had been quick to learn that the kind of thing Rubin was talking about was nonsense. "Dissolve, fade out—it's all crap. I never wrote 'close shot,' 'long shot,' 'medium shot' on anything. I told Scott Fitzgerald the same thing. It's all horseshit. You write your story; you're a storyteller; write the dialogue, where it should take place and if you have a good director he'll start with a close-up and pull back, or whatever."

Cain's assignment at MGM ended August 6, and two days later he and Elina boarded an airplane for Washington, D.C. Cain's father, now seventy-seven years old, had been in failing health for the last five years and was extremely ill. When they arrived at the family's Hawthorn Street house in Baltimore, Cain found his mother holding up and the situation such that he and Elina could feel free to leave everything in his sisters' hands and run up to Cohasset on Cape Cod, where *7-11* was scheduled for a late August production.

In Cohasset, Cain was pleasantly surprised to find his old drinking pal Sinclair Lewis, appearing on the stage in a summer stock production of his own, *It Can't Happen Here*. Both that play and Cain's *7-11* were being produced by Alexander Dean, and Lewis had aroused so much attention that *7-11* had to be held over a week. Once the excitement died down and he was no longer the center of attention, Lewis went into a sulk inspiring, among other things, a long diatribe against Dean, delivered to Cain. Cain did not agree with Lewis's assessment of Dean and said that following "my third or fourth 'I-like-him-all-right, he-always-treated-me-fine,' his manner changed and after that we rarely saw each other."

When *7-11* was finally staged in Cohasset, starring Nancy Carroll, Sheila Barrett, and Barry Sullivan, it played to sell-out crowds. Everyone was encouraged, and Cain was writing his Hollywood friends that it "looks fairly good." But, of course, it needed more revisions, so it was back to Baltimore for more work—and a grim vigil awaiting his father's death.

By early October, all revisions on the play were finished and it was sent to New York, where the producers were considering a winter opening on Broadway. Cain then started to work on "A Modern Cinderella," the serial he had put aside when he took the MGM assignment in June. He dictated the manuscript to a Baltimore secretary named Sarah Goodwin, putting it in the first-person voice of his heroine, even though the Cinderella love story was almost secondary to a complex plot involving labor difficulties and a strike.

Meanwhile, Elina had to return to Hollywood. Henrietta had fallen ill in the spring, and although she was now back in school and appeared to have recovered, Elina felt she should be with her daughter. When she returned home, she started writing Cain letters expressing concern about their financial situation and making it plain she wanted to be in the East with him. Cain wrote back: "You are not to sublet the house, or take any job, or anything else screwy, and you are not to make any more dirty cracks about my being in the East. We went all over this many times and you have repeatedly said this is the kind of life you want to lead. . . . On my end, everything has gone according to schedule; the play is done, the serial well under way. You are West and I am East for one reason only—Henrietta."

Two days later, he was a little less severe: "I think perhaps that you have some squawk," he wrote home. "But at this point, I can't get anywhere by hopping from one thing to another. In the past, we have only won by saying: This is it, and sticking to it. So let me stick with this play and do the serial while it is cooking up and soon I know we'll be better off and together again."

In mid-October, Cain's father developed pneumonia, recovered momentarily, then died when his heart gradually weakened from arteriosclerosis. "All of us felt very near him toward the end," Cain wrote Elina. "He stopped being peevish and was quite dignified and resigned and turned to us more and more. We all feel we shall remember him so much more affectionately as a result of all this, so there is nothing to wish different from what it was." His mother had prepared for what Cain said was "a state occasion," but he told her she should stop imagining a big public event, that most people probably thought he was already dead and the rest would not care. "Antonio Scotti died the other day," he said, "one of the great baritones in the history of opera; in his home city, Naples. Seven people came to the funeral."

But at the cemetery, Cain was astonished. "The old newspaper reporter" counted the crowd—1,200 people! Even more impressive was the effect the funeral and the number of people had on Mrs. Cain. They buoyed her up so, she was able to keep her own grief under control, and Cain felt chastened for what he had said the day before. To Cain, funerals had always been something of "an undertakers' and florists' fiesta," but no more. As far as his mother was concerned, "a great man had died—something she had known all along, but it helped that others thought so."

Dr. Cain had had a distinguished and admirable career: he helped build two small colleges, and when personal problems caused his break with Washington College he started anew with a major insurance company and was successful in his job until his retirement. Cain respected his father tremendously, especially for the guts he showed in starting a new career at the age of fifty-seven. However, there can be little doubt that Cain did not feel close to his father, that he even harbored a lifelong hostility for the man. He made no effort to hide his resentment at his father for encouraging him in the role of the local *wunderkind* and rushing him through school, where he had felt a "midget among giants." And he told at least one person that he always felt his father disapproved of him, both as a child and as a writer. Jamie Cain never forgave his father for that rejection.

After his father's funeral, Cain stayed for a while in Baltimore to finish "A Modern Cinderella," ignoring Elina's advice not to make any cracks about the labor leaders or unions. "Otherwise the magazines won't buy it, and after all this is purely commercial stuff," she wrote. "I hope for your sake that you win your battle. I am ready any time to meet the conqueror with the band."

Elina still had misgivings about *7-11*, and they proved well founded. The play's backers were now beginning to see problems, and their objections were summed up by director Harris and relayed to Cain by the Morris Agency: "Harris calls the plot confusing. He says the characters are not established. They're plunged into the midst of situations . . . the action plan troubles him. He can't visualize the set . . . the action piles on without breathing spells for the audience. . . ." Other than that, Harris said, it was great; it had good background and fine dialogue. But Cain was beginning to get that old feeling. "Every time I fool with a play, I get thrown out of step for God knows how long," he wrote one editor. And to a friend he lamented: "What keeps writers poor is writing plays. . . . Between the loss of income while you are writing them and the hotel expenses in New York, it is stupid to write them at all."

But Cain never could resist the lure of the theater. He met again with Harris, who convinced him the play still could be made into a success, but that the script needed more work from Cain. He estimated this would take at least another month.

Cain explained his situation: Elina was on the Coast, he was in the East, they were not too happy apart, and their money was running out. It would take at least two weeks to finish his serial, and if it did not sell at once he would have to go back to Hollywood and find a studio job. If it did sell, however, he would be all right. He would have the money to bring Elina East and finish the play. And, while it was going into production, he and Elina would take a much-needed vacation in Europe, then come back to New York for rehearsals.

He also explained the situation to Elina, adding: "I have a horror of breaking in on this serial now. . . . It is going very well and except for the unsatisfactory uncertainties of the next two or three weeks, there is no reason for abandoning it." As to the play: "Doing more picture work means nothing to me, except to make money we need to live on. Having a hit play on Broadway does." He concluded: "I am terribly lonesome for you, and am spitting on my hands to get this thing done so we can be together here, East. Neither of us cares much if it does cost something, do we, so long as we are together and enjoying the life? Write me now and tell me to go ahead, and then I promise it won't be too long before we see the whales in the Atlantic Ocean."

Cain finished the serial on November 2 and sent it to *Collier's*, then another copy to Elina, with instructions to tell Geller to get it moving at the studios at once, without waiting for *Collier's'* reaction. "Feel friendly toward me," he said, "I have really worked hard on this one." Then he went to bed and slept for two days. When he felt better, he wrote Elina that he planned to go up to New York to finish the play and expected her to come East if the serial sold immediately. "Please don't be angry at me. I have worked like a dog and had only romantic thoughts about you and the little family. I have stuck on the diet faithfully . . . and my health is much better. Now write me a sweet letter—your own handwriting, no typing—and say you love me." It was his last letter home while in the East.

These letters Cain and Elina exchanged in 1938 are among the few between them still in existence, probably the only ones. They show a remarkable closeness; she still called him Jamie, but he was now calling her Poupi, rather than Moussi, and his dependence on her and affection for her are quite clear.

Cain finished the revisions on *7-11*, but *Collier's* rejected "A Modern Cinderella," a deep disappointment after all the work Cain had put in on the serial and given his high expectations. So Cain worked two more weeks on the play, left it with Harris, and flew back to Hollywood, where Geller had found him an assignment with producer Gene Markey, who had just finished *Wee Willie Winkie* and was working on *Suez*. There is no record of whether Cain's job was on *Suez* or some other project, but whatever it was, he did not work on it long. By now he was beginning to realize that the pace he had been keeping since New Year's Day 1937, when he had decided "How you write 'em is write 'em," was exhausting. He had been writin' 'em too fast—a major novel, two magazine serials, three script jobs, and many revisions of his play. He was all written out. So when "A Modern Cinderella" suddenly sold to Universal Pictures for $17,500, he quit his job with Markey so he and Elina could take that vacation in Europe. There were some blocked funds in Nazi Germany, money which could be spent only there—and some of the trip could be written off as a promotion tour. "It is high time I surveyed some of my fields of influence," he wrote Knopf, requesting the names of his European publishers.

There was, of course, the problem of the gathering storm in Europe, and as Cain wrote one friend, "I am not fond of wars." But they decided to go anyway, to combine the European trip with a leisurely drive across America in their 1937 Buick. Before he left, Cain wrote Knopf that he was planning to start a new book when he returned, one "that has been cooking for some time." On December 26, with *7-11* apparently dead for the season, Jamie and Poupi boarded the *Normandie* in New York and sailed out into the Atlantic to see the whales.

13

FINNEY PYLORECTOMY—"A VERY GREAT EVENT"

"I'm four parts Irish," James M. Cain once said, "and yet the Irish give me a pain in the neck." Why? He did not know. But a visit to the old country would, he thought, help him find out. He and Elina arrived in England in January 1939, and after a couple of days in London they flew over to Dublin. To help him track down his ancestors, Cain hired a police sergeant, retired from Dublin Castle, the Irish equivalent of Scotland Yard, to do research, but he learned very little from the detective. He also thought fellow writer Seán O'Faoláin might help him understand the Irish. So he called O'Faoláin and said: "My name is Cain."

"K-a-n-e?" O'Faoláin asked.

"No. C-a-i-n."

There was a pause and then the writer asked: "You wouldn't be the postman?"

The two Irishmen hit it off immediately, with O'Faoláin seeing completely through Cain's outward toughness to the gentleness within. They had a fine time in Dublin, O'Faoláin rolling his *r*'s at Cain for a week and denying his accusations that the Gaelic street names were phony. Then the Cains returned to London and O'Faoláin flew over to see them. They had a few drinks in a pub, a session that ended in a violent, shouting argument. They parted friends, however, and exchanged letters for many years, although Cain never saw O'Faoláin again. And he never did find out why he disliked the Irish generally.

The Cains also flew to Paris and visited a few European cities, where Cain was surprised to learn just how famous he was in Europe. His books were translated and selling everywhere. "I remember being in Paris in 1939," Ruth Goetz recalled, "and passing the American Express Company office and seeing in the window the American celebrities . . . a picture of Jim and Elina arriving from Hollywood. They were interviewed everywhere and Cain was treated primarily as a famous author, rather than as a successful Hollywood screenwriter." One interview, however, caused them considerable trouble: A Swedish newspaper misquoted Cain in such a way as to suggest that he was violently antagonistic to Hitler—which he was, of course. But he should not have said it when he was about to enter Germany, because when the article appeared it created such a furor that the Cains decided not to risk a visit to Germany, despite the impounded funds waiting there.

They were back in Baltimore by early February, and after Cain underwent a brief stay in the hospital to see what could be done about his troublesome stomach, they began an auto trip to Hollywood, winding down through West Virginia, where Cain wanted to spend a little time among the mountain people, gathering background for a novel based on an idea that had occurred to him on one of his automobile trips in Southern California. In the early thirties, at a roadside place between the Ventura Pike and the San Fernando Road, run by a family of West Virginia mountaineers, he and another writer had been waiting to have a flat tire fixed. The mountaineers were friendly and there was a cute little child crawling around on the floor. The mother sat down and kept them company for a while, but they never did see the father. Later, back on the road, Cain's friend said: "Did something funny strike you about that family?"

"Well, they certainly were an odd bunch to be in California," replied Cain.

"I kept wondering," Cain's friend said, "who the father of the child was and if maybe the child wasn't the reason they left West Virginia, so the community wouldn't have anything to say about the child?" Cain kept thinking about this for years, trying to figure how he would handle the theme of incest in a novel. He even had a title: *The Butterfly*.

While driving around the mountains early in 1939, Cain became lost and drove into Sharples, location for the headquarters of the Boone County Coal Company, run by his old friend William Wiley. When he inquired after Wiley at the company office, a gentleman told him: "I'm sorry, but Colonel Wiley died some time ago."

"Oh," said Cain. "Where is Mrs. Wiley living?"

"Mrs. Wiley died two days before he did. In fact, he was dressing for Mrs. Wiley's funeral when he was stricken."

Commenting on Wiley's death in his memoirs, Cain wrote: "God writes stories much better than we humans are able to think of."

Back at his typewriter in his study on Belden Drive, Cain found that *The Butterfly* simply would not move. He wrote several people about the trouble he was having—but before he could resolve his block he discovered he was "hot" again at the studios. One reason was the release of *Wife, Husband and Friend*, the 20th Century-Fox picture based on "Two Can Sing." It was previewed at Grauman's Chinese Theatre on February 9 and received good reviews. With a cast including Warner Baxter, Loretta Young, Binnie Barnes, Cesar Romero, Eugene Pallette, and J. Edward Bromberg, it could hardly miss. John Stahl was the producer; the script was by Nunnally Johnson and Dwight Taylor. Frank Nugent, in the *New York Times*, called it the "pleasantest show of the week . . . good fun all the way."

But the biggest boost to Cain's fame were all the interviews in the Amsterdam, Stockholm, Helsinki, and London papers, news of which had filtered back to California. Most Hollywood writers of the 1930s were unknown east of Pasadena, and as the studio brass learned what a celebrity Cain was in Europe they treated him with a new respect. Cain could even tell one producer who wanted him to work on a little turkey: "I'm world famous without doing one of your goddamned B pictures."

He could pick and choose assignments now, at least for a while. Eventually he accepted an invitation from Universal to write (at $1,000 a week) an original comedy to take place on board ship. The idea appealed to Cain, following his return from a round-trip ocean voyage. Universal had also hired John Stahl to do Cain's "A Modern Cinderella." The serial, which still had not sold to a magazine, had been put through a typical Hollywood transformation after Irene Dunne, whom Universal had picked for the leading lady, said she would not take the role unless her co-star was Charles Boyer—the one actor in Hollywood, according to Cain, who could not play his Harvard WASP. Rather than offend or lose Miss Dunne, Universal signed Boyer and made his character a famous European concert pianist. It was also in Irene Dunne's contract that she had to sing at least one song, so they made the waitress an aspiring vocalist. This was not too bad, Cain said, because his heroine, if she did sing, would have a voice just about as bad as Miss Dunne's.

After Stahl had been working on the script awhile, Cain ran into the director on the Universal lot and told him he was glad he himself did not have to wrestle with it. Stahl nodded as if to say he was having plenty of trouble, and then Cain added that "making that guy into a hero . . . was more than I was able to do after plenty of time trying." Stahl agreed that was the problem.

Later, Cain and Stahl had another conversation about the script. Cain made several suggestions, and Stahl, indicating he had laryngitis and could not talk, whispered that he would call Cain later, but never did. Cain also was approached by Taylor, who said he wanted to get together and discuss the script. But when they met for lunch the next day, all Taylor talked about was his grievances with Stahl. Cain found it a curious lunch, but thought nothing more of it. It would be some time before he would learn what was really bothering Taylor.

A few weeks later, Cain completed his script—titled *The Victoria Docks at 8*—but was abruptly fired after the front office read it. Why, Cain never completely understood, though he was convinced it was because the script was too good. His producer was as astonished as Cain and defended him all the way. "The whole thing," Cain said, "seems to center around a general doubt as to whether the front office boys can read." A few producers rallied to his side, but they could not save him, and Cain's tour of duty at Universal was over after a little more than four weeks.

So, early in May, Cain was back in his study, chained to the typewriter and finding it hard to focus on anything. "One of the big things in writing," he wrote a friend, "is always to have a future ready; something to look forward to. When I got back from this trip I had nothing ahead."

Perhaps to help break the paralysis, he wrote Seán O'Faoláin a long letter commenting on the Irish writer's books, which he had now read, and encouraging him, as he had Wolcott Gibbs, to cash in on some of that easy Hollywood money. "How about a little number for the American trade? . . . A little story with an American hook up, a nice little job in 60,000 words, about the right length for magazine publication, book publication to follow at once, mimeographed copies to be submitted to the pictures—and then maybe I can have you and the whole O'Faoláin family out here with me, perched on the next hill, with you trying to keep your face straight while you dictate 'Fade in.' It's not art, but it's money, and the older I get the more I wonder whether the two are not the same thing." O'Faoláin never accepted the invitation.

Before long, Cain was able to break his writer's block and start two projects, both of which Morris eventually sold to *Liberty*: one of his finest short stories—"The Girl in the Storm"—about a nineteen-year-old hobo and a young girl who are trapped by a flood and take refuge in a half-built house, fixing a tasty meal with ingredients stolen from the supermarket next door; and a serial—"Money and the Woman"—which *Liberty* bought for $4,000. The serial was indirectly inspired by his old friend from the *Baltimore Sun*,

Clarke Fitzpatrick, who was now employed by the same insurance firm his father had worked for—the United States Fidelity and Guaranty Company. Fitzpatrick had asked for comments on a study he had written, "1001 Embezzlers," and Cain had responded with an excellent critique, and then came up with the idea for the serial—about a bank examiner who mortgages his house to help a woman return $9,000, which her two-timing husband had embezzled from a bank. It is a taut suspense story with a more upbeat ending than was usual for Cain. (The following year, the ending helped sell the story to Warner Brothers.)

Cain then went to work revising "A Modern Cinderella," which had now been rejected by every major magazine in the country—ten of them, according to the Morris Agency's count. Elina, Cain decided, had been right: he should have been more careful how he treated the unions; apparently his handling of organized labor in the story was preventing its sale. But even with revisions, "A Modern Cinderella" never did sell to the magazines.

Cain's stomach was now bothering him so much it was affecting his work; over the last six months of 1939 he was in and out of hospitals. And attending the premiere of *When Tomorrow Comes*, at the Pantages Theater in Hollywood in August, probably did not make him feel any better. The movie had apparently created horrendous problems at Universal. The script Stahl finally accepted had been written by Dwight Taylor, a Cain admirer, and Cain's original story was now hardly recognizable, except for one curious scene which took place in a church on Long Island during a hurricane. In that scene Irene Dunne and Boyer, although not married, make love, thinking they will not survive the storm. There was nothing like it in "Modern Cinderella"; rather, as James Francis Crow, writing in a Hollywood paper, noted, "the situation here is oddly similar to one in Cain's sensational and sinewy *Serenade*."

Cain decided the movie was a plagiarism and had his lawyers meet with Universal's lawyers. The confrontation proved a standoff, with the studio refusing to settle and Cain not wanting to undertake the expense of a trial, especially as he became increasingly convinced that his case would be hard to prove. So 1939 came to an end with Cain once again at low ebb. "I have been so harassed by illness for the last few months," he wrote Knopf, "and the consequent money problems it brought with it, that I have had to suspend work [on *The Butterfly*] and may not get back to it for some time. A magazine serial is my total output since summer and unless something breaks in pictures, I have to do still another one before I am free to go back to [it]."

Knopf was not the only one prodding him to keep at the typewriter. Seán O'Faoláin also wrote from Ireland inquiring about his work: "I devoutly hope that you are in a cheerful mood and can laugh at me, and that you aren't hard up, down in the mouth, out at heel, or otherwise bent or dented from your normal tough-guy-heart-of-a-baby-self. What the hell are you doing anyway? Here is the foremost American genius and not a peep out of him since I last heard you were about to spring a masterpiece on us. God, there's few enough of us trying our best. Don't you dare shut up and go mum."

But Cain was indeed going mum at the typewriter, and despite O'Faoláin's encouragement that he go after that masterpiece, when a studio job developed at Warner Brothers he accepted it. In January, the studio bought "Money and the Woman" for $3,500 and hired Cain (still at $1,000 per week) to work on the script. Cain wrote an outline that adhered closely to the original serial, but at an early story conference, Bryan Foy, one of Warner's low-budget directors, vetoed it on the grounds that because the heroine was married to another man, the Hays Office would never pass it. Then another director, William Jacobs, who had made one of the first Sherlock Holmes films in Hollywood, took over and, after an all-day story conference that Cain said had everyone snarling at one another, announced: "Briney, I'm going to do this thing exactly as Cain wrote it. I've been hearing too much from the readers of *Liberty* to do it any other way. Briney, did you know that 'Double Indemnity' put eight million new circulation on that magazine? It did. I checked."

So in the end it was decided to do the movie Cain's way, and the story outline managed to pass the Hays Office. And then, says Cain, to "get it exactly as Cain wrote it, they closed Cain out." The screenplay was written by Robert Presnell (who had collaborated on *My Man Godfrey*), and the movie, which they also titled *Money and the Woman*, was released in October, with Jeffrey Lynn and Brenda Marshall playing the lead roles. The film was quickly tagged a "B" picture and dismissed by *Variety* and the *Times* as dull fare—a good story to which something had happened on its way to celluloid. But at least Cain had what he needed—$10,000 to finance a return to his typewriter. Perhaps inspired by O'Faoláin, he abandoned *The Butterfly*, which was causing him nothing but frustration, and settled down to work on his first "serious" novel. Encouraged by the success of "Brush Fire" and "The Girl in the Storm," he decided to write this one in the more conventional third person. "It is a different kind of book from any I have ever attempted," he wrote Blanche Knopf, who had commiserated over problems he was having. He went on to say: "I talk as though it were some extremely new and original departure; actually it is nothing but a straight novel, but it is new for me and considerably longer than anything I have done previously."

It is curious that he shifted from *The Butterfly* to another novel, because it was at about this time that Cain met Thornton Wilder again and with his help resolved the problem he had been having with incest. The two had first met in 1929, at the reunion of the Yale class of '84, of which both their fathers had been members. Wilder had just published *Bridge of San Luis Rey*, and Cain was still a struggling playwright and editorial writer, but he and Thornton immediately took a liking to each other. Their fathers obviously believed in God, Country, and Yale, "with the distinct understanding," said Cain, "it's not whether you win that counts, but How You Play the Game. What Thornton, Miss Isabel [Wilder's sister, also present that weekend], and I believed in was obviously nothing at all, with smart-cracks."

Although they did not become close friends, the two writers remained in touch, and when Cain was in New York in 1938 they got together again. Now Wilder was in Hollywood helping with the movie version of *Our Town* and causing a furor at the Brown Derby and the Iron Lung by agreeing to work for nothing. Cain had called him immediately for dinner, but Wilder could not come.

A few weeks later, Wilder called Cain and asked him and Elina to his place for cocktails. Cain cautioned Elina to dress carefully, reminding her of the Dorothy Parker–Campbell bash they had recently attended—an intimate little affair for eight hundred people. "This is their [the Wilders'] big payback stinkaroo for everyone who's entertained them while they've been here, even for those who tried to and couldn't," he told Elina. "And this guy is much more important than Dorothy ever was so everyone's going to be there, the biggest fish in this sea." Elina put on a smart, dark blue suit and Cain put on his "grass green special," made by MacIntosh, his tailor on Hollywood Boulevard. It was made of rajah silk and had little white darts in it. "Oh, I was really turned out," he said.

They drove down to Franklin Street where Wilder had an apartment, and right away Cain knew something was wrong. There were no lanterns on the patio and no cars parked on the street. Instead of a big bash, it was just dinner for the four of them: Thornton and his sister, Isabel, and the Cains. Elina was enchanted. Cain and Wilder were soon talking shop, and when Wilder asked him what he was working on, Cain told him about the difficulty he was having with incest in his novel set in the coal mines of West Virginia. In their earlier meetings, Cain said, Wilder had always taken an "aw-shucks I just hit it lucky" approach to his work. But now he dropped that mask and showed that underneath "he was the most murderously high on the number one ball in the side pocket professional that you ever saw." Wilder listened to Cain's story idea and then said something that would eventually break the block that had been holding back *The Butterfly*. "Those nineteenth-century novelists, Jim, they knew all about incest, knew all about everything. They were professionals. But they never quite met that issue head on, and I wouldn't if I were you. Instead of the father wanting to lay Susie, it's always an uncle. They get the quality of incest, but not quite the slimy thing itself."

Cain always admired Wilder and his way of looking at things. *The Bridge of San Luis Rey* was for Cain "a quest for point, for meaning of it all, for the divine plan that explained the fall of a bridge in Peru that caused the death of five people. But at the end it is perfectly clear there was *no* point to it all, or divine plan, or anything of that kind. Thornton, I would say, was himself all the point that it needed: A rich, delightful human being." Elina also admired Wilder, and on the way home from their visit she kept calling him "ein Herr" and Miss Isabel "ganz eine Dame." All Cain could think of was what Wilder had told him about handling incest.

But for now, he was deeply preoccupied with another book: his first serious novel, about "the great American institution that never gets mentioned on the Fourth of July, a grass widow with two small children to support." The character's name was Mildred Pierce, and the novel was an outgrowth of a suggestion by Jim McGuinness when he and Cain were working at Columbia in 1932, how there was one story that never fails, the woman who uses men to gain her ends. Cain had made several starts over the years, first making the woman an airline stewardess, then a girl who had won a beauty contest and was on the make, but neither idea worked. Then he decided his story really depended on *what* woman and *what* ends. He changed her to a plain, commonplace suburban housewife with a nice figure and a way with men, but who had a weak husband and was faced with the problem of raising two girls at the beginning of the Depression. Then he decided to add an extra end—to have Mildred help her oldest girl, Veda, realize her ambition to become a singer. In the book, after Mildred throws her husband out for being too friendly with another woman in their neighborhood, she starts selling pies, takes a job as a waitress, then sells her pies to the restaurants, then she works, then buys a restaurant of her own, and finally starts a string of restaurants and becomes wealthy.

Leo thinks Mildred Pierce is based on his grandmother, who also had a weak husband and went into the hotel business in Helsinki to support herself, eventually becoming a successful businesswoman. But there was another person who played a more immediate part in the evolution of Mildred: Kate Cummings. Cain was seeing Kate regularly now; in fact, he later said it was Kate who "saw me through" *Mildred Pierce*. She was separated from her husband and had two children to support. And all during the writing of the novel, Kate made suggestions, many of which Cain did not use (to his regret, he admitted later), but many of which he did because "on such things she had great sagacity."

Despite Kate's help, the novel progressed slowly. It was a totally new subject for Cain; and there were the usual interruptions, like a request from Edmund Wilson. Wilson had written Blanche Knopf seeking background for what was to be the first literary essay by a major American critic to include a discussion of Cain. She had passed the request on to Cain, and he took the time to write Wilson a long autobiographical memorandum, which Cain stressed was strictly for his use and not to be turned over to the Knopf publicity files, as Blanche had requested. Wilson wrote back asking Cain about the influence of Hollywood on writers such as himself and John O'Hara and William Saroyan. Cain replied that he did not think Hollywood had much impact on any of the writers Wilson mentioned, and then summarized his own attitude about Hollywood, which gives us a revealing glimpse of the Cain-Hollywood connection:

> My own belief is that pictures needn't hurt a writer, but that they probably will. If he could merely work for them they would teach him a lot, particularly about concision and the necessity for building a story before trying to sell it. But he rarely stops there. Having as a rule little critical sense, he begins to believe in them, talk of the screen as a "great medium," and so on, and that sinks him. Pictures are entertainment if they entertain you, but to allow them any validity beyond that one night is to be silly. . . .
>
> Also, a writer is human, and his wife is usually somewhat subhuman, and that $1,000 a week, or $1,750, or $2,500, or whatever it is, has its effect on them both. With him, it isn't so much that he can't give up the pool, and the three servants, and the genuflections at Ciro's, as that after being paid such sums his own work no longer excites him. With luck, his novel may pay him $10,000, $25,000 if he sells it to pictures. But it will take him six months, perhaps a year, to write, and what are such buttons to a shot who could make $50,000 in the same space of time, working for pictures? His own work ceases to seem real.
>
> And—they become silly. They drink, they collect first editions, they believe the reviews about "sparkling dialogue," they become incorporated institutions, managed by agents. For myself, I'm a lucky case. I work for them now and then, rather cynically, I am afraid, and not any too successfully, though they pay me fairly well when they do send for me. The rest of the time I manage to make a living without them, and I hope retain my own ideas of what my work should be like. Also, my

taste is to live simply, and see the few friends that I care about, and call that a life. But: if a writer becomes convinced that he has no important talent, and enjoys working for pictures, why not? Nunnally Johnson puts himself in that category. For him, I confess, I have complete respect. . . .

Cain also discussed his current novel-in-progress: "I am telling it 'straight,' in the third person, that is, and am having plenty of trouble with it. The old stymie of 1922 is still at work: probably I am not really a novelist. If I can pretend it is somebody else's story, be a sort of secretary to the yarn, I do all right. But when I try to step out on the stage myself, I get red behind the ears and boot it. Well, I shall finish it, wind, weather, and tide permitting, and we shall see."

In November, he wrote Blanche Knopf that the book was two-thirds done, but there had been one major interruption. That fall, he had worked seven weeks for 20th Century-Fox on a film to be called *Lucky Baldwin*, about which very little is known, except that it was never completed. It was to be set in Virginia City, Nevada, during the gold rush days, an area and period that always fascinated Cain. In that he had never been to Virginia City, he asked the studio for two or three days to go over and absorb some background. "Oh, no need to do that," the studio people assured him, "the production department will take care of everything." But Cain felt that a man writing a picture should, if possible, visit the scene himself. So leaving on a Friday night, he went on his own to Virginia City, spending all day Saturday and Sunday going through the mines and Sutro Tunnel, "dipping my hand into the water coming out of it to make sure it was warm and in various ways getting close to the way they had mined silver back in the 1860s." The experience started Cain thinking about a novel to be laid in Virginia City at that time, when "we had whorehouses in this country, regular sho 'nuff houses with red lights over the doors."

Again, after writing a synopsis of *Lucky Baldwin*, Cain was closed out at 20th Century. Immediately he went back to work on *Mildred Pierce*. Three months later, he reported to Blanche Knopf that he was on his third rewrite, but that he was deep in debt and now "the doctors have caught up with me and are talking surgery. So I simply have to do something to get the money."

The something was the submission to Knopf of his serial "Money and the Woman," now titled *The Embezzler*, as a possible book under his 1933 contract with the publisher. Blanche replied that she thought the serial was very short for a novel, but they would give him an advance of $1,250 for it, treating it as a separate book, meaning that when he finished his current big book (*Mildred Pierce*) it should be submitted under the 1933 agreement. This upset Cain considerably, and he wrote Blanche:

> I need money, but I am not for one moment asking you for it, and I had much rather you consider *The Embezzler* on its merits, and apart from my personal position at the moment. I specifically submitted it under our agreement of 1933, and wish it considered under that agreement. You offer to publish it under a separate agreement, and yet you intimate you don't really like it. Then I have arrived at the precise result that I did not want; that is, you are proposing to do something you do not really want to do, simply to relieve my financial pressure. You may take my appreciation of your motive for granted, but it will be much better all around if you make this a business matter, rather than a personal one. If you do then I can proceed. If, as you intimate, you do not like the book, then reject it, and I can offer it elsewhere. If you want it, say so and we can proceed with plans for publication. . . . Please don't get big-hearted about this. I'll come out all right provided I know where I'm at.

So "the noose," as the Morris Agency called Knopf's effort to get a separate contract for *The Embezzler*, was not tight enough, and Cain slipped out of it. Knopf did finally accept the book as the one Cain owed him under the 1933 contract, eventually publishing it in a collection of three Cain serials, and Cain was now free to peddle *Mildred Pierce* to the highest bidder. For some time he had been sore at Knopf, not only for misjudging *Postman* but also for refusing to offer him larger advances, despite the success of his books and his emergence as a big-name writer. He told Geller to put *Mildred* out for $5,000, the amount he felt he would need for the impending surgery. Kate, particularly, had been pressing him to do something about his stomach, and everyone, Cain included, was becoming seriously concerned about his health. Often after a day's writing he would have to go to bed at five o'clock and stay there until the next morning to ease the pain and regain his strength. Finally, he began the dreary round of seeing doctors, including a Los Angeles society surgeon who was priming him for the knife, and Dr. Konrad Burchardi, whom Cain would remember as eventually going back to Germany to become Hitler's Minister of Health, though not before once and for all ruling out the liver as the source of Cain's stomach trouble. "It gould not be livach," the doctor told him, "if it wair livach, you vould now pe deat." He thought the problem was an amoeba with an incipient infection.

Then Cain had a real scare. At Kate's suggestion he went to a Dr. Robert Rathbone, and following the examination he heard the doctor say: "I think we've found a cancer in there!" Cain, understandably stunned, replied:

"I have cancer, is that what you said?" Dr. Rathbone snapped back, "I said we've found the *answer*. You have an ulcer in there."

Because Cain had gallstones as well as an ulcer, and the diet that would keep the ulcer under control would aggravate the gallstone, and vice versa, the doctor recommended a double operation, removal of both the gallstones and the lower part of the stomach where the ulcer lay.

It would be an expensive operation—but *Mildred Pierce* would come to the rescue. As his first "serious novel," however, it required telling a bigger story than one confined to a man's and a woman's lust for each other. Eventually Cain wrote four versions of *Mildred Pierce*, and each time, he said, almost on cue at page 254, the thing "fell apart right in front of my eyes."

The problem was the emergence of Mildred's daughter, Veda, who Cain considered to be one of his most notable creations. "The development of this child," he wrote in his memoirs, "is one of the things I take pride in, in my writing, for she had to be credible at all times, and yet, when her true 'talent' is finally revealed, the reader must realize and vividly believe that what he's been a witness to is the development of an opera singer, a somewhat special breed, remote from Mildred's world of pies, menu cards, and chefs, and utterly beyond her ability to understand. I feel that Veda, though cold as a person, and obviously due to tear Mildred's world apart, is a credible portrait, one that corresponds to such persons in real life."

In a sense, he had pulled it off too well. After the fourth time the book "fell apart," he took a walk around the block to talk to himself—out loud—a habit he had when he was writing. "Your trouble," he said, "is that you've forgotten what your story is about. It's not the story of a mother's devotion to an unresponsive daughter, but of a woman who uses men to gain her end. . . ." When he came back "to the key of C, and made Mildred reach for some man to help her out, it got going again."

But then, at the finish, it fell apart once more. "I banged into a climax that was a beauty—where Mildred, finding her daughter in bed with her husband, has had all she can take, and, at last, going berserk, throttles the daughter, squeezing hard on Veda's glottis, thereby destroying the one thing she loved most on this earth, Veda's beautiful voice. And then, I threw it away. . . . I let Veda, this girl who was the bane of her mother's existence, be incredibly, impossibly and needlessly smart. It got the curtain down, but that's about all I can say about it. Believe it or not, I had by that time fallen in love with Veda's totally imaginary voice, and I couldn't bear to think it was permanently gone."

Cain felt he had written ninety-nine percent of a truly fine book, then blown it in the last one percent. As for Mildred herself, "She was a peculiar study to me. I never could make up my mind if she had any brains." In fact, Cain could never really make up his mind about *Mildred Pierce* as a book. When Dorshka Raphaelson wrote Cain that she liked the novel and "couldn't put it down," he replied: "I'm glad you liked Mildred. I did and she represented an incredible amount of work." But years later he told interviewers, "I don't take much pride in *Mildred Pierce*. . . . It's not my kind of book." He also decided it had been a mistake to write it in the third person, where he felt "my hand is palsied."

Though *Mildred Pierce* may not have been Cain's kind of book, Geller found a lot of interest in it, and the publisher he eventually sold it to surprised even Cain. When Knopf heard that Geller was offering the new novel around New York, he contacted the agent and asked when he was going to see it. "Oh, let's remain friends," Geller replied. "The guy's sick, he needs a big operation, and he has to have money . . . and what he's asking as an advance for this book is five thousand dollars."

"Well," answered Knopf, "isn't my five thousand dollars as good as somebody else's?"

"What was I going to say?" Geller asked Cain.

"Yes, I hope," Cain answered.

The deal was one of the most satisfying in Cain's literary career. Even for a successful author like Cain, $5,000 was big money for a novel in those days, and the sale had "a curious psychological effect" on him. Though not much of a sulker, he admitted "I may have been a bit thrown off my step by Alfred's dislike of *The Postman Always Rings Twice*. But this $5,000, paid with no fuss at all, fixed things up fine."

Whenever Cain finished a novel, he permitted himself one "whacky indulgence," and with the completion of *Mildred Pierce* he bought himself a "snowball" machine, "like the one in the old market at Annapolis," which his father had not let him have. But then he took it home and had his Swedish maid fix him a "snowball," and it was awful. Eventually he found a use for the machine when a friend discovered that Cain had a big patch of mint by his front door. The thing was perfect for making mint juleps. Not that he could drink them himself.

Cain's ulcer was getting worse every day, aggravated, no doubt, by a very troubling situation concerning *When Tomorrow Comes*, the movie with the love scene in the church, so strikingly similar to Cain's by now famous love scene in *Serenade*. In May, after *Mildred Pierce* had been sold to Knopf, Cain accepted an assignment at Arnold Pressburger Productions, where he worked for five weeks on *The Shanghai Gesture*, an exotic suspense picture starring Gene Tierney, Victor Mature, and Walter Huston. He was having lunch at the Brown Derby one day when Dwight Taylor, who had written the final script for *When Tomorrow Comes*, came up and asked if he could join him. Cain replied yes, and after they had ordered Taylor said: "I came over to talk with you about what happened on *When Tomorrow Comes*."

"I don't know what you mean," said Cain.

"I mean all that stuff taken out of *Serenade*."

Cain said coldly: "It might interest you to know that there has been some little correspondence between attorneys on that subject, and Universal's lawyers told my lawyer that nobody in connection with the picture had ever read *Serenade* or knew anything about it." Then he told Taylor that he knew perfectly well where the scene came from but that his lawyer had finally convinced him that he did not have a legal case because he could not prove access.

Taylor was quiet for a moment, then he said: "There was access all right. Stahl came to me with that stuff and I listened to him, and after a while I said: 'Well, that is all pretty good, John, but you can't use that, it's right out of *Serenade*.' " Stahl, according to Taylor, commented it was "a hell of a good book, or something like that," to which Taylor replied: "You're damned right. But it doesn't give us the right to take stuff out of it."

Then, according to Taylor, Stahl made "one of the strangest replies I ever heard a man make. He said: 'I paid Cain a hell of a good price for "A Modern Cinderella." ' "

"That still doesn't give you a right to take stuff out of *Serenade*," Taylor told Stahl. And Stahl replied: "We had it for a while [referring to the fact that *Serenade* had been submitted to Universal and several other studios right after it came out]." So Taylor told Stahl: "O.K., providing it's understood that I'm warning you that this stuff is out of *Serenade*, I'll write it." Then he went on to explain to Cain that he had been so broke at the time he could hardly pay his bills, and that was why he had written it.

After the lunch, Cain went back to his office, a disturbed man. He hated lawsuits, and he liked Taylor and knew he would have to put him on the witness stand if he sued. The whole business made his stomach almost unbearable. But he said to himself: "Good Lord, if you won't sue after hearing that, when will you sue?" He realized that no copyright was safe unless a writer did something about piracy. So he told his lawyer, Martin Gang, he wanted to sue. Then he wrote Taylor: "As you may imagine, I tried to talk myself out of doing anything about it at all. But presently I knew this wasn't going to work. I had to do something, partly as a matter of self-respect, and partly as a matter of duty to the whole writing profession, for if all writers did nothing, there would be no protection to anybody." Then he went on to suggest that Taylor talk to Gang. Taylor may have talked to Gang, but when the time came for taking his deposition, it was obvious that he had also talked to his own lawyer and was already backing away from the story he had told Cain at lunch. By then Cain's lawyer had filed suit, and the trial was set for June 1942.

Meanwhile, Cain's stomach was being "cooled"—mostly by his giving up smoking for a while—for one of the "very great events" of his life, his operation. It was called a Finney pylorectomy and was performed by Dr. Charles Sturgeon. It removed the acid-forming part of his stomach and probably saved Cain's life, and it made it possible for him to eat and drink anything he wanted. He wasted no time in making up for the last twenty years, during which he had had to baby his stomach. Just before going into the hospital he had seen Adolphe Menjou in a gas station, and as they talked about one of his books Cain had noticed how horribly emaciated the dapper actor looked. After he recuperated from his operation, Cain saw Menjou at the Beverly Brown Derby, and the actor told Cain he had had the same operation performed by the same surgeon and was a new man. From then on, whenever they met in Perino's or Mike's or one of the Derbies, from across the room the two Hollywood Boulevardiers would raise a glass to each other and drink a toast—to Dr. Charles Sturgeon.

While Cain was in the hospital, Knopf was rushing *Mildred Pierce* into print. As usual, they were having title problems, only this time the trouble was not the inability to agree on a mutually satisfactory name—Cain and Knopf both liked "Mildred Pierce"—the problem was that so had someone's mother. After the book had been set in type, Richard Fuller, owner of the Old Corner Book Store in Boston, wrote Knopf that his wife's maiden name was Mildred Pierce and he was concerned by the coincidence. He felt his wife's name might be damaged, primarily because of Cain's reputation. Even though *Mildred Pierce* was not as shocking as *Postman* and *Serenade*, Fuller said, it was not "what you'd call Sunday School literature."

Knopf wrote Fuller that to change the name the book would have to be entirely reset. But he also asked Geller to talk to Cain about it, which he did. Cain did not think it was a problem and refused to change the name. He thought the usual disclaimer took care of it and pointed out that no matter what name they used, they would be faced with the same problem. There is always *someone* with the name of your hero or heroine. So Knopf took a firm stand with Fuller, who finally signed a waiver giving Knopf his consent to use the name, though adding that this did not include motion pictures. When Knopf told Geller of Fuller's exception, he said he was not certain how this might affect Cain in Hollywood, but "I can hardly imagine a film called *Mildred Pierce*." Cain still checked with a few Hollywood lawyers and was told that the name coincidence was no worry, not that any studio had showed much interest yet in *Mildred*.

When Cain came out of the hospital, he went East to his parents' home in Baltimore to recuperate. Why he did this is not clear, although it is possible that the tension in the Cain household was now reaching an intolerable point. In addition, Elina's mother had come from Helsinki to live with them, and it is evident from what Cain wrote about her that she was making things more difficult at home.

Cain took with him a letter from Katharine White requesting a story for *The New Yorker*, which he tried to write while resting. But he decided the story was "lousy" and wrote Mrs. White: "I never did have any skill with the kind of thing *The New Yorker* publishes, and I haven't the faintest idea why." He promised to send her a story if he could write one that satisfied him, but said he would more likely be nominating himself to do some "Profiles" for the magazine from the West Coast. "There is a dearth of regular articles out here, at least articles that I can think up, but of people to write about, a surplus."

In the exchange of correspondence, White also informed him that his old *Mercury* dialogue, "The Governor," was being included in her forthcoming *Subtreasury of American Humor*. This pleased him. "The piece . . . is one of the few things I have ever written that I have a real affection for, and it means almost more to me than I care to admit to have it in there."

Cain was also receiving recognition from another source. Just before the operation, Edmund Wilson had published his anticipated discussion of Cain, an essay in the *New Republic*, which was probably the first suggestion by a major American critic that Cain had edged his way into the front ranks of American authors. It was titled "The Boys in the Back Room," and the boys included Cain, John Steinbeck, John O'Hara, William Saroyan, and Horace McCoy. Cain, Wilson said, was the best of these writers, whom he called "the poets of the tabloid murder." But he insisted they all "stemmed originally from Hemingway," that Cain was influenced by Hollywood, that his novels were "a Devil's parody of the movies," and lamented it was a pity "such a writer [could not] create and produce his own pictures."

Mildred Pierce was published in September, and possibly because of Wilson's essay it was treated in the press as a major book by a major American writer. Still, the early reviews were disappointing. Both Ralph Thompson and J. Donald Adams in the *New York Times* gave it the back of their hands. How Cain could ever "tangle himself up with this prodigious, incredible, preposterous child," wrote Thompson, "is almost as hard to understand as Veda herself," which prompted Cain to commiserate with Knopf: "None of these critics seemed to have read the book I wrote." But as the clipping services continued to send reviews in, more and more were favorable. Many coupled *Mildred* with James T. Farrell's just published *Ellen Rogers*, finding them both realistic portraits of modern women. "Cain's tale is the hare to Farrell's tortoise," said the *New Republic*. "Unlike Farrell, he has now become readable." *Time* said that *Mildred Pierce* confirmed that Cain "is one of the most readable story-tellers in the U.S. He has broadened his subject matter and, with a cruel anthropologist's tenacity, virtually wrung it dry." And Robert Van Gelder in the *Times* reached the height of mixed praise when he said the book was ripely dramatic, well put together, and very realistic and compelling, which was understandable because "it has in it the deep, slow pull of the ancient ooze where worms and serpents crawled." Gelder did not like Mildred, Veda, Monty, or anyone else in the book, but he thought Cain had told a powerful story. The *Retail Bookseller* summed up what was perhaps the main commercial problem with *Mildred Pierce* when it said "the ultra-conservatives are likely to condemn it because of Cain's reputation for sensationalism; whereas the true James Cain fans are likely to find it decidedly mild and tame."

The most interesting review was Clifton Fadiman's in *The New Yorker*, which Knopf reprinted and used in a full-page ad. Fadiman said, "I wouldn't miss a new Cain novel any more than the Mayor [La Guardia] would miss a fire. . . ." And he concluded: "As a matter of fact, if it didn't happen to include adultery, a near rape or two, and a few other motives of comparable torridity it would make a bang-up movie." (Actually, when Hollywood got around to making *Mildred Pierce*, it had to add a murder so the movie would not disappoint the real James M. Cain fans.)

By early October, the book had sold 11,000 copies, doing particularly well in the South, and it "did a standing broad jump," as Cain put it, "onto the bestseller list." And, as with nearly all Cain books, it aroused controversy everywhere, not just with the critics. One bookseller was reported to have burned her copies, and Cain received hundreds of letters saying there could be no such woman as Mildred Pierce, that he had fabricated a lewd and incredible character. The "Talk of the Times" column in the *New York Times* wondered whether "we are going to fight a war to save the kind of characters who inhabit the books of Cain and James T. Farrell?"

To all those who said that the unattractive people in *Mildred Pierce* simply did not exist, Cain's reply was: "I can only say, as Shaw said of Pinero, 'Doesn't this fellow *meet* anybody?' " His reaction to Fadiman's review, expressed to Knopf, was that "while he still puts me in the class of potboilers, it won't hurt sales any." He also conceded that maybe the reviewers were right; that he had not written the book he thought he had. Maybe the real story was Mildred and Veda.

One friend, however, thought that no matter what kind of book Cain had started out to write, he had done a superlative job. "Just hold down the franchise," Raphaelson wrote Cain from New York, "I think it's one hell of a book. I think it marks a definitive development in you as a writer. . . . I also think the book is so close to being one of the great books of our time that you should have been horse-whipped for not having made it that . . . if you ever had any doubts about yourself, *Mildred Pierce* should lay them for good."

All in all, Cain felt optimistic about the book's sales prospects. "I think we're in better shape now than we were with *Serenade*," he wrote Knopf. "The book has no church angle or homo angle to antagonize them after they buy it, and is 100 pages longer without any padding that I know of, and is about things that concern a great many people."

Despite Cain's optimism, *Mildred Pierce* was never a runaway seller; it leveled off at slightly over 14,000 hard-cover copies. It also appeared it would have the same trouble with the Hays Office that *Postman*, "Double Indemnity," and *Serenade* were having. As a result, as the year's end approached, Cain found himself in his usual financial straits. Not only was he in debt from his operation, he was still too weak to accept a studio job. So, while recuperating, he started another serial, one he intended not only for the magazines but also the movies—the only story to become a hard-cover novel he ever wrote with a movie sale specifically in mind. He called it *Love's Lovely Counterfeit*, a "lurid title, but it was that kind of tale"—about the seamier side of city politics and involving a politician double-crossed by his chauffeur who is double-crossed by his ex-mistress.

Cain was also beginning to think about a novel to be set in New Orleans, and he hoped he and Elina could go there for the winter. But their financial situation canceled such plans. By early December he had finished *Love's Lovely Counterfeit*, and although the studios seemed excited about it there was no contract. The same for *Mildred Pierce*. Discouraged, he wrote his sister Virginia: "It has been depressing, but I make a living in a highly speculative way. I see no reason to attach much importance to it, except I assume that now and then the cards run against you."

The cards were running against America too, and although Cain seemed to be paying little attention to international affairs, he soon would: the date of his letter to Virginia was December 6, 1941.

14

IN WAR, THEY HAVE
TO SPELL "MOTHER"

Most Americans old enough to remember that Sunday morning, December 7, 1941, can recall exactly what they were doing at the time. Cain was no exception: "I was home and Henrietta came upstairs. 'The Japanese have attacked us,' she said. I went down to her room. There must have been more than one radio; it was a big house. We listened to some more news and then I said: 'Well, we're at war. This is it.' "

The war shook Cain to the core—personally and professionally. "The war is rotten and stands me on my head," he wrote one friend in early 1942. To clarify his own thinking about the conflict he started a "memoir," which he never finished, though in its introduction he said he was confused and "wholly convinced that we are getting nowhere and that nationally speaking we haven't the faintest idea where we want to go. . . . It is our lack of purpose that palsies our efforts and begets our irresolution as to whether to fight in Europe, in Australia, in China, in India, in Africa, or Siberia; whether to build ships or cargo planes, whether to defend Alaska, or half defend it, or abandon it, or issue another communiqué about the fog."

Then, trying to explain America's befuddlement, he said: "With a great many of us, a virtuously cultivated aestheticism has taken the place of the social consciousness that is the food of intellects in other parts of the world.

Indeed, we have been prone to regard a concert hall as somehow superior to a husting, and attendance at a political meeting as a gross social error."

Cain was, of course, speaking primarily for himself. Through the 1930s, many writers had been intensely preoccupied with America's domestic crisis and international conflicts. But Cain's main concern had been storytelling and that subject of subjects, Man—not man's social, political, and economic problems, but his relationships with his fellow men and to the opposite sex. In fact, it might be more accurate to say that Cain's subject of subjects was Woman. For of all the characters he created, his most vivid creations were women: Mildred and Veda Pierce, Cora Papadakis, Phyllis Nirdlinger, and the prostitute in *Serenade*, Juanita.

By the time of Pearl Harbor, Cain had written his most important works—*Postman*, "Double Indemnity," *Serenade*, and *Mildred Pierce*. The war left him "stranded," as he called it. There was no danger of his entering the service; he was forty-nine, had a wife, a family, and a history of TB, and half his stomach had been removed. But professionally, he had been stood on his head: he was unemployed, in debt, and, as usual, counting on another picture job and more serials and novels to pull him out. But now the Hollywood situation and his publishing markets were abruptly changed, and there was some truth in the thought, still being expressed in the *New York Times*'s "Topics of the Times" section, that the nation was no longer interested in the world of James M. Cain and James T. Farrell. "People are not as much in the mood for that kind of heroine," said the *Times*. Cain and Farrell both happened to be in Geller's office one day when one of the *Times* items appeared, and Farrell's reaction was: "What the hell, are we supposed to fight and die for Tyrone Power?"

Cain denied he was asking anyone to fight to save Mildred Pierce, while agreeing with Farrell that we were not fighting to save Tyrone Power either. But Hollywood was gearing up to arouse America to do just that, to fight for Tyrone Power and Robert Taylor and Clark Gable and Jimmy Stewart—except they would be wearing uniforms and dying in celluloid battles. Many of the stars and writers, of course, went off to war, although motion pictures had been declared an essential industry and valuable properties like Clark Gable were considered too important as propaganda weapons and morale boosters to be risked in battle.

Cain said the impact of the war was not so much on Hollywood *per se*, which had always been hard to define and isolate, but on eight hundred different people who reacted in different ways. "Suddenly every actor and writer had patches on his elbows—'patches by Abercrombie.' " Although most people in movieland took the war and their contribution very seriously, Hollywood was also "a very peculiar place," said Cain. "You could be having a conversation with a writer and compliment him on some war work he was doing, and he would be very pleased to hear what you had to say. And his wife would say, half-stewed, 'Give me a light,' and you'd light her cigarette and she'd say, 'My, my, but he's self-sacrificing; at three thousand dollars a week. My heart is bleeding!' "

Cain did not find day-to-day activities at the studio changed much by the war. "There was no great excitement to it; you'd have scarcely noticed any difference in the way the lots functioned with the war going on. A picture lot was run very efficiently. It had to be because there was a penalty for not being efficient. Every picture company was booked five thousand a day over-head, automatically. So everything went on greased skids. The war going on didn't change anything. You'd have hardly noticed there *was* a war going on."

Cain thought most writers, directors, and actors in Hollywood persuaded themselves that they were making a contribution. But he himself was more cynical: "I was writing for pictures which the government said they wanted written, and when the agent would sell me for $250 a week more, who was I to argue about it? Who was going to get that $250? I might as well have it because the picture company was going to keep it and I knew that they were not doing pictures wholly for patriotic reasons. Nobody even slightly pretended that a war picture was not being done for profit."

Cain had some very clear ideas about the role of a writer in war, which he expressed in a letter to Clifton Fadiman, Rex Stout, and others when they solicited his signature for a letter to President Roosevelt suggesting that the "word-men" of America should be coordinated under Elmer Davis to engage in "word-warfare." The idea appalled Cain, who replied:

I plead with you to send no such communication to President Roosevelt as you propose in your letter to me of March 26, which I have just received. The very phrase "word-warfare" is enough to bring the whole writing profession into public derision for years to come, and the idea that a coordinator should be appointed, to take charge of this kind of combat, and presumably foster it and augment it and enlarge its scope, is naïve, to say the least of it. Furthermore, you try to do something which never works and which under our system of government should never be attempted. You not only propose a new office, but demand the right to name the new officer, and right there is where you play into the hands of the very authority which you wish to improve. For naturally you can assume no responsibility for your appointee: you are private citizens, and have no responsibility. But if you name him, the incumbent executive need not assume responsibility either; he has merely passed the buck to you, and if your man doesn't prove quite the genius you think he is, we are worse off than ever. I have the utmost admiration for Mr. Elmer Davis, and quite share your belief that his conspicuous talents should be put to better use, but do not believe this is the way to go about it.

What was being proposed, of course, was the forerunner to the Office of War Information. But despite his opposition to the concept, Cain later did everything he was asked to do to help in the war effort and, in fact, spent a great deal of the war engaged in "word-warfare" through letters to various editors and columnists.

One thing that troubled Cain was the question of helping the imperial nations salvage their collapsing empires. He was against it, and soon he was writing letters to the *Los Angeles Times*, which prompted the editors of that paper to write back asking whether, as a writer of "snappy fiction," he was qualified to tell England what to do in India. Cain replied: "I do not speak as a writer of snappy fiction, but as an American disturbed about America's war and the discrepancy between our words and the facts: We do not fight for four freedoms, but for four empires. . . .These empires are really great trading corporations, dividing Europe between the stockholders, represented by the Daladiers, and the bagholders, represented by the Blums, and this so weakened her that she could not resist Germany, a country without colonies. They violate the basic law of growth which is that it proceeds contiguously. . . .The only organism that typically grows in several places at once is cancer, and we may as well face the fact that India is the great metastasis of the mortally sick world we live in."

Later, Cain started writing letters to the editors of the *Los Angeles Daily News*, who treated him with a little more respect. Manchester Boddy, the *News* editor, wrote Cain: "I have seldom encountered more stimulating, fine writing."

If the *Times* ignored his thoughts on the war, the government wanted them, and Julian Street in the Treasury Department was soon persuading him to write messages on war bonds (which appeared on the back of two of his books published in the forties) and inflation. Cain also had an idea for bringing Germany to her knees, which he passed on to Street: Turn the Treasury Department's presses loose printing phony marks to be dropped on Germany, thereby inflationing her to death.

Another thing that bothered Cain was Walter Lippmann's attitude on imperialism. "Walter, I think," he wrote Morris Markey, "is on the other side of the river from his clothes, having done a lifetime's thinking under the face of liberalism, which turns out to be an English invention, the intellectual face of Kiplingism, having thus fallen for the thank-God-for-the-British-

Fleetism and all the rest of the stuffings of the rotten punkin we now try to eat. I cannot get over the feeling that the war has passed Roosevelt, Churchill and Lippmann and other proponents of our present policy, by."

Cain's own formula for winning the war, at least in 1942, called for uniting with Canada, closer relations with China and Russia, and an eventual encirclement of Japan through Alaska and Siberia. If this could be achieved he thought Dutch Harbor in Alaska would soon become the seat of all the big war news, and he wrote Arthur Krock that he was seriously considering applying to the *New York Times* as their Alaskan correspondent.

But he never did. Except for a few fact-gathering trips for his novels, he stayed in Hollywood for the entire war. And although the war brought about the beginning of the fadeout of Hollywood's "golden years," it produced Cain's peak earning years. Including the sale of his books to the studios, in the three war years (1943–45) he earned nearly $200,000, which was big money then. But the first year, 1942, was for Cain, as it was for his country, a total disaster. He lost his home, his agent, and a plagiarism suit; the magazine serial he wrote with the movies in mind never sold to the magazines, nor did it sell to the movies until the 1950s. And with America and the movie industry suddenly tooling up for the war against Germany and Japan, Cain had difficulty at first in finding studio jobs and coming up with suitable ideas for serials or novels.

Although there was rationing and shortages of goods, the war did not impose a special hardship on the Cains. They made their contribution to the war effort; Elina eventually went to work at the Vega Aircraft factory in Burbank, helping to build twin-engine bombers, and Cain became an air raid warden, donning his metal hat and armband and joining Cecil B. De Mille, in charge of the Hollywood Hills Air Raid defense unit. They would drive up and down the steep roads in the dark, making sure everyone in the Hills had their lights out or their curtains drawn during those nervous blackouts when Southern California was certain Japanese planes were on the way to do a Pearl Harbor on Grauman's Chinese Theatre. Cain was a very conscientious warden and would often go into a strange house and pull down the black curtains himself—and perhaps accept a warming cup of spirits for the chilly night.

By now, he was drinking and eating excessively and putting on weight. After his operation, with his stomach no longer secreting acid, he made no effort to restrain his gourmet tastes or penchant for alcohol. By his own admission he went on a five-year drunk, and it was a worse drunk, he said, than any of Vincent Lawrence's, "as it was possible to convince myself, and possibly others, that it didn't mean anything, that I drank in the daytime, that it never interfered with my work, I could always drive home, etc."

Although the increased drinking apparently did not affect his work, he was having other problems with his writing. The first casualty was *Love's Lovely Counterfeit*. He had intended it to show the skulduggery that went on in Los Angeles city politics, but then, in part because his sickness had made him unable to do the research he felt necessary, and in part because the approaching war made it somehow seem in bad taste to attack a specific place, he changed the locale from Los Angeles to a fictitious midwestern city. He finished it a week before Pearl Harbor, after which it was in bad taste to attack any American city, even a fictitious one. So it was dead in the studios and with the magazines. But then Knopf saved the day, giving him a $1,500 advance and agreeing to publish it as a book.

The publisher was also planning another Cain volume—this one an anthology to consist of three of his serials: "Double Indemnity," "Money and the Woman" (retitled "The Embezzler"), and "Two Can Sing" (retitled "Career in C Major")—which led to one of their typical haggles about advances. Cain, desperate for money, asked for an additional $750 (over the $250 Knopf had already given him). Knopf agreed, but said he would rather charge the amount to Cain's general account than increase the advance. This annoyed Cain, inasmuch as the money would then be a loan rather than an advance against royalties, and he said he had never asked Knopf for a loan. "If you are fainthearted about this collection," he wrote Knopf, "say so and I can offer it to another publisher." Knopf acquiesced, and the anthology, to be called *Three of a Kind*, was set for spring of 1943 publication, with Cain to write a preface for the book.

It was fortunate for Cain that Knopf was still interested in his prewar writing because he was having a devil of a time adjusting to the war mood. Somewhat in despair, and as much as anything to discipline himself at the typewriter, he wrote a serial which he called "Galloping Dominoes." It was essentially a rewrite of his play *7-11*, though set in Reno rather than New York. The heroine is a movie star who becomes involved with the sheriff of Reno after her husband is killed in such a way as to suggest double indemnity problems, with the actress and her sister both falling under suspicion. The twist at the end is very un-Cain-like—the movie star and the sheriff turn out to be good people—and the climactic scene is disappointing. Although it never sold to either the magazines or the movies, his agent made a special effort with the studios. The story appeared tailor-made for a movie sale, and it is ironic that, considering all the flak Cain would soon be taking about being corrupted by Hollywood, when he did write something with the movies in mind, it did not sell. Cain, however, was convinced it was the war that had thrown him out of step; as he wrote Knopf, it had "swept into discard every idea I had cooking." And so, aware that he was not in tune with the patriotic wartime hysteria, he decided to focus on a prewar story. "My modern books," he said, "don't spell 'mother.' It's O.K. if your historical novel doesn't spell 'mother.' But if it's current stuff and there's a war going on and if it doesn't spell 'mother,' no publisher wants it."

His first effort to find a prewar story took him back to his newspaper days. He was convinced the studios went about it all wrong "in their never-flagging efforts to cook up a story about the end of the *New York World*. . . . It never institutionalizes the paper but makes it a sort of Hecht and MacArthur burlesque." Cain had come up with his own approach: His central character was to be a woman in constant flight from reality, a tiny, lovable creature who marries a reporter in the Washington bureau of a fictitious New York newspaper. They have a son and then the reporter is killed in Europe, where he was covering World War I. His widow goes to New York for the unveiling of a plaque in his honor and is offered a job in the library. She enters the cold, gray building on Park Row as one might a penitentiary, and soon she meets another man, like herself a dreamer, working in the library. They find a common, romantic meeting ground in their clippings, and in the excitement of providing the paper with tips, leads, and ideas for stories. Then, her son, who has also been given a job on the paper, becomes managing editor and eventually owner. He takes his mother out of her job, the one thing she loves, and moves her into a Fifth Avenue apartment. Then he proceeds to wreck the paper through his preoccupation with names, by-lines, social contacts, and practically everything except the news—Cain's version of what Swope did to the *World* before the "young master" took charge. In the end, after the paper is sold to another paper, the mother goes to work for the new paper, where her old friend is in charge of the library.

With his plot worked out, Cain was optimistically promising the completed manuscript to Knopf by the middle of July. But by then he had abandoned it and was working on another prewar story, this one about a boy who has to ride the box cars in the 1930s because of a situation at home. Then he apparently abandoned that one too to try to write a script for *Serenade*, which he hoped to sell to one of the studios. This was now becoming the thing in Hollywood: an author would write a script, thereby short-circuiting the publisher who, in those days, often took 50 percent of a movie sale. Cain was aware that Knopf might not see "the gay delightfulness" of this kind of deal, but with Cain not showing much evidence of finishing things he was starting at that time, Knopf had little interest in the project and said that if there was a script he was sure something could be worked out.

Cain never did complete a salable script of *Serenade*—and was having just as much difficulty finding any work in the studios. Geller came up with a job early in 1942, at half pay, but it lasted less than a month and there is no record of which studio hired him or of what script he worked on. Actually, he had worked only five and a half weeks since May 1941, when he came out of the operating room in debt. And his troubles were just beginning. In June 1942, Geller quit the Morris Agency and went to work for Warner Brothers, and Cain decided to find a new agent. Whether Geller's leaving the agency came before or after Cain's decision to break with Morris is not clear. Leo thinks Kate Cummings had a lot to do with persuading Cain to leave Geller, and that she convinced him another agent—H. N. Swanson—would find him the movie jobs he needed. At any rate, Cain and Swanson had lunch in July, and as Swanson recalled it, Cain's main dissatisfaction with Geller dated back to the *Postman* sale to MGM eight years earlier. He remembered seeing Cain not long after that deal and that he was "in a foaming Irish fit that he couldn't do anything about the fact the rights had been given away and he would never get another nickel out of it."

In August, Cain formally severed his relations with Morris in a letter that showed his distress not only at his decision but at his whole personal situation: "That it upsets me to leave the Morris Office, I think you know. It has figured my taxes, bought my tickets, and lent me money. I have been with it for thirteen years; it is the only agent I ever had, it has been papa, mama and whisky-soda to me, all rolled into one. Yet I have reached that certain point. I have been headed for it for some time, but put off doing anything about it partly because I thought I could piece along somehow, partly because I owed the agency money [slightly under $1,000] and I wanted to have that paid up before I did anything. But if things keep on going this way with me, I won't even be able to do that. I am in a spin, and if I don't pull the stick I am going to crash."

So Cain switched to H. N. Swanson, who is still doing business in the Swanson Building on Sunset Boulevard. "Swannie," as everyone called him, remembers Cain as "one of the greatest of our time, no question—and a great guy. Nobody ever had a fight with Jim Cain that I ever heard of. Most Irish are not always level emotionally. But he was level." Even then, Cain's (post-operation) hard drinking was becoming known around Hollywood, but Swanson said: "I'd heard he pushed the grape around a little but that didn't bother me. I've had some great drinkers on my list: O'Hara, Faulkner, Fitzgerald, Hemingway. Cain went through periods, but he held his liquor well; he was a gentleman."

By August 1942, Cain was obviously reaching another one of his periodic low points: he was $4,000 in debt, having more trouble than usual finding studio work, drinking heavily, and finding little relief at the typewriter. "I can't imagine anything with less point to it than this endless fictioneering I seem condemned to," he wrote Markey. On top of it all, or probably intricately related, the tension at home was reaching the breaking point. And on Sunday morning, August 30, two days after his formal break with his agent, he delivered his own little Pearl Harbor on Belden Drive: He walked out on Elina and Henrietta (Leo was overseas, having enlisted in the American Air Force before Pearl Harbor).

Precisely what happened to precipitate the final break between Cain and Elina may never be known. Leo thinks the main trouble was Cain's growing friendship with Kate Cummings. There is evidence that Cain started seeing Kate regularly and openly after his 1942 separation from Elina and that he had been seeing her often before the break. There is also evidence that there were men in Elina's life ("Elina's procession of hand-kissers," as Cain described them), although Leo is certain his mother was not having an affair with any of them. One who particularly annoyed Cain was Hifzi-Bey-Hadzi-Selimovitch, a Yugoslavian Hollywood bit player who took the stage name of Gene Gary. In Cain's eyes, he was a professional sponger off women, and Elina kept him around the house until he had become an intolerable nuisance. The daughter of one friend recalls that Gary would often accompany the Cains to parties, and there was one period when they were almost always together as a threesome. In June, Gary had an accident driving Cain's car, which nearly produced a lawsuit. Considering Cain's dislike for lawyers and litigation, this obviously did not help the situation. Leo is convinced that his mother's relationship with Gary was "just a friendly affair. She was a great walker and they would take walks together. He was also a great sleeper around; he must have made love to a hundred women. But my mother was just a confidante to him."

By the end of August, things had come to the boiling point. The mother-in-law was no longer a cause of immediate tension because she had become so violent around the house she had been moved into a separate apartment, at Cain's expense. But there was apparently some violence between Cain and Elina; she said at the divorce trial that for no reason Cain would often lift her by the arm and toss her across the room. "It all but drove me to the booby hatch." She claimed "he made sarcastic remarks about my speech, clothes, and manner and often insulted my friends," and he would go for weeks without speaking to her. Cain was convinced that she was "carrying on" with her men friends (and she denied it), and at one point he was considering naming one in the divorce proceedings, but changed his mind.

When Cain finally left Elina, their friends were stunned. Morris Markey, now living in New York and doing the live radio broadcasts of the opera from the Metropolitan, wrote that he was "distressed" and could not "believe that this will be a permanent break because you people have always understood each other so remarkably well. . . . I have confidence in your judgment because you are not quick-tempered or hasty in your decisions. I know the slow burns take longer to cool off, but they do cool."

This one did not. Cain moved into the Knickerbocker Hotel, a small hotel at 1714 North Ivar Avenue, which became his home for the next three years. He always felt he had no choice. "I regret it plenty, God knows," he wrote a friend. "But it was her doing, not mine." Henrietta stayed with Elina, who eventually became part owner of a Madame Louise dress shop in Beverly Hills.

Cain was truly alone and a bachelor now, and while the lawyers tried to see if a settlement could be worked out, he went back to his typewriter. As in 1936 and 1937, he seemed to be having trouble sticking with anything long enough to finish it. Nor was his general mood improved by the publication of *Love's Lovely Counterfeit*, which more or less got what it deserved from the reviewers. William Dubois, in the *New York Times*, said "it is redeemed from sheer pulp melodrama only by [Cain's] spine-tingling treatment of 'big' scenes, his wonderfully accurate ear for the rhythms of dialogue." The *Saturday Review* thought it would not add much to Cain's reputation "and it may indeed raise certain questions which he will have to answer with a better book." And *Time* pegged him as the country's "most literate pulp writer." There were a few exceptions. In *The New Yorker*, Vincent McHugh thought "the ding-dong daddy of the what-terrible-people-school" was actually moderating somewhat and that a few of the people in *Love's Lovely Counterfeit* actually had "hearts and even scruples, within reason." And Mencken wrote Cain it was one of the best things he had ever done.

But the readers seemed to share the reaction of most reviewers. By the end of the year the book had sold only 7,500 copies, and Knopf thought it was dead. To make matters worse, Cain was now involved in an expensive litigation, his plagiarism suit against Universal. A trial had been scheduled for June, but John Stahl was on location directing a picture called *Another Spring*, and the court date was rescheduled for the fall. In the meantime, depositions had been taken from Dwight Taylor and Stahl, both of whom denied completely the story Taylor had told Cain at the Brown Derby the year before. Now Taylor said that Stahl had not instructed him to use material from *Serenade*, and that he had not been influenced by Stahl in writing it. "I cannot tell and I don't think any writer on earth could tell," Taylor said to Cain's lawyer, Martin Gang, "just how much he was influenced by a conference with the producer. . . . I just can't do that. I am willing to stand by the scene that appeared in the moving picture, *When Tomorrow Comes*. I am the sole author of that scene."

Taylor's turnaround was baffling, especially in that Cain had heard from a mutual friend that Taylor had told him the same thing he had told Cain—

that Stahl had instructed him to use material from *Serenade* (Cain eventually decided that this mutual friend would not repeat his confidence in court, and so did not call him as a witness). In addition, the court case had enabled Cain to subpoena all the relevant documents from Universal, and after reading over the scripts and the memorandum he had to admit to his lawyer that the record seemed to substantiate Stahl. Gang said, "Well, you would hardly expect anything to be in writing," and since the case had already been filed, he recommended they go through with it.

At the trial, the defense began with a motion to have the case dismissed on the grounds that *Serenade* was obscene, especially the scene which was allegedly stolen. But Judge Leon Yankwich dismissed the argument, saying that although the scene in the church might be construed as sacrilegious, the final scene in the book, in which Juanita pays for her crimes with her life, "destroys all implications of immorality or impiety in the earlier scenes of *Serenade.*"

When Judge Yankwich delivered this ruling, Cain turned to Gang and whispered a remark the lawyer never forgot: "How the hell did he know what I had in my head? I hadn't the faintest idea how the book was going to end when I wrote that scene."

With the judge's ruling, Gang thought they were in good shape, but Taylor stuck to his story, and then when Stahl finally took the stand, Cain had even more doubts about his case. At one point during Gang's interrogation of Stahl, Stahl's lawyer leaped up and shouted: "Object on the grounds it is incompetent, immaterial, and irrelevant!"

"Sustained," said the judge. "Mr. Gang, you confine yourself in your little court lecture."

And then Stahl said, "Your honor, may I say something?"

"Yes, of course," said the judge.

"Your honor, I would like to thank counsel for obtaining for me all the law I'm entitled to. And your honor, for ruling in my favor. But I'd be grateful if counsel will withdraw his objection to that question and will refrain from any other objections while Mr. Gang is questioning me. Your honor, since Mr. Cain made his allegation, which I believe he made in good faith, but which is false, I have lived in the shadow of this allegation, that I deliberately encouraged writers to steal. This is the one chance I have to clear my name. I will answer any question Mr. Gang asks me, no matter how incompetent, how immaterial, or how irrelevant, or how plain silly."

"You may proceed," said the judge.

So Gang asked Stahl directly: "Who had the idea of having this couple spend a night in a church?"

"I don't remember," answered Stahl, "but if it helps any, I did."

When Stahl left the stand, Cain no longer believed in his own case. And neither did Judge Yankwich. In delivering his opinion, the judge said, "It is inconceivable that the ordinary theatergoer, who saw the chaste, idyllic church sequence in *When Tomorrow Comes* . . . would see . . . any similarity between it and the sensuous scene which Cain portrays in *Serenade*. I can see none."

Gang wanted to appeal, but Cain said they might as well drop it. Without Taylor's statement that he had been ordered by Stahl to lift material from *Serenade*, there was no case.

What had caused Taylor either to change his testimony or tell Cain a lie at the Brown Derby? Cain was never quite sure. He said he saw Taylor in the men's room after the trial and said: "Why did you tell me this goddamn cock-and-bull story? There's not a word of truth to it." Taylor stammered that Cain had misunderstood him. Cain later said friends told him that Taylor had a guilt complex and was always accusing himself of something. "Also," said Cain, "he was one of those literary guys who was much hipped on my book, *Serenade*, and he'd rather say he was directed to steal from *Serenade* than be caught snooping around my literary pants."

Another reason Cain probably abandoned the plagiarism suit is that it would cost more money, and his usual year-end financial crisis was worse than ever. His total 1942 earnings up to October were only $6,000, he was several thousand dollars in debt, and he was facing a costly legal settlement with Elina.

Then, suddenly, his luck turned, and would continue to run his way for the rest of the war. He was offered a job at his old $1,000-a-week rate with 20th Century-Fox to write a script for the Signal Corps. Things being what they were in the studios, he thought it would be a good idea to "fall into line" on government work. But he had second thoughts when the War Department began investigating him. Cain complained to producer Robert Bassler, whom he would be working for at 20th Century, that his secretary had been besieged with phone calls from a War Department investigator inquiring whether he had any "journalistic credentials." The phone calls raised two questions, Cain said: (1) whether the investigator himself might not be a spy; and (2) whether the War Department should not be advised of the ineptitude of its investigators. With a million words of his in print and on file in the public library, Cain felt the investigation was a "ludicrous travesty."

The War Department finally cleared him and he took the job with the Signal Corps, meanwhile doing his best to win the war on another front. Early in 1943, he proposed a regular column for the *Los Angeles Daily News*, and at least his approach was unique. He wanted to do the column on one subject: Imperialism, mainly British imperialism. *News* editor Manchester Boddy replied that they could not afford to pay him enough to justify a column, that it would have to be the first step toward syndication, and that a syndicated column could hardly be on one subject alone. So Cain broadened his field to include Russian imperialism and various other aspects of our war policy, and spent about three weeks writing fifteen to twenty sample columns. But even with the Cain by-line on the column, Boddy was afraid too many readers would associate his paper with Cain's diatribes against helping Britain and Russia take over the world. So he rejected the column, though suggesting they have lunch and talk the whole thing over, which they did. Boddy and Cain remained friends through the war, with Cain's contribution to the paper consisting of an occasional guest column and letter to the editor.

The Signal Corps picture had been the brainchild of Colonel Darryl F. Zanuck. The idea was to dramatize and glorify the work of the Corps with a movie laid in North Africa, and after a trip to the Signal Corps base in San Bernardino, Cain wrote a script. It was reviewed by Lieutenant Colonel H. H. Lawson, Cain's technical adviser, and although the colonel found quite a few problems concerning language and procedure peculiar to the Signal Corps, he thought it "absorbing" and was sure it would make a "very thrilling and successful moving picture." Bassler, on the other hand, had some fundamental objections to Cain's script, and in analyzing its weaknesses he provided another insight into Cain's shortcomings as a screenwriter.

"You've written forty pages of script with no reaction shot," said Bassler. By this, he was referring to the intention behind the action, the characterization, the meaning, the clarification of motives. He was talking about the "very foundation of motion picture writing," Cain admitted, and from then on maintained that it was Bassler's insight which led to his ultimate success, such as it was, with the studios. However, the Signal Corps film was never made (the script has disappeared into the Army archives, if it exists at all), and by midsummer of 1943 Cain was out of a job again—though $34,000 richer.

He would need that money to settle his matrimonial difficulties. At first, when he walked out on Elina in August 1942, she expected him to come back, but he had not. Then Cain's lawyer met with Elina's lawyer and they tried to reach a settlement. But Cain would not accept Elina's demands. And because his lawyer and hers had both become friends with Gang during Cain's plagiarism trial, Cain thought it necessary to bring in another lawyer to convince Elina he meant business. So Elina sued Cain, which was played up in the press, much being made of the fact that Cain was earning $1,000 a week scriptwriting for 20th Century-Fox while she was making 65 cents an hour working in a war factory. Finally, in June 1943, they agreed on a lump-sum settlement of $27,500, to be paid as soon as possible.

The settlement, dragging on as it did for nearly a year, was an unpleasant, ugly business, with Elina demanding far more than she finally received and Cain feeling she was making excessive demands. This made it virtually impossible for them to remain on friendly terms, although they did correspond from time to time, and Cain did see her occasionally later—such as when Henrietta married, and then when Henrietta had a daughter, Christina, with whom Cain became quite enamored. It was a large divorce settlement for 1943, but Cain could now afford it. In addition to the money from the 20th Century-Fox assignment, he was about to make a major breakthrough in his studio work, and for the next few years would be one of the highest-paid writers in Hollywood.

Much to his surprise, almost immediately after the 20th Century job ended, Cain was offered a two-week guaranteed job with Universal—the studio he had recently sued for plagiarism. His director was George Waggner, a low-budget specialist who worked on "B" pictures (*The Wolf Man*, *Cobra Woman*, etc.). Waggner gave him a script called *Gypsy Maid*, saying it was for an actress named Maria Montez and that they had to have it in two weeks. Cain set out to do his best with a script he described as "simply weird." It was full of studio lingo, and there were eight different sequences intercutting with one another at the same time.

Despite the script and the deadline, Cain was determined to make good on this one. He had been writing for the studios for ten years and still considered himself a failure at it. "They're trying to make a picture writer out of me" he wrote Edmund Wilson, "though at present the thing hangs precariously in the balance." Although several of his stories had been turned into successful movies by others, he had only one major script—*Stand Up and Fight*—and he shared credit on that with two other writers. Now, with the war on, his novel writing not progressing, and the younger writers enlisting in the services, he knew there would be good money to be made in Hollywood for the writers left behind—and he was right. More important, Cain was now taking movies more seriously, as he had since 1942, when he began to meet what he called the "cultivated kind of producer." He also felt movies had improved considerably in the early forties, and he would keep going back to the better ones—like *The Little Foxes* and *The Major and the Minor*. He would view them four and five times, then discuss them with the film cutters and editors.

He knew it was time he had a success. "You're going to do the best script they ever read," he said to himself. And for two weeks he wrote day and night, taking the script to his hotel, then bringing his work in the next day for his secretary to type. When the two weeks were up, he was not quite finished, so Waggner gave him a little more time. Then, the day after he turned in the script, he dropped by Waggner's office and was depressed to see the director furiously working over his pages. He thought: "Cain, you've fouled up again." He approached Waggner for a farewell handshake, looking down at the desk, and said: "I'm sorry you didn't like my script."

"What d'ya mean, didn't like your script?"

"I see you're rewriting it."

"Jim, she couldn't play your dialogue any more than she could fly. All I'm doing is translating your beautiful dialogue into the rotten babytalk she has to have. I liked your script. I gave you that chopped-up, confused idiotic thing because I was ashamed to offer it to any writer that had written for me. You've tightened and simplified it and tuned it and redialogued it and it's a beautiful thing, and now I can put it in front of the cameras."

Cain regarded this job as the turning point in his Hollywood career, although when the movie—titled *Gypsy Wildcat*—was released the following year, it was murdered by the critics. "Set your brain at zero when you go to see this one," said Bosley Crowther in the *Times*. He thought the farce, which involved a gypsy charmer, really the orphan of a count, who is rescued from a venal baron by a handsome athletic prince (Jon Hall), would have had possibilities if written with any wit and gaiety, but "this one is done with the humor of a guy swinging a club at your head." He added: "Among the numerous scriptwriters is the name of James M. Cain. His impact upon the picture is completely intangible—unless, of course, he was responsible for the scene in which the villain draws a bow and arrow upon the momentarily careless hero, and says: 'Stick 'em up.' "

Soon after the movie was released, Universal, Cain, and a scriptwriter named Joseph Hoffman were sued by a writer who claimed the studio had plagiarized his story for *Gypsy Wildcat*. The judge finally dismissed the case, but Cain, who remembered how alone he had felt sitting in court when he sued Universal, felt sorry for the poor writer, who obviously had no case. "Why should you have to sit there," he remembered thinking at the time, "all alone in this court, except for those attorneys, and sue me, assisted by moving picture lawyers, moving picture witnesses and moving picture money. At least some writers should have made it their business to come to your aid, to have made your case their case." After the trial, Cain suggested to Hoffman that they form a committee of the Screen Writers Guild to try to discourage writers from suing for plagiarism unless they really had a case. But if they did have a case, then the writer should go all out, with the full support of the entire writing community. Nothing came of the idea, but both this case and Cain's own suit against Universal would play an important part in inspiring Cain later to become involved in the most controversial action of his career.

Gypsy Wildcat was hardly Academy Award material, but Cain did not care. He had $2,000 for two weeks work, and almost immediately he had another studio job—this one for three weeks (at $1,250 per) at United Artists to write the script for something called *The Moon, Their Mistress*, based on Chekhov's story "The Shooting Party"—a movie that was never made. It was also about this time that he worked on the script for Thornton Wilder's *Bridge of San Luis Rey*, produced by Benedict Bogeaus and directed by Roland V. Lee. But he was on the job only about a month, contributed little, and later said: "I can't remember anything about it."

Whatever significance *Gypsy Wildcat* may have had on Cain's Hollywood career, the real turnaround of his reputation had begun the previous spring with publication of the anthology of three Cain serials, *Three of a Kind*. Despite the fact that all the stories in the book were commercial ventures written for magazines, the collection was a remarkable literary success. A. C. Spectorsky wrote in *Book Week* that "Cain's style—grit, gore and gutsy lustiness—is as timely as war news, his plots are almost as exciting"; and John K. Hutchens, in the *Times*, said: "Without much question, Mr. Cain's men and women are the most highly combustible characters in modern fiction, an aspect of his story telling that would be a little ridiculous in a lesser craftsman. With Mr. Cain, it is one device in the general scheme of a writer who holds you by the sheer, dazzling pace he sets."

Cain and Knopf were aware that collections did not sell as well as full-length novels, but *Three of a Kind* had to go back to press, putting 8,000 copies in print soon after publication. "Later, if some of my writing kicks me into prominence," Cain wrote Knopf, taking the long view, "it may be a title that will have occasional spurts of activity, as the stories are readable enough." And the book had one curious laurel: In 1949, the *Saturday Review* and the American Library Association compiled a list of books by American authors published in the past quarter-century that librarians felt were the most popular with their readers. Despite the success of *Postman* and the furor aroused by *Serenade*, the only Cain title on the list was *Three of a Kind*.

Cain always maintained that the best way for a writer to attract attention in Hollywood was to write a novel or a play that was talked about in the media and around New York. This would open doors at the studios. And now *Three of a Kind* was about to demonstrate again the soundness of this approach. "Career in C Major" and "The Embezzler" were, of course, already owned by the studios, but "Double Indemnity" was not, primarily because no studio had had the guts or the imagination to fight the Hays Office on it. In 1935, when MGM requested a Hays Office report on Cain's *Liberty* serial, Joseph Breen, then heading the Office, vetoed the story primarily on the grounds that it was virtually a blueprint for murder committed by a woman and a man who are not only in an adulterous relationship but who then get away with the crime (although they do eventually commit suicide). The report had killed the story at MGM, as well as Paramount, Columbia, Warners, and 20th Century-Fox. Cain had seen a copy of the Hays Office report, and considering all the counts against "Double Indemnity," he had come to the conclusion by 1943 that it was "the most censorable story, if any story is censorable, I ever wrote."

With all the literary attention given *Three of a Kind*, Cain and his new agent, H. N. Swanson, decided to make another effort to sell the story to one of the studios. Cain even sent Swanson suggestions for how it could be made palatable to the Hays Office. Meanwhile, Swanson had galleys from *Three of a Kind* stitched up and sent around town. One man who became particularly impressed was Billy Wilder, an Austro-Hungarian writer-director who had just finished *Five Graves to Cairo* and had already created something of a legend with his work on *Hold Back the Dawn*, *The Major and the Minor*, and *Ninotchka*. As Cain told the story, one day Wilder could not find his secretary. He kept asking for her, and finally one of the other girls said, "I think she is still in the ladies' room reading that story."

"What story?" asked Wilder.

"Some story Mr. Swanson left here," at which moment Wilder's secretary came out with the stitched galleys pressed against her bosom. Wilder took the story home to read and immediately told Joe Sistrom, a Paramount producer, that he wanted to do it. But Charles Brackett, the writer who had worked with Wilder on most of his big hits, thought the story was disgusting and said he would not touch it. Wilder decided he would write it with someone else and told Sistrom to see about buying the story. Sistrom had also read it and was equally enthusiastic. So Bill Dozier, an MGM executive, was assigned to negotiate for the rights. He called Cain and Swanson to his office and, reminding them of all the trouble they would probably have with the Hays Office, offered them $15,000—$7,500 on signing and $7,500 if the final script was approved by Breen. Swanson and Cain left the room, and as soon as they were alone the agent said to Cain: "Bud [Swanson called everyone "Bud," according to Cain], if I were you, I'd take it. You're just bidding against yourself, and if we keep this thing in suspense Wilder might just turn away." So Cain agreed—and complained for years about the $10,000 the Hays Office had cost him. Back in 1935, when Hays had vetoed the *Liberty* serial, the going price was $25,000.

Once he had the script, Wilder declined various suggestions, including Cain's, for tampering with the story, having decided he would try to stick as close to the original plot as he possibly could. Before buying "Double Indemnity," he had been contemplating doing a musical, primarily to avoid being typed as a bitter, headline-oriented dramatist. But then he saw *Cover Girl* and told one interviewer: "I realized that no matter how good my musical might be, most people would say it was no 'Cover Girl.' This 'Double Indemnity' looked like a better chance to set Hollywood back on its heels. And I like to set Hollywood back on its heels. Even my own studio said I was crazy to attempt it."

Of course, by 1943 it was a lot more difficult to shock Hollywood and the Hays Office than it had been in 1935. The Victorian morality that had dominated the 1930s was already being cracked: Clark Gable had said, "I don't give a damn" on the screen, and Edward G. Robinson and James Cagney had shot their way through two dozen gangster films. Hollywood was apparently ready for the tough insurance agent and his evil woman who would plot the murder of the woman's husband as they carried on their adulterous affair. The war had created a demand for patriotic propaganda films, but it had also helped push Hollywood into more adult films, if only for the returning GIs who had seen the world and would demand more realism in their movies.

With his desire to adhere as closely as possible to the original story, Wilder at first wanted to hire Cain as his co-writer. He greatly admired Cain; and who, after all, could write that famous Cain dialogue better than James M. Cain? But in the spring of 1943, when Wilder was first thinking about the movie, Cain was still under contract to 20th Century, working on the Signal Corps script. Bill Dozier then came up with the name of Raymond Chandler, a relatively unknown but highly respected detective story writer. Wilder had never heard of Chandler, but when he read *The Big Sleep*, given to him by Sistrom, he was sold. Dozier wrote Knopf (who also published Chandler) for the writer's address, and was surprised to learn that he was living in Hollywood, although he had never worked for a studio. When Chandler naïvely offered to write the script for a few hundred dollars, Dozier brought in Swanson to represent him. He eventually signed for $750 a week for thirteen weeks.

Although Chandler and Wilder would write a script generally considered a classic today, at first the temperamental mystery writer seemed the worst possible collaborator. In the first place, although Chandler shared agents and publishers with Cain, he did not share Wilder's enthusiasm for the author of "Double Indemnity." In a letter to Knopf, Chandler had summed up his opinion of Cain in one word: "Faugh. Everything he touches smells like a billygoat. He is every kind of writer I detest, a faux naif, a Proust in greasy overalls, a dirty little boy with a piece of chalk and board fence and nobody looking. Such people are the offal of literature, not because they write about dirty things, but because they do it in a dirty way. . . . A brothel with a smell of cheap scent in the front parlour and a bucket of slops at the back door. Do I, for God's sake, sound like that?"

Well, Wilder, for one, hoped Chandler could sound like Cain, and he kept insisting Chandler adhere closely to the original text. But for some reason it did not sound right. It looked fine on paper, but it did not read right. They even hired a group of studio actors to read scenes right out of the book, but they discovered it sounded, at least in Chandler's view, like "a bad high school play." The dialogue oversaid everything, and when spoken sounded quite colorless and tame.

This led Wilder to set up a conference with Chandler, Sistrom, and Cain. He wanted to explain (even apologize, Cain thought) why they weren't using Cain's dialogue in the script. He told Cain how much he liked it in the book, but that when the three actors read it, it did not sound right. Cain apparently was not paying much attention to what they were saying and the only thing he was to recall from the conference was a statement made by Sistrom, who was bothered by how easily the insurance agent hit on his scheme for the perfect murder. Cain explained that in the novel it was implied that he had been meditating on it for years. But Sistrom was not satisfied. He just sat there staring, then suddenly said: "All characters in B pictures are too smart." "It was a curious observation," Cain said, "putting into vivid, memorable words a principle that when a character is too smart, convenient to the author's purposes, everything begins getting awfully slack in the story, and slick. Slack is one fault and slick is another. Both are bad."

If Sistrom and Wilder were troubled at the way things were going with Cain's story, Raymond Chandler was not. In fact, Chandler, whose opinion of Cain had improved somewhat, had given a lot of thought to Cain's dialogue, and in a letter to Cain, Chandler probably came as close as anyone ever has to diagnosing why James M. Cain never developed as a scriptwriter, or a playwright. "Nothing could be more natural and easy and to the point on paper," he wrote about Cain's dialogue, "and yet it doesn't quite play. . . . It had a remote effect that I was at a loss to understand. It came to me then that the effect of your written dialogue is partly sound and sense. The rest of the effect is the appearance on the page. These unevenly shaped hulks of quick-moving speech hit the eye with a sort of explosive effect. You read the stuff in batches, not in individual speech and counterspeech. On the screen, this is all lost, and the essential mildness of the phrasing shows up as lacking in sharpness. They tell me that is the difference between photographable dialogue and written dialogue. For the screen, everything has to be sharpened and pointed and wherever possible eluded. But of course you know far more about that than I do."

It is by no means obvious that Cain did know as much about it as Chandler. But by the time he received the letter, he was signed to a long-range contract at MGM at $1,250 a week and was feeling very confident, with everyone raving about *Double Indemnity*; he was not about to admit in print that he had any shortcomings as a scriptwriter. So he wrote Chandler that he was perfectly correct in his appraisal and that the dialogue in his novels and short stories is "calculated." But, he said: "I use a completely different system in picture work when I dictate for the ear and pay almost no attention to how it appears to the eye. I have been secretly amused at picture producers who tell me: 'And don't forget to give me plenty of that fast Cain dialogue.' The truth is the fact Cain dialogue wouldn't play at all, but I think it advisable not to tell them." Then he made a significant comment about his story: "Your description of the vague, cloudy way the dialogue sounded when you had it tried with actors is wholly interesting, for in 'Double Indemnity' I was trying to capture some of those bellowing unrealities you get in a fever dream, and if the dialogue sounded as you say it did, quite possibly I succeeded."

The script for *Double Indemnity*, as finally completed, told the basic original story in a series of confrontations that do not appear in the novel. And although these scenes adhere to the basic story line, less attention is paid in the movie to the gradual deterioration of the relationship between Phyllis Nirdlinger (changed to Dietrichson in the movie) and Walter Huff (changed to Neff).

To everyone's relief—and some surprise—the script passed the Hays Office. Then it was time for casting. Again Sistrom, Wilder, and Paramount showed rare insight and judgment. For the insurance investigator they picked Edward G. Robinson, who everyone agreed was perfect. But Walter Neff was more difficult. Wilder first went after George Raft, but Raft did not like the idea of being killed at the end of his movies. So he said he would do it if Neff turned out to be an FBI agent at the end, a good guy. When Wilder laughed at this, Raft turned it down (as he had turned down Sam Spade in *The Maltese Falcon*) and, as Wilder said: "That's when we knew we had a good picture." Next he approached Brian Donlevy, who also turned it down. Then he asked Fred MacMurray, who later recalled: "I fought a long losing fight against taking the role. . . . Day after day, Billy Wilder would renew the attack by asking: 'Well, have you changed your mind yet?' Day after day, I would retreat, shaking my head. I didn't want to admit that I was refusing the part because I was afraid of it, because I feared that a guy who had played nothing but comedy roles would find this part too heavy to handle." MacMurray finally agreed to play Neff, certain that Paramount would not let him. But Paramount had heard he had signed to do a picture with 20th Century-Fox, so they let him take the role, hoping it would ruin his career.

Barbara Stanwyck also had to be persuaded to take the role of Phyllis. "When Billy Wilder sent me the script," she said, "I had played medium heavies, but not an out-and-out killer. I was a little frightened of it." She took the script back to Wilder's office and told him: "I love the script and I love you, but I am a little afraid after all these years of playing heroines to go into an out-and-out cold-blooded killer."

Wilder looked at her and said: "Well, are you a mouse or an actress?"

"I hope I am an actress."

"Then do the part," Wilder replied. And, of course, she did, and was forever grateful to Wilder, because, as with Fred MacMurray, her performance in *Double Indemnity* revealed a new depth to her talent. Wilder put a blond wig on her (because "I wanted her to look as sleazy as possible"), and when Buddy DeSylva, then production head at Paramount, saw it in the first shots, he said: "We hire Barbara Stanwyck and here we get George Washington." But the wig helped turn Barbara Stanwyck into just the woman Wilder was looking for, and there are probably movie buffs today who still believe Barbara Stanwyck is a blonde. The ending was also changed significantly. At first, Wilder had Neff die in the gas chamber; in fact, Paramount spent $150,000 to reconstruct the gas chamber, and it took five days of shooting to make the scene to Wilder's satisfaction. But at the last minute, even though he thought it was one of the best scenes he ever directed, Wilder decided it was too strong and had Chandler write another ending—also different from the original. It had the wounded Neff stagger out of his office after dictating his confession, then collapse in the corridor. Eventually, it came to be regarded as one of the most dramatic and powerful scenes filmed in that era.

The movie was shot in a little over forty days in the fall of 1943, and all winter long the talk at the Brown Derby and other bars and restaurants was about a movie, then being edited, that would rock Hollywood and the country.

Without Elina to help keep his mind focused on one project, Cain went into another period of jumping from one thing to another following his two United Artists jobs in the summer of 1943. Leo, in fact, thinks the role Elina played in Cain's writing career went far deeper than just keeping him at the typewriter until he completed something. He points out that Cain's more important works—*Postman, Serenade,* "Double Indemnity," and *Mildred Pierce*—were all written while he and Elina were living together and Cain's inability to match these stories in his later books can be traced to their separation.

In addition to Elina's absence, there were the ordinary distractions inherent in the life of a Hollywood bachelor. Cain was seeing Kate regularly now, drinking too much, and indulging his gourmet tastes. As a result he was putting on weight, which in turn necessitated periodic dieting and trips on the wagon. Cain's interest in food went back to his days as an editorial writer on the *World*. And a great many of his syndicated columns when he wrote for Hearst had been devoted to food, including a series in which he conducted a one-man campaign to start the country eating catfish sandwiches. Recalling the popular reaction to those newspaper writings, he decided now that if he was going to be a writer of popular fiction he had to learn more about food, and he became an amateur cook. He also became friends in Hollywood with the headwaiter at the Townhouse. The man's name was Alexander Perino, and he seemed so knowledgeable about food that Cain suggested he start his own restaurant, which he eventually did. Leo remembers Perino coming to Cain's house on occasion to fix spaghetti, which became one of Cain's specialties. In fact, when he was asked by author Merle Armitage to contribute to a book of recipes, Cain sent him a three-page article that included not only his own special spaghetti recipe (which had been the hit of his musical evenings) but instructions for serving it. "Spaghetti, like steak, eggs, and hot dogs," Cain wrote, "is one of the irreducible simplicities of eating, and it is precisely these simplicities which must be right to the last decimal point of each person's taste. . . ." Another Cain specialty was "Shad Roe James M. Cain." And he also applauded himself for tracking down the recipe for Guatemala black bean soup featured at Pierre's in San Francisco. When he was in Guatemala, he talked to the maître d' at the Grand Hotel, who talked to the cook, both of whom assured Cain they had never heard of black bean soup. Later, he found the "recipe" consisted of one can of Heinz black bean soup, flavored with lemon.

As for his own prowess in the kitchen, Cain maintained he was "more of an experimenter than a true virtuoso, but I keep at it until I work out what I'm after." And with his stomach mended, he could now keep at it a long time, eating anything he wanted and as much as he wanted. This was soon evident. He ballooned to 233 pounds by mid-1943, and his old friend Henry Hopkins recalled how shocked he was to see Cain when he visited him in 1943: "He was a great big, coarse, heavy man, gross."

Another distraction for Cain was his unsettled living quarters. Trying to work at the Knickerbocker was not easy. It catered to musicians such as Paul Robeson, Sir Thomas Beecham, Phil Spitalny, and "some of the sweetest-blowing (and looking) lady brass players I ever heard and saw." There were also soldiers. "The boys," he wrote his sister, "are practically every night drunk, which is what I would be, I suppose, in their places, but it is trying when you try to sleep. And their lady friends are drunk, too, and visit across the areaway with friends of the opposite side; that is they visit by yelling and giving particulars about their horizontal activities, mainly the last one and the next one. Cute, but loud."

The war and his new life were having a peculiar effect on Cain. "Time just seems to slide along without leaving a trace," he wrote his sister. Nevertheless, he considered 1943 one of the most important years of his life. He was enjoying good health and was "well along the road I have cut out for myself and, in general, have started a new life." But during the transition to this new life, writing was very difficult. In September, he wrote Arthur Krock that he had become a picture writer for the duration, but was still planning the book about the woman who worked in the *World* morgue, though "I can't be persuaded a book by me at this time is of any consequence whatever." In October, he wrote Knopf he was planning a book that would enable him to deliver a few political opinions—"a fictitious history of the Confederacy on the assumption that Beauregard held his fire at Fort Sumter, that the Confederacy attained its independence in 1861, and that the war never was fought. The narration will make use of actual persons, they will all keep their Appointment in Samarra at the indicated time and take part in the story according to their character." Three days later, he wrote Knopf again, this time that he was indeed planning to start the novel about the woman in the newspaper morgue—"probably the best idea I ever had." Later that same month, he wrote someone else that he was considering coming East to work on his play *7-11*. But by the end of the year, that agony of a play was apparently dead, once and for all, and he was writing Mencken to send him the titles of six or eight symphonies written in a minor key because a woman in a novel he was writing (probably the woman who worked at the *World*) found music in a minor key very important to her imagination.

And all during the fall, he was working on an anthology for the World Publishing Company. In August, World editor William Targ had written Cain asking him to do an introduction to a collection of stories aimed at the millions of men in uniform. It was to be called *For Men Only* and would consist of eighteen short stories by well-known authors—Hemingway, Runyon, Lardner, Steinbeck, O'Hara, Farrell, etc.—as well as one by Cain, which Targ asked him to select. He said "the name of James M. Cain, one of America's finest writers, would lend inestimable prestige and reader acceptance to our volume." Cain responded with an introduction but said he would probably write a different one if they would send him copies of the eighteen stories, some of which he had never read and most of which he had not read in twenty years. For his own contribution, he picked "Girl in the Storm"—"a variant of the two or three of mine that are reprinted until I suppose people think they are the only ones I ever wrote."

Targ sent him galleys of the stories, and Cain wrote a new introduction. He also suggested they drop Michael Arlen's "Man with the Broken Nose" and add Dorothy Parker's "Big Blonde" (which he thought "one of the great short stories in the language") as well as stories by A. Conan Doyle and Edgar Allan Poe, to all of which Targ agreed. Then, at the last minute, Targ added seven additional stories. Cain protested, saying, "Why don't you leave well enough alone," that the book as it stood was "delightful." Targ deferred to Cain's judgment and the anthology was published in 1944 and proved an attractive, successful venture. Cain received only $250 for his work, but said he did not care: "I don't count money in connection with this kind of work, and I greatly enjoy it."

Cain did, in fact, enjoy almost any opportunity to sound off in the public print with his ideas about writers and writing, and his introduction to *For Men Only* is a treasure of little nuggets on his fellow fiction writers. He concluded by praising the short story as one form of fiction that need not, to please American taste, deal with heroes. "Our national curse, if so perfect a land can have such a thing," he wrote, "is the 'sympathetic character.' . . . My friends, I take exception to this idealism, as the Duke of Wellington is said to have taken exception to a lady's idealism, when he told her: 'Madam, the Battle of Waterloo was won by the worst set of blackguards ever assembled in one spot on this earth.' The world's great literature is peopled by thoroughgoing heels, and in this book you will find a beautiful bevy of them, with scarcely a character among them you would let in the front door. I hope you like them. I think they are swell."

By 1943 it appeared as if Hollywood had also lost its idealism. When the word went around that Billy Wilder and Raymond Chandler had cleared the Hays Office with their script for *Double Indemnity*, the heels in Cain's novels became not only acceptable but sought after. Once again, the Brown Derby and Perino's were full of talk about making *Serenade* into a movie, and about the executives in the MGM dining rooms taking another look at *Postman*, which they had bought ten years earlier. Then Jerry Wald, a Warner Brothers producer, approached Cain with the idea of making a movie out of *Mildred Pierce*. But instead of toning it down, as Clifton Fadiman said would have to be done, Wald was thinking of adding a murder—an idea Cain thought had been suggested to Wald by Mark Hellinger. Monty Berrigan, the playboy Mildred married, would be murdered at the beginning of the movie, after Mildred discovers he is having an affair with her daughter. Cain objected and wrote Wald a long letter explaining why, at the same time outlining an alternative story and sketching the characters, especially a somewhat different treatment of Monty. Apparently impressed, Wald asked Cain to prepare a memorandum for him to send to Jack Warner. But Cain, after a couple of attempts, declined. "I wrote *Mildred Pierce* as a novel," he told Wald, "and it is hard for me to rethink it for a picture. Somehow, that doesn't work for me." But Wald was not discouraged and continued trying to develop a script for *Mildred*, using a treatment prepared by Thames Williamson.

At about the same time, Cain was hired to work with the man he considered MGM's best producer—Arthur Hornblow. His assignment was to write a treatment for a film to be called *Frankie from Frisco*, about California in the early 1850s. He would be paid $1,250 a week and, if the treatment was approved, he would have a job for at least a year. Cain had planned to go home to Baltimore for Christmas and even had his ticket on the Chief, but by mid-December he was writing Rosalie that he might not be able to come, that it would be "simply folly after all these years of debt and misery" to miss this golden opportunity if it should develop. He also wrote "Mamma," as he always addressed his mother, that his outline would be completed on the thirteenth or fourteenth of December and "then I know if I am a genius or a bum."

The treatment was approved by Hornblow and suddenly things were looking good. By the spring of 1944, Cain would be MGM's resident genius (at $1,250 a week), author of the hottest movie in town (Paramount's *Double Indemnity*), and several other "hot properties" that a new, daring Hollywood was considering. Everything was coming up roses—except in the one area that always gave James M. Cain trouble: women.

By the end of 1943, Cain's long friendship and affair with Kate Cummings was winding down to an unpleasant end, and there is no doubt that it hurt Cain deeply. "Kate was part of me in ways that no other woman was," he said, "and I owed her things I owed no other woman, such as my life, for what it's worth [meaning, it was Kate who persisted until he finally had his operation]." He thought Kate was shrewd and had brains and would have added something he desperately needed to his life if they had married. He has also given us one explanation why that wasn't to be. After his operation, he said, "I became God's masterpiece in the way of a drunk, the real reason Kate and I broke up, if I tell the truth about it."

However, Leo and Henrietta, Cain's stepchildren, think it was Cain who broke up with "Old Grandma," as Leo always called Kate, and Henrietta recalled that Cain seemed quite relieved when the friendship was over. But two years after the break, Cain attempted a reconciliation. Kate, however, was still bitter and would not hear of it. And so, on the rebound from this unhappy affair, Cain did what many other unhappy lovers have done: he married someone else—and it was a disaster.

RAISING CAIN WITH
THE HAYS OFFICE

Aileen Pringle was something of a legend in Holly-
wood. She had appeared on the stage with George Arliss in *The Green Goddess*, and at MGM starred in *Three Weeks* (which did for her what *It* did for
Clara Bow). She was also in *Adam and Evil*, a farce with Lew Cody, which
was followed by a series of similar comedies featuring the two stars. Her
beauty complemented an intelligence rare in Hollywood; she was described
by her close friend Gloria Swanson as "about my size with yards of auburn
hair and a scorching wit." She also had an independent spirit that made it
impossible for her to get along with the new breed of Hollywood moguls. "She
turned down a contract with Mr. DeMille," Ms. Swanson says in her autobiography, "because she had heard him berate Pauline Garon on the set one
day in front of 50 people. . . . She said DeMille had become a tyrant."

It is usually said that Aileen Pringle's Hollywood career was brought to
an end by the arrival of talking pictures, but Cain disputed this, pointing out
that she always did well on radio and "talked beautifully." According to Aileen herself, it was not talkies but conflict with a studio executive that ended
her career. "I was not much of a businesswoman," she told Hedda Hopper,
explaining her $250-a-week salary at a time when MGM was making millions
from her pictures. "I not only didn't invite my studio bosses to my parties, I

didn't care about money. My work was fun and I loved it. But when I found that one of the men who was then head of the studio misinformed me about a story he said he had bought for me, I jerked him by his tie string and said: 'I thought I was dealing with an honest man. You've spoiled this whole acting business for me. I don't care if I play Norma Shearer's maid in blackface, I'm through!' And he saw to it that I was."

After she quit films, Aileen remained in Hollywood, occasionally making a picture or working for the studios, which sometimes included meeting visiting celebrities from the East. Being witty and intelligent, she could keep a conversation going with even such brilliant conversationalists as H. L. Mencken, whom she had met in 1926 at a party given by the novelist Joseph Hergesheimer at his home in Pennsylvania. Aileen and Mencken became good friends, and after Mencken's highly publicized visit to Hollywood in 1926, their friendship blossomed to the point where they were romantically linked in the gossip columns. They did become very close, but it was a friendship carried on primarily across the continent through letters, which Mencken asked Aileen to return when he became engaged to Sara Haardt in 1930. Another friend of Cain's who knew Aileen long before Cain did was Samson Raphaelson. "She was absolutely delightful. Still good-looking well into her forties. She was literate, knew a lot about writing, and loved writing. I met her when somebody wanted to do my play *Young Love* in San Francisco. She was going to play one of the two women parts. She was hilarious. Always lots of fun."

Cain first met Aileen at a party in 1944 given by Robert Nathan, the novelist who wrote *Portrait of Jenny* and who, like Cain, spent several years in Hollywood working at the studios between novels. "This very good-looking number," said Cain, "was sitting like a Hollywood picture star when she holds court, spreading her skirt out on the floor in front of her. The adoring circle gathers around her and listens with their mouths hanging open."

Aileen's monologue was probably on the ex–movie star's favorite subject, What ever happened to show business? and probably went something like this, as she later rattled off to one reporter: "We were all friends, part of the same family. It wasn't only the money. We put on our own makeup and we kept our own faces and our own personalities. Today, these kids go into the makeup department and the guy arches their eyebrows like Dietrich, gives them lips like somebody else, and they all come out looking exactly the same. In the old days we used to be invited to sit with the writer and producer and in a friendly way talk about the story. We'd sit for hours seeing the rushes, again and again."

It was the kind of talk Cain liked, and he figured he ought to know who this woman was. Then he recognized her, and when her adoring circle began to drift away he eased over and introduced himself. Aileen had known of Cain, and soon they were having dinner together, talking about their many mutual friends, including Mencken, Jed Harris, and Arthur Krock, and the fact that they had been just missing each other at various parties and weekends all their lives. "He was a very charming man," said Ms. Pringle, "with old-world manners."

Shortly after Cain met Aileen, a tragedy hit his family, one that must have brought with it painful reminiscences of his recent marriage. In January, his stepdaughter Henrietta had married an Army pilot, Judson Holmes. Cain did not attend the wedding, and he subsequently met Holmes only once; Judson and Henrietta and one or two other service couples dropped by the Knickerbocker one night after the wedding, and they all had a visit in the bar, which Cain recalled as a very pleasant evening. Two days later, Lieutenant Holmes and his flight crew, all of whom were at the wedding reception, left California headed for Tucson, Arizona, with Holmes piloting the plane. Trying to avoid a storm, Holmes crashed the plane into the Santa Catalina mountains and everyone aboard was killed. The Army notified Holmes's mother in Danbury, Connecticut, but since Army officials had not yet been informed of the marriage, the *Los Angeles Times* carried the story before Henrietta knew about it. Cain saw it in the paper and immediately called Elina to see how Henrietta was taking the news, only to find that no one in the family had heard. It was a tragic affair for Henrietta, who had had a difficult time growing up in Hollywood but seemed to have found genuine happiness with her new husband. The few days they had in their marriage, they conceived a girl, Christine, born in November. And Cain completely fell in love with his stepgranddaughter.

In addition to Cain's complex and turbulent personal life and a full-time job at MGM, he was involved in a number of activities, all of which made working on a novel virtually impossible. He was following the war closely, doing everything asked to help in the war effort, and was constantly firing off letters to editors, columnists, and soldiers in the field offering encouragement and advice. He wrote a one-minute radio announcement for the Treasury Department to promote its fourth War Bond Drive, which the Department broadcast nationwide, the first time it had done this with a personal message from a prominent citizen. He also wrote the *Los Angeles Times* protesting the sentencing of one Captain Morrison—a flyer "who had faced Japanese bullets"—to thirty years of hard labor for rape of a woman who took several drinks with the captain early in the morning and then agreeably went on an automobile ride with him. To accuse a veteran of rape, under the circumstances, was "monstrous" in Cain's view.

In his personal correspondence, he wrote to Clifton Fadiman, saying he had become an "Exterminationist," meaning we should exterminate the Nazis. "I not only believe that Germans are Nazis but that the purpose of our post-war dispositions should be permanently to destroy their strength, rather than punish their guilt or teach them a lesson." He also wrote Mencken about this "louse of a war, producing neither words nor slogans nor music of any but the frailest kind." And he resumed his correspondence with Walter Lippmann—congratulating him on his new book, *U.S. War Aims*, but adding that being "wholly anti-imperialist and expecting little from Britain and Russia, I naturally find much in it to disagree with." Similarly, he wrote Raymond Moley of *Newsweek* congratulating him for clarifying the relationship between American domestic and foreign policies, adding that "if this country could ever get it through its head that the wheat surplus is as vital a part of our foreign policy as the agreement at Tehran, we might be getting somewhere."

After the landing at Normandy, Cain wrote a letter to his old World War I regiment, the Headquarters Troop of the 79th Division, suggesting that someone keep in mind the idea of a book about the troop's fighting in World War II (like the one he had done for his Headquarters company after the first war) and enclosing a $10 bill for the first copy of the book. Lieutenant Harry Miller of the 314th Regiment, which saw action at Normandy, never forgot Cain's letter, and three years later he wrote *Through Combat*, the story of the 314th Regiment in Europe. And he sent the first copy to Cain.

In addition to, or perhaps because of the war, Cain also became involved in something he had rarely taken an interest in: politics. In the spring of 1944, Representative John Costello, a Democrat and Cain's representative in Congress, faced an unusually ugly primary challenge from Hal Styles, a local radio announcer who had the support of the CIO. Styles also had the backing of the Hollywood Democratic Committee, which as far as Cain could see was a mixture of "fuzz-buzz pinkoes" and "straight fellow travelers." Cain contributed $100 to Costello and did minor chores for the campaign, but to no avail. Costello was defeated, and for a while Cain was active in a movement to run him anyway in a three-man race; but that plan was abandoned, and Cain turned his support to the Republican congressional candidate. He also supported Thomas E. Dewey against President Roosevelt, primarily because he felt FDR was too sick to serve another four years and his vice-presidential candidate, Harry S Truman, was "history's monstrous typographical error." In fact, Cain was a member of the Executive Committee of the Democrats for Dewey—another losing cause. But Cain came away from the 1944 campaign with his own glimpse of the future, and in a long letter to Frank Kent, the *Baltimore Sun* columnist, he predicted that labor unions would play a powerful role in practical, day-to-day postwar politics.

Cain was not doing much better at MGM than he was in politics. Although Arthur Hornblow had approved his treatment for *Frankie from Frisco*, he was not pleased with Cain's first effort at the script. He thought it lacked a central idea and was dissatisfied with Cain's heroine Frankie, feeling she did not have enough troubles to generate a successful picture. Cain agreed, probably wondering how anyone whose books were in such demand at the studio could have so much trouble writing a script himself. By now Jack Warner was convinced he could make a script out of *Mildred Pierce* and Warner Brothers had bought it for $15,000. And everyone in Hollywood was talking about *Double Indemnity*, which even Cain thought was one of the finest movies he ever saw. "After several viewings," Cain said, "I woke up to a curious fact: I was *not* ahead of the camera, waiting for heads to pop up, or anything to pop up. I was, as the saying goes, *with it*. I was on the suspense at all times, scarcely aware of photography, my mind absorbed in people and what they were doing. . . . Through some magic, whatever illusion is made of, I was caught and stayed caught." This surprised Cain, who still had a very low regard of most moviemaking. But maybe, he decided, it was time to see more films. So he began going to the theater regularly, first alone and then with Aileen, sometimes in parties of four or five. In Hollywood in 1944, the place to go for an evening was the movie theater—to see and be seen. And they saw everything—from *Andy Hardy's Blonde Trouble* and *I Love a Soldier* to *Mask of Dimitrios*, *Laura*, and *Madame Curie*—sixty movies in one year.

It was a transition period for both Cain and Aileen. Each was recently divorced and at "loose ends," as Cain put it. There was an immediate and strong physical attraction, Cain told one friend, though at least twice in the early stages of their friendship they broke off the relationship. By the beginning of summer, however, they were talking seriously of marriage, with Aileen, according to Cain, more eager to try it than he was. Cain, in fact, had real misgivings about his ability to make a go of marriage at all, and so he warned Aileen. He also pointed out that he was not the easiest man to get along with when working on a book, that he did not like "going about" when he was writing, and that his income was irregular, depending on the whims of the studios and the sale of his books. But according to Cain, all such discussions ended with Aileen saying "If we do get hungry, I'll steal the food."

For her part, Aileen made it clear she had no assets, except for her little house at 722 Adelaide Place in Santa Monica, and kept insisting, according to Cain, that they have a trial marriage of six months or so. "If I make you unhappy in any way," she told him, "I'll give you a divorce and it won't cost you a cent." Cain replied: "I'm not entering trial marriage and I don't think either of us should be in that frame of mind. So far as I am concerned, it is a life sentence and in your heart I think it is, too. But if it turns out differently,

I have no doubt you will do as you say and I am not in the least concerned on that score."

They were married in July 1944, by which time Cain was enough of a celebrity to be courted by Hedda Hopper. When she called Cain to ask him if it was true he was getting married, he replied, "I sure is." Hedda gushed: "We can forgive the famous author of 'Double Indemnity' for being ungrammatical because he was a very happy and excited gent."

The wedding was a small affair at the courthouse in Santa Monica, and at the reception Cain was particularly annoyed by the Vincent Lawrences, who brought an uninvited guest; they also brought along their chauffeur and proceeded to get drunk. This embarrassed Cain, who was moving, temporarily at least, into Hollywood society—a move that some of his old friends thought would never work. "When I heard he married Aileen Pringle I couldn't understand it," said John Lee Mahin. "She'd always been part of a Hollywood that was tinsel, the Hollywood Cain didn't like. She was very social and had to be with either Doug or Mary, that crowd. He didn't go for that."

Mencken, on the other hand, was delighted. "Of all the women extant in this great Republic," he wrote, "Aileen is probably the most amusing. You may resent it when she tries to run you as she undoubtedly will, for there is a Regular Army general hidden in her soft and disarming exterior, but you will never be bored."

Their honeymoon was in San Francisco and Sacramento, where Aileen quickly learned what it was like to be married to a writer: Cain spent much of the time researching a book at the library in Sacramento. At the start of the year, he had still been preoccupied with the novel about the woman who worked in the *World* morgue. But now he had shifted his attention back to the story of the Virginia City prostitute, which he wanted to begin in Sacramento on a river boat. As always, Cain had to have every background detail just right, and he apparently had also done personal research on at least one aspect of the story. "The prettiest girl I have met in six months," he wrote a friend in August, "was a little prostitute, whom I was on the edge of falling for, and then she went to bed with one of my friends. There is nothing wrong with a prostitute, but if she has pretty black eyes, she packs plenty of grief for anybody who gets involved with her. Anyway, enough for one book."

Cain and Aileen returned from their honeymoon just in time for the public premiere of *Double Indemnity*, and it was obviously a smash. Wilder and Chandler were nominated for the Academy Award (but lost to the writers of *Going My Way*); the *New York Herald Tribune* called it "one of the most vital and arresting films of the year" and said Wilder had made a "sensational contribution" to filmmaking. And the nation's three toughest critics—John

Lardner in *The New Yorker*, Bosley Crowther in the *Times*, and James Agee in *The Nation*—all had words of praise for it. But Louella Parsons had no reservations: " 'Double Indemnity' is the finest picture of its kind ever made," she wrote, "and I make that flat statement without any fear of getting indigestion later from eating my own words."

It was, in fact, a statement Louella would not have to eat, because there probably had never been a film quite like *Double Indemnity*. Billy Wilder maintained that it, not *The Maltese Falcon*, revolutionized Hollywood's approach to crime films, and the critics have generally agreed that *Double Indemnity* opened the door in America to what the French call the *film noir*. Philip K. Scheur, the *Los Angeles Times* movie critic, ranked it with *The Human Comedy*, *The Maltese Falcon*, and *Citizen Kane* as Hollywood trailblazers, and Alfred Hitchcock wrote Wilder that "Since 'Double Indemnity,' the two most important words in motion pictures are 'Billy Wilder.' " Wilder himself said that of all his films, "it had the fewest mistakes," adding that it "moves in the staccato manner of Cain's style." He always maintained that the two things he was proudest of in his career were the compliments he received from Cain and Agatha Christie for his handling of *Double Indemnity* and *Witness for the Prosecution*.

Cain sent all the principals involved in the movie—Robinson, MacMurray, and Stanwyck—autographed copies of his *Three of a Kind* with a note praising their work and their faithful portrayal of his characters. He thought MacMurray, particularly, had done a superb job: "The way you found tragedy in his shallow, commonplace, smart-cracking skull will remain with me for a long time and, indeed, reinforce an aesthetic viewpoint that many quarrel with; for if I have any gift, it is to take such people and show that they can suffer as profoundly as anybody else. If, harkening to clamor, I ever weaken and begin to pretty my characters up, I shall remember your Walter and be fortified."

And he wrote Barbara Stanwyck: "It is a very creepy sensation to see a character imagined by yourself step in front of your eyes exactly as you imagined her."

It was, in fact, a milestone film for each of its three principals. Edward G. Robinson's biographer wrote that " 'Double Indemnity' salvaged his [Robinson's] self-respect and career." It also demonstrated that Barbara Stanwyck, with the aid of her famous white sweater and blond wig, could play heavy, dramatic roles, and her performance won her an Academy Award nomination. And it showed that Fred MacMurray could play something besides light comedy. MacMurray always considered it his favorite role in pictures.

For Cain, although he maintained that Joseph Breen owed him $10,000 for vetoing *Double Indemnity* back in 1935 when he would have received $25,000 for its sale, the movie was especially rewarding. He wrote one friend that with the success of the film, "they have begun to wonder whether I'm so crazy after all." And in a Paramount press release for the film, he said that although "Double Indemnity" was the most censorable story he ever wrote, "it has been put on the screen exactly as I wrote it, only more so." He was aware of the impact the movie might have on Hollywood: "It may be, since the word 'adult' is the one reviewers use most frequently in connection with it, that a new field for moving pictures has been opened up."

It certainly opened up the movies for Cain and marked a victory in his ten-year war with the Hays Office, a war that began when it rejected MGM's attempt to do *Postman*. If Breen would approve a script of *Double Indemnity* that adhered so closely to the original story, he would approve anything. Warner Brothers, having bought *Mildred Pierce*, even began negotiations to buy *Serenade*. And about the same time, MGM dusted off *Postman* and writer-producer Carey Wilson quietly went to work on a script that would satisfy the new, more liberal Hays Office.

Working on *Mildred Pierce*, Jerry Wald went through several writers (Catherine Turney, Albert Maltz, Ranald MacDougall) before he finally came up with a script that satisfied him. But he never did satisfy Cain. "I'm quite startled," Cain wrote Wald about the first script the producer sent him, "to discover the adaptation has deliberately scrapped the one element in that tale which is, so to speak, its keystone. That is, the implication of having a big coloratura soprano in the family; without this, the story completely lacks point. . . . There was one basic element in *Mildred Pierce*," he continued, and "when I remembered it, it made the book go, and when I forgot, it let me in for the dreariest headaches I ever had in connection with anything I wrote. This was it: O.K., says God, you think this girl is talented. You want her to be a concert pianist. But if you want an artist in the family, why not a real one, a coloratura soprano? 'Thanks, God,' says Mildred, 'you sure are treating me swell.' But, says God, are you sure you want an artist at all? They're kind of queer, you know. Maybe Glendale is not the place for one. Maybe you're not the mother for one. I can't even hear what you say. So God says, O.K., here she is—I hope you like what you ordered."

Everything in the story, said Cain, focused on this fable. The very stature of the tale derived from the complete hopelessness of Veda's ever accepting Mildred or Mildred's ever understanding Veda. He resented Wald's transforming Veda into "a cheap little tart" and making the necessity of Mildred's getting her back "a moral question." As for the murder, he thought Wald had gone out of his way to make trouble for himself. "The poetic retribution in the story is that Mildred, having used Monty as live bait, discovers the bait has swallowed her fish." What was essential, psychologically, "is that Mildred root this overzealous affection out of her heart, and I think any murder simply beclouds the whole issue and leaves the story in an impossible situation. . . . Furthermore, the Veda in your script would never have the guts to kill Monty or the pride to want to kill him."

Cain argued that the wide appeal of *Mildred Pierce*, exemplified by the hundreds of thousands of copies sold in reprint, "rests on its subject: the aspiration that lurks in every mother's heart for the children she brings into the world, and particularly the one white-headed child who is her favorite. This book simply says perhaps a dream come true may be the worst possible thing that can happen. But before the story has any point at all, there must be a dream and it must come true. Your Mildred dreams of ham sandwiches. My Mildred, although it is constantly stated that ham sandwiches are the limit of her talent, dreams tall dreams for Veda and then has the egregious misfortune to have them come true."

He conceded it was always easier to criticize than to create, and he expressed the wish that he were in a position to do the script for Wald, as "I think we could get out one that is pretty good without much trouble." But Cain was under contract to MGM, so Wald went back to his writer and, two months later, had forty-nine pages of a new script. He also had a director—Michael Curtiz, one of Hollywood's most respected commercial hands (*Kid Galahad, Dodge City, Casablanca*, and, just released, *Passage to Marseille*). Wald sent the new script to Cain, and still Cain was not happy with it. He mailed off another long letter to Wald, stressing that *Mildred Pierce* was an attempt to develop a serious theme and objecting to Warner's attempt to exploit his literary and cinematic reputation—based, as it was, on *Postman* and *Double Indemnity*—by turning *Mildred* into that kind of Cain thriller. He told Wald that he thought the opening shots of the new script "have tingle, the promise of great photographic effectiveness, and that curious quality describable only as style, which I imagine Curtiz had a great deal to do with." But he felt the "only point developed in this footage is: Who done it? This, it seems to me, is a very thin springboard for a story which at least aims at some wider implication. For *Mildred Pierce* is one woman's struggle against a great social injustice—which is the mother's necessity to support her children even though husband and community give her not the slightest assistance."

Still against superimposing the murder on the story, he had his own ideas about the beginning of *Mildred Pierce*, an approach that would have made it a completely different picture:

I don't see why this picture can't open with Bert watering the grass, perhaps the most inane occupation any man ever had, and susceptible of a beautiful, brief comedy routine. Perhaps during this Mrs. Biederhof passes by and we see that something goes on. From then on, from his entrance into the kitchen to the end of the whole grim scene, we could move to the simple, clear springboard: Mildred is on her own. She is "that great American institution, a grass widow with two small children to support," a good-looking girl in an awful spot, the surest formula for a movie that has yet been invented. Why not tell that story, which at least has its own quality, rather than a murder story not very different from every "B" picture that has been made for the last forty years? The ending, no doubt, needs modification, because Veda's tricky little victory is all wrong. But not modification to a point of homicide. They are not that kind of people.

This was Cain's last, valiant effort to save *Mildred Pierce* from being made into "another *Double Indemnity*," and he lost. But if Wald and Warner Brothers missed the point of *Mildred*, it is only fair to say that most of the book's reviewers did too. I have not read one review that mentioned Mildred's struggle to raise two children without the aid of her husband as the book's essential theme.

When Wald finally had a script he liked, his next challenge was to pick his Mildred. Warner had tried to lure Bette Davis, but she turned down the role. The studio then sought Ann Sheridan, but director Curtiz, wanting to go with a Cain winner, was promoting Barbara Stanwyck. Wald, however, had his own ideas. *Mildred Pierce* was to be an important film for this live-wire hustler, reputed in Hollywood to be the model for Sammy Glick in Budd Schulberg's *What Makes Sammy Run?* He had just come off a series of war movies—*Objective Burma*, *Destination Tokyo*, and *Pride of the Marines*—all successful, but all dominated by men. Like Wilder, Wald knew that once you are pigeonholed in Hollywood it is the beginning of the end, and despite his reputation as a producer of "men's pictures," he was also aware that the war would not last forever and that postwar America would probably go back to its old ways, with theater audiences dominated by women. So he wanted a "woman's picture." When Jack Warner, caught up in the *Double Indemnity* excitement, gave him *Mildred Pierce* to read, he thought this was it. But he knew he had to have the right woman to play her, and he was pretty sure who she might be: Joan Crawford, the glamor girl of the thirties, now on the downside of her career. Crawford had finally separated from MGM, after eighteen years, and was in retirement during the war, living quietly at home with her two adopted children and unemployed husband, Phillip Terry. Hoping to make a comeback, she had signed a contract with Warner Brothers for $500,000 to make three films—insisting, however, on the right to pick her scripts, even to the point of telling Jack Warner that she was prepared to be taken off the payroll rather than play in a certain movie (to be called *Never Goodbye*) he was trying to force on her. "That broad must be crazy," Warner is reported to have said. But Crawford stuck by her decision. Like Wald, she knew what she wanted—a dramatic role that would be different from anything she had done in the past.

When she signed the new contract, her agent, Lew Wasserman, had taken her around Warner Brothers to meet all the producers. One of them, Wald, meeting her for the first time, was impressed, seeing something in Crawford everyone else had missed. "To me, even in that initial meeting, Crawford appealed as something a hundred times more important than glamor. I looked at that pulse-speeding face and figure and I thought, 'Here's a great dramatic actress.' " He also decided this great actress was the one to help remake Jerry Wald's reputation as a producer of a "woman's picture." So he sent her a copy of *Mildred Pierce* together with the script Ranald Mac-Dougall had finally developed, and when she read them she called Wald on the phone, exclaiming, "I love it, I love it. It's exactly what I've been waiting for!" They talked for more than an hour about directors, the cast, cameramen, and all the rest that goes into the production of a film.

When Wald told Warner he wanted Crawford and that she had agreed, the studio was enthusiastic, but now there was the problem of persuading director Curtiz: "Me direct that temperamental bitch?" he yelled, according to Crawford's biographer, Bob Thomas. "Not on your goddamn life. She comes over here with her high-hat airs and her goddamn shoulder pads. I won't work with her. She's through, washed up. Why should I waste my time directing a has-been?" Even Warner's top cameraman, Ernest Haller, resisted, saying he could not photograph her.

But Curtiz was still excited about the story, and after considerable pleading Wald persuaded his director and the cameraman to work with Crawford, though only after she had agreed to a screen test—an unprecedented step for an established star. Crawford also had to acknowledge that the director was boss on the set. So the cast was assembled: Bruce Bennett as Mildred's unfaithful husband, Bert; Zachary Scott as Monty Beragon, the playboy; Jack Carson as Mildred's partner, Wally; and Eve Arden as Mildred's faithful friend, Ida. And for Veda, Wald finally selected a promising Universal hopeful, Ann Blyth, one of twenty to thirty actresses who tried for the role, and who made it primarily because Crawford thought she was perfect and coached her through the audition.

No sooner had shooting started than it appeared as if *Mildred Pierce* would be a disaster. On the first day, when Crawford and her designer arrived on the set, Curtiz took one look at her dress and yelled to the designer:

"No, you son of a bitch. I told you no shoulder pads." Joan appeared in another dress, and Curtiz started shouting again about those "damned Adrian shoulder pads" and had the studio buy her a wardrobe of $3.97 Sears specials. Then Haller began lighting her differently than she had ever been lighted before. And finally Wald began to have some hope that the picture might be made. "For the first few days," he wrote, "the rushes looked like hell from every angle. But the dawn came before the end of the week. Mike cut himself down to swearing only in Hungarian, Ernie began smiling. Crawford stopped trying to wrap those aprons around her and let them drag. And I began sleeping nights."

So *Mildred Pierce* was off and shooting in the unlikely hands of a "men's picture" producer, a washed-up, temperamental glamor girl, and an equally temperamental director who did not like the star, working with a cameraman who said the star could not be photographed.

At the same time, over at MGM, *Postman* also appeared to be in unlikely hands. Carey Wilson was best known as the producer of the Andy Hardy series, and insiders around Hollywood were shaking their heads and saying Wilson had taken on *Postman* only because he wanted a change from the Mickey Rooney films—forgetting he had also worked on *Ben Hur* and *Mutiny on the Bounty*. But more important, and more simply, Wilson was an admirer of Cain's and thought *Postman* was one of the greatest stories he had ever read. Cain ran into Wilson one day on the Metro lot and the producer had a satanic look in his eye. "You're going to say I'm crazy, but I'm going to do your *Postman*."

Cain disagreed, saying that Joe Breen in the Hays Office, not Wilson, would be writing it. But Wilson said no. "It can be done. I'm not even worried about Breen. I'm worrying about how to tell it. But I'm going to have some fun with him."

The next time Cain saw Wilson on the lot, the producer explained what he meant by fun with Breen: "He says it can be done and he's tickled to death I'm going to try it. I wasn't there over twenty minutes, but you should have seen his face when I got up to go and hadn't said one word about *Double Indemnity*. And as I held out my hand, he said: 'Well, what are you waiting for? Why don't you say: "What about *Double Indemnity*?" ' And I said: 'Because I know you're just sitting there with your right all cocked ready to shoot it when I begin, and I'm not going to give you the chance because I'm not going to say it.' So then he laughed about it. . . . It would have been the dumbest thing in the world to have brought up the question of *Double Indemnity* because if I can't get a decent picture out of this, there could be ten *Double Indemnities* that he passed and it wouldn't make my picture any better, and he knows it and I know it. But it'll be a decent picture, or my name won't go on it."

Toward the end of the year, MGM announced that Lana Turner and John Garfield had been picked to play Cora and Frank, and the Hollywood writers were citing the revival of *Postman* as one more example of filmland's new "red meat" approach to movies, which would dominate postwar Hollywood.

With all the new action on *Mildred* and *Postman*, Cain's recently achieved status as Hollywood celebrity went up another notch, a rise which no doubt made him even more attractive to Aileen Pringle. He began receiving requests for interviews from columnists like Hedda Hopper and Philip K. Scheur, the *Los Angeles Times* Hollywood reporter, who said he "was surprised to learn that Cain had been knocking around Hollywood for the past ten years." Scheur also said he agreed with the movie director who once described Cain as looking "like an ex-Sheriff of San Bernardino," a big, "shaggy figure of a man with beetling eyebrows and hair that is close-cropped, yet somehow manages to curl."

Featured in the columns with his new, socially prominent wife, Cain now became involved in what he called "the war for the social supremacy of Beverly Hills," fought by various ladies, usually unsuccessfully, against Mrs. Edward G. Robinson. The Cains went to the parties and dinners and met the stars: Robinson, Joan Blondell, Dick Powell, Bing Crosby (when Cain asked Crosby about his singing, "the groaner" replied, "All I claim for myself is that I sing in tune"). And one day, walking back from lunch to the Thalberg Building with a young lady, he was given further evidence of this new, exalted status in Hollywood. The young lady was a writer, and she seemed especially glum. So Cain asked her what the matter was. "Oh, the usual," she replied. "My option. It's coming up tomorrow and I'm worried."

"Option!" Cain yelled. "Look who's bragging. I haven't seen an option in years. I work on a day-to-day basis. We could say hour-to-hour; we could even say minute-to-minute. Any time, any moment, the foreman could open my door, turn the light out over my typewriter, and that would be that."

"Aw for Christ sake," the girl said, disgusted.

"What did I say?" was all Cain could reply.

"Knock it off, will you, with the comical stuff about the foreman, and let somebody talk that has trouble. A fat chance you would be fired."

"Well, I have been," Cain assured her.

"Not anymore," she said. "You're Arthur Hornblow's kept intellectual and everybody knows it, and if you're not going to be fired, don't gag somebody who could be."

"What in the hell did you say?" Cain asked, blinking. "Will you repeat that?"

"It's the new status symbol—they all have one. Hunt Stromberg has Aldous Huxley, Arthur Freed has Bob Nathan, and Arthur Hornblow has you."

Cain allowed that he should have felt insulted, but he did not. In fact, when he returned to his office, he was pleased. "To discover I was an intellectual was quite a sensation."

Whatever Hornblow's reasons for keeping Cain, by the end of 1944 it appeared that once again a studio job would end in failure; the script was not going well, and Cain wrote Rosalie it was "a filthy job that drags on past all reason or sense." On another occasion, he called it "a protracted, painful, and laborious job." And by December he was reporting that "we approach the end of this dreadful tale."

When *Frankie from Frisco* was finished, Hornblow quickly rendered his verdict. "He didn't like any of it," Cain said, "and there wasn't much for him to do but bring the whole project to an end. . . . He was very cordial, brushed aside my comments of regret, and acted in every way as picture producers ought to act and seldom do." Other writers were put to work on it, and when Cain heard that later scripts were total rewrites that he had nothing to do with, he asked Hornblow to remove his name from the credits. Cain had definite views about screen credits: He did not mind working anonymously for a while on a B picture if it interested him, and he did not care whether he received a credit, feeling he did not have to rely on pictures for his public recognition; but he did feel strongly that his name should not be on anything that wasn't his, especially now that the James M. Cain credit was big enough and important enough to mean something.

Cain was taken off *Frankie from Frisco* in December 1944, enabling him to go home to Baltimore for the holidays while Aileen visited her mother in San Francisco. But his return this time was different than before. Cain went back to Baltimore a celebrity, prompting interviews in the *Baltimore Sun* and similar evidence that the hometown boy had made it big west of the Alleghenies. The *Sun* interviewer, Donald Kirkey, recalled that Cain had once worked as a reporter on the *Sun*—"a lean, dour chap, who seemed steeped in bitterness and was known to intimates in journalistic circles here as old sourpuss." Now, sitting across from him at the restaurant, Kirkey saw a huge, 230-pound man who talked about his "tin-lined stomach," the result of an operation so successful that Cain called the waitress and ordered "Two glasses of sherry, three plates of Chincoteague oysters, a crab cake dinner, two large steins of the foamy, an extra crab cake for a filler, a slab of liederkranz and coffee." After ordering, Cain commented: "I have put on forty pounds."

*Cain in the mid-thirties in a
photograph accompanying his story
"Two Can Sing" in the April 1938
American magazine.* George W.
Vassar

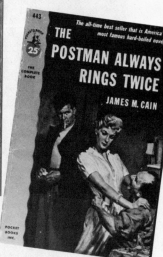

Paperback editions of Cain's most popular novels, all written in Hollywood in the 1930s and 40s. Serenade cover courtesy of Robert Jonas.

Cain's three big movies: Fred MacMurray and Barbara Stanwyck in Double Indemnity *(Warner Brothers, 1944); Ann Blyth and Joan Crawford in* Mildred Pierce *(Warner Brothers, 1945); and John Garfield and Lana Turner in* The Postman Always Rings Twice *(MGM, 1946). The Motion Picture Academy*

ABOVE: *James Montgomery Flagg
illustration for the 1936 serial "Double
Indemnity" in* Liberty *magazine.*

BELOW: *Cain and Elina in the 1930s with
Samson Raphaelson.* Courtesy of Samson
Raphaelson

H. N. "Swannie" Swanson in the 1940s. Courtesy of H. N. Swanson

Kate Cummings. Courtesy of Constance Cummings

Aileen Pringle. Motion Picture Academy

Lana Turner and Cain
lunching in the mid-
1940s.

Studio publicity shot of
Cain in the 1940s.
Cain called it his
"gangster photo."
Melbourne Spurr

House at 616 East 10th Street (now Bel Air Road) in Burbank where Cain wrote The Postman Always Rings Twice, *and front and back views of Cain's "upside-down" house at 2966 Belden Drive in Hollywood Hills.* Roy Hoopes

"Here's a natural, Manny! 'I Hope the Postman Always Rings Twice,
If He Brings Me a Letter from You.'"

Cartoons inspired by Cain's works: A caricature of the three leads in the dramatization of The Postman Always Rings Twice, *which played at New York's Lyceum Theatre,* New York Herald Tribune *(1936);* The New Yorker *(1936); and* The New York Times Book Review *(1946).*

J. M. Cain,
616 East 10th St.,
Burbank, Calif.

BAR-B-Q

By James M. Cain

They threw me off the hay truck about noon. I
had swung on the night before, down at the border, and as
soon as I got up there under the canvas, I went to sleep.
I needed plenty of that, after three weeks in Tia Juana, and
I was still getting it when they pulled off to one side
to let the engine cool. Then they saw a foot sticking out
and threw me off. I tried some comical stuff, but all I
got was a dead pan, so that gag was out. They gave me
a cigarette, though, and I hiked down the road to find something
to eat.

That was when I hit this Twin Oaks Tavern. It was
nothing but a roadside sandwich joint, like a million others
in California. There was a lunchroom part, and over that
the house part, where they lived, and off to one side a
filling station, and out back a half dozen shacks that they
called an auto court. I blew in there in a hurry and began
looking down the road. When the Greek showed, I asked if a guy
had been by in a cadillac. He was to pick me up here, I said,
and we were to have lunch. Not today, said the Greek. He
layed a place at one of the tables and asked me what I was going
to have. I said orange juice, corn flakes, fried eggs and
bacon, enchilada, flapjacks, and coffee. Pretty soon he came
out with the orange juice and the corn flakes.

"Hold on, now. One thing I got to tell you. If this
guy don't show up, you'll have to trust me for it. This was to

The first typescript page of Bar-B-Que,
which would ultimately become The Postman
Always Rings Twice. The Manuscript
Division, Library of Congress

*One of Cain's idols—Florence Macbeth, "The Minnesota
Nightingale"—in the 1920s. Although Cain did not
know her then, he would eventually meet and marry her
in the 1940s.* Godfrey Lundberg

Cain also saw his old friend Hamilton Owens, editorial page editor of the *Sun*, and discussed the possibility of writing about postwar policies and problems, an idea that he discussed further with Owens when the *Sun* editor was in Los Angeles in the spring of 1945.

Cain had a miserable return trip to California on the train, but found spring weather waiting for him in Los Angeles. He also found that despite his failure on *Frankie from Frisco*, he had not been fired by MGM. Instead, he was told to report to Carey Wilson on February 1, 1945, to work on a script, something to be called *The Common Sin*. Cain finished the script, but it never went into production, and the only record we have of it is a memorandum from Cain to Wilson discussing Wilson's reaction to Cain's first draft. It was, apparently, a typical Cain story—about a young man named Hugo Phelps who "is guilty of a folly," Cain summarized, "that is almost universal. He is a sucker for women, and had the special misfortune to fall for a girl whose only idea is to take him." And Hugo learns his lesson—"Stay away from women. Never fall for one, never trust one"—but not before he becomes so involved with her that it costs him the presidency of the company he is working for.

While writing *The Common Sin*, Cain also was on hand to consult with Wilson about *Postman*, especially how to handle the courtroom and trial scenes in which Cora and Frank are tricked into turning on each other. He had hoped to work on a novel while at MGM, but now found the studio work so demanding that even a short piece took "the most incredible time." Wilson was encouraging him not to give up his own writing, which led Cain to explore the possibility of a contract that would require him to work no more than twenty-six weeks a year—though up to forty weeks if he wished. MGM finally declined the arrangement, so Cain decided to take a leave of absence to write a novel with the understanding that MGM would have first look at it. "It is a solemn decision," he wrote Rosalie, "to give up the money they pay you, but it is still a more solemn decision to accept it, for that is writers' suicide. We have saved a little now, and I hope to write some things."

Cain's financial position was not all that precarious. His total earnings in 1944 were over $80,000, his highest income for any one year. In addition, Warner Brothers was about to close a deal for *Serenade*. There had been considerable interest in the book since the *Double Indemnity* breakthrough, and in the spring of 1944, while still trying to cast *Mildred Pierce*, Jerry Wald had inquired about the novel. Cain told Swanson he thought they should wait until *Double Indemnity* was released, because after the acclaim he felt it was sure to receive, the price would be much higher. Then, MGM showed an interest, and Cain wrote a treatment making it acceptable to the Hays Office—by substituting alcohol for homosexuality as the problem affecting Sharp's voice. The Hays Office approved it, only to have MGM back away.

Columbia was interested for a while, but finally Warner Brothers bought it for Wald, for $35,000—the highest price Cain had received for one of his books.

Cain made more suggestions for the script, telling Wald he should come out of it with a fine romantic picture, suitable for a Humphrey Bogart, with the singing dubbed in. Maria Montez was his choice for the part of Juanita. But it would be several years before Warners would develop an acceptable script and cast for the controversial book, a delay that did not surprise Cain. He always had misgivings about *Serenade* as a movie and had turned down several requests to put it on the stage, including one from Sigmund Romberg and Oscar Hammerstein to do it as a musical.

Despite the fact that he was temporarily rich with the money from the movie sale, Cain did not have a job or a regular income, so he decided to give up his office-apartment at the Knickerbocker and do his writing in Aileen's house in Santa Monica. It was not a good idea. According to Cain, Aileen complained hourly about his working in the house, that he was "underfoot" all the time and interfering with the work of her maid. When Cain asked what the maid could possibly be doing that was more important than his work, he received no answer. Aileen refused to serve his lunches, would not let the maid do it, and would not let him use the kitchen to fix his own lunch. She constantly demanded that he "get an office somewhere," and when he said he needed his library for his work, she screamed that he could take his damned books out of the house, too.

The Santa Monica house was, in fact, too small for Aileen, a maid, and a working author. And when the sale of *Serenade* had been imminent, Cain suggested they sell Aileen's house and buy a larger house in Beverly Hills, which would also be closer to the studios. But Cain said that after he saw Aileen's reaction when the first bid came in, he knew she could never sell the place and dropped the idea. Aileen later said she did not want to sell her house because she was afraid Cain would leave her and she would have nothing. But Cain never believed that. "I think she loved the house," he later told his lawyer, "and I think the damned house had as much to do with our breakup as anything else. I didn't love it, and I think that hurt her. And the fact that it was provided by the wife rather than the husband was a psychological jinx. It figured in every quarrel we had until I dreaded the very mention of it."

By the middle of 1945, the fighting in Europe was over and the war with Japan seemed to be nearing its conclusion. Already the country was full of veterans and returning soldiers, and the patriotic atmosphere to which they were returning annoyed Cain. "As usual, a great war and its prodigious emotional upheavals," he wrote one of his wartime pen pals, "produces mostly a mountain of mush—well-intended idealism, with little real validity to recommend it. Even Laurence Stallings, who is no sissy, God knows, just came in with a play called *The Streets Are Guarded*, which is about six GIs, a Wave, and the Marine who has stigmata on his hands and a halo round his head on nights when the moon doesn't rise. Just to give you an idea. When I was a GI and got demobilized, I got home on Friday, bought a new suit on Saturday, got drunk on Sunday, and went to work on Monday . . . we weren't aware of anything spectacular about it, beyond the fact that a dollar bought about half what it had bought before we went away."

Cain was distressed at all the attention given the returning soldier and said "the professional problem-solvers have taken him to their bosom like a flock of hens spying a bright new junebug." Cain thought the average American GI would get "readjusted" in the length of time "it takes to do a standing broadjump from a pair of khaki pants into a kool kloth, all-wool preshrunk."

During this time, Cain was still receiving requests from Rex Stout's Writers War Board, which he had refused to join, to enlist his typewriter in the war effort. The latest request came from Paul Gallico, who wrote: "This is an S.O.S. This is an assignment from 25,000,000 people in liberated areas of Europe. They need your pen. Just about 350 words from you will help bring them clothing they desperately need." Despite the slick approach, Cain responded with the 350 words, urging Americans to give clothes so "[we can get] our Allies out of the kitchen where they are useless and put them in the fields and factories, where they can help us win our war."

This was the last message Cain would write for the war effort. Despite his initial revulsion at the idea of mobilizing the "word-men" for word warfare, he had done his share. And he would have liked to have done more. As he wrote one friend near the end of the war: "I have had, from time to time, the big lech to put on soldier clothes again and write those immortal dispatches for some periodical with liberal ideas about expenses. But the only echelon I am attached to is the Fighting MGM. I shall probably regret it when the war ends that I took no active part in it; but I weigh 230 pounds and the idea of jeeping it dismays me."

Still, Cain had made his contribution in another way, and he knew it. His novels had been sent overseas by the millions in the cheap paperback editions supplied by the government in cooperation with publishers, and he was constantly receiving letters from soldiers and sailors commenting on how much they enjoyed them. It was a source of satisfaction, although he realized that all he gave the boys "was two hours of forgetfulness, of excitement and entertainment that had nothing to do with war, or ideologies, or indoctrination, or anything of that kind. It is the way I would like to have it."

By the summer of 1945, Cain was home every day writing. He had left MGM to resume work on a novel, but first he wrote several possible columns for the editorial page of the *Baltimore Sun*, as discussed with Hamilton Owens when Cain was in the East for Christmas. The one he proposed to open with said he was no voice in the wilderness and had accepted the national leadership as much as anyone had, but in future columns, "I expect to say, not once but often, that I believe the United Nations to be a vicious, phony, and dangerous organization that we should get out of . . . as quickly as possible." Most of the rest of the sample material was devoted to pointing out what was wrong with the U.N., in particular that there was not one instance in history where such a federation had ever worked, and that our two main allies, England and Russia, did not believe in free, independent, and sovereign states, and therefore the Big Three must inevitably part.

It was pure Cain—vintage 1945—and considered reactionary by the postwar intellectual establishment to which Hamilton Owens belonged. He declined to use the columns, saying that although they were superficially persuasive, chiefly because of Cain's style, they "clearly had no place in the *Sun*."

With the rejection of his proposal to be the *Baltimore Sun*'s resident critic of the U.N., Cain was free to do what he had planned to do when he left MGM—work on his story about the Virginia City prostitute that he had been researching ever since his trip there in 1942. It was one of his favorites: A young man from Annapolis, named Roger Duval, out in Sacramento on a spy mission for the Confederacy, falls in love with a Virginia City whore named Morina, who could be had by any man in town for ten dollars. But she will not give in to Duval because she likes him. He quits the Southern army and follows Morina to Virginia City, and when she continues to reject him, he shoots the rich miner who was not only going to marry Morina but set her madam up with a house of her own. Duval, an expert pistol shot, makes the shooting look like an accident, but the women know it was no accident and set out to kill him. He joins the Union army to save his life, but the women continue after him. Then, when Morina learns what really happened, she exclaims, "You killed a man for me!" This is the greatest compliment she has ever received, so they leave town together and go into train robbing (because Cain said he was sick to death of stagecoach robberies in Westerns). They head for Mexico with their loot. They are up in the hills in the snow and hear dogs barking and think maybe they are being followed. Duval goes off with his pistol to investigate, but decides the dogs are only barking at deer. Then he hears a twig snap and whirls to see Morina standing there, dressed in all the jewels they had stolen. But it is too late; he fired as he turned. She sinks down, bleeding in the white snow. "The end of this story," Cain said, "which compressed the whole relationship in one blazing moment, I am very proud of."

He called his new novel *Past All Dishonor*, and although he was proud of the ending, while he was working on it he became discouraged. "All my writing at this stage seems indescribably horrible," he wrote Knopf, "but I don't think the book is any worse than my others." He wrote four versions of the early part of the story, in which Morina is the niece of a Virginia City madam, then finally decided he had to make Morina a whore from the start, even if it cost him a movie sale. He set out to consciously write a "Western" with the usual cast of gunmen, gamblers, crooks, and painted ladies. But at no point in the story was there any evidence that he had his tongue in his cheek. He felt that he had written a much deeper book than the average Western, that instead of "dividing the human race conveniently into bad hombres and good, into nice girls who won't and other girls who will," he had probed into his characters and tried to bring them to life, to make them human beings rather than "moral lessons."

The book had autobiographical overtones. Cain's hero, Roger Duval, had grown up in Annapolis, had gone to St. John's College, and spent his summers swimming and sailing bugeyes in the Severn River. Cain was also proud of the research he put into the slim book. With his newspaperman's conscientious approach to facts, he found that in a period novel everything one took for granted when writing about the contemporary scene had to be researched. He had to know every last detail about mining in Nevada in the 1850s, about whorehouses, pistols and shooting, railroads and saloons, and especially life around Sacramento, in which the opening pages of the novel are set. He thought his description of this era would "come as a surprise to many, for few realize that in the 1860s, with the Civil War in mid-swing and many parts of the country wholly primitive in their ways of life, the California River boats were the last word in luxury, carrying a clientele that lived in the best hotels and ate the finest food."

Before actually writing the book, Cain spent countless hours in libraries, especially the Huntington Library in San Marino and the Pony Express Library (then in Santa Anita, but later moved to Elkins, Nevada). Carey Bliss, the curator of rare books at the Huntington, still remembers Cain as intelligent, somewhat abrupt, and "perhaps a little impatient," but never rude. Among other things, Cain wanted to know if the riverboats had showers in the 1860s, and Bliss said he doubted it. But Cain installed one in his fictional boat anyway. He was, in fact, convinced that California had not changed much since the 1860s. "I set out to do a book," he said, "that would cause people to rub their eyes and ask: Can these things be? Was this world so modern, so rich, so industrialized at the very moment Grant was taking Vicksburg?"

But most important, Cain thought *Past All Dishonor* was perhaps his most effective statement of the predominant theme in his writings: the wish that comes true and the horrors it brings to the wishers. "If you give people everything they want," he wrote in *Past All Dishonor*, "and nothing they ought to have, that'll wind them up in hell, too." Cain frankly thought many people and reviewers would think it was his best book—and by the time he had finished it, he was convinced it was.

He gave the manuscript to his MGM secretary, Barbara Lazarus, who volunteered to retype it for nothing, in return for being on full pay while sitting around idle for two months after Cain left the studio. However, Barbara was "at that certain age," as Cain put it, with young men calling on her every morning, so the typing of the manuscript dragged on while Alfred Knopf fumed and fidgeted, anxious for a fall publication of a new book by his popular Hollywood author. While waiting for his final manuscript, Cain thought he would make another attempt at his novel about incest, *The Butterfly*, having finally decided that Thornton Wilder was right: You cannot meet incest head on, you have to make it an uncle or somebody. Cain's solution was to have the father learn ultimately that the girl he was sleeping with was not his own offspring but the illegitimate daughter of her mother's boyfriend, who had caused the father to desert his family in the first place. Jess Tyler, the father, discovers this through a birthmark in the shape of a butterfly, passed from one generation to another—an idea no doubt inspired by Elina's family: Elina, her mother, Leo, and Henrietta all had a birthmark in exactly the same place.

In Cain's story, Jess kills the man who broke up his marriage and fathered the illegitimate daughter, Kady, shoving him down an abandoned mine and, with a crowbar, pulling down thousands of tons of dirt on top of him. Then he realizes he has killed the one person who could prove that Kady was not his daughter—his wife having died. When Jess and Kady are tried for incest, Jess tells the judge about the butterfly birthmark, and he believes him. But Kady does not. Humiliated at being exposed as a "pappy lover," she marries her boyfriend, and Ed Blue, the brother of the man Jess killed, comes after Jess with a rifle. As with *Past All Dishonor*, Cain wrote *The Butterfly* in the first person, with Jess Tyler telling the story while he is barricaded, waiting for Ed Blue to come after him. The reader is not exactly sure what happens at the end, but has a good idea when Jess breaks off his story in midsentence: "I'm cut off, Ed Blue is out there and. . . ."

Even using the Wilder approach, Cain had trouble beginning the novel, making as many as fifty false starts on it, he told an interviewer. Then, one day, he was telling his story to Aileen, and although she proved of little help in the writing of the book, she did make an important contribution to getting it started. After Cain had finished his story, she thought for a while, then said: "Now I understand the reason incest never gets written about, or almost never."

"Which is?" Cain replied.

"Because it's there, not in fact very often, but in spirit. Fathers are in love with their daughters. It's like what you said in *Serenade* about there being five percent of homo in every man, no matter how masculine he imagines himself to be. But if a father happens to be also a writer and cooks up a story about incest, he's in mortal terror he'll be so convincing about it all his friends will tumble to the truth. You, though, you haven't any children, and I personally think you're a fool to give this book up."

Cain was still thinking of setting the story in California, where he had first seen the mountain family that gave him the idea, but as he said to Aileen, "After the Joad family trip [Steinbeck's *The Grapes of Wrath*], if I had a Tyler family trip I'd never live it down."

"Well, if you don't mind my saying so," Aileen responded, "I think that Tyler family trip is just dull and all that California stuff so phony you'd throw it out yourself after you'd worked on it awhile. . . . That story is the story of a man's love for his own daughter, and the more it stays right up that mountain creek where it belongs and where you can believe it, the more it is going to be good." Cain decided this was sound advice.

The story then moved along very fast. In fact, Cain finished what he considered a first draft in a few weeks. Reading over his manuscript, much to his surprise, he did not find anything he wanted to change, and he said to himself: "This is it."

Eventually, he did rewrite the whole story, but for now he had two novels written, although neither was ready for the anxious Knopf. Despite all the preliminary research that went into *Past All Dishonor*, Cain insisted on sending the final manuscript to countless experts, asking them to check the details about firearms, locomotives, train couplings, riverboats, pilot houses, Nevada history, etc. (his files are full of correspondence with the Colt Fire Arms Company, the Union Pacific Railroad, and other historic sources), all of which took time. Cain even checked the roulette system Morina used to win money in the book, finding that it invariably won for him (in later years, Cain said he usually could pay expenses for his trips to Nevada if he could only get near a roulette table, which was not hard to do).

He had also done his own research on prostitutes, or "hookers" as he wanted to call them. He had heard that the term originated with the gang of women that hung around General Joe Hooker's Union Army Headquarters, but he was not sure, so he wrote Mencken inquiring about the word, also commenting that Hooker had been a reformed drunk, one of Mencken's pet hates. Mencken replied that the word "hooker" had nothing to do with General Hooker's Division Headquarters in the Civil War, that the theory was strictly a Washington legend and there was no truth to it. He pointed out that Russell Bartlett's *Dictionary of Americanisms* says "hooker" was actually in use in New York as early as 1859. "It then designated a lady who offered her professional services to sailors. It apparently came from the name of Corlear's Hook, then the red light district of the city." And he added: "I agree with you thoroughly about Joe Hooker, and I also acquiesce in the moral you draw from his disaster. There is nothing more terrible in this world than a boozer on the water-wagon. I had dinner week before last with Red Lewis and found him a mere shell of his former self. All his old liveliness was gone, and he had precisely nothing to say that was worth hearing."

Cain sent Knopf *Past All Dishonor* in August, reporting that three people had read it and liked it—including Aileen. The reaction was equally good in New York: Bernard Smith, an editor at Knopf, reported that it was "really terrific—rough, tough, fast and dirty—the Cain of *The Postman Always Rings Twice* and *Serenade.*" He anticipated an advance sale of 15,000, and an eventual sale of up to twice that figure. The Knopfs also liked it, although Blanche thought some passages should be softened. When she told Cain her reaction, he said that at first he had sulked, "wondering what Hemingway would have said to the potboiler who tried to tone down some of the stuff he gets away with. [But it] suddenly occurred to me he'd have been a hell of a sight better off if his publisher had got that stuff out, so then I got sensible."

Knopf gave Cain a $5,000 advance for *Past All Dishonor*, and prospects for a book of his never looked better. He wrote Raphaelson that (despite the fact the heroine was a whore) *Dishonor* "might make a picture, and as I am riding a wave of luck out here, I might at last get a price. I'm Dreaming of a Six-Figure Christmas."

One thing that had him dreaming was *Mildred Pierce*, which was on its way to becoming the big smash of the year. Even before the picture's release in October, there was talk (thanks, in part, to some clever leaks to the press inspired by Wald) that Joan Crawford's performance was a serious candidate for the Academy Award. Warner hyped the film with a promotion campaign built around the line: "Please don't tell what Mildred Pierce did!" The reviews were mostly raves: the *Times*, *Herald Tribune*, and even hard-to-please James Agee in *The Nation* congratulated Crawford and praised the movie. Crawford herself decided that of all her roles, this was her favorite because "it rescued me from what was known at Metro as the Joan Crawford formula." *Mildred Pierce* did win the Academy Award for her as the best actress of 1945, and it did revive her career, just as *Double Indemnity* had revived Barbara Stanwyck's career—and *Postman*, soon to be released, would revive

Lana Turner's. Cain sent Crawford an autographed copy of his novel with the inscription: "To Joan Crawford, who brought Mildred to life as I had always hoped she would and who has my life-long gratitude." Joan responded that the book with his inscription was the "nicest thing that ever happened to me" and said she could hardly wait to finish her current picture so she could invite him over "to say hello, have a drink and talk!"

Actually, Cain was never very happy with the movie version of *Mildred*. "Allowing for all the smart promotion," he wrote at the time it came out, "I still don't see in it an element to make such a smash hit. Part of the trouble is that the book wasn't really so hot—two novels in one, scrambled in a confusing way, and an idea, in addition, that I of all people ought never to have attempted, as it is something for a woman serial writer rather than a man who at least tried to work from situation. However, I should worry. It is grossing fabulously and as No. 2 smash for me, makes me quite hot in Hollywood."

But Cain also revealed where his heart really was. On the day the Academy Awards were to be given, in writing Barbara Stanwyck about another matter, he said: "Tonight Joan Crawford comes up for a possible Academy Award for her work in *Mildred Pierce*. Naturally I am pulling for her, yet the occasion makes me sad as I wanted so much that you get the award last year for your playing of Phyllis in *Double Indemnity*."

Mildred Pierce also started another round of debate as to whether characters created by James M. Cain were really what America was all about. The new controversy was kicked off by Jack McManus's review in *PM* in which he quoted Eric Johnston, the president of the Motion Picture Association, as saying: "American motion pictures are America's greatest salesmen and, in many countries, the only America that people know." McManus picked this up, citing the people in *Mildred Pierce* and asking: "Are they the American people who rallied to perform this nation's miracle of war production? Are they the American people who rose in their understanding and political strength to reaffirm Roosevelt and his world program in 1944? In a pig's eye they are! They are the slimy teratology of a literary monster-monger."

There were, no doubt, many who agreed with McManus that Mildred, Veda, and Monty were slimy characters, and that James M. Cain was indeed a monster-monger. But others noted the absurdity in McManus's argument, including Max Lerner, who wrote a rebuttal in *PM*. After pointing out the differences between wartime propaganda and art, he said:

> I am not making a pure "art-for-art's-sake" plea. But what I am objecting to is an art-for-Eric Johnston or the OWI's approach to movies. Hollywood's standards are so often irrelevant to anything remotely

approaching art that it would be a pity to drag in any more irrelevancies like FDR or the miracle of war production or what foreign people may think of us. . . . Anyone who has wrestled hard with the problem of American civilization knows that the unlovely people in *Mildred Pierce* do exist, that venom runs at times in human veins, and sawdust is stuffed at times in human hearts, in California as well as on the Rhine. An author should be able to pick for portrayal whatever segment of life he wishes, if he does it with honesty and depth. Otherwise, why not ban Dreiser and Farrell and Steinbeck and Lillian Smith and Richard Wright? Why not convert America into a paradise for the blurb writers of the NAM?

As for the movie itself, Lerner said he had become so disillusioned with Hollywood that he cheered when he saw "a film with the swiftness, economy and tension of *Mildred Pierce*."

It was a powerful and gratifying affirmation for Cain's art from a critic who was not otherwise one of his greatest fans.

After he had mailed Knopf *Past All Dishonor*, Cain took a train East to talk to his publisher about contracts for that book and *The Butterfly*, and to meet his new agent, Harold Ober. By now James M. Cain was probably the most reprinted author in the country—over one and a half million copies of his books had been sold in many different hard-cover editions and paperbacks, both in this country and abroad—and he did not feel a publisher had the right to take a full half share on his reprint, book club, and magazine sales. Knopf still remembers the day he had lunch with Cain to talk about this question. It began with Cain's coming by his office, throwing the new contracts on Knopf's desk, and saying: "I won't sign that." At lunch, however, Knopf explained to him the publisher's side, and that afternoon Cain signed the contracts, saying, as Knopf recalls: "You've given me a rationale."

After shifting to H. N. Swanson as his Hollywood agent in 1942, Cain had needed New York representation and ultimately had worked out an arrangement with Harold Ober Associates. He had not been East during the war, and now he wanted to meet Ober, which he did—leading to an awkward few minutes, as later described by Cain. "Around five one afternoon, I showed up at his office and was presently ushered in [and] there facing me, instead of a legendary agent was a legendary professor, a pink scholarly face, tall, frail slenderness, and a soft wispy, almost hesitant voice that interrupted itself at the least hint I had thought of something to say. It turned out that without business to discuss, he practically lost the power of speech. It wasn't that he was mercenary, but simply that the capacity for small talk, those vapid but sociable inquiries about wind, weather, and tide which ease most conversations, was not in him. And, being caught so badly off balance, it wasn't in me either, so we sounded like a couple of characters coached by Gracie Allen on suitable remarks to George about his notification he has been engaged by the Metropolitan Opera. . . . But this I know: Plus his savvy, over and above his erudition, shrewdness, and acumen, his honesty was the bedrock of the confidence he inspired, and that confidence was the basis of his success, his ability to close deals, to get things done. It sounds so simple, and yet probably is the rarest of human traits."

While he was East, Cain stopped in Baltimore where he showed both his new novels to his sister, Baben. After she read them, Cain was issued "a mysterious summons to her room." When he arrived, he said: "What's the matter, don't you like these books, or what?"

"I liked one of them fine," she answered, "the one about the girl in the house, *Past All Dishonor*. The other one, *The Butterfly*, I not only didn't like but didn't even slightly believe. Jamie, I want you to throw that book away. I want you to pitch it into the fireplace and forget you ever wrote it. I don't think anyone will publish it, whatever you do about it. But if they do, you're going to live to regret it."

Baben's reaction was, in fact, so intense that it shook Cain and gave him second thoughts about the novel. And it also intensified the tension between Cain and his sister over another literary matter that served to make his Baltimore stay unpleasant and would cause considerable anguish in the months ahead. Baben had written a novel and wanted to discuss it with her brother, the famous author. She had first sent it to him in May, complaining that she was having difficulty, primarily because of an "emotional upheaval." Cain said he did not think emotional upheavals had much to do with writing and tried to persuade her to take a less desperate attitude toward the project. "You are not the only person trying to write a book," he told her.

After he returned to Hollywood, he wrote her that "the novel is extraordinarily good, not only for itself but for its promise. . . . The book has such brilliant intellectual force that I hate to see something, which you could pull off for something big, go into the trunk for lack of one more good lick."

Cain's appraisal upset Baben, who showed her pique by refusing to accept money Cain sent her to help continue the book, at the same time borrowing from her sister Rosalie, to whom Cain was also sending money periodically. Cain finally wrote Baben scolding her for her childish reaction, and reminding her that she had felt no compunction about tearing into *The Butterfly*.

At the time Cain came East, immediately after the war, new automobiles were still not available and used ones were very difficult to find. But

Cain found one somewhere, because when he left Baltimore in October he drove west, down through the Appalachians, to the Gulf of Mexico and to California via Texas, New Mexico, and Arizona. His leisurely trip, taken without Aileen, had several objectives: he had not been to West Virginia since 1939, and he wanted to spend some time in Appalachia to make sure the flavor of his mountain people in *The Butterfly* was still accurate; at the same time, he wanted to get a feel of the South because he was still thinking about his nonfiction book, now titled *If Bori Had Blundered* or *If Lincoln Had Been Late*, or some such thing.

The trip was apparently very productive, although he did write how disappointed he was in the South: "I drove and read and looked and took notes. I found out one curious thing about Dixie: It's 90 to 95 percent scrub woods, and you know my conviction: poor land, poor people." But he did satisfy himself that the background he recalled for *The Butterfly* was still accurate and that his facts were solid, although after talking to Lafe Chafin, whom he had met as a reporter for the *Sun* in 1922, he decided to eliminate specific place names in the story. But he did keep it in Mingo County around the Big Sandy River.

By the time he returned to Hollywood, Cain had begun to think about a Civil War novel—in fact, a trilogy of novels. He wrote to Dr. George G. Wilson of Harvard, a Civil War authority, requesting some specific books on his subject and outlining his concept of the project. But back at his typewriter, he kept thinking of his story about the Great Depression, and he knew that once started, he would have to stick with it—or as Vincent Lawrence would tell him: "Once you start rolling that snowball, lad, you got to roll it. You go off and leave it, when you come back it'll be just a wet spot on the lawn." But he found it impossible to keep his Depression novel rolling because, all of a sudden, Paramount decided James M. Cain, the author of three hot movies, was just the man to work on another hot property it owned—F. Scott Fitzgerald's classic, *The Great Gatsby*. Hollywood had already made one *Gatsby*—a 1926 production starring Warner Baxter. But now another was being planned that would eventually star Alan Ladd and Betty Field. Although Cain felt Fitzgerald's short stories for the *American Mercury* were pretty good, he had always thought *Gatsby* "claptrap" and Fitzgerald himself somewhat overrated. To him Fitzgerald's thinking was "dull" and his writing "all diction, cadence and accent." Yet despite his lack of enthusiasm for *Gatsby*, Cain accepted the assignment and was given a play based on Fitzgerald's novel by Owen Davis, a prolific playwright most famous for the drama *Icebound*, together with an unedited script for which Cain was supposed to make suggestions. One he came up with was that somewhere in the course of the picture it would have to be made clear that Gatsby was what Fitzgerald said he was—a bootlegger. He also suggested a new ending in which Gatsby would be thought to have been killed in the famous automobile accident that kills the girl friend of Daisy's husband. "Attending his own funeral and anticipating, with excitement, the enormous crowd he thinks will be there, he stands behind a tree in the rain," as Cain describes the scene in his treatment, "to discover that only two or three people even think it necessary to show up." One who does then show up is a gum-chewing, former Gatsby girl friend from the Midwest, who (unlike Daisy) really loves him and comes to the funeral not believing the great Gatsby could have wrecked his own car. She recognizes him and leads "him off to a new life and fade-out. This, however, naturally needs thought, as well as the tricky accident," Cain concludes.

A little too tricky, perhaps. Paramount did not agree with Cain's suggestions for filming *Gatsby* and quietly dropped the idea of his doing the script.

About that time, Cain was also approached by Columbia to do a script of a different kind of classic: the opera *Carmen*, to star Rita Hayworth. Considering his love of opera, one would have thought he might have leaped at this overture. "But leave us face it," he wrote Columbia, after reading the script they had sent him, "it is a skimpy, dated little tale, and considerable work would have to be done to it to explain why Columbia Pictures Corporation saw fit to bring up the subject in connection with Rita Hayworth in this year 1945."

Meanwhile, *Modern Screen* magazine asked him to do a piece on Lana Turner, timed to come out with the release of *Postman*. This took him to Romanoff's one day for "tea" with the young actress. Cain was impressed with Miss Turner and they soon became friends. He was surprised at her height—she was taller than he'd expected—and by her total effect, which was quieter and more subdued than he would have thought from her movies. But he was most surprised by her response when he asked her what made her want to play Cora, his heroine in *Postman*. "Her honesty," Lana replied.

"Honesty, are you kidding?" Cain said, almost choking on his drink.

"Look," Lana replied. "Cora didn't pretend to herself. She knew she was a punk and that what she was going to do about it was wrong. But she wanted something out of life. She wanted something she could never get if she went along in the same old rut."

"And what did she want?" Cain asked.

"Respectability."

"I've often wondered if my readers could believe that," Cain replied.

"I believe it," said Lana. "It's what made Cora so human. She'd kill a man so she could have a little piece of property away out in the hills, a lunchroom, some cabins, and a filling station. Then she'd be something. That's what she said. Well, that's so silly you can't help feeling sorry for her. But a lot of things people do don't make any sense, and when she was so honest with herself about it, I wanted to play her."

Cain decided—at least for the *Modern Screen* piece, which he knew would promote the movie—that Miss Turner understood Cora better than he did, and concluded on a little-too-cute note that maybe "she's going to make a hit of that *Postman* yet."

When the movie was finally released Cain sent her a leather-bound copy of *Postman* with the inscription: "For my dear Lana, thank you for giving a performance that was even finer than I expected." And later, just as Joan Crawford said about *Mildred Pierce* and Fred MacMurray about *Double Indemnity*, Lana Turner said Cora in *Postman* was her favorite role. If nothing else, Cain figured he might well go down in Hollywood history for creating characters that made three very temperamental Hollywood stars happy.

The final script for *Postman* was written by Harry Ruskin and Niven Busch, the latter a friend of Cain's who had just published *Duel in the Sun*. Their script passed the Hays Office with very little trouble. "The thing the Hays Office had objected to in the original," said the film's director, Tay Garnett, "was the sort of low-level quality of the people in it. We've raised the tone of the story. I guess you could say we've lifted it from the gutter up to, well, the sidewalk."

Despite all the talent and effort that went into the film, Cain was appalled when he saw the first releases of *Postman* in Glendale. He said he crawled up the aisle on his hands and knees for fear of running into Carey Wilson, whom he considered a friend and liked too much to hand any "hokey-pokey" or gratuitous criticism. His main objection was to a scene based on Frank's running to Mexico with a girl who did a cat act. "They had this girl's cat act in the picture," Cain said, "leopards and pumas and lions and everything rolling around with each other and it had no more relationship to the story than the man in the moon."

Later, when he saw the movie at the Ambassador in Hollywood after the opening, he liked it a little better, but not much. The cat scene had been removed and there had been other retakes and editing which improved it considerably. So, knowing the director would be expecting to hear from him, he wrote Wilson telling him how much he had disliked the first version, but found the final film much better, adding: "I have been having, as you may imagine, a most unhappy time thinking about it, for nobody knew better than I did the enormous amount of work you put into it or respect more the aesthetic ideals you adhere to. There was also the circumstance that this novel, my first, lay very close to my heart. Now, it is as though a great weight has rolled away from me, and I would like you to know how happy I am." Wilson replied: "I'm awful proud of your letter. Only Jim Cain could have—and would have—written it."

The book was indeed close to Cain's heart, his one novel that he felt had a chance to stand the test of time. And he had reason to be proud of it. As Raphaelson had written him a year before, Sinclair Lewis reread the novel from cover to cover when visiting Raphaelson and "it was treated with the casualness one gives a classic." But whether or not *Postman* was in fact a classic, Cain knew that MGM's version had not captured its essence. Shortly after the picture was released, he was dining in his current favorite restaurant, the House of Murphy, when he looked up from his corned beef and cabbage and saw Harry Ruskin standing in front of him. "Well, why don't you say it," Ruskin said belligerently, his hands on his hips, feet slightly spread. "It stinks."

"Well, I don't think it stunk any worse than most of them do," Cain replied, trying to be friendly without actually praising the picture. Ruskin said they had had Lana Turner dressed in white so the public would understand that Cora was pure. "She may be playing around with the guy," said Ruskin, "but she's not taking her pants off for him." So Ruskin said he asked Carey Wilson: "Is this girl shacking this guy in bed? I know we don't put it on the screen, but I have to know."

But Wilson could never make up his mind, according to Ruskin, who paused a moment in his account and then said: "Jim, he didn't know then and he doesn't know now. That's why the central part of the thing is so fuzzy and squashy."

Cain later said that when he saw the movie "it didn't seem to make much difference." And when he was asked by interviewers, as he was by many over the years, about what Hollywood had done to his book, he would invariably say: "They haven't done anything to my book. It's right up there on the shelf."

When *Postman* was released, there was so much talk about how Hollywood had managed to "get around" the Hays Office to make Cain's three big pictures that the *New York Times* asked him to do an article explaining it. Cain responded with a revealing piece saying that despite all the changes in the scripts, Hollywood had not deviated that much from the originals. As he explained it:

> . . . I am constantly asked how these stories were "licked," as they say here in Hollywood. What did Billy Wilder do, people want to know, to get "Double Indemnity" past the Hays Office, as it was then called? What did Jerry Wald do about "Mildred Pierce"? Or Carey Wilson about "The Postman Always Rings Twice," now about to open?

In each case the answer is simply *Nothing*.

No slick tricks were employed and the stories were not toned down. Of the three I would say "Double Indemnity" stuck closest to my story, with "The Postman Always Rings Twice" next closest and "Mildred Pierce" least close. But all three stuck closer than the average picture does to the material from which it is adapted.

In each, naturally, details about sex were omitted, but they are pretty much omitted in my novels, it may surprise you to learn. People think I put stark things in my stories, or indulge in lush descriptions of the heroine's charms, but I don't. The situations, I dare say, are often sultry, and the reader has the illusion he is reading about sex. Actually, however, it gets very little footage. But, beyond this, such changes as were made, were for the sake of cinematic effectiveness, and there weren't too many of them.

No, all these gentlemen did was convince Mr. Joseph Breen, who has these matters in charge for what is now the Johnston Office, that they intended to make decent pictures. They didn't, perhaps I should explain, have extended conferences about it, with tough lumps to be ironed out, he adamant on one side, they passionate on the other. In Hollywood it isn't exactly done that way. There is a preliminary inquiry, of course, but what can Breen say? All of them know it is possible to make a salacious picture out of the Book of Genesis! It's simply a conversation piece until they "come to him with a script that we consider decent," to put it the way it is usually put.

Two weeks later, Bosley Crowther in the *Times* echoed Cain's remarks, saying *Postman* proved that the guardians of Hollywood's production code could be wrong, but also demonstrated they could rectify their mistakes, as they had by approving the film. The movie gives us hope, he said, for more truthful adult films in the future, and, in passing, he gave the movie the highest praise it received anywhere: "Mr. Cain wrote—and Metro has pictured—a Greek tragedy in modern dress, and Lana Turner and John Garfield have played it in an extraordinarily honest way."

Other reviewers were not so kind: James Agee called the film a "terrible misfortune," and *The New Republic*, *Newsweek*, and *Time* all panned it. But this did not seem to hurt the film at the box office. For years, *Postman* was among the top ten Hollywood moneymakers, before it was finally pushed off the list by the big blockbusters of the 1960s and 1970s.

While *Postman* was opening around the country and the literary-intellectual circuit was buzzing with the Hollywood achievements of James M. Cain, his name came at them again from another flank: the publication of

Past All Dishonor. The advance sales had reached an incredible 30,000, and already Lester Cowan, a producer who had just made *The Story of G.I. Joe*, was talking of a big money deal that might go as high as $225,000. Cain had planned to follow the book immediately with another best seller—*The Butterfly*—but Knopf decided to postpone publication a year, rather than have two new Cains in the store at once, even though he and Blanche had read the book and liked it (on the other hand, Bernard Smith at Knopf thought it was disappointing and was confused by the ending, which Cain, in fact, later changed).

Most of the reviews of *Past All Dishonor* were astonishingly good, considering that Cain was now one of the most popular and certainly one of the most talked-about writers in the country, the kind critics love to tear apart. Cain and Knopf were ecstatic as the notices came in. Most agreed with the *Louisville Courier-Journal* and the *Boston Herald* that this was "Cain at his best." Charles Poore, in the *Times*, called it "one of the most preposterous and entertaining books of the year." Even *Time* said it was a "well told tale." Jay Adams in the *Saturday Review* called Cain a "superb story teller," and *Newsweek* was so carried away it decided it was "timeless as a classic" and "the equal of Conrad's 'Lord Jim.' "

All in all, *Past All Dishonor* inspired probably as enthusiastic a collection of reviews as any Cain book since *Postman*. But it did produce a few vitriolic attacks, and there were two charges in particular that angered Cain: (1) that his research had been shoddy, and (2) the book was written primarily for the movies. "All the research necessary for this work could have been gathered in an afternoon at a third rate movie house," said John Parrelly in the *New Republic*. "Soft music and soft tears . . . for James M. Cain," said Malcolm Cowley, "who used to be a writer before he got so tethered in celluloid." And Edmund Wilson angered Cain more than any of them, as he hit both themes: "The characters talk straight post-Hemingway, full of phrases unknown in 1861, with occasional ladlings-in of the language of *Huckleberry Finn* when the author remembers this period. . . . Cain has been eaten alive by the movies." And taking issue with the dust jacket blurb that said that this was "Cain at his peak," Wilson concluded: "Poor fellow, he is at his nadir."

Considering how much research Cain had done on the period, how much effort had gone into checking every last detail, and the fact that by now he thought himself an expert on the language and speech of the West of this period, the attack on his research alone would have made him furious. But the charge that he had pandered to Hollywood was more than he could bear. He had made Morina a prostitute rather than the niece of a madam even though he knew this would hurt the chances of a movie sale. And he had written his earlier books the way he wanted and not the way Hollywood wanted. Hollywood finally did his pictures his way and not vice versa. He had written only one novel, *Love's Lovely Counterfeit*, with Hollywood in mind, but that was originally intended as a magazine serial, not as a book. And the Hays Office delay in approving *Double Indemnity* and *Postman* not only cost him $10,000 hard cash but quite possibly retarded his emergence as a prosperous screenwriter. He was not normally a complainer, but now he wrote Laurence Stallings about the attacks, pointing out how much research he had done, research in which, among other things, he discovered "that California and Nevada of the sixties amazingly resembled the same states today" and that his being eaten alive by the movies will be news to Hollywood, "which knows quite well how many thousands of G's I have passed up NOT conceding a point here and there." He also cited Joseph E. Jackson of the *San Francisco Chronicle*, the only reviewer, in his opinion, who actually knew anything about the Virginia City of the 1860s. Jackson not only praised the novel but said, according to Cain, that "most writers on the subject let the miners out by having them sing 'O Susannah' in the saloons, while wearing their red shirts, but that I had taken them underground and showed the dreadful life they led."

Cain had never forgiven Edmund Wilson for not using the lengthy autobiographical material he had sent him in 1940 and was under the impression most of it had come out under the by-line of Mary McCarthy, Wilson's wife, in a Cape Cod publication—although Mary McCarthy denies this ever happened and I could find no record of it in a Cape Cod paper. But Cain was convinced of it, and because of this, and the review, he henceforth had no use for Wilson, who he now decided wrote "endless reviews about a book he says is not worth reading." As for Wilson's eminence as a critic, Cain thought he was "more or less of an intellectual snob, a humorless son of a bitch."

In addition to the attacks from Wilson and Cowley there was the increasingly irritating fact that the book did not sell to the movies, although it came tantalizingly close on one occasion. MGM had first looked at it in synopsis form under the agreement Cain had made when he took a leave of absence from the studio (and to which he never returned). At the meeting in which the synopsis was discussed, one participant, at least, said he was frankly prejudiced against Cain stories and did not think MGM should be making Cain movies—despite their box office success. He felt the industry would be better off without *Double Indemnity* or *Postman*. Another executive stepped in and said the story would look much better in its final form, and someone else said everything would be all right, since the leading characters were both punished in the end. But MGM never bought it. Murder and adultery might be manageable, but how did you handle a prostitute? The columns reported that Joan Crawford wanted to play Morina in the movie, provided it survived the "Johnston Office laundry," but Cain preferred Barbara Stanwyck and sent her an autographed copy to see if she might be interested. She said she loved the story and was going to give a copy of the book to her adopted son because "I thought he ought to know about such things." However, she also felt "the red light over the door kills it for pictures." She was scheduled for a period movie at the time (*California*), but if it fell through she said she would be interested. "Ah, well," she wrote him, "help me 'kill' again, Jim. It's in my blood now thanks to you and damned if I don't like it."

The number of directors and producers who considered *Past All Dishonor* and turned it down reads like a *Who's Who* of Hollywood: Joe Sistrom, Dore Schary, David O. Selznick, Hal Wallis, Otto Preminger, Leo McCarey, Arthur Rubin, Billy Wilder, Jerry Wald, Lester Cowan, Milton Sperling. "All I need is one guy with a little dough and a glint in his eye for the property," Swanson said, but such a guy never appeared.* The book did produce one curious inquiry: a request from the State Department to do a radio version for broadcast abroad "to tell the story of America and present various aspects of American life, culture and customs." Cain was flabbergasted and gave his approval, but said "don't blame me if all you promote sounds more like a dog fight." Then he thought it over and decided the program would cause him nothing but trouble abroad and withdrew his permission.

Possibly the most significant outgrowth of *Past All Dishonor* was the encouragement Cain received as a historical novelist at a time when *Gone With the Wind* was considered the model for the genre. Many reviewers commented on Cain's special approach to historical fiction, and one writer, Oscar Lewis, was specific in his reaction. "I hope you will go back to the early West again in your fiction," he wrote Cain. "The period needs the sort of realistic treatment you can give it." In fact, it is quite possible that the response to *Past All Dishonor* and the success of *Gone With the Wind* as a book and a movie did encourage him to continue with his own Civil War novels, although he denied this when I raised the question with him, adding that he had never read *Gone With the Wind*. However, he did say, "You had to take Rhett Butler on faith, just as you had to take Jay Gatsby on faith. . . . Everybody used to write about the cotton industry in the Civil War by having their man walking around and suddenly he's got ten thousand dollars in the bank." And in his memoirs, he said that in his Civil War books "I meant to explain where Rhett Butler got his money."

When the movie *Postman* and the book *Past All Dishonor* arrived on the cultural scene, almost simultaneously, Cain was working at RKO at a salary

---

Past All Dishonor was eventually made into a film by Eric Ormer.

befitting his new status as the writer who had broken all the Hollywood codes. Swanson had negotiated $2,500 a week, his high-water mark at the studios, and his first assignment was to do a script for a film, apparently never completed, called *The Glass Heart*. One of the characters, most un-Cain-like, was a very religious girl who was starting "one of those little light-house cults, so common in California," for the benefit of returning soldiers. What Cain found interesting in the novelist's portrait was that the girl was most vital and alive when *not* quoting the Bible; her religion was in the background. This was a characteristic Cain approach to religion, as cited by Morris Markey when commenting to Cain on how effectively he had treated religion in *The Butterfly*: "Our devout and psalm-singing poor devil [Jess Tyler] never once thought of calling upon the Lord when his catastrophe closed in on him. You made a devastating commentary there, just by your silence."

The studio eventually set *The Glass Heart* aside and Cain was assigned to polishing another script; its identity remains uncertain, but it may well have been a *film noir* based on Jacques Tourneur's *Out of the Past*, starring Robert Mitchum, Jane Greer, Kirk Douglas, and Rhonda Fleming. The movie had a typical Cain plot about a gas station owner with a past and a desperate woman who becomes involved in murder. Cain was not credited on the script, and in later years he did not remember it, but the script's original writer, Daniel Manwaring, said Cain did some work on it.

Cain's next assignment was a script based on a novel by Geoffrey Holmes, *Build My Gallows High*. It was intended for Dick Powell and appears to have been the preliminary script for the movie eventually entitled *Johnny O'Clock*, which also starred Evelyn Keyes, about an honest gambler who is accused of murder. Cain had no credits and did not work on this one very long.

Although his total time at RKO was less than six months, Cain's new Hollywood status was suggested by the fact that he had hardly been on the lot for more than one week or two than he was interviewed for *PM* by Mary Morris. Ms. Morris impressed Cain as "one of the few," he wrote Herbert Bayard Swope, "who really take an interview seriously and pin you down and take notes and suck the pencil and call you up the next day for more details." She had found Cain behind door 725 in the RKO Building, which had an "atmosphere like an old wooden army barracks," where she was greeted by a "big man, middle-aged, bulky, with a rough complexion and a meaty face topped by unruly brown hair. He wore horn-rimmed glasses." The interview ranged over his career, his early failure in Hollywood, his books and his views as to why the studios paid him the money he needed to support his novel-writing career. "I get hired on, as they say, to enrich the story. Style, manner, ability to put on a cutaway."

"Cutaway?" Ms. Morris asked.

"On a story. Can I say, without sounding boastful, that I have more style than the fellow whose previous job was sending out press releases for the Shuberts or Madison Square Garden, or the fellow who covered fires for the *Daily News*? They come to me, say 'We start shootin' Monday or Tuesday, script's fair but one scene is just no goddam good.' I read it, say, 'The girl's too anxious, goes after the guy too fast. There should be something to interfere. She's gotta see an aunt off at the airport.' 'That's it,' they say. So I sit down and dialogue it in. That's style."

Cain paused and turned on his heel, his back to Ms. Morris, thinking. Then he went on, "Also they hire me for excitement, you understand. The kind of story they buy is apt to be pretty claptrap so the first thing they reach for is a little murder. I can fiddle around with it, raise the intellectual interest a bit, give it some attractiveness to cultivated people, but on the principle of high suspense.

"They show me this story—guy's dead. Nobody knows why, never bothered to figure out. Oh, they say by accidentally shooting off a gun in his hand. I want to know why he got dead at this point. Plot says he's got to be dead by beginning of chapter three. All right, we take the story elements, lay 'em out on the desk, beat 'em with a maul until they break up."

Still showing off, he also said he was only working at RKO to let the studio pay for a trip he had to take to New Orleans, where he planned to start on his Civil War novel again, though first there was the question of research, which he proceeded to explain: "Every year, you have 800 stinking books by evening meal novelists, writers who betray their ignorance by writing in, say, a book about Mexico, 'The family sat down to their evening meal.' Too damned lazy even to get out and go downtown to the Mexican consulate, find a secretary and ask questions. All I need is to read a line like 'She reeked of cheap perfume!' Preposterous! What perfume? What's the name of it? Woolworth Number 8, perhaps."

The interview came to an end with the two of them walking to the parking lot and Cain tying up the conversation, as she put it, with the remark: "This country is filled with worried souls—people who may not have education or culture, but they *ain't tepid.* My stories mirror life much more than they're given credit for."

Cain liked the interview, and so did his old friend from the *World*, Herbert Bayard Swope, who wrote from back East: "That was a good interview the Morris wench had with you in *PM*. She had sense enough to let you talk and you did, damn interestingly too, although perhaps a trifle too ritualistic—Thus are Gods made."

Aileen also read it, and she had a different reaction: she thought the references to his New Orleans trip meant he was planning to leave her, which by now must have been good news. By the spring of 1946 their marriage was finally unraveling. There appeared to be no other men or women at the root of their disenchantment with each other, just a basic temperamental difference compounded by the same irritant that had ruined Cain's relationship with Kate Cummings. As he put it, "I had become a drunk, and it made all other problems insoluble." With Aileen, these problems grew out of what Cain claimed was the denial of his lawful rights. "She refused to consult me on any question whatever that arose in the house," he wrote his lawyer, "from whether we should accept an invitation or decline it, whether we should entertain tonight or not entertain, whether I liked or did not like this, that, or the other piece of furniture she proposed to buy, and most importantly, our joint finances."

Life with Aileen, apparently, had been hard to take. At one point, when Cain had temporarily given up drinking, probably in an attempt to make the marriage work, he wrote his sister: "I have cut out drinking, which helps in one way and doesn't in another. I don't know what the hell I live for now. I have no friends I can see [and] I can't stand this collection of middle-age gold-diggers she sees." The unhappiness of their situation was underscored by the fact that with Cain's travels East and South and Aileen's visits to her mother's home in San Francisco, in the less than two years they were married, forty-seven weeks were spent apart.

For Aileen the situation had become intolerable and some idea of what she was going through can be glimpsed from a letter she wrote Mencken in 1946. "Except for one month, after I told him he would have to choose between a wife and the bottle, and he went on the wagon, I can't remember a night when he wasn't drunk, abusive, insane. I honestly think he is quite mad." He apparently abused and threatened her, and at one point she felt she could not even see Cain without another male along for protection. "He tried desperately to drag me down to the gutter and was furious because I wouldn't go along quietly," she wrote.

In later years, she told friends that Cain's drinking was at the root of their trouble, but her only public comment at the time was one remark made to a reporter: "He was moody, melancholy and grim; instead of building castles in the air he built dungeons." And she told me: "He was a monster. I was truly afraid he was going to hurt me. I would lock my door, and one night he threatened to get my bronze andirons downstairs and break it down. He was very big and strong. I remember one night we had dinner out with Rupert Hughes and his wife and Cain got drunk and embarrassed everyone. Then he wanted to drive home, but I wouldn't let him. He was a very charming man when I married him, but I never had experience with a drunk before."

After Cain's statement that he intended to go to New Orleans appeared in *PM* (and in other interviews), Aileen hired Jerry Giesler, Hollywood's most famous lawyer, to serve papers. Cain did not believe Aileen really thought he was trying to desert her, saying "why any man who was meditating such stratagems would put them in the papers is not apparent to me." Cain then hired Martin Gang to negotiate with Giesler, and Aileen's case broke down, according to Cain, when "Giesler saw the canceled checks, and learned my main cruelty consisted of stuffing $1,000 bills down her throat" (which Ms. Pringle vehemently denied). Aileen had been insisting on a cash settlement, alimony, and a share of the earnings of books Cain had written while they were living together—*Past All Dishonor* and *The Butterfly*. Cain protested on the grounds that Aileen not only had failed to contribute to his writing but actually had hindered it, and that she had already shared in the advances on the books. He pointed out that some of her own friends had convinced him that she had married him only for "mercenary motives" and were urging him not to let Aileen take him. He decided to fight back. "Sitting in this glass house, Aileen, with her usual genius for folly," he told Gang, "heaved a rock, and since she asked for it, I don't know why we don't heave it back."

The solution, in Cain's account, came from a friend. "What is hanging the thing up, I could almost bet on it," the friend said, "is your wife's suspicion that as soon as you get her name on the dotted line you are going to uncork a big movie deal. The only way to meet that is to give her a piece of it." So Cain offered her a one-third share of the two books, which he thought even the judge would consider excessive. *Past All Dishonor* had not sold to movies yet, but it appeared that it might, and for big money—which would anyway have given Cain a tax problem. And he knew *The Butterfly* probably would never sell to the movies. The attorneys agreed to the settlement, which also included a cash payment of some $6,000. Beyond that, Aileen has over the years received some royalties from each of the books.

So, in the spring of 1946, Cain moved out of Aileen's little house in Santa Monica. It should be said for Aileen that the whole affair came at a most difficult time. Her mother, with whom she was very close, had just died, quite suddenly, and Aileen felt most upset and insecure. She later wrote Cain that the whole thing was the "first and only traumatic experience" in her life.

Unable to have his old room at the Knickerbocker because of a new government regulation against living for more than five days in a transient hotel, Cain was finally found a room by a friend, at the Shoreham Hotel at Carondelet and Wilshire in Los Angeles. A few days after the settlement, Aileen called him there, and Cain recalled that "suddenly by some magic, we were the same wonderful friends that we had been before it started, that dreadful mistake we made when we decided we ought to get married. . . . If we had let it go at that, instead of trying to force it, we would both have been spared a heartbreak." In later years, Cain would say: "I don't know what it is between a man and a woman that makes a marriage go, but friendship is not one of them." What did make a marriage? "Of course I am perfect," he wrote his mother when he and Aileen had separated, "and the other two failures were surely the fault of the ladies involved, but three is getting into the funny coincidence department."

Once again Cain's life seemed to be coming apart. This time, however, he could afford the financial settlement because of the money he was making at RKO and his general status as one of Hollywood's highest-paid screenwriters. But that situation, too, seemed to be heading for stormy waters, as Cain suddenly decided to take on the studios, the courts, the Writers Guild, the Communists and anti-Communists, and eventually the entire American writing and publishing establishment in what became the most explosive experience of his turbulent career.

AAA—"THE BRAND OF CAIN"

To appreciate the ironic position in which Cain ultimately found himself after proposing his controversial American Authors' Authority in 1946, it is necessary to understand his position on Communism. As seen from the great majority of his editorials for the *New York World* and through his voluminous nonfiction for the *American Mercury* and other publications, Cain was essentially apolitical. For him the only subject was Man— or, more accurately, Man and his relation to Woman. Politics, politicians, and most national issues bored him. His analytical mind could probe quickly to the core of any such issue, and he would adopt his own position, usually "on the side of humanity" tempered with a pragmatic approach to getting along in the world; but then, with most everyone else bogged down in peripheral issues, he would lose interest. Politically, he was neither a liberal nor a conservative, but something in between. He believed religiously in democracy and was against imperialism—whether American, British, or Russian.

He was not especially sympathetic to liberal "do-gooders," though he tolerated socialistic ideas when expressed openly. He had opposed the anti-Red hysteria of the twenties and was annoyed at Mencken's Red-baiting in his *Mercury* column during the thirties. But he was also instinctively anti-Communist during the late thirties and early forties, when the issue began to _ emerge in intellectual circles. What he objected to primarily was secrecy, and the fact, ultimately established, that U.S. Communists of that era were essentially loyal to a foreign power and followed the Russian Communist party line. He was also aware of the left-wing influence in California politics and throughout American intellectual communities. Although a Democrat, he had opposed the Democratic candidate for Congress in his district because the man had been taken over by the "fuzz-buzz pinkoes," and he was likewise suspicious of the wartime Writers Board because of its leftist leanings. As he wrote *Baltimore Sun* columnist Frank Kent, when congratulating him on a column denouncing the Board: "I have begun to wonder whether this is quite such a harmless bunch of crackpots as I had thought. I think sometimes around the cocktail bar a new party line is being developed, with the atomic bomb scientists, such writers as these, and the radio thinkers forming a sort of front."

Cain was not unaware of the Communist influence among Hollywood writers, but many, including some of the now-famous Hollywood Ten, were his friends, and they got along fine socially and professionally. And he had no objection to anyone's being a Communist as long as they were open about it. As for his own view on Communism, anyone who knew James M. Cain knew how he felt. "In my opinion Communism is Communism," he said in 1947. "It is the same wherever it is encountered, and has to be fought the same way; by recognizing it for what it is and by ceasing to accept its pretension that it is something else. It is not a political party. It is a secret society and one dedicated to the interests of a foreign power. When by law we treat it as such, and not until then, will we have it under control." He also felt Communists should have to register as agents of a foreign power, with the full understanding that in time of war they would, of necessity, be placed in concentration camps.

Cain had joined the Screen Writers Guild in the 1940s, but had not been an especially active member. He was basically not a joiner, and although he supported John Lee Mahin and James McGuinness in their efforts to fight the Communist influence in the Guild, he did not take part in the intramural struggle between the Reds and anti-Reds. Mahin, who led the opposition to the Guild leadership, says: "We had stuff right from the FBI that we couldn't use, and we knew they were commies. But Jimmy didn't want to join the fight against the Communists. He was a complete loner."

The idea for an American Authors' Authority had absolutely nothing to do with Communism, fascism, politics, thought control, or intellectual monopoly, and the idea was definitely not hatched in Moscow and smuggled to Hollywood to be introduced into the mainstream of American thought by the Communist-dominated Screen Writers Guild—as many of its more hysterical critics claimed. It grew primarily out of Cain's fertile mind and was the direct result of his professional experience in publishing, movies, and courtrooms.

By 1946, his books had sold more than a million and a half copies, mostly in reprints. In fact, his books were being reprinted so often and by so many different reprint houses that he found it confusing. As he complained to Knopf: "The trouble is, the Garden City Publishing Company, the Dollar Book Club, Sun Dial, and Triangle all jumble up in my mind, and I have a suspicion there is an overlap somewhere." These reprints were controlled by the publisher, who received 50 percent of the royalties, and when Knopf tried to explain how such rights worked, saying this was the way it had always been done, Cain was still annoyed, just as he was still annoyed with the movie studios after what had happened to *Postman*. Because MGM owned all dramatic rights, he had had to fight to keep a share of his own play version of the novel, which he had spent months writing. In addition, movies of *Postman* had been made in Italy and France, and Cain felt MGM had not done enough to defend his or their rights. Also, by 1946 the studios were beginning to remake earlier pictures for which they held the rights (*Gatsby* was a good example), and Cain came to realize that someday all his stories might be remade into new movies for which he would receive nothing. In addition, he was incensed that there was no royalty arrangement for movies; by now, his three big films had grossed over $12 million, while he had been paid only $55,000 and would never receive another dime, no matter how many times they were remade into new films.

Finally, there was the question of plagiarism. As we have seen, Cain had been involved in two plagiarism lawsuits, one in which he sued Universal for what appeared to him to have been a theft of material from his novel *Serenade*, and one in which he, another writer, and Universal were the defendants. In both cases the plaintiff failed to convince Judge Leon Yankwich, who, although very literate and highly respectful of writers, had achieved such a pro-defendant reputation in plagiarism cases that members of the Los Angeles bar were advising their clients not to waste their time on plagiarism suits. In both the cases he was involved in, Cain sympathized with the plaintiff's having to sit there alone without any support from his fellow writers, pleading a case that affected the entire writing community.

So the essence of Cain's conflict with the studios was rights. Since early 1945, the Screen Writers Guild had been studying the question of leasing, rather than selling, stories to the studios, and in 1946, Cain, as a leading advocate of licensing, joined the Guild's Committee on the Sale of Original Material. While a member of this committee, he became involved in a plagiarism lawsuit, brought by David O. Selznick against a novelist by the name of Ketti Frings. Mrs. Frings had written a novel, *I Know You*, which was offered to the studios for sale. Selznick thought the story resembled Henry James's *The Wings of the Dove*, to which his studio owned the picture rights. He offered Mrs. Frings $10,000, which she refused: first, because she wanted more, and second, because she suspected that Selznick was buying her novel to keep the film from being made by another studio, with no intention of making it himself. When Mrs. Frings refused the offer, Selznick put the other studios on notice that there were "certain similarities" in the two books, the clear implication being that whoever bought Mrs. Frings's book would also inherit a lawsuit.

Selznick's action killed *I Know You* at the studios and led to Mrs. Frings suing Selznick, not only for defamation of title but also for libel, since plagiarism is a criminal act. This brought Cain into the case as a representative of the Guild's Leasing Committee. After reading the two novels, and feeling strongly that writers in such cases should have the support of other writers, he offered to testify in Mrs. Frings's behalf. He also urged the Guild to put its own treasury behind the case, rather than pass the hat, and that members attend the trial and offer to serve as supporting witnesses. He then wrote an article for the *Screen Writer* in support of Mrs. Frings, arguing that the Guild should make all litigation involving writers its solemn concern and touching on another subject that he considered critical to the rank and file: "Nobody . . . put me on any blacklist after my lawsuit [against Universal in 1942]; nobody bore me any grudges as far as I know."

There was no mention in this article (which appeared in April 1946) of the bold plan Cain was soon to launch, though there were hints of it. The title itself, "The Opening Gun," suggested the war was just beginning, and in the piece he further said the Frings case was especially important now with the Guild about to consider the question of property rights "and in the reasonably near future we are likely to see startling developments."

The "developments"—and they would, indeed be startling—concerned an ambitious scheme forming in his mind, one that he expected would settle once and for all the whole question of property rights, copyrights, royalties, and subsidiary rights with book publishers, magazines, and radio, as well as movie studios. It grew out of a conversation, probably about the Frings case, one night at a meeting of the Guild Leasing Committee. Morris Cohen, the Guild's attorney, was trying to explain to Ring Lardner, Jr., another committee member, the difference between *forbidding* members to make a certain deal and making such a deal *impossible* for them by putting the material in some kind of "repository," as he called it. "There is a profound difference," said Cohen, "between what a man is forbidden to do, but may do, if enough money is shaken in his face, and what does not lie within his power to do."

Cohen's distinction served as a catalyst, fusing in Cain's mind a number of jumbled thoughts and hunches he had been mulling on the subject of a writer's rights. And a few nights later he suddenly realized what was wrong with all writers' organizations, the reason they were invariably so feeble. "It seemed to me," he later told Mencken, "their fallacy lay in their effort to organize writers rather than properties, and that Cohen's idea . . . might furnish the key to an effective organization—a repository growing out of present forms of contract would become impossible, since the repository would execute deals only of the kind which reserved all rights intact to the writer, and would never let any part of his copyright get away from him—that is, it would lease but not sell."

Cain thought he was on to something and began having luncheon conferences at Perino's with some of Hollywood's sharpest lawyers—Cohen, Martin Gang, Norman Tyre, and Robert Kopp—as well as leaders in the writing community—Emmet Lavery, president of the Screen Writers Guild, George Kaufman, Russell Crouse, Howard Lindsay, and Sam Moore, president of the Radio Writers Guild, Dalton Trumbo, editor of the Guild publication *Screen Writer*, Herman Mankiewicz, Clarence Day, Craig Rice, and others. All professed enthusiasm to Cain, so he worked up a little brochure outlining an organization that he called the American Authors' Authority, which would serve as such a repository for all copyrights.

By now Cain had left RKO, and although the main reason had been to enable him to go to Louisiana to do research on his Civil War book, there is also evidence from his correspondence that his strong, open stand on the Frings case might have led to trouble with the front office. He saw the case primarily as a test of strength between the producers and writers, and as he told one friend: "The attitude of producers will be ferocious. . . . This is a fight, and once in a fight, before weapons, strategy, tactics or anything else can be considered, the first thing is guts."

Everyone who knew Cain was aware that the one thing he had was guts. His first instinct was to form a small group of twenty to thirty writers to launch his AAA, but the idea did not meet with much support. Then Dalton Trumbo, editor of the *Screen Writer*, talked him into reprinting his brochure about the AAA in the Guild publication, presenting the plan as something to be administered by the four major guilds. Hoping to arouse additional support for his plan, Cain agreed, though eventually he would look back on it as a mistake—not because it was Trumbo's suggestion, and Trumbo had the reputation of being a Communist, but because the organization could never be effectively administered by the four guilds. And as it turned out, identification of the plan with the Screen Writers Guild did eventually hurt him, despite the fact that, as Cain always maintained, the thinking behind the plan was 95 percent his, the work 75 percent his, and the initiative 100 percent his.

Cain's brochure was edited for publication in the July 1946 *Screen Writer* and, if nothing else, reinforced his reputation as one of the country's most persuasive and witty polemicists. He began by dramatizing the plight of the writer, not only at the hands of movie producers, but with book publishers, radio stations, magazine editors, and the United States government. One of his main complaints was that the government looked on a writer's gain as income from his labor, whereas Cain viewed it as income from his property. Thus, if a writer sells his property to a studio or a publisher, he should be taxed on a capital gain, not on income. What the writer creates is "property," Cain argued, "and he knows that he has just so many of these ova in his belly, and indeed he is never sure that the latest one he produced will not be his last; it is a special, peculiar heart-breaking business, wherein one's work, done at great labor, time, and expense, may bring almost no return, while another done with comparative ease may be a gold mine and may, more importantly, be the only gold mine the writer ever sees. And any big picture sale, even with top writers, is so unusual that it may be repeated only once or twice during their lives."

And who was the real enemy? "Stalking through the foregoing, casting his shadow over the whole dismal tale, is a villain, whether the question be magazines, publishers, theaters, movies, radio, bureaucrats, or courts. The writer has but one formidable enemy, and that is himself; like Jurgen, he lives in a hell of his own creation. It would put a much better face on the matter if it could be said that practices have grown up around him so malignantly that he is the victim of circumstances beyond his control. . . . But this would not really be true. It would be hard to imagine a profession where practice carries so little weight as it does in writing . . . practice is born with each deal as he makes it. The contract governs the case."

Writers shouldn't have to sign the deals that bind them to the publishers and producers, yet they do. Why? Because "[we] writers have certain characteristics that make it grotesquely easy to pull the wool over our eyes, to flatter us, to cajole us, to organize against us, and then to deal with us separately. To begin with, we secretly believe Judge Yankwich is right and that we are very special beings. Of course, we call it 'artists,' but we try to improve on God, so it cuts up to about the same thing in the end. Unfortunately, we have most of the defects peculiar to gods and few of their virtues, if any. We have a furious, jealous intolerance of all other gods, and indeed, each of us thinks himself the only God and holds all other gods to be phonies and their followers heretics. Thus, concerted action is completely repellent to our nature. A gang of plumbers can easily sew up a city with extortionist regulations and hang together like wolves, but anybody who has tried to get three writers to act as a unit on the simplest matter knows what the difficulties are. We feel we know everything, and when a publisher, explaining a monstrous swindle, says, 'it is customary,' rather than go to a lawyer, or to another writer, or in any way admit that we don't know whether it's 'customary' or not, we abjectly surrender whatever he wants, rarely even taking so much trouble about it as our wives would take over a questionable item in the monthly grocery bill."

The key to the whole question, he argued, was copyright! And because of the writer's inability to protect himself, let alone even understand copyright, Cain proposed an Authority that would not only control and manage *all* copyrights, but perform a number of other administrative and beneficial services. For example (and reflecting Cain's own inability to keep up with all his magazine and reprint copyrights), the Authority would protect him in and inform him of all the complicated arrangements concerning the secondary rights of popular, often reprinted and reproduced work. "Does [the author] own the radio rights?," Cain wrote, "the French rights? or were these sold as part of the 'foreign rights'? Were any of the reprint rights exclusive for a limited time? Does he still own the first serial rights? He doesn't know, and would have to search ten contracts to find out."

The AAA would take care of all that for the author. It would also represent writers in the courts and maintain lobbies in Washington and some state capitals, where it would work to have the income tax laws modified in favor of writers and to update the archaic copyright law in existence since 1909. It would be financed by levying a charge of one percent on all transactions it negotiated, and it would operate under the head of a "full-time tough mug" to be elected by four directors who would, in turn, be elected by the membership of the four literary guilds. This, in Cain's words, was how the AAA would work:

The writer will send all works to the Authority to be copyrighted in its name for his benefit. The Authority will then say, "We shall copyright for assignment no works except from writers who have become members of the proper guild." This will take care of the outlaw contributor who became so menacing to ASCAP at the time of its fight with the radio studios. It will also say we shall lease no rights except to lessors who comply with the basic agreements of the guilds. The Screen Writers Guild and the Radio Writers Guild will say, "We shall permit our writers to work on no material not leased through the Authority," and this will compel every writer in the country hoping for picture or magazine sale to send his work to the Authority for copyright before the magazines or publishers get it.

The above paragraph was, of course, the critical one. When the article was published, Cain recalled, "You would have thought I stabbed Truman."

The movie producers were, naturally enough, among the first to react; the word from the studio private dining rooms was that the moguls were talking something like this: "The writers may say that what they want is to retain their copyrights—but what they really want is to dictate to us what stuff goes on the screen, to tell us we can't change or cut material written while they are on salary to us." *Screen Writer*, in the follow-up editorial, replied this was "nonsense"—that the AAA would never have any say about what a salaried writer created.

But the most emotional reaction came from writers themselves, who simply did not want to give up their copyrights, despite the fact that they freely assigned them to publishers and other people in deals Cain insisted never favored the writer. H.L. Mencken, for example, although agreeing that AAA offered writers a way out of mounting difficulties, showed considerable foresight when he wrote his old friend: "Unhappily I doubt seriously that it would ever be possible to induce more than a small percentage of American authors to join in. Every one of them believes that he is able, single-handed and alone, to beat the whole hierarchy of Satan. I myself believe that I can do it. . . ."

One of the first to express what would soon be the main criticism against the plan was George Sokolsky, the syndicated columnist. Although he called the plan "brilliant," he also thought it would inevitably establish a supreme censor over all writers and writing in the country. "What Mr. Cain proposes is a device to get around the Constitution," Sokolsky said, claiming that Cain, in effect, would say to a magazine editor: "You want to print Westbook Pegler, all right, you can do that if you like, but Pegler declines to submit to our authority. Therefore, if you publish Pegler, you may never publish, if they join us, Clarence Budington Kelland, Lloyd C. Douglas, Ellery Queen, Dashiell Hammett, Frances Parkinson Keyes, Walter Davenport, Fulton Oursler, Octavus Roy Cohen and Joe Doakes. We won't let them. You keep Pegler out or we keep everybody out."

Sokolsky also confirmed Cain's notion that writers viewed themselves as God when he went on to argue that the most important right of the author is "to speak the truth as he sees it, against all the world, one man standing alone if necessary. A writer is not a drummer. He is a creative person with something in his mind and heart, as willing to risk the garrote as to accept the emoluments and plaudits that come to him for his work." And then the unkindest—to Cain—cut of all: "Maybe it is the preoccupation with rights and deals that has reduced American literature to its current vulgarity."

Sokolsky concluded on a high note, arguing that Edgar Allan Poe, Nathaniel Hawthorne, and Mark Twain did not recognize any authority, and shaking his head that "Mr. Cain had not thought his problem out," for Cain of all people would never submit to an authority.

Cain, of course, had never envisioned the "tough mug" at the head of his Authority being a censor. His function would be to represent the author in his contractual negotiations with publishers and movie producers. But most of the writing community agreed with Sokolsky that the AAA did pose a threat of censorship, especially since the plan came during the beginning of the Cold War against the Russian international conspiracy, when such fear of censorship was quite real. And the problem, as Cain quickly learned, was compounded by the fact that the Screen Writers Guild was rapidly being exposed as dominated by left-wing and Communist writers. Most of the men who later became famous as the Hollywood Ten were Guild members, and Cain, who had never taken much interest in the internal politics of the Guild, was, in truth, somewhat naïve in judging the difficulties he would face from those trying to make it appear that his plan was sponsored by a Red organization.

While Sokolsky, in his opening column against the AAA, did not once mention the Communist issue, there was an implication that the Authority might be Red-dominated when he suggested that such an organization would be in a position to keep the nation's most avid anti-Communist—Westbrook Pegler—from being published. It would be a while before Sokolsky would pick up the Communist theme directly, but others were not so discreet. The *Hollywood Reporter*, which Cain considered primarily a mouthpiece for the studios, supported as it was by their advertising, was quick to cry "Red!" when members of the Writers Guild met at the Hollywood Roosevelt Hotel on the night of July 29 and voted to accept the AAA. The *Reporter* headed its story about the meeting: "A Vote for Joe Stalin." It said the Guild was controlled and dominated by "avowed leftists" and that the AAA "has all the earmarks of a 'Commie' party line maneuver for the control of all writers and their writings, [and] nothing could be more to the advantage of the Communist Party in America than to obtain a complete monopoly of opinion, which will enable it to suppress the views of all other Americans."

Meanwhile, back East, the writing community, always suspicious and distrustful of eccentric California writers, was organizing for battle. People there were not so much concerned about the Communist threat—although they were willing to use that issue in their opposition—as they were about the possibility of a James C. Petrillo (head of ASCAP—the American Society of Composers, Authors and Publishers) emerging for the publishing industry. The Eastern writing establishment of that day was dominated by the Authors League, and the first indication of the size of the hornet's nest Cain had disturbed came when fifty writers—many, though not all, members of the Authors League—wrote a letter to Elmer Rice, president of the League, announcing their opposition to the AAA and the formation of an "American Writers Association" to combat the Cain plan. They acknowledged the need to correct "certain injustices and disadvantages from which authors suffer at the hands of publishers and producers," but argued that such a need "is being used to bury the entire writing profession in America under the domination of an authoritarian monopoly." The letter did not specify who would exercise the AAA's authoritarian monopoly, but it did say that the organization was "brought into the open by the Screen Writers Guild, which has a public reputation for being completely Communist-dominated." Fifty writers had already joined the AWA, including Louis Bromfield, Clarence Budington Kelland, John Erskine, John T. Flynn, Rupert Hughes, Clare Boothe Luce, Rene Kuhn, Philip Wylie, Eugene Lyons, George Sokolsky, Ayn Rand, and H. V. Kaltenborn.

Rice's first reaction was to defend the AAA in a statement denying it would create a monopolistic control or that it was Communist-inspired. The Communist issue, he said, "was a lot of moonshine," which you would expect to come "from certain of our Southern Congressmen" rather than established authors. And in an interview with reporters at League headquarters on East 39th Street, Rice said the plan would be discussed soon at a meeting of the Authors League Council. The issue, he maintained, was not whether the Screen Writers Guild was pro-Communist but whether the plan might offer greater protection to authors than some other plans being considered. The League, in fact, had been under considerable pressure to force publishers to liberalize book contracts, and almost every writer by now was protesting against publishers trying to retain a share in the movie rights. The more sophisticated writers, agreeing with Cain, were in favor of leasing to the movie studios rather than making outright sales.

Originally, Cain was scheduled to come East to explain his plan to the League meeting, but then Rice announced he had received a wire from Cain saying the he could not attend. He would, however, come East on October 9 to address the League and the Dramatists Guild. Meanwhile, in Hollywood, Cain was feeling bold and optimistic, despite the specter of Communism hovering over his plan. In a telephone interview, he told a *New York Herald Tribune* reporter that he was "simply amazed" at the support for his plan and reminded his interviewer of the peculiar history of writers. "After all, you can dress up mice to make them look like cavalry, but I have discovered that if you give a writer a peashooter to kill a tiger, he'll just sit around and talk about it. But give him a rifle and he'll go out and shoot the tiger."

Cain thought he had given writers a rifle with his AAA and was predicting that it would be accepted by all the guilds and the League by January 1. In another interview he said the talk about monopoly and Communism was "pure nonsense." The articles of incorporation for the AAA would prevent a monopoly, and he reminded his interviewer that he had worked for and contributed to Republican Governor Earl Warren's campaign and had helped organize the Democrats for Dewey in 1944. To Cain, the fact that the Screen Writers Guild was dominated by Communists was totally irrelevant. It was *his* plan, not the Guild's, and no one could question his credentials. "It is no plot," he told interviewers. "It is simply a plan to enforce our own rights. It's not the principle we're interested in, it's the money."

At first it appeared that Cain's effort to present his plan as a capitalist scheme rather than a Communist plot would succeed—or at least that the battle would be fought over the more substantive issue of monopoly control. There was a legitimate concern here. Some fuzzy thinking went into the original plan's approach to copyright law, as Cain virtually admitted in a letter he wrote to an MGM executive in which he said that much of what had bothered the executive had been in the original proposal "because various lawyers I talked to thought they knew and didn't. As my reading catches up, various details will need a lot of amending." And Emmet Lavery, president of the Screen Writers Guild, conceded in an interview with Thornton Delehanty of the *New York Herald Tribune* that concern about the AAA's acting as a monopoly in restraint of trade was a legitimate issue. But far from freezing out writers, he said, the AAA would want to bring them in, because the more influence writers had the more effective the Authority would be. As for control on ideas, he said this would be as unlikely as it was in the Dramatists Guild, and who could imagine that Guild dictating ideas to a playwright? Lavery also reminded his interviewer that he was an avowed, practicing Catholic, not a Communist.

But the opposition continued to build back East, and Cain knew he had a fight on his hands when James T. Farrell came at him from another flank, suggesting that the real conflict was between those who cherished their freedom and those who had sold out to commercial interests. Farrell wrote Rice urging that the forthcoming meeting of the Authors League's Executive Committee reject AAA because it was "reactionary and bureaucratic." Farrell pointed out that the plan had been sponsored by the Screen Writers and Radio Writers Guild (which had adopted the plan shortly after it was first proposed), and "while they are the most highly rewarded writers in America, they are also the most unfree. . . . They have very little free expression in their own work. The bureaucratic board of 'tough guys' which they want is one which will, in the main, concern themselves with monetary questions." Farrell also objected to Rice's "cavalier" dismissal of allegations that there was a Stalinist influence in the plan and asserted that such political charges could not be ignored. He closed by urging that the League's meeting be open to the press.

It was a curious agrument. Farrell seemed to be saying that the writers who had shown no hesitancy to sell themselves to American commercial interests would also be easily taken in by a Communist bureaucratic board. Rice dismissed Farrell's letter, saying no one group was going to dominate the League and assuring that the plan would be debated fairly by the Council, then voted on by the full membership, although the Council meeting would not be open to the press, since they would also be discussing authors' grievances. He then denied a request from the dissident AWA (which had now organized and elected novelist John Erskine as its national chairman) to send representatives to the Council meeting, although it did invite one AWA member, Rene Kuhn, to attend. She declined, because she was not allowed to bring a lawyer with her.

The League's Executive Council met in September. Cain did not attend, but his representative, William Pomerance, executive secretary of the Screen Writers Guild, spoke for fifteen minutes, saying that the Cain plan was being offered primarily as a "springboard" for action by the writing community. Rice stressed that the League was concerned with many of the grievances to be dealt with by the AAA and that the League wanted to give the plan a fair hearing. After three hours, the Council decided no action would be taken "without a complete survey and study of every aspect of the proposal and of its application," and a committee was appointed to study the plan. The feeling in the League was expressed by Rice, who told reporters after the meeting that it was "extremely unlikely" that the League or any of its guilds would adopt any plan that would entail a surrender by authors of copyrights. Nor would it approve the establishment of "any administrative official or board who would have arbitrary or dictatorial powers or would tend to place any restrictions upon freedom of thought or expression or create a monopolistic control that would deprive any author of his means of livelihood." Cain now knew that some modifications would have to be made in the plan before it would be acceptable to the rank and file.

Shortly after the meeting, another heavyweight opponent entered the ring: the *Saturday Review*, edited by Norman Cousins. Cain had expected most magazines to be against him because "magazines copyright in their own name, and in such a fight as the Authority would face, the question of who gets there first, or who holds this scrap of paper, is of the essence." But he had hoped that publications representing the writing community would be on his side. As it turned out, the *Saturday Review* did come out on the side of the writing community—the Eastern wing, as dominated by the Authors League and the New York literary community. In an editorial, *SR* said Cain's plan was a "blue sky" proposal "written with all the enthusiasm and confidence of a wildcat oil company prospectus." It went on to voice a reaction probably shared by most writers, not only in the East but around the country: "It is obvious that any all-embracing Authority of this nature, owning the copyrights to the works of a majority of American writers, advising them and perhaps controlling their contracts and negotiations with publishing here and abroad, with the theatre, motion pictures, and the radio, financed by percentages taken from every sale of any kind, could without much difficulty strangle free speech and free literary enterprise."

SR also cited Cain's threat (designed to counteract the repeated statements by the studios that they had several years' backlog of scripts, hence did not have to worry about writers getting tough or going on strike) that if the writers were to unite the day might come when screenwriters would announce that "at a certain date, they will not work on any material except that whose copyright is owned by the Authority." *SR* argued that this was only one or two steps "from telling a magazine editor or publisher that a member of the Guild will not sell his work to him if he publishes other writers whose copyrights are not owned by the Authority." It also mentioned the Communist overtones and concluded that the AAA was "dangerous and unworkable."

The stage was now set for Cain's trip East to present the plan at a meeting of the Authors League. But first he wrote a brief article for the *Screen Writer* explaining in more detail what the AAA was and taking the occasion to back away from the one point in his plan that bothered friend and foe alike: the threat of monopoly in the original plan forcing all participating authors to join one of the four guilds. He now acknowledged his mistake and said "the Authority would accept any property from anybody at all and utterly regardless of its content, but that any writer who wishes a voice in the management of the Authority must naturally join the proper one of the four guilds."

Cain also took time to dispel the charge that his plan was "a cat's-paw of Communism" and had been conceived in Moscow. He cited a remark made by one of the leaders of the opposition, when the plan was first adopted at the meeting attended by more than four hundred Hollywood writers. "After thinking about it," the man had said, "and learning more about it, I'm in favor of this thing, because I've become convinced it has no political purpose of any kind, but is simply one gang of capitalists trying to get more dough out of another gang of capitalists." Cain concluded his somewhat self-consciously witty piece by saying that eventually "this view of things might make good Republicans of us all."

Having finished the article, Cain headed East in mid-October to do battle, but while he was en route, Elmer Rice was taken to the hospital, and Louise Sillcox, executive secretary of the League, thereupon canceled the meeting, even though members on both sides of the issue insisted the meeting could be held without Rice. When Cain arrived and learned of this turn, he was furious and held an impromptu press conference at 5:00 P.M. on a Friday in the cocktail lounge of the Gotham Hotel. It was, to say the least, a confused session. Cain accused the Authors League of a "double-cross" and announced that he had hired a hall himself at the Henry Hudson Hotel and would address the League and anyone else who wanted to attend. The playwright Marc Connelly, author of *Green Pastures*, appeared unexpectedly and said that he, not Cain, represented the Guild and that he had just spoken to Emmet Lavery, Guild president, who saw no objection to the League's canceling the meeting.

"You are alibiing," said Cain.

"I am alibiing nothing," Connelly replied, and then accused Cain of a "usurpation of authority."

With this, Stefan Heym, vice-chairman of the League's Action Committee and author of the much-discussed *Hostages*, a novel about the Nazi occupation of Prague, came to Cain's defense, saying that he was essentially right in suspecting that League officials were trying to sabotage the AAA and that the rank and file were eager to hear what Cain had to say.

Cain, meanwhile, was entertaining reporters and arguing with Harrison Smith of the *Saturday Review*, who objected to Cain's statement that "publishers' contracts are the worst gyps on earth." Smith said they were becoming "more standardized" all the time. Cain denied the AAA would create a monopoly and left the group, insisting that he would organize his own meeting the next day, October 20.

Cain was unable to obtain the Henry Hudson Hall until eight o'clock the night of October 21, but meanwhile the members of the AWA, opposing Cain, held their own meeting, on the twentieth, in the St. James Theatre on West 44th Street, where the musical *Oklahoma!* was playing. The group chose Dorothy Thompson to speak against the AAA but also invited Cain to attend. Aware that the Authors League did not recognize the dissident group, and feeling he should not either, Cain declined. Instead he accepted an invitation to be interviewed over radio station WNYC. There he found himself transmitting his views at the very time Dorothy Thompson was telling the seventy-five or so writers assembled at the St. James that all authors would be "coerced into joining the authority by boycotts of the organized writers against publishers or producers who take the work of the unorganized." This, said Miss Thompson, then acknowledged as the journalist most expert on the Nazis, was the way Dr. Goebbels had forced German writers into a single organization that throttled their freedom. Cain had now succeeded in drawing fire from all flanks. His plan was considered both Communist and Fascist.

In his radio interview, Cain said "writers fear this thing because it is new, as people once feared banks and lightning rods and surgery. Writers resent all discussion of literature in its economic aspects and think it completely below them. It was not below Giuseppe Verdi, one of the first businessmen in the history of music, and it was not below George Bernard Shaw, a genius at literary business. But it is below three-quarters of American writers."

The next night Cain was at the Henry Hudson, and even he was amazed at the turnout. Over six hundred writers were there, most of them boisterously favoring Cain and shouting down anyone who tried to criticize the AAA. The meeting was under the direction of Carl Carmer, the upstate New York regional writer, who was chairman of the League's Action Committee sponsoring the meeting. Cain accused Elmer Rice, Marc Connelly, and Louise Sillcox of being "enemies of free speech" and introduced a new issue—that the Authors League had refused to grant him and supporters of the AAA their membership list so that details of the plan could be sent to all the members. He announced that the League was being sued in court to obtain the list and charged that "it is these reactionary, almost incomprehensibly censorious writers, some of them in this so-called AWA, others of them a clique which runs the Authors Guild and the Authors League, who are guilty of a monstrous campaign against the right of a writer to say what he thinks."

Despite efforts to silence him, James T. Farrell managed to hold the floor for some questions, including a request that Cain explain why, as Farrell had heard, Cain had put the threat of coercion in his original plan. Cain replied that at the time he felt this would give the AAA greater strength, but withdrew the idea when it was obvious that forcing writers to join the AAA was not agreeable to the Screen Writers Guild. But to make certain Farrell knew where he stood, Cain said: "I mean power here, no mistake."

Some members wanted the meeting to pass a resolution in favor of the Authority, but both Cain and Carmer were opposed, arguing that the plan should be passed on by the League's four guilds. Still, despite the obvious enthusiasm on the part of so many writers, curiously enough it was at this meeting that Cain, at least as he tells it, had his first hint that maybe the plan had some inherent weakness. One reporter there was young Harvey Breit, who wrote a long, thoughtful analysis of the plan and the controversy it had aroused for the *New York Times Book Review*. Cain remembered seeing Breit at the meeting, and years later wrote him that he had made quite an impact on him that evening. "Every time I'd get a lull in the whoop-de-do, I'd glance at you, and the look on your face of baffled, bewildered boredom told me something of the phony nature of what I was doing."

The next blow in the fight was struck by Byron Price, vice-president of the Motion Picture Association, who came at Cain from both the right and the left. Price said no writer could have any manuscript accepted without first clearing it with the AAA, "precisely as German writers were required to do under Nazism and Russian writers must do under Communism."

The next round was fought on the pages of the *Saturday Review*, where Harrison Smith, after witnessing the crazy goings-on while Cain was in New York, especially the treatment given James Farrell at the Henry Hudson, invited Farrell and Cain to "debate" the plan in the pages of the magazine. Farrell went first, stating his objections to the plan, and Cain followed with his comments in rebuttal to Farrell's arguments. Farrell continued to harp on Cain's original intent to force every writer to join AAA, arguing that it showed the authoritarian nature of Cain's thinking and that, furthermore, most of the proponents of the plan were not authors in a "desperate plight" but wealthy, overpaid screenwriters. He maintained that these commercial screen and radio writers would ultimately gain control over the independent writer with five tough mugs and a million-dollar kitty controlling all copyrights. The essence of his argument was this: "Organization, collectivization is good on the economic front: but only anarchy, freedom to struggle toward untrammelled freedom in expression of ideas, and the creation of art can be our guide."

Farrell did not make a good case or argue it well. Cain's rebuttal was not only devastating but also went to the core of his thinking about literature and art. He said he did not know how to reply to Farrell, "as I have been unable, after several readings of his article, to understand clearly what he is trying to say, if anything. He uses the gobbledygook of the professional leftist and makes much of the fact that some Hollywood writers make $100,000 a year, though not noting that the majority of them make $60 a week when they make it, which isn't any too often. He insists on a far-fetched, political interpretation of the American Authors' Authority, though he doesn't state what is wrong with the obvious commonsense view of it that is designed to give a writer better terms from publishers, employers, government and everybody else, than he gets at present."

Then, quoting Farrell's remark about collectivization and the creation of art, Cain said:

> If this twittering nonsense is what the editors of this magazine expect me to dignify with something in the way of a reply, all I can say is I don't know how to do it. That somebody, in this age and time, still believes in anarchy, that freedom can be struggled for without making contact with the realities as they exist, that art can be consciously "created" any more than a baby can be consciously created—these ideas, to me, are simply weird, and downright silly. I don't believe freedom is successfully pursued by cranky theorists riding farfetched obsessions. I believe free speech is uttered by free men, and that men become free by fighting repression as it exists, and not by ignoring repression as it exists to tilt at phantom windmills. I believe the conscious creation of art is a form of literary smugness.

Cain won this round by a wide margin, and a week later the supporters of AAA won another round: New York State Supreme Court Judge Bernard Shientag ruled that the Authors League had to turn over its list of 2,150 members, as well as the minutes of the previous year's meeting (to reveal how Council members had voted), to the League's Action Committee. This would enable the committee to inform the League's entire membership of the details of Cain's final plan, whenever that plan was ready.

Although a victory for Cain and his forces, this did not mean that they had the support of the League's Action Committee, as appointed by Rice to study the AAA. The committee did favor leasing material, and it did claim that League officials were resisting its effort to modernize, but the committee was also developing a plan of its own, while staging an internal struggle to oust the League's old guard, and it was making progress. By the end of the year, Elmer Rice announced he was retiring for health reasons, and word filtered out that although the committee acknowledged Cain's "helpful cooperation," it was proceeding on a plan that would eliminate what most writers felt was the authoritarian nature of the AAA.

By early 1947, the battle over AAA settled down to a nervous truce, awaiting the preparation by the Screen Writers Guild of a revised, formal plan that would be sent to League and Guild members and all other writers for whom it could find an address. The issues continued to be debated in the nation's press, inspiring an incredible volume of editorial comment not only in the expected publications but in newspapers that rarely considered such esoteric subjects as an intramural struggle in the writing community. For several months, the *Screen Writer* ran a sampling of press comment—it was approximately 90 percent against Cain's plan and 10 percent for, with favorable comments appearing mostly in left-wing publications. The majority opposition revolved primarily around the authoritarian concept, with some commentators fearing the AAA would produce not just another Petrillo, but a *Communist* Petrillo. The P.E.N. Women also came out against it, as did most national writers' organizations. The opposition was hardening as well in the Authors League. Oscar Hammerstein II had replaced Elmer Rice as president, and one of his first acts was to appoint a new Licensing Committee, consisting of Edna Ferber, Paul Gallico, Marc Connelly, Eric Barbouw, and Kenneth Webb. Emmet Lavery, representing the West Coast Guild writers, had been a member of the original committee appointed by Rice, and Marc Connelly had acted as his representative on the committee, but Hammerstein's new committee, while including Connelly as a member, did not include Lavery or any other West Coast Guild member. Neither Hammerstein nor Connelly told Lavery he had been excluded. The revised formal concept of the AAA was reprinted as a "Special Supplement" in the March 1947 issue of the *Screen Writer*, with a supporting article by Cain and an opposing one by Louis Bromfield. Cain's article consisted mostly of a repetition of his earlier arguments, a scornful account of the attacks on the plan as being Communist-inspired or designed to produce a new Petrillo, criticism of the Authors League for not doing anything about licensing for thirty-five years, and the argument that what writers needed was a professional team that could get tough with publishers, movie studios, and Congress. Bromfield's opposition was based on his fear that the potential for evil in the plan outweighed the potential for good, primarily because of the surrender of copyright and the inherent possibility of boycott and control.

By now, although most people did not realize it, Cain was backing away from identifying himself with the Guild or the AAA. He still believed in his plan, but he was beginning to suspect the Guild. As a result, he had very little to do with the actual drawing up of the By-laws and Articles of Incorporation of the revised plan.

The supplement was mailed to the nine thousand members of the four guilds, plus four thousand writers not affiliated with any guild. The package included a questionnaire designed to test support and understanding of the plan, and it was assumed that the membership of all four guilds in the Authors League would eventually vote on AAA.

Meanwhile, the Authors League's new Licensing Committee was quietly studying the AAA without the Screen Writers Guild being represented in the deliberations or even knowing they were taking place. When the committee finally released its "Report" in May, it was clear not only that the League was firmly opposed to the plan but that the report was being offered to its members as a thoughtful rejection of what it called "an oversimplified approach" to the idea of licensing, which it still endorsed. The wording also suggested a final rejection of the AAA, implying there was no need for a full membership vote.

Despite the fact that its proponents insisted the AAA would operate under League jurisdiction, the committee obviously considered the AAA a challenge to the League's authority. It stressed that the By-laws and Articles of Incorporation of the AAA included rights "now within the purposes and objectives for which the Authors League of America was originated." In addition, the report listed ten specific provisions of the plan—from the "vague proposal" that the Authority was to preserve and protect rights arising out of copyright to the "potential risk in vesting copyright ownership in another"—that gave the committee concern.

When the Guild finally received the report, Lavery was furious at not having been included in the committee and wrote Hammerstein a strong protest. Hammerstein replied, telling Lavery of the formation of the new committee and saying he had thought one of the members of the old committee had told him what had happened. At the same time, he explained that the League hierarchy had some real concern about the AAA, although it was as eager as anyone on the West Coast to do something about copyright. "I have heard that we have been accused of being emotional and sentimental about our copyrights," Hammerstein wrote. "I have a feeling that you out there are being emotional and sentimentally loyal to the AAA. I feel that we have some very hard-headed reasons for not rushing into an immediate embrace with AAA. I think we have to approach this as a fundamental fight with producers, notably with the motion picture producers—they are no crowd of sissies. The copyrights they own are listed as among their most valuable assets. They are not going to lightly have this wrested from them. . . . Please don't think, therefore, that we in the East are a bunch of slow-moving fuddie-duddies clogged with fear or laziness or conservatism. We are honestly doubtful about your AAA as the best instrument for winning the licensing fight."

The letter convinced Lavery that Hammerstein, although opposed to the League's AAA, wanted it to have fair treatment in the League. But this opinion quickly evaporated when Hammerstein resisted mailing to the League membership a rebuttal to the committee's report. In it the Guild offered a point-by-point analysis of the committee's objections, concluding with the argument that the Guild was not wedded to the AAA as the only solution to the licensing problem and pleading with the League to come up with something, anything, in its place.

As the tension between the East Coast and the West Coast guilds mounted, Lavery complained that the League, as it often had, was "treating the Screen Writers Guild as if we were merely the country cousins who needed constant correction and disciplining." Hammerstein countered that, quite the contrary, he repeatedly heard the phrase that the "tail is wagging the dog," meaning the Screen Writers were "trying to dominate the League and the three other guilds." He said this had contributed to the stampede into the dissident American Writers Association and was seriously retarding the recruitment of new members.

At the same time, a curious little flap developed involving George Bernard Shaw, who, virtually alone, had won liberalized contracts from British publishers and producers. Lavery had sent Shaw a copy of the AAA proposal together with a long letter outlining the struggle to achieve the licensing plan (including the problems with the Authors League). The British playwright responded with an article for the *Screen Writer*, which amounted primarily to an attack on the Authors League as ineffectual and a promise to support the AAA *if* it adopted a number of provisions he suggested *and* disassociated itself immediately from the League. Coming as it did at the height of the tension between the Screen Writers and the League, and at a time when the West Coast Guild was insisting the AAA was not a challenge to the League but would operate under its direction, the Shaw article was an obvious embarrassment. Lavery decided to run it in the *Screen Writer* anyway, though he included the disclaimer that Shaw was speaking for himself and that the Guild would not withdraw from the League. He also gave Hammerstein the opportunity to reply to Shaw in the same issue, and the League president wisely dismissed the Shaw tirade as unrealistic and pointed out that Shaw was not offering to join the AAA, but permitting it to join G.B.S.

By the summer of 1947 the fight to establish a central depository for copyrights had slipped almost completely out of Cain's hands and had become the focal point of a bureaucratic struggle between the Authors League and one of its member guilds. This was not a situation in which one would expect to see James M. Cain, a loner for much of his life, involved. Bored by organizational struggles for control, he was rapidly losing interest in the fight, and not just because the AAA was disappearing in the bureaucracy of the guilds. More important, he had become aware, not only from Hammerstein's correspondence but also the early response to the AAA questionnaires, that there was real opposition in the writing community. The response was "extraordinarily disappointing," Cain wrote Mencken, "revealing that . . . writers as a breed have no comprehension of the basic questions involved by their work."

By now the chairmanship of the AWA had been taken over by Rupert Hughes, who had organized a group of right-wingers that was attacking Cain and the AAA unmercifully, mostly with the "Communist!" club. Hughes was something of a legend in the Hollywood writing fraternity, having been a successful novelist, playwright, and historian since 1911. And in the 1920s he wrote a book that endeared him to Cain—a biography of George Washington that attempted to strip the founding father of the myths and legends surrounding his life while preserving his greatness. Hughes also had had some success as a movie writer, though by the mid-1940s his best work was behind him.

Cain's attitude toward Hughes and the right-wingers he attracted was now mostly one of contempt, and he said "just how this outfit of picture actresses, magazine editors, Socialist candidates for president and similar professional space seekers are expected to save literature from me I don't exactly know." He realized that most AWA followers had joined up because Hughes was screaming "Commie," despite the fact that to accuse James M. Cain of being a Communist was manifestly a joke. All in all, said Cain, these people, who have "for years called themselves 'Tories' as a good comfortable excuse to settle back with the 5:30 old-fashioned and do nothing about anything," were getting on his nerves.

And well they might. Since the *Screen Writer* had published its special supplement proposing the AAA, the cries of "Communism" had intensified, despite the fact that the plan now proposed nothing more revolutionary than a revocable trustee for an author's copyright. The hysterical, including many big names and publications, were crying "Red!" John Dos Passos, a member of AWA, charged that the AAA plan had been Communist-inspired and was basically a political maneuver foisted on "willing dupes" working with the Screen Writers Guild; James Burnham, emerging as one of the country's leading professional anti-Communists, in an article called "The Goal of Soviet Policy," published in the *American Mercury*, included the AAA among several Soviet-pact and pro-Soviet organizations that were "simply part of [Russia's] preparation for war" with the United States; Hearst editorials said the AAA was a "Red device for getting the stranglehold" on all writing in America, and although Cain was not himself a Commie, he had been taken in by them; the *New York News* quoted movie actor Richard Arlen, who said the "real Reds [in Hollywood] are among the writers" and then linked this remark to the AAA, an organization designed to "regiment literary talent all over the United States"; Roscoe Drummond, in the *Christian Science Monitor*, said the new plan did nothing more than "remove all of Mr. Cain's blunt language and retain all of his bad provisions," and attacked it as Communist; a syndicated columnist named George Peck said "Biblical Cain slew his brother Abel. Today a gentleman of the same name is out to slay American writers and, in so doing, choke off the free voice of press, screen, radio and theater.

The Communists don't miss a trick." Philip Wylie also attacked the AAA in a clever article in which he used the story of Cain and Abel, signifying envy and greed, without ever once mentioning the name of James M. Cain, although all the writing fraternity knew whom he was talking about. Wylie did, however, raise one point that was rarely discussed in the press when he pointed out that "if such an Authors' Authority ever came into existence our Supreme Court would smash it as the greatest American indecency to freedom."

Cain could take most of this, but he was finding it difficult to cope with Hughes and the argument that he had been taken in by the Communists and was perhaps himself a secret fellow traveler. Hughes was attacking him incessantly in speeches around the country and in a series of newspaper articles. "The Cain plan bears the brand of Cain," Hughes said on one occasion, "though he himself is not a communist." But then he added: "Of course it is very hard to find anyone who will openly admit that he is one though the sprawling world known as Hollywood is lousy with holders of cards and their side-kicks." At other times Hughes would say he didn't know whether Jim Cain was a Communist or not, but "all I say is if anyone runs with Communists and preaches Communism, he's one, whether he calls himself a hypochondriac or a Zulu."

The reason Cain was finding it so difficult to combat Hughes's charges was that, like the rest of Hollywood, he was waking up to the fact that there were indeed some real, live, card-carrying Communists in their midst—and most of them were members of the Screen Writers Guild. This was at the beginning of the post–World War II hysteria over Communism, and when the word began to spread that there might be some actual members of the party in Hollywood, the House Un-American Activities Committee was on its way. Early in 1947, J. Parnell Thomas, chairman of the committee, Representative John McDowell of Pennsylvania, and two committee staffers, Robert Stripling and Louis Russell, appeared in Hollywood interviewing "friendlies" in support of the committee's investigations. Soon nineteen "unfriendlies" would be on their way to Washington to testify, or rather refuse to testify, before the committee, and ultimately ten of them would go to jail. Among them were several of Cain's colleagues at the Guild and in the AAA fight—Dalton Trumbo, Ring Lardner, Jr., Lester Cole, and Albert Maltz. The AAA was caught up in the middle of this hysteria, and as was becoming increasingly obvious, many of its critics were interested in it only as an issue with which to attack the Hollywood Communists.

Hollywood was now split into two camps—pro-Communists and anti-Communists—and Cain was somewhere in between, with friends in both. He decided it was time to have a long, hard look at the situation. At the time he first became involved with the Guild through his membership on the Committee on the Sale of Original Material, he had been inside their offices only twice in ten years, on each occasion to tell them how ineffectual he thought they were. He had heard the rumors about "Reds" in the Guild, but discounted them, having heard the same thing in the 1920s when it turned out to be mostly hysteria. Now he suspected that where there was so much smoke there might be a little fire. So in the spring of 1947, he accepted Lavery's invitation to join the Guild Board. He also read back issues of the *Screen Writer*, which he decided was nothing but a "Communist propaganda sheet." Then, after attending several meetings of the Board, he felt the evidence was inescapable, as he wrote Mencken, that the Guild was "red as Stalin's nose, so that at present I would not assign the copyright of a he-and-she joke to any organization it controlled or helped control."

As he explained it, "at the risk of admitting I had been somewhat naïve, I had to do some hard thinking. It was a temptation to bull along anyway, for I don't back down so easy." But on the Communist issue he felt that was not possible. He had lunch one day with a friend who tried to console him by saying that if the Communists were in favor of the same things he was, it was all right to go along with them on certain issues. Cain did not agree: To him, Communism was Communism, and he was against it.

Considering this feeling, and what he saw now as overwhelming evidence that the Guild was dominated by Communists, Cain was simply at a loss as to how he might refute Hughes and the other critics attacking the AAA. And so, by the summer of 1947, an obviously bitter Cain came to a very difficult decision: For an organization such as his AAA, he wrote Mencken, "the guilds of the Authors League are too crooked, too ridden by an office clique, too timid and silly, as Shaw says of them, to be trusted with control, and the Radio Writers and Screen Writers Guild have let this Party line possess them to a point they can be trusted with nothing."

His disillusionment with the writing community was complete and absolute. "I have come to the conclusion," he wrote Hedda Hopper, "it is impossible to organize writers. Plumbers, yes, or scene shifters, or electric chair operators. In these will be found some sense, some comprehension of the solidarity they owe each other. But writers . . . are idiots and may be expected not only to turn on each other at every conceivable point, but to pursue any whacky idea that catches their fancy, regardless of whether it is in their own interest or not. At the moment they have tied themselves to the kite of leftist labor. I have tried to convince them they are not labor but in their small way capital, and that when they organize their properties through some such plan as I proposed they will be getting somewhere. They scream for it, then keep on doing the one thing that stultifies it, which is march in the Red parade."

Cain had given up on the Guild for good. Later, after the Hollywood Ten had rocked the movie community by their defiant attitude at hearings before the House Un-American Activities Committee in Washington, Cain would have one final battle with the Communists in the Guild, which will be discussed in the next chapter. As for the AAA, he tried, for a while, to develop what he called a "small cadre" of writers to band together and start their own AAA, to be open to any and all. But nothing came of this, and by 1948 Cain was, once again, deep in his writing, without the time, energy, or inclination to give the AAA his attention.

Still, the idea and the tempest Cain had generated continued to move the Eastern literary community. By July, most commentators and everyone connected with the Authors League agreed that the AAA, as such, was dead, but the League was still studying ways of achieving many of its objectives. Late in the year, the Authors Guild negotiated a "model contract" with Random House, the first in history that liberalized the reprint rights, although, curiously enough, it also permitted publishers an increased share in movie rights. Book club rights remained, as they are today, on a fifty-fifty sharing basis. The following year, Authors League president Paul Gallico announced League intentions to work for leasing rather than sale of motion picture rights. And the struggle has continued through the years, until today an author, if he is successful enough, can negotiate individually most of the things Cain was trying to achieve for every author, regardless of how successful the author might be. In later years, Cain did not talk much about the AAA. He felt he had given it a fair shot, but "There's no use devoting your life to a lost cause, so I dropped it." But he remained proud of one thing: the meeting at the Henry Hudson Hotel in New York, attended by six hundred writers—"the largest number," he liked to boast, "ever assembled in one spot in the history of literature."

17

PLEASANT HARBOR

The spring of 1946 was a difficult period for Cain. He left Aileen and his $2,500-a-week job at RKO at about the same time and immediately began planning a research trip to New Orleans. He had also met an English film producer in a Beverly Hills bar, which led to serious conversations and, later, an exchange of letters about Cain's going to England in late summer to work on a movie. His interest in going abroad may have been stimulated by a warm correspondence with a woman in Ireland, which cooled somewhat after the subject of the woman's husband arose. Personally, he told one friend, he was beginning to wonder if he was even capable of sustaining a close relationship with a woman. He felt he was in a "nose-dive," one that was having a serious impact on his work.

Then, quite by accident, in July he met the woman he would remain with for the next twenty years, who would provide the peace and tranquillity he at least professed to need. He had been invited to a tea party at the home of Mrs. La Nora Griffith, a well-known Hollywood singing coach, but on the afternoon of the party he found himself feeling depressed and decided not to go. He dropped by the house of a friend, Bert Parks, also invited to the party, to ask him to give the hostess his regrets. Parks was on the phone, talking about the party, as it happened, and Cain sat down to wait, not paying much attention to the conversation. Then he heard Parks say: "Yes, it looks like a pleasant afternoon—all kinds of interesting people will be there. Florence Macbeth and . . ."

Florence Macbeth! The Chicago opera star who had been the divinity of Cain's youth when he studied to be an opera singer. He could still remember her pictures in the Wagnerian costumes from the music magazines he had read so religiously. When Parks hung up, instead of asking him to give his regrets Cain said: "Are you ready to go?"

When they arrived at the party, Cain's earlier instincts not to attend were confirmed: it was one of those large, chic affairs that he could not stand. He did not recognize Miss Macbeth and was in no mood to ask people which one she might be. But there was one woman who, for some reason, caught his eye. She was pouring drinks, though not really taking part in the activities. As Cain described her, she had "a pale face and a strangely haunting beauty. Her figure when once or twice she got up was pretty but a little stocky." Because of her withdrawn manner and the fact that she took no interest in the party, Cain assumed she was one of those social registerites who had gone into business and was catering the affair. In a few minutes, he was talking to the hostess just as the woman he took to be the caterer passed by, and he asked Mrs. Griffith who she was. "Oh," she replied, "that's my very good friend Florence Macbeth, and I do want you to meet her."

La Nora introduced them and they started to chat. It turned out Florence Macbeth was living in a small cottage on the Griffith property and had agreed to "pour" at the party on the condition that she not be asked to take part in the activities. "It's not my party," she told Cain, "and no one is interested in me."

They hit it off very well, and the next day Cain called to invite her to join him for dinner. She hesitated at first, then accepted, and "it was quite an evening," recalled Cain, who was surprised that "two middle-aged people who had both known dark days could sit in a car by the sea and watch the moon come up." They had a lot to talk about, and among other things Cain learned that she was recovering from a nervous breakdown and was living on Mrs. Griffith's property because the singing coach had become obsessed with her making a comeback. She was coaching her voice, which Miss Macbeth had not used for several years.

Florence Macbeth was born in Mankato, Minnesota, in 1891. Her mother was Alice Monfort and her father, a successful meat packer, was Charles J. Macbeth. Florence, a sensitive child who was shy, gentle, and reticent around people, oddly enough developed an urge to go into show business. Her father was a close friend of the Ringling Brothers, especially

John, and Florence was always around the big tents. She said there was never any doubt about her going into the circus, only "whether I would rather be a bareback rider, galloping with grace and dash around the ring, or one of those marvelous ladies in tights and with a whip, who tame the lions and make the savage jungle beasts march around like little kittens."

The decision was never made. Her urge to ride bareback and tame the big cats shifted to the stage when Marie Tempest, appearing in *The Fencing Master*, came to the Mankato Opera House. Her mother had trouble controlling little Florence in the theater because she insisted on standing on her seat imitating Miss Tempest. The next day Florence disappeared, and when her mother finally found her in her bedroom she was posing in front of a long mirror wearing a chiffon scarf she had taken from her mother's dresser. When asked what she was doing, Florence said: "I'm going to do what that pretty lady did when I grow up."

With Florence's mother being a talented pianist, it was apparent to almost everyone in Mankato that young Florence also had musical abilities. She had a beautiful voice, but her mother tried to discourage Florence from using it; in fact, when Florence at the age of thirteen went to Faribault to attend St. Mary's Hall, her mother told the headmistress: "We know this child has a voice, but want nothing done about it. She may study piano, that's all."

In 1909, Florence went East with her family, preparing to finish her education at Wellesley College. But at a party one evening Florence, accompanied by her mother at the piano, sang, and Yeatman Griffith, a retired voice teacher who was present, pleaded: "Let me have this voice, now." Her father did not know what to say, but her mother did—she changed her mind and agreed to let Florence pursue a singing career. The next few years she studied under Griffith and others in Pittsburgh, Italy, and London, before she was finally displayed by Griffith at a "critics' audition" in England. The critics raved about her, praising not only her coloratura soprano voice but also her beauty and well-bred, gentle manners. The audition produced a flurry of rave reviews that Cain, seeing them years later, said were some of the most sensational press notices he had ever read. The audition also brought her an agent, and within days Miss Macbeth was scheduled to debut with the Lamoreaux Orchestra in Scheveningen, the Netherlands. This was in 1912, and the concert was a sensation. She made her opera debut in 1913 as Gilda in *Rigoletto* in Darmstadt, Germany, where she also gained an enthusiastic sponsor in Richard Strauss. The following year she made her London debut singing with Thomas Beecham's Queen Hall Orchestra. This concert created another sensation, inspiring the *London Daily Telegraph* critic to write: "In many years we have not heard [a voice] that has throughout its whole extent the same warmth of tone, the same astounding roundness, the same absolute accuracy of pitch and the same beautiful quality from its lowest note to its topmost height; and doubt if such a voice has been heard since Madame Patti first appeared."

From London, Miss Macbeth went home to make her American debut on January 14, 1914, with the Chicago Opera Company as Rosina in *The Barber of Seville*. It was the year that young Jamie Cain, sitting on a bench in Lafayette Park across from the White House, made his decision to become a writer—when Florence Macbeth was just a distant idol. Cain never did hear her sing.

From 1914 to 1931, Miss Macbeth sang with the Chicago Opera Company and in concert tours from one end of America to the other, as well as in Canada and Europe. She sang with Mario Chamlee, Pasquale Amato, Charles Dalmores, and Titta Ruffo, but her most constant operatic companion was Tito Schipa, who liked to sing with her because she was that rarity for an opera prima donna, a petite woman. By 1927, she had given 1,500 concert performances, crisscrossing the country by train, year after year, when the Chicago Opera Company was not performing. In 1923, she made headlines when the St. Paul Railroad gave its crack train, the Olympian, the green light, nonstop all the way from Chicago to St. Paul, so that Miss Macbeth could be on time for a concert in Minneapolis. Many critics said she was the greatest coloratura America ever produced. She was called the "Minnesota Nightingale" and sang regularly in Chicago and in Ravinia Park, about fifty miles north of Chicago. She also made more than two dozen records for Columbia, mostly Scottish and French songs, as well as the big coloratura arias.

Florence Macbeth's meteoric career peaked in the twenties, but then, as with so many American lives, came crashing down in the 1930s following a string of misfortunes. During the First World War, she had married an English captain, Edward Whitwell, a member of the British financial mission to the United States. Captain Whitwell was an engineer and had designed structures for amusement parks in England. This, combined with Florence's interest in circuses, led to his taking charge of the Starlight Amusement Park in New York City, when they were living there. While she traveled, he ran the park and supervised the investment of Florence's singing income—hundreds of thousands of dollars, most of which were lost in the stock market crash of 1929. Then, when still living in New York, Florence fell from a horse while riding in Central Park, an accident that prevented her from ever having children. In 1931, strep throat forced a temporary retirement, and by the time she recovered, the Chicago Opera Company had dissolved. She sang for a while with Paul Whiteman and the St. Louis Opera, but never could regain the voice and fame she had in the 1920s. Then her mother died, and Florence's husband suffered a stroke and needed constant attention. The couple eventually moved to California, where Captain Whitwell died in 1942. Florence took his death very hard, eventually suffering a nervous breakdown herself. After recovering, and at the urging of La Nora Griffith, wife of her first teacher, she began to study for a radio career—when she met James M. Cain.

Although they quickly became close friends, marriage did not come for some time. For one thing, California law decreed that Cain's divorce from Aileen would not be final for a year. In addition, there was Cain's doubt that he had the capacity to make a marriage work. And Florence herself, recently widowed after twenty years of a happy marriage, was not sure she wanted to "joggle her memories," as Cain put it. She also had a cynical disbelief in "cuckoos nesting in autumn," her phrase for middle-age love.

But Cain was happy with Florence, who he found never got on his nerves. "Physically, she delighted me, and I don't mean just sexually. Something more elusive than that—some chemical harmony of touch, sound and even smell, that makes for peace and tranquillity. . . . She unkinked me in all sorts of strange ways."

By the end of the summer he was hinting to his sister of marriage and described his new love to Rosalie as about his age, "small, red-headed, Scotch-looking, and pretty. The Scotch is important, after the shellacking I have taken the last twenty years; good solid; thrift is part of her and, indeed, with good solid sense at my side and plenty of business experience along with it, my affairs suddenly go very well, especially my financial deals; I have an easy comfortable feeling, drink less, weigh less, work more, and better."

It appeared as if Cain had not only found his "pleasant harbor," as he described Florence, but a business manager as well, and now he was able to restore some semblance of order to his writing career. When leaving RKO in June he had hoped to go down to New Orleans to continue research on his Civil War novel, but his preoccupation with the AAA controversy, and possibly his blossoming affair with Florence, delayed the trip. He did, however, find time for a variety of projects, including a short novel called *Nevada Moon*, which he hoped to sell to the magazines and a studio. It was about an insurance agent and a beautiful woman involved in a complicated divorce action in Reno. The characters included Keyes, played by Edward G. Robinson in *Double Indemnity*, and numerous references to the film, among them the fact that Keyes looked like Robinson. Cain did this partly as a joke and partly at Swanson's urging, since Robinson had asked if Cain had another script featuring Keyes which might be suitable for a movie. Cain finally finished the story, but Robinson did not like it, and it never sold to the studios or a magazine. Cain put *Nevada Moon* away in the trunk, where it stayed for several years.

Late in 1946, Vincent Lawrence died, and Cain wrote a tribute to his old friend for the *Screen Writer* in which he tried to capture Lawrence's screwball character, at the same time stressing the debt both Hollywood and James M. Cain owed him. Lawrence was the first writer in Hollywood, Cain said, "to articulate the philosophy of the love story into the intellectual whole," and the core of his thinking "is also the core of my novels. . . . I have hardly written the symbol -0- which closes all my stories in the last twenty years without wondering what Lawrence was going to think of it."

Cain revealed his thoughts about the movie industry in another piece called "A Free Lance for Hollywood," written for the London magazine *The New Theatre*. They had requested a piece that they apparently hoped would portray the Hollywood writer as a suffering, sensitive artist, several intellectual cuts above the producers and directors he worked with. But Cain said at the beginning of his article that he was going to have to disappoint them. There was a new breed of producer, he said—reflecting the impression Bob Bassler, Arthur Hornblow, and others had made on him—and they were every bit as smart and sensitive as the writers; generally they would listen to what the writer had to say and often improve on his ideas.

He also gave his views as to why the British public did not like British movies. On his visit to England in 1939, he could not find British movies playing anywhere in London. All he found were American movies. The reason, he said, was that the British movies, so admired by the critics and ignored by the public, failed to solve the problem that lay at the center of every script—the love story. "Somewhere along the line," Cain wrote,

> the English nation, or the more intellectual part of the English nation, which handles aesthetic matters, decided to be quite casual about love. Any open emotion became distinctly bad form, and matter-of-factness a sort of cult. Now this certainly has charm . . . if we know that under the calm, great volcanoes are smoldering. . . . But if under the calm there is nothing but more calm, then we have only a set of very hollow people betraying their complete futility. Well, I don't see any futility in the English people. But I see complete futility in the English movie, for what the English producer has done is mistake the appearance for the substance, and depicted a world so false and so dull that even its own public cannot stomach it.

He conceded that what Hollywood did might not be worthwhile, but he knew it was what the people liked and, furthermore, he had some suspicion that what people liked "is what has life in it, i.e., what is good."

The article was a precise summary of Cain's view on the relationship between public taste and art, although it was hardly calculated to land him that scriptwriting job in London—in fact, he never did go to England to work on a British movie, although there is nothing to indicate why the job did not materialize. The article also demonstrated again Cain's feeling that movies, like magazine fiction, do not count; they are commercial ventures that should cater to, not defy, public tastes. The only creative efforts that counted were for the stage and books, and for these the artist was free to follow his own muse.

With his Civil War novel shelved because of love story problems and months of research still to be done, Cain returned to *The Butterfly*. At least three people had mentioned the similarity between its conclusion and that of *Past All Dishonor*, so he decided to change the ending. He also decided to do a preface, as he had done for *Three of a Kind*, which he assumed had contributed to that book's remarkable success. He particularly wanted to answer Wilson and Cowley, who had charged that he had been devoured by the movies and that *Past All Dishonor*'s slick and inaccurate portrayal of Western life in the 1860s proved it. "I think, now and then, a preface is indicated," Cain wrote Knopf, "particularly with reviewers who tend to assume the author is as ignorant as his characters."

The preface was 12 pages long—one-tenth of his 120-page novel. It begins with Cain tracing the origins of the story back to his efforts to write a novel about West Virginia in 1922, all to let the critics know how much thought and work over the years had gone into *The Butterfly*. Then he launched into "the Hemingway thing," as he put it. "I belong to no school, hard-boiled or otherwise," he wrote, "and I believe these so-called schools exist mainly in the imagination of critics." He acknowledged that young writers often imitate older writers, as he had imitated Ring Lardner's short stories. But no writer, he said, can write a book by "peeping over his shoulder at somebody else, any more than a woman can have a baby by watching some other woman have one. It is a genital process. . . . Schools don't help the novelist, but they do help the critics; using as mucilage the simplifications that the school hypothesis affords him, he can paste labels wherever convenience is served by pasting labels and although I have read less than twenty pages of Mr. Dashiell Hammett in my whole life, Mr. Clifton Fadiman can refer to my hammer-and-tongs style and make things easy for himself." And on behalf of all writers: "I say to these strange surrogates for God, with their illusion of 'critical judgment' and their conviction of the definitive verity of their wackiest brainstorm: You're really being a little naïve, you know. We don't do it that way." He said he owed no debt to Ernest Hemingway, would admit it if he did, and that two writers could hardly be more dissimilar in content: "He writes of God's eternal mayhem against Man, a theme he works into great classic cathedrals, but one I should be helpless to make use of." He did acknowledge that he and Hemingway both had an excellent ear, that both shuddered at the least hint of the highfalutin, the pompous or literary, and that both had people talk as they do talk, although Hemingway used four-letter words and he had never written one. He also said they both cut the "he saids" and "she saids" to a minimum, but that he went much further in that direction than Hemingway and explained how this came about in the writing of *Postman*.

Then he took on the Hollywood issue, arguing that although he was close to the picture business and worked in the studios, he had not been particularly successful in Hollywood. He conceded that some of his stories had been made into big successful movies, but pointed out that he had only three fractional credits in the fourteen years he had been working in Hollywood. The successful movies associated with him were all made from scripts written by other writers, but his scripts were never accepted by the studios! "Why, I don't know and they [the other writers] don't, for . . . many of them are my friends and we discuss the riddle freely. Moving pictures simply do not excite me intellectually, or aesthetically, or in whatever way one has to get excited to put exciting stuff on paper. I know their technique as exhaustively as anybody knows it. I study it but I don't feel it." He said he wrote four versions of *Past All Dishonor* in which Morina was not of the oldest profession, but rather the niece of the lady who ran the brothel, and each laid an egg until he realized that the girl had to be "a straight piece of trade goods." He had known that putting the red light over the door would cost him a picture sale, and "so far it has; it is there just the same and it made all the difference in the world with the book."

He also went on at length outlining all the research he did on *Past All Dishonor* and concluding on a personal note, very possibly designed to dilute the talk going around in the wake of his controversial AAA proposal that James M. Cain was a crazy Red: "Yes, I have actually mined coal, and distilled liquor, as well as seen a girl in a pink dress and seen her take it off. I am fifty-four years old, weigh 220 pounds, and look like the chief dispatcher of a long-distance hauling concern. I am a registered Democrat. I drink."

Knopf read Cain's preface and had some doubts about such a long introduction to such a short novel. But in letters to both Blanche and Alfred, Cain was adamant, stressing that the piece had very little to do with the novel and that he had to say something about "this gang of hatchet men which leaps at my throat in New York." He also held that "this Hemingway thing" had about gone far enough, and over Blanche's protest he insisted on leaving in a remark about Hemingway's being better than he was. "Why kid myself," Cain said. "He is. And it seems to me by saying so I forestall a lot of jeers in the first place and create an impression of candor that the thing must have if I am to be believed about my remarks on pictures."

Knopf finally gave in and said the preface would stand. But then, when the galleys were ready and circulated, the publisher began to have much more serious concern about the book, which he set forth in a letter to Cain: "I am myself pretty immune to shock and I confess to having read and re-read *The Butterfly* without feeling in any way outraged. But as we approach a publication date and hear from more and more people who have also read the book, I think I ought, as your friend and publisher, to tell you that there may be breakers ahead. A surprising number of people in the book trade really dislike the book intensely—think it shocking, that it oversteps the line of what is permissible to deal with in fiction. Of course, incest is the ugly word, and though it turns out not to have been incest in the end after all, they don't see it that way. Don't misunderstand me; I certainly don't anticipate legal trouble of any kind, but I am prepared and want you to be prepared, for possible unpleasant talk in print and out, and a considerable amount of sales resistance. You once said in a long letter to me that your stories would always deal with 'plain and fancy fornicating.' I don't think we ought to have it too fancy." Knopf also thought the "fancy fornication" would sell: the first printing would be 30,000.

Cain replied that he was well aware of the explosive potential of the novel, especially after his sister tore into it the year before. But he was encouraged that the Knopfs liked it and that others who did were personally enthusiastic, stressing that it achieved a clean, engaging literary quality in handling a very difficult theme and was completely devoid of any material that might have been aimed at Hollywood. Cain, in fact, thought he had set a trap for the reviewers, writing a novel that was anti-Hollywood and including a preface that quite candidly assessed his literary approach and style.

And it worked: Most reviewers commented favorably on the preface— which made Knopf happy, and now he thought the piece was one hell of a brilliant idea. "I have had many a chuckle," he wrote Cain, "at the way these birds swallowed the hook you baited so carefully for them." Hamilton Basso in *The New Yorker* commented on Cain's statement that writing a novel is a genital process and said that "nowhere in the whole field of aesthetic inquiry can this paragraph be matched. Mr. Cain, unlike Tolstoy in 'What Is Art?' and various other writers who have attempted to understand the creative impulse, does not waste his time, or ours, in useless speculation. And his central argument is, of course, irrefutable. *Can* a woman have a baby by watching another woman have one? Think about it." *Time* magazine said the preface was so spirited that readers were likely to start the new novel with respect and sympathy.

Most reviews, in fact, whether favorable or unfavorable, devoted as much space to the preface as they did to the story. Not that the story was ignored. Also as Cain had anticipated, the reviewers were either violently pro or con, but surprisingly enough the favorable reviews outnumbered the negative. On the latter side, *The New Yorker* said it could no longer be denied that Cain was the "best comic-strip artist in the country," although perhaps the creators of Dick Tracy and Steve Canyon were more creditable and more skillful in writing the English language; *Time* said *The Butterfly* was "about as incestuous as *Tarzan and the Apes*"; and columnist Ashton Stevens in the *Chicago Sun* said "the whole book is a phoney scare." But the *New York Herald Tribune*, the *San Francisco Chronicle*, the *Saturday Review*, A.C. Spectorsky in the *Philadelphia Record*, William Targ in the *Philadelphia Inquirer*, the *Chicago Tribune*, and the *St. Louis Post-Dispatch* all had words of praise for the novel or Cain, and one reviewer—Lloyd Lewis in the *Chicago Sun*—was beside himself: "*Butterfly* had me at its end turning out my study light and crawling on hands and knees to my bedroom, butting my head into chairs and hall walls, all for fear someone would wing me with a hillbilly rifle bullet through a window."

The publication of *The Butterfly* and *Past All Dishonor*, back to back, brought Cain to the height of his reputation as a novelist who specialized in shocking his readers. Both books sold well, with *Butterfly* achieving his second-highest hard-cover total—45,000 copies. But more and more the critics were beginning to deplore the trend in hard-boiled literature, of which James M. Cain was acknowledged to be the leading practitioner, despite all his efforts to avoid the "tough-guy" label. Robert Gorham Davis, while praising *The Butterfly* in the *New York Times*, devoted most of his review to questioning whether "hard-boiled fiction" might not only be training people to accept violence and perversion, but to take pleasure in them. "Hard-boiled literature makes entertainment out of suffering," Davis wrote, "by de-humanizing it. The important question is whether it can succeed in this without de-humanizing its audience," a theme J. Donald Adams in another *Times* essay endorsed. And Roger Bourne Linscott, commenting in the *New York Herald Tribune* on the reviewers who agreed that Cain characters had now disposed of all the Ten Commandments, said he called Knopf's office to discuss this, only to be told that Cain critics were in error. "To date no Cain character had been found guilty of making a graven image." There was also another cardinal sin Cain had missed: seducing a child. He would deal with that delicate subject in his next novel.

By early 1947, Cain and Florence were talking of marriage, and Cain was a new man. His correspondence to his friends and family reflected the peace and tranquillity he had found and for which, he thought, he had been waiting all his life. At least one of his friends disagreed. "You weren't designed for a life of protected contentment," Morris Markey wrote him. "Unless somebody gives you a legitimate excuse for heaving a skillet now and then you get restless."

The advancing years and Florence were mellowing Cain, who was still in the middle of his vicious fight with the movie studios, the publishing industry, the writing community, and the Communists and anti-Communists over his controversial AAA plan. Gradually Cain was coming to a decision that it was time to concentrate on writing novels. "Either I'm going to wind up a picture writer or I'm going to get back on novels and amount to something," he told Florence in 1947.

His "little opera singer," as he often called her, encouraged him to go on with his novels, which led to one of the most important decisions in his life: In his mind and his approach to writing, he shifted from a newspaper man and movie script writer who occasionally did a novel on the side to "a plain, professional 100 per cent novelist." And it was a curious decision, motivated as it was by the desire to "amount to something," because whatever place James M. Cain achieves in American literature, it will be based on the books he wrote prior to 1947. He decided to amount to something at the peak of his creative life, and from then it was all downhill.

Cain's decision to quit screenwriting may also have been motivated by an instinctive feeling that Hollywood itself was headed for hard times. The movie industry still had not completely recovered from the antitrust suit brought by the Justice Department in 1939 against the eight major studios, an action which broke up the monopoly the studios held in the distribution of films. The cozy relationship between the majors and the theaters across the nation had, the government argued, prevented theatergoers from having any choice in what movies they would see. And now there was a new threat: television. By 1947, 14,000 homes had television sets to carry the opening of the Eightieth Congress, President Truman's State of the Union address, and the World Series between the Yankees and the Dodgers. And, by 1948, Howdy Doody, Kukla, Fran and Ollie, Douglas Edwards, Milton Berle, John Cameron Swayze, and Ed Sullivan would soon compete with Clark Gable, Joan Crawford, Jimmy Stewart, and Barbara Stanwyck, many of whom would, in time, also be appearing on television programs.

In the spring of 1947, Cain and Florence were anticipating a joint writing career and making "high and exciting plans," as he wrote Florence's Aunt Jenny, "not only as to the book we shall do about her, but other books we shall do on ideas of mine, some of them novels." In April, he began one of the novels that he considered to be the most ambitious, important contemporary novel he ever attempted—*The Moth*. But he had a hard time sticking with it because of several interruptions. In addition to his preoccupation with the AAA, which lasted well into the summer, he also became involved in writing a profile of the director John Ford, for which he was paid $3,000 by Ford's studio. It was called "Minstrel Boy" and was a pure promotional effort designed to hype Ford's latest movie, *Fort Apache*. The idea was that Cain would sell the article to a magazine, though on three separate occasions he warned the studio—Argosy Films—that the article would not be bought. He wrote the piece anyway, took the $3,000, for which Swanson received 10 percent, then insisted on giving Harold Ober $300 for trying to sell it, which he never did.

Another project eating into his time was the research on Florence's career. He had amassed a huge file of 4-by-9 cards on her autobiography, which they had decided to call *La Picina*, Campanini's name for her. As Cain read more and more of Florence's press notices, he found "the riddle is how a singer could evoke such respect, which often verges on reverence, without becoming one of the big vocal legends."

He also became involved in yet another writing project, growing out of a piece he did in 1945 for the *Chicago Daily News*. The *News* book review section had an annual feature in which distinguished authors recommended Christmas books, and in 1945 it asked Cain, the inveterate frequenter of libraries, to do a piece focused on reference books as gifts. His favorite was *Who's Who in America*, which he said he had been devouring since he first came across it as a boy in his father's study in 1903. This led to an extensive correspondence with the publisher of *Who's Who*, Wheeler Sammons, who eventually asked Cain to write a preface for the 50th Anniversary Edition, to be published in 1948. Cain said he would consider it an honor and spent months corresponding with Sammons and gathering material for a piece. He finished it in June and felt it was a solid, scholarly essay befitting the publication in which it appeared—and although he was not paid for his contribution, it did give him recognition in places he rarely appeared: The Honorable Emanuel Celler of New York, commenting on the 50th Anniversary Edition of *Who's Who* on the floor of the House, said that "since James M. Cain has lent his genius to . . . this anniversary edition," he wanted to enter Cain's preface in the *Congressional Record*.

Meanwhile, as Florence assumed more and more influence on Cain's life, the two moved closer and closer to the inevitable. One night after dinner they were driving back to Florence's house in Cain's big Packard when the idea of marriage came up and Florence said: "You go home now and hold your head under the pump—I don't want to see you for a week. You think things over, and if you still want to marry me, come back, and we'll talk. You don't have to marry me! Do you hear what I say? You don't have to. If you don't want to, just don't call anymore and that'll be that."

"I wish I could tell the whole female gender what a difference that makes," Cain said later. "Because the truth is, on this problem of marriage, the man rarely has a full fair chance to say no—once the question comes up, he is a rat if he backs out, and that may be one reason why our divorce rate is so high."

As soon as he reached home, he called Florence and said he did not need a week; he knew how he felt. He wanted to get married. So they made their plans: They would wait until he finished *The Moth*, be quietly married in October, then put the announcement in the mail somewhere on Route 66 on their way to Louisiana and Washington, where Cain wanted to do research on his Civil War project in the Library of Congress. Then they went into virtual seclusion, seeing no one because Florence did not want to meet Cain's friends in an anomalous situation while he was waiting for his divorce from Aileen to become final. Florence also gave up her idea of a musical comeback, which would be impossible now with all the travel they were planning for the next few years.

The divorce from Aileen brought Cain's domestic life back into the press, and when it became known that he was now dating the former opera star Florence Macbeth, "Walter Winchell practically married us on the air," as Cain put it, and congratulatory phone calls began coming in from her friends and his. "So here she was," Cain said, "a widow by the city records, but a bride by community acclamation. With my usual inspired resourcefulness, I stepped into the breach and reminded her there was no law we couldn't get married," which they quickly did, in a little church in San Marino on September 19, 1947. It was a poetic experience for Cain, who would always remember going to the Marriage License Bureau in Pasadena and the clerk looking up at Florence and saying, "Hello, Olympia," alluding to her role as the doll in *Tales of Hoffmann*; nor did he ever forget the San Marino church and the comic argument they had that night when Florence said "I was a sap," and finally, the three-day honeymoon in the Hinghonton Hotel at San Marino.

The marriage was a milestone in Cain's life. As he told friends, it was great to discover that "given the right woman, I was as normal as anyone else." He also said, rather enigmatically, that the marriage "turned back the clock many years and let me start over again. That is a psychological matter, relating to my childhood, . . . nothing scandalous, Freudian, or even interesting, but to me, important." What, precisely, he was referring to we will probably never know, but he did say now that he had "entered calm and beautiful waters, where it turns out you can achieve the greatest intensity inside you, which is all that counts on paper." The waters may, in fact, have been a little too calm—at least in the opinion of some of his friends, one of whom met Florence shortly after they were married and was appalled. "I thought he was terribly tame compared to what I had known of him," she said. "There were so many things that Jim liked to talk about; he liked history, he liked music, he had a very lively mind. And when I met him with that cold, fat lady, I thought she's daunted him! I found her so really off-putting . . . and rather pompous."

But James M. Cain did not seem to mind being tamed, and now that he was in calm waters he could devote more time to his writings. Their financial situation seemed secure. Florence had a small income from investments not lost in the Depression, and Cain was now looking forward to a steady and substantial income from the reprint sales of his books, plus additional income from new books. In 1947, his earnings from Knopf amounted to $22,500, most of that from reprint sales (by the end of the year, the total sale in all editions of *Mildred Pierce* alone was 733,000 copies). The sum included a $3,500 advance for *The Moth*, which had touched off another one of Cain's periodic contract squabbles with Knopf, this one entirely of Cain's doing. He kept waiting for the $3,500 he knew the contract called for, and when Knopf did not send it Cain became miffed. He finally mentioned it in a letter, to which Knopf responded that the contract called for the $3,500 "to be paid at the author's wish and discretion." Since Cain had not asked for it, Knopf naturally had not sent it to him. After Cain then got out the contract and read it, he wrote Knopf that there, "sure enough, it was exactly as you said it was." And he added, "Some day, God willing, I shall know what is in a contract."

Cain had first started thinking about elements of *The Moth* in the early thirties, when he was planning his story about a California drifter working in the oil fields. At that time, he had been moved by the spectacle, seen two or three nights a week driving home to Burbank, of young hoboes riding the freight cars headed for nowhere, perched like crows silhouetted against the sky. So he conceived a story about a young boy growing up in Baltimore and "letting the Depression happen to him," as Cain put it. But he decided that to interest the reader he had to have the boy plummet to a fall, so he made him a boy soprano in his church, a high-school football star, and a success in vaudeville who hits the skids when his father invests the boy's money only to lose it in the stock market crash. Then his father runs him out of town because of an incident involving a girl. This, of course, had to be a serious offense, to turn a father against a son whose money he had already lost. And it was: Cain's hero, Jack Dillon, is dating a local girl, but is also very friendly toward—and secretly in love with—her twelve-year-old sister. Although he never makes love to her, gossip results from an incident on the bank of the Severn River, across from Annapolis, and soon everyone from the Naval Academy to the suburbs of Baltimore is certain that twenty-two-year-old Jack Dillon has seduced twelve-year-old Helen Legg. Jack is forced to leave Baltimore at the beginning of the Depression and spends the next several years riding the rails and being involved in a series of adventures. He finally settles down in California, where he marries a woman who owns an oil field; he revives her dormant well, then breaks up with her when she discovers that he is still in love with Helen Legg, his former twelve-year-old girl friend. Jack heads East, to find that his father is dying. But the love story has a happy ending, climaxing a long, picaresque novel unlike anything James M. Cain had ever written, or ever would.

It was the broader canvas he had talked about in the closing paragraph of his preface to *Three of a Kind*, an authentic, realistic account of what life was like in the 1930s. The only violence in it involves the shooting of a hobo friend during the robbery of a gas station, and the sex is mostly alluded to, as in all Cain novels. It is a good story, well told, that moves along, holds one's interest, and is easily Cain's most autobiographical effort. The title and opening paragraph were taken from an incident centering on the first thing Cain could remember in his childhood—the big luna moth, with its "pale blue-green, all-filled-with-light color" as it fluttered through the trees after escaping a boy who was whacking it with a stick. The moth keeps reappearing in the novel as the story moves through Baltimore, Annapolis, the Eastern Shore, World War I with the 79th Rainbow Division, and the South. And even the love story seems to have had an autobiographical origin, judging from one of Cain's letters to a woman, recalling how smitten he had been with her one night on a hill in Chestertown, when she was fourteen and he was twenty-two.

There is no preface to this novel, but there is an acknowledgments page of the kind you would expect to find in a nonfiction book, indicating the painstaking research Cain, as always, put into a novel. Among those mentioned is Jim Moran, a tramp who hung out at the Los Angeles Mission. Cain had given Moran some old clothes and money and had ridden around with him in Los Angeles for a month, even visiting a hobo jungle, where one day Cain saw a hobo who moved him deeply—"an elderly man with the remains of a decent suit, and a pleasant friendly manner, . . . who must have been a bookkeeper or something of that kind, but now was just a thing, sitting in this horrible place by the railroad track. He didn't seem bitter—was quite resigned, in fact, and utterly, hopelessly beaten. I kicked in with such cash as I had, and went on my way, shaken to the heels."

It took from April until December to finish the first draft of *The Moth*, "eight solid months of plugging along, until by the end of it you get that white look around your gills of a shad that went upriver to spawn." It was his longest novel, one that he let run on, as he wrote Blanche Knopf, because he thought a thick book would help sales. "The trouble with my books," he wrote her, "has usually been that they are neat little things, tense and lean and compact, perhaps, but $2.00 books just the same, with no great vitality in the stores." At the same time, he had misgivings as it neared 500 pages. "No story requires that much telling," he wrote Raphaelson.

Cain finally sent the manuscript off to Knopf, biting his fingernails as usual, and then was relieved to hear that both Knopfs liked it—though they felt that considerable work had to be done on it. And after showing the first draft around to several people, Cain agreed. One studio Swanson took it to turned it down, calling it "a filthy book," and several women, including Cain's sister Rosalie, said Jack disappointed them, falling for a twelve-year-old girl. Cain knew that to drop the relationship would scuttle the book, but he also felt it would be a good idea to rework it to stress the "big brother" relationship. "It was never for one moment," he wrote Rosalie, "meant that Jack and Helen had got physical when she was twelve years old, but some people assumed so, and I had to know why." Rosalie explained why, and Cain tried to eliminate the implications in the rewrite. Not only did he hope to sell this one to the movies, but he also had hopes of a book club sale. The James M. Cain who had written about adultery, murder, homosexuality, prostitution, and incest without caring what the studios or the book clubs thought was mellowing.

The rewriting of *The Moth* continued to delay the Cains' trip South; and while sweating out the final stages, Cain also was carrying on a running battle with the Communists in the Screen Writers Guild, as an aftermath to the promotion of his AAA plan, now virtually abandoned. In that lingering dialogue, the absurdity of the charge that James M. Cain could ever have been a Communist or fellow traveler became more apparent. With postwar politics increasingly dominated by the Communist issue and the Cold War, Cain's own politics remained as hard to pinpoint as ever. He definitely was not a liberal, which he defined as "a Republican who believed the slaves should have roast pig at Christmas." In reality, he thought a liberal was "an imitation Englishman," as exemplified by the fact that the hotbed of liberalism was Harvard University, which he considered an imitation English school.

Cain had always been a registered Democrat. And judging from his writings, the kind of Democrat he admired most was the practical city political boss, a hard-headed realist whose first allegiance was to the people of his ward. In 1944, Cain had helped organize and run Democrats for Dewey in his district, which he said was a fine idea except that there were not very many of them. As the campaign of 1948 approached (in which he did not expect to participate because he would be traveling), his candidates, in order of preference, were Governor Earl Warren of California, Thomas Dewey, and Harold Stassen. He was also aware that General Douglas MacArthur was a candidate and had been "ever since that historic day in 1865 when Arthur MacArthur [Douglas's father] became the Boy Colonel of the Civil War." The idea of a MacArthur presidency did not bother him, but his man was Warren, primarily because of his stand on racism, which to Cain was the most important issue. On that, Warren "is as leftist as Stalin," Cain said, "and maybe a little more so. As race is the essence of leftism in this country at the moment, I regard this as important, not only with regard to my own implacable convictions on the subject, but as an element in the responsibility of electing him."

Considering Cain's pragmatic political views, combined with his personal dislike of duplicity and hypocrisy, it is not surprising that he resisted the Communists' efforts to take over the Screen Writers Guild. After the Hollywood Ten had defied the Thomas Committee and returned home, there were proposals to use Screen Writers Guild funds to defend Guild members cited by the committee. But Cain was opposed and became one of the leaders of the group prepared to go to court to prevent such usage. At one meeting, Cain asked Albert Maltz: "Are you or are you not a Communist?" Cain did not expect him to answer the same question he had refused to answer in Washington, but neither did he expect to be ruled "out of order" by the chairman or hissed down from the floor, as he was. So he went home and wrote a strong letter to the Guild protesting that the chair had no authority under the Guild constitution to rule him out of order, that a person's convictions were his own but his politics were a public matter, and that the Congress, in seeking information on which to base its laws, had every right to ask Guild members if they were Communists. He also pointed out that the members had been cited not as writers, but as witnesses refusing to obey the law, that it would amount to a misappropriation of funds to use Guild money to defend them, and that he would sue if the Guild did. He ended his letter by asking again: "Are you or are you not Communists?" To the letter he attached a notarized affidavit that he was a registered Democrat.

Cain did not receive a reply to his letter, and the issue in the Guild was eventually settled by an election. The anti-Communists ran on the All Guild ticket, headed by screenwriter Sheridan Gibney. Among other things, the ticket promised it would discontinue the *Screen Writer*, which, Cain argued in literature he wrote for the campaign, was nothing more than a Communist propaganda sheet costing the Guild $2,000 a month. He also argued that defending Guild members who had been cited for contempt was a job for the Communist party, not the Guild. The All Guild ticket won a sweeping victory, and Cain could report to columnist Hedda Hopper than the Screen Writers Guild was now 100 percent clean. Actually, he thought its rank and file were never more than 3 percent Communist, but that this small minority had managed to gain all the important offices. As for the Red hunt now preoccupying the country, Cain thought it was phony. "The politicians investigating Communism," he said, "don't really mean business; they want to hit it in the press, and miss it in the precincts, so the CIO won't get too sore." And by 1948, Cain was contributing money to the Committee of One Thousand to Abolish the House on Un-American Activities Committee. On the other hand, he defended the controversial studio blacklisting designed to prevent the hiring of Communists or fellow travelers in Hollywood. He persisted in his belief that a person's political views should be a public matter, "and since political conviction is surely a ponderable factor in deciding a writer's qualifications for an assignment, if writers insist on keeping this matter to themselves, they can thank only themselves if the studios . . . bow out."

With his decision to concentrate on his novels, Cain was, in fact, losing interest in studio work. "I think I am through with pictures forever," he wrote Helen Markey. But then, late in 1947, he took up one picture assignment with a writer-producer named Lou Brock, who had done *Flying Down to Rio* and *Top of the Town*. Brock hired Cain to write a treatment for an original script to be called *Forbidden Game*, revolving around an American couple down in South America who become involved in an obscure game called Pato. Cain finally finished a 110-page synopsis about the first of March 1948, and was ready to head East. Brock had assured Cain that any studio in Hollywood would be eager for a story that would enable them to put James M. Cain's name on the marquee, but when he showed it around there were no takers. But Cain did receive $5,000 for his work, the last money he would ever earn for screenwriting.

Finally, the Cains left California and drove down through Tucson, Roswell, New Mexico, Texarkana, then to Memphis, Chattanooga, Bristol, and Charlottesville, ending up in a motel on the outskirts of Washington, where Cain planned to start reading about the Civil War in the Library of Congress. He also went to Baltimore and New York, visiting friends and having one interesting dinner at Sardi's with Leonard Bernstein. The composer had written Cain just before he left California, requesting permission to try to make a grand opera from *Serenade* and suggesting that Cain do the libretto. Cain replied that he had had several proposals to adapt the novel for the stage, most of which were "obvious theatrical claptrap." However, he thought Bernstein might just pull it off, although he declined to do a libretto. When Bernstein persisted in urging him to write the book, Cain suggested Bernstein himself should do it. Eventually Bernstein teamed up with writer Arthur Laurents, and producers Martin Gabel, Robert L. Joseph, and Henry Margolis bought an option on the novel. Now the idea was to do a musical, rather than an opera, but that was put aside when Laurents and Bernstein started to work on what would eventually become *West Side Story*.

In late June, Cain and Florence headed South again for Louisiana, by way of Parkersburg, West Virginia, and Marietta, Ohio, where Cain wanted to study the steamboats in the River Museum. As he traveled from town to town and library to library, he took notes on 3-by-5 cards in a system he had learned from H.L. Mencken. It was Mencken, in fact, who had instilled in Cain his obsession with accuracy in his novels. One time in their Baltimore days, he was having lunch with Mencken and complaining about how someone had peeled his hide in the evening *Sun*, probably about one of his magazine articles. "Forget it," Mencken said. "It happens to anybody who writes for newspapers. And anyway, tomorrow is another day's paper, and it's amazing how quickly such things are completely forgotten. But," said Mencken, and Cain never forgot the look that came into his eye with his next statement, "for God's sake, never go up on your lines if it's a book you're going to do. It's on somebody's shelves forever, and for twenty years somebody'll be taking it down to show his friends, at your expense."

There are more than two thousand 3-by-5 cards in the file demonstrating that Cain researched his subjects with the thoroughness of a historian. But with a difference, "for while the historian," Cain said, "need only concern himself with who won the battle, and how, the novelist has to know which road his character took after it was over, what he ate while stumbling along, the local names of all sorts of small things, and what the people were doing with themselves as the action proceeds. Who could know, for example, nowadays, that in Civil War times well water was so dangerous in Alexandria [Louisiana] that people drank water trapped in cisterns from the rain on the roof, and that this was the reason water failed the federal Army—since so few places ever had wells—and they had to drink Red River water by then fouled with dead horses and filth, and came down with dysentery. You'll find little about it in the dispatches, except for the dysentery, and have to read travelers' accounts to discover the reasons."

Cain read the dispatches and the travelers' accounts and every document he could lay his hands on about life in and around Alexandria in 1863–64, and although his trip was invaluable and essential to his researches, he said for every single document of value he found traveling in the South, he found twenty-five in the Library of Congress. Still, he was seeing things with the eye of a novelist. The mulatto country around Simon Legree's McAlpin Place, he said, was "a frightening place of stillness, mud and gloom, with a strange inbred eye, small, black and snakey, that stares at you wherever you go." And the people in the Southern mansions baffled him. "I don't know how you do Southern mansions," he wrote Joseph Pennell, author of *The History of Rome Hanks*. "The people who live in them seem stuffed with straw, and on the Teche, in Louisiana, a curious idea occurred to me, in one of these places. Talking with an elderly owner, I got to wondering if he *was* stuffed with straw, or, if that was too springy, at least with cotton." He also could not stand Louisiana food, and he wrote Perino in Hollywood that you had to travel the U.S.A. to know just how good Perino's restaurant was. Except for one or two places in New Orleans and Degaan's in Shreveport, the lard and "indigestible roux" were impossible, and Cain reported becoming literally ill from a bowl of "court bouillon."

During the time Cain and Florence took their Southern trip, *The Moth* was published, so Cain was interviewed on many occasions by local reporters. The girl who interviewed him for the Parkersburg, West Virginia, *News* saw "a dynamic individual with a profusion of grey hair, eyebrows and friendliness." Cain told her he hated all forms of work, particularly disliked the arduous research that went into a historical novel, but that "if you are going to be a writer of novels, nothing will stop you." The *Houston Press* reporter thought Cain resembled "a refined, middle-aged Irish bricklayer." In that interview, Cain complimented the Houston librarian, Miss Louise Franklin, saying, "I barely mention a subject and she pops up with a paragraph from some ancient or little-known book," and explained that the reason he was on this trip, among other things, was to find out how his hero would travel. "There was a [railroad] line from Galveston to Houston in those days, but, you know, sure as I'd write that he rode it someone would recall—after the book was out—that the line in the month I mentioned was shut down because there wasn't any firewood."

He had coffee one afternoon with a *Houston Post* reporter named George Fuermann and was obviously feeling rather talkative. "I simply wouldn't write another story in the *Serenade*, *Postman* idiom," he told Fuermann. "For one thing, it would just cause people to ask why I couldn't find another string to my bow. I'm still writing to entertain people, and I'm not searching for any of this social awareness in my stories." He said that both the Civil War novel he was working on and *The Moth*, just published, were something new for him. "I have made an effort in these two books to examine the chief characters' surroundings and environments and their effects on the characters more than I have ever done before."

Whether he would achieve this goal in his Civil War book remained to be seen. But *The Moth* was out now for critics to assess, and Cain's effort to examine a broader canvas was not being judged an overwhelming success. The critics were still divided about Cain: some thought he was a great artist; some thought he bordered on being a pulp writer; and some thought maybe he was both. Since *The Moth* was promoted by Knopf as the tale "of wider implication" Cain promised in his preface to *Three of a Kind*, it was given a respectful reception by the critics, but the great majority of the reviews were disappointing. There were, however, a few who thought that Cain had at last lived up to his promise and written his big book. "No living writer," said Stephen Longstreet in the *Los Angeles News*, "has Cain's eye, detail, or brutal truth; a talent for making the habits and vices and virtues of our streets and heart say something that is readable and art, at the same time. . . . *The Moth* is American to the core, no other nation, no other time, no other story could have been told any place. . . . This is a great book by a great artist. . . . James M. Cain is nearer to the truths of our lives than any other novelist writing today." Sterling North, in his syndicated book review column, said: "There is a streak of authentic poetry in James M. Cain. There is also a real love for humanity hidden under his cynical, self-protective shell. But never before has he written a book in which both these latent qualities were as evident as in *The Moth*. Some sense of security in the author has given him the courage to reveal to his readers a more tender and mellower facet of his personality." North concluded that Cain was showing distinct signs of growth and, if he "can hold his sensation-hungry audience with his new and quieter approach to realism, he is headed for the first rank of American novelists."

But the negative reviews were his worst yet. Merle Miller, in the *Saturday Review*, said that "occasionally James M. Cain writes like an angel—a slightly malicious, dyspeptic, and ribald angel with a lust for gore. More often he writes the way you think Rocky Graziano might if he were more literate." The *Houston Post* thought the novel was "dull to the point of irritation"; *PM* thought the story lacked gusto and meandered. *The New Yorker* praised its reporting but was disappointed in it as a psychological study; James MacBride, in the *New York Times*, said he had been a Cain addict since his "wonderful raucous column in the old *World*, but it was sad to report that his latest, most ambitious book was also his dullest." But the most devastating critique came from *Time*, which devoted almost two columns to cutting up the book and Cain. Commenting on Cain's first-person approach to storytelling, *Time* said it absolved "the author from having to write in English. Cain's command of the I'm-telling-you-brother vernacular has been compared with Lardner and Hemingway, but it is neither as inventive as Lardner's nor as selective as Hemingway's. It often sounds like what it often is—something the movies picked up pure and handed back to Americans as if it had been their own."

Finally, the one critic who had never been able to make up his mind about Cain was more confused than ever. Lewis Gannett, who wrote a regular "Books and Things" column for the *New York Herald Tribune*, had hated *Postman*, but said he could never stop talking about it; *Serenade* was revolting, but he thought its glimpses of the human subconsciousness gave it much dignity; and he compared Cain to Hemingway. Now, approaching *The Moth*, he said, "I sniffed it, as reviewers do at beginning and end, and decided it was hooey and I would not read it, and then picked it up to read myself to sleep, and read on and on, far too wide awake for comfort. Mr. Cain uses the American language as skillfully as any living writer, he paces his vernacular in a hard, nervous rhythm that makes Hemingway's dialogue seem stilted and self-conscious. . . . He knows his material and he never forgets that the business of the novelist is to keep his story moving." But *The Moth*, Gannett finally decided, moved too fast, and "you finish it with a sense of excitement and sit back to wonder just why the promise of *The Postman Always Rings Twice*—published fourteen years ago—has not been fulfilled in any of the six books that have succeeded it, and why Mr. Cain continues to be almost a first class writer." Gannett thought the answer might be found in a statement Cain made in *The Moth* that "the art of writing consists in having something to say"—and he came to the conclusion that Cain did not.

The poor reviews were hurting the book, and by August it had sold fewer than 25,000 copies, which was disappointing to both Cain and Knopf after the back-to-back successes of *Past All Dishonor* and *The Butterfly*. Cain was beginning to have second thoughts about broader canvases. As he told one of his friends, "if you ask me, a simple tale, told briefly, is what most people really like."

The Cains were back in Washington by early September 1948, with Cain planning to start writing the Civil War book immediately. He knew that research problems would develop during the writing, and he wanted to remain near the Library of Congress, where he was set up to do his work. He and Florence were also still thinking about her autobiography, and there remained a lot of research to be done on that project. So they asked a friend in California, Frances Burroughs, to move their belongings out of La Nora Griffith's Hacienda Place cottage, which Florence still rented, and put them in storage. Then they rented a small white frame house at 6707 44th Avenue in

Hyattsville, Maryland, for $165 a month. It was on a quiet street in a conveniently located middle-class suburb called College Park. Cain was only about twenty minutes from the District line, dividing Maryland and Washington, D.C., on the Library of Congress side of the Capitol. And by driving twenty-five minutes in the opposite direction, he could visit his mother in Baltimore. He told H. N. Swanson and many of his friends that he planned to stay in Washington only a year. And he wrote Swanson that despite his declining interest in studio work, if he heard of an assignment that might be right for him, "don't be bashful about letting me know. We would dote on a trip West. This Maryland climate is almost setting us insane."

Although he could hardly have realized it at the time, James M. Cain would never see Hollywood again. It was the end of one of the most remarkable careers the town, famous for bizarre, unusual careers, had ever known. Despite the fact that Cain left California as one of Hollywood's most famous screenwriters, and had made more than $380,000 in his seventeen years in Hollywood, he had received credit (in each case, shared with other writers) on only three films—*Algiers*, *Stand Up and Fight*, and *Gypsy Wildcat*.

Cain's fame as a scriptwriter and about half the money he made in Hollywood came from films based on stories that were adapted to the screen by someone else. From 1933 to 1945 he sold to the studios seven stories that were made into movies. Still to come was the movie version of *Serenade*, a second version of *Two Can Sing*, and the sale of *Love's Lovely Counterfeit*, which would eventually be made into probably the worst picture with which Cain's name was ever associated. Of course, Cain's real fame rested primarily on three big movies—*Double Indemnity*, *Mildred Pierce*, and *Postman*—credited with having had a significant impact on Hollywood's approach to films.

But Cain, by his own admission, was a complete failure as a scriptwriter, and the various reasons for this failure have been touched on previously. Yet they went much deeper than the fact that "he didn't realize what the camera told and overdialogued," as John Lee Mahin diagnosed them, or that his dialogue did not play to the ear, as Raymond Chandler discovered, or because of his inability to come up with trick plot situations, which Cain once said was all Hollywood wanted. "Even working in a whorehouse," he had complained years ago, "the girl has to like the work a little bit, and I could not like pictures." His basic dislike of pictures went all the way back to the first movie he ever saw, *The Great Train Robbery*, after which he and his friend came out of the theater laughing, with utter contempt for Hollywood. Of course this was before World War I, but Cain's attitude toward the movies did not change much in the 1920s, even when sound was added and movies became more sophisticated. On the *New York World* in the twenties he wrote dozens of editorials ridiculing Hollywood, and he was part of that generation of American writers which looked down on Hollywood with scorn, another reason why it infuriated him when Edmund Wilson and Malcolm Cowley accused him of being corrupted by Hollywood. But, as we have seen from his two articles about screenwriting, he was ambiguous in his approach to the movies. He conceded that Hollywood catered to the public taste, but he wasn't about to say that this was wrong; people liked stories that had life in them and, in the long run, he thought what they liked was probably good. Art, of course, was not for critics to determine; that task was left up to Posterity.

At the same time, he recognized the need for freedom in the creation of art, and because of the nature of the motion picture business, the filmwriter could never achieve the freedom he needed and would never gain complete satisfaction from his work. "Imagination is either free or it is not free, and here [in pictures] it is not free." In filmmaking, imagination and performance by actors, guided by a director, were inseparable. But where Cain really found fault with pictures was not with the techniques and demands of the medium, or the need to cater to public taste; the problem was the mentality of the men making the pictures. Not until the 1940s did he meet what he considered to be a few civilized, cultured producers, but still he thought picture-making was essentially in the hands of dopes. He held these moguls and their product—not movies *per se*—in utter contempt, and it was on their account that he believed he flopped in Hollywood. "I wanted the picture money," he said. "I worked like a dog to get it. I parked my pride, my aesthetic convictions, my mind outside on the street, and did everything to be a success in this highly paid trade. . . . The only thing I could not park was my nose."

Despite all his protests, there is probably more truth to the charge that Cain was influenced by Hollywood than he ever cared to admit. Acknowledging all the conventional complaints about Hollywood, he also argued that the motion picture industry's primary goal was to produce good entertainment, and that it did better in this pursuit than other businesses. And if there was any one man who knew how to do it, it was Vincent Lawrence, an expert on what the public wanted. Lawrence was Cain's mentor in the writing of *Postman* and probably influenced his work more than any other person, as Cain recognized by dedicating *Postman* to him.

There was still another aspect of Cain's writing that suggests Hollywood may have had more of an impact on his work than he realized: "I care almost nothing for what my characters look like," he wrote in the preface to *Three of a Kind*, "being almost exclusively concerned with their insides. . . . The movie writer's description of a character's externals, 'a Clark Gable type,' would do perfectly well for me. And if you don't like the appearance of the gentlemen in these pages you are quite free to switch off to Clark Gable or Warner Baxter . . . or whoever you like. . . . In women's appearance I take some interest, but I pay much more attention to their figures than I do their faces—in real life. Their faces are masks more or less consciously controlled. But their bodies, the way they walk, sit, hold their heads, gesticulate, and eat, betray them. But here, again on paper, I am more concerned with what goes on inside them than with what they look like. So if you want to put Loretta Young . . . or Brenda Marshall [in place of one of the characters in "Career in C Major"] it will not affect things in the slightest."

Cain also said: "The truth is that movies are about the boy, the girl, and the final fade, and that is all they are about, until somebody comes along with an idea that is a big hit in a book or a play, and then for a time they are about that until they revert to type." The truth is, James M. Cain's best books were also about the boy and the girl (not always admirable) and the final fade (usually involving death). But then he came up with a couple of big ideas, like the Depression and the cotton racket in the Civil War, and before he could revert to type, it was too late.

Cain was as ambiguous about life in Hollywood and California as he was about writing for the movies. He was never really part of the Hollywood social life, and he did not try to hide his contempt for it. He was sensitive to the fact that when one of his books hit the headlines, everyone would invite him out to dinner and fuss over him, and then later, during periods when he had drifted out of favor with the studios and was deep in the writing of a novel, the invitations did not come and people who had had him out to dinner acted as if they scarcely knew him. It was almost like life in official Washington. Perhaps as a protective front, Cain prided himself on living "in the Hollywood no one ever heard about, made up of perfectly sensible people who led well-bred lives and paid almost no attention to the whoop-de-do." But then, as he wrote one correspondent: "I wasn't really of Hollywood, and wasn't widely acquainted. I had friends in the picture business, but not many. Actually I was a bit of a bust as a picture writer, and I suppose when you're a failure at something, you don't go around too much putting on the phony front."

At the same time, Cain enjoyed the life he led in Hollywood—at least during the years he and Elina were happily married. He liked those spontaneous Hollywood parties to which "you are invited because you are wanted," not, as in society Hollywood, or the East, where "evenings are cold-blooded jobs of entertaining" and you are invited for many reasons other than because the host and hostess would like to see you.

But most of all, it was California itself that Cain liked. One time, when *Life* magazine published an article on California that did not seem adequate to Cain, he wrote a long letter to the magazine's West Coast representative itemizing aspects of the state the author failed to mention that reads as if it had been written by the Los Angeles Chamber of Commerce. And in an effort to persuade a friend who was thinking of moving from Minnesota to Maryland to change his mind and consider California, he wrote: "It does have a winter, a patch of brisk weather with occasional storms, from December 15 to February 15. But in between it is sunny, and for the rest you live in a climate of constant springtime, balmy in the daytime, cool to blanketish at night. In summer, it is not hot, just pleasant, and the nights are cool. I spent three hot days in seventeen years in California. . . . Poetically or mentally, or whatever you want to call it, it is the center of the universe. It has five big universities with proper libraries and serious staffs." He also said it was inhabited by "the most courteous, agreeable people on earth," the roads were dream roads, and the prices no higher than elsewhere. And to sum it up, he quoted a Hollywood friend: "There is just one place on earth for those who want to work or those who want to loaf, and that is California."

It is little wonder, then, that Cain deplored returning to Maryland, "the churlish little state from which I fled."

PART FOUR

HYATTSVILLE

TWO TRIALS
AND MANY
TRIBULATIONS

Although Cain was not happy about settling down in Hyattsville, Maryland, he was too preoccupied with his Civil War novel to really care where he lived. He felt confident he could bring his own brand of realism to the historical novel—a belief encouraged by his old colleague from the *World*, Allan Nevins, by now one of the country's leading historians. After reading Nevins's *Ordeal of the Union*, Cain wrote the historian about his idea for a story based on the assumption that the Civil War was never fought. Nevins wrote back disputing his theory but saying how much he liked Cain's books and urging him to write a straight-out historical novel. "You have all the gifts, and here you could be both fascinating and convincing."

Cain himself thought his style of fiction, applied to the historical novel, might just produce another best seller. "It will be quite a romantic tale," he wrote Joseph Lisser at Knopf, "full of skulduggeries involving large sums of money, and it has a current topical interest in the difficulty of coordinating different arms of the military services. I imagine it could do very well commercially. . . . I have higher hopes for it than anything I ever wrote."

The tale he had in mind centered on the ill-fated 1864 Red River expedition into western Louisiana commanded by Union General N. P. Banks. In Cain's opinion it was "the great story of the Civil War." Months of research had confirmed his hunch that the expedition set up a struggle between the Union Army and the Union Navy over hundreds of thousands of dollars' worth of cotton; it also, as previously indicated, showed him "how men like Rhett Butler had made their fortunes."

Cain now had three hard-cover books—*Past All Dishonor*, *The Butterfly*, and *The Moth*—bringing in money, plus the reprint sales for his earlier works, which appeared as if they would go on forever. His income from Knopf in 1948 was nearly $30,000, in addition to which Avon had recently given him a $500 advance for his short novel *The Galloping Domino*, based on his play *7-11*, and planned to bring it out as an original paperback, to be called *Sinful Woman*.

This upset Knopf, who thought it was bad business to have original paperbacks of Cain's floating around while he was publishing him in hardcover. Cain did not mean to fast-deal Knopf, but after the publisher had turned down *7–11* in its original form a couple of years earlier, Cain had assumed he would not be interested in it again, after he rewrote it as *The Galloping Domino*.

Cain could see that his basic research on the Civil War novel was going to continue for some time, so as the year ended he wrote his landlord, David Watkins, asking him to extend his lease until August 1950. Then he plunged into the Red River campaign, taking time off only to follow the 1948 election on the radio.*

During the winter of 1948 and into 1949, Cain went to the Library of Congress almost every day, which he wrote his mother "gets to be like toddling off to the office, as most of the nation does." But it was hard going. Not only was he bogged down in the historical mud of the Red River basin, but his mind did not seem to be operating with its usual sharpness. By now, with his heavy eating and drinking, he had ballooned to nearly 250 pounds, and there is evidence in his letters and other writings that the alcohol was affecting his work. From time to time he would go on the wagon, then slip off and resume the heavy drinking, which usually took place before, during, and after dinner.

The seriousness of the problem was brought home to him one evening

---

*The day after, he wrote Mencken a long postmortem, the last letter of substance he would write his friend from Baltimore. He recalled that once, having breakfast on their weekly run from Baltimore to New York, Mencken had said that what delighted him most in life was exposure of a fraud. Now Cain, reversing his earlier opinion of Truman, rejoiced at Truman's "exposure of 10,000 frauds, the experts, the pollsters, the columnists, the thinkers, the saviours, a whole cocksure crew, not one of whom, it is now revealed, had a shadow of the sagacity they laid claim to. . . . It sticks to the ribs and rolls under the tongue. I never heard of a defeat more richly deserved or a victory more decently earned, if we concede that kicks in the belly are the only solid decencies of politics."

when he wanted to tell Florence a story his friend, the baritone Mostyn Thomas, had told him about another baritone, John Charles Thomas, with whom Florence had once sung. It concerned an aria, "Di Provensa Il Mar," from *La Traviata*. As Cain told the story to Florence, he also tried to sing the Italian of the second verse, which he had known by heart. But it would not come. He was horrified: "Something you learn when you are nineteen years old is part of you and you know it until the day you die." The following week, he came down with the flu, which prevented his having a drink for several days. One morning after he had recovered, he was shaving when, all of a sudden, the words he had tried to recall came to him, in Italian! He had to give up drinking! He thought of that old principle which he so devoutly believed, that an alcoholic is never more than one drink from disaster. And then he came up with what he thought was the equivalent of Einstein discovering his theory of relativity: An alcoholic was also never more than one drink from salvation! Instead of stopping forever and a day, he would just skip the next drink.

It happened one night when Florence, who was not drinking much then but would join Cain so he did not have to drink alone, reached for an orange to make his regular evening old-fashioned, and he said: "Why don't we skip that?"

She said, "All right." Then after dinner she asked, "The usual—the pink drink?" (gin and Dubonnet), and Cain said, "Let's skip that, too." He kept skipping them, and by the end of his second year on the wagon he had lost sixty pounds and was beginning to think about another novel—the story of a woman who had weighed three hundred pounds and then took off her excess weight, making her extremely attractive to men.

At about the same time he gave up drinking, he went into the hospital for an operation, and although it was a minor one, it was very painful and kept him away from the typewriter for weeks. Then it was Florence's turn. The trip through the South and settling in their new home had also been a strain on her, and she began having health problems, which at first were diagnosed as "tension." But of all the distractions that hit Cain in those first years in Hyattsville, by far the most annoying and time-consuming were back-to-back lawsuits, filed in January and February 1949, which dragged on the rest of the year and into the next. One lawsuit, filed by the attorney general of the state of Massachusetts, charged that Cain's novel *Serenade* was obscene. The other was filed by a woman who said Cain had stolen material from an unpublished story she had sent him and had used it in *Mildred Pierce*.

The Massachusetts charge was brought also against Erskine Caldwell's *God's Little Acre*, but the two books were tried separately. The judge in both cases was Justice Charles Fairhurst, and Cain's lawyers (hired by Knopf) as well as Bernard DeVoto, who followed the cases from his editor's "Easy Chair" in *Harper's*, thought his conduct was eminently fair. For example, the attorney general contended that *Serenade* contained a passage (the love scene in a Catholic church) that must necessarily offend "the sensibilities and religious feelings of a large section of the community." Judge Fairhurst, a Catholic himself, agreed, but said this was irrelevant to the question of obscenity. DeVoto stressed that "the importance of that Ruling at the present time cannot be overestimated, for the most alarming feature of the current attack on freedom of speech is the effort of minority, racial and religious groups to suppress expression at the source."

At the same time, however, De Voto was critical of the current trend in paperback publishing, which was to flood the newsstands with books carrying lurid, sexy covers, implying that almost any story, from *Treasure Island* to *Tom Sawyer*, had racy passages in it. It was, in fact, the New American Library copy of *Serenade* that had been picked up by the Massachusetts state police. The strategy of the defense was to play up the book as a Knopf hardcover, rather than as a New American Library paperback, which, among other things, meant building up the testimony of Harold Strauss, the book's editor at Knopf, and playing down that of Victor Weybright, publisher of NAL. The lawyers, from the New York firm of Stern and Reubens, also brought in three distinguished "experts"—Theodore Morrison, professor of English at Harvard; Ralph Thompson, book reviewer of the *New York Times*, and Robert Gorham Davis, a former Harvard professor, then teaching American literature at Smith College—all of whom provided a strong defense for the novel. They said the sexual episodes were an integral and necessary part of the story, that *Serenade* was a literary effort, that Cain was an extremely proficient representative of the so-called hard-boiled school, which had evolved from the realistic tradition in literature, and that *Serenade* was well thought out and representative of the school.

Judge Fairhurst ruled in favor of *Serenade* and *God's Little Acre*, but a year later the Massachusetts Supreme Court overturned the judge's decision in the case of the Erskine Caldwell novel, while upholding his decision on *Serenade*. Under the terms of his contract with Knopf, Cain was obligated to pay the legal fees, which came to over $3,000, but Knopf agreed to assume half the amount and to carry Cain's half as an advance against his next book.

The suit against *Mildred Pierce* was more complicated and nerve-racking. In the fall of 1948, an undated letter from Miss Mae Caro of Los Angeles finally caught up with Cain in Hyattsville. Miss Caro charged that the movie *Mildred Pierce* was based on a script she wrote, called *Nothing to Live For*, which, in soliciting advice and a possible sale to Cain, she had delivered to his New York office in 1937. She threatened a lawsuit over the alleged piracy but concluded that she felt sure they could "straighten this matter out amicably."

Cain's long letter of reply began with a little lecture on the hazards of a plagiarism lawsuit. He then said he had not had an office in New York since 1931, that even if Miss Caro had delivered the manuscript to someone he would not have accepted it because he had a habit of never reading or offering advice on manuscripts submitted by amateurs, that the origins of *Mildred Pierce* went back to the conversations he had had with James McGuinness on the Columbia picture lot in 1932, and that when the novel appeared in 1941, he had sent McGuinness an autographed copy acknowledging his contribution to the original concept. He said that the moving picture differed in several respects from the novel and that before she took legal action she had best read the book and compare it to the movie. He concluded by saying that he was writing her primarily to acquaint her with the facts and that he declined to "straighten this matter out amicably" because there was nothing to straighten out.

Cain thought the whole thing was ridiculous, that stealing *Mildred Pierce* was about like stealing a ball park, and he assumed that would be the last he would hear from Miss Caro. He was wrong. In January she filed suit against him and Warner Brothers. Cain was informed of Miss Caro's action by her New York lawyer, who said that he was being served with a summons and that failure to answer the summons would result in a $100,000 judgment against him. Cain, a veteran of the courtrooms, knew he had trouble, and he quickly wrote Warner Brothers about his letter from Miss Caro, sending a copy of his reply and asking them to recommend a New York lawyer. He then wrote Knopf, asking the publisher if he would pay him all the money in his account, in the event that Miss Caro tried to attach his assets. Knopf responded to his request and Cain settled down to studying the *Mildred Pierce* scripts, aware that any mistake they might make in handling what he considered a preposterous lawsuit could ruin him financially.

Through Warners, Cain engaged the New York firm of O'Brien, Driscoll, Raftery and Lawler. Then he went into the hospital for another minor operation while George Raftery rushed to obtain the first deposition and plot his legal strategy, which included a claim that the statute of limitations had negated the case and that if it did go to court the case should be tried by a judge rather than a jury, inasmuch as a woman going against a wealthy author and movie studio was likely to receive undue sympathy from a jury. Cain obtained a copy of Miss Caro's *Nothing to Live For*, which he read with great relief. He had thought there was a chance, through some fluke, that he might have seen it, but he immediately knew he had never laid eyes on it. It was, in his description, the "quite familiar pattern of the feminine autobiographical tale, in which the writer is perfect and feels persecuted by somebody, usually a husband who is a drunk or a crook or a chaser, in this case a husband plus a daughter." He also thought, from the tone of the story, that Miss Caro would be very effective in front of a jury (if the case went to a jury) and that her actions since filing the suit showed that although she might be a chiseler, she was a "fanatic believer in the assumption that she was wronged."

As the case developed, it also became apparent that Warner Brothers was going to seek immunity behind the warranty of the original sale and leave Cain to hold the bag. The studio was quite open in its position, a fact Cain thought might work to his advantage, changing the case from that of "a poor working girl against a big picture company," to that of "a poor working girl plus a big picture company attempting to ride on the back of one fairly hard-working author."

By June, Cain was completely recovered from his operation and spending considerable time on the case, which clearly had him distressed. Even if he won the case, he could receive a grudge verdict, because some members of the jury would almost certainly be offended by the book (he still remembered the passionate hatred it had aroused in 1941), or there might be "the $5,000 verdict the jury gives anyhow just because it can't make up its mind, because Warner Brothers is rich and can afford it." Even $5,000 would ruin him in his present financial situation.

At the end of the year, both lawyers agreed to postpone the case until the following May, and then it was postponed again, all of which Cain interpreted as a sign that Miss Caro was backing off, that she was now dreaming of no more than a $2,500 nuisance settlement. In January 1951, she turned down an offer of $500 to settle out of court, and then Richard Mackey, her attorney, dropped out of the case. He told Cain's lawyer that, frankly, he had taken the case without reading Miss Caro's script, and now that he had he felt she had no case whatever. He also said that Miss Caro had no proof that she had given the manuscript to Cain in 1937, only her oral testimony.

Within a few weeks, another attorney called and told Raftery that after reading the story he saw certain similarities and that he thought the settlement should be $10,000. When Raftery asked him what the similarities were, the attorney said the "ungrateful child"—at which point Raftery hit the roof, saying if there was any one topic in the public domain, from the Bible on down, it was the ungrateful child. He said Cain was ready to go to trial and that their defense would take considerable effort, time, and money, a point not lost on Miss Caro's lawyer: their suit was in a federal court, where they would be liable for all court expenses if they lost. Shortly thereafter, the attorney came back with an offer to settle for $1,000, but Raftery still said no. At this point Warner Brothers wanted out, with their lawyer saying that the studio would put up another $250 (over the earlier offer of $500) if Cain would chip in. Raftery said no, and thereupon Miss Caro settled for $750, all paid by the studio. Cain was still left with substantial legal expenses, and he had spent countless hours at the typewriter composing long letters and memos to Raftery.

All in all, the two lawsuits added up to nearly two years of unnecessary harassment at a time when his writing was not going well and his income was steadily declining. Barbara Stanwyck had written him, pleading, "Where the hell is the story you promised me two or three years ago—come on, hurry up and write one for me. A nice juicy murder." But, as his letters to friends and relatives show, he was having trouble with "this dreadful book, which I shall call *Ghost Riders on the Red River*." Invariably, he would report to someone about the difficulty he had been having but now the problem was licked, only to write someone else two months later about all the difficulty he was still having—but then, again, the problem was licked and he could glimpse the end.

Fortunately, Cain's book and movie properties were still in demand, and some were producing significant income; others were at least keeping the Cain by-line alive. The most pleasing to Cain (and least remunerative) was 20th Century-Fox's remake of *Wife, Husband and Friend*, based on Cain's story "Two Can Sing." The new movie (*Everybody Does It*), written by Nunnally Johnson, was by almost every reviewer's appraisal a hilarious comedy. Bosley Crowther, in the *Times*, called it a historic milestone for Hollywood in that it marked Paul Douglas's first starring role (as the husband of a would-be opera singer who discovers that he is the one who has the voice in the family). The cast included Linda Darnell, Celeste Holm, and Charles Coburn, and the movie and the rave reviews must have been the highlight of an otherwise glum year for Cain.

The flood of paperback sales also rushed on, fed by new titles being added all the time, including two more that had not appeared in hard-cover. He received a $1,000 advance from Avon for his old, unpublished serial "Nevada Moon," now with Cain having tightened the opening pages and eliminated all references to Edward G. Robinson and *Double Indemnity*. He had agreed to the sale partly because he was feeling pinched for money, but more to the point was his old belief that anything written for newspapers or magazines did not matter, and that since paperback books were not reviewed, appeared mostly on the newsstands, and soon disappeared from sight, they were no more significant than a magazine sale. Avon gave the book a new title, *Jealous Woman*, which Cain hated as much as he hated *Sinful Woman*. But he went along with the titles because he was assured they helped sales. Apparently they did, because the next year Avon was dickering for "The Modern Cinderella," his 1937 serial that had been made into the movie *When Tomorrow Comes*. Again Avon did not like Cain's title, so this time he came up with one over lunch with Maurice Diamond: *The Root of His Evil*. This was his third original novel for Avon, all of which, in paperback, are rare items now. The most consistent seller of the three remained the first, *Sinful Woman,* which Cain thought was due to the upbeat ending. He was not very proud of any of them, but in defense of their publication he once said, "There is only one book that really hurts a writer, and that is no book."

Meanwhile, New American Library paid him $2,000 for reprint rights to *The Butterfly* (which he and Knopf split, fifty-fifty, and then Avon expressed interest in a collection of Cain short stories. Cain was not very enthusiastic about the idea. He thought he had a half-dozen stories that were pretty good, including "Pastorale," "Dead Man," "Brush Fire," "Coal Black," and a few others. But the rest, in his opinion, "were little stinkers written with the hope *Liberty* or some such magazine might buy them." He felt Hemingway had made a mistake in bringing out his collection of forty-nine stories, despite the fact it contained "Fifty Grand," "The Snows of Kilimanjaro," and "The Short Happy Life of Francis Macomber." He never did get around to assembling an anthology for Avon, and the project was abandoned. However, New American Library brought out an abridged version of *The Moth*; and "Career in C Major" and "The Embezzler" were combined to make one 25-cent paperback titled *Everybody Does It*, to capitalize on the Paul Douglas movie. And of course his earlier books were still selling well in paperback, especially *Postman*, for which he was awarded a "Silver Kangaroo" by Pocketbooks in 1950 when it passed the million-copy sales mark. At the awards ceremony in New York, he was amused that Dale Carnegie, author of *How to Win Friends and Influence People*, was being watched over "by this very good-looking number in her early thirties," to prevent a very unsure-of-himself and obviously bored author from demonstrating his inability to make friends.

Obviously James M. Cain was still "hot," but being hot in Hyattsville was not the same as being hot in Hollywood. He did hear from a producer named William Dozier, who invited Cain to New York to talk about a story idea he had for Rita Hayworth, and for which he thought Cain might be just the right man. Cain went to New York, saw Dozier, then wrote Swanson that he was interested, but instructed him to drive a hard bargain: $10,000 to start, $10,000 on completion, and $10,000 for four weeks' employment in Hollywood to incorporate changes that would no doubt be wanted in the script. Cain said he had plenty of money in the bank and a steady income from his properties, so "don't give ground because you think I need it. I would rather lose it than make a poor deal." He lost it.

Actually, Cain's financial situation, for life in Hyattsville, *was* sound, though there was no escaping the fact that his income was dwindling: in 1949, it was $17,000, half of what it had been the year before; and in 1950 it was $12,000. In both years the money came mostly from Knopf in the form of hard-cover and reprint royalties. Obviously he needed new titles, and the Civil War book was dragging on and on. At one point he wrote Swanson that he and Florence were giving serious thought to returning to Hollywood, and did Swanson see any hope of a job for him out there?

Although Cain was losing weight and regaining his pep, he was complaining that he needed a rest. There were plans to visit Florence's home in Minnesota, but then she was not feeling well and complained of fatigue, which the doctors decided was due to a blood pressure problem.

Cain and Florence had reached those years when friends begin to drop away, one by one, and each death brought its anguish—and an immediate letter of condolence from Cain. And over in Baltimore, time was slipping away for Henry Mencken. He had been in declining health since 1947, and by late 1949 he had suffered a serious stroke and was in and out of hospitals. Cain talked to him on the phone and sent him little notes, but did not go over to see him. "I don't exactly know why," he wrote the Knopfs, "perhaps for fear he'll have no idea who I am . . . and I fear I would put him under a strain. . . . I have little patience with people who cheerfully and chirpily go about what they conceive to be their duty, only to cause the patient more upset." Eventually he did visit Mencken in Baltimore and was delighted at how well his old friend looked and acted. Mencken was mostly cheerful, although at one point he lapsed into introspection and announced calmly to Cain, as though stating a fact rather than voicing a bitterness, that he was through, an old man, nearly seventy, and would be dead within a year.

But the biographers were not waiting for Mencken's death: by 1950 books about Mencken began to appear. Francis Brown at the *New York Times Book Review* asked Cain to review *The Irreverent Mr. Mencken*, by Edgar Kemler—and Cain agreed, although he found the job difficult. "I got a case of the shakes," he wrote Brown, "for fear of Henry's reaction, I having, as you may understand, an intellectual reverence for him that is all mixed up with a wrenching personal affection. To cause him an upset, to lose him as a friend, at this late hour, would indeed have been a blow. And yet, one dare not fill the inkwell with goosegrease, one owes the reader a fair report."

And a fair report was what he gave, which pleased not only Brown but Mencken and his friends as well. He said that in his day Mencken was a sort of "neon goldfish, shining like an Aurora Borealis," and hence almost impossible as a subject for a biography. But he felt Kemler had succeeded, and he concluded his review by asking what with the censor, the patrioteer, and the bigot in full cry once again, "who the big bull elephant will be to smash at them hard once more, and whether there will ever be another one quite as big, quite as brave, quite as mad, as this one."

Mencken, in turn, thought Cain was the most competent writer the country had ever produced. In 1940, he wrote someone who had inquired about Cain that "he is a man of extraordinary gifts, and at the same time of sharp limitations. I have never known him to write anything downright bad." A few years later, he told Ward Morehouse, in a *Baltimore Sun* interview, that "the only author I ever knew who never wrote a bad article was James M. Cain. I never turned down a piece by him." When the interview appeared, Cain thanked Mencken and said the only reason he wrote those articles was because "it was always such a delight to get your letters of acceptance, and I still have most of them as treasured mementos."*

Mencken lingered on for several years after his first series of strokes. A more abrupt and tragic end—under very mysterious circumstances—came to another old friend of Cain's, Morris Markey, who had helped him find a job on *The New Yorker*. Markey was special to Cain, who always considered him something of a substitute for his brother Boydie. Markey too had spent time working in Hollywood, although Cain never felt he had the temperament to be a successful screenwriter. Cain was right, and after failing in Hollywood, Markey returned to New York, where for years he did the notes for the Texaco radio opera broadcasts on Saturday afternoons and wrote magazine articles. But his letters to Cain revealed an increasing unhappiness with the city, and when his daughter, Sue, graduated from college, the family moved to Halifax, Virginia, a sleepy little Southern town very near the North Carolina border, only eight miles from where Markey's mother lived and where he had grown up. There he planned to finish a novel, which he called *Doctor Jeremiah*.

Then, one morning in early July, Helen Markey called Cain to tell him that Morris was dead and the funeral was to be the next day, if he wanted to come. Cain felt he had to go. Thirteen years later, he wrote a four-page single-spaced account of his trip to Halifax and the strange death of Morris Markey in a letter to their mutual friend, Laurence Stallings—an account, as Stallings described it, that reads like a combination of Tennessee Williams and Mickey Spillane.

Helen had not said how Markey had died, and it was not until Cain reached Petersburg and bought a Richmond paper that he learned Morris had

---

*Unfortunately, they did not turn up in Cain's or Mencken's papers. Mencken made a point of not keeping carbons of *Mercury* correspondence; and Cain said that in 1938 his secretary lost a box of his papers, including his Mencken correspondence.

been shot. There was some question as to how it happened and why, just enough mystery to start a little Southern town such as Halifax buzzing with gossip and speculation, which goes on to this day. Markey's body was found in the hall at the foot of the stairs. A .22-caliber rifle was nearby, with one cartridge fired from it. No one saw the accident, and after the county coroner and the district attorney spent most of the day talking with members of the Markey family, they decided there was not enough evidence to issue a verdict of homicide, suicide, or even accident. The official report was "death from causes not determined," and there it stands today.

Cain learned more about what happened from Marvin Markey, Morris's brother, after he arrived at the Markey home, where the atmosphere was still tense because of the persistent questioning of the coroner and district attorney. On the day before his death, as Cain recounted it, Sue had driven to the store and along the way had seen four little puppies on the side of the road, where someone had abandoned them. Deciding they should have a merciful end, she took them home, got out the family .22, and shot them. When she went to bury them, she left the .22 in the hall. This was a mistake, for they had been keeping the rifle hidden in the fear that Morris, despondent over his health and drinking heavily, might use it to take his life. And he did. The trouble was, he did not do it the usual way. He jammed the rifle against the back of his head—probably, the family assumed, to make it appear an accident, but unfortunately it did not appear an accident at all, but as though someone had held the gun from behind.

After the funeral, as sundown was approaching, Cain had a few minutes with Helen Markey. In a moment of letdown, Cain thought, she said: "Why all the talk, Jim? We know what happened, of course—he had cirrhosis of the liver and couldn't stop drinking. He drank to deaden the pain—at least for an hour or two. It went on all the time, it gave him no peace." And she went on to recall Morris's promise to her that when he came to the end of his days, it would be an accident—which Cain took to be a reference to an insurance policy. Then Cain left, driving into a tremendous thunderstorm on the way home.

It was a tragic affair, a sad end for one of Cain's warmest friends, and the day he drove down to the funeral, to be confronted with that Tennessee Williams scene in the small, southern Virginia town, was one he would never forget.

Two months after Markey's death, Cain and Florence were off on another research trip down through the South, still studying the riverboats used to transport cotton during the Civil War. After they returned to Washington, he went back to the book, which had now become "an Old Man of the Sea, almost, around my neck," but again, he could see the end of it. However, in the spring of 1951, he was interrupted with a tempting offer to write a radio (and possibly TV) series inspired by the interest in the Kefauver hearings on organized crime and the country's fascination with its underworld. Harold Ober had been approached by a man named Roy Winsor, with the Biow Advertising Company in New York, to see if Cain would be interested in writing a radio script for a continuing series to be called "Congressional Investigator." They had requested treatments from other writers, but were unhappy with the scripts they received, feeling they were too similar to programs already on the air—"District Attorney," "FBI," and "Counter-Spy." They wanted a program with more civil responsibility, one that put the emphasis on the reasons a crime was committed rather than the crime itself.

Cain went to New York, met with Ober, Winsor, and some others, came back to Hyattsville, and spent a couple of weeks writing a twenty-page outline for what, in treatment form at least, seemed like a substantially above-average radio series. The Biow people liked Cain's proposal, but Cain and Ober did not like the financial arrangement, and Cain finally decided it was just "one more fly-by-night radio idea." Ober apologized for getting him into it, and nothing ever came of Cain's proposed program.

It was another disappointment for Cain, whose income was still falling. He had not sent Knopf a new book to add to the list for four years, and it looked as if he never would, so hopelessly was he lost in the historical records of the Civil War. His total income for 1951 was a little over $11,000, more than half from his fading reprint sales. He did write one short story— "Pay-Off Girl," not one of his better efforts—which he sold to *Esquire* for $400. But two other short stories he wrote that year did not sell to anyone. And then the author of stories about murder, adultery, homosexuality, prostitution, and incest must have rocked the Ober offices in New York when he wrote them that he had been meditating "a sort of neighborhood series, with an eight-year-old boy, his squirrel, his eight-year-old lady-friend, his mother who wins diving contests, his father who teaches Greek, and his uncle who tells the stories. . . . I have a gift at this kind of thing," Cain said, "and used to make the *Ladies' Home Journal*, believe it or not."

Ober believed it and did not discourage Cain, but he did ask that he let each story stand by itself, not using the same characters in each one, because magazines were no longer buying series stories. This probably killed the idea for Cain; he never wrote any stories about the eight-year-old boy and his pet squirrel.

He was also approached by the producers of the Theater of Famous Authors TV series to contribute an original story for $2,000, and although he told Ober he was skeptical about such projects because they rarely worked out, he would do one if the producer got serious, although "I prefer not to be pulled into an endless raz-ma-tazz trying to suit him with something original." Cain much preferred adaptations. But nothing ever came of that project either, or of another radio script he was invited to write, which prompted him to tell one friend: "I couldn't count the number of hot deals that have blown up in radio which are to make me rich overnight and which, for one reason and another reason, all of them good, come to nothing."

In addition to his writing misfires, he had a personal mishap. One day he was driving along a slippery road on the Eastern Shore in a drizzling rain and, attempting to pass another car, slid into an army truck. Although it could have been serious, nobody was hurt, and Cain wrote the headquarters commending the soldiers for taking charge of everything at a time when Cain was still dazed and disorganized. The accident rattled Cain more than he cared to admit, making him and Florence wonder whether his advancing years were affecting his ability to handle a car. "I have had, now, two collisions in my life," he wrote a friend, "and in each case it has taken all sorts of damnable wrestling with myself to admit that both were my own fault."

The Cains were also finding the sweltering Maryland summers impossible, more aware than ever that "every book you read going back to colonial times harps on the dank, dismal, unhealthy climate of Maryland." Florence was now drifting back into the black despair she had suffered from when they first came to Hyattsville in 1948, and the doctor was warning Cain that if he himself did not let up and get some rest he would probably have a nervous breakdown. This presented Cain with the difficult task of writing his mother to tell her that, for a while at least, he would have to stop sending her the money he had been relaying regularly. He said he had been driving himself to finish his book but the doctor had said that if he did not take a rest, he would probably break down first. So he and Florence took a brief trip to Lake Champlain, which for benefit of the I.R.S. at least, he said was for the purpose of gathering background for a play about Benedict Arnold, though there is no record that he ever tried to write such a play.

When he returned from the lake country, he settled down for one final effort to finish his Civil War novel. He wrote at least three drafts for which he had various titles—*The Lady Is a Pirate*, *The Slim Girl*, *The Silver Mountain*—"each one worse than the other," he said. "And if the cotton made two miles a day in those Texas caravans creaking across the desert, it still moved faster than my story did."

At first he had planned a three-part saga of the war, and "it must have been a saga," he wrote one publisher years later, "because it sagged all over the place." Then he focused on one story, but bogged down in the intrigues between the Army and the Navy and President Lincoln in the closing days of the war. He also got caught up in the military campaign, and carried away by the local color accumulated on his thousands of 3-by-5 research cards—particularly "this stinkhole of the western world, Baghdad, the most colorful place you ever saw. I had all the background and I knew the name of every whore and Mexican general who was cutting in on the gravy and everything else down there. I probably knew more about Baghdad and the cotton racket during the Civil War than anybody that ever lived."

But after three drafts, he said, "I simply could not bring it to life. It just lay there in pieces and I did not know why." He had written Raphaelson that he wanted him to read it, complaining it had been a murderously long haul and probably would not be much of a book when it was done. "But it's like a hen with an egg in the tube; maybe it's not any jumbo, extra-size select, but until it is laid nothing else can come through."

Even when he at last finished it, he felt he had indeed laid an egg, and wrote Raphaelson that the mere fact he wanted him to read it showed something was wrong with it. Cain finally decided that, for him at least, no novel could come to life without concentration on the love story. But now he was exhausted on the subject of the Red River campaign and he needed money quick, so he turned to a contemporary tale growing out of his decision to quit drinking in 1949.

It was crushingly obvious by now that Cain was not making a success of the serious writing career he had intended to pursue when he turned his back on those $2,500-a-week studio jobs and came East to immerse himself in the Red River campaign. And this failure must have contributed to his deteriorating mental state as well as Florence's despair. In addition, with Cain now almost sixty years old, it was questionable whether he *could* find work in Hollywood.

It is not clear when the Cains made their final decision not to return to California. As early as 1949, Cain had written his friend Edward Sirich that they were thinking of staying in Maryland, partly because they were dug in and could not face another move. "Making this trek," he said, "has been a God-awful wrench, to both of us, and leaves us somehow suspended in mid-air because we really don't accept this dreadful little state, take no pride in it, and want no piece of it."

But in 1950, he was writing Swanson that one thing was certain: "In this neck of the woods, except as a base for research, I don't fit in at all." Furthermore, because of the war clouds gathering over Korea, both he and Florence were uncomfortable in Washington. Hence, would Swanson keep a watch out for something in Hollywood?

But Swanson did not find anything—and Florence knew why. One day, after Cain had decided he had completed his Civil War researches in the

Library of Congress, he said to Florence: "Well, I suppose we're going back now?"

"Back where?" she asked.

"Well—Hollywood. It's home."

"Have you kept track of what's happened to Hollywood while we've been here?"

"So? Has anything?"

"It's not there anymore," she answered.

"Oh—you mean TV?"

"Yes, TV. The Hollywood we knew does not exist anymore, so that big money you used to earn, and that sometimes I used to earn, won't be coming in. That I don't mind, but if we have to make do on a reduced income, I'd a lot rather make do here, where everyone's income will be pretty much like our own, than out there, where all our friends are Beverly Hills millionaires."

So they decided to stay, and in later years Cain said it was the worst decision he ever made. "California is a neck of the woods everyone is fascinated with," he told me. "It was El Dorado. You can put it in your book, 'It was nothing but a wayside filling station—like millions of others in California' and that's O.K. Any piece of California, no matter how drab, prosaic or dull, is California just the same, the Land of Golden Promise. And I don't know anyone who is holding his breath over Prince Georges County, Maryland."

He was soon to find out, with his next book, just how true that was. Maryland was not El Dorado, and no one seemed to care about Prince Georges County—or James M. Cain.

19

"A KIND OF MOUSE
IS BORN"

For Cain, as for the nation, 1952 was a pivotal year. In the presidential election the country rejected Adlai Stevenson, perhaps the most articulate, literate candidate since Woodrow Wilson, and elected the hero of World War II, General Dwight D. Eisenhower. Although Cain had little use for those he regarded as liberal do-gooders, he admired Stevenson's literacy and intelligence and was angered at what he felt was the press's effort to play down Stevenson's candidacy while dignifying Eisenhower's ineptitudes and trying to lift his campaign rhetoric "above the level of the Abilene creamery."

Cain took no active part in the campaign of 1952, perhaps because he could not afford to. Income from his books was now critically small, amounting to only $5,700 in 1952—his lowest earnings since 1933. His health was deteriorating—perhaps, though he couldn't be sure, the reason he was having more and more trouble writing—and, more critically, Florence was not well. She was showing alarming spurts in her blood pressure, which would shoot up two or three times a week. The doctors began to hint that Florence was doomed, but Cain was determined to prove them wrong. "I quickly decided," he later wrote a friend, "that blood pressure was partly exhaustion, and began relieving her of *all* chores, except a few that gave her an interest in living. Particularly, I decreed that after fixing my dinner, which I ate . . . around three in the afternoon, she was 'washed up for the night,' as they say in show business. She had nothing to do but nap the rest of the afternoon, come down, have a snack, watch TV with me, hold hands, relax, and then later snack again—and then to bed. It worked."

It worked all right, and probably saved Florence's life. But it also changed his; for the next fifteen years Cain nursed Florence in her prolonged battle with a blood pressure condition that caused her to grow weaker day by day, month by month, year by year—until it finally made her an invalid and imprisoned Cain. The strict regimen he set up for her, refusing to let anything come into their daily lives that might upset or pressure her, resulted in their gradually becoming recluses in their little house in Hyattsville. It was one of the reasons that the man who left Hollywood in 1948 as one of the nation's most popular authors gradually drifted into obscurity in the 1950s, until people began to wonder "Whatever happened to James M. Cain?"

But nursing Florence was not the only reason for his slow fadeout. Since 1934, when *Postman* exploded in the nation's bookstores, the name of James M. Cain had been continually before the public—novels, short stories, articles and serials in the national magazines, the American Authors' Authority, and movies based on his fiction came out one after another, almost all of them arousing controversy. But since 1948, when *The Moth* was published, little had been heard from James M. Cain. Only the paperbacks on the newsstands had been keeping the Cain name alive, and they were rarely mentioned in the media.

By 1952, however, a number of things were providing some hope that James M. Cain would soon be emerging from obscurity. First, there was the Civil War novel, which had been through a number of rewrites, enough to fill ten normal books, as he told his sister Rosalie. "[I] have been tempted more than once to call this one off and start another," he wrote. "It is a frightening thing to do, for it is notorious that a writer who [does this] is an ex-writer."

There was also a promising project developing in Hollywood: John Garfield, who had made such a hit in the movie version of *Postman*, was now giving some thought to bringing the play back to the stage in a summer stock production in which he would also star. Cain, however, refused to do any work on it unless Metro returned the play rights to him. So Swanson went to MGM and pointed out that since they were not play producers they might as well give Cain those dramatic rights. Furthermore, since MGM would own the picture rights to any improvements Cain made in the script, and would benefit from the publicity surrounding a successful play, Cain would be increasing the worth of their basic property. MGM agreed, provided that a play be produced by May 1954. Then, before Cain could get started on the play,

Garfield died suddenly, and the project seemed to die with him. But by then Cain had come down with the playwright virus again, so now he turned his attention to a project he had earlier proposed to broker Leah Salisbury. The play was to be called *The Guest in Room 701*, and he worked on it sporadically throughout 1952.

In addition, there was the possibility of a new novel. Cain had been hoping for some time that as soon as he could remove the Civil War albatross from around his neck he would "pop off a couple pretty quick, as I did before, for example, after taking God knows how long . . . on *Past All Dishonor* and doing *The Butterfly* in five weeks."

Now he proposed to pop off a quickie novel based on an idea he first had out in California, but which did not really jell until he began losing weight dramatically. The story, set in southern Maryland, concerned a boy, Duke Webster, who specializes in training fighters for the ring. To keep out of jail and to pay back $86 he has stolen, Webster is ordered by a judge to work for a Southern gentleman who owns a restaurant and has a wife so large she has to use two bathroom scales to weigh herself. A former beauty who is encouraged to indulge her insatiable appetite because her husband would like nothing more than to see her eat herself to death, she is drawn to Duke, who hits on the idea of putting her in training, as he did fighters, and reducing her down to normal. The plan works and they fall in love, which leads to a climactic scene in which Duke impulsively kills his creation. Cain called the novel *Galatea*, after the statue in Greek mythology sculpted by Pygmalion, the king of Cyprus, and brought to life by the goddess Aphrodite.

Cain finished *Galatea* in late 1952 and was so unsure of it that he asked Knopf to send his reactions to him at Room 26 in the Library of Congress, so that if it was rejected, Cain would not have to immediately face Florence with the bad news. He had led her to believe he was still working on the Red River book at the library, not having had the courage to tell her he had given up on that project, at least temporarily, while trying to bring in some quick money with a commercial success.

Knopf surprised Cain, writing him at the library that "*Galatea* is all right—not up to your best in my opinion, but I think we will do well enough to make it worth everybody's while." Blanche also thought it was a good story and was happy about publishing it. However, both expressed misgivings about the ending, which gave Cain a sleepless night, stirring up his own doubts and making him realize that "I liked this book deeply." So he changed the ending, explaining to Blanche: "It may be a fine irony, full of literary logic, that a man creates a woman, then compulsively kills her, but to the reader, and especially the American reader, what this totes up to is the punishment not of evil but of good. . . . Some time during the night, I came up with an idea that will involve only a few pages of copy . . . which will result in a happy ending. . . . The reader, as the saying goes, can 'root' for Duke and Holly, and feel they earned their happiness."

The new climax took place on a ladder to a water tower from which Holly, at one time, had planned to leap to her death. Instead, there is a confusing scene in which Holly's husband is killed, leading to an even more confusing trial and courtroom scene in which Holly and Duke are acquitted, after which they move to Nevada and live happily ever after. There is still the Cain theme—the wish that comes true: "We all get what we pray for," Holly says at the end. "The trouble is we get it all." But this time, the wish that comes true is apparently not a frightening thing.

With Knopf willing to publish *Galatea*, Cain decided to do a rewrite, but not until he straightened out his finances with Knopf. The publisher still had him on the books for a $1,600 debt from Cain's share of the legal fees in the *Serenade* suit. Knopf agreed to cancel that and charge it against a $3,600 advance for *Galatea*; in other words, offering to pay Cain another $2,000 in cash. But Cain was desperate for money and replied that he wanted $4,000 cash—and would write Knopf a check for $500 against his debt, which he would pay off from future royalties. Knopf agreed.

Cain may have thought he was drifting into obscurity—suffering from an inability to write, low morale, and a declining income—but he was still a celebrity, at least to some publishers who were writing nice, glowing little jacket blurbs about first novels by the "latest James M. Cain." And his alma mater, Washington College, was after him to be more active in college affairs. But Cain declined. President Daniel Gibson also dangled an alumni citation in front of him, saying he had "survived a very severe screening by an alumni committee." This approach, naturally, did not sit well with Cain, who declined again. Undaunted, Gibson invited him to a Class of 1910 reunion and, later, a rally, and Cain replied: "I long ago came to the conclusion I wasn't the reunion type." Then Gibson tried to tempt him with a citation for "outstanding achievements in the field of journalism"—to which Cain said that although his achievements were quite substantial, they all had taken place twenty years ago, so he would "preclude an element of absurdity by declining the honor." The following year, Gibson shifted his approach, offering Cain a citation for his achievements in literature. Again Cain declined: "To put it in plain words, I am highly controversial, some people thinking I'm fine, but others thinking just the opposite, in caps."

Cain was more receptive to invitations from television stations, and agreed to sit still for an interview on WBAL-TV in Baltimore. But one occasion in which he surprisingly did not participate was a banquet in New York for Herbert Bayard Swope, to be attended by as many former staffers of the

New York *World* as could be located. One reason for declining may have been the pressure of the intensive schedule he had set up for himself after getting rid of his Red River albatross. He had developed an idea for a new novel that involved research in the coal mines of Pennsylvania and a "big river"—the Susquehanna. This took him and Florence on a trip to Harrisburg, where he also had a chance to get together with his World War I buddy, Gilbert Malcolm, now provost of Dickinson College. From Harrisburg, Cain went immediately to Norfolk, Virginia, for a lecture at a branch of the College of William and Mary (now known as Old Dominion University). The head of the English department was professor William W. Seward, an admirer of Cain's who had modeled his own novel—*Skirts of the Dead Night*—on Cain's style, convinced that Cain could "say more in a few words than any other living novelist." Since 1950, Seward had been after Cain to address his creative writing class, and Cain finally agreed to come down in April 1953, although he ended up addressing the full graduating class and never did discuss creative writing. Instead, he chose to discourse on world affairs, confusing the students with his 1920s view of the world. He told them America should revert to the Monroe Doctrine, called the United Nations Charter "the windiest document I ever read," said Dean Acheson's explanation as to why we were in Korea was "absurd," that Wendell Willkie "took a trip around the world and discovered it was round," and called the notion that peace is indivisible "a silly idea."

Cain considered the whole lecture a disaster, and for most of the students and faculty no doubt caught up in the internationalism of the postwar world, it probably was. After Norfolk, Cain went back to Hyattsville and began writing short stories, during which he had a brief flirtation with the Dictaphone. "Mechanically, the machine is pure magic," he said, "but by the time I dictate, redictate, shuffle records, shift the treadle and do all the other things, I am in a state." Besides, when he played it back he said he sounded too much like a city editor barking at himself. Although he soon gave up on the machine, he did get at least one good line out of the experience for one of the short stories he was writing: "I tried to act natural, but my voice sounded like a bark from a dictating machine." The story was "Two O'Clock Blonde," one of two (the other one was "Cigarette Girl") that appeared in *Manhunt*, a now defunct magazine that specialized in hard-boiled fiction. Ober had reservations about Cain's appearing in an obviously second-rate men's publication, but Cain persisted, telling Ober: "The fact is it's the first magazine in a long time that has shown much interest in my writings, and I think it is worth cultivating for a good many reasons." One of the reasons was that it did not take advertising, which, Cain thought, "let writers really lean on it, without having to radiate sweetness and light." And, as with novels, Cain still felt that the only story that hurt a writer was no story.

But even *Manhunt* was disappointed in Cain. Although it had published those two stories, the editor returned three others, complaining that they were fuzzy in style, diffuse and confusing, and that he was genuinely concerned with the quality of Cain's work—which he thought might have been due to his trying to write on a dictating machine. But the fact was, Cain was having increasing trouble with his work. The rewriting of *Galatea* did not come easily, and when the book came out in the summer, the reviews must have been unsettling to the sixty-year-old writer. "This new Cain novel," said Saul Pett, in a widely syndicated Associated Press review, "has 242 pages. I read all of them, I reread some 2 and 3 times, I still don't know quite what Cain is talking about." The *Harper's* reviews concurred. "I read and reread these scenes [on the water tower] and could never understand what really happened." "James M. Cain . . . is running down," said *The Nation.* Perhaps the unkindest cut of all came from Charles Lee, in the *Saturday Review*: "James M. Cain achieves the dubious distinction of writing dully enough to make the authors of the *Congressional Record* seem the very models of clarity and charm."

There were a few kind words: David Dempsey in the *New York Times Book Review* said that Cain was still "a master craftsman within the zone of psychological cheekiness that he has staked out." The *Washington Post* called the book "James M. Cain at his best." And Stephen Longstreet in the *Los Angeles Daily News* said the kind of things they used to say about James M. Cain back in the good old Hollywood days: "*Galatea* is the best novel he has written. As a matter of fact, as an American story teller he has no peer, and I think in time Cain will be rated just under Faulkner and Hemingway as a master story teller of the hard, dark minds and adventures of our times. . . . That Cain is one of our best writers has been hidden from us by our critics, who are often snobs and log rollers. . . . [*Galatea*] is the best tough yarn of the year, maybe of the decade."

But the cheer from Longstreet, an obvious Cain loyalist, was not enough to drown out the boos, which were disturbing. No one had ever called James M. Cain dull before, and no one would have dared call him confused and unclear. Cain had had high hopes for the book, primarily because, as he had learned in his days on the *World*'s editorial page, food and diets are subjects that obsess Americans. But *Galatea* did not become a best seller, although it sold around 12,000 copies by the end of the year and eventually went into paperback. There was also a flurry of interest in Hollywood, with Louella Parsons carrying an item that Otto Preminger had bought it. He did eventually put up $1,000 for an option, but let it lapse, and *Galatea*, which obviously presented problems to a filmmaker, never did sell to the movies, although another option was taken in 1979.

Fortunately, by the time *Galatea* was published, Cain was preoccupied with another project. After John Garfield's death, Joseph Bernard, his director on *Postman*, took up the revival of *Postman* as a play, planning a road tour as well as summer stock. With MGM's consent, he and Cain worked out a standard Dramatists Guild contract, with Cain to receive 5 percent on the first $5,000 of box office receipts, 7½ percent on the next $2,000, and 10 percent thereafter. So while working on *Galatea*, Cain also did a minor rewrite of his *Postman* play, and when he finished the novel, he became involved in the play's production, taking trips to Connecticut and New York to work with Bernard. He was in the audience when it opened in Pittsburgh and toured with it for a while, until it became obvious that he had fathered a financial, aesthetic, and personal disaster.

The cast was picked by Bernard and producer Clifford Hayman. To replace Garfield as Frank Chambers, they chose Tom Neal, who had appeared in more than a hundred films in ten years, including *Another Thin Man*, *Something About a Soldier*, and *The Great Jesse James Raid*. He had also starred in the 1950 Broadway production of *Laura* with Miriam Hopkins. For Cora, they chose Neal's co-star in *Jesse James*, Barbara Payton, a former model whose most successful Hollywood roles were with James Cagney in *Only the Valiant*, Gregory Peck in *Trapped*, and Gary Cooper in *Dallas*. Both Payton and Neal were box office attractions in 1953, and Cain was optimistic about the chances of making some money. But it was soon obvious he was wrong. The two stars, in Cain's appraisal, pulled out all the stops, and the stopper, too, in their portrayals of Frank and Cora. Fortunately for Cain, most of the reviewers put the blame for the play's failure on them, but not all. *Variety* said the new production proved again that Cain was a "pedestrian playwright," although it conceded he was a first-rate novelist and *Postman* a minor classic in book form. Before it closed, the play moved on to Chicago and St. Louis, and although it had an occasional favorable review, most critics agreed with Claudia Cassidy in the *Chicago Tribune* who said that "the crude dramatization suggests that if the theater isn't dead, someone ought to arrange a mercy killing."

In addition to being an embarrassment, the play earned Cain only $593.84, after expenses, and one-fourth of that went to Knopf under the extremely complex contractual arrangements governing *Postman*. So Cain began a protracted hassle with Knopf, maintaining again that Knopf had relinquished *all* dramatic rights in 1934, hence was not entitled to the one-fourth share of stage rights. Eventually Cain became so worked up that he said unless Knopf returned the money he had paid the publisher from the royalties earned by the 1936 stage production of *Postman*, he would take his books elsewhere. The amount was only $148.46, but Cain insisted it was a matter of principle. He added that he had only the friendliest feeling toward Knopf personally. "I like to eat lunch with you, I like your jokes. I ask no better publisher, and you have one thing that for me is of great importance, which is nerve. Cardinals don't frighten you and nobody does, which is a tremendous thing. But this damned cockleburr sticks in my craw."

Knopf's correspondence indicates that he was bewildered by the whole thing and immediately offered to pay Cain the $148.46, which Cain accepted, with characteristic apologies for his ill humor. "I am no bargain on such a subject," he wrote Knopf, "I just as well own that right now."

Cain returned from Pittsburgh sick and disgusted. "It was even more of a fiasco than before," he wrote his mother, referring to the 1936 production, "and I hope, if I ever make the slightest move to have it done again, somebody takes a gun and puts an end to the nonsense."

It took Cain most of 1953 to recover from his return to the theater, but by early 1954 he was ready to rework his Civil War novel. By now, however, he was having serious problems at the typewriter. As he described them to a friend: "1. Sluggish memory. I began fumbling for names . . . out of the past. 2. Typos in my work. Letters would get twisted up, many more than the normal. 3. Opaque in summer, when the dog days hit, and sensitivity to cold in the winter. 4. Confusion in thinking, inability to unkink a story, so it would roll. 5. Inability to care whether guy got doll or not."

Although his new Civil War novel still revolved around the Red River campaign of 1863, Cain had apparently decided that the question of whether the guy got the doll was indeed, still and all, the most important thing in a story. He would now focus on a love affair between a young Union soldier named William Cresap and the daughter of a Southern businessman, Mignon Fournet, and on their struggle to sell thousands of dollars' worth of cotton claimed by both the North and the South. He called the book *Mignon* and, once again, he went South to do research and absorb local color—this time to Brownsville and Port Isabel, Texas, and Matamoros, Mexico. By May, he was back at his typewriter, writing friends in Texas for more information.

He worked on *Mignon* off and on for three more years, but despite the fact that he was telling the story in the first person of Lieutenant Cresap, it still did not jell. He began to think that maybe he had become incapable of writing a novel. And yet, as he wrote William Koshland at Knopf: "I started all this on the basis of *Past All Dishonor*, which had the biggest sale of any of my books—so maybe it is my racket and we'll come out of it with something that goes."

But as the months dragged on, the work became tougher and tougher. He complained to Knopf: "God deliver me from a period book. But I know no way to finish them, but to finish them."

He finally did finish it in early 1957, and after he sent it off to Knopf, the publisher's reaction must have come back as a crushing blow.

The story is altogether too complicated, and yet perhaps not involved enough. The point is that it is much too short. Three of us have read the book and none of us really get the hang of it. It became a little more intelligible to me when I looked up the Red River campaign in a couple of reference books. After all, you hit on a little backwater episode in the Civil War which is completely unfamiliar to almost everyone likely to read your book. The answer, I am sure, isn't to write a preface explaining what the Red River campaign was, but to give, in more detail, the setting. I think your lady character is weak. . . . Cain enthusiasts will expect a little more sex than you have given here. Also . . . the motivations of the hero and heroine are by no means always clear. Whose side is each on, and why? You may answer that all this is very clear to you. I can only say that it isn't clear to the reader. I am sure there is better stuff in the Red River campaign than you have worked into this book.

There was, however, one bright note: Ober liked it now and was prepared to offer it to the magazines. But Cain decided to follow Knopf's advice and rewrite it. And, once again, he thought he knew where the trouble was: "Nothing ever really ails any book but the lovers, and it is here where your letter is most valuable to me," he wrote Knopf. "Cresap, whatever heart of gold he finally achieves, is at the start too nice a guy and his errand takes too much telling. She is too full of improbable convictions, and has the opposite fault—she is too patly cynical."

Cain promised to have the rewrite done soon—but once again he was tragically and disastrously wrong. It would be almost three more years before the next version of *Mignon* would be sent off to Knopf.

During his last rewrite, Cain had become interested in another project calculated to lead to frustration—the rewriting of his play *The Guest in 701*, which he had been working on for several years. *The Guest in 701* reads like a James M. Cain novel—almost impossible to put down until you reach the end, tense and exhausted. And although the characters are from a higher walk of life than those in most of his books, they are—typically Cain—less than admirable. The entire play takes place in one room of a New York hotel, called the Dijon and resembling the Gotham, where Cain often stayed. Two of the leading characters—Harold and Helen Reed—are in town from Buffalo. Reed is a successful lawyer, successful enough to have his picture in the papers with a story reporting that he is staying at the Dijon. He has to give a speech, and obviously it has been years since they have been in New York, where he was once a law student at Columbia. The publicized return to the city inspires a procession of people out of their past and into their suite, 701: Helen's old boy friend, who is now a multimillionaire, still wants to marry her, and spends most of the play trying to convince Harold, literally, to sell him his wife; Harold's old girl friend at Columbia, who now runs a high-class bar; Harold's pal from college, who is now an ex-alcoholic with a heart condition and information with which he intends to blackmail Harold; and a mysterious woman who spends most of the play quietly reading the Sunday *New York Times* in the anteroom, waiting her turn to see Harold. Gradually Harold becomes involved in a complex web of his own weaving, mostly out of events that took place ten years earlier. Before it is all over, Harold is blackmailed, he agrees to sell his wife to the rich socialite, and he finally meets with the mysterious woman, who eventually shoots him, before she is shot by the police. Tenny, the rich socialite who wants to marry Helen, ends up in the last scene ready to marry Harold's old girl friend.

When Cain finished rewriting it in 1955, the first thing he wanted to do was show it to Samson Raphaelson, so he accepted a long-standing invitation to visit the Raphaelsons in their Bucks County, Pennsylvania, home. Another purpose of the trip, at least as far as Raphaelson was concerned, was to make portrait photographs of both Cain and Florence—though Florence was not able to go along. Raphaelson had gone "camera mad," as he wrote Cain, and no nonsense—five cameras, a dozen lenses, a darkroom. He had even given up writing for five years while he indulged his passion. "Cain arrived," as Raphaelson later described the visit, "and we sat up half the night and had one of our violent discussions, agreeing on very little, enjoying it enormously. The next morning, after breakfast, while he was sitting on the terrace, I drifted out with the camera. He knew about me and my photography, but he had hardly glanced at the framed photographs in every room, including kitchen and bathrooms; and now on the terrace he told me he had been deeply worried, that he was afraid I had abandoned writing. I told him I was head over heels in a new play, and this cheered him up. Still, he didn't like that camera in my hand. I'm sure he was thinking, 'I don't trust you anymore, not with that maniac look on your face when you hold a camera.' "

Later Raphaelson sent him a print and Cain responded: "I guess it must be good, as I keep studying it, seeing a total stranger and trying to fathom what I think of him. The sloppy shave I guess came from using an unfamiliar mirror, plus we can assume lack of character to some extent. The rest of it utterly baffles me. Just why, on your terrace, at that hour of day, I had such a strained expression, I don't know, but at least it does seem concentrated."

One reason Cain may have thought he had such a strained expression was that Raphaelson thought *The Guest in 701* was a bad play. "I had to tell that to Jamie," he said, years later, "not in those words, but where it wouldn't work, where it was way off. Jamie wasn't a playwright, and he wanted to be one." Cain was stagestruck, said Raphaelson, understandable because he wrote such superb dialogue in his books. But "structurally, he didn't know how to get into a play. If only he had taken a course at any reputable school where fundamentals of dramatic structure were discussed, he would have learned all he needed to know. But he would not do it. And I could not bring myself to tell him the A, B, Cs—he was the last man in the world you could do that with."

Raphaelson's criticism of *The Guest in 701* did not discourage Cain, who continued, off and on all during 1955, and the next two years, trying to persuade producers to take an interest in it. At one point the Theatre Guild and various independent teams, including Robert Joseph and Jay Julien, and Oscar Lerman and Martin Cohen, appeared ready to produce it, and Cain earned a little over $1,000 in option money. He rewrote the play several times and continually sought advice and suggestions as to what might be wrong with it. The best critique came from H. N. Swanson, who felt that the focus, right at the beginning, should be on Tenny, who ends up the closest thing to a hero the play has—"a great big friendly dog looking for someone to rub up against," said Swanson. He considered Tenny a kind of Jay Gatsby— very rich and in love with another man's wife—and recommended that Cain go back and reread Fitzgerald's novel. *The Guest in Room 701*, however, was never produced, taking its place in Cain's papers along with *7-11*, *Give Me One More Day*, and other unproduced plays as testimony to his continuing frustration as a playwright.

Cain may have felt he could afford the luxury of writing a play on speculation because of a temporary improvement in his financial situation. His income in 1955 was over $21,000, more than in any year since he had come East, due primarily to the sales of *Galatea* to paperback and *Love's Lovely Counterfeit* to the movies. The 1942 novel about corruption in a Midwestern city was given a new title, *Slightly Scarlet*, and adapted for the screen by Robert Blees (*Magnificent Obsession*). Barbara Stanwyck was originally scheduled to star in the film, but at the last minute she backed out. John Payne, Arlene Dahl, and Rhonda Fleming were eventually cast in the lead roles. And it was just as well Miss Stanwyck withdrew because it was possibly the worst movie ever made from a Cain story. Bosley Crowther, in the

New York Times, called it "an exhausting lot of twaddle about crime and city politics, an honest mayor, his secretary-mistress, her kleptomaniac sister and the fellow who wants to get control of the gang." But he took Cain off the hook by saying that any relationship between *Love's Lovely Counterfeit* and *Slightly Scarlet* was "unrecognizable."

Even more unrecognizable was the relationship between what was finally released in 1956 as the movie version of *Serenade* and the novel Cain wrote in 1937. Cain had always maintained that *Serenade* was almost impossible to produce as either a movie or a stage play, although he had been happy to accept the $35,000 Warner Brothers paid for it after *Double Indemnity* demonstrated that Cain's toughest stories could be filmed. And all during the fifties, his agent was still dickering with various people associated with Leonard Bernstein about some kind of Broadway production of the novel. When Warner Brothers bought it, Cain suggested to Jerry Wald how it might be dressed up for the studio, which was primarily interested in the singing and the Mexican background: "Why don't you switch it from a *man* wrecking this man's life to a woman wrecking his life—because he has a weakness for liquor which she disregards because she is ruthless." Liking Cain's approach, Wald went on from there, but it was years before the film would be brought into the theaters. At first there was thought of casting Ann Sheridan in the role of the Mexican who befriends the opera singer, but Cain argued that although Sheridan could speak Spanish, she had no accent, and that would just manufacture trouble. "Get a girl who speaks with an accent naturally," he told Wald, "and your scriptwriters won't have to break their back establishing the character." Cain thought Maria Montez would be right for the part, but they tested her and found, to nobody's surprise, that she could not handle the acting. "All her dialogue had to be written in baby talk," said Cain, recalling his experience with *Gypsy Wildcat*. Then Wald left Warner Brothers, and as late as 1953 a studio executive was writing Cain saying they were thinking of Katy Jurado, who had just created a sensation in *High Noon*, and pleading with him to read the script to see "where the boys went wrong." He promised to read Cain's answering memo, "even if it is over 100 words."

There is no record of Cain's response, but the script problems were evidently resolved, for Cain began to hear that the movie was being shot, much of it in Mexico, although the churches were being used primarily for praying and marriage, rather than candlelight meals of iguana soup and lovemaking by the altar. And it was apparent the studio had stuck to Cain's original idea of making alcohol and women the singer's basic hang-up, rather than homosexuality. Now the problem was Joan Fontaine, playing a rich society woman who sponsors the opera singer, but then loses interest, turns to other men, and leaves him to his bottle and a Mexican enchantress, played by Sarita Montiel (who had just finished a starring role in *Vera Cruz*). For the opera singer, the obvious choice was Mario Lanza, now on the downside of his meteoric Hollywood career. Like Cain, Lanza had had an eating, drinking, and weight problem. He had not appeared in a movie since *Because You're Mine* in 1952, and it was thought by some that the obvious similarity between his attempted comeback and the comeback of the singer in *Serenade* would make the movie a natural for promotion. But the coincidence did not help. The only things that saved *Serenade* from being a total disaster were Lanza's singing of at least fifteen operatic arias and Vincent Price, who gave a good performance as Lanza's manager. The reviews were fair, acknowledging Lanza's singing and the difficulty the writers and director—Ivan Goff, Ben Roberts, John Twist, and Anthony Mann—had translating the story from the world of James M. Cain to Hollywoodland.

Cain never did see *Serenade* on the screen. Years later, when it was on television, he watched fifteen minutes of it and then asked Florence if she objected to his turning off this "ghastly thing." But Cain's final attitude toward what Hollywood had done to his novel was typical of his views on the relationship between literature and the movies: "They're entitled to do whatever they want," he said, "because they paid me the money."

Bad as they were, both *Serenade* and *Slightly Scarlet* did all right at the box office. But the money they made the studios did not help Cain, because there were no royalties for him over the original purchase prices. And after his reasonably good year in 1955, things were again looking bleak: In 1956, his total income was a little over $6,000, and the following year, it dropped to under $3,000.

His friends were also decreasing. Henry Mencken died in 1956, and the loss was a heavy blow. The funeral was unceremonious and Spartan, following Mencken's wishes that only a few old friends should be present to see him off on his last journey. Cain's reaction to the starkness of the occasion was summed up in a letter to Arthur Krock: "He could have remembered, I thought, that though he disbelieved he was entering the next world, he was at least taking leave of this one, and permitted some sort of rites that would have served as a memorial to what he did, which was considerable. Somehow, we were made to subserve a gag, and the effect wasn't so much bleak as blank. The minute of silence didn't quite say it."

After the funeral, Frank Kent took Cain, Hamilton Owens, and Alfred Knopf over to Marconi's, and they all sat around reminiscing, with everyone talking so much, Cain recalled, he could hardly get a word in. He did remember one stray bit from the conversations: Kent's remarking about having seen Swope recently, and how the red had gone out of his hair and he didn't "asservate all over the conversation" the way he used to. Cain thought this was the most perfect characterization in five words he had ever heard.

By the mid-1950s, Cain had drifted into a period of depression and relative inactivity. But it was not a "midlife crisis" in the conventional sense—at least, not as Cain saw it. "Those middle-age crises," he said in his eighties, "generally boil down to a girl with pretty legs that a guy wants to shack up with, and his wife decides that he's having a menopause of his own. I'd say these crises are overpsychologized." Not only was Cain showing no interest in shacking up with young girls, but he and Florence rarely even went out of their little house or had people in. When friends came to town, Cain would meet some for lunch, but others would be put off with polite letters saying Florence's health did not permit *any* kind of excitement or activity. His other work was also suffering. He was invited by Carey McWilliams to contribute to *The Nation*, but declined, saying he thought "my slant these days would not exactly be the magazine's." He was keeping in touch with Katharine White at *The New Yorker*, but there was no talk of Cain's contributing. She did ask him for a recommendation for a new fiction editor, but he replied: "I have no one to nominate for obstetrician, nurse, teacher, dress designer and speech coach to *New Yorker* fiction writers—and only one person that I know of has ever filled that job. I give you one guess who she is."

He was also taking little interest in politics, although he did write to the *Washington Post*, taking it to task for treating Harold Stassen contemptuously in his effort to knock Vice President Richard Nixon off the ticket. Cain pointed out that when Eisenhower won, which was most likely, the certain presidential candidate in 1960 would be Richard Nixon, unless someone did something to stop him—and even Harold Stassen was preferable to Richard Nixon as the 1960 Republican nominee.

Despite his troubles at the typewriter, Cain was still trying to bring in some money with his writing, though with little success. He wrote one short story ("Death on the Beach") for *Jack London's Adventure Magazine*, but received only $200 for it. This did not concern him, for as he pointed out to Ober, stories like Hemingway's "Fifty Grand," and his own "Pastorale" and "Dead Man," often went on bringing in money for years, and "perhaps this is no masterpiece but we'll see what we see." He was half right. "Death on the Beach" was no masterpiece and, as far as I could find, was never reprinted. For that matter, it is impossible to find a copy of *Jack London's Adventure Magazine*, even in the Library of Congress.

Cain had also been doing quite a bit of book reviewing. He reviewed several novels, despite the fact that he looked down on fiction reviewers and generally did not trust his own critical judgment in fiction, always maintaining that he did not read contemporary authors because "I might like one of them too well and start copy-catting." But this was something of a pose because, judging from his correspondence and interviews, he apparently read widely in contemporary fiction and had strong opinions about some contemporary books and authors. *Lolita* was "a true masterpiece of closely observed character, smart plotting to deliver the point and simple, unliterary writing." Hemingway's *A Farewell to Arms* he thought "very fine," and his short story "The Killers" was a "very craggy thing . . . that sticks with you." In fact he thought Hemingway was a "Matterhorn of literature," though he was annoyed at his "total disregard for boatsmanship" in *The Old Man and the Sea*, which he believed Hemingway had written for boys without realizing it. Gore Vidal's *Burr* put him under a spell, and he wrote Vidal that "after your reappraisal of figures like Washington, Jefferson and Hamilton, American biography can hardly be the same any more." Norman Mailer he thought pretty good, "but I wish he'd take a walk around the block and get rid of the smell of the privy that's on him." Truman Capote: "I like that guy, but I don't want to write like him." He liked Rex Stout and called Nero Wolfe "a masterful creation"; but he would not read Dashiell Hammett or Raymond Chandler.

When he did not like a novel, Cain would not hesitate to act like a literary critic, despite all the suffering he had experienced in the hands of those "strange surrogates of God." He said *We Fished All Night* by Willard Motley (who had also written *Knock on Any Door*) was "one of the most tormentingly bad books I have any memory of," although he acknowledged Motley was a talented writer, even as he wished he would try to "emulate Flaubert a little more and Farrell less." He did not have much good to say about Graham Greene's *Our Man in Havana*, which he found confusing, or Eric Ambler's *Passage of Arms*. Greene and Ambler were clearly not his kind of writers; and of *Passage of Arms*, he said, "I found myself wishing, I confess, that someone, somewhere in this book would find a girl to seduce." On the other hand, the kind of sex that dominated Gerald Walker's *Cruising*—the story of a psychopathic homosexual killer cruising around looking for pickups—repulsed him. He said he came from Annapolis, "where we can cuss in meter," so he was not offended by strong language; but the kind of "small, slimy words in this book [were] aesthetically offensive." He also reviewed Budd Schulberg's novel about Scott Fitzgerald, *The Disenchanted*, which he thought a better novel than any Fitzgerald ever wrote. He had to revise the review at Francis Brown's request, for being too rough on Fitzgerald—as it was, he said it was questionable whether Fitzgerald was "the sweet prince of narrative prose"; Schulberg's hero seemed to think he was, and it was a point many (especially Cain) took exception to, "particularly on the score of workmanship." Cain always felt that Fitzgerald did not rewrite enough and that

"*Gatsby* could have been a great book," as he wrote Brown, "and it wasn't, through sheer sloth."

Cain was much more comfortable reviewing nonfiction. He praised *The Mystery of Marie La Farge*, a book by Edith Saunders about a nineteenth-century Frenchwoman who could have been a model for many heroines in nineteenth-century French fiction, so similar was her life to that of Madame Bovary and other French fictional heroines. He was less impressed with Charles Angoff's *H. L. Mencken*, saying that although he acknowledged the accuracy of much of what Angoff had to say, he wished he had "started out with a ten-inch block of marble instead of a one-gallon bucket of clay. Allowing for all verisimilitude, I remember Mencken bigger than this, and finer and sensibler."

All in all, although Cain reviewed books for several years, he was not very good at it, and he conceded more than once that "reviewing is not my racket." Apparently Francis Brown, editor of the *New York Times Book Review*, agreed, because he stopped sending him books, by which act Cain later claimed Brown "fired" him. At the root of the problem, according to Cain, was the fact that he still could not write well when he had to be himself—and book reviews had to express the personal opinion of the reviewer. Cain still had to pretend to be someone else.

When Knopf rejected *Mignon* in 1957, Cain was sixty-six. He had been trying to develop a book out of the Red River campaign for nearly ten years. He had not worked steadily, of course, having been idled or sidetracked for long spells by periods of declining health, by having to nurse Florence, and by other projects which he felt would bring in some quick money. And, as each year dragged on, his problems grew worse. There was now little chance that Florence would ever recover her health; the most Cain could hope for was to prolong her life, and the couple became more and more reclusive. Then, in 1957, Florence suffered a dislocated shoulder, which gave her considerable pain and made it impossible for her to dress. Cain's income also continued its steady decline; 1958 was the second straight year in which he earned less than $3,000, although he now had an income of approximately $5,000 from the government, a combination of social security and military pension for being "a hero in World War I," as he put it. The Cains did look at some property on the South River ("a most enchanting spot," Cain wrote a friend), and in 1958 they seriously discussed buying their rented house, on which they were paying $165 a month. But Cain's ability to buy was based on anticipation of big money coming in from a possible *Mildred Pierce* television series, which failed to materialize—so that idea had to be abandoned, at least for a while.

Of the many problems slowly pressing in on him, the deaths of his mother at the age of ninety-five and of two sisters, Virginia and Genevieve, in 1958, hit him the hardest. They came within six months of each other and, combined with his own failing health and Florence's invalidism, made working impossible. His only living relative now was Rosalie, and he had very few old friends left. He did renew his friendship with Walter Lippmann in 1958, with a visit to the columnist's home on Woodley Road in Washington, but by now the two lived in such different worlds, and Cain was so restricted by having to care for Florence, that any close relationship was impossible.

And as if things were not going badly enough, their little cat Nickie died in 1958. Like so many childless couples, the Cains had become overly attached to their pet, as revealed in this description of one gloomy Christmas: "We did nothing about it at all except to light our little tree, hold hands and watch the wonder of our little cat, who would creep up on it, stare, and begin to touch the ornaments with his paw. When it would fall down on the rug, he would edge up to it warily, then begin popping it with his paw and then of course it would disappear into a little pile of tinsel, and this he couldn't understand. Florence, delighted in his bewilderment, felt Christmas to be a birth, a reawakening of all created things, including the animals that gave up their manger, even little cats."

Nickie was buried in the Bonheur Memorial Park in Elkridge, Maryland, and Cain wrote the park's manager: "From you, I needn't conceal this was a bereavement that wrenched us both in the deepest part of our nature, and we are not over it, not by any means." They eventually replaced Nickie with another cat—and Florence still had "Mr. Cardinal and Mrs. Cardinal," two little birds she fed regularly in her backyard.

There was, however, one encouraging development. In the spring of 1959, Cain discovered what had been making him feel so rotten and, perhaps, write so poorly. He read an article in *Newsweek* about cholesterol, which sent him to his doctor, who put him on a no-eggs, no-butter, no-fatty-foods diet that stressed corn oil margarine—"a therapeutic agent," as Cain put it. It cured him, in forty-eight hours—and he immediately started writing everyone from Alfred Knopf to Bob Rathbone about how great he felt and how easy the writing was coming to him with his new diet.

But he still could not hide the fact that he was growing old. Ruth Goetz had not seen Cain since he left Hollywood, and one day, about this time, she came down to Washington and had lunch with him at Harvey's—and was shocked. "My God, he has aged so terribly," she thought to herself. KTLA, a Hollywood radio station, wrote requesting an interview for a program it was developing called "Living Legends." And Walter Lippmann was celebrating his seventieth birthday, for which occasion a book was being planned by Marquis Childs and James Reston. Cain had lunch with Childs to talk about the old days on the *World*, and when the commemorative book—*Walter Lippmann and His Times*—was published, Childs said in the introduction that the *World* and its staff set the pace for the New York and America of the twenties. "The *World*," he wrote, "was a constellation of men, witty, brilliant, sometimes even searching and profound. Their names, Rollin Kirby, Heywood Broun, Arthur Krock, James M. Cain, Franklin P. Adams, and many others, evoke a time that today seems more distant than the Stone Age."

Cain may have begun to feel like he was from another age, but it was not the Stone Age. The Civil War had become his era, his albatross, and with his new diet making him feel better and his mind functioning more clearly, he set out once again to rewrite *Mignon*. And he had a special incentive: Jerry Wald, now head of his own Company of Artists, affiliated with 20th Century-Fox, had written him asking if he was working on a new book and, if so, requesting to see it. "Since I am a charter member of the James M. Cain Fan Club," he wrote, "I am more than interested in anything you are doing or contemplating doing." He went on to write of having worked with MacKinlay Kantor on *Andersonville* and Grace Metalious on *Peyton Place*, glowingly accounting how he had helped Metalious get $265,000 for the reprint rights to her *The Return to Peyton Place*. "As far as I am concerned," he wrote, "James M. Cain means far more than Metalious and is far more worthwhile merchandising to the world audience."

In many ways, Cain still did live in the Stone Age of publishing, and Wald's letter, putting him in touch with the new world of movie-book hype, must have been a tonic. So Cain replied that he was a "charter member of the Jerry Wald fan club" and that his letter had arrived just as he was making a double breakthrough—on his health and on his novel. "And so you know what we're talking about," he wrote Wald, "this is a Civil War story, Louisiana in 1864, and deals with the cotton intrigue there, the $50,000 racket that men lost their lives for—with plenty of color, music, dancing and, of course, sex. I think it better that nothing is done in the way of promotion until we have a script, but that won't be too long now, as a great deal is on paper. By 'script,' I mean the script of a novel. This is not a movie 'original,' one of those things in a blue cover about a Clark Gable 'type.' "

He promised Wald he would have a completed novel by the end of August, but once again *Mignon* defied him. Most of 1959 and 1960 were spent trying to get her to resubmit to being put down on paper, and now he became totally obsessed with this "endless period book," as he wrote more than one friend, this "pot at the end of the rainbow" that prevented him from even thinking about anything else.

Finally, near the end of 1960, after two years of incomes around

$2,000, he finished *Mignon*, only to receive another crushing disappoint-
ment: Knopf turned it down again! But this time, Cain did not agree with his
publisher. Instead of starting another rewrite, he told his agent to look for a
new publisher. "There is no pretending that any rejection is good," he wrote
Ivan von Auw, who was now handling Cain's affairs after the death of Harold
Ober in 1959, "but in this case it may not mean as much as it might from
somebody else. He [Knopf] has had from the beginning some notion that the
Red River expedition was just a 'small backwater' of the Civil War, as he
called it—though what that has to do with a novel I don't exactly see. Also, I
have yet to hear from him any expression of enthusiasm for a book of mine
[this was not true; Knopf thought *Serenade* was a masterpiece, and praised
other Cain novels] and this faint-heartedness has been reflected pretty much
in his advertising, or lack of it. Also he turned down my first novel, *The
Postman Always Rings Twice*, until Walter Lippmann stuffed it down his
throat, but it led the best-seller lists in 1934, and has sold steadily since in
reprint as well as translation. So he could be wrong, and if he's the wrong
publisher for me, we're not worse off to know it."

Obviously Cain was deeply hurt by Knopf's rejection. But von Auw,
too, had some reservations about *Mignon*, and made some suggestions for
changes—the most helpful, Cain said, he had ever had from an agent. Cain
incorporated them and did some "tinkering" of his own, which took him well
into March 1961. He changed the ending, which was originally set in Annapolis, and eliminated much of the legal ramifications of the cotton trade—all
of which made the book shorter and, he felt, gave it much more drive. The
changes were so extensive that he thought it worthwhile to let Knopf see it
again, but the publisher's feelings were unchanged. As Cain wrote von Auw:
"*Mignon*, apparently, is no such winner as I had hoped . . . it got no better
reception than the version I sent you earlier. All I can say is, if you can get a
buyer, I shall be most grateful. I would hate to confess how much time, labor
and money it represents, and something to show for it would be a help, psychologically. I have a horror of abandoning something after getting so deep
into it."

Von Auw did finally find a buyer—Richard Baron at Dial liked *Mignon*
and agreed to publish it, providing Cain would make some changes to be
suggested by Jim Silberman, Dial's editor in chief. Cain agreed, but then,
hearing nothing from Silberman for weeks, he went into a period of nervous
nail-biting. "What I fear," he told von Auw, "is that he'll send me one of
those memos of 22 pages, with 379 objections to the script as it stands, the
way Katharine White used to deal with writers of Profiles for *The New Yorker*.
But I don't think *Mignon* can be revised on that basis. I think, as you wrote,
that its trouble is not in detail, but in shaping to give it point."

When Silberman finally did come through in July with his suggestions, Cain was impressed; he thought they were "shrewd, sensible and helpful in every way . . . [and] on an intellectual level that commands respect."

He told Silberman that most of his suggestions paralleled his own feelings about the novel. But it was December before he finished what turned out to be "practically a new book." Now, however, he thought it so much better there was no comparison. He also planned another preface, this devoted primarily to a little background on the Red River expedition and his exhaustive research, an idea he eventually abandoned. His main problem was still the same one he had had with *Postman*, *Serenade*, and *Past All Dishonor*: the ending. "The heroine has to die," he said, "but I can't bear to kill her, and so I come up with a far-fetched finish that makes no sense. You'd think she was really alive instead of something out of my head." But he knew the ending— especially a Cain ending—had to have a special impact. He wrote Silberman, recalling his paperback novel *Sinful Woman*, which always, year in and year out, outsold his other two paperback originals two to one. He had become curious why this was so and on rereading the book had found out: "Right at the end, forgotten by me, came a smashing emotional surprise. It explained everything and impressed endings on my mind."

Cain was still anticipating big things from *Mignon*, writing people that he had finished something that would mean "considerable income." His need was greater than ever. In 1961, his earnings consisted mostly of the $1,000 advance Dial had given him for *Mignon* and $700 from *Esquire* for a short story, "The Visitor." *Mignon* was going to put him on "sugar hill," as he called the big money.

Mignon was finally published in the spring of 1962, and if it had been just another novel, it would have been considered a success. It eventually sold 15,000 hard-cover copies, and Dial sold the reprint rights to Dell for $15,000, half of which went to Cain. But *Mignon* was not just another novel. It had been written and researched over a period of twelve years, with Cain hoping to produce another *Gone With the Wind*—not in form, but in commercial success. It was also his only major work since leaving Hollywood to "go back to novels and amount to something." *Galatea* had been a quickie, written to make money, but *Mignon* was a major work. Yet not only was it a literary failure, Jerry Wald, still a charter member of the Cain fan club, did not feel that *Mignon* had movie potential, and Swanson was never able to sell it to a studio. All in all, the failure of *Mignon* was perhaps the low point of Cain's life.

Actually, the reviews were mixed: Quite a few praised the book, agreeing with the *Chicago Tribune* that the special Cain approach could be translated to a historical novel: "It would be difficult to imagine a writer further removed than James M. Cain from the usual civil war fictioneer," said H. T. Kane in the *Tribune*, "nevertheless, Cain has carried off his subject quite well. As might be expected, his narrative has a swifter pace than many others, Confederate, Union or otherwise. . . . Cain gives us a highly colored, sharply focused, sometimes complex narrative."

Others thought it was too highly colored and complex, and many agreed with Martin Lewis in the *Times*, who said he preferred Cain in modern dress. Still others were cruel and must have cut the heart of a sixty-nine-year-old writer who had spent twelve years researching and writing a book he hoped would revive not only his bank account but his reputation. Cain's hometown *Baltimore Sun* said it was "hard to imagine what Cain had in mind with this mishmash of goings on in the Red River section of Louisiana during the civil war" and that the book was "too confusing for mindless entertainment and anachronistic and sketchy as to background for enlightenment." As for his research, *Library* magazine called Cain's attempt to re-create the Civil War "inept" and "ludicrous" and said it was "not even for libraries that buy everything."

These indictments may have been too harsh, but *Mignon* is clearly a confused novel, especially considering the research and rewriting that went into it. Cain read over four hundred books about the Civil War and countless documents, in addition to traveling over much of the ground on which the battles were fought and his plot unfolded. The story itself was solid enough and could have been made into a good movie: a beautiful Southern spitfire, widowed by the war, meets a dashing Union lieutenant, who has been discharged from the Army after being wounded and is in New Orleans to set up a construction business. He falls in love with her, gets her father out of jail, saves her from the clutches of her father's evil business partner, and eventually becomes involved with both of them in a complex scheme to sell "hoodooed" cotton to the North, a scheme frustrated by the fortunes of war. The story ends with an emotional punch, characteristic of Cain's best novels.

But *Mignon* does not come off, for any number of reasons. For one thing, despite all the research, what the reader learns about the Red River campaign is very sketchy. Everything in the book is authentic, but Cain's story, told by Bill Cresap, the Union lieutenant, moves along too fast for the reader to pick up much background and atmosphere about the war. The story is sometimes confusing and difficult to follow—possibly because of the over-tautness of Cain's prose, especially the dialogue—and the ending, despite its impact, is gimmicky, which serves to make the story seem pointless.

The book's failure puzzled Cain. "*Mignon*, I one hundred per cent don't understand," he wrote Virginia Riffaterre at Dial. He knew he should have realized that a book that had resisted writing so much must have had something terribly wrong with it—but what? At one point, in the middle of the night, he felt he had the answer: "This girl [Mignon] hit on a scheme to get rich and failed. That I think is what made it pointless." But a year later, he was writing Stallings that although *Mignon* had laid an egg, "when I re-read it, I can't see why—to me it seems all right. Why this astigmatism?"

He never did have the answer—but he knew the book had hurt his already sagging reputation. And amortized over twelve years, its modest financial success had to be counted a disaster. "It was just 'a lotta goddamn research,' " Cain said; and, ironically, most of that research was never used in the book—at 246 pages, slim for a historical novel. The success of *Past All Dishonor*, which had the highest sales of any of his hard-cover books, had led him into thinking he could write period books—probably the most serious miscalculation of his career. *Past All Dishonor* was published in 1946— at the height of his fame as a Hollywood writer, a fame resting primarily on the back-to-back releases of three big movies, all contemporary stories that were also best sellers. It is more than likely that most of the 55,000 hard-cover copies of *Past All Dishonor* were bought because James M. Cain's name was on the cover and not because of his ability to write a period novel. In fact, it is quite possible that many readers were disappointed that *Past All Dishonor* was not a typical Cain story set in present-day California; certainly some of the reviewers were. Yet Cain, even in the postwar period, was still looking for subjects outside the contemporary scene, and he interpreted the success of *Past All Dishonor* as confirmation of his ability to write historical fiction—a conviction he held right up to the publication of *Mignon*. And he knew it had to be written, like so many other novels. "They are like children," he wrote a friend. "Though runty, ill-favored and weak, they have to be born, and then you get perfectly furious, as all parents do, when the world doesn't see them as beautiful."

Nobody but James M. Cain ever saw *Mignon* as beautiful—and eventually he came to have his own doubts. "All that reading and labor," he told Luther Nichols in a *New York Times* interview when *Mignon* was published, "and a kind of mouse is born."

20

TWILIGHT TIME

By 1962, when *Mignon* was published, Cain and Florence had settled into domestic seclusion in their little Hyattsville home. Cain's long periods of poor health, their lack of money, and Florence's virtual invalidism all contributed to a desire to cut themselves off and "live within these four walls," as Florence put it. The previous year had been another bad one financially, with Cain's professional income amounting to just over $2,000. And his mobility was restricted even more when he had his second automobile accident in twelve months. He figured his car was costing him approximately $250 a year, during which he drove only 250 miles. "You're not only paying a dollar a mile," Florence said, "your accident rate is around one every hundred miles—a little too high for comfort. You can get rid of that car or me." So Cain sold what was left of his Packard for $35 and the rest of his life traveled by taxi or was chauffeured by friends.

Although the couple socialized very little, they had established friendly relations with their neighbors in University Park. On one side, when they first moved in, were Carroll and Frances Lewis, both from the South. The Lewises were particularly fond of Florence, "a charming woman." They thought Cain a little eccentric and blustery, and he did not always get along with Carroll Lewis, who was a construction contractor. They had one especially stormy argument about a drainage ditch in their adjoining backyards—but then Cain sent Lewis a Stetson hat to apologize for his behavior.

On the other side, at first, were a naval officer and his two sons, of whom they did not see very much. Then a large, likable family with eleven children—the Kisielnickis—moved in, and they and the Cains became fast friends, with several Kisielnicki children doing odd jobs for Cain over the years. Ted Kisielnicki, a government laboratory technician, and Cain got along fine, and Cain especially liked Mrs. Kisielnicki, whom he described as "a very pretty lady, who takes a lot of pride in the ease with which she pops one [child] out every two years"—a facility that reminded him of his mother.

Obviously, University Park was a new world for Cain, altogether different from Hollywood Hills, where his neighbors had included Bela Lugosi, Marie Wilson, Lawrence Tibbett, several other writers, and the composer George Antheil (who was forgiven his musical deficiencies, in Cain's estimation, when one day he rushed from his house in his underwear to save a young girl from being washed down a storm sewer in a flash flood—a story Cain told many times over the years). But Cain enjoyed his new environment, and people who knew him at the time recall him as a very likable man, though sometimes gruff and abrupt, who refused the celebrity status some of the local people wanted to confer on him. William Reading, who worked in the Suburban Trust Company and eventually became Cain's banker, always looked up to Cain as a very successful author. He called him "Mr. Cain," until Cain insisted, "Don't call me Mr. Cain—you call me Jim." He often took Reading to lunch, especially after a much-publicized robbery of the bank, and quizzed him about the details of the banking business—no doubt during the period when he was trying to develop one of his TV programs (never produced) about an insurance investigator.

Florence, by all accounts, was not an easy person to know or get along with. She could be very standoffish and did not like to converse, except with people who would let her talk about the things she wanted to talk about—mostly animals and her childhood, never her opera career. Cain did not try to force a social life on her, although he'd had a quiet social life with friends in Hollywood. Consequently, and with no children (because of her accident, Florence always insisted, not because she had not wanted them), they drifted into a lonely life. She was devoted to their pets, and after Nicki died, they bought a new cat, Mittens, to keep them company. There was also television. "It used to be that all we knew was what we read in the papers; but now it's what we see on TV," Cain said. In addition to the news, they watched musical programs and series—"Dr. Kildare" and "Peyton Place"—partly because Cain was hoping that someday he might still develop a TV series of his own and partly to see old Hollywood friends, such as Robert Sinclair's wife

Heather Angel, on the tube. Cain also produced perhaps the rarest fan letters in the history of television, complimenting the singers of singing commercials when he and Florence felt they were good. He would write the company to find out, for example, the name of the girl who sang the Valley Forge Beer commercial—"Buy it by the Bottle or Buy it by the Can"—and when he learned it was a Miss Rose Marie Jun, who had once sung with the Rome Opera Company, he wrote her a fan letter and followed her career for years.

They began to move out of their enforced seclusion a little after the publication of *Mignon*—partly because they were both feeling a little better and partly because Cain had to make a few appearances to promote the novel. He was interviewed by various radio and TV stations as well as newspapers and magazines, and one interview—for *Newsweek*—proved an embarrassment for him. The reporter, Cain later had to explain to his sister, spoke with a thick Slavic accent and did not seem to understand English. And "he was obsessed," Cain said, "by his instructions from New York, which were obviously to smoke me out and get me to own up I'd been on a ten-year drunk." In trying to explain the real reason for his literary silence, Cain blamed his illness, caused by too much cholesterol, and admitted he was frightened. "My father died a blithering idiot and for a time I thought the same thing was happening to me," Cain told the reporter, who used the quote in *Newsweek*. "Blithering idiot" was not exactly the way he wanted his father remembered, and from then on he was wary of interviews.

He was feeling well enough now to accept a citation from a college—but not Washington College, where he continued to decline all efforts by the president either to give him an award or to persuade him to speak. But Cain did accept a "Distinguished Service Award" from the University of Maryland in 1963, buoyed by the effects of his noncholesterol diet, which he considered miraculous. Commiserating with Katharine White about her own illness, Cain said he "was getting more brains" than he had had in a long time and, as a result, his "writing seems to be coming to life all over again."

With his old brains at the typewriter and even before *Mignon* was published, he was hard at work on another book. By the middle of 1962 he had more than a hundred pages completed of a story about a woman—the buyer for a big Maryland department store—"who attempts through her daughter to gain the place in the sun she herself has never attained to." Obviously, the character was not unlike Mildred Pierce, and consequently he considered it almost clairvoyant when he received a long letter from Jerry Wald, who by now had turned down *Mignon*. "The other night," he wrote Cain, "while Joan Crawford and I were having dinner, we got to talking about 'Mildred Pierce' and our line of conversation finally drifted around to the source of the novel. I told Joan I'd write you and see whether we couldn't get you started thinking

about a woman's story—a contemporary one—in the same vein. We naturally do not want to do a repeat of that story, but I have been thinking of the
possibility of doing a story about a woman who runs a big department store in
New York, who has a family, a husband and a daughter, who, because she
devotes so much time to her job, are neglected until the daughter finds herself in a terrible crisis."

Wald went on for four single-spaced pages, outlining the plot and elabo-
rating on what he thought was wrong with the movies in 1962, one fault being
"the failure of many writers to create characters who can make a valid claim
on the intellect." The reason for the success of *Mildred Pierce*, Wald
thought, was that "she presented a full-blooded human being with passionate
convictions and strong feelings."

Cain was excited after the letter and put it aside until he could come up
with something that would clinch Wald's interest in the new novel. Then, the
next day, when he opened the paper, he was stunned to read that Wald had
died. Cain immediately wrote Joan Crawford, telling her about Wald's clair-
voyance and the novel he was working on, which included a woman who
worked for a big department store, "an ominous creature." He concluded by
saying that Miss Crawford occupied a special place in his life and, more dis-
ingenuously, "the last time I saw my favorite picture, it seemed as exciting as
ever."

Miss Crawford replied ("James Dear"), agreeing they both suffered a
great loss with Wald's death, that the "ominous creature" sounded wonderful, and that she would be delighted to read the new novel. She had just
finished filming *The Caretakers*, with Robert Stack, and was about to start on
Whatever Happened to Baby Jane?

Mignon, despite its rejection by the critics, was doing reasonably well
in the bookstores. But Dial, adhering to tradition, was reluctant to pay Cain
any more money until the royalty statement was due, even though he was in
desperate straits. But finally the company gave him an additional advance
against royalties, and 1962 eventually turned out to be his best year since
1955, with earnings amounting to $12,000.

Two hundred dollars of that money was an option put up by producer
Ramon Gordon to dramatize *The Butterfly*, a story Cain was convinced could
never be made into a play or a movie. Curiously enough, he approved the
idea. He went to dinner with Gordon on one of his trips to New York and
thought him "well-bred, well-heeled and well-dressed, although he didn't
seem like a guy who could write a play." But Cain still agreed to let him go
ahead with it, and Gordon sent him a script which Cain felt was "utterly
naïve." Cain made some suggestions, which prompted Gordon to come to
Washington to see him. Now Cain was even less impressed. He was also

deep in his post-*Mignon* novel and "terrified" of Gordon and the thought of becoming involved in another play. So he refused to see the producer and then, characteristically, felt bad about it and asked von Auw to extend Gordon's option for another year, without charge, if requested. But nothing ever came of the project, which took its place alongside the many efforts by stage, radio, and TV producers in the 1950s and 1960s to dramatize Cain properties.

He did, however, become involved with Max Gissen, the editor for Time-Life books, in something of a literary tempest. It all started pleasantly enough with Gissen writing Cain to inquire whether he might be interested in doing a 2,000-word introduction to *The Treasure of Sierra Madre*, which Gissen planned to publish in the Time Reading Program. He was inspired to ask Cain because of *Serenade* and thought he would be just the man to introduce readers to this minor classic set in Mexico. He also thought Cain might know the novel's author, a very mysterious fellow who wrote under the pseudonym B. Traven.

Cain responded that *Treasure* was "indeed a dilly" that fascinated him and he would like to write an introduction. He did not know Traven, but in his usual investigative fashion set out to learn what he could about the man. Gissen's first approach was on May 7, 1963. A week or so later, he wrote Cain setting a June 5 deadline. Cain sent him his piece on May 27, then heard nothing from Gissen for a week, which led him to believe everything was fine. In truth, he had written one of his poorer nonfiction efforts, obviously rushed and containing some of his favorite colloquialisms. And although he did include quite a bit about Traven, he made it clear that all writers who conceal their identity "are a pain in the neck to me." Actually, he felt Traven was a "fourth-rate nitwit."

Gissen, however, thought Cain's piece was dreadful, although he did not say so in his first response, which he wrote Cain on June 3. Instead, he said it was "too casual for an introduction, a piece written almost on the run, 'I kid you not' and 'So you pays your money and takes your choice,' etc., give it the air of discussing a book that hardly matters, and I chose *Treasure* because I think it does matter." He also asked Cain if he would "care to have another go at it," and made a few suggestions for the rewrite. "All this is tiresome, I know, but if you do decide to tackle it again, I'd appreciate a word to that effect and an approximate date of arrival."

Cain, in fairness, had made it quite clear that *Treasure* mattered, but Gissen's response ruffled him. He refused to rewrite the piece, which is surprising because usually Cain responded to requests for rewrites, especially such a courteous one. It was too bad, because it probably could have been salvaged with a little work. Instead, Cain wrote Gissen that he must want something resembling a sales pitch, which he thought was not desirable. "Everywhere," he said, ". . . there is a rising clamor of protest against over-blurbing by publishers." And he concluded: "If you don't like it, you don't like it," but "I don't work for nothing. You owe me $500."

This really irritated Gissen, who replied that there was "no question here of a 'sales pitch.' Writers like Graham Greene, Justice Douglas, Lewis Mumford and Aldous Huxley do not write 'sales pitch' copy, and all of them have given me an introduction." Then he really unloaded on Cain: "What you have here is simply an astonishingly poor piece of copy, and if you do not wish to try to improve it, that is your decision. While no jury of writers and editors could be persuaded that one could 'owe' $500 for this kind of work, a check for that amount is being forwarded."

The gauntlet was down, and now Cain exploded, explaining that he had been primarily irked at Gissen's handling of the matter—i.e., waiting for a week on a piece that had a "hurry up" deadline and then declining Cain's suggestion that he call him if he wanted any rewriting, responding instead with a letter requesting a rewrite, but which did not say what it was Gissen objected to—a letter that was furthermore stiff in tone and made no allusion to payment. "That was coming a bit thick, considering you started it all, and as a matter of principle I stood on my rights and demanded payment." He concluded: "Now that self-respect has been satisfied, I hereby return the check . . . and trust that this will wind up a most unpleasant episode." But three days later, he had a change of heart and wrote Gissen with less passion, trying to explain his approach to such pieces, discussing other approaches to the introduction, and offering to revamp it. "Call me, I don't bite. My number is still Warfield 8-1963 and the cost will be less than $5, something Time can easily stand."

Obviously, a seventy-year-old writer who had once lived and worked in the same world as Gissen just wanted to make a connection and be treated like he was still part of it. But Gissen had had it and wrote back that there was no point starting over again. "What bothered me most was the writing itself, and I suppose that we'd get nowhere trying to negotiate it." But he offered to send the $500 check back to Cain.

Cain was hurt; Gissen had said, in effect, that the piece was hopeless because of the writing, and that is one thing you can't tell any professional writer—let alone James M. Cain. Cain came back saying he had written a number of prefaces for top publications and that having reread his piece, "I don't see that it differs one decimal point from the writing I've done before. And the simple explanation seems to be that through the motions of insisting

I take this money, you hope all the time and conduct yourself in such a fashion that I'll be so disgusted I'll decline. If so, your hopes are fulfilled, as I meant to do just that for precisely that reason."

When Gissen finally sent him the check, Cain returned it with a one-line letter: "Let's have an end to it."

It was a sadly revealing episode, probably indicating more than just an aging writer's pique at having a piece rejected or even his desire to be pampered a little. The truth is that Cain had not really had one piece of writing go well since *The Moth* in 1947—sixteen years of declining powers and unsatisfactory work. He thought he had regained his touch with the cholesterol discovery, but the Gissen rejection may well have provided the first realization that he had truly become the thing he feared most—an ex-writer.

If he was, he was an ex-writer who did not know how to stop writing. Every morning he was still pounding out five pages, his 1,200 words. But, as in 1937, he had a hard time focusing for long on any one project. By early 1963 he had put aside the novel he had started when Wald wrote him and, strangely enough—considering all the anguish *Mignon* had caused him, and the fact that he had sold off his 1,000-book Civil War library—was making another effort to get a novel out of the Texas-Mexico cotton trade during the Civil War, "an in-close, first-hand account of what it was like." He tried to build history around a man and a woman turned loose on the Desierto Muerto between Texas and Matamoros, Mexico, and having a dreadful time fighting the elements and cotton racketeers. He called it *The Pink Buttercup* after the little flowers in Texas, and spent months trying to make it come to life. "I started it," he wrote one of his research sources, "got around 250 pages, then rewrote, got the same distance again, and then rewrote it still again. It always broke in the same place, down toward the end, and, at last, it dawned on me that this was a very bad sign. Books should be building, at that point, if they are soundly imagined, and that this one should be feathering out thin at that point didn't look good." He also decided it was too much like *Mignon*, and finally gave up *The Pink Buttercup*, though he still thought he would come back to the Civil War someday.

He then turned back to his novel about the department store buyer whose daughter was unhappily married. But he was soon having trouble with this one, too, and was further upset when Jim Silberman suddenly left Dial in mid-1963 to work for Random House. Although Cain liked Richard Baron well enough and thought his wife and assistant, Virginia, one of the loveliest people he had ever met, Silberman, he felt, was one of the few people he could really talk to and, more important, one of the few who was willing to listen to him. But Dial had an option on his next book, which he intended to honor. Henry Robbins had replaced Silberman at Dial, and Cain was soon writing Robbins explaining why he had not delivered the novel he had promised. As with his best books in the past, the first draft of this new one was written in the first person, but then he happened to reread *Past All Dishonor*, *Postman*, and *Mildred Pierce*, and found that, oddly enough, the only one he enjoyed and took any satisfaction in was *Mildred Pierce*, written in the third person. "So I may be about to abandon the first-person style and am in the process of recasting this book in the third person," he told Robbins.

He called the new novel *The Magician's Wife*, and it was finally finished (in the third person) in November 1963. As soon as he had sent the manuscript to von Auw, he wrote Dorothy Olding in the same office about another idea for a period story. This one concerned the battle of New Orleans, the sesquicentennial of which would be celebrated in January 1965. He envisioned a tale of around 45,000 to 50,000 words, suited for magazine publication, growing out of a "little nugget" he had unearthed in reading about Andrew Jackson. As outlined to Ms. Olding, the plot revolved around a Mrs. Livingston, wife of a big New Orleans lawyer, who "compassionately took in a wounded British officer, and then the word got around that such a man in the house was indeed a prize, as he might be able to save the ladies . . . from the consequences if the British should gain the city—of the toast then being drunk: 'Beauty and Booty.' Then all of a sudden, every house in town wanted a wounded Britisher, and that's what my story's about. . . . The end of the book is the battle, a colorful thing, indeed, that lasted 20 minutes and cost 1,500 British lives."

Cain's letter was written with the hope of receiving encouragement, but instead he got back a large bucket of cold water. There was, Ms. Olding said, hardly any market for serials now, or historical fiction, and since most magazines were aimed at the young feminine reader, she wondered with whom, in Cain's story, the reader would identify. Cain at first accepted her opinion, but then changed his mind and decided to write his War of 1812 story anyway, calling it "Beauty, Booty, and Blood." When he sent it to Ms. Olding, she wrote back that there was no chance to sell it to a magazine and it would take a major rewrite to make a novel of it. Cain said he would do the rewrite, but he never did.

Meanwhile, he was "gnawing his fingernails" awaiting von Auw's reaction to *The Magician's Wife*, which he thought he had given his "best lick." But, on rereading his copy, he found it gave him "a bad taste in my mouth"—primarily because of the ending, which he had made a happy one for his hero. His dissatisfaction prompted a long session of introspection about just what he stood for as a novelist. "And I came up with the conclusion that what I try to do is satisfy a theme, the fault of this novel being it didn't do that, but satisfied a character. That is, it provided a man with a

happy ending, while turning its back on the demands of the theme itself. . . .
Trying to do nice by the character, it did dirt by the reader by denying him
his expectations." Just about this time he received a note from von Auw saying that although the book was readable and had the usual Cain pace, he had
been unable to become involved with the characters and questioned their
credibility. However, von Auw went on to say, he was still ready to submit it
to Dial as the option book, unless Cain wanted to work on it a little more.

Cain quickly wrote back urging him not to do anything until he added a
new ending and made a few other changes that would remove von Auw's reservations. It took him until the spring of 1964 to finish it, but then he thought
he had "a really good book"—happy now that his hero's fate was unhappy.
Von Auw agreed that Cain had improved it and sent it immediately to Dial,
producing one of the most curious and maddening waiting periods in Cain's
long publishing career. Part of the problem was due to the chaos at Dial created by the exit of Silberman, followed soon by the departure of Henry Robbins, plus the fact that Dial appeared to have cooled on Cain after the
disappointing sales of *Mignon*. Cain, at least, was convinced Baron wanted
out from under and began writing Silberman at Random House: "Let us by
the dark of the moon and noiselessly keep in touch." He thought *The Magician's Wife* might well arrive on Silberman's desk one morning; in addition,
he had an idea for a semiautobiographical nonfiction book about his own experience giving up smoking, based on the premise that "nobody was ever
born with a taste for tobacco."

It took Dial three months to give von Auw a decision on *The Magician's
Wife*, but when it finally came, it was favorable, although the publisher said
a few suggestions for changes would be in the mail. Meanwhile, Cain had
decided to give it still another ending, which he thought would "change the
book over from an almost thing to a possible success," suggesting he still
really lacked confidence in the novel. The new ending was in New York by
the middle of August, and this produced another curious waiting period, with
Dial saying nothing to him for several months about a book they had agreed
to publish—after he had made a few changes, though still without their editorial suggestions.

Extremely annoyed with Baron and his "notions of courtesy," Cain told
von Auw, "I don't know who he thinks he is, or who he thinks I am, that he
acts as though I were some office boy whose letter he needn't bother to answer." It had now been seven months since Cain had submitted *The Magician's Wife* to Dial and three months since Baron had said he wanted to
publish it and that somebody would be writing him about the suggested
changes. Cain was straining to get started with a rewrite incorporating his
own further ideas, but not until he heard from Dial. In addition, his finances

were once again stretched precariously thin; 1963 had been another bad year—with a total professional income of a little over $3,000. And 1964 was not any better, with less than $3,000 coming in. There had been some promising developments in Hollywood: Swanson thought he had a studio sale of *Past All Dishonor*, for $30,000, and Broderick Crawford and Kraft Theatre had done a pilot based on the character Keyes, but nothing came of either of these projects. Cain had now had one good year in the past ten.

Then, suddenly, Dial resolved its apparent internal problems and Cain heard from E. L. Doctorow (who would one day achieve literary fame with his own novels, most notably *Ragtime*), Dial's new editor in chief. Doctorow wrote Cain a long memorandum suggesting what he thought needed to be done to *The Magician's Wife*, most of which Cain said was cogent and paralleled his own thinking. But in truth he was a little stunned and surprised at the detailed analysis of the book's weaknesses, though he bowed to what he later called a "red-faced acceptance of a writing lesson from Doctorow." Even before his note from the Dial editor arrived, however, he had reread the script for the "umpteenth time" and decided "all four of the main characters needed a great deal of shaping, and the dialogue needs a hair cut—pretty much along the lines you suggest." The story, Cain felt, still held up, and the suspense had found the "phantom circuit." He was eager to start another rewrite, which he thought would be done after the first of the year—1965.

But try as he might, he could not make the book read the way he wanted, and at the end of January he wrote Doctorow that he was still having trouble, deep trouble. He had read Doctorow's memorandum over and over and decided both of them had been pulling their punches on what ailed the novel. "Our genteel talk about 'character' and so on simply ignored the fact that characters derive from situation and that mine were not only shaky, but showed all the overcomplication that is caused by an effort to pep weakness up with motion."

He realized he had "the same old situation I had started this story with, the one that caught me in the first place, that I abandoned for no good reason." So he virtually started over again, promising Doctorow the final script in three weeks. There was no reply from Doctorow—in fact, Cain had not heard from him since his original memo back in November and was beginning to feel once again that Dial did not care whether he ever finished *The Magician's Wife* or not. But then, suddenly, New York rediscovered James M. Cain, and it came through no effort on his part.

When Norman Mailer's *American Dream* was published by Dial, Tom Wolfe wrote an essay-review of it for *Book Week*. In the process of damning Mailer with faint praise, Wolfe said some of the better passages in the new novel were almost as fast-paced as James M. Cain's and that "in much of the book Mailer moves, probably unconsciously, in the direction of Cain and shows great promise." He said Mailer, like Cain, had a gothic attitude toward sex, but unlike Mailer's approach to making love, it was not embarrassing in the context of a Cain novel like *The Postman Always Rings Twice*.

And Wolfe concluded his essay:

> Of course, Mailer cannot match Cain in writing dialogue, creating characters, setting up scenes or carrying characters through a long story. But he is keener than Cain in summoning up smells, especially effluvia. I think Norman Mailer can climb into the same ring as James M. Cain. He's got to learn some fundamentals, such as how to come out of the corner faster. But that can be picked up. A good solid Cain-style opening goes like this:
>
> "They threw me off the hay truck about noon. . . ."

Tom Wolfe was the darling of the "new journalism," having contributed to the creation of a fresh style of magazine writing, most of which had appeared in *Esquire* and *This Week*, the *New York Herald Tribune*'s influential Sunday magazine supplement. So Wolfe's praise of Cain did not go unnoticed. Several of Cain's friends sent him clippings of the Wolfe essay, and the Raphaelsons wired him to be sure to read the review—A FINE TRIBUTE TO YOU. It also stirred his publisher. As Cain told the Raphaelsons, after doing his rewrite on *The Magician's Wife* and going all winter without "one peep" from Dial, "no letter of inquiry, no what-ho, what-ho, no anything, when that review reached them, they came to life with a bang, with phone calls from the editor, the publisher's wife, etc., as well as gifts." He finished *The Magician's Wife* and sent it off to Dial with the hope that just maybe James M. Cain was hot once again. Dial moved quickly, accepting the rewrite as well as still another ending Cain sent along ten days later.

In many ways, *The Magician's Wife* is one of Cain's most interesting—but exasperating—books. First, it returns to his favorite story, developed in "Pastorale," *Postman*, and "Double Indemnity"—a man driven to conspire with a woman to murder her husband. The man's motive is lust, confused in his mind with love; the woman's is money. Clay Lockwood, a rising executive in a large meat company, meets Sally Alexis, wife of a performing magician. He tries to resist falling under her spell, but finally gives in, agonizing through a complex plot involving murder, several twists, a trial, and a grim climax. And it is obvious why Cain had so much trouble with the ending; his hero eventually finds himself in such a bind that the only way out is suicide. It is also obvious why von Auw could not believe in the characters. Even in

Florence Macbeth in a 1920s
portrait. St. Paul Pioneer Press

These three novels, all written as magazine serials, were published by Avon in the late 1940s and early 1950s as paperback originals. In 1980, Gregg Press reprinted them in one hardcover edition called Hard Cain.

Portrait of Cain taken by Samson Raphaelson on a 1955 visit to the Raphaelson farm in Bucks County. Raphaelson had recently taken up photography, a subject that seemed to bore Cain. "He hardly glanced at the framed photographs in every room," Raphaelson said. Later, when Raphaelson sent Cain the photo, Cain replied that "it utterly baffles me, just why, on your terrace, at that hour of day, I had such a strained expression. But at least it does seem concentrated." Samson Raphaelson

In 1950, Cain received a "Kangaroo" trophy from Robert F. deGraff, Chairman of the Board of Pocket Books, Inc., for the one-million-copy sale of The Postman Always Rings Twice.

Cain out for a stroll in University Park in the 1950s with his leashed cat, Nickie. When Nickie died in 1958, Cain wrote the manager of the park where he was buried: "From you, I needn't conceal that this was a bereavement that wrenched us both in the deepest part of our nature."

After years of bitter feelings about his alma mater, Washington College, Cain finally accepted its recognition in the 1950s. In bottom left photo he poses in front of his house on 44th Avenue in Hyattsville with Frederick Dumschott (left), Vice-President, and Joseph H. McLain, President. He eventually donated his collection of foreign editions of his novels to the college library, and in 1978 the college honored him with a posthumous citation (below). Roy Hoopes *(second and third photos)*

Washington College
Alumni Citation

awarded to

James M. Cain '10

in recognition of outstanding achievements and services

in the field of

Literature

which reflect honor upon this College

on this twenty-first day of May

at Chestertown, Maryland

1978

*Movies based on Cain's books continued to appear
long after he left Hollywood and on after his death.
Most recently: Jessica Lange and Jack Nicholson in*
The Postman Always Rings Twice *(Lorimar, 1981);
and Stacey Keach and Pia Zadora in* The Butterfly
(Par-Par Productions, 1981).

Mrs. Alice Piper, the executrix of Cain's estate, at the American Film Institute in 1975, when AFI was showing Cain's three classics: The Postman Always Rings Twice, Mildred Pierce, *and* Double Indemnity.

*Cain in 1975 in
Lafayette Park across
from the White House,
where sixty years earlier,
sitting on a bench, he
decided "out of the
blue" to become a
writer.* Roy Hoopes

Cain's obsession with writing continued until the very end, kept up daily in a corner of his bedroom on his Underwood standard. "Every now and then I used to say: 'For Christ's sake, why don't you become a carpenter or something,' but I'm still at it." Roy Hoopes

the twice-rewritten version, they are guilty of improbable actions. Clay Lock-wood is simply not portrayed as a man who would enter into a murder conspiracy, particularly with a woman he seems to dislike half the time. Nor are his actions in the last few pages convincing. Then there is Sally, the hardest to swallow of any of Cain's bitches.

There is one character in the book—Grace Simone, Sally's mother—who is very provocative and attractive, and who Cain had hoped at one time would interest Joan Crawford. She was reminiscent of Mildred Pierce, with an evil daughter and cunning business ability—and Cain admitted he "fell for her." So does his hero, Clay; he marries her. When the book was in galley form, he had Swanson send Joan Crawford a copy, as she had requested. "I wouldn't be telling the truth," he wrote her, "if I didn't admit that your note had a great deal to do with my moving this story from the if-as-and-when position to the get-at-it-&-do-it column."

He also wrote Dial to send her a nice, fresh-off-the-press, bound copy, with a note from him. "Those people out there," he wrote Bill Decker, Dial's managing editor, "especially the big ones with gold stars on the dressing rooms, expect things to be done in a certain way, and they're first-edition conscious, very much so. The note I write her must appear to be dashed off casually, but at the same time be done with due regard to the amenities she's accustomed to—she might, just possibly, want to buy it or have it bought for her."

Cain, as always, did his research thoroughly, drawing on his early experience with Swift and Company in Baltimore, updated with visits to their plant in the early 1960s. The locale of the book is an agglomeration of the Annapolis, Curtis Bay, Silver Spring, and South River areas of Maryland, with the road on which the murder takes place transplanted from the Eastern Shore. He would have preferred to use a real geographic location, as he had in his earlier books, but he said that after you have "been on the receiving end of a lawsuit, as I have, and found out how gruesomely much one costs, you'll take simple precautions."

The Magician's Wife was written when Cain was over seventy, but despite its deficiencies it contains perhaps some of his best writing, and the story moves along with the unlaydownable quality Franklin P. Adams had noted in Cain's narrative style forty years earlier. There is not one flat page or passage in *The Magician's Wife*, as there were in *Galatea* and *Mignon*. His characters might annoy more than usual, but Cain had refound his famous momentum.

Cain was now in excellent mental and physical health, although in 1963 a tumor developed under his arm that began to worry him considerably. "As time went by, in spite of my best efforts to kid myself, it got to the size of half a grapefruit," he wrote a friend. So he finally decided to have it removed. Fortunately, it was benign, and after recovering from the operation he felt better than ever. "I've called myself Peter Panski, the boy that never grew up," he told his sister, "and I wonder if it's really a good thing." Still, with all his newfound zest, he knew he was aging. "So, with me," he wrote a friend, "life isn't so dull exactly, but it begins to resemble a bowl of cherries that stay green all the time and resemble typewriter keys. Books, with me, take longer and longer and no doubt one day will take really long." But in an upbeat note he wrote to another: "I don't get sick. I don't fall down. I don't do anything much, except get one day older every 24 hours. Every so often, by processes unexplained, I get out a book."

Florence, on the other hand, was not doing well. She too was over seventy and, after a brief period of relatively good health, was gradually and perceptibly weakening. She would occasionally see their friend from next door, Mrs. Kisielnicki, who would come over and let her talk about her childhood and pets. But that was all Cain would allow. One day she had a few friends in and her blood pressure soared and for a week things hung in the balance. "I couldn't even keep her company," Cain said, "for fear some subject would come up that would get her all excited, and that would be it. She was saved, I felt, by her cat, who stayed with her the whole time and nipped and talked and purred at her, until she began to calm down." But Florence had drifted into a period of utter misery and dared not walk without hanging on to something, due, Cain said, to a neuritis condition that disturbed her sense of balance. Then, in late 1965, Florence had a serious fall and her situation deteriorated. The doctor wanted to put her in the hospital, but Cain would not let him.

Cain's protective attitude toward Florence as she continued to decline was the subject of much talk in the neighborhood. She was seldom seen, and on one occasion when she did come outside, she fell, seemed confused, and had to be helped back into the house by one of the neighborhood boys. Cain insisted in all his letters to friends that Florence's high blood pressure was the reason for their becoming such recluses. But there was another factor: As Florence's condition became worse, she had started drinking brandy to help ease the pain and, apparently, she came to rely more and more on it, until finally she must have been drinking to the point where it affected her conduct and behavior. Cain did his best to cover this up, restricting her callers and activities. He even refused to let workmen come into the house, although it was in disrepair, with the wallpaper literally hanging in shreds and the kitchen plaster cracked. And it was because Florence could not have her brandy in the hospital that he let her have her way and stay home after her fall.

None of this was known to outsiders while Florence was still alive, but Cain did tell a few close neighborhood friends after her death. Not once in the dozens of letters about Florence's declining health and the isolated life they led does he mention Florence's condition, even to his closest friends. He was determined that Florence Macbeth, one of America's truly great opera stars, would go to her grave with her reputation intact.

It was not a pretty situation: two childless people in their mid-seventies who had both known fame and fortune, living as virtual recluses in an old house that was slowly falling apart, while concerned neighbors watched and talked and tried to help, with little encouragement from this eccentric old gentleman who kept everyone away.

Almost every week, Cain and Florence were faced with news of departing friends. Galli-Curci's death particularly upset Florence, and Cain was hit hard by the death of Malcolm Ross, his New York roommate; of Edward Sirich, from St. John's days; and of Gilbert Malcolm, his World War I buddy. Of course, both Cains were demoralized by that "ghastly thing," as Cain called the Kennedy assassination. He admired young Kennedy and wrote his sister that at the time of the inauguration, for a gag, "I was going to write a song, 'An Irishman loves a silk hat, oh how he loves its silken sheen,' " remembering how his father used to love to dress up in his silk hat and cutaway and parade around the Chestertown campus. "And then, as though to mock me, there they all were [at the Kennedy funeral] in their one-button cutaways we remember so well."

During the period Dial was trying to make up its mind about *The Magician's Wife*, Cain had turned to reading the Bible, and he wrote Raphaelson that he wanted to have a session about it. "I have to confess," he said, "it doesn't impress me as much as I thought it would, Old Testament or New. The baffling part isn't so much the complex dreams, hopes, hates, and repressions it brings to light on the part of a lot of pious chroniclers, but the taste of the human race in accepting such stuff and enshrining it as something to live by."

Cain had his own ideas about God. "I find it impossible to believe in life after death," he wrote one friend, "and if you don't accept that, the Christian theology goes up in smoke. . . . To me, God is life, and if no immortal soul figures in, then all must be included in the concept. So animals to me take on a mystic meaning, more perhaps than they do to most people."

It was evident that, as Cain's life began to slip away, religion and the Bible would not be a solace. Life on earth and man's achievements were of much more concern to him than the hereafter, and if there was any one publication that was Cain's bible, it was his boyhood favorite, first read in his father's study, *Who's Who in America*. At seventy-three, with his friends slowly leaving this earth and his wife seriously ill, he was becoming more and more conscious of a man's life work and place in history. "It seems equally incredible that I am seventy-three," he wrote his sister on the 105th anniversary of his father's birth. "I am running out the references in a book I am reading on political parties in the U.S. by looking all sorts of people up in the *Dictionary of American Biography* [another one of Cain's basic books], and in case after case they are dead by the time they are as old as I am."

He could not help but be conscious of mortality considering the number of people constantly approaching him for interviews and information about former friends and colleagues themselves becoming subjects of biographies—Dale Kramer and Allan Churchill wanting information about Harold Ross; Mark Schorer inquiring about his friendship with Sinclair Lewis; Carlos Baker writing him about Hemingway; E. J. Kahn asking him to recall his days on the *World* and his memories of Herbert Bayard Swope. Then, of course, there was the Mencken industry, which inspired numerous requests for interviews and letters, especially for an ongoing biography by Cain's friend from the University of Maryland, Carl Bode, whom he had first met in the early 1950s when they were both doing research at the Library of Congress. In all cases, Cain responded generously with long, substantive, and often beautifully composed letters and memoranda that have been as helpful to me, his biographer, as they were to their recipients. Arthur Krock, for example, thought Cain's contribution to Kahn's *The World of Swope* "the best of any provided by HBS's contemporaries."

Cain always considered biography "the mother of history." He read biographies avidly and thought them the one literary pursuit in which Americans excelled. James Parton's *Andrew Jackson*, Douglas Southall Freeman's *Robert E. Lee*, Carl Van Doren's *Benjamin Franklin*, Carl Sandburg's *Abraham Lincoln*, and Allan Nevins's *Grover Cleveland* he included among the great American books. He felt Americans not only excelled at the scholarship biography required, but had raised the literary level of biography. An important contribution in this evolution was being made by *The New Yorker* Profile writers. Cain was particularly impressed with Kahn's biography of Swope, which he said "is probably going to be known as one of the great biographies."

Cain thought a good biography had two elements: "One, the biographee, the subject; two, the biographer, the man telling the tale and his capacity to make it interesting." He professed not even to understand what a "critical biography" was and thought a biographer should concentrate on the man rather than an appraisal of his work. He also thought biographies of singers were terribly difficult because everything that matters is locked in the singer's throat and "there is a limit to description's power." Part of the trick with biography was "knowing whom to do a biography about," for he had, from time to time, given thought to writing a biography himself. The people who intrigued him were James K. Polk ("a generally neglected figure who nevertheless had an enormous effect on our history"), General N. P. Banks ("one of the tough-luck boys of the Civil War"), J. N. Cortina ("a bandit, a sort of Mexican Robin Hood, who affected the course of events, especially in our Civil War, much more than anyone has admitted"), and Ulysses S. Grant ("who has been copiously written about, but never, so far as I know, with sufficient emphasis on his third great talent, which was writing"). By his seventies, Cain had, in fact, become so preoccupied with biography that it would eventually become the subject for a new novel.

Cain had no objection to people writing memoirs, if they were candid, but an autobiography was a special breed. Years earlier, when his friend Phil Goodman was thinking of writing his own story, Cain told him he could never do it. "Why?" asked Goodman, to which Cain replied: "Because an autobiography must be susceptible to the subtitle, *Or, Up From Slavery*. You were never down, so there's no story to you coming up. Memoirs, perhaps— but no autobiography." Goodman was amused by this, and Cain never wavered from that approach, making the same remark in many interviews in his later years.

His one friend who he felt was justified in writing an autobiography was Samson Raphaelson, the dramatist, screenwriter, and short story writer who wrote "The Jazz Singer," "Skylark," "Jason," "Hilda Crane," and "Accent on Youth." "You have a story to tell," he wrote Raphaelson. "It is, in effect, the story of the Jazz Singer: a Jewish boy who alternates all his life between being a high-toned imitation goy, and being what he is, a Jew. It is a story 100,000 Jews share in and I for one would greatly enjoy reading it."

But, for himself, Cain did not think he had a story to tell, and he resisted all requests from his agent and publishers to write an autobiography— although he did start, late in his life, to write his "memoirs." To him, an autobiography was the detailed story of a man who had a life that warranted telling; memoirs were just reminiscing by someone who had the capacity to make his nostalgic recall interesting and readable.

One thing that must have disturbed him was that no one was coming around to inquire about doing his biography. One person did appear, though, who wanted to do a critical study, including a biographical sketch. He was David Madden, an aspiring novelist and playwright who taught English at Centre College. Madden was one of a breed of young writers-in-residence at various universities whom Cain thought were more interested in studying literature and writing reviews and critical essays than writing novels.* In 1959, he wrote an essay on Cain for Norman Holmes Pearson's American literature course at Yale, which was eventually printed in *The University Review*. It was probably the first literary study to approach Cain as an American writer worth considering seriously since Edmund Wilson's 1940 essay "The Boys in the Back Room." By 1959, Cain had been dismissed by the academics and literary essayists as a popular, commercial writer. James T. Farrell, W. M. Frohock, and Albert Van Nostrand all found him overrated, with Farrell and Van Nostrand feeling his main fault was the instinct to write for the movies, and Frohock concluding that nothing he wrote "is outside the category of trash." But Madden thought Cain was one of the most important of a school he called the "Tough-guy Writers of the Thirties"—Cain, Raymond Chandler, Horace McCoy, Dashiell Hammett. His thesis was that these writers should not be ignored by students of American literature merely because they were popular or tough. They had something to say about America, a fact European writers and academics had already discovered.

Madden's essay and other writings on the popular culture of the 1930s and 1940s helped make Cain and other tough-guy authors respectable subjects for study in the universities. A few years after his essay appeared, Madden gave a speech on Cain "in fear and trembling," he said, "to a group of Ohio English professors; to my surprise, that lecture conjured up in them a latent literary interest mingled with a passionate nostalgia. I discovered that while a professor of medieval literature may not have found time to read William Styron, Wright Morris, John Hawkes, Walker Percy, Flannery O'Connor, Saul Bellow, John Barth, he has read and remembered fondly *The Postman Always Rings Twice*."

Madden also discovered that of all the popular writers of the 1930s being studied in the 1960s, Cain was probably the most admired. "I have only to speak for ten minutes to young writers about you," Madden wrote Cain, "and they read you and praise you right away." Madden had already written a book on Wright Morris for the Twayne series of studies on American writers, and now he proposed a book on Cain. The Twayne editors agreed.

Despite the fact that the last thing in the world James M. Cain wanted was to be categorized in any literary "school," especially one stamped with a label he had spent most of his life trying to avoid, he cooperated with Madden in preparing his essay; and when he first read it, he said it made him "feel as though I had paraded myself in the police line-up in a bikini suit or

---

*Madden was actually a fiction writer first and critic second, having already written *The Beautiful Greed*; he later wrote *Bijou*, *The Suicide's Wife*, and *Pleasure Dome*.

less. But it touches me nevertheless, indeed shakes me up. If I am worth all this close analysis, I don't know, but it is very penetrating, and nails the truth in more places than I would like to admit."

No doubt flattered and pleased that one of the young university critics was regarding him seriously, Cain developed a pleasant, professional relationship with Madden after the essay appeared, with Cain reading, commenting on, and writing a publisher's blurb for Madden's first novel, *The Beautiful Greed*, and Madden inviting Cain to give a speech at a 1962 Writers' Conference at Morehead College in Kentucky (an invitation that appealed to Cain until he learned the subject would be "creative writing"; then he declined).

Cain was less than enthusiastic at first about Madden's doing a book-length literary study on him. He hemmed and hawed and stalled around for a few days after Madden had written him to inquire whether he would cooperate on what Cain viewed as "one of those critical things 1/10 bio and 9/10 guff." Then one night he was voicing his displeasure at the thought of a literary study to Florence, and she said: "Well, I don't see anyone else coming around wanting to write a book about you."

Cain had to admit she was right. So he wrote Madden a nice note, saying "how could I decline such an honor?" He promised to help in any way he could, but added: "It's only fair to warn you that in some ways I'm an utterly crass Philistine—as I scarcely ever save clippings about me, or old articles, or the various things you might want, such as film scripts." Madden wanted to visit him that summer (1964) for interviews, but Cain said no, that he was too preoccupied with his writing and nursing Florence. Instead, he offered to write Madden a series of autobiographical notes, as he had done for Bode on Mencken. By summer, he was well into his memorandum, which eventually amounted to over one hundred pages of autobiography. And he was still pretending to be someone else—he wrote them all in the third person as if he were talking about a writer named James M. Cain.

Madden had a grant from Kenyon College to do the Cain study and a deadline from Twayne of September 1965, which he had to delay because Cain did not finish the autobiographical notes until January 1966. Actually, Cain thought Madden's "obvious motivation is to get something between covers that will lead to a better job, rather than a passion to do a good book." It was an unfair rap, because in several letters to Cain (and in later conversations with me) Madden demonstrated a disregard for academic promotion together with a genuine enthusiasm for Cain and his writing, and he was obviously excited about the project. He also made several efforts to promote anthologies of Cain's short stories and nonfiction with publishers.

Meanwhile, Dial was ready to publish *The Magician's Wife*, and when

Cain sent Madden a copy, Madden wrote back that he thought it was his best since *The Butterfly*. Since Cain agreed with Madden that *The Butterfly* was indeed his best book, his expectations were set off again. But when the reviews started coming in, he was crushed. In many ways the unfavorable reaction to *The Magician's Wife* hit him even harder than *Mignon*'s failure. He had rewritten his latest book at least a half-dozen times, even before his final "best lick" rewrite for Doctorow. He also thought *The Magician's Wife* represented a new development in his writing. "In the last few years," he wrote Madden, "in my mind, and on the sheet as I type, there has come a new beat, or cadence, or accent, or whatever it might be called, that I fought off at first, as probably a sign of old age. But then I began to realize it was me, trying to push through. So I'm letting myself be me, and don't have anything like the compulsion I used to have, to put it in somebody's mouth. It goes rather deep, I think, and is already conditioning my ideas . . . so that they're branching out, or enlarging, or whatever it might be called. . . . I can still do the garrulous punk with my eyes shut, of course, but isn't it time for a change?"

He thought *The Magician's Wife* marked the change to the new Cain capable of dealing with complex human relationships in the third person. But the reviewers did not agree. Some were friendly, such as Martin Levin, in the *Times*, and at one point the favorable notices were running 2–1. But the bad ones were again devastating. The *Time* reviewer, who had no doubt read his Frohock, said: "For 30 years, novelist James M. Cain has worked a literary lode bordering on a trash heap. Even his best works reeked of their neighborhood." Now, with *The Magician's Wife*, *Time* said he had achieved a breakthrough—it was "pure trash."

So, despite the favorable reviews and the fact that David Madden, Tom Wolfe, and Dial (with its extensive advertising) had tried to revive Cain from literary obscurity, *The Magician's Wife* had to be considered another failure. The sales were disappointing; Joan Crawford did not like it; and despite herculean efforts by Swanson in Hollywood, the studios rejected it as being "too much like *Double Indemnity*." Cain thought he knew why the book flopped. "It had a 1 and a 2," he said, referring to Vincent Lawrence's theory of plotting, "but where it went after the somewhat successful murder, I could never invent. The man's suicide at the end is simply the confession I had no 3, for suicide is an ending few readers accept." Perhaps suicide was more accepted as a way out of an impossible situation in other countries—Italy, Germany, and Japan, for example—for there the book sold very well.

The Magician's Wife brought down the curtain on Cain's efforts to make something of himself as a serious writer after leaving Hollywood. It would be ten years before a resurrected James M. Cain would publish another novel. But he kept churning them out. Even before *The Magician's Wife* was published, he had started a new one—motivated at least in part by a desperate need for money, to the point of having to borrow $1,000 from von Auw. This book was a story about a little girl who was given a pet Siberian tiger to raise and the problems it caused in the family when they discovered, too late, that it had become "the genie that looks like a cat and won't go back in the bottle." The story seemed, as they all did at the beginning, like a simple chore, "a little fairy tale I could do with one hand," he wrote a friend. Then the tale itself began to seem like a genie he could not get back in the bottle. "So I suppose I'll fight it out along this line if it takes all summer," he moaned. "Aren't there any easy ones?"

Not for Cain, especially now. In fact, writing was becoming harder and harder; by November, he had written four or five versions of the new novel, none satisfactory. And before the following summer, he would be confronted with a crisis unlike any he had ever faced. Florence's condition was becoming worse every day, and the gloom that dominated the home was expressed by Cain in a letter commenting on what turned out to be their last Christmas together: "We have reached a time of life when Christmas . . . brings sadness too. . . . It is a time for totting scores, and not all of them are plus."

Cain's own letters totting the score were increasingly depressing. He figured he was getting ready to die because the Library of Congress had been after him to donate his papers, a sure sign. His letters also told of the continuing effort to keep Florence, now seventy-six, alive—cooking meals, running the house, playing valet to their cat, counting the laundry, writing checks, ordering the groceries, and carrying her upstairs every night, which was usually preceded by this little scene Cain described to a friend: Florence would be sitting on the sofa rocking back and forth, trying to lurch to her feet, and Cain would say: "Now what is it, what do you want?" With a touch of self-pity, Florence would reply, "Oh never mind, I don't ask anything," and she would get up. "Do you want more toast, is that it?" Cain would ask, and she would say: "I can get it myself." Then he would put his arm around his wife, sit her down again, kiss her, and say, "I'll get it, no trouble, service with a smile—but I'm not a mind reader, you know." Florence would kiss him back and he would get the toast.

Florence could be hard to get along with, as Cain was the first to concede. "All she lived for was to sing," Cain said, and when she no longer could, "she crawled into a hole and pulled it in after her." But he considered opera singers "a separate breed," one he admired. "It so happens that opera is ten times as tough as any other challenge to a singer, and it also happens that I respect it more than any other singing." Cain paid his respects to opera singers by nursing Florence her last fifteen years, protecting her reputation, and loving her for herself, which he thought brought happiness to her life.

Although there was little pain in Florence's last months, she was in utter misery, weakening little by little every day and unable to do anything about it. Cain thought she half prayed that the final day would come, but he battled to the end to prolong her life. And then, one morning, May 5, 1966, he tiptoed into Florence's room and found her dead. "A shock I'll never forget," he said.

The depth of his shock and grief was obvious from his letters. As they gradually aged together, he and Florence appeared to have become as close as two people possibly could: in fact, in her last years, she had begun calling him "Jamie," and he thought it was a measure of their closeness that he did not object. "I was hooked on her, but bad," he told his sister. "Both of us were screwballs, but our wackiness matched up, so we got along and needed each other."

But, Florence was gone now, and Jamie was alone—seventy-five years old and just possibly an ex-writer. The future did not look promising.

21

RESURRECTION

Cain buried Florence at Mankato, where he spent three or four gloomy days. Then he returned to Hyattsville and had to write all of their friends about Florence's death. In her effort to keep out of the public eye, she had refused to let him list them in the telephone book. As a result, the local papers could not call to obtain information for a proper obituary and the Associated Press had nothing to put on the wires. The lack of an obituary bothered Cain, and he made an effort to generate a few articles about her, without much success. So it appeared "as though the waves had closed over her," although he conceded "she was responsible, as her withdrawal from the world was almost an obsession with her."

With the post-funeral affairs taken care of, Cain had to face the reality of living alone, probably for the rest of his life. "I'm knocked apart worse than I try to show or want to admit—but little by little I get readjusted," he wrote Ruth Goetz, who had written him a compassionate letter expressing genuine concern at how he would be able to manage with Florence gone. A few months later, he told her: "I don't feel lonely, yet have little gregarious desire. The thing takes the form, I find, of surges that sweep over me, futile strugglings to bring her back. I'm not, as you know, the soft, sentimental type, so the answer must be, I was hooked."

Gradually he began coming out of his depression. He decided to stay in his house in Hyattsville, although he had given up any thought of buying it. A year before, he had written the owner to express an interest should one of the Hollywood deals for *Past All Dishonor* or *The Magician's Wife* materialize. But he was not optimistic and told his landlord about the big deal "with contracts all signed and cigars passed out, after which not one cent was paid." He then asked for a year's rent extension on the lease and even reconditioned the living room, which now looked fine except for "the damned drapes." The new ones shut out light and "I have to admit the living room looks like the prayer nook in a high-class mortuary"—which might have been appropriate because, for a while after Florence's death, Cain closed himself in a "shrine," as he called it. He admitted this bordered on the neurotic, but he did not want people in the house who might lead the conversation around to Florence.

The memories, however, could not be stifled; little things would come up, like two identical form letters within three weeks requesting autographs from James M. Cain and Florence Macbeth. There were also the holidays. Halloween: "I dread it. I used to get such a lift, listening to the music of that voice as she would step out and talk to the kids, and tonight she won't be there." And much worse, the Christmas season, which depressed him because "I'm sure all sorts of things will be sent me on the basis of compassion for an old goat living alone." Then, "with everybody and his brother-in-law dropping in to cheer me up, I guess I was cheered, but they all had to be eggnogged, and by [the] last week, I was so cheerful I wanted to cut my throat."

He made one effort to break out of his mourning by putting his name in the phone book. And after receiving a host of person-to-person calls, he printed his phone number in large numbers at the bottom of his stationery, adding the line: "Station-to-Station Does it—I'm the only one here."

But he found that the telephone world had changed considerably and was baffled by the recording he would often get when he called Ruth Goetz. "All I can say," he wrote her, "is that record of yours numbs me the way a beautiful anaconda numbs a frog he's about to swallow. I sit there trying to think of something friendly to say, something funny to say, something serious to say, and then when the time comes I sound like John the Baptist in the cistern, before his head is cut off." On top of that, he realized the answering machine completed the call and he had to pay for it—although he did not get to talk to the party on the other end. "Baby, your friends may be dumb, but they're not so damned dumb that they couldn't figure out that if you're not answering the phone you're out. And if they love you, they'll call again."

As with many people in bereavement, Cain found the best antidote was work, and shortly after Florence's death he was telling friends that he still seemed to be able to write. But writing was one thing and writing publishable novels, another. For five years—from 1966 to 1971—Cain wrote regularly, and the result was one failure after another.

His first effort was to finish the novel about the little girl and her pet tiger, which he began after *The Magician's Wife*. He called it *Jinghis Quinn*, wrote it in the third person, and sent it off to von Auw with high expectations, saying "it is the kind of story which in Hollywood's present humor, after the smash of *Born Free* and the success of various animal pictures, might be wanted there." Von Auw disagreed, and Cain rewrote the book. Then Dial turned it down and so did Jim Silberman at Random House. It was a crushing blow to Cain. "I thought a law had been passed that when I wrote a book it sold," he told a friend.

The manuscript of *Jinghis Quinn* was returned to Cain in October 1967. Over the next four years, through fits and starts and, in general, experiencing a hard time focusing on any one project, Cain wrote three new novels, each one of which returned the shock of proving unpublishable.

First, after vacillating between several ideas—including one about a girl who stows away on a spaceship to Mars—he settled on a novel about a woman in her thirties who marries a boy not yet out of his teens. He set the book in suburban Maryland, having made his peace with the East. And he wrote David Madden, "As Suburbia, where I live, begins to cast its spell, or take its toll. . . . I'm beginning to realize, it's the new frontier, and as such worth anyone's attention." Titled *Kingdom by the Sea*, the book came back from William Koshland at Knopf with a rejection letter as difficult for Koshland to write as for Cain to read: "With the best will in the world, Jim, and even knowing the story you have set in this manuscript, I can't see it as coming off. . . . Something tells me, even though your failure to get this published will knock you off schedule, that it ought to be put aside."

Next came an effort called *Cloud 9*, another Eastern novel with a large cast and an intricate plot dealing mainly with sex and Maryland real estate, and containing an attempted murder, an actual murder, a thread of mystery, and a glimpse of Washington's world of embassies, lobbyists, and caterers— all leading to a bloody, brutal climax. It too was rejected by Koshland: "I read *Cloud 9* as soon as Ivan and Dorothy submitted it . . . I'm sorry but I just can't warm up to the book, the characters who people it, or the shenanigans through which you put them. It would make no sense for me to go into detail, Jim, I hate like hell to turn you down, but it's gotta be."

It was beginning to look as if James M. Cain was through—*Galatea*, *Mignon*, *The Magician's Wife*, three books that were not successful; and now three rejects in a row. "Everything I've done since I came to Maryland seemed to misfire," a very discouraged old man wrote his sister Rosalie. He also wrote von Auw apologizing to him and Dorothy Olding for imposing a bad book on them. But he would not quit. "I'm still at the same old typewriter," he wrote, "and if you can stand it, I'll be sending something else on fairly soon. I think I'm in a new phase, so don't scrub me, just yet."

Cain's announcement of a "new phase"—typical of his drastic swings from dejection to euphoria over his later career, and of his repeated attempts to pick up the pieces and convince himself that he was actually writing "better than ever"—did indeed herald an extraordinary shift for his next novel, though not a fortunate one. With everyone from psychiatrists to politicians to parents expressing an inability to understand the younger generation, or the gap between society and adolescent youth, James M. Cain, a man without children of his own, decided to write about a young girl in her teens in conflict with her father. He called it *The Enchanted Isle*, and this time the manuscript did not even reach William Koshland's desk. Neither von Auw nor Dorothy Olding thought it was publishable.

Cain was deeply perplexed, thinking he had made this one come to life and unable to understand what he had done wrong. He was convinced, however, that the problem was not old age, but his new direction. Ruth Goetz agreed. "I think you must come away from this idea of doing what you call quick little situation books," she wrote him, "and get back to those wonderful seedy, lousy no-goods that you have always understood so wonderfully and written so superbly. . . . Anyway, 'situation' is a hangover from Vinnie [Lawrence], and Vinnie's kind of storytelling is far behind us now."

Cain conceded she was right and wrote von Auw: "I shall now go on to a book I've been contemplating for years—one that I'll play straight without any cock-eyed melodrama."

This one, apparently, was to be a sequel to *Past All Dishonor*, in which Biloxi, the madam ruined when Duval kills the man who was going to set her up in a new whorehouse, goes off and starts one of her own. Cain was intrigued with the idea for a while, but then, discouraged and convinced that the Civil War was no better for him than teen-agers in the Maryland suburbs, he stopped writing—at least for a while.

For all their lack of success, these books gave Cain a great deal of comfort as he entered old age. They were his creations, his children in a sense, and they helped him adjust to the lonely life of a widower. There was little else in his life. He bought "the damnedest collection of wine glasses, liquor glasses, champagne glasses, julep glasses, and, of course, the booze to go with them, all on ice and all ready to serve. And no one ever comes, for the reason I never invite them." He would sit for hours, in dour silence.

In July 1967 he had his seventy-fifth birthday, and the occasion left him depressed. Hardly calculated to cheer him was a campaign initiated by Henrietta and Leo to reunite Cain and Elina. Cain tried to discourage it, feeling that too much time had elapsed and too much had happened for their chances together again. The constant telephoning during the attempted reconciliation led to a scene which might have been amusing, but for its nearly tragic consequences. One time when Henrietta called Cain from California, he was coming down the stairs and, instead of waiting until he got to the bottom of the staircase, he reached down over the banister for the phone. When he learned it was Henrietta, long distance, he tried to shift his feet so he could continue talking and, losing his balance, fell over the banister and landed on his back, knocking the wind out of him. He was sure he had broken his neck. The phone was dangling in front of him, but he was unable to move. He yelled for Henrietta to hang up, then lay there and tried to gather his wits. After managing to get to his feet, he decided he did not want to go to the hospital and submit to the ordeal of X rays and tests; he would just sweat out the pain. It took weeks, and when he finally got back to the typewriter he found it tired him to sit for long periods. The fall seemed to have irritated a chronic bladder condition. So he wrote mostly standing up, shifting to yellow pads and longhand, and had his work transcribed by a typist. His eyes were all right—at five feet; but at twenty feet, he was virtually blind.

Cain continued to discourage relations with his family, even vetoing a visit from Henrietta's daughter, Christine, whom he had doted on when she was a little girl. "But allowing for all that," he wrote Elina, "allowing for Auld Lang Syne and all things I naturally feel, I have had a crippling, stunning disastrous loss, and I am not in the humor for socializing. I live alone, I see no one except one or two neighbors. I go nowhere. I am seventy-five years old."

Although leery of attempting a reconciliation with Elina, Cain did, briefly, entertain ideas of making up with Aileen. Eight months after Florence died, he wrote Aileen that he could now act more naturally in his letters. Then, when he had his fall, Aileen called, and her warmth and friendliness moved him. His subsequent letters to her discussed reconciliation—but in a passive way, giving her a chance to pick up the cue if she was so inclined, which she was not.

Cain kept wondering about living with a woman again. Alfred Knopf, who was only two months younger, had remarried. But then Cain began having dizzy spells, finally diagnosed as angina pectoris, and he speculated on how a man with heart disease could consummate a marriage in the bedroom—a disturbing thought, but one which evoked the germ of an idea for another novel.

The days came and went, through Christmas, 1967, when "everybody and his brother-in-law called by long distance from California, New York, Pennsylvania, and places in between, to cheer me up—and when somebody gets your number from information, dials, and gets you on the line, you have to talk. So, that's all I did, talk, and try to sound cheerful." The digitalis prescribed for his heart seemed to help, but it also produced a drowsiness that practically put him into near-coma and induced a continuing sense of lethargy, which he decided was worse than the disease. Then, in July 1968, Carol Kisielnicki, one of the children next door, took him to a shopping center in Hyattsville to buy a new suit—and suddenly his heart stopped beating for a few seconds and he passed out, producing quite a suburban scene, as described by Cain: "Ambulance, doctor, crowd, boy yelling 'Hey skinny, come get a load of what's stretched out on the pavement!' " And what was stretched out on the pavement was the writer—or maybe ex-writer—James M. Cain, who, by his own description, looked "like an old wharf rat."

When he came to, he was looking into blue sky and the eyes of Carol Kisielnicki. Stunned and scared, he did not know what had happened, except that he had seen death "and there were no angels." He had had a serious fall, which literally grated his bones and fractured his skull. Again he refused to go to a hospital, but stayed in bed at home until the doctor felt he was able to get up and around. He insisted that the digitalis had caused the blackout. This upset the doctor, which made Cain more convinced than ever of his self-diagnosis. Then, after a cold put him on Achromycin, his energy returned and he discontinued the digitalis and began touting Achromycin to his fellow heart patients, much to the distress of his doctor. But he never took digitalis again, although he did carry nitroglycerin tablets in case he had another attack.

Despite his poor health, Cain kept at his writing, though at times his correspondence seemed to be taking more of his time than his fiction. All his life, Cain had been a prodigious letter-writer—to friends, professional colleagues, editors, columnists, radio and television commentators, people whose work or art he admired, or stores or clerks he wished to congratulate or criticize. He also appeared to be much more interested in current events in the sixties and seventies than he had been in the twenties and thirties. And, in his final years, he seemed to be writing for a future biographer. Many of his last letters drift off into anecdotes about his youth and career, beyond just the nostalgic reminiscing of a man in his twilight years. Cain had read enough biographies to know the importance of letters in re-creating a man's life, and I suspect he just wanted to make sure some of the best stories were not forgotten.

But, of course, there was more to his letter-writing than the thought of making it easy for his biographer. He was a lonely man, and letters—and the telephone—were now virtually his only link with the outside world. Being a former editorial writer, he could hardly refrain from commenting on subjects that concerned him—the Vietnam war, the civil war in Ireland, gun control, politics, Israel, the Cold War, black rioting, to mention just a few of the issues covered in Cain's voluminous "letters to the editor" file. There was also in his letter-writing a bit of the Wise Elder of the human tribe obligated to set the record straight—correcting an editor about a long-forgotten fact in American history, or telling someone what it was like on the Eastern Shore at the beginning of the century, in France in 1918, New York in the 1920s, or Hollywood in the 1930s.

Then there were the letters to David Madden—a huge file of correspondence not only about himself and his views on writing, but also concerned with Madden's career, in which Cain had taken a special interest. Several of these letters from Cain were devoted to one of his pet literary subjects: academia versus the real world. Madden was young and still in the formative stage of his career; he had published a novel, a book on Wright Morris, a collection of short stories, and a few very perceptive essays for the university quarterlies. In addition, his interest in Cain had led to four books—the Cain study for Twayne and three anthologies of essays by various literary critics on modern American literature—and in 1968 he had been asked to join the faculty at Louisiana State University as writer-in-residence. But he had also written some popular short stories for *Playboy* and one of its imitators, *Adam*, and in these Cain thought he saw promise of a real writer. He wrote Madden that it was Phil Goodman who had shown H. L. Mencken the real world and encouraged him to be something other than a Baltimore *wunderkind*. And he, Cain, wanted to be Madden's Phil Goodman and lead him out of academia into deep waters—as, in fact, Mencken had done for him. He said he suspected Madden looked on his magazine stories as "hack" writing done for money but, Cain pointed out, "they are a different kind of writing from this stuff for the think magazines, that you get off with your other hand. 'Publish or Perish'; so goes the campus slogan—they're all hell for these alliterative mottos, like 'Endow or Die' forty years ago. But in the name of this shibboleth, some awful gunk was written. . . . The real pay is for *Adam* or publications out to hook readers and hold them. David, why this obsession with the literary: After all, you can go just so far on writers." He thought Madden's campus experience had "loused you up as a fiction writer. Fiction won't stay on campus. It is pelagic stuff, it gets translated into dozens of languages, it reaches out. Getting oriented to college publication is equivalent to little theater production in the drama—it will constrict you if you let it. . . . Break loose from that tradition. It'll be worth it to you—because on the campuses you'll amount to just as much, even more, if you do it as a hard-boiled professional, potboiling writer who plays it to win."

To Cain, it was a sin to write for the professors and not for the general reader. "It's tougher, writing for people, don't let anyone tell you different. And it's *better*. These academic dissertations have been bad for 100 years. I've had occasion, quite a few times, to order up some book in the American Statesman series, which was put out in the 1880s—and had eminent contributors, like William Graham Sumner and Henry Cabot Lodge. But they had the same defect of being written for *scholars*, not for *people*, and they laid an egg, most of them. But look at the historical writers, like Barbara Tuchman and Margaret Leech and John C. Miller who are gathering thousands in royalties for writing so people can read them."

Madden says Cain's admonitions had very little impact on his development, that the direction of his career was by then well established; he intended to write and teach at the same time, and he has been successful at both. He says Cain's books also had only an indirect effect; that his appeal was initially through movies made from his novels and a dim recollection of some of his paperback books in the 1940s, especially those with Robert Jonas's artistic covers.

Another subject of their correspondence was Cain as a "tough-guy" writer. He fought Madden constantly on the label, thinking it not very complimentary. But Madden argued: What was wrong with being "tough"? It didn't exclude other qualities. Still, Cain did not think he could be included in any school, and he denied vigorously that the so-called tough-guy writers had had any influence on him. However, after much thought, he did concede that Madden's concept of Cain as the writer of "pure novels" in which the author never intruded on the narrative to make a thematic point was valid. He told Madden he concluded that by "pure novel" he meant one "whose point is developed from the narrative itself, rather than from some commentary on the social scene or morality of the characters, or economic or political aesthetic preachment. If that is what you mean you hit my objective directly, for I try to let the fable . . . deliver its own 1, 2 & 3."

On the other hand, he thought the essay on him by Joyce Carol Oates (in Madden's anthology) was highly critical, although Madden insisted it was friendly and, as further proof, pointed out that the response to the anthology had been tremendous and that most people felt Cain was the most important writer discussed in the book. But Cain persisted that not only was it not a favorable essay, but she had not understood what he was trying to do. "Her criticism is not only captiously adverse," he wrote Madden, "but to me at least just plain intellectual jibber-jabber. She insists and persistently refuses to see, or even give me the right to see, what I am trying to do. She keeps harping on my amoral characters, but reminds me somehow of what Shaw said of Sir Arthur Wing Pinero, and the far-fetched characters of his plays: 'Doesn't this fellow ever *meet* anybody?' Has she ever met a hobo and talked with him? Since when is a hobo moral? Well so, O.K., Stanley Walker complained about one of my books that 'it contains no admirable characters,' to which I say: 'Since when is Don Quixote admirable?' Am I restricted to admirable characters? To moral characters? Or what the hell is her squawk?"

Oates's main squawk was that "though he deals constantly with the Artistic, Cain, it will be said, never manages to become an artist; there is always something sleazy, something eerily vulgar and disappointing in his work." But Ms. Oates insisted she admired Cain and even wrote him a note saying she was "surprised" that he thought she did not like him and maintaining she wrote critical essays only about writers she liked and admired.

Cain's attitude obviously made it difficult for Madden, who genuinely admired Cain as a writer and wanted to promote serious study of his work. But he felt Cain did not understand the assumptions and concepts of literary criticism, as opposed to reviews, "that a job had to be done by critics if he was to have his work considered seriously as literature. He wanted it both ways—popularity and commercial success, and critical acclaim, and never understood his status somewhere in between . . . [and] he never understood that you don't have to read a writer to write somewhat like him."

To his credit, Cain never let his annoyance with Madden and academia stand in the way of their relationship, and he genuinely tried to help Madden in his own career as well as cooperate in his writing about Cain. He also understood that Madden was trying to help him—at a time when he needed all the outside help he could get, because his own writing was going so badly and his financial situation was once again deteriorating. Swanson did not think the story about the girl and the tiger had movie possibilities, but had tried Disney anyway, without success, all of which made Cain's sense of its failure as a novel even more discouraging.

Then, suddenly in 1968, he was given a lift from two unexpected sources: Swanson reported still another option on *Past All Dishonor*, this one from James Harris, working with CBS films; and the Book-of-the-Month Club, at Knopf's suggestion, decided to bring out a new collection of Cain novels. *Postman*, "Double Indemnity," and *Mildred Pierce* were pulled together into a volume called *Cain X 3*, for which Cain received an advance of $5,000. It was a wonderful break.

Knopf, recalling Tom Wolfe's praise of Cain in his review of the Mailer novel, picked Wolfe to do the introduction, and when the piece came in it was pure music to all ears. Wolfe recalled his advice to Norman Mailer and said, "Cain was one of those writers who first amazed me and delighted me when I was old enough to start looking around and seeing what was being done in American literature . . . *momentum* was something he had a patent on. . . . Picking up a Cain novel was like climbing into a car with one of those Superstockers which is up to 40 by the time your right leg is in the door." And, after rereading the three novels in the collection, Wolfe said he was amazed and delighted "partly because I can see how complex Cain's famous 'fast-paced' 'hard-boiled' technique really is."

But what really pleased Cain was not so much what Wolfe said about him as the fact that it was Wolfe who was saying it. Cain was thought, even by many who remembered him, to be an outdated storyteller of the 1930s and 1940s, and here was the darling of the "new journalists" telling everyone that old Jim Cain was still an exciting writer and that contemporary novelists like Mailer could learn a thing or two from him. With this kind of send-off, it was hard to see how the anthology could miss—and it did not. The response revealed that the three Cain novels had now become little gems of American literature. Ross Macdonald, in a lead review in the *Times*, thought *Postman* and "Double Indemnity" were "a pair of native American masterpieces, back to back." Kenneth Lamott, in *The Nation*, thought *Mildred Pierce* was a serious American novel and that "watching Cain at work can still give the reader that particular pleasure that comes from watching a master craftsman." Robert Kirsch in the *Los Angeles Times* said Cain may be "the novelist par excellence of Southern California" and that not only had the three novels not dated, "they capture and compel with all the illusion of the original experience." William Hogan, in the *San Francisco Chronicle*, recalled that when these books first appeared, he thought Cain "was the greatest writer in the business," but now they read like "poetry." Pete Hamill, in the *Village Voice*, said the three novels showed what Hemingway *should* have done, that Cain's famous style came from his journalism days, and although Cain was not a great writer, he was a good one and *Postman* "might be a great one." But perhaps the most significant comment of all came from Robert Sorenson in the *Minneapolis Tribune*, who lamented that Cain had listened to the critics in the 1940s and that when he went off "and tried to become *serious* and *significant*, we lost an exciting, if not an important, writer."

The anthology proved again what the publishers of the millions of reprints of Cain's novels already knew: that James M. Cain did not date, his best books went on selling. And people were talking about him once again. The book inspired numerous interviews, and with James M. Cain now probably the most illustrious literary lion in the Washington area, the editor of the *Washington Post Potomac* magazine, John Carmody, decided to play up the new collection into a major cover story. He ran Tom Wolfe's introduction in its entirety and also went out to Cain's house to interview him, ending up taking Cain to lunch at the Olney Inn in Maryland.

"James M. Cain at Twilight Time" was the title of the resulting article, and it captured perfectly the flavor of a relic from Hollywood's golden age living as a recluse in Hyattsville, Maryland. "Jim Cain is scrunched down in the front seat of the car," Carmody wrote. "The brim of his old felt hat is turned up. He is wearing what he calls his 'undertaker's coat.' A 10-year-old double breasted gray suit. A faded Pendleton plaid shirt and a solid red tie peer from the top of an old nubby brown sweater. He has Wayne Morse eyebrows and a wide, toothless smile that is almost always there. He speaks in a gruff 'city room' voice of which he is proud . . . [a] heart attack has shrunk and enervated him. But the Sunset Boulevardier is still there in the old costume. And he turns to look at every pretty girl the car passes." At the Olney Inn, Cain entertained Carmody with old Hollywood stories and then "broke into the Paramount Fight Song—'Fight on for old B.P.'—his arms waving and his face laughing, as the restaurant begins to empty, except for one couple who stare, fascinated. Then you realize," said Carmody, "that this is one of these men you used to read about who really *did* go to lunch with F. Scott Fitzgerald at the MGM commissary . . . who in one guise or another probably flickered through the Schulberg novels and maybe Nathanael West and certainly Fitzgerald and John O'Hara, all those people who went to Hollywood and saw a journeyman screenwriter out of the New York milieu—and sneered just a little, though Cain had outlasted them all out."

Cain X 3 produced a flurry of publicity across the country that reminded the whole World War II generation of readers that the author of *Postman*, "Double Indemnity," *Serenade*, and *Mildred Pierce* was alive and well and living in, of all places, Hyattsville, Maryland. It also produced letters from all over the country and turned Cain into a local celebrity who was asked to autograph books, speak to some group or other, and be interviewed by the students in Room 9A in the Hyattsville Junior High. Even the pooch next door, Cain said, seemed to treat him with more respect.

At about the same time, Cain received a boost from still another source. David Madden's *James M. Cain* was finally published, and after much agonizing and anguish, Cain came to the conclusion he liked the book and that Madden had done a good job. The study had been ready in the fall of 1965, but due to a variety of obstacles was not published until late 1970. Cain was fidgety all during the delay, convinced Twayne was taking its time because James M. Cain was no longer a popular writer and therefore not important enough to justify such serious treatment (which was not the case for Twayne, as Madden tried to assure him). And he still resented being categorized a "tough-guy writer." "You'd think, instead of A.M. Washington College, I was H. DC. [Honorable Discharge] from Sing Sing," he told one friend. But all ended well, and after publication Cain wrote Madden: "I'm not only pleased, but pleased as punch and accept this book as well as like it."

In the book, Madden expanded on his theme that Cain was one of our leading writers of the "pure novel," a novel that does not depend on a genre such as "crime" for its existence. He saw Cain as a novelist who had pursued the American dream to its manifest destiny: "Cain went to the scene of the last-ditch stand of western romance—the shores of the Pacific—to deal in broken American dreams. On this landscape of decaying dramatic scenery he continued to depict man's innate desire for the drama which life seems to deny the average man." Cain's art, Madden concluded, "more than anything else, moves even the serious reader to almost complete emotional commitment to the traumatic experiences Cain renders."

Madden also discussed the impact Cain and the other "tough-guy" American writers had had on American literature, as well as on European intellectuals, especially Albert Camus and the Italian and French movie-makers of the postwar period. The book sold only 1,500 copies and was not widely reviewed, but it enhanced Cain's standing in academia. And during an interview with Cain on a Washington TV station, the host held up the Madden book and praised it as signifying Cain's acceptance in American literature.

Despite all the excitement—or perhaps because of it—Cain was not sleeping well at night. His angina was bothering him and he was increasingly concerned about growing old. "So many die," he wrote one friend, "it leaves you rather frightened. I no doubt will go soon—I'm nearer seventy-seven than seventy-six, and I hardly know myself, or quite understand how I got that way." He also found that when he set the alarm clock for an early appointment he would lie awake all night waiting for its ring. So he stopped making morning engagements and, because he had become afraid of blackouts after his shopping mall attack, he cut down on his social life in general. As he wrote one friend he felt he should have invited over, "you and a passel of friends could easily have had crisis stretched out on the floor to deal with—and you couldn't very well have gone kiting off to your car and left it lying there."

And he missed Florence terribly. "Every night, I touch a little memento of my Florence that I keep at the head of my bed," he wrote one friend. "It seems only yesterday since I let myself go to sleep watching the light from her door and yet it's been nearly three years." Now, he would often doze off watching the Huntley-Brinkley newscast, and one night when he did, he woke up with a start to find Florence sitting in the chair across the room. "If you're so tired, why don't you go to bed?" she said.

"I guess I should," he replied. But then he got to wondering why Florence was not sitting beside him so she could see the TV too. "And suddenly, in terror, I realized she wasn't there at all. . . . I was utterly alone."

END OF THE
RAINBOW

After his resurrection by *Cain X 3* and David Madden's study, Cain made some effort to become more accessible professionally. He still declined offers of an honorary degree from Washington College, insisting that he was "not the kind of writer learned degrees were intended for." But he did agree to participate in the dedication of a gymnasium center named after his father, although at the last minute he had to withdraw due to a mild angina attack, which left him conjuring visions of passing out in the college procession. He gradually became good friends with President Dr. Daniel Gibson, and then, when Gibson retired, with the succeeding president, the late Joseph H. McClain. And eventually he got over his anger at his alma mater and donated fifty paperback editions of all his foreign language reprints to the college library.

Despite his periodic concern about his heart, three months after the Washington College gymnasium dedication Cain agreed to go up to New York and accept a Grand Masters Edgar awarded by the Mystery Writers of America. His willingness to make the trip might have been influenced by MWA's decision to put him in the hands of a very attractive Washington mystery writer named Patricia McGerr. Miss McGerr helped him get ready for

New York, even buying him a razor at the last minute and making sure he got to the dinner on time.

Cain entertained the audience with his acceptance speech, and while in New York took the opportunity to have dinner with Ruth Goetz and her family, as well as Arthur Hornblow, Jr. In all, he thoroughly enjoyed the trip, coming to the conclusion that he had more pep than he thought.

With all this newfound energy, he even agreed to take part in a Catholic University symposium on "Literature and the Cinema," and then a more extensive writing project sponsored by the Maryland Art Council, in which he participated with Dr. Carl Bode, James Backas, and novelist Jack Salamanca in a writing course for the winners of a Maryland literary composition. Cain worked in the program three consecutive years, though at first, as always, he thought he had made a mess of it. "Refreshed by two hours sleep, dolled up in a Hollywood suit and perfumed with Charbert cologne, I laid my usual, extra-fancy, guaranteed fresh jumbo-select egg." But the students thought differently; in fact, the session in which he selected a simple plot idea from one of the students and prodded the class into developing it into a screenplay was thought to be one of the best. Cain finally pulled out, though, after developing "a bad case of the Doubts about the whole project—as to whether we aren't dangling a chimera in front of those kids, encouraging them to do something most of them will not have the talent for, ever. *If* it's a talent. Personally, I think it's a disease, and the fact it produces books that people buy doesn't make it any more healthy."

In the early seventies, he also started sending pieces on random subjects to Philip Geyelin, editorial page editor of the *Washington Post*. Although occasionally one would be used on the op-ed page, most were returned, and finally Cain confessed to Geyelin his reason for submitting the pieces: he wanted to work up a close enough relationship with Geyelin to make the real pitch—"to be taken on as an if-as-&-when editorial writer for the *Post*, contributing pieces on nonpolitical subjects, like holidays, sporting events, book hits, and so on. . . . My trouble as a columnist is a psychological block I've never surmounted: On paper I can't be myself, always having to put my novels in the mouth of some characters or else be stiff-self-conscious and queer. But pretending to be the corporate awfulness of the newspaper, I'm in my element." Cain was not proposing a regular job or salary arrangement, just piecemeal work to be done at home. He would send in weekly memos on the subjects he would like to discuss, then Geyelin would have a brief conversation with him every morning about what he was to write on the next day. Editorial writers on major papers have worked this way, but it is a relationship the writer usually develops after twenty years or more in his editorial cubbyhole serving the page. Such plush assignments are seldom handed out to outside writers, no matter how big the name or how good the writer. Geyelin declined Cain's offer.

Although still leading a lonely life, Cain was now less reclusive than he had been before Florence died. He also had a new cat—Snobby—a stray tom he had come by on Christmas Day, 1969, and which he had planned to send to the animal hospital to be put to sleep; but then after feeding him, nursing, and giving him Kaopectate with an eyedropper, he could not bear to part with him. So Snobby stayed, and Cain took up a quiet life with his new pet: "I wake up every morning feeling utterly pooped . . . tell myself I owe it to myself to take a day off. I get up, put on my bathrobe, go down in bare feet and let in the cat . . . he is as God created him, without any surgical improvements, and he's going to stay that way if I have anything to do with it. But it means he has to be let out at night, and so around 8 a.m. I go down and let him in. Then for ten minutes we have a snuggle, which he looks forward to and insists on. Then [after feeding Snobby] I read the paper a few minutes. Then I come up, bathe, shave, and dress. Then I go down, finish the paper, broil up my breakfast, and eat it. Then I go to work. After three or four hours of that, I suddenly remember my decision not to work and ask myself what happened to it. I always seem to forget about it. But one of these days, I'll take a day off. In the evening, sometimes people come in—I have a few friends who live nearby and we crack jokes."

Cain's new friends included a widening circle of people from around his neighborhood who gradually came to dote on him. Ted and Thelma Kisielnicki, next door, and their eleven children were especially close. But he could be a trying friend and neighbor. "I loved him dearly," says Thelma Kisielnicki, "but there were times he would feel like a stone around my neck. Most of the time he could be a very charming man, but he could also be very difficult. One time I was out in my front yard and my dog took after a stray cat and he got very angry and wanted to know why I let my dog chase after that cat. So I went in the house. But I knew the next day there would be flowers from the florist—and there were—always with a little note saying he was doing penance."

There were also Keith and Leona Dunklee up the street. They had moved down from Rochester in 1965 and had known Florence only briefly. "I knew she did not accept the neighbors," said Leona Dunklee, "so I stayed away." But after Florence died and Cain began gradually to emerge from his shrine, he and the Dunklees became good friends. Keith was in the auto leasing business and would do favors for Cain and take him for drives on Sunday afternoons. Then, Leona started chauffeuring him around, helping him gather background information for the story he was working on. Keith had always had an interest in music and was a baritone, which helped bring them together, although Cain assured them he could not sing.

In the late 1960s, Cain went along with the Dunklees to a Christmas party at the home of Jim and Dorothy Youniss, and he developed a strong relationship with the Younisses that lasted the rest of his life. "I remember the first couple of meetings were not pleasant," says Jim Youniss. "He felt he had to tell us his Hollywood stories and all that. And then we met straight on and it was very pleasant." It became a weekly habit to get together. Cain would call up about five o'clock in the afternoon with some pretext such as: "Did you hear what Nixon said today? We gotta talk about that," which meant Dorothy was supposed to pick him up at eight o'clock. So she did, Youniss says, and "he'd come in the house with his Australian hat pulled down over his bushy eyebrows, and in one hand he'd have a bone for the dog and the other held some candy for the kids."

When Leona Dunklee subsequently went to work, Dorothy Youniss took over the chauffeuring and drove Cain to places where he had to speak, or to lunch at Trader Vic's with some of the *Potomac* writers, with whom he eventually became quite friendly. At first, Jim Youniss says, he was never quite sure why Cain wanted to talk with him, and then they began to realize that he was hungry for good conversation. According to Dorothy, Cain used to say "Jim reminds me of Lippmann and you remind me of Mencken." And when she asked why, he replied: "Because when I talked with Lippmann, I always felt I had heard something. And you remind me of Mencken because he was always on time."

One thing that impressed all his neighbors was the interest and concern Cain showed for the children. The Kisielnickis had eleven children, the Lewises next door had two, the Dunklees had three, and the Younisses had four. And Cain always knew where each one was in school and how they were doing. He had candy for them every Halloween, and every Christmas he would send them a card with $5 in it, until finally he decided "you can't do anything with $5 these days," so he started sending them $10. One neighborhood boy whom Cain had taken an interest in was Eric Piper, who used to go by Cain's house and listen to his tales about Hollywood. And when Eric was going abroad and wanted to say good-bye to Mr. Cain, his mother, Alice Piper, said she would like to go along and meet him.

Alice Piper worked in the Adult Education Program at the University of Maryland, where her husband was an engineering professor. She was impressed by Cain and enjoyed hearing him talk. Having had some experience taking care of older people in her own family, she began to inquire if there was anything she could do for him. He seemed to enjoy her company, so she began calling him up to ask if she could bring him a casserole or something, and usually he agreed. So, gradually, Alice Piper started looking after him. She found his endless storytelling fascinating, as well as his talk about music and writing. "But I liked mostly his sense of humor and the fact that he was most often in a good humor. He was very considerate of others, always a gentleman. And he did not put others down, never intellectually arrogant or impatient with people of lesser intellect. His most irritating quality for me was the way he would use slang, although you knew he could speak much better. 'Leave us face it' was one of his favorites that always annoyed me."

From the early 1970s until Cain's death, these friendships became closer and closer—and remained genuine. Cain also made a few amusing, and sometimes poignant, attempts to meet or court younger women. In 1972, the name of Dita Beard emerged in the media as the woman who wrote an office memo that seemed to substantiate the accusation that the Nixon administration had settled some antitrust cases in favor of ITT for a $400,000 contribution to the 1972 Republican presidential campaign fund. Cain thought Mrs. Beard had been wronged because a private memo from one officer to another in a private corporation had been made public. He thought she had grounds for a lawsuit, and so he wrote her when she was in the hospital in Denver, suffering from a heart condition. He also said he thought she was "very good-looking," and that her writing style was "enchanting."

This led to a lengthy correspondence between Mrs. Beard and Cain, through which he became more and more infatuated with her. He told her he had the same heart condition and advised her how to treat it. Then, finally, they met. Mrs. Beard's daughters agreed to take her out to Cain's house to meet him one Saturday afternoon, and Cain immediately called the Younisses for moral support. They agreed to help and arrived early. For the occasion, Cain made some of his famous mint juleps, which were to be savored and oohed over if one did not wish to offend the host. The Beards arrived, and Cain's jaw dropped perceptibly: the woman who had inspired such passionate letters did not look at all as she had in the media. And when she started to speak, which was "steadily," according to Jim Youniss, she must have used every cussword in the book, which, coming from a woman, offended Cain. Finally, the ultimate offense. She took one of his mint juleps, asked what it was, said "good" when he told her, and gulped it down, almost in a single swallow. Cain slumped down in his chair and did not come to life until about 4:40 P.M., when Mrs. Beard announced she had to be leaving. It was a case of mutual disenchantment.

His affair with Robin Deck, however, was more enduring. Ms. Deck worked on Capitol Hill and was interested in the theater. One day she was taken by a friend to hear Cain talk at Catholic University, where he was participating in a seminar on "Literature and the Cinema." An acquaintanceship was established, and a few months later Robin's friend, an aspiring writer, suggested they go out to see Cain. It was an enjoyable afternoon, followed by Cain's calling Robin several days later and inviting her out by herself. She went, and thus began a period of about nine months in which Robin saw Cain constantly—often spending the day at his house and going to parties and other social affairs with him. She was not working at the time and found it very exciting and stimulating talking with Cain, who advised her on her life and career. The friendship finally came to an end when she left for Guam, where she planned to marry a man who worked for the governor. She and Cain exchanged several letters and phone calls while she was away. Then, three years later, after her marriage plans had fallen through, she returned to Washington. Cain had asked her to come and stay with him after her return, but they never did resume their close relationship.

During this period Cain was also engaged in continuing correspondences with Aileen Pringle, Constance Cummings, and Ruth Goetz, none with romantic overtones, but all suggesting Cain's overwhelming desire for acceptance by women. Although most of his fictional heroines are portrayed as bitches, in life Cain was drawn to women in a basic, passionate way, as Winthrop Sargent once noted in a letter to him, to which Cain replied: "Curious you should have used the word 'passion' as describing my attitude, in writing, toward women. It is the secret word I use to myself, though never, of course, would admit publicly, as it might get volleyed around. To me, I mean seriously, not merely as a pat formula I have found convenient, love may be many things but first of all, before it is anything, it must be desire, and without desire, it is nothing. But desire, of course, if you can get it incandescent enough, is passion—something aimed at, seldom reached, but at least you sense it."

He always summed up his own attitude toward women by differing with Mencken, who had said: "Love is the illusion that one woman differs from another." Cain's view was: "Love is the discovery that one woman does differ from another."

One of Cain's few remaining pleasures was snatched from him after his cat, Snobby, wandered away for five days and returned with a fractured jaw. Dorothy Youniss drove them to the vet, who wired the cat's jaw, but there was nothing more to be done. One afternoon, Cain dozed off for a nap with Snobby at his side. When he awoke, Snobby was dead. "Few things in my life have upset me so," he wrote Rosalie. His relationship with Snobby had been an education, he said, "and, as always in my relation to other created things, brought me closer to God. The love and devotion that this little creature has shown is an inspiration."

Along with a more outgoing social life and an attempt to become more accessible professionally, Cain had also changed his attitude toward interviews. As he neared eighty, he became more agreeable to being on TV and talking with reporters, and the venerable old goat, as he often called himself, began appearing in the media. Thomas Chastain, a novelist who had always been a Cain fan, came down from New York to interview him for *Publishers Weekly*, just prior to his eightieth birthday. "James Cain is six feet tall and big-framed," Chastain reported, "the hair and memorably bushy eyebrows are still gray rather than white, giving him, overall, a bit of the look of the southern Colonel. Most of all, the vitality of the writing is evident in the man, even after eight decades, four wives, seventeen years as a screenwriter in Hollywood and, not least, sixteen novels which most critics of his work agree virtually assure him a place in world literature."

Cain told Chastain that "my eyes are not on the past. I can honestly say I have no consciousness of any sense of achievement. I'm excited for the future, for the new book, the book I'm working on now."

Despite his four straight rejected novels, by 1972 Cain was writing again. He had several reasons for continuing at his typewriter or yellow pad every morning. In the first place, there was his diehard unwillingness to admit he was an ex-writer. Second, there was the old need for money. *Cain X 3* had brought in some royalties, but it also, for a while at least, hurt his reprint sales. His situation finally became so desperate that he had to discontinue the monthly check he sent regularly to his sister Rosalie and ask his agent Ivan von Auw for a $1,000 advance on his next novel, which he knew was asking a lot "because you and Dorothy wouldn't be human if you hadn't begun to wonder if I'm through as a novelist." Also, he had received an unexpected lift from H. N. Swanson in Hollywood, to whom he had sent *The Enchanted Isle*. Swanson, who was about Cain's age, thought Cain had shown real understanding of the generation gap. "This is Cain at his suspenseful best," he wrote. "I plan to sell it by pointing out that this girl is typical of the kids who run away from home these days." Swanson put a new title on it— *The Mink Coat*—Xeroxed ten copies, and started sending them around to the studios. His enthusiasm made Cain happier than the latest option sale of *Past All Dishonor* to a producer named Jerry Gershwin. Reminded of the time Knopf had turned down *Postman* before Walter Lippmann intervened, Cain now thought maybe it would happen all over again with a little sleeper named *The Mink Coat*. But the story never sold to the movies, or to a publisher— and Gershwin never made a movie from *Past All Dishonor*.

So Cain started to work again on a novel he had begun after *The Magician's Wife*, "the story of a modern Don Juan, a biographical sort of thing," he said. "It has been in my mind for years and always hung up on a basic snag." In his unpublished memoirs, Cain describes his problem with the novel at some length: His Don Juan was to go on chasing women successfully "until he meets a filthy rich widow, with a teen-age son, realizes he can get her, and with her, her money, and proceeds to do it, leaving her ecstatically happy—the teen-age son not so much. But having made the killing of a lifetime, he realizes that to hang on to the money he'll have to be true to the wife, something he's never been, to any woman, something he knows, or fears, he's utterly incapable of. So he clenches his fist and tries. But the teen-age son is no help. He has friends, and they tell him his stepfather's proclivities, so he presently brings on a confrontation. He tells the guy he knows what kind of rat he is, knows what he means to do, which is kill his mother for the money. He says: 'O.K., I've tried to beat some sense into her head, tried to get her to call it off, this insane thing with you. But I'm warning you: You kill her and I'll kill you.'

"So, I had a thing rolling that seemed really to have a kick—a guy had his dream come true and then found out he had to live with it. I worked out all kinks, set the whole tale against the Maryland countryside, put together a mansion, an acre of grass, a countryside . . . came up with an outline as good as I could possibly want—and I knew I was off."

The enthusiasm was brief, as he came to realize he had a plot that would not work. As he explained it, "Lurking in this book was something I couldn't make myself swallow. I'd written about heels, and in fact seem mainly to have chosen heels as my central characters. But this particular heel, for some reason, I found myself unable to take any interest in. He much too much resembled that other heel celebrated for the same weakness, Jacques Casanova. Now, Casanova, as I think, was the great literary figure of the eighteenth century. Thackeray himself admitted it was Casanova's account of his adventures in London that gave him the idea for *Vanity Fair*, and if there had been no Casanova we can question whether Dumas Père would have come into flower in quite the way that he did. But personally, Casanova was contemptible, verging on sickening. In the case of my guy, he had to be just as much of a crook, just as much without conscience, and worst of all, for me, just as vain, just as proud of himself for the successes he had with women, as Casanova was as a matter of habit. So, I had a fine novel, with nice, exact algebra going for it, and an explosive, cracking climax awaiting me that really gave great promise. I couldn't write one word of it. It just died from a slight case of stomach sickness. I had never had that happen, though it came close to happening in *Mignon*."

But Cain hated to give up all the work he had done to create the Maryland atmosphere, and he was intrigued by the character of the widow, as he always was by someone with a great deal of money. Furthermore, he felt he was back in the old Cain groove. "Somewhere along the line," he wrote a friend in 1972, "I got the idea that happy endings were tougher and for that reason a 'greater challenge.' But when I began trying to carry this idea out, and came up with things that were neither one thing nor the other . . . [I made] the resolve to get myself back to first principles, and let the guy lose everything, if that's what the theme says he should do."

For years Cain had been meditating on doing a story that dealt indirectly with the subject of biography, so now he started the novel over with a not-too-young English professor at the University of Maryland who goes to Wilmington, Delaware, to persuade a conglomerate millionaire to put up $20 million for an Institute of Biography—to be located in Washington near the Library of Congress. The English professor would be the director, and the millionaire, of course, would have a good-looking wife who quickly becomes involved in a love affair with the professor. The millionaire, in turn, is having an affair with the only woman in the world who can arouse him sexually—his Swedish housekeeper. But if he were to get divorced, he would have to marry her, and he does not want to marry a servant. To this foursome, Cain added an oversexed University of Maryland coed who is willing to go to bed with the professor for love and with the millionaire for mink and who brings this complex—and at times even suspenseful—plot to an improbable conclusion, with all his people acting out of character. He also injected one of his pet theories, by conveniently making it the subject of the Maryland professor's Ph.D. thesis—that the mysterious woman in Shakespeare's sonnets was actually Anne Hathaway. The sonnets, according to Cain, were written by a very young genius in love with himself, and the "W.H." which the Thorpe edition says was "the true begetter of these sonnets" was none other than "Will Himself." Cain was convinced he had made a significant discovery, one that would ensure the book wide attention.

Cain called this one *The Institute*, and immediately after finishing it he sent it off to Dorothy Olding, who submitted it to Knopf. Again it was Bill Koshland who had the painful job of turning down another Cain effort, although this time his letter went to Ms. Olding: "I just can't persuade myself that we should publish this and I'm terribly afraid no one else will either. Jim, alas, lived too long and can't adapt his own considerable gifts to today's modes." Other readers of *The Institute* were having the same reaction. Both Ruth Goetz and a Washington friend thought the dialogue was dated, and Cain said he did not know what he could do about it. "I have to write as I write, and can't young it up."

He did have to write—in fact, it seemed that nothing could discourage James M. Cain from writing. Despite five straight rejections, he went immediately into another novel—this one about "the mystical nonexistence of hijacking." He had a hijacker parachute out of an airplane with $100,000 and an airline stewardess as hostage, perhaps inspired by the news story of a hijacker who did bail out over the Rockies with a lot of money and was never found—although some of the money was. The two land on an island in the Muskingum River in Ohio, where they disrupt the lives of two mountain folk—a mother and her son living on a farm near the river. In a piece of vintage Cain, he had the airline stewardess and the son begin to jockey for the money. He also added a touch of forbidden sex as, reaching back to *The Butterfly*, "I stole an element out of mountain mores. It's not uncommon for Mom, who's probably still in her twenties, with a good-looking boy and nothing to do with herself up there in the hollow where they live, to get a letch for this boy. . . . But she was not the *real* mother. I put that in to make it palatable."

Cain became very excited about this one, and even went prancing full of vim and vigor out to Marietta, Ohio, to gather background, or "dope," as he always put it. Marietta gave him the red-carpet treatment, including interviews in the *Marietta Times*, during one of which he met *Times* reporter Melinda Howes, whom he took out to dinner and quickly fell in love with, causing her considerable embarrassment. But perhaps the most significant thing about this meeting is that Ms. Howes remembers him as very alive, alert, and active, although he was by then eighty years old.

Meanwhile, things were happening in New York. Thomas Chastain had sold a mystery novel to the new publishing house of Mason and Lipscomb and, in the course of conversations with one of the young partners in the firm, Thomas Lipscomb, Chastain showed him his Cain interview in *PW* and mentioned *The Institute*. Lipscomb asked Chastain to see what he could find out about its status. Chastain called Cain, who told him Knopf had turned down *The Institute* and that he was writing a new one, the story of the hijacking, which he now called *Rainbow's End*. Chastain reported this back to Lipscomb, who was very interested, having always been a fan of Cain's. But he also wondered "whether Jim Cain was still in fighting trim or was this just a last gasp."

To find out, Lipscomb went to see Cain in Hyattsville. He was impressed by his alertness, professionalism, and stream of ideas for books. He did not especially like *The Institute*, but he was enthusiastic about Cain's description of *Rainbow's End*. But then Cain told Lipscomb he would never let any publisher see a work-in-progress. They finally agreed to a two-book contract (the second book being *The Institute*) calling for $7,500 per book, the largest contract Cain had ever received. Mason and Lipscomb was a young house with lots of money and few authors, and a resurrected James M. Cain would give them just the by-liner they were looking for. In addition, Lipscomb had had talks with film and paperback people, all of whom expressed interest in a new James M. Cain title, and Lipscomb passed this word along to Cain, urging him to finish *Rainbow's End*.

Cain sent the manuscript up to New York in late summer, and while he awaited Lipscomb's reaction he began to rewrite *The Institute*. Lipscomb's reaction to *Rainbow's End* came quickly. He thought Cain had done a beautiful job for the first three-quarters of the book. But he did not like the happy ending; it was not consistent with the characters or the story Cain had originally outlined to him. He told Cain what he thought in a letter couched in perfect editorialese: "To put it in a nutshell, you've built something fascinating and strong, but I think you've left a lot of the scaffolding up so it makes it hard for me to see the whole structure."

Cain said he did not know what Lipscomb meant by the scaffolding showing, so Lipscomb followed with a more detailed analysis, to which Cain did not object. He decided the whole novel needed extensive work and began the usual rewriting, which lasted well into early 1974. But he did not change the ending, much to Lipscomb's displeasure. In fact, Lipscomb made one attempt in galleys to alter the ending dramatically, eliminating the double wedding Cain had put in and having the hero lose the girl and the money. This sent Cain into a rage. "In fifty years of writing, for newspapers, magazines and book publishers, I never had anything like this happen to me," he wrote Dorothy Olding. Then he thought it over and decided the double wedding should indeed be eliminated, but that was all. He wrote Lipscomb that his idea that the boy shouldn't get the girl "is so fantastically wrong I've disregarded it."

Lipscomb consented and said later "for all I know, history may prove him right." But he still would have preferred the downbeat ending, and thought he had failed in not fighting hard enough for it.

Cain finished *Rainbow's End* with his characteristic mixture of trepidation and optimism. "I'm pleased to report," he wrote Lipscomb, "that though I'm generally nauseated by what I write, in this case I realized it was holding me—I have done better than I realized." The novel was published in late 1974, as Lipscomb was about to leave the publishing house; and it was agreed a new novel by the resurrected James M. Cain was enough of an occasion to justify a press conference. It was, in fact, not a bad idea to remind people once again just who James M. Cain was; a year before, ABC television had made a not very good version of *Double Indemnity*, starring Lee J. Cobb, Richard Crenna, and Samantha Eggar, and not only did Cain receive no money for the remake, it was advertised as "based on Raymond Chandler's suspense classic," to the understandable annoyance of Cain and all his friends.

The press conference was held during the Association of American

Booksellers annual meeting in Washington. Dorothy Youniss drove him over, and Orlando Petrocelli (who worked for the finance department of Mason and Lipscomb), seeing Cain for the first time, remembers him "as an old man who could hardly walk." It was only the year before that Melinda Howes at the *Marietta Times* had remarked on his agility. Jim Cain had aged perceptibly in his eighty-second year. But he could still captivate an audience, amusing them with such remarks as, "You usually can tell when a writer is going down hill by the size of his liquor bill," and "A woman never remembers the pain of childbirth and a writer never remembers his plots." Most of the people present were too young to remember the James M. Cain who wrote *The Postman Always Rings Twice*, and as one reporter said to Larry Swindell of the *Philadelphia Inquirer*, when told about "Double Indemnity," "Oh, yeah! I saw the movie on TV. Didn't know it had been a book." Cain also told them about Hollywood, Lana Turner, and the reason for his literary silence all these years. It was because sitting at the typewriter wore him out. "Now I lie on a couch and write longhand and a girl types it for me," he said, neglecting to mention the succession of unpublishable books he had written in the nine years since *The Magician's Wife*.

By the time *Rainbow's End* was published, Cain was convinced he had not put in enough work on the ending, perhaps agreeing with Lipscomb that a happy ending was a mistake—although he never conceded the point. He just said the ending was full of kinks and that the editors had changed all the dialogue "so they didn't sound like mountain people in Ohio." But he was tired of the book and wanted to get on with *The Institute*, which, in his opinion, was far more important.

The reviewers, however, preferred *Rainbow's End*, and most of them applauded the return of the old master of mayhem and murder. "In Maryland," wrote John Barkham, in his syndicated review, "James M. Cain is still very much alive, and though you saw his 'Mildred Pierce' and 'The Postman Always Rings Twice' as very old, very late movies . . . 'Rainbow's End' is written with the same drive, the same energy, the same lean hyped prose with not a word wasted. If there's any trace of mellowness with age, it's in the happy ending." Charles Witteford, in the *Miami Herald*, said *"Rainbow's End*, I'm happy to say, is vintage Cain, and it's all here—the big money, the unusual circumstances, the spare, tight style and the staccato dialogue."

The *Boston Globe* was also happy to report that James M. Cain was "alive and still writing, at 83, and *Rainbow's End* could have been a crackerjack novel were it not for too many goodies at the end." Richard Fuller, in the *Philadelphia Inquirer*, said, "Cain has the old momentum, and you keep turning the pages to find out what in thunderation is going to happen."

The resurrection of James M. Cain was now acknowledged nationwide, after having been known by Washingtonians and a few New Yorkers for some time. In 1974, John Carmody, the *Post* editor who had written the *Potomac* piece on Cain, and Marian Clark, a young assistant editor on *Potomac*, went out to visit Cain in Hyattsville. They had champagne and all got along well. Marian, especially, was taken with Cain. She had read his novels in college and enjoyed listening to him talk. This led to occasional lunches at Trader Vic's in Washington, attended by Cain, his chauffeur for the day (usually Dorothy Youniss), and a small James M. Cain fan club of *Post* staffers: Carmody, Clark, *Potomac* editor Shelby Coffey, and writer Kenneth Turan. Cain was in his element. The *Post* writers knew they were lunching with a legend and loved to hear his Hollywood stories and ask him questions about writers and the old days, which Cain answered candidly. "He shot so straight," as one of them put it. This led to Coffey's asking Cain to contribute short pieces to a couple of special issues of *Potomac*—on "Fame" and "Christmases Past." In time Cain began doing regular articles, mostly light, amusing pieces on such subjects as tape-recorded answering services, working in Kann's Department Store in 1914, and a trip to a nearby animal farm. To gather "the dope" for these articles, he would call on one of his volunteer chauffeurs, insisting on giving them 20 percent of whatever he made on the articles. When Dorothy Youniss drove him out to see the animal farm, he told her to bring the kids along, and afterward they went to McDonald's, where he amazed the Youniss children by knowing all the answers on the Question Cards McDonald's was giving out, enabling the kids to stuff themselves with free dessert. He also baffled the counter girl when he placed his order for dessert. "What's a pie-a-la-mode?" the young thing asked.

But the most impressive reminiscences were done sitting alone at the typewriter. One, in particular—a piece on Walter Lippmann at the time of the former columnist's death in 1975—aroused considerable attention. Cain called it "Walter Lippmann Had Style," and in it said it was Lippmann's "obsession with style and its basic principles" that got Cain his first job. He also wrote that, as he used to say of Lippmann, "he can't be frightened and he can't be bought." Carey McWilliams, editor of *The Nation*, read the piece and wrote Cain urging him to write something for his magazine. Cain replied that he would meditate on it, and that he had been pleased while writing the article on Lippmann to find "the old fire horse could still jump to the sound of the bell, and send it out in two days, that being *Potomac*'s deadline they slapped on me." He added that magazine writing was not his forte. The piece also evoked a little nostalgia in *The New Yorker* offices, from which Andy Logan wrote Cain, complimenting him and saying: "It's the only account I ever read that made him [Lippmann] seem living and real rather than a disembodied and occasionally wrong-headed philosopher. I ran down the hall and gave it to Dick Rovere, who was similarly delighted, and an hour later he was sharing it at lunch with Arthur Schlesinger, Jr. I passed it on to Shawn and Vic Navasky at the *Times*."

After the Lippmann piece appeared, I had a meeting with Cain, the first of several during which I would interview him for a *Washingtonian* article. When I went out to his house, I was greeted cordially by the aging six-footer. His advanced age was accentuated by the thick glasses he wore, lenses that magnified the deeply receding, tired eyes. He still had the beetle eyebrows, though they were gray now. His face was lined and his shirt collar had been drawn tightly around his neck by his necktie. He did not smile easily, but when he thought something was funny he would come up with a good knee-slapping laugh. He was a very gentle man, and his mind was sharp, especially when he talked about writing. His anecdotes about Hollywood and his old literary friends were inexhaustible, although he often repeated himself.

After several interviews, I asked Cain if he would let me take his photograph in Lafayette Park, across from the White House, where he had first made his decision to become a writer—sixty years earlier. At first he said he would, then he said he would not, then he changed his mind again and said, "Hell, I guess if you want to do it, it's all right with me." I said fine, but when I called him back to set the date, he said, "Roy, I've been thinking it over. It's too much like a publicity stunt. I have never gone in for personal publicity, and as a newspaperman I have a distrust of people who do things for publicity. Another thing, I have often been accused of being a sensationalist in my books. And I suppose some of them have been on sensational subjects. But I have always been able to say that although my books might have been sensational in their day, I have never once sought personal publicity by doing anything sensational or that smacks of a publicity stunt. That also has something to do with my feeling about taking that picture."

I tried to convince him the photo would have historical significance, but he still resisted. But a few days later, I telephoned him about some points in the article, and he said: "I've been meaning to call you. I finally decided to go ahead and let you take that photo if you still want to." So we went, quickly, and I shot several rolls of film in Lafayette Park. After a while Cain obviously was tiring and wanted to leave. "I haven't been completely honest with you," he said on the way home in the car, "about why I did not want to go to Lafayette Park. After such trips I get tired. I begin to fade." But he was fine when we got back to the house. I had a beer and he talked for a while about his writing. "I don't know how I'm finally going to come out as a writer. God hasn't made up his mind yet." And when I asked him if he ever regretted his decision to write, he said, "Hell, yes, a hundred times. Every now and then I used to say, 'For Christ's sake, why don't you become a carpenter.' But I'm still at it."

Incredibly, after sixty years, he was still at it, and when *Rainbow's End* was published in 1975, the reviews poured into Mason and Lipscomb, where copies were made and sent down to Cain, who was delighted. Mason and Lipscomb was also happy; the book sold well in hard-cover and Berkley brought out a paperback. But *The Institute* was a different story. After Lipscomb left Mason and Lipscomb (and it became Mason-Charter), Cain was handled by Orlando Petrocelli, now an editor. Petrocelli had agreed with Cain that *The Institute* was a more important book and that it should come out first, but had been overruled by Lipscomb. However, Petrocelli also saw the flaws in the novel, and the first thing he did was in effect to rewrite it. "But then I refused to give it to him because I would be insulting the man," Petrocelli said later. "Who the hell do you think you are, I said to myself. Here is a man with a great reputation—who unfortunately time has passed by." So he made some editorial changes, but far fewer, he said, than Cain later imagined. Still, his editing could not hide the sad fact that time had, indeed, passed Cain by. The sex episodes simply did not read right, and Cain's handling of the Washington scene was embarrassingly uneven.

Cain was thoroughly convinced, however, that no matter what its faults, the book would be widely reviewed because of the "Shakespeare element"—given his conviction that most reviewers considered themselves Shakespeare experts. But he was wrong. The book reviewers of the 1920s and 1930s might have been Shakespeare experts, but in 1976 they showed little interest in Cain's theories about the bard's sonnets. And, although some reviewers, such as Mark Stuart of the *Hackensack Record*, who had missed *Rainbow's End*, greeted "a new novel by James M. Cain" with "You've got to be kidding," most of the critics assumed it was now firmly established that Cain was alive and well and still writing—but lamentably not the way he once did. David Madden, in his review, did call *The Institute* the best of Cain's recent novels, but felt the conversation was dated. And John D. MacDonald, in the Sunday *Times*, had some high praise for the old Cain and acknowledged the debt all writers owed him, Dashiell Hammett, and Raymond Chandler, but said *The Institute* was a "faint and embarrassing echo."

The poor reception of *The Institute* was taken as just one more in a long series of rebuffs at the hands of reviewers. But it was probably harder to take than the others, and not just because of Cain's age and the failure of his Shakespeare thesis to receive any attention. *The Institute* was Cain's first real attempt to write about contemporary people in what might be called his walk of life: that is, upper-middle-class people from the universities, business, law practices, politics, and journalism. Perhaps the contrast in the responses to *Rainbow's End* and *The Institute* gives us a clue to the problem Cain faced as a writer. Both were written when he was in his eighties and both were told in the first person. But the story told by an Ohio mountain boy was applauded by reviewers as sounding like the old Cain; the one told by a University of Maryland Ph.D. was thought by almost everyone who read it to ring false— even in the dialogue, which was James M. Cain's strong suit. This discrepancy worried Cain so much that when David Madden mentioned in his review that Cain's dialogue was "dated," he wrote Madden asking him to cite specific examples, saying "this is a new sin for me to be committing." He thought the sins might have been the fault of the editors at Mason-Charter. Madden responded with a long list of citations, and indeed they read like vintage Cain. But they did not sound right coming from the pen of a university professor or the mouths of people in his walk of life. Cain was a master at capturing the dialogue of Eastern mountain people, the California roughneck, and the Glendale suburbanite, but he could not make educated Easterners sound—or act—right, any more than he could make James M. Cain sound right when writing under his own by-line.

The sale of *Rainbow's End* and *The Institute*, combined with a sudden spurt of interest in his back titles, made it seem almost like the old times in Hollywood, when he went like a yo-yo from rich man to poor man. In 1973, Cain's professional income doubled from $6,000 to nearly $13,000, and in 1974 it was over $10,000. Then it began to decline steadily, and he never had another big sale. The long, incredible literary career of James M. Cain had finally come to an end—after a brief resurrection inspired by David Madden, a collection of earlier novels, and Tom Wolfe, and given life by a few articles in the *Washington Post* and two novels written in his eighties. But the resurrection had come too late; the world had indeed passed him by. No longer was it shocking just to write about incest, adultery, murder, prostitution, and homosexuality; you had to describe the acts in detail—and that gentleman Jim Cain could not do.

James M. Cain, however, could never stop writing. After he finished his final rewrite of *The Institute*, he went immediately into another novel, and before long, it was giving him the usual trouble. He called this one—his last, as it turned out—*The Cocktail Waitress*, and it was a subject to which he had obviously given a lot of thought, and one that probably had autobiographical overtones. It concerned a girl forced to find a job when her husband is killed in an automobile accident. As Cain describes the story in his memoirs: "She lands in a cocktail bar, as a waitress, and within a short time a man comes in whom she met at the funeral . . . he attracts her, the more so since she obviously attracts him, so he leaves her a $20 tip. Some weeks later, when he has sent his driver to bring her to his house, and then, without asking her in, has come out to hand her an envelope, with a check for $45,000 in it, through the window of the car, she is quite agreeably jolted, and at the same time annoyed at the queer way it was done. That night, in the bar, she thanks him, but . . . tells him: 'Well, if you like me that much, $45,000 worth, you could show it the way other people show it—like making passes, like making noises about getting married, something like that. I'm not too bashful to say what I mean, not at all. The $45,000 is fine, but how about that wedding ring?'

"He reacts with pathetic eagerness, telling her he would ask nothing better than to be married to her, but dare not even think of it. He has angina, and the doctor has assured him he dare not get married. Sex would kill him, from the strain it would put on his heart. He loves her, insanely—but he doesn't want to die."

Cain thought he had developed a nice situation, but where did he go from there? "If she persuades him to marry her, and agrees to do without sex, the story has an impossible blank in it. If she marries him and a slip-up occurs, he dies and the story is over." Then there was the old first-person, third-person trouble. Initially Cain tried it in the third person, anticipating the problems of telling it in the first person of a young woman having to talk about her intimate relations with an older man. But after reading the first hundred pages back from the typist, he found it cold and dull and finally decided—*once and for all*—that he could not work in the third person. He started rewriting the story as told by the cocktail waitress—"in her lingo," as he put it—"and it has come off the floor astonishingly." As for the sex, "I had her tell enough so that what happened was clear and, at the same time, not go into details."

It took Cain most of 1975 to finish *The Cocktail Waitress*, and it was hard going. "I always intend not to work; then I do work. I go upstairs about eleven, although sometimes I sit down here thinking about what I'm going to write, clarifying my dialogue. That can often be more laborious than what I actually do at the machine; it can go on for an hour. Then I go up and start to work at the typewriter. I get about six pages a day now at the typewriter, and that poops me out. But six pages is about 2,000 words, and that's what any writer regards as a day's work. When the exhaustion comes you are not giving the reader anything. You get two or three of those highs when it begins to send you, you begin to feel it, and that's exhausting, and after two or three of them you have to quit; you just don't have any more writing in you. I finish writing about two o'clock. Then I come down and sit twiddling my thumbs for about twenty minutes, then I fix my lunch."

After finishing *The Cocktail Waitress*, Cain sent it off to Dorothy Olding, who promptly sent it to Orlando Petrocelli. Still dissatisfied with the ending, Cain wrote Petrocelli that he was going to rework it. "If you're dealing with me, you may as well get used to it," he wrote. "I work on an ending ceaselessly, believing it to be the most vital part of a story." It took him a couple of months to finish the new ending, but to no avail: Petrocelli returned *The Cocktail Waitress* to Olding, saying that "this would only get us in trouble." Ms. Olding agreed and decided not to send it to anyone else.

The rejection of *The Cocktail Waitress* seemed to convince Cain finally that if he was not an ex-writer, he was at least an ex-novelist. So, rather late in his career, he decided to become a children's book writer. The idea grew out of his correspondence with E. B. White, who had told him how well his own children's books were doing. "If White can do so well with children's books, then I have a children's book," he told the Younisses. He dug out his old story about the girl and her pet tiger, *Jinghis Quinn*, and tried to revive it, but with no success. The agent's record shows that it spent close to six months bouncing around from publisher to publisher before it was finally retired—and Cain decided he was not a children's book writer either.

Next, encouraged by all the compliments he had been getting on his reminiscent pieces in the *Washington Post*, he decided to try writing his memoirs, as Dorothy Olding and others had been urging him to do for years: He thought he would develop his story through a series of vignettes about friends and acquaintances from his Hollywood, New York, and Baltimore days, when the going was good—although he was always quick to point out that the "good old days" were not really as good as everyone thought.

Cain worked on his memoirs off and on until his death, and although they are fascinating in spots, they remain disjointed and were never completed to the point where they could be considered for publication. They have, however, been quoted extensively in this book.

Cain's pieces for the *Washington Post*'s *Potomac* section, written partly because he liked one of its editors, Marian Clark, and partly because of the attention they brought him, were remarkably good articles, written in a tight, breezy style and full of the personalization that was now characteristic of much of the "new journalism." It would be hard to tell they were written by a journalist whose first such piece had been published in the *Baltimore American* in 1917—except that Cain did not hestitate to remind readers of his longevity: "Of course, I look like a boy, talk like a boy, and act like a boy, but actually am in my eighties."

There were personality pieces about Jack Benny, W. C. Fields, Charles Laughton, and H. L. Mencken. Others were on subjects he had written about as a *World* editorial writer: how to make a real mint julep; mockingbirds; how to sing "The Star-Spangled Banner" (preferably in a key lower than C, he had finally discovered); treason; and one amusing piece about a molester of his garbage can, which concluded: "God save me, I now have a pet raccoon." He claimed it was the worst-organized piece he had ever written and yet "got the biggest reaction of anything I ever wrote in this reincarnation," or even in the time he was writing for the *World* or Hearst. Animals, he had proved again, would bring more letters to the editor than any other subject with the exception of food. In fact, the dozen or so *Post* articles he wrote on many subjects proved so popular and so pleasing to him personally that at one point he was talking about publishing a collection of them.

One of the *Post* pieces in 1977 led off: "As I begin to write, it is early summer, and for a month I have been an object of curiosity to passers-by in their cars, as I stand in front of my house, here in University Park, Maryland, my mouth hanging open, my head tilted back, my eyes staring up toward the sky. To my neighbors, however, I am a comprehensible spectacle, for they all know what I am doing here." He was simply "drinking in the most beautiful music the morning knows, and trying to locate its source"—the song of the mockingbird.

His neighbors and friends knew exactly "what he was doing" because James M. Cain was now the adopted "granddad" of a small, middle-class Maryland suburb, and it was the business of the neighborhood to know what he was up to at all times. "There are three or four ladies around here," he told one Maryland University audience, "that pretend they come over to tell me a funny thing that happened on the way to the market or wherever they are going, but, actually, they come over to check if I'm still breathing."

The four ladies who took care of him were Thelma Kisielnicki, next door; Leona Dunklee, up the street; and Dorothy Youniss and Alice Piper, who lived a few blocks away. Mrs. Piper had become so close to Cain that he finally persuaded her to become the executrix of his estate.

Cain was now very conscious that time was running out. He posted signs in two or three places around his house which read: "In case of death, Please notify the Maryland Board of Anatomy." And when he made an appointment for someone to visit him, he would often add with a laugh: ". . . if you don't see any crepe on my door."

Thelma Kisielnicki and another lady across the street always watched for his raised window shade in the morning to make sure he was up, especially after the summer of 1977, when he became mentally upset. "For the first time in my life," he told me during this period, "I feel the undertaker breathing over my shoulder." He would also break off in the middle of a telephone conversation, saying he could not talk anymore, that he had to rest. Once, in the middle of the night, he called Alice Piper and asked her why his paper had not been delivered yet. Another morning, when his paper was still on the front doorstep at 11:00 A.M., the neighbor across the street called Thelma Kisielnicki. "So I left work right away and came home, and I thought I was going to find a corpse," says Mrs. Kisielnicki. She let herself in with a key Cain had given her and called to him, and he answered with a muffled noise. She went upstairs and found him. He told her, "I just don't know what's happened to me. I can't seem to get the distance between here and my feet." Kisielnicki insisted on calling a doctor, who gave Cain some medication that seemed to improve his condition.

One day, late in October, Leo Tyszecki called Cain from California to discuss coming East to have Thanksgiving dinner. Cain thought that would be a good idea, but sounded tired and weak and said: "Leo, I'm losing out to them." The next day was cold, miserable, and rainy. Steven Bernard, a rare book collector, had to go out to Cain's house on his lunch hour to pick up some books. They had met three years earlier when Cain autographed some first editions of his novels, and the following year Bernard had been out again for some autographs. This time, his wife had received a call from Cain saying that he was not able to sign the books Bernard had mailed him and would he please pick them up. When Bernard arrived at 6707 44th Avenue and Cain answered the door, Bernard was shocked at his appearance. He looked like Howard Hughes in his last days—"much thinner, and his hair was wild and unruly, shooting straight back," says Bernard.

"I can't take on a job like that," Cain said, pointing to the unopened box of books on the floor. "I'm too old." Bernard apologized for having imposed on him, and Cain said: "If I promised to sign those books for you, I'm sorry to break the promise. That's my problem—I have a flaw in my character. I let people down."

Bernard said he did not believe that, and hurriedly he retrieved the books and left in order to bring an end to what was obviously an embarrassing moment for both of them. When Bernard returned home that evening, he remarked to his wife that Cain must have been quite ill to act so uncharacteristically gruff.

That same evening, about six o'clock, the Kisielnickis went over to Cain's with two trays of food for his dinner. They did not find his condition particularly alarming. He was sitting in his chair, this courtly gentleman who until recent weeks had always risen to his feet when a lady entered the room, but, as always, he tried to force a drink on Ted Kisielnicki. Thelma Kisielnicki fixed a tray in front of him and said: "Here is your dinner; we're going to leave you to eat and we'll be back to take your tray away, so don't try to get up with it."

About twenty minutes later, Mrs. Kisielnicki returned. Cain was not in the chair and everything was deathly quiet. She called and there was no answer. So she went into the kitchen and there she found him slumped in the corner, where he had apparently slid to the floor after washing the dishes. Mrs. Kisielnicki knew what had happened. She walked next door to call her children and husband, who telephoned for the ambulance. The hospital report said James M. Cain had died from "natural causes."

Cain said in 1968: "I used to add my father's age at his deathbed, which was seventy-eight, and my mother's, which was ninety-five, and divide by two, as tradition says you should, and came up with eighty-six, as the age I could look forward to. I'll never make it."

He missed it by only one year. And he was writing until the very end, on his memoirs. Four days after he died, the *Washington Post* published a short article Cain had written for them in October, about bunions in America at the turn of the century. This last published piece of his opened on a nostalgic note: "At the closing days of the last century, when I was a boy and you, I imagine, weren't yet a gleam in your romantic father's eye, all barber shops had a sign in the window: CHIROPODIST." And the day after he died, Steven Bernard received a letter from Cain with the $3 he had sent him earlier to cover the return postage on his books. Mailing that letter must have been one of Cain's last acts.

Cain had said he did not want a funeral service, that he would prefer a cocktail party. Like Mencken, he did not think he was going to a Hereafter, but then he always felt Mencken had erred in playing down his exodus from this world. Cain wanted old friends to gather and have a good, warm time, talking about his departure. And thanks to Alice Piper, Carl Bode, Ruth Goetz, Jim Backas, Jack Salamanca, and Jim Youniss, they did. Hundreds of good, warm folks from the Maryland suburbs—as well as a few people, Ruth Goetz and Constance Cummings among them, from out of town—attended a memorial tribute at Maryland University, where drinks were served after several friends paid tribute: Jim Backas talked about Cain's love of music; Jack Salamanca said he regarded the days and hours he had spent with Cain as meaning more to him than any he had spent with other artists; Carl Bode said Cain was unlike any other American writer; Jim Youniss recalled the warmth Cain had added to their family life; and Ruth Goetz talked about the shy young man she had met in New York in the 1920s. Samson Raphaelson was not able to come, but Ruth Goetz read a letter he had sent for the occasion:

I have been helpless, from the day I heard of his death, as if I had never written before. How do you write about someone who, no matter where he happened to be, the moment you thought of him you knew he was with you, on your side, thinking it out for you, ordaining great things for you, creating an image of you so much more vivid than the image you have of yourself—and often so charmingly different—that you couldn't help loving him.

Loving him for the grace he bestowed on you and on those others who had the luck to be his friends—and it seemed like luck, for there was no rhyme or reason in it. If there was, it was his secret. He had less of the vice of prejudice than any man I ever knew. Without putting on the airs of "tolerance," he always found something amusing, engaging, forgivable, and even worthy, now and then, of his profound respect, in the damnedest imaginable variety and assortment of bums, misfits, pillars of society, friendly and unfriendly neighbors and amicable and glowering aliens. His respect was usually wrapped in a grin—a grin indescribable to anyone who has not seen it on the homely, craggy, unforgettable face of Jamie.

He was a great host to life—particularly hospitable to life's blunders, sins, imbecilities, crimes, and to all the vanities which go hand in hand with virtue, decency, loyalty, and good citizenship.

His feeling for language was imbued with elegance, and his taste was so above cultural display that the elegance was hidden deep beneath his apparently offhand way of writing and speaking—his style.

He was full of opinions—opinions that seemed crotchety, cantankerous, cynical. These opinions somehow never really hurt anyone. They were spontaneous, unexpected, and they came like bubbles, floating, caressing, from his outrageous and loving need to surprise and delight the party of the second part.

He was a man of music. Almost every paragraph of his was the complex product of an orchestral inner ear. Nobody, in my opinion, wrote quite as well as did Jamie when he was going good, and thank God that it is all there, in one book after another, forever, to be found and refound.

THE NEWSPAPERMAN
WHO WROTE YARNS
ON THE SIDE

"I am probably the most misread, misreviewed and misunderstood novelist now writing," Cain wrote in his preface to *Three of a Kind*. One reason for this critical confusion was expressed by University of Maryland professor Carl Bode at the Cain memorial service: "The critics do their damnedest to put writers in pigeonholes, but James M. Cain wouldn't pigeonhole. He was not a tough-guy writer. He was not a detective story writer or a writer of hard-nose mystery as exemplified in the works of Raymond Chandler and Dashiell Hammett. And he was not a Hemingway. He was his own person. There has never been any writer quite like him, and the kind of work he did will be with us for a long while."

This would make Cain happy, because in his opinion the only real measure of a book was "the test of the *Grand Vin*. It lasts." He said critics were nothing more than "posterity's bookmakers," and book reviews were irrelevant. He always professed to follow the practice of fellow novelist Arnold Bennett, who once said of reviews: "I don't read 'em, I measure 'em."

Cain did not especially trust his own critical judgment in fiction, but he had strong opinions about writers and books. Usually he presented his views as one man's opinion rather than as judgments about literary significance. Several writers helped him along the way, and he acknowledged their special contributions: Ring Lardner, H. L. Mencken, Walter Lippmann, and Vincent Lawrence. He also devoured *Sherlock Holmes* and considered A. Conan Doyle another writer he owed a debt to: "That easy intimacy with the reader, the first-person style that seems to get on without effort, that selection of some microscopic thing that explodes the whole situation." He recalled that in writing *Postman*, "when I was thinking of putting in that business about the echo of Nick's voice [heard in the canyon after he died] I had just about decided not to until I remembered an incident in one of the Holmes stories, and I decided to go ahead."

Cain never wrote a literary essay, but in his collected letters and writings we are given a glimpse of his favorite authors and books as well as a few he did not like. Mark Twain, he thought, "goes marching on, almost as alive today as he was when he died," whereas "Hawthorne, Poe, Hart, Wharton, Lewis, Dreiser, all begin to look fly-blown and to be read mainly in American literature courses." He thought *The Red Badge of Courage* by Stephen Crane was "one of the worst novels ever set on paper." And he said the "only writer I consciously cannot stand is Charles Dickens," who is "so dreadful head-on and obvious that I do frow up on the carpet when I think of him." Coleridge he thought the most widely read English poet, and although he acknowledged the faults of "The Ancient Mariner," none of them offset "the fact that certain spots in the middle are livid projections of horror, as good as any ever written."

Most people attribute the famous Cain style and momentum to the fact that he was a newspaper reporter and to the assumption that he was influenced by Ernest Hemingway. Often forgotten is the fact that after Cain made his decision to become a writer in 1914, he went home and taught English and writing for three years at Washington College in Chestertown, Maryland. This was before he had ever worked for a newspaper. And his teaching experience taught him something else he never forgot: "Language wants to be read—in fact, being read is its main object." He soon became so caught up in his study of language that he put together a book on grammar and punctuation with examples from world literature. But he never submitted it to a publisher.

So James M. Cain's preference for clear, fast-paced prose was not simply a case of a newspaperman learning style and structure from the copy desk. Cain was an authority on style and language, a fact that won him his most important newspaper job (on the editorial page of the *New York World*) and helped develop his close friendship with H. L. Mencken. In the 1920s, on train trips between New York and Baltimore, Cain and Mencken would talk for hours about the craft of writing.

Cain's obsession with simplicity in language went back to his conversations with Ike Newton and his childhood arguments with his father, when young Jamie Cain would insist that in writing people should talk as they do talk, whereas his father would insist that people be made to talk as they *should* talk.

Cain's own style can be traced not only to an early fascination with the speech of the average workingman, but to Ring Lardner's free and easy colloquialism (which Cain copied in letters he exchanged with his brother in World War I) and the somewhat refined language of the Western roughneck he later encountered in California.

While admitting he was always conscious of style, Cain denied any effort to be "tough" or that he belonged to any school, hard-boiled or other. He did own up to a little "muscle flexing" in his books, blaming this not on a conscious desire to be tough but to "a morbid fear of boring the reader to death . . . a result of my first fiasco at novel writing [in 1922]." He admitted he was in the habit of "needling a story at the least hint of a letdown." But as for his characters being tough, he said "all my guys are a bunch of yellow-bellied rats. I thought if I ever met Hemingway I would ask him, 'How long do you boil them to make them so tough?' "

He denied that violence was a distinguishing characteristic of his novels. "I take no interest in violence. There's more violence in *Macbeth* or *Hamlet* than in my books." Sex, however, was something else. "Why not?" he wrote a book reviewer. But it had to be justified. "I go on the assumption that I have to earn the right to it—thus devise a situation that inevitably leads to it, that develops its emotion, that has its livid color—and having done this I don't go into details. The idea that it can be omitted or played down, or that it must be regarded as dirty, is nonsense. It is the dominant drive in most human beings, male or female. If it is not there, then something must be wrong with them." But it should be subtly expressed. *Time* once quoted him as saying: "People think I just put stark things in my stories . . . but I don't. The reader has the illusion he is reading about sex. Actually, however, it gets very little footage." A close reading of Cain's most controversial novels bears this out.

Of all the misunderstanding about his work, the charge that annoyed him most was that he had been corrupted by Hollywood. In his 1940 essay, Edmund Wilson said Cain's early novels were "produced in his off-time" from scriptwriting, that they are "a kind of devil's parody of the movies." But at least he liked Cain's earlier novels; by 1946 he thought Cain had been "eaten alive by the movies." Malcolm Cowley said pretty much the same thing that same year.

In rebuttal, Cain took great pains to point out that he was not a successful Hollywood writer, but rather a novelist and newspaperman. He also said that with one exception he never wrote a novel with Hollywood in mind. The one exception was *Love's Lovely Counterfeit*, written first as a magazine serial and conceded by even his admirers to be perhaps his worst hard-cover novel. Certainly he was not trying to please Hollywood with *Postman*, "Double Indemnity," and *Serenade*, considering all the problems the studios had getting them produced. And Hollywood had to add a murder to *Mildred Pierce* to give it a certain "cinemagic."

There is probably, however, some truth to the charge that Hollywood and a desire to please the studios affected his writing, more than Cain would have liked to admit. But as Billy Wilder and Raymond Chandler found out, Cain's dialogue would not adapt to the screen. Like John Cheever's, it was written to be spoken inside the reader's head, not aloud. Yet in the final analysis, it was not so much Hollywood that gave Cain's novels their distinctive cinematic flavor as something else he decided late in life: His first loves were dialogue and the theater, and he never really gave up his ambition to be a playwright. "I am not a novelist at all," he said, "but a playwright who casts his plays in novel form." It was not for the movies Cain was writing his novels, as Wilson and Cowley thought, but the stage—or at least that was how Cain saw it.

But if Cain was an unsuccessful screenwriter, he was an abysmal failure as a playwright. In an attempt to assess Cain as a dramatist, his lifelong friend and colleague, the playwright Samson Raphaelson, says: "My hunch is that Cain was so damn good at dialogue in his novels and he was so inventive when he needed a dramatic scene that he never got it into his head that the very structure of a play was different. He understood the architecture of a novel, but he never even grasped how different architecturally a play was." Movies, Raphaelson points out, often flow like a novel, and when that was called for, Cain was in his element. "But when a playwright's instincts were needed he underestimated the time and effort involved in the exercise of that special skill. Five pages to a novelist are five pages. To a playwright they are a SCENE it might take weeks to solve."

The most characteristic aspect of Cain's best novels is the fact that they are all written in the first person. Only three are not: *Mildred Pierce*, *Love's Lovely Counterfeit*, and *The Magician's Wife*. And this, too, he related to the fact that he was primarily a novelist who was really a playwright. "You see," he told one interviewer, "the playwright can be the other character . . . at no point does he speak for himself and . . . I guess I'm kind of a bastard type, a playwright who is half novelist and a novelist who is more than half playwright."

In Cain's first-person novels, the person telling the story is usually someone not gifted with a graceful literary style, but a "low-life person," as he called him, who would not be expected to write very well. And what makes these first-person stories unusual is that despite what Cain said, they are written narratively, not as the person would write but as he would talk. If most of the characters who tell Cain stories were *actually* to write them out, they would probably use a very stilted, wordy prose, as many uneducated people do, trying to show they are capable of writing formal English. This contradiction causes, I think, some of the confusion in appraising Cain's style. A story actually *written* by Frank Chambers or John Sharp would, I suspect, read a lot differently than *Postman* or *Serenade*. What Cain did was make their written stories sound as if they had been talked into a tape recorder—long before Sony had made its contribution to literature.

Cain always said he considered himself "a newspaperman who writes yarns on the side." But the yarns would keep stirring him up until he could get them down on paper. "You hire out to do other kinds of writing that leaves you more and more frustrated, until one day you burst out, say to hell with it all and go sit down somewhere and write the thing you truly want to write." But you did not do it for self-expression. The main purpose of writing was to entertain, which is why Cain was not ashamed to admit he wrote for money. If people would not buy a book, it was a waste of time writing it. "All books are potboilers," he told one interviewer. "A man who says he wrote a book for any purpose except money and recognition (which leads to more money) does not know what he is saying." To another interviewer he said, "I'm like old man Verdi. When somebody told him that the first performance of one of his operas was sublime, he said, 'Fine. What was the ticket sale?' "

From that day in 1914 when he decided what he wanted to do with his life, he spent sixty-three years involved in some form of writing. It was his sole, lifelong occupation. But writing did not come easily to Cain, and if he indeed wrote for the money he earned every penny of it. He usually made false starts on his novels, sometimes as many as fifty (as on *Past All Dishonor*) before he felt the thing right. He threw out 80,000 words of the first draft of *Postman* because he thought they slowed the story down. "A novel is something that has to be endured by the writer," he said. "Anybody who can't go back for the fourteenth and fifteenth revision with freshness and enthusiasm ought to get out of the business."

Still, putting his own novels through one rewrite after another was an agony. "I always know that when I get a good night's sleep, the next day I'm not going to get any work done. If you're not lying awake at night worrying about it, the reader isn't going to either." He said there are "1,000 reasons, all of them good, for not writing novels. There isn't one good reason for writing them"—except the money, of course, and he sometimes wondered whether the agony was worth the reward. "I never knew a writer who regarded it [writing] as anything but a refined form of crucifixion."

At the same time, Cain agreed with the old saying: "Those who can write must write." But he considered it a disease, not a gift. "Who but a nut would be worrying about a boy, a girl, and a villain who do not exist, who have no problems except as they exist in his head, but at the same time, lo and behold, people are supposed to worry about them."

But for Cain, writing was at least a disease he could live with—in fact, he relished it. In sixty-three years of continual writing, he never tired of his trade. "I seem to have a zest for writing," he said at eighty-three. "It excites and possesses me. I have no sense of it possessing me any less today than it did fifty years ago." He also let people know that he would never take a rest, that he would never retire. And he never did.

Cain thought there was something peculiar about him that explained his first-person approach to writing: "I simply can't imagine why I know what the character is thinking of. What am I, God or something?" He said this late in life, then cited a contemporary best-selling author, Peter Benchley. "That boy who wrote *Jaws*, he knows exactly what was going through the girl's head when she got bitten by the shark, though she never gets to shore and talks to anyone about what she thought. How does he know?"

Cain felt about the third person the way Dorothy Parker felt about the camera. "I think it's a terrible medium," she said. "It sees anything." And he questioned what ability he had to "see everything." The third person was "pretentious." The first person enabled him to write with "salty, pithy expressions." And he thought his inability to be himself was not unusual: "Actors have it, and markedly so."

He did concede, however, that it caused him problems as an author, and not solely because it made his literary facility suspect with the critics. First, why would his main character, "this gabby boy, be telling the story at all?" Second, "if the outline says he must die, as it not infrequently does, how can he from the grave tell how he got that way?"

Cain had to solve these problems by inventing ways and reasons for his first-person narrator to be relating his story or, more often than not, his confession. "It doesn't have to be a very important reason, it can be the most cock-eyed reason in the world that wraps it up in a sentence or two. But just the same, I have to have that or I can't tell the story."

For Cain the story was everything, as he emphasized in his letters from Hollywood to Sally Benson. But you needed predicament to make a good story. "All other technical summaries of what the story teller is up against, like 'little girl in trouble,' which is Hollywood's favorite, or 'guy in a spot,' which is Broadway's, or 'character trapped,' which is the professors', leave out the essence of the whole matter, and particularly the essence of suspense, which is: What is the character going to do about it?"

The predicament Cain most often had in mind when he sat down at the typewriter was how could two people in love get off their love rack. And the love rack was usually murder. "Books ought to be about personal relations rather than broad issues," he said out of his horror of becoming a writer with a MESSAGE. *Alice in Wonderland* was his guide; he always tried to "remember this book as something to steer by. I . . . remind myself it is about a little girl who followed a white rabbit down his hole—about as unpretentious an idea as could be imagined. It is, so far as I see now, devoid of any significance, any lesson to be imparted, any wisdom—those pitfalls for every writer. Whenever I feel an impulse to be important, I remind myself of Alice."

The important thing was not only to have a good story but to tell it in an interesting fashion, one that would not put the reader to sleep. As for motivation, he thought it should be obvious in his character's actions, and that there should be no need to explain the "why." His early critics considered this one of Cain's faults as a writer, and by mid-career he thought there might be some justification to the charge. He began to think more about motivation: "Before, I thought why my characters did certain things was completely obvious because they acted from basic emotions. Now I realize there can be a whole lot of other motivations." Still, it never became a deep concern. Later in life, he admitted: "I have no consciousness of ever developing a character in any particular way. I think it's something I should be concerned about, but I'm not." He felt he had little capacity to analyze character either in fiction or in real life.

Cain believed the typical pattern of his mind was tragic. "I may not have the literary stature to be given credit for 'tragedy,' that pretentious word, and yet my thinking seems to veer in that direction. Tragedy in America," he said, "is usually interpreted to mean the forces of circumstances driving the protagonist to defeat, or frustration or death or ruin or something of this sort. This is a superficial, academic idea. I once heard my father give a better definition: 'Tragedy is that force of circumstances driving the protagonist to the *commission of a dreadful act!*' I didn't hear him say this until I had written *The Postman Always Rings Twice*, and I had never theorized much about tragedy, Greek or otherwise. Yet it will apply to most of my writing, even my lighter things."

Cain eventually came to the conclusion that in his novels he tried to satisfy a theme, whereas most novelists, he thought, regarded the principal character as a theme. By "using characters off the top of the pile, plain average people scarcely worth describing in detail," he adhered to a theme, sometimes with astonishing results. "When I finished *Past All Dishonor*," he wrote David Madden, "I hadn't any idea why I wanted Morina to die in the snow. Then [Florence] said: 'But I know why, and it seems funny that the snow, to you, was merely something that "wanted in," as you put it. It was symbolic, don't you see, of Morina's obsession that here now at last, by blood and theft and brilliantly managed escape, she was purged of all evil, becoming at last pure. That's why the snow wanted in.' I began to suspect that she was right."

It has been observed that Cain's novels were musical in their structure, that he could develop his climax the way a composer develops a coda. And indeed Cain thought there was a relationship between music, especially out of his preference for thematic music, and his novels: "Beethoven, Mendelssohn, Puccini, Mascagni, Bizet . . . are my favorites, all different emotionally, but similar in the logic of their musical approach. Wagner, Richard Strauss, Debussy . . . who depend on overpowering gush of tone, harmony and color, tend to bore me. It even carries over to the popular side, for Vincent Youmans interests me more than any American composer, as he is the only one I know of who makes tunes out of themes, as such. 'Tea for Two' is built out of three notes treated as a theme. It therefore, to my imagination, is exciting, all the more so because of its leanness. [My] novels which were thematically worked up . . . were hits—*The Postman Always Rings Twice*, *Past All Dishonor*, *The Butterfly* and 'Double Indemnity'—whereas those which proceeded more from character and character destiny, *Mildred Pierce*, *The Moth*, *Serenade*, and *Mignon*, didn't do so well."

Over the years, Cain was besieged by requests for advice from would-be writers seeking guidance on how to write a novel. He always responded graciously, and most of his nuggets of wisdom have been preserved in correspondence, ranging from fundamental advice to amateurs, such as his sister Genevieve, to more professional tips to such established writers as Sally Benson. If one were to summarize his message on how to write a novel, it would be in one word: Write! Just sit down at the typewriter and start writing—and see whether you have it in you. Don't spend a lot of time thinking about "being" a writer. "If someone says he's going to write the life of Shakespeare," he wrote one eager correspondent, "or a History of England, or a novel about a sharecropper, then probably he means it and eventually will get the thing out. If he merely intends to 'write' without quite knowing what, he may be kidding himself."

To Cain, the art of writing was simply a matter of "having something to say and wanting to say it." Asking yourself whether you had it in you to write a novel was "a form of introspection closely tied up with all amateurs' highly exaggerated ideas of the sanctity of art, and the rarity of the talent required to produce it." Such introspection got one nowhere. "One might hesitate to make the decisions necessary for a writing career, but once the decisions have been made, and the financial sacrifices accepted . . . these uncertainties are not in order. . . . Maybe it's not a work of genius. There's no such thing as a book which is gold and another which is brass. Some are better than others, that's all that can be said, but how much better is a matter of opinion."

The distinguished editor Saxe Commins once said: "In all the years I have worked with creative men [among them Theodore Dreiser, Sherwood Anderson, W. H. Auden, Eugene O'Neill, Sinclair Lewis, William Faulkner] there has never been a hint of what some critics insist is the creative process; it is something of which these writers were for the most part unaware." And so it was with Cain. "Novelists," Cain once wrote to a writing teacher, "feel that their craft is pretty well covered by the saying about singing coloratura music, 'You can or you can't.' In other words, the talent, the bias of mind, the aesthetic secretions necessary to doing a novel are congenital, and not to be acquired. As to formal education—if college degrees, etc., are meant—I know of none of them who attach the least importance to it whatever. The truth is that many novelists (London, Dreiser) were almost illiterates, if formal education be counted: their styles were involuted, their sentences did not parse, their background was spotty, encyclopedic in some directions, a total blank in others. The aesthetic gift is . . . a process that begins with conception, often exciting, goes through gestation, usually exhausting, and ends with birth, which is invariably laborious, protracted, and painful. Just what a college education would do to help it [this cycle], whether the parent be a novelist or a woman, is a little hard to see, except to get respect from onlookers. It reminds me of the story told by the Princess Virgilia Sapeia, in *Polish Profile*, of the Viennese obstetrician who said to her, after labor started: 'Would your Highness be kind enough to push?'

"There is no preparation I know of or experiences that will help a novelist. He is well advised to stick to things he knows about, in a journalistic sense. . . . But so far as that prestudy business, like the four years in medical school as prestudy for medicine, it would be just as helpful to aim a peashooter at the moon. Somerset Maugham in *The Summing Up* remarked that while most people gave the novelist credit for exhaustive knowledge of human nature, and no doubt he needed some, he knew of no way to go around studying it. Technique is necessary, and studied by every novelist morning, noon, and night, by reflection, painful trial and error, and discussions with other novelists and interested friends. Every book is in part the test of a new experiment in technique. But the best that can be said is that while it can be learned, it cannot be imparted, and a man will acquire only what he can use."

When the recipient of this advice wrote back, asking him to elaborate on certain points, Cain replied exasperatedly: "The muses I have often said are the most immoral of women. All they ask is to be thrown on the bed, after which they will shower their base attackers with fame, riches, everything they have. But they won't settle for less. And I know of no preparatory course for the crime of rape. It takes (1) a nature of that peculiarly wanton kind, and (2) an irresistible desire for the lady. It still comes down, as I told you, to: You can or you can't."

James M. Cain could. He wrote the English language with the best of them, as even his severest critics concede, and he could concoct and tell a story that the reader would stay awake to finish until 2:00 A.M. if necessary. He was, indeed, a writer's writer, but with it all, he was vaguely dissatisfied with his career. "As a novelist, I am still an uncertain quantity, for I have had dreadful stylistic difficulties to overcome. . . . My trouble is that I have never had any sense of accomplishment whatever. . . . What have I done? Nothing that gives me the slightest lift. I work, I sell something occasionally, I make a living. That's about all there is to tell. I have the same blank in my mind standing in front of an audience, trying to get a kick out of the round of applause, trying to feel something—utterly without success."

This sense of a lack of accomplishment was somehow tied up with the fact that he could write only in the first person, and that even then he had to pretend to be someone else. Why this was so, we will probably never be certain, but after reading all his nonfiction and thousands of his letters, it is clear that when he wrote as himself, as James M. Cain, he had a tendency to be too cute, often the trait of an insecure person. In his unpublished memoirs, he said: "Until now, I have seemed incapable of being myself. Now I can take my shoes off, wobble my toes, and let go, so the tale comes to life."

Cain, being himself at the typewriter, unfortunately liked to wobble his toes a little too much. Pretending to be someone else restrained him to some extent, but his invariable preference to pretend he was some "low-life" character contributed to his problems with the critics, who often complained that he did not write about "significant people," that his characters were all bums, losers, and criminals. This always infuriated Cain. He considered the critics snobs and liked to cite something Carey Wilson, the Hollywood producer who made *Postman*, said to him. "What I like about your books," Wilson told Cain, "is that they're about dumb people that I know I bump into every day in the parking lot. I can believe them. And you put them in interesting situations. After all, how much do I care about a goddamn hobo and a waitress out there in that place you put them in your first novel? But for chrissake, I couldn't put it down for two hours when I read that book."

Most of Cain's characters were like people, "you bump into every day"—or at least you used to in the 1930s. And if they were dumb losers, so were most Americans in the 1930s, or at least they felt pretty dumb and hopeless in the face of a collapsed economy and deteriorating society. Cain might have paraphrased Lincoln and pointed out that God must have liked these dumb people because he made so many of them. Or he might have noted that when Henry Fielding, Laurence Sterne, and Tobias Smollett began writing their realistic novels in the eighteenth century, critics said the same things they later said about him, that these authors were interested primarily in "entertainment" and their characters were all "low-life."

Of course, Cain also drew to some extent on the life around him for his novels. His stepson says that Mildred Pierce's success in the restaurant business was patterned somewhat on the life of Cain's second wife's mother, a very prosperous hotel owner in Helsinki. And Leo thought he knew a woman who was the model for Phyllis Nirdlinger in "Double Indemnity," and a singer who was the model for John Sharp in *Serenade*. But Cain was never comfortable using his personal life and relationships in his fiction, nor could he write about his professional peers. It would have been too obvious who the narrator was. "I never write about newspapermen," he once told me. "It would be transparent that I am writing about myself."

As aware as he was of his limitations as a novelist, on only one occasion did Cain come close to trying to explain them. This was in a 1940 letter to the critic Edmund Wilson, in which Cain said, almost apologetically, that one of his problems as a writer was that writing was "not my first choice as a trade." He recounted his early ambition to be a singer and the discovery that he had no voice. "This was the worst blow of my life, and at the lowest point in my woe I decided to be a writer. . . . Writing to me was distinctly a consolation prize, and I am afraid I so regard it still. I wish I didn't. If I could get one tenth the excitement from the prospect of a book coming out as I used to get from an invitation to sing at some amateur entertainment, I would probably write more books and feel happier about them. But I don't. To me, writing is mainly work, and the fact that I write a lot better than I sing doesn't quite fix things up."

Cain did not believe in philosophizing or moralizing in his stories. Instead, he wrote about what he called "the wish that comes true, for some reason a terrifying concept. . . . I think my stories have some quality of the opening of a forbidden box, and it is this, rather than violence, sex or any of the things usually cited by way of explanation, that gives them the drive so often noted." He also said "money turns out to be death personified in much of my writing because that's the way I see it." And whatever his reluctance to philosophize in his novels, he did say: "My body of work expressed my view of life. I've been accused of being this or that, but never an optimist."

Despite the fact that James M. Cain always felt he was misunderstood, he could say, "I don't lack for at least as much recognition as I deserve." But he was annoyed at reviewers who spent columns pointing out why his books were no good while the public was buying them by the thousands. "I think to myself," he told me, "that the aim of art is to cast a spell over the beholder. Oscar Wilde said that. Well, if the book casts a spell, you can't put it down, and if that's the only object the book has, to say it's no good because it achieves its end . . . I'm bewildered."

CHRONOLOGY

1892   July 1, James Mallahan Cain born in Annapolis, Maryland. First of five
            children born of James W. and Rose Cain. The other children were
            Rosalie, Virginia, Genevieve, and Edward. James W. Cain was a pro-
            fessor at St. John's College.

1903   Family moved across the Bay to Chestertown, where Dr. Cain became
            president of Washington College.

1910   Graduated from Washington College at the age of 17.

1910–14   Held a series of jobs in Maryland and studied voice in Washington,
            D.C., before deciding "out of the blue" to become a writer, while sitting
            on a bench in Lafayette Park, across from the White House.

1914–17   Lived at home in Chestertown, where he tried unsuccessfully to sell
            short stories to magazines. He also taught English and mathematics at
            Washington College, where he received a master's degree in drama.

1918   Reporter for the *Baltimore American* and then the *Sun*, before enlisting
            in the Army as a private. He served in France with the 79th Division and
            saw action in the Meuse-Argonne campaign. His brother was killed in a
            plane accident just after the war ended.

1919   Edited his company newspaper, *The Lorraine Cross*, before returning to
            the states in mid-year and resuming his old job on the *Baltimore Sun*.

1920   Married Mary Rebekah Clough, a college sweetheart.

1922   Covered the treason trial of William Blizzard in Charleston, West Virginia, as a reporter for the *Sun*. Wrote articles about the trial for the *Atlantic Monthly* and *The Nation* as well as by-lined feature pieces for the *Sun*. During this period, he met H. L. Mencken, with whom he enjoyed a lifelong friendship.

1923 Attempted to write a novel growing out of his experiences in West Virginia, but abandoned it deciding he was not a novelist. In the fall, he quit the *Sun* and took a job teaching English and journalism at St. John's College in Annapolis.

1924 Wrote his first article—"The Labor Leader"—for H. L. Mencken. It appeared in the second issue (February) of the *American Mercury*. He also separated from his wife Mary, was forced to resign from St. John's College after a dispute with the president, and entered a tuberculosis sanitarium in Sabillasville, Maryland. He spent the summer in the sanitarium, continuing to write articles for Mencken. Then he went to New York where, with Mencken's help, he found a job writing editorials for Walter Lippmann, editorial page editor of the *New York World*.

1925 Wrote his first dialogue for *Mercury*, "Servants of the People," appearing in the April issue.

1926 First play produced by Philip Goodman, "Crashing the Gates." It was staged in Stamford, Connecticut, and Worcester, Massachusetts, but closed before reaching Broadway.

1927 Divorced Mary Clough and married Elina Sjosted Tyszecka of Finland, mother of two children, Leo and Henrietta.

1928 First short story, "Pastorale," published in the March issue of the *American Mercury*. In September, he began a by-lined column for the Metropolitan section of the *New York World*.

1930 *Our Government*, a collection of satirical dialogues, many of which had appeared in the *Mercury*, published by Alfred A. Knopf.

1931 Lost his job with the *World* when the paper was bought by Roy Howard and discontinued. From February to November he was managing editor of *The New Yorker*. In November, he took a job with Paramount Studios in Hollywood, and for the next 17 years he worked off and on as a scriptwriter for a number of studios (for list of studios, see page 652).

1933 His third short story, "Baby in the Icebox," published in the January *Mercury* and the following year was made into the first movie based on a Cain story—*She Made Her Bed* (for complete list of Cain movies, see Filmography). Also began writing syndicated column for Hearst.

1934 *The Postman Always Rings Twice*, first novel, published by Alfred A. Knopf.

1935 Discontinued Hearst column.

1936 "Double Indemnity" began as a serial in *Liberty* magazine. Adapted *Postman* to the stage and it ran for 72 performances on Broadway.

1937 *Serenade* published by Alfred A. Knopf.

1938 "Two Can Sing" published in *American* magazine (later made into two movies and appeared in hard-cover as *Career in C Major*). Play *7-11* produced by summer stock company in Cohasset, Maine. Father died.

1940	"Money and the Woman" appeared as serial in *Liberty* (later made into movie) and appeared in hard-cover as *The Embezzler*.
1941	*Mildred Pierce* published by Alfred A. Knopf. Cain underwent major operation for ulcer and gallstones.
1942	*Love's Lovely Counterfeit* published by Knopf. Divorced Elina Tyszecka.
1943	*Three of a Kind* (containing "Double Indemnity," "Career in C Major," and "The Embezzler") published by Alfred A. Knopf.
1944	*Double Indemnity* appeared as movie. Cain married Aileen Pringle.
1945	*Mildred Pierce* produced as movie.
1946	*The Postman Always Rings Twice* appeared as movie. *Past All Dishonor* published by Alfred A. Knopf. Cain attempted to launch his American Authors' Authority, which preoccupied him for most of a year. Separated from Aileen Pringle.
1947	*The Butterfly* published by Alfred A. Knopf. Divorced Aileen Pringle and married Florence Macbeth. *Sinful Woman* published by Avon.
1948	*The Moth* published by Alfred A. Knopf. Moved to Hyattsville, Maryland, where he and Florence would spend the rest of their lives.
1950	*Jealous Woman* published by Avon.
1951	*The Root of His Evil* published by Avon.
1953	*Galatea* published by Alfred A. Knopf. Adapted *Postman* for the stage; performed in Pittsburgh, Chicago, and St. Louis.
1958	Cain's mother and his sisters, Virginia and Genevieve, died.
1963	*Mignon* published by Dial.
1965	*The Magician's Wife* published by Dial.
1966	His wife, Florence, died.
1968	Suffered near-fatal heart attack in a Hyattsville shopping mall.
1969	*Cain X 3* published by Alfred A. Knopf.
1974	Wrote first of a series of articles and reminiscences for the *Washington Post*.
1975	*Rainbow's End* published by Mason-Charter.
1976	*The Institute* published by Mason-Charter.
1977	On October 27, James M. Cain died at the age of 85 at his home in Hyattsville, Maryland. His sister, Rosalie, died a few months later in Baltimore.

A C K N O W L E D G M E N T S

A project of this magnitude is impossible without the assistance of many people in many different ways, and I therefore wish to express my sincere appreciation to everyone who had a hand in making this book possible—first and foremost, James M. Cain himself. Before his death, he loaned me twelve cartons of papers and granted me numerous interviews; in addition, his unpublished memoirs, prolific letter writing and carefully kept carbons, from which I quote extensively, have obviously been essential to the development of this manuscript. I also wish to extend my deepest thanks to Mrs. Alice Piper, literary executrix of Cain's estate, for permitting me to quote from Cain's correspondence and papers and otherwise assisting me in a variety of ways during my research and writing.

In addition, a number of people deserve a special show of appreciation: Leo Tyszecki, Cain's stepson, for showing me around James M. Cain country in Hollywood, submitting to interviews, spending hours writing letters, and telephoning me to answer my many queries about his early life in the Cain household; Mrs. Ethel Buyer for loaning me Gilbert Malcolm's World War I diary and locating the only remaining copies, as far as I am aware, of *The Lorraine Cross*; Dorothy Olding, with Harold Ober Associates, Cain's New York agent, William Koshland, with Alfred A. Knopf, and H. N. Swanson, Cain's Hollywood agent, for their complete cooperation in tracing Cain's literary and Hollywood life; Samson and Dorshka Raphaelson and Ruth Goodman Goetz, for reaching back into their memories for recollections of an old friend; my brother David Hoopes and my wife Cora for reading the manuscript in its first draft, suggesting cuts and changes, and polishing; and my editor, Don Hutter, for significant editorial contributions. I also wish to thank my editor in the very early stages, Danny Moses, for his support and encouragement, Dr. Howard M. Merriman, who first introduced me to Cain in my George Washington University days, and Ron Steel, for leading me to invaluable material in Walter Lippmann's papers. David Madden, who wrote his own study of Cain and is cited often in these pages, also played an important part in the evolution of this book, and my debt and gratitude to him are unlimited.

Many other people granted me interviews, assisted me in my researches, or otherwise provided counsel and guidance along the way: James and Margot Backas, Richard Baron, Nicholas Benton, the late B. A. Bergman, Steven Bernard, Lynn Bloom, Carl Bode, Joan Brittain, John Carmody, Thomas Chastain, Shelby Coffey, Judge Stephen Collins, George Harmon Cox, Constance Cummings, Richard Dabney, Robin Deck, Hurt Deringer, E. L. Doctorow, Frederick Dumschott, Keith and Leona Dunklee, Harlan Ellison, James T. Farrell, Suzi Frazier, Martin Gang, Bernard Gessner, Ethel Gibbs, Max Gissen, Maurine Higgenbothan, Mrs. Henrietta Holmes, Henry Powell Hopkins, Melinda Howes, Riley Hughes, Paul Hume, John K. Hutchens, Mary LaFogg, Richard Lebherz, John Leonard, Alfred E. Lewis, Carol and Francis Lewis, Richard Lingeman, Thomas Lipscomb, John Lee Mahin, Ronald Martinetti, Stan Marx, John McAleer, Mary McCarthy, Winzola McClendon, Patricia McGerr, William McGhee, Wilbur McGill, Joseph McLain, Felix Morley, Katherine Myrick, Herbert Nusbaum, Orlando Petrocelli, Richard Powers, Aileen Pringle, Helen Purcell, Donna Schrader, William Seward, Alix Seymore, Virginia Shaffer, James Silberman, Mrs. O. Perry Simmons, John Slonaka, Christine Spilsbury, Chris Steinbrunner, Miriam Strange, W. G. van Sant, John T. Ward, Deanna Wilcox, Billy Wilder, Alan Williams, Mrs. Edmund Wilson, Tom Wolfe, Stephen Wright, James and Dorothy Youniss, David Zinsser, and Maurice Zolotow.

Finally, special thanks to Cora Hoopes and Beverly Unsworth for typing, retyping, and typing again this ever-shrinking manuscript.

SOURCES AND NOTES

SOURCES

By far, the most important source for this book was James M. Cain himself. In one way or another, over the years, he left an exhaustive record of his life, a fortuity that sometimes made this project seem more like the editing of an autobiography than the writing of a biography. His autobiographical record appears in many different forms:

Letters: Cain was a prolific letter writer. He was also a careful retainer of carbon copies of letters he wrote, most of which are now on file in the Library of Congress. When I first met Cain and he agreed to cooperate with me on his biography, he arranged to have the library lend me ten boxes of those letters, and he gave me two additional cartons from his house, which I eventually gave over to the Library of Congress. In addition, the library had nineteen boxes of letters and other material that it could not let out of the library. And after Cain's death, Mrs. Alice Piper, executrix of Cain's estate, added four or five boxes of material from files still in Cain's possession.

Not only are the letters an invaluable source of information for a biographer, they are, as would be expected, carefully written and make good reading whether they are addressed to H. L. Mencken or Cain's plumber. In addition, Cain was an inveterate letters-to-the-editor writer, and these letters provide an extensive and reliable guide to his thinking on a variety of subjects. Finally, in his later years, I am certain Cain wrote much of his correspondence with his biographer in mind. Many of his letters, written after 1965, drift off into anecdotes about his youth and career that are more deliberate and detailed than the nostalgic reminiscing of a man in his twilight years. Unfortunately, in 1938, Cain's assistant misplaced some of his files and they were never found, so many of his early letters have been lost; some of these, however, are in the Alfred A. Knopf files in New York, and the Mencken letters are in the New York Public Library. Another excellent source of Cain letters is the Harold Ober Associates file in the Princeton Library.

Autobiographical writings: Late in life, after steadfastly maintaining that he would never write an autobiography, Cain began work on his memoirs. He did not complete this work, however, and the manuscripts are unfortunately not suitable for publication. But they have graciously been made available to me by Mrs. Piper. The memoirs are in three forms: a first draft, a more polished draft, and a separate memoir begun in 1942, written primarily to explain, possibly to himself, why he had paid so little attention to the international events leading up to World War II. Late in his life, he also wrote a long interview with himself, which, it seems, he intended for publication but never submitted. These later memoirs are disjointed and sometimes at variance with Cain's writing on identical subjects in earlier accounts, but they were invaluable to me, especially as sources for the early years. In fact, it is unlikely that anything but the sketchiest outline of Cain's life in Annapolis and Chestertown could have been made without his memoirs.

In addition, when David Madden was writing his study of Cain for the Twayne Literary Series, Cain sent Madden approximately one hundred pages of autobiographical material written in the detached third-person manner, in which he said, in effect: "Cain did this and Cain did that." Both Madden and Mrs. Piper made this material available.

Book prefaces: Cain wrote prefaces to a number of his books; they are not only autobiographical but contain perceptive and informative analyses of his work and, in some cases, his views on writing and other writers.

Memoranda concerning friends and acquaintances: Late in life, Cain was repeatedly approached for information about friends and professional acquaintances who were to be the subject of some biography. Cain invariably responded with long letters or memoranda about the person. The subjects included H. L. Mencken, Herbert Bayard Swope, Harold Ross, Walter Lippmann, and Sinclair Lewis. He also wrote articles about Walter Lippmann and screenwriter Vincent Lawrence that contain much autobiographical information.

Magazine and newspaper writing: Most of Cain's by-lined articles in newspapers and magazines were autobiographical. For example, his *American Mercury* article "The Taking of Montfaucon," although written in colloquial first-person style that did not reflect how Cain actually talked, was a pure autobiographical account of his nightmarish night of September 26, 1918, in France, at the beginning of the Meuse-Argonne offensive. And many of his signed pieces and columns in the *Baltimore*

Sun, *New York World*, and for the Hearst Syndicate are rich with autobiographical insight.

My one disappointment with Cain as a source is that, unlike most writers, he did not keep a scrapbook of his newspaper writings. Thus, his *Baltimore Sun* pieces, his *World* by-line pieces, and his Hearst columns had to be laboriously hunted down through yards of microfilm, and I am sure I missed some. One great find came to me by way of Ronald Steel, Walter Lippmann's biographer, who had discovered that all of the *World*'s editorial pages under Lippmann's direction (which spanned Cain's entire career on the *World*) had been saved and annotated by Lippmann's secretary—that is, every editorial on the page had the name of its author penciled over it. These pages are preserved on microfilm at the Yale University Library, and they were so valuable to me that I purchased four microfilms from the library (for $80), rented a microprinter from the NEC Micrographics Company in Hyattsville, Maryland, and spent days reading (and reprinting in many cases) Cain's editorials in my own library.

Interviews: Although Cain might protest the point, he was an excellent interview subject, being both outspoken and quotable. In his later years, he granted many interviews, some of which were the basis of magazine and newspaper articles about him. I had three long interviews with him in person and several shorter ones. Other good interviews, which have been cited frequently in the notes section, were obtained by a friend of his, Margot Backas; Thomas Chastain for *Publishers Weekly*; Chris Steinbrunner for the Mystery Writers of America; and David Zinsser for *Paris Review.*

Other sources: In addition to the voluminous source material in Cain's own files, there is valuable information in the traditional sources: *Twentieth Century Authors*, *Current Biography*, *Book Review Digest*, etc. Unlike Herbert Bayard Swope, whose name, according to his biographer Alfred Allen Lewis, turns up in almost every book written by or about an important person of letters in the first half of the twentieth century, Cain's name appears rarely in books of the 1920s and 1930s. He is, however, mentioned briefly in some of the biographies or autobiographies of such men of the times as Theodore Dreiser, H. L. Mencken, Harold Ross, Raymond Chandler, Arthur Krock, and Swope himself. Whenever such books are the source of information, they are cited in the chapter notes that follow. One other excellent source is David Madden's *James M. Cain* (Twayne Publishers, 1970). It contains a brief biography of Cain (based primarily on the material furnished Madden by Cain). But, more important, Madden, a novelist himself, provides an excellent, balanced appraisal of Cain the writer and his place in American literature. Some material on Cain also exists at St. John's College in Annapolis and at Washington College in Chestertown, Maryland. In addition, Cain and Gilbert Malcolm's *History of the 79th Division Headquarters Troop* and the *History of the 79th Division During the World War: 1917–1919*, edited by J. Frank Barber, were helpful for the World War I years, as was Gilbert Malcolm's World War I diary, generously made available to me by Mrs. Ethel Buyer (formerly Mrs. Gilbert Malcolm). Articles often cited in the notes section include Peter Brunette and Gerald Perry's "Tough Guy," based on a long interview with Cain for *Film Comment*; John Carmody's "James M. Cain at Twilight Time," from *Potomac*, a former title of the *Washington Post* magazine section; Donald Kirkley's "The Tin-Lined James M. Cain Can Stomach Hollywood" for the *Baltimore Sun*; and Mary Morris's "He Ain't Tepid," an article based on an interview with Cain written for *PM* in the mid-1940s but apparently never published (a copy is in Cain's files). Also informative was Mary McCrory's *Washington Star* column of January 15, 1950.

Newspaper sources were essential in documenting reaction to Cain's efforts to establish the controversial American Authors' Authority in the late 1940s, as well as for reviews of his books.

Court records were valuable for information on Cain's three divorces and his involvement in two lawsuits concerning copyright problems.

SOURCE ABBREVIATIONS
JMC Memoirs I: first draft of Cain's unpublished memoirs
JMC Memoirs II: second draft of these memoirs
JMC Memoirs III: separate unpublished memoirs begun in 1942
JMC Self-Interview
JMC memo to DM: autobiographical account written to David Madden for use in the latter's book.

Complete information about Cain's publications is in the "Publications by James M. Cain" section of this book. In the notes, I only refer to "JMC" and the name of the work.

ABBREVIATIONS OF INDIVIDUAL NAMES
Many of the individuals cited as sources in the notes are repeated several times, hence initials are used to refer to them. For example, JMC to AK, August 12, 1969, refers to a letter from Cain to Arthur Krock. The initials used in the notes are listed below:

MB	Margot Backas
BAB	B. A. Bergman
EC	Elina Cain
GC	Genevieve Cain
JMC	James M. Cain
CC	Constance Cummings (Mrs. Constance Levy)
MG	Martin Gang
RGG	Ruth Goodman Goetz
EH	Edith Haggard
RH	Roy Hoopes
AAK	Alfred A. Knopf
BK	Blanche Knopf
WK	William Koshland
AK	Arthur Krock
WL	Walter Lippmann

TL	Thomas Lipscomb
DM	David Madden
EM	Mrs. Ethel Malcolm (now Mrs. Ethel Buyer)
GM	Gilbert Malcolm
MM	Morris Markey
RMc	Rosalie McComas
HLM	H. L. Mencken
HO	Harold Ober
DO	Dorothy Olding
DR	Dorshka (Mrs. Samson) Raphaelson
SR	Samson Raphaelson
JS	James Silberman
LS	Laurence Stallings
HNS	H. N. Swanson
LT	Leo Tyszecki
IvA	Ivan von Auw

1 "A MIDGET AMONG GIANTS"

page
3   hired a retired sergeant: JMC to John J. Shea, March 9, 1969.
3   "I hated Ireland . . .": JMC to SR, October 12, 1969.
3   "A massive, handsome man . . .": JMC memo to DM.
4   Jim Cain graduated . . .: *Who's Who in America* (Chicago: Marquis, Who's Who, Inc., 1977).
4   Then he moved down . . .: St. John's College Catalog, 1977–78.
4   Rose Mallahan Cain . . .: JMC memo to DM.
4   she was related to the Irish pirate: JMC Memoirs II.
6   "He was a bit over six feet . . .": JMC Memoirs II.
6   "In her adolescent pictures . . .": JMC Memoirs III.
6   The year 1892 . . .: JMC, "James W. Cain—A Memoir," written by JMC for Washington College; in JMC files.
6   The birth was a difficult one . . .: JMC memo to DM.
7   the nation's second most: M. V. Brewington, *Chesapeake Bay: A Pictorial History* (Cambridge, Maryland: Cornell Maritime Press, 1956), p. 12.
7   the clipper ship *Josephine II:* Carl Bode, *Maryland* (New York: W. W. Norton, 1978).
7   "The colored help . . .": JMC Memoirs III.
7   "Virginia was next to me . . .": JMC Memoirs II.
8   "a feeling I imagine": JMC, *The Moth.*
8   a footrace was immediately organized: JMC memo to DM.
9   When Jamie was six . . .: RH interview with Henry Hopkins, May 28, 1978.
9   Jamie only once remembered . . .: JMC, "Tribute to a Hero."
9   Two of his short stories . . .: "Everything but the Truth" and "The Birthday Party."

9   His first teacher . . .: JMC Memoirs II.

10   "Apologize!": JMC Memoirs II.

10   he would have apologized: JMC memo to DM.

10   "I was in some spot . . .": JMC to Bushrod Howard, December 7, 1945. Jamie's first romance came in the third grade, where his teacher was Anna Brady, whom everyone called Nannie. The girl was a naval officer's daughter with a round, pretty, somewhat freckled face and a graceful little figure, just the least bit fat. Her most noticeable aspect, which Cain usually noticed first in a woman, was a round, bouncy bottom, inside a pleated dark blue skirt. She and Jamie were Miss Brady's star pupils, and as a climax to the end of the year, Nannie scheduled a spelling bee. The prize was to be a "portfolio," although Jamie did not know what a portfolio was. But he did not worry about that; when he won it he would find out what it was. Except he did not win. He spelled "rhinoceros" with an *a* before the *s* and had to sit down. The love of his life sidled up and offered to show him the portfolio, but he made no move to take it or even to look at her. He just stared at his feet. He had always excelled in class; now, not only had he been beaten, he was humiliated by his love. His infatuation was over, and he was determined to prove that he was the brightest pupil in his class. JMC Self-Interview.

10   Professor Clarence W. Stryker . . .: JMC memo to DM.

10   His father thought he was a little nutty . . .: JMC to Arthur Hornblow, January 12, 1970.

10   "Roosevelt and Sampson and Schley . . .": JMC, Preface to 50th Anniversary Edition, *Who's Who in America*, 1948.

11   Jamie was continually coached . . .: JMC Memoirs III.

11   His mother also spoke . . .: JMC Memoirs II.

11   he later suspected his father: JMC memo to DM.

11   "double promotion": JMC Memoirs III.

12   In the fifth grade . . .: JMC memo to DM.

12   "Those eleven-year-old girls . . .": JMC Memoirs II.

12   Miss Tate's methods . . .: JMC Memoirs II.

13   the momentous decision: JMC Memoirs II.

13   What young Jamie should get . . .: JMC to editor of (Annapolis) *Evening Capital*, undated.

13   he was more intrigued: JMC Self-Interview.

13   The professor—now "Dr. Cain" . . .: JMC Self-Interview. Those who played football at St. John's around the turn of the century remember Jim Cain well. Years later, Ned Duvall, who played for the "professor," remembered him as a lean, tall, dignified, almost immaculate, extremely virile coach, with a clear enunciation and a dramatic sort of tone, which held the attention and inspired his players. "His cold, austere reprimand was awakening and ingratiating, as his 'Ah, Ned!' and warming smile and hearty handshake were gracious, when you did something worthwhile. He had the ability to foresee the various difficulties the team might encounter in the game and while his instructions were definite, he also, by thought or word, suggested alternatives that might fit the situation. . . . Time and observation have convinced me

that he was one of the very greatest of the pioneer coaches. More than any two men he helped to make St. John's an institution of high spirit, loyalty, traditions and courage in those early years." Ned Duvall to JMC, October 27, 1949.

13 Senator Clarence W. Perkins: Speech by Frederick Dumschott, *Washington College History*, October 30, 1937.

14 what was even more exciting: JMC Memoirs II. Jamie was sure he helped his father's negotiations for the Washington College job when he found a four-leaf clover and had it in a glass of water waiting for his father at the station one night when he came back from Baltimore.

14 "I think we all felt . . .": JMC, "Tribute to a Hero."

15 "the familiar symptoms of yokelry": JMC Memoirs II.

15 Their furniture was carted . . .: JMC Memoirs II.

16 ". . . the most celebrated drunk . . .": JMC to Dr. Daniel Gibson, May 24, 1966.

16 But he did write Cain . . .: Dr. Daniel Gibson to JMC, May 27, 1966.

16 where the ladies: JMC, "James W. Cain—A Memoir."

17 What fascinated Jamie . . .: JMC Memoirs II.

17 He hung on his every word . . .: JMC memo to Frederick Dumschott in JMC papers.

17 Jamie did not realize it then . . .: JMC Memoirs II.

18 Then came the news . . .: JMC Memoirs II. Although Cain recalls the amount his father received from the legislature as $110,000, the *Washington College History* records it was $30,000 and that the new building would cost an estimated $35,000.

18 The next day, when the papers . . .: Carl Bode, *Mencken* (Carbondale, Illinois: Southern Illinois University Press, 1969), pp. 39–40.

18 "Only two or three of the candidates . . .": JMC, "Tribute to a Hero."

18 There were no stands . . .: JMC memo to Frederick Dumschott.

18 "skying it up in the air": JMC to Charles Gibson, March 10, 1966.

19 "to get on the same side": JMC to Hedda Hopper, September 3, 1947.

19 "They never saw me at all . . .": JMC Memoirs II.

19 his voracious reading: JMC to Evelyn Burne, August 14, 1967.

19 fudgemaking parties and musical evenings: At the fudgemaking parties, Jamie acquired the reputation as quite a cutup, with such antics as putting trash in his sister's fudge when she was not looking. RH telephone interview with Suzi Frazier.

19 "local option": Katherine Myrick to RH, November 20, 1978.

20 Jamie was given his evening "toddy": JMC to EM, August 7, 1966.

20 The family practiced . . .: JMC, "Tribute to a Hero."

20 "hick operation": JMC memo to DM.

20 he did not believe: JMC to SR, October 12, 1969.

20 his father replied: JMC, "Tribute to a Hero."

22 "a midget among giants": JMC Memoirs II.

22 In his freshman year . . .: JMC memo to DM.

22 seventeen-year-old: *Baltimore Sun*, March 29, 1970.

22 "He was kind of devilish . . .": RH interview with Ethel Gibbs, October 12, 1978. Jamie told his story about Ethel sixty years later to a group from Washington College who visited him in Hyattsville and it made the *Kent County* (Maryland) *News*—for which gentleman Jim Cain apologized to Ethel in a letter, saying it was unintentional and that he was sure the legs were as beautiful as ever. JMC to Ethel Gibbs, December 16, 1973.

23 ". . . the Torrens System . . .": JMC to Robert Gill, December 15, 1961.

23 ". . . hindlegs and bark": JMC to William Seward, September 27, 1965.

23 He also liked Dr. J. S. William Jones . . .: JMC to Mrs. William Jones, September 28, 1944.

24 "I'm sorry, it doesn't interest me": JMC Memoirs II.

24 "In all those years . . .": JMC memo to DM.

24 he even entertained the idea: JMC to John Parz, February 10, 1967.

24 considered one of the bright students: Jamie was also something of a prankster in college, although the legend, which still exists, that Jamie and Eddie Crouch tied a cow to the door of Professor Seronde's house never actually happened. Jamie was sixteen at the time and was ready to do it, until he learned that Crouch, who was twenty-one, had been stringing him along and never planned to go through with it. JMC Memoirs II. He did, however, join those members of the church choir who instead of singing "hallelujah" in Handel's "Hallelujah Chorus" would sing, "You're a liar," to which the basses would reply, "You're another, you're another." JMC Self-Interview.

25 "once had the distinction . . .": *Pegasus*, 1910.

25 "Run, Jamie, run!": Harvey Russell in *Kent County* (Maryland) *News*.

25 "complete indifference . . .": JMC memo to DM.

25 the yearbook shows: *Pegasus*, 1909 and 1910.

25 At the end of his junior year . . .: JMC Memoirs II: At one point in college, Jamie read a 350-page abridgment of the 2,100-page *Les Misérables*, and later, when he read the uncut version, was convinced that Victor Hugo could have profited with a good editing.

26 "If I and the other players . . .": JMC Memoirs II and Vaughan Truitt Memoir in Washington College Library.

26 strictly regulated: Vaughan Truitt, "Washington College 50 Years Ago," in Washington College Library.

26 "Social intercourse": Ethel Gibbs to RH, June 29, 1978.

26 duet on the piano: J. S. W. Jones, "Co-Education at Washington College," Washington College *Bulletin*, April 1932.

26 "sociable shacking": JMC Memoirs II.

26 Early in his college years . . .: JMC Memoirs II.

26 "If you can look at him . . .": Grace Riggin to RH, July 1978.

27 For most of their college years . . .: RH interview with Ethel Gibbs, October 12, 1978.

27 ". . . she was interested in him": Ethel Cooper to RH, July 12, 1978.

27 ". . . a very nice match": RH telephone interview with Suzi Frazier, undated.

27 In the summers . . .: JMC Memoirs II.

27   thought he had lost his head: RH interview with W. G. Van Sant.

27   Mary seemed to like him . . .: JMC Memoirs II.

28   "My father . . .": JMC Self-Interview.

28   "I had been out of this country . . .": JMC, "Prophecy," *Pegasus*, 1910.

28   JMC, "Auld Lang Syne." In later years, Cain said he was not very happy about this poem and declined all requests to reprint it. JMC to Dr. Daniel Gibson, February 22, 1970.

2 CONSOLATION PRIZE

page

30   "At last . . . I became . . .": JMC Memoirs II.

30   "Never once, in our house . . .": JMC memo to DM.

30   his father would remark: JMC Memoirs II.

31   "The girl who had been so friendly . . .": JMC memo to DM.

31   an evening at the Rennert Hotel: JMC Memoirs I.

31   He dressed in corduroy suits . . .: JMC memo to DM.

32   "It'll be O.K. . . .": JMC Memoirs I.

32   "small as a whorehouse beer": David Zinsser, with JMC, *Paris Review*, Spring-Summer 1978.

32   But he was ready for the real thing: JMC Memoirs II.

33   "SORRY TO BREAK OUR DATE": JMC Memoirs II.

33   raised to $75 a month: JMC memo to DM.

33   "I became the worst engineer . . .": JMC to Mrs. J. S. William Jones, September 28, 1944.

33   One day he was coming out . . .: JMC Memoirs II.

34   He began to admire them . . .: JMC Self-Interview. The Maryland State Highway Commission informed me that the files that might have contained JMC's reports to the home office in 1912–13 no longer exist.

34   Cain decided to invite John Monroe: JMC Memoirs II.

35   he landed a job as principal: JMC, "Remembrances of Kann's Past." The Vienna, Maryland, High School no longer exists nor do the school records for years before 1923.

35   "office to office": JMC Memoirs II.

36   one of his divinities: JMC to Mrs. Charles Fox, November 4, 1951.

36   *Captivating Mary Carstairs*: Henry Sydnor Harrison, *20th Century Authors* (New York: H. W. Wilson).

36   so Cain went down: JMC Self-Interview.

36   finding himself sitting on a bench: JMC Memoirs II.

37   "But it was no clarion call . . .": JMC to Edmund Wilson, June 29, 1940.

37   ". . . the wrong end of the telescope . . .": JMC to Paul Watson, December 7, 1969.

37   once again, Cain went home: JMC Memoirs II.

37   "is what you were born for": JMC memo to DM.

37   "a good stock of quotations": JMC Self-Interview.

38   if anyone in the family was destined: JMC memo to DM.

38   Rosalie was pretty . . .: JMC memo to DM.

38   Cain never felt close to his parents . . .: JMC to RMc, April 5, 1953.

38   only two things she taught him: JMC to Louis Gavin, April 2, 1967.

39   "We didn't worry about him . . .": JMC memo to DM.

39   "black magic": JMC to RMc, December 3, 1966.

39   to remain a little girl: JMC to RMc, March 10, 1958.

39   "get so furious": JMC to RMc, October 29, 1970.

39   any writing talent he had: JMC memo to DM.

39   in which music or a singer: RH interview with JMC, undated.

39   a convivial man: JMC to RMc, May 21, 1967.

39   a bad case of ergophobia: Two examples of Dr. Cain's writing are in Cain's files in the Library of Congress: a long lecture entitled "The Bible as Literature" and a manuscript of an unpublished book, "The Financial History of the United States," which JMC recorded in the library card catalog. Both of Dr. Cain's manuscripts are confined in the straitjacket of academic prose, and if Jamie Cain rebelled against anything in his family it was his father's literary style. JMC Memoirs II.

39   little Virginia was burned: JMC to RMc, September 1, 1968.

39   There were barriers . . .: JMC to RMc, May 28, 1964.

39   Jamie's disinclination: JMC to Frank Gavitt, August 24, 1966.

39   afraid of his father: JMC Memoirs I.

40   ". . . likable rake . . .": JMC Memoirs II.

40   "Remember, I'm the one . . .": JMC to RMc, September 16, 1968.

51   About the time he started writing . . .: JMC Memoirs II. Unfortunately, there are no traces of any of Cain's early stories in his files, but apparently they were primarily efforts to project color and background.

51   "I intend to live . . .": David Madden, *James M. Cain* (Boston: Twayne Publishing Co., 1970), p. 30.

51   "a very efficient teacher . . .": RH interview with George Bratt, November 1978.

51   "a big mistake": JMC Memoirs I.

53   What can be taught . . .: JMC memo to DM.

53   Dr. Cain's first real conflict . . .: JMC memo to Frederick Dumschott in Cain papers.

53   discussing the eligibility: JMC Memoirs II.

53   ". . . his father liked to drink": RH interview with Ethel Gibbs, undated.

54   Another former student . . .: RH interview with George Bratt, November 1978.

54   "I remember the night . . .": JMC to unidentified friend, August 23, 1970.

54   seeing Mary Clough again: JMC Memoirs II.

54   hard at work on his short stories: JMC Memoirs I.

55   suddenly, one day early in the summer: JMC memo to DM.

55   he saw a big sign: JMC to "Merlin," undated.

55   For his first two days . . .: JMC memo to DM. We will never know what it was about Cain's first *American* story that caught the editor's eye. Cain never kept

scrapbooks, as most writers do, and none of his early newspaper stories are in his files. It is impossible to find the by-line "James M. Cain" in the *Baltimore American* for 1917 because at that time the paper did not carry by-lines.

56   One interview from this period . . .: JMC, "Remembrances of Kann's Past."

56   he had to go back: JMC Self-Interview.

56   "And then in one . . .": JMC Memoirs II.

57   back at his old assignment: JMC memo to DM.

57   a disturbing incident: RH interview with JMC, undated.

58   considered military service: JMC memo to DM.

58   When he arrived home . . .: JMC Memoirs II.

58   "Without the good work . . .": Letter from Dr. Paul Titsworth in JMC files, undated.

58   "a catastrophe": JMC Memoirs II.

3 DOUGHBOY EDITOR

page

60   Doughboy Editor: The term "doughboys"—the American infantry sent to France in World War I—grew out of the name mounted troops in Texas gave to the foot soldiers on duty along the Rio Grande. Tramping in the adobe soil of Texas all day, troops would be covered with a white dust, so the cavalry dubbed them "adobes." It did not take long for this to evolve into "dobies" and then, by the linguistic process, "doughboys." Laurence Stallings, *The Doughboys* (New York: Popular Library, 1964), p. 15.

60   a period of standing around waiting: JMC to EM, February 25, 1966.

61   Cain did not see Malcolm again . . .: JMC memo to DM.

61   Cain wandered around . . .: JMC to EM, May 1, 1966.

62   Cain's father and mother . . .: JMC to EM, May 1, 1966.

62   Mary Clough also came . . .: JMC Memoirs II.

62   On July 6 . . .: JMC and GM, *History of the 79th Division Headquarters Troop.*

62   "one gray and overcast morning": JMC Memoirs II.

63   Cain's 79th Division landed at Brest: JMC to EM, June 12, 1966.

63   "the rats run races . . .": *History of the 79th Division Headquarters Troop.*

63   They were having lunch . . .: JMC Memoirs II.

64   the supply sergeant handed Cain: JMC, "Americana My Foot."

65   Orders finally came . . .: JMC to EM, August 21, 1966.

65   Three days later . . .: *History of the 79th Division Headquarters Troop.*

65   He could see the whole battlefield . . .: JMC, "It Breathed," *New York World*, no date.

66   "the nightmare of September 26": JMC to EM, August 28, 1966.

66   It was a time for heroes: Laurence Stallings, *The Doughboys*, pp. 275, 279, 291.

66   the night of September 26: JMC Memoirs I. A full account of the night of September 26, 1918, is also given in JMC, "The Taking of Montfaucon."

67 Cain and his troop . . .: *History of the 79th Division Headquarters Troop.*

67 We're in sight of the end!: JMC, "Christmases Past—Silent Night 1918."

68 At Vacherauville . . . : JMC Memoirs II.

68 They were at Moleville Farm . . . : Appendix, JMC and GM, *History of the 79th Division Headquarters Troop.* The account given in the troop history (written by Cain and Gilbert Malcolm) was slightly different from the one Cain gave in his memoirs. In the history, the officers were holding their watches on the booming guns and exactly at 11:00 A.M. the artillery fire was stopped. But Cain insists, in his memoirs and in other writings, that there was no firing at Moleville Farm that morning: "No guns were sounding—the legend that they were is completely false. Both sides knew what was coming and lest even one man get needlessly killed, all gunners held their fire, so the front was still as a church." Oddly enough, Cain apparently contributed to the legend in the history he wrote with Malcolm.

69 the night of November 11, 1918: JMC Memoirs II.

69 the morning after the Armistice: JMC, "Christmases Past. . . ."

69 Cain approached the corporal: JMC to EM, September 8, 1966.

70 he had delivered the goods: JMC Memoirs II.

70 the beautiful autumn faded: JMC to EM, January 1, 1965.

70 sitting on a wall of the bridge: JMC, "Christmases Past. . . ."

71 And the rumors began: JMC and GM, *History of the 79th Division Headquarters Troop.*

72 "By New Year's . . .": JMC to EM, August 18, 1966.

72 summoned by Captain Madeira: JMC to EM, September 18, 1966.

72 The first thing . . . : JMC to EM, August 18, 1966.

73 Cain's brother Boydie . . . : Unfortunately, there are no letters between JMC and Boydie in JMC's files.

73 Cain would write Boydie . . . : JMC memo to DM.

74 Two men helped see him through . . . : JMC to RMc, February 22, 1964.

74 their first expedition there: JMC to Sergeant Sam B. Lyons, August 19, 1945. The Army Historical Division was unable to find any copies of *The Lorraine Cross*, but Appendix VIII of the *History of the 79th Division AEF During the World War: 1917–1918* by JMC and GM contains several selections from the paper. There were also a few pages in JMC's files, and EM gave me several copies.

75 L'Envoi: JMC poem in memo to DM.

75 Sergeant Alexander Woollcott . . . : JMC and GM, *History of the 79th Division Headquarters Troop.*

75 The next time Cain was in Bar-le-Duc . . . : JMC to EM, November 6, 1966.

76 developing into an operator: JMC to Sergeant Sam B. Lyons, August 10, 1945.

77 He also had to have trucks . . . : JMC to EM, September 18, 1966.

77 Cain always felt . . . : JMC memo to DM.

77 "a hick celebrity . . .": JMC to Wesley Hartley, November 17, 1957.

78 They began immediately . . . : JMC to EM, January 22, 1967.

78 a little brochure: JMC to Sergeant Sam B. Lyons, August 10, 1945.

78	By now the division headquarters . . .: JMC to EM, January 22, 1967.
78	arriving just in time: JMC to Sergeant Sam B. Lyons, August 10, 1945.
78	the big day: JMC and GM, *History of the 79th Division Headquarters Troop.*
79	The lunch was successful . . .: JMC to EM, January 22, 1967. JMC's story in the *Times* was a long, dramatic account of the 79th in France, tracing its action from the time it entered the line on September 14, almost kilometer by kilometer to the taking of Wavrille, Gibercy, and several stubbornly held hills, just before the armistice of November 11.

4 "TREASON" DID NOT A NOVEL MAKE

page
84	a letter to a friend: JMC, "Talking Queer Lingo," *Baltimore Sun*, November 14, 1918.
84	"a combat newspaperman": JMC to Arnold Schwab, August 30, 1957.
84	"the bullets were really flying": RH interview with JMC, undated.
85	Cain had changed his mind: JMC Memoirs II.
85	"ill-starred venture": JMC Memoirs II.
85	In the center . . .: RH interview with John Ward, September 28, 1978.
85	As junior man . . .: JMC Memoirs II.
86	"old sourpuss": Donald Kirkley, "The Tin-Lined James M. Cain Can Stomach Hollywood," *Baltimore Sun*, January 7, 1945.
86	One incident typified . . .: JMC Memoirs II.
86	"I told these people . . .": JMC Memoirs II.
87	one day late in 1920: JMC to EM, April 10, 1965.
87	One man he came to know . . .: RH interview with JMC, undated.
87	Cain began to question: JMC to EM, August 26, 1965.
88	wrangling labor assignments: JMC memo to DM.
88	The steel companies . . .: Frederick Lewis Allen, *Only Yesterday* (New York: Harper & Brothers, 1931), p. 38.
88	What first attracted Cain . . .: JMC memo to DM.
89	"the most powerful influence . . .": Allen Churchill, *The Literary Decade* (Englewood Cliffs, New Jersey: Prentice-Hall, 1971).
89	During the war . . .: Carl Bode, *Mencken* (Carbondale, Illinois: Southern Illinois University Press, 1969), p. 191.
89	Cain immediately wrote Mencken . . .: JMC Memoirs II.
89	typhoid fever: JMC to RMc, September 1, 1968.
89	his legs went to sleep: JMC to Professor Melvin R. Yoken, August 16, 1970.
90	one of the most important stories: JMC, "Treason—to Coal Operators."
90	a glorified riot: JMC, "The Battle Ground of Coal"; JMC, "West Virginia: A Mine-field Melodrama"; JMC, "Treason." The conflict in the West Virginia coal mines was the culmination of a bitter struggle that had been taking place between the coal operators and the unions since the end of the war. The focal point of the conflict was the nonunion mines operating in Logan and Mingo counties. The wages in the coal mines were governed by an agreement that set

the pay scale in what was known as the Central Competitive coal fields in Pennsylvania and Maryland. Wages in all other fields used the central wage as a base, making allowances for different operating conditions and freight rates, etc. This worked for a while until large new fields were discovered in West Virginia and the mines there began operating with nonunion members. There were no problems during the war because union and nonunion mines alike had no trouble selling their coal. But after the war, when the coal miners went on strike, the new nonunion mines sold 4 million tons of coal in six weeks when consumption averaged 8 million tons a week. It was obvious that these nonunion mines were a threat not only to the union mines but the union miners. The new mines used cheap, nonunion labor—mostly West Virginian mountain people who were indifferent, at first, to the unions and very poor at organizing. As a result, the West Virginia miners could undersell the union mines and continued to operate when the union mines were shut down because of a reduced market for coal. Naturally, the unions realized they had to organize the West Virginia mines. The mine owners resisted, and in the climate of the Big Red Scare the public was on their side. The mine owners up north in Pennsylvania and western Maryland were caught in the middle. On the one hand, they favored unionization of the West Virginia mines because it would make them competitive with their unionized mines; on the other hand, if the unions could be kept out of the West Virginia mines, it might help them break the unions in their state.

91   "He didn't believe . . .": JMC, "Coal Baron," unpublished article in JMC files.

91   the first to be tried: Coverage of the Blizzard trial is from *Baltimore Sun*, April 25, 1922, and May 28, 1922. Cain's reports appeared in the morning *Sun* under the by-line "from our staff correspondent," although most (but not all) of his dispatches carried the initials "J. M. C." at the end.

91   lost the first round: The defense did win one point in the early rounds: Judge J. M. Woods ruled that the prosecution must bring a bill of particulars against Blizzard. It did, and the charge was that he had allegedly induced union officials to put up large sums of money to finance the "war against the state of West Virginia," and that Blizzard also allegedly led the troops.

91   On the second day, John L. Lewis . . .: Lewis issued a statement that the coal miners in West Virginia had been denied the right to organize and protect their interests by the coal operators to whom "profits in dollars and cents is the all-consuming principle." Lewis also stressed that the miners on trial were all native sons, descendants of the pioneers, "good American citizens."

The defense, it was learned, would not only deny the charges but would contend that Blizzard actually made attempts to send the armed miners home. It was also argued that the miners' fight was not against the state of West Virginia but against the armed guards hired by the coal operators.

At the same time, there was the fear that witnesses would be intimidated, and accusations that armed deputies in the courtroom were already threatening witnesses. There were no serious incidents of that sort at the Charleston trial, but the charges were not taken lightly because in an earlier trial at Matewan, four witnesses had been murdered.

92   After a few days . . . : JMC, "Treason."

93   listened to both sides: The tone of the prosecution argument was set by A. M. Belcher with his opening statement: "Gentlemen of the Jury, there were two flags flying while that armed march was in progress. One was the Stars and Stripes, the flag of your country and mine. That flag flew over the defenders of Logan County, the men who opposed that army, and said, 'they shall not pass.' The other flag, flown by members of that army, the army that was raised by the United Mine Workers of America to overthrow the sovereignty of our State, was the red flag of anarchy." The most dramatic argument for the defense was made by Harold W. Houston. He stressed that the act that "touched off the rebellion" was the murder by armed guards of two miners on the courthouse steps in Sharples the previous August. In reaction, the miners "simply adopted a petition which they presented to the Governor of the State asking for a redress of their grievances," which were: that they wanted a twice-a-month pay day and that 2,000 pounds should make a ton (both points already provided by law in West Virginia). They further proposed a joint arbitration board to settle their differences. "And these gentlemen call that treason! Think of it— treason that 2,000 pounds should make a ton! Strange treason, indeed."

93   he saw a beautiful girl: Donald Kirkley, "The Tin-Lined James M. Cain."

93   But his trouble was deeper . . . : JMC Memoirs I.

94   a cautious green light: Ellery Sedgwick to JMC, June 8, 1922.

94   Mencken replied: HLM to Ellery Sedgwick, June 8, 1922

94   Then he received a letter . . . : JMC Memoirs I.

94   "The Battle Ground of Coal": *Atlantic Monthly*, October 1922.

95   a bold stand: Because of the country's mood, created by the Big Red Scare, and the fact that young JMC had already acquired the reputation of a controversial writer, Sedgwick also felt obliged to explain in his "Contributors Column" that the *Baltimore Sun* was a "paper of conservative character, respected by friends and enemies alike." Sedgwick concluded his comments by saying: "Radicals the country over continually accuse newspapers of a bias in favor of capitalism. But the *Sun*'s general course in this and in other matters is strong testimony to the power and probity of the press." JMC, "Treason." The article left little doubt how he felt about the trial: "By a jury of his peers, packed against him and bearing instructions virtually proclaiming his guilt; on the flimsiest sort of evidence and with not the ghost of a chance at a fair trial from start to finish, Walter Allen, union miner, has been solemnly judged to be a traitor to that section of coal operators' real-estate known as the sovereign state of West Virginia."

      He also said it was absurd to confuse the paid guards of the coal mines (who also were sworn in as state deputies, an act of questionable legality) with the solemn state of West Virginia and even more absurd to consider the mountaineers, nine-tenths of whom were native Americans, who marched against the mine owners' forces, as entertaining thoughts of treason.

95   "a pelagic fish": JMC Memoirs I.

96   "In those days": Allen Churchill, *The Literary Decade*, p. 3.

96   he conceded: David Zinsser, interview with JMC, *Paris Review*, Spring-Summer 1978.

96   go down to work in the mines: JMC, "Coal Baron," unpublished article.

96   Another motivation . . .: MB interview with JMC, August 28, 1975.

97   the current Gilbert and Sullivan vogue: JMC, "Gilbert and Sullivan vs. Jazz," *Baltimore Sun*, August 21, 1922

97   talked for about ten minutes: Memo on HLM in JMC files, undated.

97   a rich voice: JMC to Carl Bode, October 9, 1963.

97   he had not impressed: MB interview with JMC, August 28, 1975.

98   the mountain people: JMC, Preface to *Three of Hearts*.

98   a card-carrying member: Correspondence between JMC and John L. Lewis, 1944.

98   Cain worked underground . . .: JMC Self-Interview.

98   took time to investigate: JMC, "Hunting the Radicals," *Baltimore Sun*, January 3, 1923.

99   shopping in the company store: JMC Memoirs I.

99   "The owner . . .": JMC, Preface to *Three of Hearts*.

99   When Cain reached Sharples . . .: JMC, "Coal Baron," unpublished article.

100   The novel he planned . . .: JMC Memoirs I. Unfortunately no other copies of Cain's first three drafts of his first effort as a novelist exist.

100   "That last one": JMC to MG, July 4, 1946.

101   part of the problem: JMC, Preface to *Three of a Kind*.

101   He also decided . . .: JMC, Preface to *The Butterfly*.

101   ". . . slinking back to work": David Zinsser, interview with JMC, *Paris Review*.

5   DEEP WATER AT LAST

page

103   "I could never quite believe": JMC Memoirs I.

103   He also felt . . .: JMC to Mrs. Hamilton Owens, April 22, 1967.

103   The only redeeming factor . . .: JMC to Mrs. Mark Watson, March 26, 1966.

104   the year he spent teaching: JMC Memoirs I.

104   It was obvious by now . . .: JMC Memoirs II.

104   aware of his mannerism: JMC memo on HLM in files.

105   Virginia Shaffer . . .: RH interview with Virginia Shaffer, August 8, 1978.

105   Cain had also become friends . . .: Mary Clough affidavit in *Cain* v. *Cain*. Equity No. 2696, in Centreville, Maryland, courthouse, May 7, 1927.

105   Cain also had . . .: JMC Memoirs I.

105   Elina was born in Turku . . .: Ulli von Wendt, "Visitors from Sunny California," in the Finnish magazine *Astra*, translated by LT, January 1939.

105   their three-month-old son, Leo: RH interview with LT, undated.

105   "seeing how well we hit it off . . .": JMC Memoirs II.

106	He had not seen Mencken . . .: MB interview with JMC, August 28, 1975.
106	The week before Cain was to start . . .: JMC memo to DM.
106	Cain appeared promptly . . .: Memo on HLM in JMC files.
106	a title Cain did not think much of: JMC memo to DM.
106	a long conversation: MB interview with JMC, August 28, 1975.
107	"the enemy of literature and mankind": JMC memo to DM.
107	"liberated me from the village pump": JMC to Ronald Martinetti, August 26, 1969.
107	Major Garey: JMC Memoirs I.
107	the fastest speed-reader: RH interview with Bernard Gessner, undated.
108	a big burly fellow: RH interview with Felix Morley, undated.
108	Mencken answered the door . . .: JMC to Sarah Mayfield, August 19, 1968.
109	But as the weeks slipped by . . .: JMC Memoirs I.
109	"as we couldn't have them dictating . . .": JMC memo to Professor M. K. Singleton in JMC files, undated.
110	Sinclair Lewis . . .: Carl Bode, "Let's Lift a Glass to James M. Cain," *Baltimore Sun*, June 25, 1978.
110	"He is recruited . . .": JMC, "The Labor Leader."
111	Cain continued to drink: Mary Cain affidavit.
111	A showdown . . .: Transcript of trial *Cain* v. *Cain*.
112	"There's no such thing . . .": JMC Memoirs I.
112	At about that time: JMC Memoirs II.
113	"The man is a Priest": JMC, "The Editorial Writer."
113	"But there the gentleman is . . .": JMC, "Pedagogue: Old Style."
114	Mencken had prescribed: JMC invitation into Sunday Night Club, May 10, 1924, in Mencken letters in Enoch Pratt Library, Baltimore.
114	He actually did not mind . . .: JMC memo to DM. One reason Cain did not regret leaving St. John's was his conviction that it had no future under Major Garey. Garey remained as president at St. John's for several years, and in the long run, the thing that annoyed Cain most about Garey was a decision during his administration that led to the construction of the Maryland (State) Hall of Records. At the front of the campus, this huge building, Cain felt, not only detracted from the campus and had no business being there, but more important, it obstructed the view of the historic Paca-Carroll house in which he was born. JMC to Rebecca Wilson, September 5, 1976.
114	A Baltimore doctor confirmed . . .: JMC Memoirs I.
115	the state tuberculosis sanitarium: Sabillasville is a little town in northern Maryland, very near the Pennsylvania border. The sanitarium is no longer in existence, and the medical records have long since been destroyed.
115	the female politician: Cain's attitude toward women politicians is not surprising, considering he had a rather dismal view of all politicians, male or female. On the other hand, for an iconoclast, he showed a very conventional approach to women and feminism. He said that the man in the street will invariably say that "a woman's place is in the home" and, ignoring the angry rebuttals, even the hastiest reflection reveals there is some truth in the statement. The reasons were distinctly Cain: Women excel in the business of liv-

ing, not in the business of providing the means and bulwarks of living. And when they become involved in politics, they are concerned not with the only variety of politics that really counts—"where cold, sordid gain is the stake and the game is played by intrigue, counter-intrigue, and every known kind of sweaty, shifty-eyed artifice"—instead, she concerns herself with "pale, wan issues . . . mothers' bills, children's bills, better babies' bills," etc., and "out of politeness the men usually pass the whole proposed crop at every session." By contrast, Cain cited a well-known woman he did not name who lived in Washington and wielded real power by the influence she exerted—as a woman—on the men in authority.

115   American male political leaders: In contrasting American and European statesmen, JMC wrote that Europeans "were adventurers. There was not one among them who did not, at one time or another, shoot the bones for the whole pile. There was more than a suggestion of the sinister about them; they were in unusually close touch with brute reality; they faced the fact of a cruel, senseless world without being oppressed . . . they were unfettered by timidity, the 'morals' that give ordinary men pause. It was not so much that they were unscrupulous as that they were cynics, magnificent cynics, cynics on a heroic and shocking scale."

116   his roommate asked: RH telephone interview with JMC, undated.

116   "at the end of the plank": JMC Memoirs I.

117   he still wanted to write: Donald Kirkley, "The Tin-Lined James M. Cain Can Stomach Hollywood," *Baltimore Sun*, January 7, 1945.

117   there was also Elina: Ulli von Wendt, "Visitors from Sunny California."

117   "one of Henry's . . .": AK, *Memoirs* (New York: Funk & Wagnalls, 1968), p. 65.

117   you never apply: MB interview with JMC, August 28, 1975.

117   He was impressed . . .: JMC Memoirs I.

118   By 1924 . . .: George Juergens, *Joseph Pulitzer and the New York World* (Princeton: Princeton University Press, 1966), p. 14.

118   it was drafty: E. J. Kahn, *The World of Swope* (New York: Simon and Schuster, 1965), p. 236.

118   Swope's office . . .: Richard O'Connor, *Heywood Broun* (New York: G. P. Putnam, 1975), p. 80.

118   the *World*'s distinctive reporting: Morris Markey, "Reporter at Large," *The New Yorker*, March 14, 1931.

119   the quality of these sections: E. J. Kahn, *The World of Swope*, p. 238.

119   "The Insatiable Telegraph": editorial by Maxwell Anderson, *New York World*, September 24, 1924.

120   He thought Lippmann . . .: JMC memo to DM.

120   Lippmann later explained . . .: JMC memo to DM.

120   When Cain reported . . .: RH interview with JMC, undated.

121   Cain went upstairs to the office . . . .: JMC memo to DM.

121   "as soon as I find out . . .": David Zinsser, interview with JMC, *Paris Review*, Spring-Summer 1978.

121   everyone's in favor of motherhood: MB interview with JMC, August 28, 1975.

121   "Leave us never forget": JMC to Charles Addams, January 25, 1968.

121   "slunk down the circular stairs . . .": JMC to editor of *Newsweek*, August 29, 1966. JMC's first published editorial (*New York World*, September 26, 1924) ought to be preserved somewhere; here it is:

> In his patriotic efforts to find out what the Volstead Law means, Representative John Philip Hill of the 3rd District of Maryland has finally been indicted. May he speedily be brought to trial. Not that we want to see him jailed, but we confess a hankering to see the show.
>
> When he began his manufacture of wine and cider in his Baltimore home, he gave notice by a series of fearful and wonderful proclamations in the newspapers. He tested his brew with devices bearing strange but apposite names, and as the bubbles rose he recorded the mounting alcoholic content upon great charts, looking like thermometers, in front of his home. He besieged the Prohibition Commissioner with pathetic pleas for information as to whether he was breaking the law or not. Finally, to add a subtle touch, he revealed that he was using formulas furnished regularly upon application by the Department of Agriculture.
>
> In brief, without ever losing sight of his point, he staged fine comedy, conducting his fight always good-humoredly and like a gentleman. What is in store for him next is not apparent, but it seems safe to say that Hill will be equal to the emergency and that the show will be worth seeing.

122   so he walked around Greenwich Village: JMC Memoirs I.

122   a nice, lighthearted piece: *New York World*, October 1, 1924.

122   When the ball struck . . .: Shirley Povich, *The Washington Senators* (New York: G. P. Putnam, 1954), p. 132.

122   "It is given to some cities . . .": *New York World*, November 5, 1924.

122   His edits . . .: JMC editorial in *New York World*, late 1924.

123   early in 1925: JMC, "Walter Lippmann Had Style."

123   counterattacking in *The Nation*: JMC, "The World Hits the Trail."

123   It was Krock . . .: MB interview with JMC, August 28, 1975.

124   things are all right: JMC memo to DM.

124   and wrote that a man: *New York World*, December 24, 1924.

125   "the pale color of health": JMC, "Walter Lippmann Had Style." Lippman had one peculiar trait that baffled Cain. Often when Cain went to check over with Lippmann what he would write about that day, he sat on the near side of his desk with his list of subjects, neatly typed in a column, in front of him. Lippmann would lean back on the far side of his desk and tell him: "I see you have Coolidge down there. Yes, I think he has a rap on the knuckles coming for that nonsense he came out with yesterday." Or: "Yes, by all means do a piece on the World Series—but I warn you, if the game goes to extra innings, as it very well may, you'll have to work pretty late."

He was reading Cain's subject list upside down. Cain once asked him how he acquired this habit and Lippmann said he did not know; he had learned to read this way when he was four and he just assumed that was how it was done. JMC Memoirs II.

Lippmann had a very large head, but his voice, according to Cain, was distinctive for what singing teachers called "escapement," meaning it was slightly breathy and, on the phone, just a bit ghostly. He was solidly built, however, and despite his massive hands, he wrote such microscopic script that sometimes his handwritten editorials could not be typed by his secretary and had to be sent directly to the composing room to be deciphered under a reading glass. Cain once asked Lippmann why he had not learned to type, and he said: "I play the typewriter just as you do. I type fine, but I won't do my copy on a typewriter. I fall in love with the neat perfection of it and hate to make corrections." But in his longhand copy, he made dozens of corrections, in the margins, with lines running in showing where they went—and they were almost impossible to read by anyone except his secretary, Miss Lashin. JMC undated memo to Allan Nevins and MB interview with JMC, August 28, 1975.

125 "he was courtesy itself . . .": JMC, "Walter Lippmann Had Style."

6 BOMBING OUT IN STAMFORD AND WORCESTER

page
126 "How the Finns Keep Fit": *New York World*, January 1, 1925.
126 Elina was still working . . .: Ulli von Wendt, "Visitors from Sunny California," in the Finnish magazine *Astra*, translated by LT, January 1939.
126 "insanely happy": JMC to Edmund Wilson, June 1940.
126 Felix Morley remembers: RH interview with Felix Morley, undated.
127 Elina had to return: JMC Memoirs I.
127 in New York in the 1920s: James Boylan, ed., *The World and the 20s* (New York: The Dial Press, 1973), p. 86.
128 Their members were interchangeable . . .: Allen Churchill, *The Literary Decade* (Englewood Cliffs, New Jersey: Prentice-Hall, 1971), pp. 130–33.
128 As Broun said . . .: Richard O'Connor, *Heywood Broun* (New York: G. P. Putnam, 1975).
128 There was also Burton Rascoe . . .: Allen Churchill, *The Literary Decade*, pp. 130–33.
128 the most notable list: Allen Churchill, *The Literary Decade*, pp. 179–80.
129 "the angry man . . .": RGG to JMC, undated.
129 "the typical American man of God . . .": JMC, "The Pastor."
129 "the Sage of Potato Hill": *20th Century Authors* (New York: H. W. Wilson), pp. 675–76.
129 "in a literary style . . .": *E. W. Howe's Monthly*, May 1925.
130 ". . . the bacillus of Service . . .": JMC, "The Pathology of Service."
131 a county almshouse: JMC, "Servants of the People."
131 Scotty Akers: JMC, "The Hero."
132 "so I guess . . .": JMC to WL, September 26, 1925
132 While he was in the hospital . . .: JMC to Sara Mayfield, August 20, 1968.
132 Twice a month . . .: JMC memo to HLM in JMC files.
132 Cain was also . . .: JMC Memoirs II.

133 "Cain will be at my house . . .": HLM to BK, July 19, 1925.

133 On one of their train trips . . .: JMC Memoirs I.

133 And when Cain went . . .: JMC Memoirs II.

133 his father was a publisher: RH interview with RGG, undated.

133 Goodman's real interests: Carl Bode, *Mencken* (Carbondale, Illinois: Southern Illinois University Press, 1969).

133 It was a Goodman stroke . . .: JMC to David Wayne, March 13, 1972.

133 Through his membership . . .: RH interview with RGG, undated.

133 *The Old Soak*: Edward Anthony, *O Rare Don Marquis* (Garden City, New York: Doubleday, 1962).

133 a young pantomimist and juggler: JMC memo to DM.

134 everyone drove out: JMC Memoirs II.

134 The story evolves . . .: Description of *Crashing the Gates* is from *Variety*, February 7, 1926, and a clip from an unidentified paper in clipping file, Lincoln Center Library, New York.

135 Goodman invested: RH interview with RGG, undated.

135 One man who liked . . .: JMC to JS, June 27, 1962.

135 *Crashing the Gates* opened . . .: JMC Memoirs II.

135 the most interesting story: JMC to James Cagney, October 25, 1970.

135 In Stamford . . .: JMC Memoirs I.

136 "The stylish thing . . .": *Worcester* (Massachusetts) *Telegram*, February 19, 1926.

136 "little short of a mess": *Variety*, February 7, 1926.

136 "Jim, if you ask me . . .": JMC Memoirs II.

136 "You should never jeopardize . . .": JMC memo to DM.

136 an editorial for the *World*: *New York World*, September 2, 1928.

137 Cain's first meeting with Lawrence: JMC Memoirs II.

137 "it would be most surprising . . .": JMC, "Vincent Sargent Lawrence."

137 Then one night . . .: JMC Memoirs II.

138 He walked out of the apartment . . .: JMC Memoirs I.

138 "the dream that comes true": JMC to RGG, December 21, 1964.

138 The first dialogue . . .: JMC, "Hemp."

138 the Towanda, Ohio: JMC, "Red White and Blue."

139 "The Man Merriwell": JMC, "The Man Merriwell"; footnote: JMC to HLM, December 13, 1932.

139 Patten told Cain: JMC memo to DM.

139 a few close friends: RH interview with RGG, March 9, 1979.

139 "I've had many conversations . . .": JMC memo to DM.

139 one story Cain told: JMC memo to AK in JMC files.

139 much-quoted incident: JMC to Mrs. LS, September 17, 1968.

140 "I have to listen to Stallings . . .": AK, *Memoirs* (New York: Funk and Wagnalls, 1968), p. 65.

140 Stallings had catapulted: *20th Century Authors*, p. 1325.

140 Eventually it was said . . .: Joan Brittain, *Laurence Stallings* (Boston: Twayne Publishers, 1975), p. 17.

151 Cain was convinced: JMC to RGG, February 11, 1971.

151 A story Cain . . .: JMC to Joan Brittain, February 12, 1971.

151 Cain greatly admired Markey . . .: JMC memo to DM.

151 Markey's attempt: JMC to MM, June 8, 1945.

151 lure him away: Dale Kramer, *Ross and The New Yorker* (New York: Doubleday, 1951), p. 87.

151 he was drawn to Markey: JMC to Mrs. LS, July 29, 1963.

152 respect for Cain's writing: RGG at JMC memorial service, November 11, 1977.

152 ". . . paprika-haired figure": Allen Churchill, *The Literary Decade*, pp. 30–31.

152 Mencken, his sandy hair: JMC Memoirs II.

152 Goodman, a huge . . . Jew: JMC memo to Philip Alan Friedman, in JMC files, undated.

153 Lewis, tall: Mark Schorer, *Sinclair Lewis* (Englewood Cliffs, New Jersey: Prentice-Hall, 1962).

153 "ag'in everything": JMC to Hamilton Owens, September 16, 1964.

153 "green swill": JMC memo to Philip Alan Friedman.

153 "a gay companion drunk . . .": JMC to Mark Schorer, January 7, 1957.

153–155 Lewis first took an interest: JMC memo to Philip Alan Friedman.

155 "Jim, I read that book": JMC memo to Philip Alan Friedman in JMC files.

155 helped Hamsun win: *20th Century Authors.*

156 Lewis was there: JMC memo to Philip Alan Friedman, in JMC files.

156 "This was the one time": JMC memo to DM.

156 Cain, on the other hand: JMC to Professor Melvin Yoken, August 16, 1970.

156 around 1927: JMC to RMc, May 22, 1971.

157 to consider a reconciliation: Ethel Cooper to RH, July 12, 1978.

157 "While she was an intellectual": JMC Memoirs II.

157 her thesis: Washington College *Alumnus Review.*

157 "I am sure . . .": Mary Clough to Dr. Jones, January 10, 1942, in Washington College Library.

157 "Don't think that Mary . . .": JMC Memoirs I.

157 (In fact, Leo says . . .): RH interview with LT, undated.

157 Cain also suspected . . .: JMC Memoirs I.

157 Ruth Goodman remembers . . .: RH interview with RGG, undated.

158 Elina learned to speak English: RH interview with RGG, February 27, 1978.

158 "She had a beautiful mind . . .": JMC Memoirs II.

158 Ruth remembers one night: RH interview with RGG, undated.

158 on July 2, 1927: JMC Memoirs I.

7 THE CORPORATE AWFULNESS

page

159 "Many years ago . . .": Heywood Broun, "It Seems to Me," *Atlanta Journal*, December 18, 1937.

160 John Lee Mahin . . .: RH interview with John Lee Mahin, undated.

160 "The corporate awfulness . . .": JMC, "Are Editorials Worth Reading?"

161 "One feels . . .": JMC, "High Dignitaries of State."

161 In a self-appraisal . . .: JMC Memoirs III.

162 he learned what really interested: JMC memo to DM.

162 His first big hit . . .: *New York World*, July 12, 1925.

162 a woman reporter: JMC to Nora Sayre, March 8, 1973.

162 "the hog editor": JMC Memoirs I.

163 The reaction . . .: JMC, "Are Editorials Worth Reading?"

163 QUERY: JMC memo to DM.

164 ". . . the very first concert . . .": JMC to Herbert Bayard Swope, November 16, 1937.

164 Arthur Krock, however, remembers . . .: AK, *Memoirs* (New York: Funk and Wagnalls, 1968), p. 71.

164 the Scopes trial: Frederick Lewis Allen, *Only Yesterday* (New York: Harper & Brothers, 1931), p. 188.

164 "a clown's show": JMC memo to Allan Nevins in JMC files.

164 Cain took one crack: *New York World*, July 25, 1925.

164 "the greatest moment": JMC, "Are Editorials Worth Reading?" The Battling Siki editorial is in *New York World*, December 16, 1925.

164 ". . . the Pulitzer Prize . . .": It was only a rumor; Cain was not nominated for the prize in 1925. Rose Valenstein of Pulitzer Committee to RH, August 22, 1978.

165 In the spring of 1926 . . .: JMC, "The End of the World."

165 Cain arranged . . .: JMC Memoirs II.

165 Cain always liked Swope . . .: JMC to Allan Nevins, November 14, 1968.

165 "his pink hair streaming . . .": JMC memo to E. J. Kahn in JMC files, undated.

166 a delicate position: AK, *Memoirs*.

166 In 1927 . . .: Frederick Lewis Allen, *Only Yesterday*

166 Lippmann was apparently unable . . .: JMC, "Walter Lippmann Had Style."

166 If Cain was unhappy . . .: Richard O'Connor, *Heywood Broun* (New York: G. P. Putnam, 1975), p. 146.

167 in Cain's opinion: JMC, "Walter Lippmann Had Style."

167 analyzed the Lowell Report: JMC to *The Nation* in JMC files.

167 The next morning . . .: JMC, "Walter Lippmann Had Style."

168 Within four months . . .: Richard O'Connor, *Heywood Broun.*

168 until one day: "It Seems to Heywood Broun," *The Nation*, May 23, 1978.

168 inept, stupid: JMC to *The Nation* concerning Heywood Broun, undated. The letter was either never sent or not published if it was sent. I suspect the latter.

169 creating a sensation: Donald Friede, *The Mechanical Angel* (New York: Alfred A. Knopf, 1948), pp. 50–51.

170 Cain's version . . .: MB interview with JMC, August 28, 1975.

170 a tingling lead editorial: James Boylan, *The World of the 20s* (New York: The Dial Press, 1973).

170 Then he wrote . . .: *New York World*, May 24, 1927.

170 In another piece . . .: *New York World*, September 10, 1927.

170 In still another . . .: *New York World*, March 4, 1927.

171 Cain closed out the year: *New York World*, May 13, 1927.

171 Cain was given: JMC memo to DM.

171 Cain's only editorial achievement . . .: JMC Memoirs I.

172 the most home runs: *New York World*, May 14, 1928.

172 1928 Yankees: *New York World*, May 3, 1928.

172 sudden and dramatic departure: E. J. Kahn, *The World of Swope* (New York: Simon and Schuster, 1965), p. 308.

172 One of the problems . . .: JMC Memoirs I.

172 One of the speakers . . .: JMC memo to E. J. Kahn, undated.

172 Alexander Woollcott: E. J. Kahn, *The World of Swope*, pp. 312–13.

173 fellow editorial writers: JMC Memoirs II.

173 In fact, he realized . . .: JMC to Louise M. Starr, December 23, 1971.

173 despite Nevins's eccentricity: JMC to Ellen Hoffmann, March 6, 1971.

173 By contrast . . .: JMC to Frank Kent, May 18, 1944.

173 Through that basic education . . .: JMC memo to DM.

174 the letters column: JMC Memoirs I.

174 which intrigued Lippmann: John Leonard, "The Wish of James M. Cain," *New York Times*, March 2, 1969.

174 the editorial page: JMC Memoirs III.

174 Lippmann's attitude . . .: JMC memo to DM.

174 As Cain described . . .: JMC, "Walter Lippmann Had Style."

174 It was on writing . . .: *New York World*, August 30, 1929.

175 MISTAKE IN AN UNFORTUNATE PLACE: *New York World*, August 31, 1929.

175 he was rather pleased: JMC, "Walter Lippmann Had Style."

175 finest stylist writing: JMC to Allan Nevins, undated.

175 "He never tried to dictate . . .": MB interview with JMC, August 28, 1975.

175 our expert on stuffed shirts: Memo on JMC in WL's files, Yale University.

175 "He was a realist": JMC, "Walter Lippmann Had Style."

176 "And yet, when most . . .": JMC to David Weingeast, October 1, 1947.

176 Cain's favorite example . . .: JMC, "The End of the World."

177 "He cannot be frightened . . .": JMC, "Walter Lippmann Had Style."

177 "I have no capacity . . .": MB interview with JMC, August 28, 1975.

177 "This newspaper job": RH interview with JMC, undated.

8   THE LITERARY LIFE

page

178 finding another way: JMC memo to DM.

179 Knopf wrote: AAK to JMC, July 1928.

179 He shifted the locale . . .: JMC memo to DM.

180 he had now found: JMC, Preface to *Three of a Kind*.

180 "The only way I can keep . . .": JMC, "Reflections on Ideas and Where They Come From," *New York World*, February 22, 1931.

181   copied from Ernest Hemingway: JMC, Preface to *The Butterfly*.

181   he remembered all the excitement: JMC to Carlos Baker, July 24, 1963

181   he did not read Hemingway: JMC to Francis Russell, February 8, 1969.

181   It was that of Roxy Stimson . . .: JMC to John Lardner, May 19, 1958.

182   including Hemingway's biographer: JMC to Carlos Baker, June 24, 1963. I asked Baker if he had ever tried to confirm this theory and he said he had not, but his hunch was that it was not correct, which Cain himself had said might be the case. But Baker wrote me that Cain's theory "still remains to be proved or disproved." Carlos Baker to RH, June 1, 1978.

182   ". . . I'd say she influenced me plenty": For a sample of Roxy Stimson's dialogue, see Mark Sullivan, *Our Times*, Vol. 6, pp. 233–36, and David McCullough interview with JMC in Book-of-the-Month Club *News*, February 1975.

182   wanted Cain to try a novel: Robert Linscott to JMC, April 23, 1934.

183   one of his finest articles: JMC, "The Solid South."

183   Cain, meanwhile, had not forgotten . . .: JMC to AAK, December 10, 1928.

183   from Blanche Knopf: BK to JMC, November 11, 1928.

183   Alfred Knopf wrote: AAK to JMC, March 7, 1929.

183   Cain responded immediately . . .: JMC to AAK, March 10, 1929.

184   reprinted in 1929 and 1942: *Infantry Journal*, December 1942.

185   Cain's first meeting with Alfred A. Knopf . . .: RH interview with AAK, December 14, 1979.

185   "a brutal photograph . . .": *New York Post*, January 4, 1930.

185   "The serious framework . . .": *New York World*, January 4, 1930.

185   the sardonic thrust: *Baltimore Sun*, January 25, 1930.

185   "just that touch . . .": *Outlook*, January 29, 1930.

185   ". . . the height of clever satire": *New York Times*, September 6, 1930.

186   Thirteen years later . . .: HLM to JMC, October 24, 1933.

186   earning only $250: AAK to JMC, February 25, 1933.

187   "But she didn't like . . .": JMC to EM, September 10, 1966.

187   Ruth Goodman Goetz recalled: RH interview with RGG, undated.

187   Cain left her alone . . .: RH interview with L T, undated.

187   Cain spent many evenings . . .: JMC Memoirs II.

187   The talk would usually . . .: RH interview with RGG, undated.

187   "the most competent writer . . .": Ward Morehouse interview with HLM, *Baltimore Sun*, June 5, 1946.

187   "Belief in you . . .": JMC memo to DM.

188   One time . . .: JMC Memoirs I.

188   So Cain suggested . . .: JMC, "The Gentle Side of W. C. Fields."

189   a piece by John O'Hara: *New York World*, December 13, 1927.

189   Cain reprinted it: *New York World*, December 25, 1927.

189   Cain asked O'Hara: JMC to Mathew Bruccoli, April 14, 1974 and April 17, 1974.

189   "I used to bounce . .": MB interview with JMC, August 28, 1975.

190   "The man is bigger . . .": JMC memo on HLM in JMC files, undated.

190   ". . . the incomparable language . . .": JMC to Ronald Martinetti, August 26, 1969.

190 he would compare: JMC to Carl Bode, February 1, 1966.

190 Mencken's shallow thinking . . .: JMC to Mrs. Barry Wood, June 10, 1951.

191 You could search back . . .: JMC memo on HLM in JMC files, undated.

191 "When I would write . . .": JMC to John Lardner, February 24, 1956.

191 "But you couldn't argue . . .": JMC to John Lardner, December 24, 1956.

191 One person: JMC to Ronald Martinetti, September 4, 1969.

191 "I was a big boy then . . .": JMC Self-Interview.

192 ". . . a pet rabbit": JMC to John Lardner, February 24, 1956.

192 shocked to learn: JMC to Hamilton Owens, September 9, 1964.

192 ". . . at his own evaluation": RH interview with JMC, undated. Cain shared
Mencken's discomfort with anything British. This led to Cain's being mentioned in Mencken's monumental *American Language*, which Cain said assured his own immortality. Quoting a 1931 article Cain wrote for the
American Mercury, Mencken wrote: "To the common people everything English, whether an article of dress, a social custom or a word or a phrase has
what James M. Cain has called 'a somewhat pansy cast.' "

192 Cain started out . . .: JMC memo to HLM in JMC files.

192 he was leery: JMC Memoirs II.

192 "I often thought": JMC to Wesley Hartley, November 17, 1957.

193 The times . . .: Allen Churchill, *The Literary Decade* (Englewood Cliffs, New
Jersey: Prentice-Hall, 1971), p. 296.

193 As Cain wrote . . .: JMC to Mrs. Harry Wood, March 9, 1952.

193 "With Henry . . .": JMC to Dale Kramer, November 5, 1950.

193 Mencken insisted on: JMC memo on HLM in JMC files.

194 ". . . embittered Georgia intellectual . . .": JMC to RGG, October 12, 1976.

194 on the day of the crash: RH interview with RGG, undated.

194 When the marriage was announced . . .: Sara Mayfield, *The Constant Circle*
(New York: Delacorte Press), p. 163.

194 "She could see through people": JMC Memoirs II.

9 END OF THE *WORLD* AND THE TWENTY-SIXTH JESUS

page

195–96 Cain's editorials appeared in the *New York World* on the following dates: in
favor of the hot dog: February 3, 1929; big lobsters were superior: September
1, 1929; bridge: January 8, 1929; radio: February 12, 1929; Sacco-Vanzetti:
March 9, 1929; bike race: April 1, 1929; doctors' suggestion: April 6, 1929;
presidential handshakes: June 14, 1929; ex-Presidents: April 13, 1929; Yankee pennant: April 15, 1929; Floyd Gibbons: April 24, 1929; Robert Hutchins: April 29, 1929; roadside signs: May 1, 1929; arithmetic: May 3,
1929; "Miss Universe": May 20, 1929; Yale: September 24, 1929; talking
pictures: March 26, 1929; morality in the movies: September 24, 1929; a patient recovering: September 30, 1929; Senator Millard Tydings: October 31,
1929.

196 Goodman continued to argue: JMC, "The End of the World."

197 "lacked the ability . . .": James Barrett, *Joseph Pulitzer and His World* (New York: Vanguard Press, 1941).

197 Another sign . . .: JMC, "The End of the World."

197 the *World* was for sale: James Barrett, *Joseph Pulitzer and His World*, p. 415.

197 "Nothing the young master did": JMC Memoirs II. There is no space to recount the complex efforts of people other than Howard, including Swope, to buy it or the negotiations that led up to the sale; they have been described in a number of places, including E. J. Kahn's biography of Swope and James Barrett's book on the *Joseph Pulitzer and His World*. Joseph Pulitzer's will specified that the stock of the *World* could not be sold by its trustees, the Pulitzer brothers. But the lawyers had figured out a way to get around this: (1) the will said the stock of the *World* could not be sold, but nothing about the newspaper; (2) courts had held, in similar cases, that trustees were obliged to exercise judgment to protect an estate; they could not be compelled to keep property that was losing money. Just how much money, if any, the *World* was losing is not clear, but the courts decided it would abide by the judgment of the Pulitzer brothers that holding the *World* would jeopardize their estate.

197 snapped Lippmann: JMC Memoirs II.

197 finally persuaded Lippmann: JMC memo to Allan Nevins in JMC files, undated.

198 "I don't see . . .": JMC to HLM, March 11, 1930.

198 The spirit of . . .: James Barrett, *Joseph Pulitzer and His World*, p. 418.

199 made his contribution: JMC, "The End of the World."

199 Markey had been lured away . . .: Dale Kramer, *Ross and The New Yorker* (New York: Doubleday, 1951), p. 87.

200 ". . . smile of relief": JMC to Robert Hunter Pierson, April 25, 1953.

201 "Auld Lang Syne": JMC, "Auld Lang Syne," *The New Yorker*, December 20, 1930.

201 meeting Raoul Fleischmann: JMC memo to DM.

201 Cain did recall: JMC Memoirs I.

201 from the fear: Brendan Gill, *Here at The New Yorker* (New York: Random House, 1975), p. 40.

201 Charles Morton . . .: *Atlantic Monthly*, April 1962.

202 James Thurber reported . . .: James Thurber, *The Years with Ross* (Boston: Little, Brown, 1959), p. 148.

202 During the nine months . . .: RH, Survey of *The New Yorker*, March 1931–November 1931.

202 "Of all the idiots . . .": JMC to Charles Angoff, September 23, 1954.

202 His two contributions . . .: *The New Yorker*, May 23, 1931 and November 21, 1931.

202 "As he passed by . . .": JMC Memoirs I.

203 "We gotta get this place awganized": RH interview with JMC, undated.

203 "The main reason": JMC Memoirs I.

203 "If I'd told him I had leprosy . . .": RH interview with JMC, undated.

203 regarded secretaries: JMC to Charles Cooke, June 27, 1969.

203 "Plugs, Cain, plugs": RH interview with JMC, undated.

204 hire one more secretary: John Dorsey, "The Writer Never Gives Up," *Baltimore Sun* magazine, March 29, 1970.

204 Another thing . . .: JMC Memoirs I. The system to which JMC objected worked as follows: *The New Yorker* would advance writers and artists regular weekly salaries, then reduce the debt every time one of their pieces or drawings was used. "It puts these people," he told Ross, "in the position of working for nothing, of paying for dead horses. The result, as we've seen only too often, is that they pay for one dead horse with another—what they write or what they draw is not so sharp as it would be if it were bringing in good hard cash." Cain suggested that he scale down the deduction, so out of every payment due the writers and artists they would have quite a nice sum to show. Ross let him work it that way—but then he would give advances on top of advances, so before one was wiped off the books, another would come. They never did hit on a real solution. And occasionally, as with Dorothy Parker, "who seemed to have as much business sense as a half-grown June bug," said Cain, he would wipe the slate clean just to get more work out of her. JMC Memoirs I.

204 "He got along well . . .": BAB to RH, August 11, 1978.

205 liked Dorothy Parker: James Bready interview with JMC, *Baltimore Sun*, June 18, 1967.

205 "Aw, Harold . . .": JMC Memoirs I.

205 a compulsively neat man: E. B. White to RH, July 7, 1978.

205 White was always . . .: E. B. White to JMC, June 29, 1975.

205 to live without her: JMC Memoirs I.

205 his mother told him: RH interview with L T, undated.

206 the absence of children: JMC Memoirs I.

206 "It would be pleasant . . .": JMC to L T, March 28, 1972.

206 James Thurber said . . .: James Thurber, *The Years with Ross*, p. 147. Cain said that "for years I couldn't read Thurber's book on Ross out of utter terror of what he might have said about me. The other night, however, a lady brought it over, assuring me his comment was really quite friendly, and so, at least—I read it." JMC to E. B. White, June 22, 1975.

206 "cared not a hoot . . .": JMC to Harrison Kinney, June 20, 1971.

206 "always talking . . .": JMC to P. J. Wingate, April 16, 1970.

206 Thurber recalled that . . .: James Thurber, *The Years with Ross*, p. 148.

206 "Having myself": JMC to Harrison Kinney, June 10, 1971.

206 ". . . I went to him . . .": JMC to Harrison Kinney, June 20, 1971.

207 Cain remarked to Thurber: MM to JMC, May 18, 1945.

207 One question of libel . . .: JMC Memoirs I.

209 Cain was also proud . . .: JMC to Allen Churchill, August 13, 1947.

211 remembered their few social meetings: JMC Memoirs I.

211 "as safe as Lillian Gish . . .": MB interview with JMC, August 28, 1975.

211 did not seem important: JMC Memoirs I.

211 he told one former *New Yorker* hand: JMC to Joel Sayre, May 6, 1968.

212 He also thought . . . .: JMC to Eugene Kinkaid, May 25, 1969.

212 He felt that Ross . . . .: JMC to J. M. Lalley, December 14, 1951.

212   when Ross died: JMC to Joel Sayre, May 6, 1968.

212   ". . . a prodigious admiration . . .": JMC to Allen Churchill, August 13, 1947.

212   "He illustrated the principle . . .": JMC memo to DM.

212   "Whether in magazine editing . . .": JMC to Allen Churchill, August 16, 1947.

212   two "great editors": JMC to Clay Blair, Jr., May 6, 1962.

212   "never took a peeve home . . .": JMC to Allen Churchill, August 13, 1947.

212   He found it impossible . . .: JMC to BAB, October 29, 1961.

212   a little package of entertainment: JMC memo to DM.

212   Although he always . . .: JMC Memoirs I.

213   Eileen Collins: JMC memo to DM.

213   but he did learn: JMC to Mrs. Harry Wood, March 15, 1952.

213   He also remembered . . .: Peter Brunette and Gerald Perry, "Tough Guy," *Film Comment*, May 6, 1967.

213   Benchley had mentioned: JMC to DO, September 20, 1975.

213   used to be "appalled": JMC memo to DM.

213   ". . . as miserable a human being . . .": BAB to RH, August 7, 1978.

213   ". . . so little qualified . . .": JMC to Charles Cooke, July 27, 1969.

213   "my last days . . .": JMC to E. B. White, June 22, 1975.

213   Cain's break with Ross: RH interview with JMC, undated.

214   early in November: JMC Memoirs I.

214   Fleischmann wrote: Raoul Fleischmann to JMC, December 13, 1951.

214   "For God's sake . . .": JMC to Sally Benson, August 25, 1934.

214   ". . . by the time I thought up . . .": JMC to Wolcott Gibbs, August 13, 1934.

10   MURDER ON THE LOVE RACK

page

217   "I'd been gradually coming . . .": JMC Memoirs II.

218–20 "She was the one factor . . .": JMC Memoirs II.

220   One night, he told it to . . .: JMC to Erle Stanley Gardner, undated.

220   After a few more days . . .: JMC memo to DM.

221   Taking Doran's advice . . .: JMC Memoirs II.

221   He told them . . .: RH interview with JMC, June 12, 1975.

222   "Boy, oh boy . . .": JMC Memoirs II.

223   one of Mankiewicz's stories: JMC to Joel Sayre, February 25, 1945.

223   After about three months . . .: JMC Memoirs II. *Hot Saturdays* was made without Cain.

223   "usually been the white-haired boy . . .": JMC, Preface to *Three of a Kind*.

223   his health was not good: RH interview with LT, undated.

223   He had no idea . . .: JMC to Will Shuster, April 9, 1945.

223   "It is obvious": JMC to HLM, October 31, 1932.

224   Elina settled the matter . . .: JMC Memoirs II.

224   "Unconsciously," he said: Knopf publicity copy for *Past All Dishonor* by
       JMC.

224   Cain loved to drive . . .: RH interview with L T.

225   "Always this bosomy-looking thing . . .": Mary Morris, "He Ain't Tepid,"
       unpublished interview for *PM*, mid-1940s.

225   He and Elina . . .: JMC memo to DM.

225   he had learned: JMC, Preface to *Three of a Kind*.

225   It would be about . . .: JMC, "The Baby in the Icebox."

225   sold it for $250: HLM to JMC, October 27, 1932.

226   The movie . . .: Paramount press book for *She Made Her Bed*, Lincoln Center
       Library, New York.

226   a short piece: JMC, "Don't Monkey with Uncle Sam."

226   "the first really good article . . .": HLM to JMC, December 21, 1932.

226   Ralph Thompson . . .: *New York Times*, December 1, 1937. "Paradise" pro-
       vides an excellent insight into Cain's attitude toward California when he first
       moved out there. On the positive side, he lists the friendliness of the people,
       in part because they have no roots in California (and roots, Cain thought, dis-
       couraged hospitality); the fact that people in all walks of life speak good En-
       glish and are well educated; the good schools, roads, traffic control, and
       recreational facilities, including an abundance of swimming pools, to say
       nothing of the Pacific Ocean; the culture—singing, dancing, music recitals,
       and exhibits of paintings. "I am not particular here."
           On the negative side, Cain included the architecture and the food, which
       was undistinguished, especially the seafood. On the other hand, he noted
       there was very little hunger. "Ten cents will buy an incredible amount of food
       and hardly anybody lacks for ten cents." But most important, he said, was
       what "we laughingly call my intellectual life." There was a dreadful vacuity to
       the place, and what he missed most was something—anything—that "pricks
       my imagination a little, gives me some sort of lilt, makes me feel that today I
       heard something. And I am the sort that is as likely to get this from the
       common man as his more erudite cousin, the highbrow. But what do I get:
       Nothing."
           And what bothered Cain about southern California was "the piddling oc-
       cupations to which the people dedicate their lives." The trouble was there was
       no significant work in California, which created all kinds of problems, one of
       the most significant being that "it is unusual to find a man who is doing the
       same thing now as he did last year. If he has a poultry farm, a few months ago,
       he fixed flats and a few months before that had a newsstand." They are not
       inferior people out here in California, Cain concluded, but they "suffer from
       the cruel feebleness of the play which the economy of the region compels
       them to take part in."

227   "a broken, beaten . . .": JMC to Mrs. Vincent Lawrence, March 26, 1972.

227   Ruth thought . . .: RH interview with RGG, undated.

227   Leo recalls . . .: RH interview with L T, undated.

227   "Three extra girls . . .": JMC, "The Widow's Mite, or Queen of the Rancho."

228 the former Dorothy Wegman: Dorshka (Wegman) Raphaelson's story is recounted in her book *Glorified* (New York: Brentano's, 1930).

228 Cain first met: JMC, "Charles Laughton."

229 Knopf . . . wrote him: AAK to JMC, November 21, 1932.

229 "Your note . . .": JMC to AAK, December 4, 1932.

229 Mencken, who wrote Knopf: HLM to AAK, December 14, 1932.

229 Knopf wrote Cain: AAK to JMC, December 15, 1932.

229 for $200 a week: JMC to HNS, January 16, 1950.

230 "He has another side": JMC Memoirs II.

230 Maurice Zolotow: Maurice Zolotow, *Billy Wilder in Hollywood* (New York: G. P. Putnam, 1977), p. 56.

230 He and . . . McGuinness: JMC Self-Interview.

230 Cohn asked one of his writers: JMC Memoirs II.

231 This was in February 1933: When Robert Riskin died, Cain felt such a debt that he knew he must write Fay Wray, Riskin's widow, and did. Though he met Miss Wray only once, he didn't expect an answer, but to his astonishment she wrote him back, a very warm letter, recalling the evening they had met, and also recalling that Riskin had often spoken of him, and wondered if the talk had had any result. JMC memo to DM.

231 "the boy who . . .": JMC, Preface to *Three of a Kind*.

231 the kind of guy: RH interview with SR, undated.

231 Leo remembers him: RH interview with L T, undated.

231 He wore $45 suits: JMC, Preface to *Three of a Kind*.

232 Lawrence's effect . . .: RH interviews with SR, undated.

232 Cain always thought . . .: JMC, Preface to *Three of a Kind*.

232 "the love rack": David Zinsser, interview with JMC, *Paris Review*, Spring-Summer 1978.

232 Raphaelson had . . .: RH interview with SR, undated.

232 And then, one time . . .: JMC memo to DM.

233 "That jells the idea . . .": JMC to Mrs. Danber, March 11, 1959.

233 But the love story . . .: JMC, "Vincent Sargent Lawrence."

233 "Get her out of there . . .": JMC to Mrs. Danber, March 11, 1959.

234 "Hell, it not only . . .": JMC to WL, July 31, 1933.

234 "Christ, we didn't only . . .": JMC memo to DM.

234 Cain found that: JMC, Preface to *The Butterfly*.

234 "While this may seem . . .": JMC to AAK, August 17, 1933.

234 "If Jake is . . .": JMC, Preface to *The Butterfly*.

234 He titled it . . .": JMC Memoirs II.

235 "You have a curious gift . . .": JMC to WL, November 11, 1933.

235 But Cain did not send it . . .: JMC to WL, July 31, 1933.

235 Cain finally decided: JMC to WL, July 21, 1933.

235 A few days . . .: AAK to JMC, February 25, 1933.

236 wire from Lippmann: WL to JMC, July 31, 1933.

236 Cain wired back . . .: JMC to WL, July 31, 1933.

236 "I don't know . . .": JMC to AAK, July 31, 1933.

236 Next he wrote Lippmann . . .: JMC to WL, July 31, 1933.

236   "I was playing golf . . .": RH interview with AAK, December 14, 1979.

236   the columnist wired: WL to JMC, August 8, 1933.

237   wire from Knopf: AAK to JMC, August 8, 1933.

237   Cain wired Lippmann: JMC to WL, August 8, 1933.

237   a phone call from Lippmann: JMC Memoirs II.

237   The deal Knopf offered . . .: WL to JMC, August 9, 1933.

237   "I am very glad . . ." JMC to AAK, August 17, 1933.

237   The next day . . .: JMC to AAK, August 18, 1933.

237   Within a few days . . .: AAK to JMC, August 22, 1933.

237   Knopf did not like . . .: AAK to JMC, September 14, 1933.

237   Around this time . . .: JMC memo to ABC-TV program "Book Talk" in JMC files, undated.

238   Knopf had decided: AAK to JMC, October 6, 1933.

238   "There is only . . .": JMC to HO, December 11, 1949.

238   So he wrote Knopf . . .: JMC to AAK, October 14, 1933

238   Knopf replied . . .: AAK to JMC, October 22, 1933.

238   Leo recalls: RH interview with LT, June 5, 1979.

239   "More than five hundred novels": JMC Memoirs I.

239   His first effort . . .: JMC, "The Widow's Mite, or Queen of the Rancho."

239   When Cain sent . . .: JMC to Carroll Lewis, December 28, 1961.

239   "You have heard . . .": JMC, "Camera Obscura." In later years, JMC thought his piece on the Hollywood studio had dated (JMC to DM, June 12, 1966), but, at the time, it amounted to a significant defense of the studio moguls' attitude toward writing, which he felt was much maligned. And those Eastern intellectuals and critics, who would later charge that Cain had "sold out" to Hollywood, might well have made their original judgment on the basis of his 1933 *Mercury* article. He said that the most inaccurate of all the legends about Hollywood was the one that suggested the "studios don't want good work from a writer, but only the cheapest stuff he can think up, and the more stereotyped, mawkish and salacious the better." Cain said this idea is held not only by the outside world, but the Hollywood writers themselves, that it was their favorite out and what they blamed their troubles on. "Well, I don't believe it," said Cain. "I sat in a good many moving picture conferences; I have yet to hear an executive say: 'Boys, it ain't sexy enough'; what they usually say is: 'Boys, it's no goddamn good. Maybe you need more time. Take it. But it's got to be a whole lot better if we're going to schedule it.' . . . When the boys go back to their office [after a story conference in which their script has been rejected], no doubt they feel hurt. No doubt they feel this is a story about a sensitive young something or other and as such must be pretty good. No doubt they feel that they are sensitive young somethings or others themselves, and couldn't possibly have anything but a masterpiece. No doubt they feel the movies are run by a lot of ex-buttonhole makers who wouldn't know something good if it was handed to them on a silver platter. No doubt they pity themselves handsomely, but I'll tell you why their effort was turned down. It was no goddamn good, and that was the beginning of it and the end of it."

    There were, however, real reasons, Cain said, why writers were unhappy in Hollywood, even cynical, less sensitive professionals. And the most important was that the actors and directors had more impact on the movie than a writer, which the critics knew. The critic is concerned with what in telegraphy is known as "the phantom circuit, that electrical area which exists apart from all wires, models, all costumes, all effects: the imagination." But when he looks for it on the screen where does he find it? And if he spots it, who does he credit—the actor, the director, the writers? He concluded that any writer who had "his mind on Bigger and Better things" will be unhappy working in Hollywood. But he said the studios were still right in their effort to produce entertainment, not art, and that "there are worse trades than confecting entertainment and if you realize clearly that you are at work on entertainment, something that lives tonight and tomorrow is forgotten, then the suspicion that you are a prostitute of the arts loses much of its sting."

240 went to work on another piece: JMC, "Tribute to a Hero."

240 nothing so much as: Harry Russell, "Tribute to an Author," *Kent News*, Chestertown, Maryland, date unavailable.

240 Knopf felt . . .: Carl Bode, *Mencken* (Carbondale, Illinois: Southern Illinois University Press, 1969), p. 228.

240 "knocked me for a loop": JMC to HLM, October 16, 1933.

240 Mencken wrote back . . .: HLM to JMC, October 24, 1933

241 Cain said: JMC to Hamilton Owens, April 3, 1934.

241 He wrote Cain . . .: BAB to RH, November 8, 1978.

241 It began . . .: JMC, "Wanted: A Western Story," *New York American*, November 11, 1933.

242 "It has become quite hard . . .": JMC, "Romance under the NRA," *New York American*, December 5, 1933.

242 picked up on such subjects: JMC, *New York American* columns, November 23, 1933 to March 26, 1934.

243 Knopf questioned . . .: AAK to JMC, December 7, 1933.

243 but Cain said: JMC to AAK, December 13, 1933.

243 Cain was seriously: JMC to AAK, November 1, 1933.

243 Knopf liked the idea . . .: AAK to JMC, November 7, 1933.

243 The first sign . . .: JMC Memoirs II.

243 Then Cain received . . .: JMC Memoirs II.

11 THE "UNLAYDOWNABLE" BOOK LAUNCHES
A STRANGE CAREER

page

244 "Six Minute Egg": Harold Strauss, *New York Times*, February 18, 1934.

245 any single review: Franklin P. Adams, *New York Herald Tribune*, February 18, 1934. Regarding *The Postman*, Hal Borland in the *Philadelphia Ledger*, February 19, 1934, wrote: "The next time anyone tries to tell you that newspaper work spoils a writer for serious or artistic work tell him to read *The Postman Always Rings Twice*." He also said "there is a strong possibility that

[Cain] will look back a few years hence and see that novel standing out as an achievement and its influence comparable to Hemingway's *The Sun Also Rises*." Gilbert Seldes commented on the excitement caused by *Postman*, when he wrote in his *New York Journal* review, February 24, 1934: "It is a long time since I have heard so many people of so many different tastes say that a book is 'great.' " And although Seldes himself did not think *Postman* was great, he did think it was a good story and acknowledged Cain's ability to tell it. William Rose Benét, in the *Saturday Review of Literature*, February 24, 1934, also applauded Cain's literary style and dialogue and thought Cain would go far as a novelist. "We have what is technically termed a 'Wow!' " said *The Nation*, April 4, 1934. T. S. Mathews, in the *New Republic*, February 28, 1934, said: "It does not pretend to tell the whole story, but it does pretend to tell nothing but the truth." Hamilton Owens, at the *Baltimore Sun*, February 17, 1934, mistrusting his own judgment because Cain was a Baltimorean and an old friend, said he loaned his copy to three people and each reported he was unable to lay it down until it was finished. Edith Riley in the *Houston Post*, June 3, 1934, praised Cain and said, "If you would learn what goes on in the mind of a murderer; if you would see life stripped bare; if you would be absorbed in reading a dramatic and intense tale of a stratum of life with which the average reader is not familiar; you will find an end to your quest in *The Postman Always Rings Twice*." Herschel Brickell, in his syndicated book review column, February 19, 1934, said, "This is strong men's meat and not for those who mind blood and raw lust. It has vigour and economy of method among its more admirable qualities, but its artistic merit won't keep it from giving the sensitive nightmares." Even the *Junior League Magazine*, May 1934, acknowledging *Postman* was "rapidly becoming the book of the hour about which everyone is either complaining or eulogizing," gave it a cautious endorsement: "If you can stomach all that [realism and sex] and if your sensibilities aren't too devitalized by *Saturday Evening Post* fiction, you will find this good strong stuff."

245   "I hate the book!": Lewis Gannett's review, *New York Herald Tribune*, February 1, 1934.

245   ". . . several disgusting scenes . . .": Gertrude Atherton, "Words and Deeds," *New York American*, January 1935.

246   "Brutal and shocking": *London Times*, May 25, 1939.

246   "One day last week . . .": *London Daily Express*, May 31, 1934.

246   ". . . American conte . . .": *London Telegraph*, May 6, 1934.

246   "pride of ownership": Clarke Fitzpatrick to JMC, March 27, 1934.

246   "If you read . . .": JMC to Mrs. Dorothy O'Donnell, March 14, 1939.

246   Arthur Krock . . .: Ad in March 1934 *American Mercury*.

246   The *Mercury* review . . .: *American Mercury*, April 1934.

246   Raphaelson sent a copy: RH interview with SR, undated.

246   "Well, there's all . . .": JMC Memoirs I.

247   Morris Markey, wired: MM to JMC, undated.

247   " 'Nothing less than . . .' ": RH interview with L T, June 5, 1979.

247   "That's all right . . .": JMC to AAK, February 3, 1957.

247   *Redbook* said . . .: *Redbook*, May 1934.

247   One writing teacher . : .: Setting Cain's dialogue to poetry was done by Clement Wood, in *Author & Journalist*, January 1949.

> "Well, what the hell? We're together, ain't we?"
> "I guess so. But I thought an awful lot, Frank.
> Last night. About you and me, and the movies,
> and why I flopped, and the hashhouse,
> and the road, and why you like it.
> We're just two punks, Frank.
> God kissed us on the brow, that night.
> He gave us all that two people can ever have.
> We had all that love, and we just cracked up under it.
> It's just a big airplane engine
> that takes you up to the sky,
> right to the top of a mountain.
> But when you put it in a Ford,
> it just shakes it to pieces.
> That's what we are, Frank, a couple of Fords.
> God is up there laughing at us."

247   H. L. Mencken pointed out . . . .: HLM, *The American Language* (New York: Alfred A. Knopf, 1919).

248   stepson and friends: RH interview with LT, undated.

248   "Though it is fastened . . .": *New York Times*, February 28, 1934.

248   an excellent short story: *Bradenton* (Florida) *Herald*, April 27, 1934.

248   Three book houses . . .: Several letters in files between JMC and Houghton Mifflin, Farrar Rinehart, and Raoul Fleischmann, representing Smith Haas.

249   soon he had requests: Mrs. William Brown Meloney to JMC, January 30, 1934.

249   as did *Redbook*: William Lengel to JMC, February 27, 1934.

249   and *The New Yorker*: Wolcott Gibbs to JMC, August 2, 1934.

249   "Please don't go in . . .": EH to JMC, August 3, 1934.

249   One of the first things . . .: JMC to RMc, March 14, 1934.

249   ". . . I can't sell ideas . . .": JMC Memoirs II.

249   *The Traitor*: RH interview with JMC, undated.

249   Cain's story . . .: JMC to Lewis Milestone, August 16, 1934.

249   *Aida*: James Geller to JMC, June 20, 1934.

249   "preposterous . . .": JMC to CC, July 5, 1970.

249   Geller insisted . . .": JMC to DO, December 31, 1965.

249   One of the first things . . .: JMC to Alan Wycherly, June 11, 1963.

250   "Gable is a prospector . . .": JMC to Walter Wanger, April 8, 1934.

250   So he went back . . .: JMC memo to DM.

250   returning the $3,333: Louis Sobol, "The Voice of Broadway," *New York Journal*, December 6, 1934.

250   "You're crazy": JMC, "That Was Hollywood," unpublished article in JMC files.

250   *San Francisco*: John Douglas Eames, *The MGM Story*.

251   In May, he went East . . .: JMC Memoirs II.

251   "It makes me feel . . .": JMC, "The Bosky Dells," *New York American*, June 11, 1934.

251   "shoved off in my usual . . .": JMC to HLM, May 21, 1934.

251   "I don't know . . .": JMC to Marjorie Sirich, May 21, 1934.

251   "When I wrote it . . .": JMC, "Baghdad's People," *New York American*, June 1, 1934.

252   The trip to Centreville . . .: JMC Memoirs II.

252   "The Western virus": JMC, "Western Virus," *New York American*, June 29, 1934.

252   Cain returned to California . . .: JMC Memoirs II.

252   "It was so hot . . .": JMC, "The Bosky Dells."

252   "Hollywood looks exactly . . .": JMC to EH, May 21, 1934.

252   "I wanted to write . . .": JMC, "Literary Osmosis," *New York American*, June 20, 1934.

253   one "treatment": MGM files on *Postman* in Hollywood.

253   But when Geller heard . . .: JMC memo to DM.

253   by the sale: AAK to JMC, June 7, 1934.

253   a two-acter: JMC, "The Postman Is Below."

253   "the impressionistic style . . .": JMC memo to DM.

253   Cain sent the play off . . .: JMC to AAK, February 3, 1957.

253   writing for the magazines: JMC Memoirs II.

253   "If stenography was abolished . . .": JMC, "The Influence of Stenography on Literature," *New York American*, October 24, 1934.

254   "Working like a wildman": JMC to EH, July 29, 1934.

254   Cain's reaction . . .: JMC to EH, August 13, 1934.

254   "You have made me . . .": EH to JMC, September 4, 1934.

254   Cain worked in . . .: RH interview with L T, undated.

254   When he was chilly . . .: JMC, "Stifling," *New York American*, January 29, 1935.

255   After reading Lippmann's . . .: JMC to WL, July 16, 1934.

255   he was also trying: JMC to HLM, May 26, 1934.

255   according to Cain: JMC to Ronald Martinetti, August 11, 1969.

255   a little crusade: JMC to Sally Benson, August 25, 1934.

256   "I wish you . . .": JMC to AAK, August 3, 1934.

256   Knopf wrote . . .: AAK to JMC, August 6, 1934.

256   "Because his dialogue . . .": RH interview with DR and SR, undated.

256   Once Cain and Raphaelson . . .: JMC, "Other Guy's Play," *New York American*, July 20, 1934.

257   In 1933, Rafe . . .: SR, "Tragedy and Comedy," *New York Times*, January 6, 1935.

257   One night . . .: RH interview with SR, undated.

257   I like it better: JMC, "Film Capital," *New York American*, November 9, 1934.

257 He had recalled . . .: JMC to AK, August 21, 1944.

258 "This stuff of yours . . .": JMC to W. M. Flynn, March 9, 1936.

259 sometime before the Cains moved: RH interview with L T, June 5, 1979.

259 Charles Angoff: JMC to Charles Angoff, August 31, 1934.

259 For another . . .: The three food articles were "How to Carve That Bird," "Them Ducks," "Oh, les Crepes-Suzettes."

259 He deduced this . . .: JMC, "Upgrade Note," *New York American*, August 13, 1934.

259 "upside down house": RH interview with JMC, December 9, 1975.

259 It even had a "ghost": JMC, "The Ghost," *New York American*, December 19, 1934.

260 words of encouragement: James Geller to JMC, September 11, 1934.

260 in late November: JMC to Thelma Helburn, November 20, 1934.

260 Miss Helburn replied . . .: Thelma Helburn to JMC, December 7, 1934.

260 revisions in the mail: JMC to Thelma Helburn, December 19, 1934.

260 He saw Mencken . . .: JMC to Marjorie Sirich, March 12, 1935.

260 "At the end of three days . . .": JMC, "Stifling."

260 One night at a party . . .: RH interview with John Lee Mahin, undated.

261 He had been assigned . . .: JMC to James Geller, March 1, 1935.

261 Cain did make $5,000 . . .: JMC income tax return, 1935, in JMC files.

261 a story, which he sent: JMC to EH, March 13, 1935.

261 "Hip, Hip, the Hippo": JMC, "Hip, Hip, the Hippo," *Redbook*, March 1936.

261 "I never had . . .": JMC to EH, March 27, 1935.

261 They were trying . . .: JMC, "The Cat's Meow," *New York American*, October 6, 1934.

262 which Cain took as: RH interview with L T, undated.

262 "your favorite flower": Mary Morris, "He Ain't Tepid," unpublished interview for *PM*, mid-1940s.

262 "spiritual history": JMC, "Spiritual History," *New York American*, February 7, 1935.

262 Leonard Schuster . . .: Leonard Schuster to JMC, February 7, 1935.

262 Cain's own favorite . . .: JMC to BAB, August 12, 1967 and August 9, 1967.

263 he never did invite Cain: JMC Memoirs I.

263 "Get rid of Cain . . .": James Thurber, *The Years with Ross* (Boston: Little, Brown, 1959), p. 154.

263 "It's the same old round": JMC to WL, April 17, 1935.

263 he wrote Knopf: JMC to AAK, April 17, 1935.

263 He began to see a relationship . . .: JMC testimony in *Cain* v. *Universal*, USDC (Los Angeles) 1755Y.

264 did not like Hollywood parties: JMC memo to DM.

264 "Dr." Mencken: HLM to JMC, August 27, 1930.

264 "some sort of mumbled explanation,": JMC, "No Proteins," *New York American*, February 20, 1934.

264 Meyers had studied music: JMC, "Close Harmony."

265 "a darling host . . .": RH interview with DR and SR, July 24, 1978.

265 the ideal group: JMC, "Close Harmony."

265   The regulars . . .: RH interview with L T, June 5, 1979.

265   One night . . .: Tanya Graham to JMC, April 19, 1935.

265   Cain himself: Ralph Hayes to JMC, December 31, 1943.

265   He discovered . . .: JMC to Ralph Hayes, March 28, 1936.

266   "At last, I begin to see . . .": JMC to Henry Meyers, October 20, 1935.

266   Mahin recalled: RH interview with John Lee Mahin, June 13, 1979.

266   really great male singers: JMC testimony in *Cain* v. *Universal*.

266   "Naturally, I . . .": JMC to Paul Hume, September 29, 1948.

267   "Oh, I don't know . . .": JMC to CC, undated.

267   Dr. Hirshfeld's endorsement . . .: JMC to Dr. Samuel Hirshfeld, April 17, 1944.

267   "It's a new writer . . .": EH to JMC, June 24, 1935.

267   "It would be hard . . .": Day Winn to EH, July 2, 1935.

267   "I have no interest . . .": JMC to EH, July 12, 1935.

267   Mrs. Haggard said . . .: EH to JMC, July 15, 1935.

268   "swell yarn": JMC to AAK, October 9, 1935.

268   Geller had had five copies . . .: RH interview with JMC, undated.

268   written it over twenty times: Peter Brunette and Gerald Perry, "Tough Guy," *Film Comment*, May 6, 1967.

268   "It was enough . . .": JMC, unpublished portion of Preface to *Three of a Kind* in JMC files.

268   for $5,000: JMC income tax records, 1935.

269   "shilly-shally way": JMC to AAK, October 9, 1935.

269   the Guild had decided: JMC to Thelma Helburn, October 20, 1935.

269   friendship with Charles Laughton: JMC, "Charles Laughton."

270   Cain was also seeing: MB interview with JMC, August 28, 1975.

270   met one day at the Raphaelsons': JMC to CC, August 1, 1971.

270   "It's important for us . . .": AAK to JMC, October 17, 1935.

270   he began to wonder: JMC to Mr. Grayson, March 18, 1936.

271   "those Mama-knows-best letters": JMC to Maureen Daly, November 17, 1968.

271   an article for the *Mercury*: JMC, "Close Harmony."

271   "driving like a wild man": JMC to Henry Meyers, October 20, 1935.

271   college education: JMC to Paul Palmer, October 9, 1935.

272   a dreadful experience: JMC to RGG, June 9, 1936.

272   just before Christmas: JMC to EC, December 12, 1935.

272   "We don't have chinchilla . . .": JMC, "Fit for a Queen—Worth a King's Ransom."

12   "HOW YOU WRITE 'EM IS WRITE 'EM"

page

273   "Mencken does not seem . . .": JMC to EC, December 27, 1935.

273   Cain wrote Elina: JMC to EC, June 9, 1936.

274   "the miracle man": JMC, "The Postman Is Below."

274   "the audience got . . .": JMC, "The Postman Is Below."

274   Barthelmess was given: JMC to Mary Porter, March 19, 1936.

275   chilled sales: JMC to Paul Palmer, March 6, 1936. Most of the reviews of *Postman* are in the Lincoln Center Library for the Performing Arts in New York; they are not dated. Widella Waldorf, in the *New York Post*, came closest to summing up the problems the critics had in assessing two performers they liked in a story they found distasteful with characters they found shoddy, when she said that Barthelmess and Philips "bring to the play a quality it probably shouldn't have, but which is nevertheless welcome indeed." And Burns Mantle, reporting on the 1935–36 season in New York, summarized Broadway's reaction by saying the fault with *Postman*, despite its technical perfections, was that it "is hard to write an appealing story about repellent human beings." Burns Mantle, *The Best Plays of 1935–36* (New York: Dodd Mead, 1936), p.12.

275   one of the policemen: JMC memo to DM.

275   "wrought wonders": Hollywood Reporter, March 9, 1936.

275   "The real trouble . . .": JMC to RGG, June 9, 1936.

275   While working . . .: JMC to Maureen Daly, November 7, 1968.

275   is considered: JMC memo to DM.

275   "All I could see": JMC to EM, undated.

276   "a complete bust": JMC to Gertrude Sayre, August 19, 1936.

276   where he discovered: *Providence* (Rhode Island) *News Tribune*, March 23, 1935.

276   I get stuck . . .: JMC to AAK, June 30, 1936.

277   Knopf replied . . .: AAK to JMC, July 7, 1936.

277   he declined the offer: JMC to AAK, July 19, 1936.

277   Knopf replied . . .: AAK to JMC, July 22, 1936.

278   a very good father: RH interview with LT, undated.

278   Cain's health: JMC to AAK, October 9, 1935.

278   The Raphaelsons . . .: RH interview with DR and SR, undated.

278   Leo recalls: RH interview with LT, undated.

278   "He was not . . .": RH interview with SR, undated.

279   "Anyone who . . .": JMC memo to DM, October 9, 1966.

279   "is driving me nuts . . .": JMC to Heinrich Bucholtz, December 14, 1936.

279   a miserable trip: JMC to AAK, January 18, 1937.

279   "How you write 'em . . .": JMC to Dorothy Rouses, May 23, 1938.

279   a major turning point: JMC to Stephen Wright, September 13, 1970.

279   began to take shape: JMC memo to DM.

280   for $8,000.: JMC to Collector of Internal Revenue, February 28, 1937.

280   "Bright Gold": JMC to James Geller, February 4, 1937.

280   on April 3: Pan Am travel schedules in JMC files.

280   he found her in La Locha's: JMC Memoirs I and II.

281   he checked with Mr. Gallo: JMC testimony in *Cain* v. *Universal Studios*, USDC (Los Angeles) 1755Y.

281   rented a car: JMC Memoirs II.

281   "I never quite had . . .": JMC Memoirs II.

282   ". . . backward country": JMC to WL, September 20, 1937.

282   began to have trouble: JMC to AAK, May 1, 1937.

282   "It turns out . . .": JMC to Mr. Simon, June 29, 1939.

282   flop into his bed: JMC to CC, August 11, 1974.

282   "I hated it while . . .": JMC to HLM, undated.

282   Even today . . .: RH interview with L T, undated.

282   nor Constance Cummings: RH interview with CC, undated.

282   he wrote of occasionally: JMC to CC, August 11, 1974.

283   in a letter to Mencken: JMC to HLM, December 8, 1937.

284   Mencken replied . . .: HLM to JMC, December 10, 1937.

284   "SUPERB": BK to JMC, July 23, 1937.

284   "I AM PROUD . . .": AAK to JMC, July 23, 1937.

284   "a masterpiece": HLM to JMC, September 11, 1937.

284   working title: JMC to AAK, July 28, 1937.

284   Knopf was stumped . . .: AAK to JMC, July 26, 1937.

284   "put on a campaign . . .": JMC to IvA, November 12, 1965.

284   "For Rafe: without whose belief . . .": RH interview with SR, undated.

284   Actor-producer . . .: Anton Bundsman to JMC, July 23, 1937.

284   The gossip columnists . . .: New York Times, September 19, 1937.

285   sold to the American: JMC to Robert Goodhue, June 2, 1937.

285    $1,000 a week: JMC income tax statement, 1938. It may have been as a pre-
liminary to going to work for MGM that he had his most memorable meeting
with Sam Goldwyn. Cain's agent, Geller, arranged an hour for him to discuss
a sequel to Hurricane, a 1937 picture made by MGM. And for the meeting,
Goldwyn had cut his calls: "He talked with the greatest intelligence," said
Cain. "I didn't have to talk down to him. Usually when a writer talks to another writer he makes it short and sweet; but with someone else, he uses a
slightly different vocabulary and he elaborates a bit. With Goldwyn, I didn't
have to put it into words of one syllable at all. He was with it all the way and
very interested, obviously. Suddenly a male secretary knifed into the room.
'Mr. Goldwyn, you said you weren't to be disturbed unless (mentioning some
agent) called, and he's on the wire now.' Goldwyn said O.K., he'd talk to him.
And then: 'At 500 you haf a deal, at 750 I vill not pay, I vill not pay!' he
said."

    While Goldwyn talked on the phone, Cain was thinking to himself: "Now,
who could argue with that accent?" And by the time he had left Goldwyn's
office, he had come to the conclusion that the legend who had inspired the
"mucus of a good idea" and "include me out" was no dumbbell and that the
accent and the stupid act was a put-on. "Goldwyn acquired his accent and
slipped in his role of Hollywood ignoramus when it was time to close a deal."
Peter Brunette and Gerald Perry, "Tough Guy," Film Comment, May 6,
1967.

285   Cain was assigned . . .: RH telephone interview with Herbert Nausbaum at
MGM in Hollywood.

285   One morning around nine-thirty . . .: JMC to Sara Mayfield, February 2,
1969.

285   "Well, nice seeing you": Peter Brunette and Gerald Perry, "Tough Guy."

285   Paul Palmer . . .: Paul Palmer to JMC, March 23, 1937.

285   not because he was opposed: JMC to Coleman McCarthy, July 3, 1973.

286   He went into a sulk . . .: JMC to Martha Duffy, August 13, 1973.

286   a big success: Paul Palmer to JMC, May 13, 1938.

286   Cain agreed: JMC to WL, September 20, 1937.

286   Lippmann responded . . .: WL to JMC, October 21, 1937.

286   exchanging thoughts: JMC to HLM, August 10, 1936.

286   confessed to Palmer: JMC to Paul Palmer, August 10, 1936.

286   "how a man can manage . . .": JMC to Heinrich Bucholtz, August 13, 1936.

286   He paid $1,240 . . .: JMC income tax statement, 1938.

286   the first production: *Hollywood Reporter*, January 8, 1938.

286   Fred Keating . . .: *New York Evening Post*, December 11, 1937.

286   a frantic search: *New York American*, December 19, 1937.

286   "third-act trouble": *New York Daily News*, January 2, 1938.

286   delayed until March: *New York Times*, January 25, 1938.

286   until fall: *New York Times*, January 17, 1938.

287   it had substance: *New York Times*, December 5, 1937.

287   And Lewis Gannett . . .: *New York Herald Tribune*, November 30, 1937.

287   "the sensationalism . . .": *Pittsburgh Post Gazette*, December 5, 1937.

287   "literature of a high order": *Pittsburgh Post Gazette*, December 11, 1937.

287   The *Chicago News* reviewer . . .: *Chicago Daily News*, December 15, 1937. Additional comment on *Serenade*: Ralph Thompson, in his "Books of the Times" column (*New York Times*, December 1, 1937), said, "James M. Cain's new novel is an amazing performance, a piece of great story-telling. It carried me away as few other books have ever done." Dawn Powell, in *The New Republic* (December 8, 1937), wrote: "Just as one begins to suspect that his hero is being dealt more aces than are in the deck, Cain performs the trick of which he is the only living master, of sawing a novel in two. A sentence does this trick, throwing all that has preceded into a totally new light and creating a double theme—of the story told and of the real story. . . ."

The *New Yorker* (December 4, 1937) noted it had been published, recommending it as "beautifully contrived hokum, guaranteed to thrill," and giving Cain a cautious pat on the back for his knowledge of music and singing. In fact, friend and foe alike praised Cain's musical knowledge. For example, in a generally critical review (*Huntington* [West Virginia] *Herald Advertiser*, January 9, 1938), H. R. Pinchard commented that its pages included "arguments about Beethoven and Rossini and about the music of Mexico and about John McCormack singing Handel, and the surprising thing about it is not the fact that it has an authentic ring but that it is absorbing and interesting even to one who never before suspected that Handel had been sung by John McCormack," and William Soskin in the *New York Herald Tribune* (December 5, 1937) thought Cain's feeling for the less ponderous composers, such as Rossini, actually helped bring a certain musical feeling to his style—"a gaudy, rhapsodic, Lisztian quality, a magical concoction of complex suspense and recurring climax that leaves the reader silted and hugely entertained."

The British reviewers of *Serenade* were less enthusiastic than their colleagues across the ocean, and it did not overwhelm them as *Postman* had done. But there was some warm praise, particularly from Frank Swinnerton (*London Observer*, no date). He said Cain's style "is brilliant in its colloquial certainty. And he knows as Defoe knew, exactly what detail to give. . . . I regard this book as both a tremendous dramatic success and a score for Modern American letters." And J. D. Beresford (*Manchester Guardian*, no date), after recommending the book and warning his readers to avoid it, said, "I must admit that the book has a tremendous drive and vigour."

287 And Dr. James Nielson . . .: JMC Memoirs II.

287 "For a while": Peter Brunette and Gerald Perry, "Tough Guy."

287 ". . . It is abnormal . . .": JMC to David Watmour, October 20, 1970.

287 she was approached: Sterling Bagby to RH, April 23, 1979.

288 "You advertise . . .": JMC to Donna Schrader, June 16, 1965.

288 "Could be that . . .": JMC Memoirs II.

288 "So, two body blows": JMC to AAK, March 13, 1938.

288 Knopf wrote back . . .: AAK to JMC, March 2, 1938. Cain always denied that he ever wrote about actual people and in *Serenade*, especially, all the characters were fictitious. But in his unpublished memoirs, he did admit there was one singer "whose voice got me to thinking that its special quality might have this simple explanation." Cain knew him in Hollywood and said they were all sitting in his living room one night and suddenly the singer blurted out: "I read your goddamn book!"

"Which book?" asked Cain.

"This new one, *Serenade*."

"Did you like it?"

The man sat for a moment, staring at Cain. Then he said, with a detectable growl, "It scared the Jesus out of me!" JMC Memoirs II.

288 "I look back . . .": RH interview with MG, June 13, 1979.

289 Goodhue thought: Robert Goodhue to JMC, February 14, 1938.

289 *Pepe le Moko*: *Variety*, June 29, 1938.

289 "This was impossible": JMC to George William, June 8, 1969.

289 four $1000 weeks: JMC income tax statement, 1938.

289 He always felt . . .: Peter Brunette and Gerald Perry, "Tough Guy."

289 "If you are interested": JMC to Wolcott Gibbs, April 16, 1938.

290 "I guess I'm better off . . .": Wolcott Gibbs to JMC, April 22, 1938.

290 "What to do . . .": JMC to Wolcott Gibbs, April 27, 1938.

290 He could hardly . . .: Albert Benjamin to JMC, April 6, 1938.

290 He queried . . .: JMC to Merritt Hubbard, May 19, 1938.

290 "How about a Cinderella . . .": JMC to Dorothy Rouses, May 25, 1936.

291 "There was a man . . .": JMC Memoirs I.

291 The story was based on . . .: The description of *Stand Up and Fight* is from the reviews (mostly unidentified) in the Lincoln Center Library in New York.

291 his old friend: Joan Brittain, *Laurence Stallings* (Boston: Twayne Publishers, 1979), p.22. Although he did not receive a screen credit, Stallings's name is on the script in the Amerian Film Institute Library in Hollywood.

292 Cain learned: JMC to AK, August 31, 1971.

292 The two writers discussed . . .: RH interview with JMC, December 9, 1975.

293 Mahin told Cain . . .: RH interview with John Lee Mahin, June 13, 1979.

293 Lewis had aroused; Mark Schorer, *Sinclair Lewis* (Englewood Cliffs, New Jersey: Prentice-Hall, 1962), p.640.

293 "my third or fourth . . .": JMC to Mark Schorer, January 7, 1957.

293 "looks fairly good": JMC to Milt Gross, September 19, 1938.

293 Elina had to return: JMC to LT, May 21, 1938.

294 expressing concern: JMC to EC, October 5, 1938.

294 "All of us felt . . .": JMC to EC, October 11, 1938.

294 "Antonio Scotti died . . .": JMC to EM, March 5, 1967.

294 They buoyed her up . . .: JMC to Lewis Burris, March 22, 1970.

294 "of an undertakers' . . .": JMC to EM, May 22, 1967.

294 Cain did not feel close: RH interview with Robin Deck, February 11, 1980.

295 "Otherwise the magazines . . .": EC to JMC, October 18, 1938.

295 by the Morris Agency: William Morris Agency to JMC, October 10, 1939.

295 "Every time . . .": JMC to Paul Palmer, May 23, 1938.

295 "What keeps writers poor . . .": JMC to Marjorie Sirich, March 31, 1938.

295 He met again with Harris . . .: JMC to EC, October 18, 1938.

296 "Feel friendly . . .": JMC to EC, November 2, 1938.

296 "Please don't be . . .": JMC to EC, November 4, 1938.

296 Geller had found: JMC memo to DM.

296 Wee Willie Winkie: *New York Times Directory of Films* (New York: Random House, 1971). While Cain was in the East, WL tried to arrange a dinner at the River Club with the Markeys, but Cain missed it and, in fact, was annoyed that he did not see WL in Washington at all during the time he was working in Baltimore, having forgotten, as he wrote his friend, that "you had moved your tepee there." He also noted that *Time* picked the damnedest pictures of WL to print, "only surpassed by their annual portrait of me, which looks like a retired truck driver." Cain, in fact, was very conscious of his looks and rarely saw a photograph of himself he liked. JMC to WL, November 18, 1938, and December 4, 1938.

296 for $17,500: JMC income tax statement, 1938.

296 "It is high time . . .": JMC to AAK, December 4, 1938.

297 "I am not fond of wars": JMC to Tris, May 21, 1938.

297 "that has been cooking . . .": JMC to AAK, December 4, 1938.

13 FINNEY PYLORECTOMY—"A VERY GREAT EVENT"

page

298 "I'm four parts Irish": JMC to H. Alan Wycherly, February 2, 1969.

298 So he called O'Faoláin . . .: EM, "James M. Cain as Novelist," unpublished paper in JMC files.

298 O'Faoláin seeing: Seán O'Faoláin to JMC, January 21, 1941.

298   rolling his *r*'s: JMC to Joseph Lalley, January 7, 1949.

299   "I remember being in Paris . . .": RH interview with RGG, undated.

299   A Swedish newspaper . . .": RH interview with L T, undated.

299   a brief stay: JMC to Seán O'Faoláin, May 13, 1939.

299   In the early thirties . . .: RH interview with JMC, April 16, 1975.

299   Cain became lost: JMC, "Coal Baron," unpublished article, in JMC files.

300   the trouble he was having: JMC to BK, March 26, 1939.

300   ". . . pleasantest show . . .": *New York Times*, February 25, 1939.

300   "I'm world famous . . .": John Carmody, "James M. Cain at Twilight Time," *Washington Post Potomac*, January 19, 1969.

300   (at $1,000 a week): JMC income tax statement, 1939.

300   Universal had also hired . . .: JMC deposition in *Cain* v. *Universal*, USDC (Los Angeles) 1755Y.

300   she would not take: Peter Brunette and Gerald Perry, "Tough Guy," *Film Comment*, May 6, 1967.

300   according to Cain: MB interview with JMC, August 28, 1975.

301   Cain ran into: JMC deposition in *Cain* v. *Universal*, USDC (Los Angeles) 1755Y.

301   *The Victoria Docks at 8*: Script of *Victoria Docks at 8* is in Stuart and Roger Birnbaum's private collection in Hollywood.

301   Cain never completely understood: JMC to Seán O'Faoláin, May 13, 1939.

301   "The whole thing": JMC to RMc, April 30, 1939.

301   "One of the big things . . .": JMC to Virginia Dean, April 30, 1939.

301   he wrote Seán O'Faoláin: JMC to Seán O'Faoláin, May 13, 1939.

301   indirectly inspired: Clarke Fitzpatrick to JMC, February 24, 1937.

302   Cain had responded: JMC to Clarke Fitzpatrick, June 22, 1937, and February 10, 1942.

302   ten of them: William Morris Agency memo to JMC, May 10, 1939.

302   *When Tomorrow Comes*: Reviewing *When Tomorrow Comes*, Frank Nugent in the *New York Times* (August 17, 1939) said the story of "transparent fortuitousness" could not be excused by Dunne's and Boyer's "willingness to repeat for the ladies' matinee trade the type of star-crossed romance more happily expressed a few months back in 'Love Affair.' " To make matters worse, Nugent put much of the blame on Cain, who had virtually no responsibility for the final script.

       When Tomorrow Comes was remade into a little tearjerker in 1957. It starred June Allyson, Rossano Brazzi, and Jane Wyatt, and the only reason Cain was aware of this was that late in his life he was still receiving royalty checks for something called *Interlude*, the name of the remake. Peter Brunette and Gerald Perry, "Tough Guy."

302   There was nothing like it . . .: James Francis Crow, "Dunne and Boyer in Star Roles," in unidentified clipping in JMC files.

302   Cain decided the movie . . .: JMC to BK, January 4, 1940.

302   "I have been so harassed . . .": JMC to AAK, January 4, 1940.

302   Seán O'Faoláin also wrote . . .: Seán O'Faoláin to JMC, January 21, 1940.

303   the studio bought: JMC income tax statement, 1940.

303 Cain wrote an outline . . .: JMC Memoirs II.

303 ". . . from the readers of *Liberty* . . .": *Liberty*'s circulation in 1936 was only 3 million, so it is unlikely that "Double Indemnity" added a circulation of 8 million. The Liberty Library Corporation feels that what Jacobs heard was that a total of 8 million extra readers bought the magazine during the entire run of the eight-part serial. Pamela Tiernam to RH, August 28, 1979.

303 "I talk as though . . .": JMC to BK, April 12, 1940.

304 The two had first met . . .: JMC, "Thornton," unpublished article in JMC files. In the article, JMC described his New York meeting with Wilder: "There was something collegiate about him—not student collegiate or professional collegiate, rather I would call him tutorial collegiate, the eternal instructor in the English Department, who helps the boys with their problems and monitors the monthly tests, but not in a snoopy way."

Most of the talk was about Wilder's new play, then in rehearsal. Wilder was apparently insisting on doing the play in a way Dean disapproved of. The only prop on the stage would be a stepladder, with people sitting on their own graves and a stage manager walking around explaining everything. But what struck Cain was Wilder's reaction to Dean's insistence that his idea would not work. "He listened with the utmost good humor and utter immovability—he meant to do his play the way he meant to do it, that was plain to be seen."

When Wilder left, Dean shook his head, more in sorrow than anger, and said, "You can't tell him anything. He was born bullheaded and there's nothing you can do about it. Well, when the thing flops he'll learn his lesson—perhaps." The play, of course, was *Our Town*, which made theatrical history and would soon bring Wilder to Hollywood.

304 ". . . I just hit it lucky": RH interview with JMC, December 9, 1975.

305 "saw me through": JMC to CC, October 13, 1974.

306 Wilson had written . . .: BK to JMC, June 24, 1940.

306 My own belief . . .: JMC to Edmund Wilson, June 29, 1940.

307 In November . . .: JMC to BK, November 6, 1940.

307 *Lucky Baldwin*, about . . .: Although I could find out very little about *Lucky Baldwin*, this interesting little passage from one of JMC's unpublished novels—*Cloud 9*—suggests the story stuck with him: "Don't forget what Lucky Baldwin told them out in California when they complained they were charging too much for the land around Santa Anita: 'The land,' he roared at them, 'hell, we give the land away. I'm selling climate.' "

307 worked seven weeks: JMC income tax statement, 1940

307 Lucky Baldwin: M. Weinstock, "Town Talk," *Los Angeles Times*, November 20, 1940.

307 he asked the studio: JMC Memoirs II.

307 The experience . . .: RH interview with JMC, undated.

307 Cain was closed out: Harry Joe Brown to JMC, December 11, 1940.

307 reported to Blanche Knopf: JMC to BK, March 29, 1941.

307 Blanche replied . . .: BK to JMC, April 8, 1941.

308 I need money . . .: JMC to BK, April 10, 1941.

308 "the noose": William Morris Agency to JMC, April 12, 1941.

308   He told Geller . . .: JMC Memoirs I.

308   and everyone: JMC to Mrs. Robert Rathbone, November 5, 1968.

308   after a day's writing: JMC to RMc, May 27, 1965.

308   a Los Angeles society surgeon: JMC to Mrs. Robert Rathbone, February 5, 1967.

308   "It gould not be . . .": JMC to MM, 1948.

308   Cain had a real scare: JMC to Mrs. Robert Rathbone, February 5, 1967.

309   gallstones as well: JMC memo to DM.

309   the doctor recommended: JMC Memoirs II.

309   "fall apart right . . .": JMC memo to DM.

309   "The development of . . .": JMC Memoirs II.

309   "I banged into a climax . . .": JMC Memoirs I.

309   ". . . I threw it away . . .": JMC to Jerry Wald, September 15, 1943.

309   "She was a peculiar . . .": Winzola McClendon interview with JMC, *Washington Post*, undated clipping in JMC files.

309   "I'm glad you liked Mildred . . .": JMC to DR, October 16, 1941.

310   But years later . . .: Peter Brunette and Gerald Perry, "Tough Guy."

310   "my hand is palsied": JMC to SR, June 19, 1946.

310   When Knopf heard . . .: JMC Memoirs I.

310   "a curious psychological effect": JMC Memoirs II.

310   "whacky indulgence": JMC to RMc, October 24, 1944.

310   he took it home: JMC, "Spirits."

310   at the Brown Derby: JMC deposition in *Cain* v. *Universal*, USDC (Los Angeles) 1755Y.

311   After the lunch . . .: RH interview with JMC, undated.

311   He realized that no copyright . . .: JMC, "The Opening Gun."

311   he told his lawyer: Cain also asked Knopf to join him in the suit, sharing one-fourth of the expenses, but said that if he did not, Knopf should put in writing that he renounced all claim to whatever damages they might win. Knopf declined to be a party to the suit. JMC to AAK, July 31, 1941, and AAK to JMC, August 6, 1941.

311   Then he wrote Taylor: JMC to Dwight Taylor, August 26, 1941.

312   trial was set: *Daily Variety*, September 4, 1941.

312   "cooled": JMC to GM, September 6, 1963

312   Finney pylorectomy: JMC Memoirs II.

312   so had someone's mother: Most popular writers, no doubt, are plagued by coincidences involving the names of their principal characters. But Cain seemed to suffer more than most: After "Double Indemnity" appeared, it turned out there was an insurance agent in Los Angeles with the same name as one of Cain's insurance agents (Walter Huff), and Cain had to write a long letter to *Liberty* explaining how he arrived at the name. JMC to W. M. Flynn, March 9, 1936. He had the same problem with Leonard Borland in "Two Can Sing," and he had to explain to Dr. Borland in Chicago how he derived that name. JMC to Dr. Leonard Borland, May 16, 1938.

312   Richard Fuller: Richard Fuller to AAK, August 10, 1941

312   Knopf wrote Fuller . . .: AAK to Richard Fuller, undated.

312 finally signed a waiver: Richard Fuller to JMC, August 24, 1941.

312 "I can hardly imagine . . .": AAK to James Geller, August 24, 1941.

312 Cain still checked . . .: JMC to AAK, August 26, 1941.

313 he went East: JMC to AAK, August 26, 1941.

313 the Cain household: JMC to GC, March 18, 1945.

313 "I never did have . . .": JMC to Katharine White, September 5, 1941.

313 "The piece . . .": JMC to Katharine White, December 6, 1941.

313 Edmund Wilson had: Edmund Wilson, "Boys in the Back Room," *New Republic*, November 11, 1940.

313 Ralph Thompson: *New York Times*, October 5, 1941.

313 J. Donald Adams: *New York Times*, September 25, 1941.

313 "None of these critics . . .": JMC to AAK, September 26, 1941.

314 "Cain's tale is . . .": *New Republic*, October 6, 1941.

314 "is one of the most readable . . .": *Time*, September 29, 1941.

314 Robert Van Gelder: *New York Times*, October 5, 1941.

314 "the ultra-conservatives . . .": *Retail Bookseller*, November 1941.

314 Clifton Fadiman's: *The New Yorker*, September 27, 1941.

314 11,000 copies: JMC to AAK, October 2, 1941.

314 ". . . standing broad jump": JMC to Mr. Houghland, October 13, 1941.

314 One bookseller . . .: *Retail Bookseller*, November 1941.

314 Cain received hundreds: JMC to Jean Morris, March 31, 1942.

314 "Talk of the Times": *New York Times*, September 26, 1941.

314 "I can only say . . .": JMC to Jean Morris, March 3, 1942.

314 while he still puts me: JMC to AAK, October 2, 1941.

314 One friend . . .: SR to JMC, November 6, 1941.

315 better shape now: JMC to AAK, October 2, 1941.

315 slightly over 14,000: AAK to JMC, November 5, 1941.

315 a lurid title: JMC to Marjorie Sirich, October 13, 1941.

315 Cain was also beginning . . .: JMC to Virginia Dean, November 23, 1941.

315 he wrote his sister: JMC to Virginia Cain, December 1, 1941.

14 IN WAR, THEY HAVE TO SPELL "MOTHER"

page

316 "I was home . . .": RH interview with JMC, December 9, 1975.

316 "The war is rotten . . .": JMC to RGG, January 23, 1942.

316 "wholly convinced that . . .": JMC Memoirs III.

317 "Topics of the Times": *New York Times*, September 26, 1941.

317 Cain denied . . .: JMC to Vincent Schefmeister, January 9, 1966.

317 Cain said the impact . . .: RH interview with JMC, December 9, 1975.

318 "There was no great . . .": JMC Memoirs II.

318 "I was writing . . .": JMC Memoirs II.

318 Cain, who replied: JMC to Clifton Fadiman, Rex Stout et al., March 28, 1942.

319   "snappy fiction": JMC to editor of the *Los Angeles Times*, August 19, 1942.

319   "I have seldom encountered . . .": Manchester Boddy to JMC, December 10, 1942.

319   soon persuading him: JMC to Julian Street, August 15, 1942.

319   Cain also had . . .: JMC to Julian Street, August 17, 1942.

319   "Walter, I think": JMC to MM, August 3, 1942. JMC's differences with Lippmann on policy were compounded by what he considered a personal affront. As he explained to MM, he had "detected leanings toward sassiety in our Harvard friend . . . and had a suspicion that when they dropped over two or three years ago, that they, or she at any rate, were slumming. It gave me a fine cordial feeling. Forgetting it, I dropped him a note at the time he was on the subject of neutrality unsupported by arms, reminding him that three of our border states in 1861 declared themselves 'neutral' and referring him, to save him time, to Jefferson Davis's account of it. I got a note from his secretary saying that he was too busy to write but thanks. Of course, that made me feel swell, too. I don't know what one does after that."

320   he wrote Arthur Krock: JMC to AK, March 2, 1942.

320   contribution to the war effort: LT to RH, September 6, 1979.

320   "as it was possible . . .": JMC to SR, October 29, 1947.

320   ". . . I could always drive . . .": JMC to MM, 1948.

321   changed the locale: JMC to Alvin Levin, June 26, 1946.

321   Knopf saved the day: AAK to JMC, July 28, 1942.

321   typical haggles: JMC to AAK, July 23, 1942.

321   ". . . I can offer it . . .": JMC to AAK, August 1, 1942.

321   with Cain to write a preface: JMC to AAK, July 23, 1942.

321   he wrote a serial: JMC to AAK, October 4, 1967.

321   "swept into discard . . .": JMC to AAK, May 23, 1942.

322   "My modern books": RH interview with JMC, undated.

322   His first effort . . .: JMC to AK, March 2, 1942.

322   his own approach: JMC to Mrs. Smith, March 2, 1942.

322   optimistically promising: JMC to AAK, May 23, 1942.

322   was working on another: JMC to AAK, August 17, 1942.

322   abandoned that one: JMC to AAK, August 15, 1942.

322   Knopf had little interest: AAK to JMC, August 21, 1942.

323   five and a half weeks: JMC to unidentified lieutenant, May 5, 1942.

323   Leo thinks . . .: RH interview with LT, undated.

323   "in a foaming Irish fit . . .": RH interview with HNS, undated.

323   "That it upsets me . . .": JMC to William Morris Agency, August 28, 1942.

323   remembers Cain: RH interview with HNS, undated.

323   he was $4,000 in debt: JMC to GC, August 22, 1943.

323   "I can't imagine . . .": JMC to MM, August 3, 1942.

324   Leo thinks the main . . .: RH interview with LT, undated.

324   Elina's procession: JMC to RMc, November 9, 1964.

324   In Cain's eyes . . .: JMC to H. K. Travers, June 6, 1942.

324   The daughter of one . . .: RH interview with Lynne Bloom, undated.

324   Gary had an accident: JMC to John Wade, June 6, 1942.

324   a separate apartment: JMC to MG, October 12, 1942.

324   "It all but drove . . .": Newspaper clipping in *Los Angeles Times* morgue, June 3, 1943.

324   he was "distressed": MM to JMC, December 11, 1942.

325   "I regret it plenty . . .": JMC to Dr. E. H. Sirich, May 24, 1944.

325   part owner: RH interview with LT, undated.

325   "it is redeemed . . .": *New York Times*, October 11, 1942.

325   "and it may indeed . . .": *Saturday Review*, October 24, 1942.

325   "most literate pulp . . .": *Time*, October 12, 1942.

325   "the ding-dong daddy . . .": *The New Yorker*, October 10, 1942.

325   Mencken wrote: HLM to JMC, November 27, 1942.

325   Knopf thought: AAK to JMC, November 30, 1942.

325   Now Taylor said . . .: Dwight Taylor's deposition in *Cain* v. *Universal*, USDC (Los Angeles) 1755Y.

325   Cain had heard: Memo re conversation with Dwight Taylor in JMC files.

326   "Well, you would hardly . . .": JMC Memoirs II.

326   dismissed the argument: Judge's opinion, *Cain* v. *Universal*, USDC (Los Angeles) 1755Y.

326   "How the hell . . .": RH interview with MG, undated.

327   "It is inconceivable . . .": Judge's opinion, *Cain* v. *Universal*, USDC (Los Angeles) 1755Y.

327   "Why did you tell me . . .": Peter Brunette and Gerald Perry, "Tough Guy," *Film Comment*, May 6, 1967.

327   only $6,000: JMC income tax statement, 1942.

327   "fall into line": JMC to Robert Bassler, November 6, 1942.

327   he proposed: JMC to Manchester Boddy, January 11, 1943.

327   one subject: Imperialism: JMC to Manchester Boddy, January 19, 1943.

328   Boddy replied: Manchester Boddy to JMC, February 9, 1943.

328   The Signal Corps picture . . .: Lieutenant Colonel Alfred Larabee to General C. M. Milliken, November 4, 1942.

328   "absorbing": Colonel Lawton, critique of JMC script in JMC files.

328   "You've written forty pages . . .": Mary Morris, "He Ain't Tepid," unpublished interview for *PM*.

328    $34,000 richer: JMC income tax statement, 1942.

328   reach a settlement: JMC to Martin Gang, June 26, 1943.

328   Cain was earning: *Los Angeles Times*, March 26, 1943.

328   Finally, in June 1943 . . .: *Cain* v. *Cain*, Los Angeles District Court D-234-689.

329   Cain feeling: JMC to GC, August 22, 1943.

329   Cain was offered: JMC Memoirs II.

329   "simply weird": Peter Brunette and Gerald Perry, "Tough Guy."

329   "They're trying . . .": JMC to Edmund Wilson, May 11, 1943.

329   not progressing: JMC Memoirs II.

329   "cultivated kind . . .": Mary Morris, "He Ain't Tepid."

329   "You're going . . .": JMC Memoirs II.

329   the day after: RH interview with JMC, undated.

330   Cain regarded . . .: JMC Memoirs II.

330   "this one is done . . .": *New York Times*, October 5, 1944.

330   Soon after the movie . . .: Joseph Hoffman to RH, August 28, 1978.

330   "Why should you . . .": JMC, "The Opening Gun."

331   *The Moon, Their Mistress*: *Los Angeles Daily News*, September 11, 1943.

331   *Bridge of San Luis Rey*: *Film Comment*.

331   remarkable literary success: Cain also wrote a preface for *Three of a Kind*, an effort, Cain said, to explain to his readers why he felt he was "the most misread, misreviewed and misunderstood novelist now writing." The explanation added up to a review of his literary career, dating back to his first efforts to write a novel in 1922, and in his *Times* review, John Hutchens called it "uncommonly interesting"—and many critics agreed. He also said that he would probably not write any more of the "intense tales" of the kind usually associated with him and that in the future, he would "tell tales of a little wider implication than those which deal with one man's relation to one woman."

331   Cain's style—grit: *Book Week*, May 9, 1943.

331   "Without much question . . .": *New York Times*, April 18, 1943.

331   "Later, if some . . .": JMC to AAK, May 26, 1943.

331   In 1949 . . .: *Saturday Review*, August 6, 1949.

331   In 1935, when . . .: Murray Schumach, *The Face on the Cutting Room Floor* (New York: William Morrow, 1964), p.64.

332   The report had killed . . .: JMC memo on "Double Indemnity," February 25, 1946, in JMC files.

332   "the most censorable . . .": JMC, "Double Exposure," a publicity release for Paramount.

332   Swanson had galleys: JMC to HNS, February 9, 1943.

332   As Cain told the story . . .": RH interview with JMC, undated.

332   But Charles Brackett . . .": Maurice Zolotow, *Billy Wilder in Hollywood* (New York: G. P. Putnam, 1977).

332   He called Cain and Swanson . . .: RH interview with JMC, undated.

333   told one interviewer: Philip K. Scheur in *Los Angeles Times*, May 6, 1944.

333   Wilder at first wanted: Maurice Zolotow, *Billy in Hollywood*, pp.111–12; Frank McShane, *The Life of Raymond Chandler* (New York: E. P. Dutton, 1976), pp.106–07. The struggle between Chandler and Wilder is a story in itself, well told in biographies of Chandler and Wilder by McShane and Zolotow. For Chandler it was exhausting and aggravating, and he said it probably shortened his life. Wilder paid tribute to Chandler's creative talent, but acknowledged that he had problems working with Chandler and, in fact, was so displeased with the first script that he is said to have thrown it in Chandler's face with a few well-chosen expletives.

334   He wanted to explain . . .: MB interview with JMC, August 28, 1975.

334   He told Cain how . . .: JMC to Frank McShane, May 30, 1975.

334   "All characters in B pictures . . .": Peter Brunette and Gerald Perry, "Tough Guy."

334 "Nothing could be more . . .": Raymond Chandler to JMC, March 20, 1944.

335 So he wrote Chandler . . .: JMC to Raymond Chandler, March 25, 1944.

335 told the basic original story: Frank McShane, *The Life of Raymond Chandler*.

335 Wilder first went . . .: John Henley, "Program Notes," *Cinema Texas*, Spring 1978.

335 Then he asked Fred MacMurray . . .: Fred MacMurray, "The Role I Liked Best," *Saturday Evening Post*, July 19, 1947.

335 But Paramount . . .: John Henley, "Program Notes."

336 "When Billy Wilder sent me . . .": Ellen Smith, *Starring Miss Barbara Stanwyck* (New York: Crown, 1973), p.169.

336 Without Elina to help . . .: RH interview with LT, undated.

337 He also became friends . . .: RH interview with LT, undated.

337 a book of recipes: JMC, "Spaghetti," Merle Armitage, ed., *Fit for a King* (New York: Longman, 1939), p.33.

337 "Shad Roe James M. Cain": JMC to Leila McLaughlin, April 24, 1949.

337 Guatemala black bean soup: JMC to Myra Waldo, November 24, 1968.

337 "more of an experimenter . . .": JMC to BAB, 1961.

337 "He was a great big . . .": RH interview with Henry Hopkins, undated.

337 unsettled living quarters: JMC to Virginia Cain, August 23, 1943.

337 "some of the sweetest-blowing . . .": JMC to GC, August 23, 1943.

338 "I can't be persuaded . . .": JMC to AK, September 15, 1943.

338 In October . . .: JMC to AAK, October 6, 1943.

338 Three days later . . .: JMC to AAK, October 9, 1943.

338 writing Mencken: JMC to HLM, undated.

338 In August . . .: William Targ to JMC, August 19, 1943.

338 Cain responded . . .: JMC to William Targ, September 8, 1943.

339 Targ sent him galleys . . .: William Targ to JMC, August 23, 1943.

339 He also suggested . . .: JMC to Anne Lund, October 23, 1944.

339 "Why don't you leave . . .": JMC to William Targ, January 10, 1944.

339 "I don't count money . . .": JMC to William Targ, January 10, 1944.

339 a treasure of little nuggets: JMC, Preface to *For Men Only*.

339 instead of toning it down: JMC to Jerry Wald, September 15, 1943.

339 murder—an idea: Peter Brunette and Gerald Perry, "Tough Guy."

340 "I wrote *Mildred Pierce* . . .": JMC to Jerry Wald, September 22, 1943.

340 now using a treatment: Thames Williamson, "Treatment for Mildred Pierce," Warner Brothers papers, University of Wisconsin Library.

340 *Frankie from Frisco*: RH interview with JMC, undated.

340 even had his ticket: JMC to RMc, December 12, 1943.

340 his outline would be: JMC to Rose Cain, December 12, 1943.

340 "Kate was part of me . . .": JMC to CC, May 28, 1970.

340 He thought Kate . . .: JMC to CC, January 9, 1972.

340 "I became God's masterpiece . . .": JMC to Benn Levy, September 5, 1970.

340 "Old Grandma": RH interview with LT, undated.

340 Cain attempted a reconciliation: JMC to CC, March 12, 1973.

341   which did for her: Corporal Robert Wenzel to his parents, September 19, 1944.

341   she was described: Gloria Swanson, *Swanson on Swanson* (New York: Random House, 1980), p. 182.

341   "talked beautifully": JMC to Corporal Robert Wenzel, November 1, 1944.

341   "I was not much . . .": Hedda Hopper's interview with AP, March 3, 1949.

342   she could keep: Carl Bode, *Mencken* (Carbondale, Illinois: Southern Illinois University Press, 1969), p.157.

342   "She was absolutely . . .": RH interview with SR, July 24, 1978.

342   "This very good-looking . . .": RH interview with JMC, undated.

342   "We were all friends . . .": AP interview with Hedda Hopper, March 3, 1949.

343   soon they were having dinner: JMC to AK, August 22, 1944.

343   ". . . a very charming man": RH interview with AP, June 8, 1981.

343   a tragedy hit: JMC to Howard Lewis, January 26, 1969.

343   Holmes crashed the plane: Unidentified clipping in JMC files.

343   Cain saw it in the paper: RH interview with LT, undated.

343   completely fell in love: JMC to Eero, November 14, 1945.

343   He wrote a one-minute . . .: Julian Street to JMC, February 5, 1944.

343   He also wrote . . .: JMC to *Los Angeles Times*, June 14, 1944.

344   "Exterminationist": JMC to Clifton Fadiman, January 5, 1944.

344   "I not only believe . . .": JMC to Clifton Fadiman, January 17, 1944.

344   "louse of a war . . .": JMC to HLM, May 23, 1944.

344   "wholly anti-imperialist . . .": JMC to WL, July 7, 1944.

344   clarifying the relationship: JMC to Raymond Moley, October 24, 1944.

344   After the landing . . .: Unidentified clipping in JMC files.

344   "fuzz-buzz pinkoes": JMC to Hon. Norris Poulson, October 7, 1944.

344   "history's monstrous . . .": JMC to Manchester Boddy, August 3, 1945.

344   long letter: JMC to Frank Kent, May 24, 1944.

345   he was not pleased: JMC to Voldemar Vetlugia, January 19, 1944.

345   even Cain thought: JMC to David Hanna, February 5, 1944.

345   "I was, as the saying goes . . .": JMC memo on Billy Wilder in JMC files.

345   And they saw everything . . .: JMC income tax statement, 1944.

345   Cain told one friend: RH interview with Robin Deck, undated.

345   Aileen, according to Cain: JMC to MG, February 15, 1946.

345   "If I make you unhappy . . .": JMC to MG, April 3?, 1946.

346   "I sure is": Hedda Hopper column in *Los Angeles Times* morgue.

346   Cain was particularly annoyed: JMC to RGG, March 5, 1945.

346   "When I heard . . .": RH interview with John Lee Mahin, undated.

346   "Of all the women . . .": HLM to JMC, July 25, 1944.

346   he had shifted: JMC to Mrs. John Bowie, January 4, 1944.

346   "The prettiest girl . . .": JMC to Rob Wagner, August 31, 1944.

346   one of the most vital: Ellen Smith, *Starring Miss Barbara Stanwyck* (New York: Crown, 1973), p.177.

347   John Lardner: *The New Yorker*, September 16, 1944.

347   Bosley Crowther: *New York Times*, September 7, 1944.

347   James Agee: *The Nation*, October 14, 1944.

347   Billy Wilder maintained . . .: David Madden, *James M. Cain* (Boston: Twayne Publishers, 1960), p.119.

347   *film noir*: John Henley, "Program Notes," *Cinema Texas*, Spring 1978.

347   ranked it with: Philip Scheur, "Film History Made by Double Indemnity," *Los Angeles Times*, May 6, 1944.

347   Wilder himself . . .: RH interview with Billy Wilder, undated.

347   "The way you found . . .": JMC to Fred MacMurray, February 4, 1944.

347   "It is a very creepy . . .": JMC to Barbara Stanwyck, February 4, 1944.

347   Edward G. Robinson's biographer . . .: James Robert Parish, *The Tough Guys* (New Rochelle, New York: Arlington House, 1976), pp.475–76.

347   MacMurray always considered . . .: Fred MacMurray, "The Role I Liked Best," *Saturday Evening Post*, July 19, 1947.

347   although he maintained: JMC, "The Postman Rings Thrice."

348   they have begun: JMC to Rob Wagner, August 22, 1944.

348   "it has been put . . .": JMC to Paramount Publicity Department, July 24, 1944.

348   "It may be . . .": Paramount Publicity Release in JMC files.

348   even began negotiations: JMC to AAK, February 8, 1945.

348   "I'm quite startled": JMC to Jerry Wald, September 5, 1944.

349   another long letter to Wald: JMC to Jerry Wald, November 10, 1944.

349   "I don't see why . . .": JMC to Jerry Wald, November 10, 1944.

350   to lure Bette Davis: Leroy Carr, *Four Fabulous Faces* (New Rochelle, New York: Arlington House, 1970), p.292.

350   Wald, however, had . . .: Jerry Wald, "I Took One Look at Her," *Photoplay*.

350   a series of war movies: Undated clipping in American Film Institute file in Los Angeles.

350   Hoping to make a comeback . . .: Philip Scheur, "James M. Cain Novel Selected as Her Vehicle," *Los Angeles Times*, October 29, 1944.

351   "To me, even in . . .": Jerry Wald, "I Took One Look at Her."

351   she called Wald: Bob Thomas, *Joan Crawford* (New York: Simon and Schuster, 1978), p.203.

351   on the first day . . .: Jerry Wald, "I Took One Look at Her."

352   Carey Wilson was best known . . .: Philip Scheur, "Postman Finally Rings Screen Bell," *Los Angeles Times*, July 15, 1976.

352   one of the greatest: RH interview with JMC, undated.

352   "You're going to say . . .": JMC, "The Postman Rings Thrice."

353   "red meat" approach: Fred Stanley, "Hollywood Crime and Romance," *Los Angeles Times*, November 19, 1944.

353   "was surprised to learn . . .": Philip Scheur, "Writes Film Whodunnit," undated clip in *Los Angeles Times* morgue. During the entire Scheur inteview, Cain paced the floor and "in two hours plodded through a whole range of sub-

jects, from 18th century Spanish history to labor unions, in the saltiest language imaginable. It was funny," Scheur said, "to hear him interspersing an erudite discourse on Thornton Wilder's The Bridge of San Luis Rey with cuss words, aint's and dropped gs."

353   "the war for the social . . .": JMC memo to Marian Clark in JMC files.

353   And one day, walking back . . .: JMC, "Fame and Hot Hollywood."

354   "a filthy job . . .": JMC to RMc, October 23, 1944.

354   "we approach the end . . .": JMC to RMc, December 11, 1944.

354   "He didn't like any . . .": JMC to Francis Martin, undated.

354   he asked Hornblow: JMC to Arthur Hornblow, May 13, 1946.

354   but he did feel strongly: Peter Brunette and Gerald Perry, "Tough Guy," *Film Comment*, May 6, 1967.

354   The *Sun* interviewer . . .: Donald Kirkley, "The Tin-Lined James M. Cain Can Stomach Hollywood," *Baltimore Sun*, January 7, 1945.

365   saw his old friend: Hamilton Owens to JMC, May 29, 1945.

365   not been fired: JMC to Carey Wilson, March 31, 1945.

365   *The Common Sin*: JMC to Carey Wilson, February 14, 1945.

365   a typical Cain story: JMC to Carey Wilson, April 23, 1945.

365   consult with Wilson: JMC to Carey Wilson, May 11, 1945.

365   He had hoped to work . . .: JMC to HNS, December 4, 1944.

365   "the most incredible time": JMC to H. B. Patten, March 19, 1946.

365   Cain decided to take: Memo in MGM files in Hollywood.

365   "It is a solemn decision": JMC to RMc, May 20, 1945

365   over $80,000: JMC income tax statements, 1944 and 1945.

365   Cain told Swanson . . .: JMC to HNS, May 4, 1944.

365   Cain wrote a treatment: JMC to Frederic Stephani, October 6, 1944.

366   Warner Brothers bought it: HNS to JMC, October 23, 1944.

366   Cain made more suggestions . . .: JMC to Jerry Wald, November 7, 1944; April 11, 1945; and April 24, 1945.

366   Sigmund Romberg: BK to JMC, May 17, 1940.

366   give up his office-apartment: JMC to Lieutenant Colonel D. N. Nott, April 9, 1945.

366   "underfoot": JMC to MG, July 4, 1946.

366   Cain suggested they sell: JMC to MG, February 5, 1946.

366   "As usual, a great war . . .": JMC to Corporal Robert Wenzel, December 8, 1944.

367   the professional problem-solvers: JMC to Corporal Robert Wenzel, February 13, 1945.

367   "This is an S.O.S. . . .": Paul Gallico to JMC, February 3, 1945.

367   ". . . our Allies out . . .": JMC, "Give Clothes," written for Treasury Department.

367   "I have had, from time to time . . .": JMC to Joel Sayre, February 28, 1945.

367   "was two hours of forgetfulness . . .": JMC to Thomas Shaw, November 14, 1945.

368   several possible columns: Sample columns JMC wrote for *Baltimore Sun* in 1945 are in JMC files. About this time, JMC also wrote Bob Bassler at 20th

Century-Fox suggesting a remake of his serial "Two Can Sing," which Fox had already made into *Wife, Husband and Friend*, starring Loretta Young. Cain wanted to do it again the way the original story was written and starring a young woman who had impressed Cain considerably. "The actress," he wrote Bassler, "is Mary Anderson [who had appeared in *Gone With The Wind*], and she has never had a chance in pictures to do what she regards as her forte and which she did so successfully in *Guest in the House* on the stage, which is a melting, sweet little bitch . . . The picture, as made before, left something to be desired, because naturally for Loretta Young, they didn't do a bitch at all and the thing is somewhat pointless from any other point of departure. I don't like to work on my own stories, but it makes a difference. I am not working at a studio at the moment and later, if a polish job on the script would help get in touches which might improve it, I would be free to undertake it, though prefer not to." Fox eventually did remake "Two Can Sing" but starring Linda Darnell, not Mary Anderson, and Cain was not hired to polish the script. JMC to Robert Bassler, June 9, 1945.

He also wrote a piece called "Coal Baron" about his friend William Wiley, who headed a West Virginia coal mine company—a beautiful, moving piece intended for *Reader's Digest*. It never sold and is still in the JMC files. JMC to Paul Palmer, June 15, 1945.

368 It was one of his favorites: JMC, *Past All Dishonor*.

368 he was sick to death: JMC to Genevieve Kneiss, February 23, 1945.

368 "The end of this story": JMC Memoirs II.

369 "All my writing . . .": JMC to AAK, June 4, 1945.

369 if it cost him: JMC, Preface to *The Butterfly*.

369 a much deeper book: JMC, Knopf's publicity copy for *Past All Dishonor*.

369 Carey Bliss, the curator . . .: Carey Bliss to RH, June 27, 1978.

369 Among other things . . .: Carey Bliss to RH, July 6, 1978.

369 "I set out . . .": JMC to SR, June 19, 1946.

370 his most effective statement: JMC Memoirs II.

370 "at that certain age": JMC to BK, August 3, 1945.

370 While waiting for his . . .: JMC Memoirs II.

370 Wilder was right: RH interview with LT, undated.

370 Cain had trouble: RH interview with JMC, undated.

371 "Now I understand . . .: JMC, Preface to *The Butterfly*.

371 "This is it": JMC Memoirs II.

371 Cain even checked . . .: JMC to Professor A. E. Hutcheson, November 22, 1945.

371 so he wrote Mencken: JMC to HLM, May 4, 1945.

371 Mencken replied . . .: HLM to JMC, May 8, 1945.

372 really terrific: Bernard Smith to BK, September 7, 1945.

372 wondering what Hemingway: JMC to BK, September 19, 1945.

372 might make a picture: JMC to SR, November 12, 1945.

372 clever leaks to the press: Bob Thomas, *Joan Crawford*.

372 "Please don't tell . . .": "Program Notes," Dartmouth Film Society, Fall 1971.

372 *Times*: *New York Times*, September 29, 1945.

372 *Herald Tribune*: *New York Herald Tribune*, September 29, 1945.

372 *The Nation*: *The Nation*, October 13, 1945.

372 "it rescued me . . .": Joan Crawford, "The Role I Liked Best," *Saturday Evening Post*, December 2, 1946.

373 Joan responded . . .: Joan Crawford to JMC, March 15, 1946.

373 "Allowing for all . . .": JMC to Rob Wagner, November 14, 1945.

373 "Tonight Joan Crawford . . .": JMC to Barbara Stanwyck, April 7, 1946.

373 "American motion pictures . . .": *PM*, October 4, 1945.

373 "Are they the American people . . .": *PM*, October 11, 1945.

374 After he had mailed . . .: JMC, "The Opening Gun."

374 Knopf still remembers . . .: RH telephone interview with AAK, undated.

374 an awkward few minutes: JMC, "Harold Ober," a memoir in JMC files. Ober represented Cain until the agent's death in 1959, after which Cain remained with Harold Ober Associates, represented by Ivan von Auw and Dorothy Olding (who still handle Cain's literary works) as Swanson still handles his movie sales in Hollywood.

375 "a mysterious summons . . .: JMC Memoirs II.

375 Cain said he . . .: JMC to GC, May 10, 1945.

375 showed her pique: RMc to JMC, March 18, 1946. Although Baben's novel was eventually submitted to a publisher, it was never published.

375 Cain finally wrote Baben . . .: JMC to GC, March 22, 1946.

376 *If Bori Had Blundered*: JMC to MM, April 3, 1945.

376 "I drove and read . . .": JMC to SR, November 12, 1945.

376 he decided to eliminate: JMC to Mrs. William Blizzard, April 19, 1946.

376 he did keep it in: JMC to Lafayette Chapin, August 19, 1947.

376 He wrote to Dr. George . . .: JMC to Dr. George Wilson, November 22, 1945. In his letter, Cain outlined the first concept of the novel that would eventually prove one of the great disasters of his career:

This novel was to move against the background of General Banks's expedition up the Red River in 1864, and as paprika to the tale, I was going to use the skulduggery that Admiral Porter dragged out into the open in his naval history of the war, the suspicion, which is hard to resist after reading some of the federal and confederate orders as reprinted in the Official Record of the war, that cotton speculation, with some army officers getting a rake-off, had more to do with the expedition than strategy had. I designed my story from that angle, with the Navy virtuously heading off Army graft, as the Admiral intimates it did, when I make a startling discovery. The very boats he took up the river, a short time later, whacked up $400,000 or more between them, as their share of prize cotton they had captured, which puts a totally different light on the whole matter. And now, rereading his account of the expedition, I find the gunboats took nearly 1,000 bales of cotton from Army detachments by main force, claiming it as prize to the Navy. It wasn't sold, apparently, as it had to be used as stuffing for a bridge of barges; but the whole episode compels me to find out a lot more about prize law at this time, and its application to this expedition, than I had at all supposed was involved. For if some twist of the law actually made this campaign a contest between Army and Navy for hundreds of thousands of dollars' worth of cotton, to be divided up between officers and crews—this is indeed an amusing tale, too comic to be lost through perfunctory research.

376   "Once you start rolling . . .": JMC, "That Which I Should Have Done I Did Not Do."

376   "claptrap": JMC to H. Alan Wycherley, July 8, 1963.

376   "dull": JMC to H. Alan Wycherley, July 4, 1963.

376   *Icebound*: *20th Century Authors* (New York: H. W. Wilson).

377   A little too tricky: "Gatsby Treatment," mailed to Mr. Doran, November 13, 1945.

377   "But leave us face it": JMC to Eve Ettinger, November 17, 1945.

377   a piece on Lana Turner: JMC, "Lana."

378   Lana Turner said: Lana Turner, "The Role I Liked Best," *Saturday Evening Post*, October 4, 1947.

378   a friend of Cain's: JMC to Niven Busch, April 7, 1944.

378   "The thing the Hays Office . . .": Thornton Delehanty, "James M. Cain Amazes Hollywood by Becoming Top Screenwriter," *New York Herald Tribune*, August 26, 1945.

378   "I have been having . . .": JMC to Carey Wilson, March 13, 1946.

379   "I'm awful proud . . .": Carey Wilson to JMC, March 15, 1946.

379   "it was treated with . . .": SR to JMC, October 11, 1945.

379   "Well, why don't you . . .": Peter Brunette and Gerald Perry, "Tough Guy."

379   As he explained it: JMC, "The Postman Rings Thrice."

380   The movie gives us hope . . .: Bosley Crowther, "For Better and For Worse," *New York Times*, May 5, 1946.

380   "terrible misfortune": James Beaver, Jr., *John Garfield* (South Brunswick, New Jersey: A. S. Barnes, 1978), p. 37.

381   as high as $225,000: JMC to Lester Cowan, May 1, 1946.

381   but Knopf decided: AAK to JMC, November 27, 1945.

381   he and Blanche: BK to JMC, November 21, 1945.

381   thought it was disappointing: B. Smith to BK, November 26, 1945.

381   "Cain at his best": *Louisville Courier-Journal*, July 28, 1946, and *Boston Herald*, May 13, 1946.

381   "one of the most preposterous . . .": *New York Times*, May 25, 1946.

381   "well told tale": *Time*, May 27, 1946.

381   "superb story teller": *Saturday Review*, June 1, 1946.

381   "timeless as a classic": *Newsweek*, May 27, 1946.

381   "Soft music and soft tears . . .": *The New Republic*, June 24, 1946.

381   "The characters talk straight . . .": *The New Yorker*, May 25, 1946.

382   California and Nevada of the sixties: JMC to LS, June 18, 1946.

382   most writers on the subject: JMC to Gale Research Co., August 14, 1974.

382   never forgiven Edmund Wilson: RH interview with JMC, undated.

382   Mary McCarthy denies this: Mary McCarthy to RH, August 11, 1978.

382   no record of it: Helen G. Purcell (curator, Wellfleet Historical Society) to RH, September 28, 1979.

382   "endless reviews . . .": JMC to GC, July 7, 1945.

382   At the meeting . . .: Memo in MGM files in Hollywood.

383   Joan Crawford wanted to: Danton Walker, "Broadway," *Washington Times Herald*, April 27, 1946.

383   Cain preferred: JMC to Barbara Stanwyck, March 7, 1946.

383   "I thought he ought . . .": RH interview with JMC, undated.

383   "help me 'kill' again . . .": Barbara Stanwyck to JMC, March 13, 1946.

383   The number of directors . . .: HNS to JMC, February 6, 1947.

383   "All I need . . .": JMC to Phyliss Demares, June 14, 1947.

383   The book did produce . . .: Department of State to JMC, December 3, 1946.

383   don't blame me: JMC to Department of State, February 1, 1947.

383   withdrew his permission: JMC to Department of State, February 15, 1945.

383   "I hope you will go . . .": Oscar Lewis to JMC, November 3, 1947.

383   "You had to take Rhett . . .": RH interview with JMC, undated.

383   "I meant to explain . . .": JMC Memoirs II.

384    $2,500 a week: JMC income tax statement, 1946.

384   *The Glass Heart*: JMC to Rose Cain, January 14, 1946.

384   ". . . little lighthouse cults . . .": JMC to GC, January 14, 1946.

384   "Our devout and psalm-singing . . .": MM to JMC, March 4, 1947.

384   it may well have been: Peter Brunette and Gerald Perry, "Tough Guy."

384   next assignment: Mary Morris, "He Ain't Tepid," unpublished interview for *PM*, mid-1940s.

384   he was interviewed: JMC to Mary Morris, May 14, 1946.

384   "one of the few": JMC to Herbert Bayard Swope, June 18, 1946.

385   Cain liked the interview . . .: JMC to Mary Morris, May 14, 1946.

385   "That was a good interview . . .": Herbert Bayard Swope to JMC, April 29, 1946.

386   "I had become a drunk . . .": JMC to Aileen Pringle, May 2, 1967.

386   "She refused to consult . . .": JMC to MG, May 27, 1946.

386   "I have cut out drinking . . .": JMC to RMc, December 15, 1945.

386   forty-seven weeks were spent apart: MG to Jerry Giesler, June 14, 1946.

386   "Except for one month . . .": Aileen Pringle to HLM, undated.

386   "He was moody, melancholy . . .": *Los Angeles Times*, September 5, 1946.

386   "He was a monster . . .": RH interview with Aileen Pringle, undated.

387   intended to go to New Orleans: JMC to Virginia Cain, June 20, 1946.

387   "Giesler saw the canceled checks . . .": JMC to MG, July 12, 1946.

387   Ms. Pringle vehemently: RH interview with Aileen Pringle, undated.

387   attorneys agreed to: *Pringle* v. *Cain*, USDC, Los Angeles District Court Case D-313-068.

387   "first and only traumatic experience": Aileen Pringle to JMC, undated.

387   Cain was finally found: JMC to Aileen Pringle, September 12, 1967.

387   suddenly by some magic: JMC memo to DM.

388   "I don't know what it is . . .": RH interview with JMC, undated.

388   "Of course I am perfect": JMC to Rose Cain, April 19, 1946.

16 AAA—"THE BRAND OF CAIN"

389   He had opposed . . .: JMC to Paul Palmer.

390   "I have begun to wonder . . .": JMC to Frank Kent, December 15, 1946.

390   Communism is Communism: JMC to Hedda Hopper, September 3, 1947.

390   he supported John Lee Mahin: RH interview with John Lee Mahin, undated.

391   "The trouble is . . .": JMC to AAK, April 12, 1944.

391   Cain was still annoyed: JMC, "An American Authors' Authority."

391   Cain sympathized: JMC, "The Opening Gun."

393   "It seemed to me . . .": JMC to HLM, July 18, 1947.

393   began having luncheon: *Screen Writer*, July 1946.

393   "The attitude of producers . . .": JMC to Oliver Garrett, February 18, 1946.

393   His first instinct . . .: Oliver Garrett to JMC, February 19, 1946.

393   Then Dalton Trumbo . . .: Oliver Garrett to JMC, February 14, 1946.

394   Cain always maintained: JMC to Hedda Hopper, September 6, 1947.

394   Cain's brochure . . .: *Screen Writer*, July 1946.

396   "You would have thought . . .": JMC to Cyril Clemens, August 18, 1947.

396   "The writers may say . . .": *Screen Writer*, September 1946.

396   "Unhappily I doubt . . .": JMC to HLM, July 8, 1946.

396   "What Mr. Cain proposes . . .": George Sokolsky, "These Days" (syndicated column), August 28, 1946.

397   "A Vote for Joe Stalin": *Hollywood Reporter*, July 29, 1946.

398   a letter to Elmer Rice: *New York Times*, September 13, 1946.

398   Fifty writers . . .: *New York Times*, September 18, 1946.

398   "was a lot of moonshine": *New York Times*, September 14, 1946.

398   "simply amazed": *New York Herald Tribune*, September 14, 1946.

399   "It is no plot": Unidentified clipping in JMC files.

399   Cain virtually admitted: JMC to E.J. Mannix, August 10, 1946.

399   And Emmet Lavery . . .: *New York Herald Tribune*, September 15, 1946.

399   from another flank: *New York Times*, September 16, 1946. Before he died, Farrell said: "I told the author I never doubted Jim Cain's sincerity in that plan, but the others involved—they were something else again—at least in my mind." James Farrell to RH, February 26, 1979.

400   He then denied a request . . .: *New York Times*, September 18, 1946.

400   met in September: *New York Times*, September 19, 1946.

400   Cain now knew . . .: JMC to HLM, July 18, 1947.

400   entered the ring: *Saturday Review*, September 28, 1946.

401   "at a certain date . . .": JMC, "Just What Is the A.A.A.?"

402   "You are alibiing": *New York Times*, October 19, 1946.

402   held their own meeting: *New York Herald Tribune*, October 21, 1946.

403   The next night Cain . . .: *New York Times*, October 22, 1946.

404   a long, thoughtful analysis: *New York Times*, November 17, 1946.

404   "Every time I'd get . . .": JMC to Harvey Breit, July 13, 1957.

404   The next blow . . .: *New York Times*, October 24, 1946.

404   The next round . . .: *Saturday Review*, November 16, 1946.

405   to turn over its list: *New York Times*, November 27, 1946.

405   Elmer Rice announced: *New York Times*, December 25, 1946.

406   Emmet Lavery, representing . . .: Emmet Lavery to Oscar Hammerstein II, May 13, 1947.

406   but Hammerstein's new committee: Oscar Hammerstein II to Emmet Lavery, May 19, 1947.

406   Cain was backing away: JMC to Hedda Hopper, September 6, 1947.

406   the committee finally released: Confidential Report of the Authors League Licensing Committee to Authors League Council Rejecting the A.A.A., in JMC files.

407   Lavery was furious: Emmet Lavery to Oscar Hammerstein II, May 13, 1947.

407   Hammerstein replied . . .: Oscar Hammerstein II to Emmet Lavery, May 19, 1947.

407   when Hammerstein resisted: Memo from Emmet Lavery to Executive Board of the A.A.A. Committee, May 21, 1947, in JMC files.

408   "treating the Screen Writers . . .": Emmet Lavery to Oscar Hammerstein II, June 9, 1947.

408   "tail is wagging the dog": Oscar Hammerstein II to Emmet Lavery, June 17, 1947.

408   The British playwright . . .: *Screen Writer*, April 1947.

408   "extraordinarily disappointing": JMC to HLM, July 18, 1947.

409   1920s he wrote a book: *20th Century Authors* (New York: H.W. Wilson).

409   "just how this outfit . . .": JMC to John Tunis, August 27, 1947.

409   The hysterical . . .: *New York Times*, April 9, 1947.

409   "The Goal of Soviet Policy": James Burnham, "The Goal of Soviet Policy," *American Mercury*, January 1947.

409   "Red device for getting . . .": Hearst syndicated editorial, May 12, 1947.

409   "real Reds [in Hollywood] . . .": *New York News*, May 16, 1947.

409   "remove all of Mr. Cain's . . .": *Christian Science Monitor*, May 3, 1947.

409   "Biblical Cain . . .": *Indiana Herald*, June 18, 1947.

410   Philip Wylie also attacked . . .: Philip Wylie, "The Right to Starve," *Miami News*, June 22, 1947.

410   ". . . the brand of Cain": Rupert Hughes, "The Brand of Cain," *The New Leader*, February 15, 1947.

410   "all I say is . . .": *New York World-Telegram*, June 18, 1947.

410   Early in 1947 . . .: Bruce Cook, *Dalton Trumbo* (New York: Charles Scribner's Sons, 1977), p. 174.

410   Soon nineteen "unfriendlies" . . .: John Cogley, *Report on Blacklisting* (New York: Arno Press, 1956), p. 86.

411   he had been inside: JMC to Hedda Hopper, September 3, 1947.

411   red as Stalin's nose: JMC to HLM, July 18, 1947.

411   Cain did not agree: JMC to Hedda Hopper, September 3, 1974.

411   simply at a loss: JMC to Cyril Clemens, August 18, 1947.

411   "the guilds of the Authors League . . .": JMC to HLM, July 18, 1947.

412   "I have come to the conclusion": JMC to Hedda Hopper, September 3, 1947.

412   most commentators: *New York Herald Tribune*, December 7, 1947.
412   The following year . . .: *New York Times*, April 6, 1947.
412   "There's no use . . .": RH interview with JMC, June 28, 1975.
412   "the largest number": JMC memo to DM.

17   PLEASANT HARBOR

page
413   He had also met . . .: Anthony Havelock-Allen to JMC, January 15, 1946.
413   an exchange of letters: JMC to Anthony Havelock-Allen, January 25, 1946.
413   "nose-dive": JMC to Arthur Hornblow, August 14, 1966.
413   He had been invited . . .: JMC memo to DM.
413   "it was quite an evening": *Mankato Free Press*.
414   she was recovering: JMC to MG, September 13, 1948.
414   Her mother was Alice Monfort . . .: Florence Macbeth, "I Remember Mankato," unidentified clipping in JMC files, July 3, 1952.
415   Florence also had musical abilities: La Donna Olson, "Who, What, When?" *Mankato Free Press*, June 8, 1966.
415   a flurry of rave reviews: JMC to Mrs. Robert Rathbone, June 4, 1966.
415   the *London Daily Telegraph* critic: Excerpts from "World Press" in a Florence Macbeth concert program in JMC files.
416   "Minnesota Nightingale": "Florence Macbeth Rushed to City," *St. Paul Dispatch*, November 24, 1923.
416   During the First World War . . .: JMC, "Florence Macbeth: Statistics," in JMC files. I am also indebted to Paul Hume for facts about Florence Macbeth's career.
416   While she traveled . . .: "An Opera Singer Who Longed to Be an Opera Star," *St. Paul Pioneer Press*, June 20, 1926.
416   lost in the stock market crash: JMC to Ruth Schontall, April 22, 1968.
417   She sang for a while . . .: "An Opera Singer Who Longed."
417   Captain Whitwell died in 1942: La Donna Olson, "Who, What, When?"
417   "joggle her memories": JMC to Arthur Hornblow, August 14, 1966.
417   "Physically, she delighted me . . .": JMC interview with RH, undated.
417   small, red-headed: JMC to Rose Cain, July 13, 1946.
417   including a short novel: JMC to HNS, May 12, 1949.
417   partly as a joke: JMC to Edgar Carter, November 17, 1959.
418   Cain wrote a tribute: JMC, "Vincent Sargent Lawrence."
418   Cain revealed his thoughts . . .: JMC, "A Free Lance for Hollywood."
419   "I think, now and then . . .": JMC to AAK, August 3, 1946.
419   It begins . . .: JMC, Preface to *The Butterfly*.
420   had some doubts: AAK to JMC, August 30, 1946.
420   Cain was adamant: JMC to AAK and BK, September 5, 1946.
421   Knopf finally gave in . . .: AAK to JMC, September 9, 1946.
421   "I am myself pretty immune . . .": AAK to JMC, January 13, 1947.

421 Cain replied . . .: JMC to BK, January 17, 1947.

421 one hell of a brilliant idea: AAK to JMC, April 11, 1947.

421 "nowhere in the whole field . . .": *The New Yorker*, February 17, 1947.

422 were likely to start: *Time*, January 27, 1947.

422 "the whole book is a phoney scare": *Chicago Sun* clipping in the JMC files, no date.

422 But the *New York Herald* . . .: *New York Herald Tribune*, January 26, 1947.

422 *San Francisco Chronicle*: *San Francisco Chronicle*, January 27, 1947.

422 *Saturday Review*: *Saturday Review*, February 1, 1947.

422 *Philadelphia Record*: *Philadelphia Record*, January 19, 1947.

422 *Philadelphia Inquirer*: *Philadelphia Inquirer*, January 26, 1947.

422 *Chicago Tribune*: *Chicago Tribune*, January 26, 1947.

422 *St. Louis Post-Dispatch*: *St. Louis Post-Dispatch*, January 29, 1947.

422 *Chicago Sun*: *Chicago Sun*, clipping in JMC files.

422 45,000 copies: JMC to Robert Bassler, February 5, 1967.

422 *New York Times*: *New York Times*, February 9, 1947.

422 "To date no Cain character . . .": *New York Herald Tribune*, February 23, 1947.

423 "You weren't designed . . .": MM to JMC, January 31, 1947.

423 "Either I'm going to wind up . . .": MB interview with JMC, August 28, 1975.

423 encouraged him: JMC to Raymond Tompkins, November 7, 1948.

423 The movie industry still . . .: Ezra Goodman, *The 50 Year Decline and Fall of Hollywood* (New York: Charles Scribner's Sons, 1961), p. 125.

423 By 1947, 14,000 homes . . .: Arthur Shulman and Roger Youman, *How Swell It Was: The Television Years* (New York: Shorecrest, 1966), p. 66.

424 "high and exciting plans": JMC to Mrs. Charles Fox, May 23, 1947.

424 a profile of the director: HO to JMC, July 20, 1949.

424 insisted on giving Harold Ober $300: JMC to HO, July 29, 1949.

424 the riddle is how: JMC to Wheeler Sammons, April 7, 1947.

424 who eventually asked Cain: Wheeler Sammons to JMC, March 27, 1947.

424 finished it in June: JMC, Preface to 50th Anniversary Edition, *Who's Who in America*, 1948.

424 "Since James M. Cain . . .": *Congressional Record*, February 16, 1948.

425 "You go home now . . .": JMC memo to DM.

425 "Walter Winchell practically . . .": JMC to SR, October 29, 1947.

425 "Hello, Olympia": JMC to EM, July 30, 1966.

425 given the right woman: JMC to Arthur Hornblow, August 14, 1947.

426 entered calm and beautiful waters: JMC to SR, October 29, 1947.

426 "I thought he was terribly tame . . .": RH interview with RGG, July 27, 1978.

426 $22,500: JMC income tax statement, 1947.

426 733,000 copies: AAK to JMC, January 14, 1948.

426 He finally mentioned it . . .: AAK to JMC, August 12, 1947.

426 Cain had first started . . .: JMC, "Vagabonds," unpublished article for *Potomac* in JMC files, undated.

427   visiting a hobo jungle: JMC, "The Vagabonds."

427   "an elderly man . . .": JMC to Mrs. Gordon Layne, November 12, 1947.

428   "eight solid months . . .": JMC to MM, December 18, 1947.

428   "The trouble with my books": JMC to BK, May 27, 1947.

428   "No story requires . . .": JMC to SR, October 29, 1947.

428   "a filthy book": JMC to BK, February 17, 1948.

428   Jack disappointed them: JMC to BK, February 19, 1948.

428   "It was never for one moment": JMC to RMc, February 27, 1948.

428   hopes of a book club sale: JMC to BK, February 22, 1948.

428   "a Republican who believed . . .": JMC to Marjorie Sirich, February 24, 1947.

429   "ever since that historic day . . .": JMC to Raymond Moley, July 29, 1947.

429   "is as leftist as Stalin": JMC to Marjorie Sirich, February 24, 1947.

429   Cain asked Albert Maltz: "A Public Question," statement by JMC to Screen Writers Guild, in JMC files, undated.

430   literature he wrote: "Vote the All Guild Ticket," a statement by JMC.

430   "The politicians investigating . . . : JMC to Hedda Hopper, September 3, 1947.

430   he defended the controversial: Paul Ziporkis to JMC, October 1, 1948.

430   "and since political conviction . . .": JMC to Executive Board of Screen Writers Guild, in JMC files, February 16, 1948.

430   "I think I am through . . .": JMC to Mrs. Morris Markey, February 27, 1948.

430   late in 1947: Lou Brock to JMC, August 9, 1948.

430   *Forbidden Game*: Stuart Birnbaum's private inventory in Los Angeles.

430   Cain finally finished . . .: JMC to Lou Brock, September 29, 1948.

430   dinner at Sardi's: JMC to Leonard Bernstein, October 1, 1947.

431   "obvious theatrical claptrap": JMC to HO, November 19, 1948.

431   but that was put aside: *New York Times*, June 1, 1955.

431   headed south again: *Marietta* [Ohio] *Times*, undated clipping.

431   It was Mencken . . .: JMC to HLM, June 30, 1947.

431   "for while the historian": JMC to J.W. Ferguson, November 13, 1949.

432   "I don't know how you do . . .": JMC to Joseph Pennell, November 21, 1948.

432   bowl of "court bouillon": JMC to Alexander Perino, July 24, 1949.

432   "a dynamic individual . . .": *Parkersburg* [West Virginia] *News*, June 30, 1948.

432   "a refined, middle-aged . . .": *Houston Press*, August 14, 1948.

432   "I simply wouldn't write . . .": *Houston Post*, August 22, 1948.

433   "No living writer": Stephen Longstreet, quoted in Knopf ad for *The Moth*.

433   "There is a streak . . .": Sterling North syndicated column, undated clipping.

433   "occasionally . . . Cain writes . . .": *Saturday Review*, July 10, 1948.

433   "dull to the point . . .": *Houston Post*, August 11, 1948.

433   the story lacked gusto: *PM*, August 11, 1948.

433   praised its reporting: *The New Yorker*, August 11, 1948.

433   "wonderful raucous column . . .": *New York Times*, July 11, 1948.

433   write in English: *Time*, July 26, 1948.

434   "I sniffed it . . .": *New York Herald Tribune*, July 14, 1948.

434   poor reviews were hurting: AAK to JMC, August 24, 1948.

434   "if you ask me . . .": JMC to Mrs. G. Ellis Porter, February 11, 1948.

434   asked a friend in California: JMC to La Nora Griffith, September 15, 1948.

435   "don't be bashful . . .": JMC to HNS, September 22, 1948.

435   which Cain once said: JMC to HLM, August 10, 1937.

435   "Even working in a whorehouse": RH interview with JMC, undated.

436   "Imagination is either free . . .": JMC, "Camera Obscura."

436   1940s did he meet: JMC memo to DM.

436   "I care almost nothing . . .": JMC, Preface to *Three of a Kind*.

437   "The truth is that . . .": JMC to unidentified lieutenant, in JMC files, April 29, 1942.

437   one of his books hit: MB interview with JMC.

437   "in the Hollywood . . .": JMC, "Hot Hollywood."

437   "I wasn't really of Hollywood . . .": JMC to Carroll Schoenwolf, March 9, 1970.

437   "you are invited . . .": JMC, "Film Capital," *New York American*, November 19, 1934.

438   a long letter: JMC to Dorothy LaFollette, November 27, 1943.

438   "It does have a winter . . .": JMC to Edward Sirich, September 29, 1948.

438   "the churlish little state . . .": JMC to AAK, undated.

18   TWO TRIALS AND MANY TRIBULATIONS

page

441   Cain wrote the historian: JMC to Allan Nevins, December 15, 1948.

441   "You have all the . . .": Allan Nevins to JMC, December 30, 1948.

441   "It will be quite . . .": JMC to Joseph Lisser, September 3, 1948.

442   nearly $30,000: JMC income tax statement, 1948.

442   a $500 advance: HO to JMC, August 19, 1948.

442   This upset Knopf . . .: AAK to JMC, October 21, 1947.

442   Cain had assumed: JMC to AAK, October 4, 1947.

442   follow the 1948 election: JMC to HLM, November 3, 1948.

442   ". . . like toddling . . .": JMC to Rose Cain, December 7, 1949.

442   brought home to him: RH interview with JMC, undated.

443   into the hospital: JMC to C.E. King, June 5, 1949.

443   a strain on her: JMC to Rose Cain, December 11, 1948.

443   The Massachusetts charge . . .: *Francis E. Kelly* v. *Serenade*, Superior Court of Massachusetts No. 61046.

444   thought his conduct was: Bernard DeVoto, "The Easy Chair," *Harper's*, July 1949.

444   The strategy of the defense . . .: Summary of case by firm of Stern and Reubens for AAK, Case No. 61046 decision May 2, 1949.

444   Knopf agreed to assume half: AAK to JMC, November 14, 1950.

445   She threatened a lawsuit . . .: *Mae Caro* v. *Warner Bros. and JMC*, USDC (New York City) Civ. case No. 49-106A.

445   Cain's long letter . . .: JMC to Mae Caro, September 30, 1948.

445   he quickly wrote Warner: JMC to Warner Bros., January 7, 1949.

445   He then wrote Knopf . . .: JMC to AAK, January 16, 1949.

445   ruin him financially: JMC to Warner Bros., February 19, 1949.

445   Through Warners . . .: George Raftery to JMC, March 22, 1949.

446   "quite familiar pattern . . .": JMC to George Raftery, April 30, 1949.

446   "a poor working girl . . .": JMC to George Raftery, May 25, 1949.

446   "The $5,000 verdict . . .": JMC to George Raftery, May 12, 1949.

446   Cain interpreted: JMC to George Raftery, December 31, 1950.

446   He told Cain's lawyer . . .: JMC to George Raftery, January 18, 1951.

446   Within a few weeks . . .: George Raftery to JMC, January 16, 1951.

446   "ungrateful child": George Raftery to JMC, February 9, 1951.

447   Miss Caro settled for $750: Dismissal Action in U.S. Civil case No. 49-106A.

447   "Where the hell . . .": Barbara Stanwyck to JMC, December 4, 1950.

447   dreadful book: JMC to HNS, June 19, 1949.

447   historic milestone: *New York Times*, October 30, 1949.

447   must have been the highlight: JMC to HLM, November 30, 1949.

448   Apparently they did . . .: HO to JMC, July 26, 1949.

448   rare items now: JMC memo to DM. Again, Knopf protested Cain's permitting these cheap editions of inferior works to appear, arguing that they hurt his prestige as a hard-cover author. But Cain replied that although he agreed, he needed the money and pointed out that Knopf had turned down "Modern Cinderella." All three Avon paperback originals were brought out in 1980 by G.K. Hall in a collection called *Hard Cain*.

448   The most consistent seller . . .: JMC to Mr. and Mrs. James Keefe, May 25, 1949.

448   due to the upbeat ending: AAK to JMC, April 13, 1951.

448   "There is only one book . . .": JMC to AAK, April 17, 1951.

448   paid him $2,000: AAK to JMC, July 8, 1949.

448   "were little stinkers . . .": JMC to HNS, March 5, 1949.

448   *The Moth*; and "Career in C Major": WK to JMC, August 30, 1949.

448   "The Embezzler": WK to JMC, December 16, 1949.

448   ". . . very good-looking number . . .": "People," *Time*, June 26, 1950; Peter Brunette and Gerald Perry, "Tough Guy," *Film Comment*, May 6, 1967.

448   invited Cain to New York: JMC to HNS, January 16, 1950.

449    $17,000: JMC income tax statement, 1949.

449    $12,000: JMC income tax statement, 1950.

449   Cain was losing weight: JMC to La Nor Griffith, January 21, 1950.

449   to visit Florence's home: JMC to Mrs. Charles Fox, November 12, 1950.

449   complained of fatigue: JMC to Bert Parks, January 21, 1950.

449   in declining health: Carl Bode, *Mencken* (Carbondale, Illinois: Southern Illinois University Press, 1969), pp. 369–70.

449   "I don't exactly know . . .": JMC to AAK, September 11, 1949.

449   Eventually he did visit . . .: JMC to BK, October 23, 1949.

449   dead within a year: JMC to BK, January 8, 1950.

449   "I got a case of . . .": JMC to Francis Brown, April 23, 1950.

449   "neon goldfish . . .": JMC, "The Irreverent Mr. Mencken," book review in JMC files.

450   ". . . a man of extraordinary gifts . . .": Memo on JMC, July 5, 1940, in HLM papers in Enoch Pratt Library in Baltimore.

450   "the only author I ever knew . . .": Ward Morehouse, "Report on America," *Baltimore Sun*, June 5, 1946.

450   ". . . always such a delight . . .": JMC to HLM, June 19, 1946.

450   substitute for his brother: JMC to Mrs. LS, July 29, 1963.

450   radio opera broadcasts: JMC to Wolcott Gibbs, April 27, 1938.

450   moved to Halifax: MM to JMC, September 27, 1949.

450   one morning in early July: JMC to LS, July 14, 1963. After writing Stallings about Markey's death, Cain requested that Stallings burn the letter, which Stallings did. But a copy remains in JMC files.

451   spent most of the day: *Richmond* (Virginia) *Times-Dispatch*, July 12, 1950.

451   as Cain recounted it: JMC to LS, July 14, 1963. The fact that the death of Markey is still an item for discussion in Halifax was confirmed by my own trip down there in 1979 in search of information.

451   "an Old Man of the Sea . . .": JMC to Mrs. Charles Fox, November 12, 1950.

452   unhappy with the scripts: Roy Winsor to JMC, April 3, 1957.

452   He planned to send . . .: JMC, outline for "The Investigator," in JMC files.

452   liked Cain's proposal: HO to JMC, April 26, 1951.

452    $11,000: JMC income tax statement, 1951.

452   "Pay-Off Girl": HO to JMC, March 12, 1952.

452   "a sort of neighborhood series . . .": JMC to HO, July 28, 1951.

452   did not discourage: HO to JMC, August 2, 1951.

452   "I prefer not . . .": JMC to HO, October 14, 1951.

453   "I couldn't count . . .": JMC to Clarke Fitzpatrick, August 12, 1951.

453   Cain wrote the headquarters: JMC to Commander Company C, 75th Anti-Aircraft Battalion, Ft. Meade, Maryland, undated.

453   "I have had . . .": JMC to Wilbur Hubbard, January 29, 1951.

453   "every book you read . . .": JMC to Edward Sirich, September 2, 1951.

453   stop sending her: JMC to Rose Cain, July 8, 1951.

453   a brief trip: JMC travel expenses, 1951, in JMC files.

453   "And if the cotton . . .": JMC Memoirs II.

453   "it must have been a saga": JMC to JS, March 10, 1961.

453   bogged down: JMC to Irvin Ward-Steinman, June 15, 1962.

454   "this stinkhole . . .": RH interview with JMC, March 10, 1961. By now Cain had focused his story, as he outlined to one of his research sources, Wilbur Hubbard, January 29, 1951:

A Union officer, as a result of the operations on the Teche in 1863, sees what can be done, not only financially but also politically, by cotton-trading in 1864. He becomes a part of the movement, almost a conspiracy, to elect

General Banks president in 1864. The idea was to use the cotton, and the money to be made from it, as bait to the people of the Attakapas and Texas country, so they would fall back and let Banks march through as a peaceful conqueror. And then on the wave of popular acclaim sweep him into the White House. The movement envisaged a continuation of the military movement to Mexico, and the annexation of that country, an idea even Banks was sold on, as admitted by his biographer, F. H. Harrington. In my story, the girl has such traits of character that she is tempted to advance the career of her husband, a Secessionist, to join the Union officer in his plans. When the husband is killed she and the hero are confronted by something utterly unexpected, and then are completely smashed when the Union navy seizes the cotton as a prize. Just before the battle of Mansfield they see another chance for riches and glory, and lose again. In the building of the dam, which the man helps with, they find what they feel to be regeneration and finally get each other. The story is a tale of an adventure in treason, really.

454   ". . . like a hen . . .": JMC to SR, July 13, 1952.
454   wrote Raphaelson: JMC to SR, March 29, 1953.
454   ". . . a God-awful wrench . . .": JMC to Edward Sirich, June 19, 1949.
454   "In this neck . . .": JMC to HNS, September 11, 1950.
455   "Well, I suppose we're . . .": JMC Memoirs II.
455   "California is a neck . . .": RH interview with JMC, undated.

19 "A KIND OF MOUSE IS BORN"

page
456   "above the level . . .": JMC to Professor Walter Agard, August 25, 1952.
456   only $5,700: JMC income tax return, 1952, in JMC files.
456   His health was deteriorating . . .: JMC to Huntington Cairns, May 14, 1952.
456   "I quickly decided": JMC to Sara Mayfield, July 17, 1969.
457   "[I] have been tempted . . .": JMC to RMc, July 1, 1952.
457   now giving some thought: John Garfield to JMC, April 28, 1952.
457   So Swanson . . .: JMC to AAK, February 3, 1957.
457   Cain would be increasing: JMC to HNS, May 10, 1953.
458   "pop off a couple . . .": JMC to BK, August 14, 1951.
458   after the statue: JMC to Ernest Lang, November 15, 1953.
458   he asked Knopf: JMC to AAK, November 8, 1952.
458   "It may be a fine irony . . .": JMC to BK, November 29, 1952.
459   Knopf agreed to cancel . . .: AAK to JMC, November 26, 1952.
459   Cain was desperate: JMC to AAK, November 28, 1952.
459   to some publishers: Coward McCann to JMC, February 8, 1952 and E. P. Dutton to JMC, January 16, 1952.
459   But Cain declined: JMC to Daniel Gibson, April 1, 1952.
459   ". . . a very severe screening . . .": Daniel Gibson to JMC, September 11, 1952.

459 declined again: Daniel Gibson to JMC, September 14, 1952.

459 "I long ago came . . .": JMC to Daniel Gibson, May 1, 1953.

459 "preclude an element . . .": JMC to Daniel Gibson, September 9, 1952.

459 "To put it . . .": JMC to Daniel Gibson, May 1, 1953.

459 an interview on WBAL-TV: JMC to Arnold Wilkes, July 13, 1952.

459 a banquet in New York: JMC to Earl Evan, May 20, 1953.

460 an idea for a new novel: JMC to EM, April 5, 1953.

460 where he also had a chance: JMC to EM, April 25, 1953.

460 "say more in a few words . . .": Professor William Seward to JMC, July 21, 1950.

460 never did discuss: *Norfolk Virginia-Pilot*, April 24, 1952.

460 Cain considered . . .: Professor William Seward to RH, January 22, 1979.

460 "Mechanically, the machine . . .": JMC to William Carey, April 6, 1953.

460 when he played it back: JMC interview in *Norfolk* (Virginia) *Ledger Dispatch*, April 23, 1953.

460 "The fact is . . .": JMC to HO, April 19, 1953.

460 "let writers really lean . . .": JMC to C. A. Tulman, May 24, 1953.

461 Cain still felt: JMC to HO, May 24, 1953.

461 returned three others: John McCloud to DO, June 6, 1953.

461 "This new Cain novel": Associated Press review in *Indianapolis News*, August 29, 1953.

461 "I read and reread . . .": *Harper's*, November 1953.

461 ". . . is running down": *The Nation*, September 5, 1953.

461 ". . . the dubious distinction . . .": *Saturday Review*, August 28, 1953.

461 "a master craftsman . . .": *New York Times*, August 16, 1953.

461 "James M. Cain at his best": *Washington Post*, August 16, 1953.

461 ". . . the best novel . . .": *Los Angeles Daily News*, September 21, 1953.

461 12,000 copies: AAK royalty statement, (in JMC papers) period ending October 31, 1953.

461 Louella Parsons: *New York Journal-American*, October 10, 1953.

462 $1,000 for an option: JMC income tax statment, 1954, in JMC files.

462 presented problems: JMC to HNS, February 2, 1966.

462 standard Dramatists Guild contract: Edgar Carter to O. Joseph Bernard, February 5, 1953.

462 trips to Connecticut: JMC expense sheet for 1953 production of *Postman*.

462 The cast was picked . . .: Playbill for *Postman*, 1953.

462 pulled out all the stops: JMC to RMc, November 26, 1953.

462 "pedestrian playwright": *Variety*, October 7, 1953.

462 "the crude dramatization . . .": *Chicago Tribune*, October 19, 1953.

462 So Cain began . . .: JMC to AAK, February 3, 1957.

462 so worked up: JMC to AAK, May 5, 1957.

463 Knopf's correspondence . . .: AAK to JMC, May 7, 1957, and May 9, 1957.

463 "I am no bargain . . .": JMC to AAK, May 16, 1957.

463 "It was even more . . .": JMC to Rose Cain, November 1, 1953.

463 described them to a friend: JMC to SR, December 21, 1961.

463 back at his typewriter: JMC to Mr. Gidden, May 10, 1955.

463   "I started all this . . .": JMC to WK, July 13, 1957.

464   "God deliver me . . .": JMC to AAK, undated.

464   the publisher's reaction: AAK to JMC, March 28, 1958.

464   Ober liked it . . .: HO to JMC, May 17, 1957.

464   "Nothing ever really ails . . .": JMC to AAK, April 1, 1958.

464   interested in another project: JMC, *Guest in Room 701*, manuscript in JMC files.

465   so he accepted: SR to JMC, June 19, 1953.

465   "Cain arrived": Samson Raphaelson, "People We Like," *Film Comment*, December 1977.

465   "I guess it must be . . .": Samson Raphaelson, "People We Like."

466   "I had to tell . . .": RH interview with SR, undated.

466   all during 1955: *New York Herald Tribune*, May 29, 1956.

466   At one point . . .: *New York Times*, September 28, 1956.

466   over $1,000: JMC income tax statement, 1956.

466   The best critique . . .: HNS to JMC, June 24, 1958.

466   *The Guest in Room 701*: Stuart Birnbaum to RH. *7-11* was changed to *The 49-ers* when Cain learned that someone had opened a New York bistro called 7-11. *Give Me One More Day* consists of an extensive outline of the play's characters and notes for acts one and two. *Galahad Rides Again* concerns a football player, a coach, the team, and a secondary plot about a black maid. The papers acquired by Stuart Birnbaum include *The Life Line* (with Morris Markey), about boxing, and *$50,000,000 Can't Be Wrong*. RGG to JMC, September 21, 1968.

466   over $21,000; JMC income tax statement, 1955, in JMC files.

466   at the last minute: Barbara Stanwyck to JMC, November 4, 1955.

467   "an exhausting lot of twaddle . . .": *New York Times*, March 17, 1956.

467   "Why don't you switch . . .": JMC interview, "The Third Degree," newsletter of the Mystery Writers of America, November 1977.

467   ". . . over 100 words": Walter MacEvery to JMC, April 14, 1953.

467   much of it in Mexico: *New York Times*, November 15, 1955.

468   "ghastly thing": Peter Brunette and Gerald Perry, "Tough Guy," *Film Comment*, May 6, 1967.

468   over $6,000: JMC income tax statement, 1956, in JMC files.

468   under $3,000: JMC income tax statement, 1957, in JMC files.

468   "He could have remembered . . .": JMC to AK, February 1, 1956.

469   "generally boil down . . .": RH interview with JMC, undated.

469   "my slant these days . . .": JMC to Carey McWilliams, September 6, 1956.

469   She did ask him . . .: Katharine White to JMC, July 25, 1956.

469   "I have no one . . .": JMC to Katharine White, July 29, 1956.

469   write the . . . *Post*: JMC to *Washington Post*, August 16, 1956.

469   perhaps this is no: JMC to Elizabeth Christman, November 9, 1957.

469   "I might like one . . .": JMC to H. Alan Wycherly, February 23, 1969.

470   a true masterpiece: JMC to Polly Davis, May 4, 1962.

470   Hemingway's . . .: JMC to John Aldridge, June 20, 1965.

470   after your reappraisal: JMC to Gore Vidal, November 19, 1973.

470 I wish he'd take: JMC obituary by John Leonard, *New York Times*, October 29, 1977.

470 "a masterful creation": JMC to John McAleer, October 7, 1973.

470 most tormentingly bad books: *New York Times*, November 7, 1951.

470 Greene and Ambler . . .: Undated clippings from *New York Times* in JMC files.

470 *Cruising*: *New York Times*, September 6, 1970.

470 The Disenchanted: *New York Times*, October 29, 1950.

471 " . . . a great book": JMC to Francis Brown, July 2, 1950.

471 *H. L. Mencken*: *New York Times*, June 17, 1956.

471 "reviewing is not my racket": JMC to Arthur Bell, August 14, 1969.

471 "fired" him: JMC to Helen Yglesias, April 24, 1969.

471 Florence suffered: JMC to Robert Pierson, September 23, 1957.

471 approximately $5,000: JMC income tax return, 1958, in JMC files.

471 military pension: Veterans Administration to JMC, December 16, 1949.

471 "a hero in World War I": RH interview with JMC, undated.

471 "a most enchanting spot": JMC to John E. Chamberlin, January 27, 1957.

471 buying their rented house: JMC to Donald Watkins, April 1, 1958.

472 renew his friendship: JMC to WL, February 10, 1958.

472 "We did nothing about it . . .": JMC to Mrs. Maurice Bernstein, December 21, 1968.

472 I needn't conceal: JMC to H. S. Potee, September 21, 1958.

472 "a therapeutic agent": JMC to SR, December 21, 1961.

472 started writing everyone: JMC to Robert Rathbone, December 28, 1960, and JMC to AAK, May 28, 1959.

472 "My God . . .": RH interview with RGG, undated.

472 requesting an interview: Richard Lamparski to JMC, June 3, 1959.

472 Cain had lunch . . .: JMC to Marquis Childs, April 9, 1959.

473 ". . . a constellation of men . . .": Marquis Childs and James Reston, *Walter Lippmann and His Times* (Freeport, New York: Books for Libraries Press, 1968), p. 10.

473 "Since I am a charter member . . .": Jerry Wald to JMC , June 17, 1959.

473 So Cain replied . . .: JMC to Jerry Wald, June 21, 1959.

473 He promised Wald . . .: JMC to Jerry Wald, July 2, 1959.

473 after two years of incomes: JMC income tax statements, 1959 and 1960, in JMC files.

474 "There is no pretending . . .": JMC to IvA, December 3, 1960.

474 the most helpful: JMC to IvA, January 9, 1961.

474 He changed the ending . . .: JMC to IvA, March 7, 1961.

474 eliminated much: JMC to IvA, February 16, 1961.

474 "*Mignon*, apparently . . .": JMC to IvA, April 23, 1961.

474 Richard Baron at Dial: IvA to JMC, May 17, 1961.

474 "What I fear": JMC to IvA, June 27, 1961.

475 "shrewd, sensible . . .": JMC to JS, December 1, 1961.

475 "practically a new book": JMC to IvA, October 30, 1961.

475 planned another preface: JMC to JS, December 1, 1961.

475   "The heroine . . .": JMC to JS, December 6, 1961.
475   "Right at the end . . .": JMC to JS, December 1, 1961.
475   "considerable income": JMC to William Freedman, September 11, 1960.
475   "sugar hill": JMC to Allen Rivkin, October 18, 1959.
475   "It would be difficult . . .": *Chicago Tribune*, May 27, 1962.
476   Martin Lewis: *New York Times*, May 6, 1962.
476   "hard to imagine what . . .": *Baltimore Sun*, undated clipping, in JMC files.
476   As for his research . . .: *Library*, April 15, 1962.
476   ". . . one hundred percent . . .": JMC to Virginia Riffaterre, May 29, 1962.
477   he was writing Stallings: JMC to LS, July 4, 1963.
477   ". . . 'a lotta goddamn research' ": RH interview with JMC, undated.
477   "They are like children": JMC to Mrs. Ena J. L. Cain, April 16, 1963.
477   "All that reading and labor": *New York Times*, May 13, 1963.

20 TWILIGHT TIME

page
478   ". . . these four walls": JMC to Mrs. Maurice Bernstein, January 9, 1966.
478   over $2,000: JMC income tax statement, 1961, in JMC files.
478   "You're not only paying . . .": JMC to RMc, May 29, 1962.
478   Packard for $35: JMC income tax statement, 1962.
478   "a charming woman": Mrs. Frances Lewis interview with RH, undated.
479   "a very pretty lady . . .": JMC to H. F. Miller, July 22, 1962.
479   his neighbors: RH interview with L T, undated.
479   He called him "Mr. Cain": RH interview with William Reading, undated.
479   "It used to be . . .": JMC to Henry Myers, July 1, 1962.
480   the name of the girl: JMC to Valley Forge Co., November 13, 1955.
480   "he was obsessed": JMC to RMc, April 18, 1962.
480   "My father died . . .": *Newsweek*, April 23, 1962.
480   but not Washington College: JMC to Daniel Gibson, December 6, 1963.
480   Cain did not accept: University of Maryland Honors Convocation, November 8, 1963.
480   "was getting more brains": JMC to Katharine White, December 8, 1961.
480   hard at work: JMC to Henry Myers, April 16, 1961.
480   ". . . attempts through her daughter . . .": JMC to Joan Crawford, July 15, 1962.
480   "The other night": Jerry Wald to JMC, July 11, 1962.
481   "an ominous creature": JMC to Joan Crawford, July 22, 1962.
481   Miss Crawford replied . . .: Joan Crawford to JMC, July 22, 1962.
481    $12,000: JMC income tax statement, 1962, in JMC files.
481   "well-bred, well-heeled . . .": JMC to IvA, January 8, 1963.
482   interested in doing: Max Gissen to JMC, May 7, 1963.
482   "indeed a dilly": JMC to Max Gissen, May 12, 1963.
482   set out to learn: JMC to HNS, May 12, 1963; JMC to AAK, May 9, 1963; JMC to Fulton Brylanski, May 10, 1963.

482   setting a June 5 deadline: Max Gissen to JMC, June 3, 1963.

482   ". . . a pain in the neck . . .": JMC to Anthony West, July 22, 1967.

482   "too casual for an introduction . . .": Max Gissen to JMC, June 3, 1963.

482   could have been salvaged: Unpublished Foreword to *Treasure of Sierra Madre*, in JMC files.

483   "Everywhere," he said . . .: JMC to Max Gissen, June 5, 1963.

483   "no question here . . .": Max Gissen to JMC, June 13, 1963.

483   now Cain exploded: JMC to Max Gissen, June 17, 1963.

483   three days later: JMC to Max Gissen, June 20, 1963.

483   "What bothered me most . . .": Max Gissen to JMC, July 17, 1963.

483   "I don't see that . . .": JMC to Max Gissen, July 21, 1963.

484   "Let's have an end . . .": JMC to Max Gissen, July 26, 1963.

484   sold off his 1,000-book: JMC to Dan Kilgore, March 28, 1963.

484   "an in-close, first-hand . . .": JMC to Dan Kilgore, February 24, 1963.

484   "I started it": JMC to Dan Kilgore, February 25, 1964.

484   he still thought: JMC to Dan Kilgore, June 24, 1964.

484   left Dial in mid-1963: JMC to JS, April 20, 1963.

484   one of the few people: JMC to Virginia Baron, July 13, 1963.

484   the only one he enjoyed: JMC to Henry Robbins, August 6, 1963.

485   it was finally finished: JMC to DO, November 17, 1967.

485   "little nugget": JMC to DO, November 22, 1963.

485   a large bucket of cold water: DO to JMC, November 9, 1964.

485   "gnawing his fingernails": JMC to DO, November 14, 1964.

485   "a bad taste in my mouth": JMC to IvA, December 7, 1963.

486   a note from von Auw: IvA to JMC, December 5, 1963.

486   urging him not to do: JMC to IvA, December 7, 1963.

486   "a really good book": JMC to JS, January 6, 1964.

486   "Let us by the dark . . .": JMC to JS, January 19, 1964.

486   "nobody was ever born . . .": JMC to JS, January 28, 1964.

486   it was favorable: IvA to JMC, July 29, 1964.

486   "change the book over . . .": JMC to IvA, August 1, 1964.

486   was in New York: JMC to Richard Baron, August 13, 1964.

486   "notions of courtesy": JMC to IvA, November 27, 1964.

487   over $3,000: JMC income tax statement, 1963, in JMC files.

487   less than $3,000 coming in: JMC income tax statement, 1964, in JMC files.

487   for $30,000: JMC to Aileen Pringle, June 15, 1963.

487   Kraft Theatre: JMC to HNS, June 21, 1963; *Los Angeles Times*, June 19, 1963.

487   stunned and surprised: JMC to E. L. Doctorow, November 28, 1964.

487   "red-faced acceptance . . .": JMC to IvA, April 2, 1966.

487   "Our genteel talk . . .": JMC to E. L. Doctorow, January 3, 1965.

488   concluded his essay: Tom Wolfe, "Son of Crime and Punishment," *Book Week*, March 14, 1965.

488   "A FINE TRIBUTE TO YOU": SR to JMC, March 15, 1965.

488   "no letter of inquiry . . .": JMC to SR, March 15, 1965.

488   "in comfortable waters again": JMC to IvA, April 9, 1965.

488   another ending: JMC to E. L. Doctorow, March 21, 1965.

499   "fell for her": JMC to Joan Crawford, May 10, 1965.

499   "Those people out there": JMC to William Decker, May 19, 1965.

499   "been on the receiving end . . .": JMC to John Chamberlin, January 1, 1967.

500   "As time went by . . .": JMC to GM, undated.

500   "I've called myself . . .": JMC to RMc, undated.

500   "So, with me": JMC to Robert Sinclair, January 3, 1965.

500   "I don't get sick . . .": JMC to Mostyn Thomas, December 29, 1965.

500   was not doing well: JMC to Mrs. Cecil Garvin, December 14, 1970.

500   her blood pressure soared: JMC to Viriginia Baron, March 7, 1965.

500   But Florence had drifted . . .: JMC to Mrs. William Blizzard, December 7, 1965.

500   dared not walk without: JMC to Glendy Culligan, December 29, 1965.

501   subject of much talk: RH conversations with Mrs. Alice Piper and Mrs. Thelma Kisielnicki, undated.

501   Galli-Curci's death . . .: JMC to RMc, August 29, 1963.

501   "ghastly thing": JMC to Aileen Pringle, November 28, 1963.

501   "I was going to write . . .": JMC to RMc, December 8, 1963.

501   "I have to confess": JMC to SR, January 3, 1965.

501   "I find it impossible . . .": JMC to Arthur Hornblow, August 22, 1966.

502   "It seems equally incredible . . .": JMC to RMc, August 26, 1965.

502   "the best of any . . .": JMC to AK, October 2, 1965.

502   "the mother of history": JMC to Edmund Wilson, May 11, 1943.

502   "is probably going to be . . .": JMC to AK, October 1, 1965.

502   "One, the biographee . . .": JMC to Henry Myers, January 26, 1969.

502   "critical biography": JMC to *New York Times Book Review*, June 30, 1957.

503   biographies of singers: JMC to Paul Hume, September 13, 1967.

503   "knowing whom to do . . .": JMC to Mary Ruth Yoe, January 13, 1974.

503   The people who intrigued . . .: JMC to Thomas P. Lewis, September 3, 1962.

503   "Because an autobiography . . .": JMC to RGG, August 10, 1967.

503   "You have a story . . .": JMC to SR, December 6, 1975.

503   at Centre College: DM to RH, February 21, 1980.

504   an essay on Cain: *The University Review*, Winter 1963.

504   Cain had been dismissed: James T. Farrell, "Cain's Movietone Realism," *Literature and Morality* (New York: Vanguard, 1947); Albert Van Nostrand, *The Denatured Novel* (Indianapolis: Bobbs Merrill, 1960); W. M. Frohock, "The Tabloid Tragedy of James M. Cain," *The Novel of Violence in America* (Dallas, Texas: Southern Methodist University, 1950).

504   "Tough-guy Writers . . .": David Madden, ed., Introduction to *Tough Guy Writers of the Thirties* (Carbondale, Illinois: Southern Illinois University Press, 1968).

504   "in fear and trembling": DM to JMC, March 25, 1964.

504   "feel as though . . .": JMC to DM, May 12, 1961.

505   with Cain reading: DM to JMC, May 12, 1961.

505   invitation that appealed: JMC to DM, February 18, 1962.

505   he declined: JMC to DM, March 2, 1962.

505   "one of those critical . . .": JMC to Aileen Pringle, February 15, 1967.

505   ". . . I don't see anyone else . . .": RH interview with JMC, undated.

505   "how could I decline . . .": JMC to DM, March 8, 1964.

505   but Cain said no: JMC to DM, March 22, 1964.

505   By summer . . .: JMC to DM, July 19, 1964.

505   Madden had a grant . . .: DM to JMC, January 8, 1965.

505   "obvious motivation . . .": JMC to Donna Schrader, February 18, 1966.

505   genuine enthusiasm: DM to RH, February 21, 1980.

506   Since Cain agreed . . .: JMC to DM, February 26, 1960.

506   final "best lick" rewrite: JMC to William Decker, October 7, 1965.

506   "In the last few years": JMC to DM, August 5, 1965.

506   He thought *The* . . .: JMC to Donna Schrader, February 28, 1966.

506   Martin Levin: *New York Times*, August 8, 1965.

506   running 2–1: JMC to RMc, August 26, 1965.

506   "For 30 years . . .": David Madden, *James M. Cain* (Boston: Twayne Publishers, 1970).

506   Joan Crawford did not: JMC to Joan Crawford, June 13, 1965.

506   "too much like *Double* . . .": JMC to HNS, October 28, 1965.

506   "It had a 1 and a 2": JMC memo to DM.

506   in other countries: RH interview with JMC, April 16, 1975.

507   "the genie that looks like . . .": JMC to Mrs. William Mann, November 2, 1965.

507   "a little fairy tale . . .": JMC to Hamilton Owens, March 24, 1966.

507   "So I suppose . . .": JMC to SR, December 30, 1965.

507   he had written four: JMC to IvA, November 25, 1965.

507   ". . . a time for totting scores . . .": JMC to Mrs. E. J. Connor, January 9, 1966.

507   getting ready to die: JMC to RMc, February 27, 1966.

507   to keep Florence: JMC to RMc, September 1, 1968.

507   "Now what is it . . .": JMC to George Roberts, June 23, 1966.

507   "All she lived for . . .": JMC to Edward Waters, December 13, 1966.

507   "It so happens . . .": JMC to George Roberts, August 10, 1966.

508   she half prayed: JMC to Mrs. Cecil Garvin, August 28, 1968.

508   "A shock I'll never forget": JMC to DR, June 5, 1966.

508   in her last years: JMC memo to DM.

508   "I was hooked on her . . .": JMC to RMc, July 5, 1966.

21   RESURRECTION

page

509   three or four gloomy days: JMC to Mrs. Cecil Garvin, October 16, 1970.

509   she had refused: JMC to Mrs. Martin V. Farmer, December 9, 1966.

509   "as though the waves . . .": JMC to RMc, July 5, 1966.

509 "I'm knocked apart . . .": JMC to RG, June 17, 1966.

509 who had written him: RGG to JMC, June 13, 1966.

509 "I don't feel lonely . . .": JMC to RGG, September 22, 1966.

510 A year before . . .: JMC to David Watkins, October 9, 1965.

510 with contracts all signed: JMC to David Watkins, May 6, 1966.

510 "the damned drapes": JMC to EM, November 2, 1966.

510 a "shrine": JMC to EM, February 11, 1966.

510 "I dread it . . .": JMC to Robert Sinclair, October 13, 1966.

510 "I'm sure all sorts . . .": JMC to RMc, December 3, 1966.

510 "with everybody and his . . .": JMC to Robert Rathbone, January 12, 1967.

510 "All I can say": JMC to RGG, January 12, 1967.

511 sent it off to von Auw: JMC to IvA, May 21, 1967.

511 ". . . the kind of story . . .": JMC to IvA, July 29, 1967.

511 Von Auw disagreed . . .: IvA to JMC, May 19, 1967.

511 Then Dial turned it down . . .: IvA to JMC, June 12, 1967.

511 so did Jim Silberman: IvA to JMC, October 2, 1967.

511 "I thought a law . . .": JMC to Arthur Hornblow, October 27, 1967.

511 a woman in her thirties: JMC to DO, December 17, 1967.

511 "As Suburbia . . .": JMC to DM, May 5, 1969.

511 "With the best will . . .": WK to JMC, June 8, 1970.

511 "I read Cloud 9 . . .": WK to JMC, April 19, 1971.

511 "Everything I've done . . .": JMC to RMc, May 23, 1971.

512 ". . . the same old typewriter": JMC to IvA, June 6, 1971.

512 "better than ever": JMC to RMc, August 23, 1970.

512 Neither von Auw nor . . .: IvA to JMC, November 19, 1971.

512 Cain was deeply perplexed . . .: JMC to HNS, December 17, 1971.

512 "I think you must come . . .": RGG to JMC, November 24, 1971.

512 "I shall now go on . . .": JMC to IvA, undated.

512 "the damnedest collection . . .": JMC to Aileen Pringle, May 28, 1967.

513 Cain tried to discourage . . .: JMC to RMc, September 7, 1967.

513 One time when Henrietta . . .: JMC to EC, March 26, 1967.

513 managing to get to his feet: JMC to Robert Rathbone, May 12, 1967.

513 It took weeks . . .: JMC to Robert Rathbone, September 19, 1967.

513 it tired him to sit: JMC to Mrs. Cecil Garvin, October 8, 1967.

513 "But allowing for all that": JMC to EC, February 26, 1967.

513 act more naturally: JMC to Aileen Pringle, January 10, 1967.

513 discussed reconciliation: JMC to Aileen Pringle, March 23, 1967.

513 finally diagnosed: JMC to AK, June 5, 1967.

514 ". . . and his brother-in-law . . .": JMC to RMc, September 24, 1967.

514 produced a drowsiness: JMC to RGG, March 10, 1965.

514 "Ambulance, doctor . . .": JMC to RGG, June 19, 1968.

514 "like an old wharf rat": JMC to Arthur Fried, June 30, 1968.

514 "and there were no angels": RH interview with Carol Kisielnicki and Dorothy and James Youniss, undated.

514 This upset the doctor . . .: JMC to Dita Beard, April 16, 1972.

514   touting Achromycin: JMC to AAK, January 10, 1969.

514   he did carry nitroglycerin: JMC to AAK, January 17, 1969.

515   He wrote Madden . . .: JMC to DM, May 19, 1968.

515   ". . . different kind of writing . . .": JMC to DM, May 5, 1968.

515   "loused you up . . .": JMC to DM, March 14, 1966.

516   "It's tougher . . .": JMC to DM, May 11, 1968.

516   Madden says . . .: DM to RH, December 30, 1979.

516   But Madden argued . . .: David Madden, *James M. Cain* (Boston: Twayne Publishers, 1970), pp. 153–61.

516   "whose point is developed . . .": JMC to DM, July 10, 1967.

516   "Her criticism . . .": JMC to DM, March 24, 1968.

516   "though he deals . . .": Joyce Carol Oates, "Man Under Sentence of Death: The Novels of James M. Cain," DM, ed., *Tough Guy Writers of the Thirties* (Carbondale, Illinois: Southern Illinois University Press, 1968), pp. 110–28.

517   even wrote him a note: Joyce Carol Oates to JMC, April 2, 1970.

517   Cain did not understand: DM to RH, June 10, 1968.

517   ". . . don't have to read a writer . . .": RH interview with DM, Feburary 27, 1980.

517   Swanson did not think . . .: HNS to JMC, November 28, 1968.

517   Cain's sense of its failure: JMC to RMc, January 21, 1968, and February 28, 1968.

517   Swanson reported . . .: HNS to JMC, June 18, 1968.

517   Book-of-the-Month: James Ellison to JMC, February 26, 1969.

517   an advance of $5,000: JMC income tax statement, 1969, in JMC files.

518   "Cain was one of those . . .": Tom Wolfe, Introduction to *Cain X 3*.

518   Ross Macdonald: *New York Times*, March 2, 1969.

518   Kenneth Lamott: *The Nation*, June 16, 1969.

518   Robert Kirsch: *Los Angeles Times*, February 7, 1969.

518   William Hogan: *San Francisco Chronicle*, February 3, 1969.

518   Pete Hamill: *Village Voice*, May 29, 1969.

518   Robert Sorenson: *Minneapolis Tribune*, February 16, 1969.

519   "Jim Cain is scrunched down . . .": John Carmody, "James M. Cain at Twilight Time," *Washington Post Potomac*, January 19, 1969.

519   Even the pooch . . .: JMC to BAB, May 1, 1971.

519   came to the conclusion: JMC to DM, November 27, 1969.

520   "You'd think . . .": JMC to RGG, November 18, 1966.

520   "Cain went to the scene . . .": David Madden, *James M. Cain*.

520   The book sold only . . .: DM to RH, December 30, 1979.

520   And during an interview . . .: JMC to DM, February 1, 1971.

520   "So many die": JMC to Mrs. Ruth Ford, February 16, 1969.

520   So he stopped . . .: JMC to BAB, May 18, 1969.

520   "you and a passel . . .": JMC to Sara Mayfield, June 18, 1969.

520   "Every night . . .": JMC to Mrs. Mario Chamlee, March 23, 1969.

521   "If you're so tired . . .": JMC to Mrs. Cecil Garvin, December 4, 1968.

page

522   "not the kind of writer . . .": JMC to Daniel Gibson, January 25, 1970.

522   But he did agree . . .: JMC to Daniel Gibson, February 3, 1970.

522   Miss McGerr helped . . .: RH interview with Patricia McGerr, undated.

523   Cain entertained the audience . . .: "The Third Degree," newsletter of the Mystery Writers of America, November 1970.

523   opportunity to have dinner: JMC to George Roberts, May 19, 1970.

523   "Literature and the Cinema": Catholic University Symposium Program, March 8-13, 1970, in JMC files.

523   Maryland Art Council: A Report on the First Maryland Arts Council Literary Competition, spring 1971, in JMC files.

523   "a bad case of the Doubts . . .": JMC to Victoria Wyatt, September 15, 1973.

523   finally Cain confessed: JMC to Philip Geyelin, October 3, 1971.

524   a stray tom: JMC to LS, April 4, 1971.

524   "I wake up every morning . . .": JMC to DR, June 20, 1970.

524   "I loved him dearly": RH interview with Mr. and Mrs. Theodore Kisielnicki and their daughter Carol, undated.

524   "I knew she did not accept . . .": RH interview with Mr. and Mrs. Keith Dunklee, undated.

525   "I remember the first . . .": RH interview with Mr. and Mrs. James Youniss, undated.

525   Cain would call . . .: James Youniss remarks at JMC Memorial Service, November 11, 1977.

525   One neighborhood boy . . .: RH interview with Mrs. Alice Piper, undated.

526   $400,000 contribution: The Staff of the New York Times, *The End of the Presidency* (New York: Dell Publishing Co., 1974), p. 165.

526   "very good-looking": JMC to Dita Beard, undated.

526   lengthy correspondence: JMC correspondence with Dita Beard and her daughter in JMC files, undated.

526   His affair with Robin . . .: RH interview with Robin Deck, February 11, 1980.

527   Sargent once noted: Winthrop Sargent to JMC, December 8, 1959.

527   "Curious you should . . .": JMC to Winthrop Sargent, December 11, 1949.

527   "Love is the illusion . . .": JMC note in JMC's files.

527   Snobby, wandered away: JMC to Mrs. Vincent Lawrence, March 28, 1971.

528   "James Cain is six feet tall . . .": Thomas Chastain, *Publishers Weekly*, July 24, 1972.

528   Cain was writing again: JMC to Mrs. LT, December 23, 1971.

528   ". . . you and Dorothy . . .": JMC to IvA, November 21, 1971.

528   "This is Cain . . .": HNS to JMC, December 14, 1971.

528   "the story of a modern Don Juan . . .": JMC to DO, November 23, 1971.

528   In his unpublished memoirs . . .: JMC Memoirs II.

529   "Somewhere along the line": JMC to Benn Levy, February 13, 1972.

530   started the novel over: JMC Memoirs II.

530   English professor at the University: JMC, *The Institute*.

530   "I just can't persuade myself . . .": WK to DO, March 6, 1973.

530   "I have to write . . .": JMC to RGG.

530   "the mystical nonexistence . . .": RH interview with JMC, undated.

531   Howes remembers him: RH interview with Melinda Howes, undated.

531   Chastain showed him: RH interview with Thomas Chastain, undated.

531   "whether Jim Cain . . .": RH interview with TL, undated.

532   "To put it in a nutshell . . .": TL to JMC, undated.

532   Cain said he did not . . .: JMC to TL, December 17, 1973.

532   more detailed analysis: TL to JMC, December 17, 1973.

532   Lipscomb made one attempt: TL to JMC, June 27, 1974.

532   "In fifty years of writing . . .": JMC to DO, June 30, 1974.

532   "is so fantastically wrong . . .": JMC to TL, July 8, 1974.

532   "for all I know . . .": RH interview with TL, undated.

532   "I'm pleased to report": JMC to TL, February 9, 1974.

532   "based on . . . Chandler's . . .": MG to JMC, October 16, 1973.

533   "as an old man . . .": RH interview with Orlando Petrocelli, undated.

533   only the year before: RH interview with Melinda Howes, undated.

533   "You usually can tell . . .": *Washington Post*, June 4, 1974.

533   one reporter said: Larry W. Swindell, "The Postman Still Rings for Big Jim Cain," *Philadelphia Inquirer*, June 30, 1974.

533   Cain was convinced: JMC to TL, June 16, 1974.

533   although he never conceded: RH interview with JMC, undated.

533   John Barkham: *San Francisco Chronicle*, March 23, 1975.

533   Charles Witteford: *Miami Herald*, March 23, 1975.

533   "alive and still writing . . .": *Boston Globe*, June 1, 1975.

533   "Cain has the old momentum . . .": *Philadelphia Inquirer*, March 9, 1975.

534   In 1974 . . .: RH interview with Shelby Coffey, undated.

534   20 percent of whatever: James Youniss at JMC memorial service, November 11, 1977.

534   piece on Walter Lippmann: JMC, "Walter Lippmannn Had Style."

534   Carey McWilliams . . .: Carey McWilliams to JMC, February 18, 1975.

534   Cain replied . . .: JMC to Carey McWilliams, March 2, 1975.

534   "It's the only account . . .": Andy Logan to JMC, Feburary 8, 1975.

535   "But then I refused . . .": RH interview with Orlando Petrocelli, undated.

536   "Shakespeare element": JMC to DO, March 27, 1974.

536   Mark Stuart: *Hackensack Record*, July 20, 1976.

536   David Madden: *Louisville Courier-Journal*, August 26, 1976.

536   John D. MacDonald: *New York Times*, August 22, 1976.

537   ". . . a new sin . . .": JMC to DM, January 24, 1972.

537   Madden responded . . .: DM to JMC, April 18, 1977.

537   from $6,000: JMC income tax statement, 1973, in JMC files.

537   over $10,000: JMC income tax statement, 1974, in JMC files.

537   began to decline: JMC income tax statements, 1975, 1976, in JMC files.

537   "She lands in a cocktail bar . . .": JMC Memoirs II.

538   "in her lingo": JMC to RG, February 2, 1975.

538   "I had her tell . . .": Peter Brunette and Gerald Perry, "Tough Guy," *Film Comment*, May 6, 1967.

538   "I always intend not . . .": RH interview with JMC.

539   "If you're dealing . . .": JMC to Orlando Petrocelli, November 22, 1975.

539   "this would only . . .": DO to RH, January 17, 1980.

539   "If White can . . .": RH interview with Mr. and Mrs. James Youniss, undated.

540   Kisielnicki and another lady: RH interview with Thelma Kisielnicki, undated.

541   late in October: RH interview with LT, undated.

541   rare book collector: Steven Bernard to RH, June 6, 1978.

541   That same evening . . .: RH interview with Thelma Kisielnicki, undated.

542   "I used to add my father's . . .": JMC to AK, October 27, 1968.

542   a short article: JMC, "Americana My Foot."

542   the day after he died: Steven Bernard to RH, June 6, 1978.

542   Hundreds of good . . .: JMC memorial service, taped by RH, November 11, 1977.

542   read a letter: SR to Alice Piper and friends, November 6, 1977.

AFTERWORD: THE NEWSPAPERMAN WHO WROTE YARNS ON THE SIDE

page

545   "The critics do their damnedest . . .": Carl Bode at JMC memorial service, November 11, 1977.

545   "the test of the *Grand Vin* . . .": JMC article for "Booknotes," intercompany newsletter published by Random House, Spring 1970.

545   "posterity's bookmakers": JMC to E. M. Forster, August 15, 1947.

545   "I don't read 'em . . .": JMC to Donna Schrader, September 1, 1965.

546   "That easy intimacy . . .": JMC to JS, June 12, 1963.

546   "goes marching on . . .": JMC to George Steiner, August 25, 1973.

546   "one of the worst novels . . .": JMC to John McAleer, August 23, 1976.

546   Coleridge . . .: JMC to George Steiner, August 25, 1973.

546   "Language wants to be read . . .: JMC Memoirs I.

547   Cain denied any effort: JMC, Preface to *The Butterfly*.

547   "muscle flexing": JMC, Preface to *Three of a Kind*.

547   " 'How long do you boil them . . . ' ": *Washington Post* obituary, October 28, 1977.

547   "I take no interest . . .": *Washington Elm* (Washington College alumni magazine), May 2, 1969.

547   ". . . the dominant drive . . .": JMC to Ronald Martinetti, August 11, 1969.

547   "People think I just put . . .": *Time*, April 28, 1946.

547   "produced in his off-time": *The New Yorker*, May 25, 1946.

547   Malcolm Cowley said . . .: *PM*, June 2, 1946.

548 Like John Cheever's . . .: Interview with John Cheever, *Washington Post*, October 8, 1979.

548 "I am not a novelist . . .": JMC Memoirs II.

548 "My hunch is . . .": SR to RH, December 9, 1979.

548 he told one interviewer: MB interview with JMC, August 28, 1975.

549 "low-life person": JMC, Preface to *The Butterfly*.

549 "a newspaperman who writes yarns . . .": JMC to Bushrod Howard, October 10, 1946.

549 "You hire out . . .": James Bready interview with JMC, *Baltimore Sun*, June 18, 1967.

549 "All books are potboilers": Katherine Gresham interview with JMC, *Washington Post*, June 11, 1950.

549 "I'm like old man Verdi . . .": Mary McGrory interview with JMC, *Washington Star*, January 15, 1950.

549 "A novel is something . . .": JMC to Ross Lane, March 15, 1969.

549 "Anybody who can't go back . . .": Mary McGrory interview with JMC.

549 "I always know that when . . .": David Zinsser, interview with JMC, *Paris Review*, Spring-Summer 1978.

550 "I never knew a writer . . .": JMC to Mrs. G. R. Tankersley, September 20, 1970.

550 "Those who can write must write": JMC to CC, November 1, 1970.

550 a disease, not a gift: JMC to Mrs. Robert Rathbone, January 21, 1968.

550 "Who but a nut . . .": JMC to Mr. Melsamo, August 23, 1968.

550 "I seem to have a zest . . .": RH interview with JMC, undated.

550 ". . . a terrible medium": JMC to Julia LaMuniere, undated.

550 "this gabby boy . . .": Glendy Culligan interview with JMC, *Washington Post*, August 17, 1965.

550 "It doesn't have to be . . .": Peter Brunette and Gerald Perry, "Tough Guy," *Film Comment*, May 6, 1967.

550 ". . . technical summaries . . .": JMC to GC, May 18, 1945.

551 "Books ought to be . . .": RH interview with JMC, undated.

551 "remember this book . . .": JMC to Evelyn Byrne, August 14, 1967.

551 The important thing . . .: JMC, *The Moth*.

551 "Before, I thought why . . .": Mary Morris, "He Ain't Tepid," unpublished article for *PM*, 1946.

551 "I have no consciousness . . .": David Zinsser, interview with JMC, *Paris Review*.

551 little capacity to analyze: JMC to John McAleer, November 8, 1976.

551 "I may not have . . .": JMC to Edmund Wilson, June 1940.

552 "When I finished . . .": JMC to DM, January 20, 1964.

552 It has been observed . . .: Jack Salamanca at JMC memorial service, November 11, 1977.

552 "Beethoven, Mendelssohn . . .": JMC to DM, January 20, 1964.

552 "If someone says . . .": JMC to Fulton Catten, January 28, 1962.

552 ". . . something to say . . .": JMC, *The Moth*.

552 "a form of introspection . . .": JMC to GC, June 21, 1945.

553 "In all the years . . .": Saxe Commins, *Publishers Weekly*, April 17, 1978.

553 "The muses . . .": JMC to Paul Marian, May 1979.

554 "As a novelist . . .": JMC to Mrs. L T, November 29, 1970.

554 "Until now . . .": JMC Memoirs I.

554 "What I like . . .": RH interview with JMC, undated.

555 His stepson says . . .: RH interview with L T, undated.

555 "I never write about newspapermen": RH interview with JMC, undated.

555 "not my first choice . . .": JMC to Edmund Wilson, June 1940.

555 "the wish that comes true . . .": JMC, Preface to *The Butterfly*.

555 "money turns out . . .": Larry Swindler, "The Postman Still Rings for Big Jim Cain," *Philadelphia Inquirer*, June 30, 1974.

556 "I don't lack . . .": JMC, Preface to *The Butterfly*.

556 "I think to myself": RH interview with JMC, undated.

BOOKS

Our Government. New York: Alfred A. Knopf, 1930.

Most, but not all of the chapters of *Our Government* appeared first in the American Mercury, under different titles. The table of contents, with the original source of the chapter indicated, is as follows:

Chapter

I   The President
    Appeared in October 1927 *American Mercury* as "Red White and Blue."

II Congress
    Extracted from the *Congressional Record*, Vol. LXVIII, Part 6, pp. 6358–61.

III State Government: The Governor
    Appeared in December 1929 *American Mercury* as "Citizenship."

IV State Government: The Legislature
    Appeared in April 1929 *American Mercury* as "Will of the People."

V   The Administration of Justice: Counsel
    Original dialogue.

VI The Administration of Justice: The Judiciary
    Original dialogue.

VII   The Jury
      Appeared in January 1928 *American Mercury* as "Trial by Jury."
VIII County Government: The Commissioners
      Appeared in April 1925 *American Mercury* as "Servants of the People."
 IX   The School System
      Original dialogue
  X   The Sheriff
      Appeared in April 1927 *American Mercury* as "Hemp."
 XI   Town Government: The Commissioners
      Appeared in September 1925 *American Mercury* as "The Hero."
 XII The Military Force
      Appeared in June 1929 *American Mercury* as "The Taking of Montfaucon."

The Postman Always Rings Twice. New York: Alfred A. Knopf, 1934.

Serenade. New York: Alfred A. Knopf, 1937.

Mildred Pierce. New York: Alfred A. Knopf, 1941.

Love's Lovely Counterfeit. New York: Alfred A. Knopf, 1942.

Three of a Kind. New York: Alfred A. Knopf, 1943. Contains "Career in C Major," "The Embezzler," and "Double Indemnity," with Cain's Preface.

Past All Dishonor. New York: Alfred A. Knopf, 1946.

Sinful Woman. New York: Avon, 1947.

The Butterfly. New York: Alfred A. Knopf, 1947, with Cain's Preface.

The Moth. New York: Alfred A. Knopf, 1948.

Three of Hearts. London, Robert Hale, 1949. Contains *Love's Lovely Counterfeit*, *Past All Dishonor*, and *The Butterfly*, with Cain's Preface.

Jealous Woman. New York: Avon, 1950.

The Root of His Evil. New York: Avon, 1951.

Galatea. New York: Alfred A. Knopf, 1953.

Mignon. New York: The Dial Press, 1962.

The Magician's Wife. New York: The Dial Press, 1965.

Cain X 3. New York: Alfred A. Knopf, 1969. Contains *The Postman Always Rings Twice*, *Mildred Pierce*, "Double Indemnity," with Preface by Tom Wolfe.

Rainbow's End. New York: Mason-Charter, 1975.

The Institute. New York: Mason-Charter, 1976.

Hard Cain. Boston: G. K. Hall & Company, 1980. Contains *Sinful Woman*, *Jealous Woman*, and *The Root of His Evil*, with Preface by Harlan Ellison.

The Baby in the Icebox and Other Short Fiction. Edited and with an Introduction by Roy Hoopes. New York: Holt, Rinehart and Winston, 1981. Contains several dialogues and short stories by Cain, plus the magazine serial "Money and the Woman" (later titled "The Embezzler").

SHORT FICTION

"Pastorale," *American Mercury*, March 1928.

"The Taking of Montfaucon," *American Mercury*, June 1929.

"The Baby in the Icebox," *American Mercury*, January 1933.

"Come-back," *Redbook*, June 1934.
"Double Indemnity," serial, *Liberty*, 1936.
"Dead Man," *American Mercury*, March 1936.
"Hip, Hip, the Hippo," *Redbook*, March 1936.
"The Birthday Party," *Ladies' Home Journal*, May 1936.
"Brush Fire," *Liberty*, December 5, 1936.
"Coal Black," *Liberty*, April 3, 1937.
"Everything but the Truth," *Liberty*, July 17, 1937.
"Two Can Sing," *American*, April 1938.
"The Girl in the Storm," *Liberty*, January 6, 1940.
"Money and the Woman," serial, *Liberty*, 1940.
"Pay-Off Girl," *Esquire*, August 1952.
"Cigarette Girl," *Manhunt*, May 1953.
"Two O'Clock Blonde," *Manhunt*, August 1953.
"Death on the Beach," *Jack London's Adventure Magazine*, October 1958.
"The Visitor," *Esquire*, September 1961.
(Several unpublished stories are also in the files of Mrs. Alice Piper in Hyattsville, Maryland, and Stuart and Roger Birnbaum in Los Angeles.)

POETRY
"Auld Lang Syne," *The New Yorker*, December 20, 1930.
"Gridiron Soliloquies," *The New Yorker*, November 21, 1931.

DIALOGUES AND SKETCHES
From 1928 until 1931, Cain wrote a weekly by-lined column for the "Metropolitan Section" of the *New York World*. Most of the columns consisted of short sketches or dialogues about New York and New Yorkers, and Eastern Shore yokels. At the same time, he was writing a series of dialogues (many of which appeared in *Our Government*) for the *American Mercury*. His last dialogue was written in 1933 and appeared in *Vanity Fair*.

"Servants of the People," *American Mercury*, April 1925.
"The Hero," *American Mercury*, September 1925.
"Hemp," *American Mercury*, April 1927.
"Red White and Blue," *American Mercury*, October 1927.
"Trial by Jury," *American Mercury*, January 1928.
"Theological Interlude," *American Mercury*, July 1928.
"Will of the People," *American Mercury*, April 1929.
"Citizenship," *American Mercury*, December 1929.
Appeared originally in *Our Government*:
    "The Administration of Justice: Counsel."
    "The Administration of Justice: The Judiciary."
    "The School System"
"Don't Monkey with Uncle Sam," *Vanity Fair*, April 1933.

PLAYS

Crashing the Gate, produced by Philip Goodman. Played in Stamford, Connecticut, and Worcester, Massachusetts, in February 1926, but closed before reaching Broadway.

The Postman Always Rings Twice, produced by Jack Curtis, directed by Robert Sinclair. Played 72 performances at the Lyceum Theatre in New York in 1936.

7-11, produced by Richard Aldrich, directed by Alexander Dean. Played one week in summer stock in Cohasset, Massachusetts, 1938.

The Postman Always Rings Twice, produced by Clifford Hayman and Viola Rubber, directed by Joseph Bernard. Performed on road tour in Pittsburgh, Chicago, and St. Louis in 1953.

The Guest in Room 701. Never produced.

PREFACES, INTRODUCTION, MISCELLANY

Prefaces to: *Three of a Kind* (Alfred A. Knopf, 1943), *The Butterfly* (Alfred A. Knopf, 1947), *Three of Hearts* (Robert Hale, 1949), and the 50th Anniversary Edition of *Who's Who* (1948). He also wrote an Introduction to *For Men Only* (Cleveland, Ohio: World, 1944), and contributed a chapter on "Spaghetti" to *Fit for a King* by Merle Armitage (New York: Longman, 1939).

MAGAZINE ARTICLES

"Treason—to Coal Operators," *The Nation*, October 4, 1922.

"The Battle Ground of Coal," *Atlantic Monthly*, October 1922.

"West Virginia: A Mine-field Melodrama," *The Nation*, June 27, 1923.

"The Labor Leader" *American Mercury*, February 1924.

"The Editorial Writer," *American Mercury*, April 1924.

"Pedagogue: Old Style," *American Mercury*, May 1924.

"Politician: Female," *American Mercury*, November 1924.

"High Dignitaries of State," *American Mercury*, December 1924.

"The World Hits the Trail," *The Nation*, March 4, 1925.

"The Pastor," *American Mercury*, May 1925

"The Pathology of Service," *American Mercury*, November 1925.

"The Man Merriwell," *Saturday Evening Post*, June 11, 1927.

"Are Editorials Worth Reading?" *Saturday Evening Post*, December 24, 1927.

"The Solid South," *The Bookman*, November 1928.

"The End of the World," *The New Freeman*, March 11, 1931.

"Sealing Wax," *The New Yorker*, May 2, 1931.

"Paradise," *American Mercury*, March 1933.

"The Widow's Mite, or Queen of the Rancho," *Vanity Fair*, August 1933.

"Camera Obscura," *American Mercury*, October 1933.

"Tribute to a Hero," *American Mercury*, November 1933.

"How to Carve That Bird," *Esquire*, December 1934.

"Them Ducks," *Esquire*, January 1935.

"Oh, les Crepes-Suzettes," *Esquire*, February 1935.

"Close Harmony," *American Mercury*, October 1935.

"Fit for a Queen—Worth a King's Ransom," *McCall's*, March 1937.

"Lana," *Modern Screen*, April 1946.

"The Opening Gun," *Screen Writer*, May 1946.

"An American Authors' Authority," *Screen Writer*, July 1946.

"Just What is A.A.A.?" *Screen Writer*, October 1946.

"Do Writers Need an 'AAA'?" *Saturday Review of Literature*, November 16, 1946.

"A Free Lance for Hollywood," *New Theater*, London, 1947.

"Vincent Sargent Lawrence," *Screen Writer*, January 1947.

"Respectfully Submitted," *Screen Writer*, March 1947.

NEWSPAPER ARTICLES AND COLUMNS

New York Times: The June 8, 1919, issue of the *Times* carried a long piece by Cain (with no by-line) on the "History of the 79th Division."

"The Postman is Below," March 8, 1936.

"The Postman Rings Thrice," April 21, 1946.

Baltimore Sun: From 1920 to 1923, in addition to his regular reporting (sometimes under his by-line, sometimes under the initials JMC), Cain also contributed occasional feature columns under his own by-line.

New York World: In addition to his regular editorials (which are preserved and identified in the Walter Lippmann collection in the Yale University Library), Cain also wrote a regular column for the *World*'s Sunday Metropolitan Section, from September 1928 until February 1931.

Hearst Syndicate: From November 1933 until March 1935, Cain wrote a three-times-a-week column for the Hearst Syndicate.

Washington Post: Late in his life, Cain wrote several articles for the *Washington Post*. Most of them appeared in the *Post* magazine, then known as *Potomac*. A few appeared in the "Style" section of the paper. *Potomac*: "Hot Hollywood," June 16, 1974; "Christmases Past—'Silent Night 1918,' " December 22, 1974; "Walter Lippmann Had Style," February 2, 1975; "Remembrances of Kann's Past," July 6, 1975; "Word-Doubter," October 26, 1975; "The Raccoon," February 15, 1976; "That Which I Should Have Done I Did Not Do," May 2, 1976; "Spirits," May 9, 1976; "Treason," January 3, 1977; "Stalking the Wild Kudu," April 13, 1977: "O, Say," July 3, 1977; "To Keep a Mockingbird," August 14, 1977. "Style" section: "Charles Laughton," August 22, 1976; "The Gentle Side of W. C. Fields," September 26, 1976; "Americana My Foot," October 31, 1977.

FILMOGRAPHY

CAIN'S STORIES THAT WERE MADE INTO FILMS

CAIN STORY	ORIGINAL FORM/DATE	STUDIO	PRICE	MOVIE, CAST, DATE
"The Baby in the Icebox"	Short story; *American Mercury*, 1933	Paramount	$ 1,000	*She Made Her Bed*, Richard Arlen, Robert Armstrong, Sally Eilers (1934)
The Postman Always Rings Twice	Novel; Alfred A. Knopf, 1934.	MGM	$25,000	*The Postman Always Rings Twice*, Lana Turner, John Garfield (1946) *Le Dernier Tournant* (French) *Ossessione* (Italian)
"Two Can Sing"	Novelette; *American Magazine*, April 1938. Also included under title "Career in C Major" in *Three of a Kind*, Alfred A. Knopf, 1943.	20th Century-Fox	$ 8,000	*Wife, Husband and Friend*, Loretta Young, Warner Baxter, Binnie Barnes, Cesar Romero (1939). *Everybody Does It*, Paul Douglas, Linda Darnell, Celeste Holm (1949).
"The Modern Cinderella"	Written as a magazine serial but never sold. Eventually appeared in an original	Universal	$17,500	*When Tomorrow Comes*, Irene Dunne, Charles Boyer (1939). *Interlude* (1957).

The "Money and the Woman" row also carries the note above its title: *paperback published by Avon, 1951, under title The Root of His Evil.*

Title	Publication	Company	Price	Film
"Money and the Woman"	Originally appeared as a magazine serial in *Liberty*, 1940. Also included under title "The Embezzlers" in *Three of a Kind*, Alfred A. Knopf, 1941.	Warner Bros.	$ 3,500	*Money and the Woman*, Jeffrey Lynn, Brenda Marshall (1940).
"Double Indemnity"	Originally appeared as magazine serial in *Liberty* beginning on February 15, 1936. Also included in *Three of a Kind*, Alfred A. Knopf, 1943.	Warner Bros. ABC (for TV)	$15,000	*Double Indemnity*, Fred MacMurray, Barbara Stanwyck, Edward G. Robinson (1944). *Double Indemnity*, Lee J. Cobb, Richard Crenna, Samantha Eggar (1973).
Mildred Pierce	Novel; Alfred A. Knopf, 1941.	Warner Bros.	$15,000	*Mildred Pierce*, Joan Crawford, Ann Blyth, Zachary Scott, Jack Carson (1945).
Serenade	Novel; Alfred A. Knopf, 1937.	Warner Bros.	$35,000	*Serenade*, Mario Lanza, Joan Fontaine, Vincent Price, Sarita Montiel (1956).
Love's Lovely Counterfeit	Written as a serial and possible movie, but never sold to a magazine. Published as a novel, Alfred A. Knopf, 1942.	RKO-Benedict Bogeaus Production	$10,000	*Slightly Scarlet*, John Payne, Arlene Dahl, Rhonda Fleming (1956).

THE CAIN REVIVAL

After his death, there was renewed interest in Cain in Hollywood, and recently several movies based on Cain's novels were either made or planned:

- Lorimar made another version of *The Postman* starring Jack Nicholson and Jessica Lange.
- Zee Productions made *The Butterfly*, starring Stacy Keach, Pia Zadora, and Orson Welles.
- Peter Bogdanovich is producing *Past All Dishonor*.
- Avco Embassy Productions purchased an option on *The Magician's Wife*.

SCREEN CREDITS

Algiers, 1938. A Walter Wanger Production; Universal. Director: John Cromwell. Other writer: John Howard Lawson. Stars: Hedy Lamarr, Charles Boyer.

Stand Up and Fight, 1939, MGM. Director: W. S. van Dyke. Other writers: Jane Murfin and Harvey Ferguson. Stars: Wallace Beery and Robert Taylor.

Gypsy Wildcat, 1944, Universal. Director: Roy William Neill. Other writers: James Hogan and Gene Lewis. Stars: Maria Montez and Jon Hall.

WORK IN STUDIOS

Tracing Cain's screenwriting career is extremely difficult. However, a partial account of his work in Hollywood from 1931 to 1948 is outlined below:

YEAR	STUDIO OR PRODUCER	FILM OR SCRIPT	ESTIMATED LENGTH OF TIME
1931-32	Paramount	*Ten Commandments*	6 months
		Hot Saturdays	
1933	Columbia	*The Story of Samuel Insull*	6 weeks
1934	MGM	*Duchess from Delmonico*	8 weeks
1935	Paramount	*Dr. Socrates*	5 weeks
1937	Universal	*Algiers*	3 weeks
1938	MGM	*Stand Up and Fight*	8 weeks
1939	Universal	*The Victoria Docks at 8*	4½ weeks
1940	Warner Bros.	*Money and the Woman*	10 weeks
	Universal	*Lucky Baldwin*	7 weeks
1941	Arnold Productions	*Shanghai Gesture*	5 weeks
	Warner Bros.	not known	1½ weeks
1942-43	20th Century-Fox	Signal Corps film	22 weeks
1943	Universal	*Gypsy Wildcat*	3 weeks
1943	United Artists	*The Moon, Their Mistress*	3 weeks
1943	United Artists	*Bridge of San Luis Rey*	4 weeks
1944	MGM	*Frankie from Frisco*	1 year

1945	MGM	*Common Sin*	6 months
	Paramount	*The Great Gatsby*	?
1946	RKO	*The Glass Heart*	5 months
		Build Your Gallows High	
1947	Lou Brock	*Forbidden Game*	?

INDEX

AAA. *See* American Authors' Authority (AAA) (proposed)

"Accent on Youth" (Raphaelson), 503

Accent on Youth (play), 257

Adam and Evil (film), 341

Adams, Franklin P., 128, 159, 182, 197, 226, 473, 499; column: "Conning Tower," 96, 119, 189; review of *Postman*, 245

Adams, J. Donald, 287, 313, 422

Adams, Jay, 381

Agate, James, 246

Agee, James, 347, 372, 380

Aldrich, Richard, 286

Algiers (film), 289, 435

Algonquin Round Table, 127, 129, 132, 159, 211

Alice in Wonderland (Dodgson), 10, 174, 191, 551

Allen, Elizabeth, 135

Allen, Walter, 90, 93, 94, 95

Amato, Pasquale, 100, 416

Ambler, Eric: *Passage of Arms*, 470

American Authors' Authority (AAA) (proposed), 389–412, 428, 457

American Dream (Mailer), 487–88

American Language, The (Mencken), 77, 89, 247, 286

American Magazine, 249, 285, 290

American Mercury, 106, 108, 109–11, 164, 248, 286, 376, 409; Cain published in, 14, 20, 22, 74, 84, 113–275 *passim*, 389; Cain's criticism of, 191–92; first issue, 109; review of *Postman*, 246

American Writers Association (AWA), 398, 400, 402–03, 408–09

Anderson, Maxwell, 118, 119–20, 124, 140; *Outside Looking In*, 135; *What Price Glory?*, 120

Anderson, Sherwood: "Caught," 110, 553; *Dark Laughter*, 128; *Winesburg, Ohio*, 96

Angoff, Charles, 202, 241, 246, 255, 259, 260; *H. L. Mencken*, 471

Antheil, George, 169–70

Arden, Eve, 351

"Are Editorials Worth Reading?" (Cain), 139

Argosy Films, 424

Arlen, Michael: "Man With the Broken Nose," 339

Arlen, Richard, 226, 409

Arlen, Richard, Jr., 226

Arliss, George, 341

Armitage, Merle, 337

Armstrong, Robert, 226

Arno, Peter, 286

Arnold Pressburger Productions, 310

Arrowsmith (Lewis), 110, 129, 153

ASCAP, 398

Association of American Booksellers, 532–33

Atherton, Gertrude, 245; *Crystal Cup*, 128

Atkinson, Brooks, 275

Atlantic Monthly, 181; Cain published in, 94–95, 102, 117, 120

Auden, W. H., 553

"Auld Lang Syne" (Cain), 28–29, 201

Aussey, Germaine, 286

Authors Guild, 403, 412

Authors League, 403, 405, 411, 412; Action Committee, 405; Cain to address re AAA, 401–02; East Coast Guild, 407–08; Licensing Committee, 406–07; opposed Cain's proposed AAA, 398, 399–400, 401, 406–07; West Coast Guild, 406, 407–08

Avon, 442, 447–48

AWA. *See* American Writers Association

Babbitt (Lewis), 156

"Baby in the Icebox, The" (Cain), 225–26, 229, 231; film version: *She Made Her Bed*, 248

Backas, James, 523, 542

Baker, Carlos, 502

Baker, Ray Stannard, 25

Balmer, Edwin, 261

Baltimore American, 55–56, 57

Baltimore Sun, 25, 65, 73, 185, 354, 368, 476; Cain at, 57–58, 84, 85–93, 96, 97, 102, 103

Bar-B-Que (Cain). See *Postman Always Rings Twice*

Barbouw, Eric, 406

Barkham, John, 533

Barnes, Binnie, 300

Baron, Richard, 474, 484, 486

Baron, Virginia, 484

Barrett, James W., 163, 197, 198

Barrett, Sheila, 293

Barthelmess, Richard, 248, 272, 273–74, 275

Bartlett, Michael ("Mike Swartz"), 265

Bartlett, Russell: *Dictionary of Americanisms*, 372

Bassler, Robert, 327, 328, 418

Basso, Hamilton, 421–22

Baxter, Warner, 300, 376

Beach, Rex, 96

Beadle, Erasmus, 241

Beals, Carleton, 110

Beard, Dita, 526

Beautiful Greed, The (Madden), 505

"Beauty, Booty, and Blood" (Cain), 485

Beecham, Sir Thomas, 190, 337, 415

Beery, Wallace, 291, 292

Benchley, Peter: *Jaws*, 550

Benchley, Robert, 128, 202, 211, 213, 274, 285

Benjamin, Albert, 290

Bennett, Arnold, 545

Bennett, Bruce, 351

Benny, Jack, 539

Benson, Sally, 202, 214, 255–56; Cain's correspondence with, 550–51, 552; *Junior Miss*, 256; *Meet Me in St. Louis*, 256

Bercovici, Konrad, 128

Bergman, B. A., 204, 213, 214, 241, 242, 253, 262, 263

Bernard, Joseph, 462

Bernard, Steven, 541, 542

Bernstein, Leonard, 430–31, 467

Bickford, Charles, 135, 219, 291

Biddle, Troy, 74

Bierce, Ambrose, 241

Big Sleep, The (Chandler), 333

"Birthday Party, The" (Cain), 267

Blees, Robert, 466

Bliss, Carey, 369

Blizzard, William, 90–93

Blyth, Ann, 351

Boddy, Manchester, 319, 327–28

Bode, Carl, 502, 505, 523, 542, 545

Bogeaus, Benedict, 331

Boni and Liveright (publishers), 128

Book of Burlesques, A (Mencken), 89

Book of Prefaces, A (Mencken), 89

Book-of-the-Month Club, 517

Bottoms Up (Nathan), 133

Bowers, Claude, 182

Bowie, Jack, 36

Boyd, Ernest, 109, 113, 153

Boyer, Charles, 279, 289, 290, 300, 302

Boylan, James: *World of the 20s, The*, 170, 171

Boyle, Kay, 202

"Boys in the Back Room, The" (Wilson), 313, 504

Brackett, Charles, 332

Branham, Juliet, 105

Bratt, George, 51

Breen, Joseph, 331, 347–48, 352

Breit, Harvey, 404

Bridge of San Luis Rey (Wilder), 304, 305; film, 331

Brock, Lou, 430

Bromberg, J. Edward, 300

Bromfield, Louis, 398, 406; *Possession*, 129

Brooks, Van Wyck, 129, 262

Broun, Heywood, 119, 128, 159, 166–69, 182, 197, 473

Brown, Francis, 449, 471

Brown, Herb, 250

"Brush Fire" (Cain), 276*n*, 303, 448

Buck, Frank, 262–63

Build My Gallows High (Holmes), 384

Bundsman, Anton, 284

Bunny, John, 22, 64

Burchardi, Konrad, 308

Burke, Bill, 116

Burnett, W. R., 261

Burnham, James: "The Goal of Soviet Policy," 409

Burr (Vidal), 470

Burroughs, Frances, 434

Busch, Niven: *Duel in the Sun*, 378

Butterfly, The (Cain), 39, 101, 186, 299, 300, 302, 303–04, 370–71, 374, 375, 376, 384, 387, 419–22, 442, 458; Cain thought his best book, 506; publication of, postponed, 381; sales, 422; stage version, 481–82; thematic structure of, 552

Cabell, James Branch: *Rivet in Grandfather's Neck, The*, 238

Cagney, James, 135, 333, 462

Cain, Aileen Pringle (wife of J. M. Cain), 341–43, 345–46, 353, 366, 371, 372, 385–88, 413; break-up, settlement with Cain, 387, 425; Cain considered reconciliation with, 513; Cain's correspondence with, 527

Cain, Edward ("Boydie") (brother of J. M. Cain), 8, 15, 19, 38, 39–40, 151; in World War I, 73–74

Cain, Elina Tyszecka (wife of J. M. Cain), 3, 105–06, 117, 126–27, 193, 194, 260, 265, 370, 437; Cain relied on, 278, 302; Cain's settlement with, 327, 328–29; children's attempt to reunite with Cain, 513; divorced and free to marry Cain, 156; keeping Cain at work, 231, 247,

Cain, Elina Tyszecka (wife of J. M. Cain) (cont'd)

251–52, 254, 336; learned English, 158, 205; life with Cain, 157–58, 186–87, 205–06, 228, 230, 234, 239, 256, 278, 304, 305, 324–25; mother of, came to live with, 313; move to California, 217–18, 223, 224; part owner of dress shop, 325; returned to Hollywood, 293–94; traveling with Cain, 280–82, 293, 297, 298–99; worked in factory, World War II, 320

Cain, Florence Macbeth (wife of J. M. Cain), 414–17; Cain mourned, 509–10, 520–21; death of, 508; drinking, 500–01; health problems, 443, 453, 454, 456–57, 465, 471–72, 500, 507–08; life with Cain, 423–26, 434–35, 442–43, 449, 451, 454–55, 458, 478–81, 505; planned autobiography, 424, 434; recluse, 469, 471, 479, 500–01

Cain, Genevieve ("Baben") (sister of J. M. Cain), 8, 38, 375, 472, 552

Cain, James M.: AAA proposal, 389–412, 420, 423, 424, 428; acknowledged his debt to certain writers, 545–46; advice from, sought by would-be writers, 552–54; agents, 249, 320, 323, 337, 374, 474 (see also Geller, James; Haggard, Edith; Morris Agency; Swanson, H. N.); aging, 472–73, 500; alcohol, drinking, 19–20, 104, 110, 116, 264, 323, 340, 386, 442–43; answer to critics, 419–21; answered charge of Hollywood corruption, 381–82, 420, 421; approached to do radio, TV scripts, 452–53; association with American Mercury, 106, 108, 109–11, 113–14, 115–16, 117, 129–33, 138 (see also American Mercury); attempt at singing career, 35–36, 37–38, 555; attempted column for Washington

Post, 523–24; attracted to women, 22, 25–28, 32–33, 54, 58, 115, 526–27, 531; authority on style and language, 546–47; autobiographical elements in works of, 8, 33, 37–38, 101, 369, 427, 537; awarded "Gertrude," 248; awarded Grand Masters Edgar, 522–23; awarded "Silver Kangaroo," 448; battle with Communists in Screen Writers Guild, 428–30; believed pattern of his mind was tragic, 551; biographical studies re, 503–05; birth, early years, 6–22; break with Catholic Church, 20; career as screenwriter, 430, 435–38 (see also Cain, studio jobs); cats, 472, 479, 500, 524, 527; childless, 205–06; cinematic education, 292–93; considered himself a journalist, 199; could not take adverse criticism, 257; criticism of American Mercury, 191–92; death of, 541–42; debate with Farrell in SR, 404–05; decision to be like Mencken, 95, 103; decision to become a children's book writer, 539; decision to become a writer, 37, 40; decision to concentrate on novels, 423, 430; decision to stay in Maryland, 454–55; declined honors from Washington College, 459, 480, 522; denied Hemingway influence, 419–21; denied hard-boiled label, 244, 256, 419, 422, 444, 504, 516, 520, 547; depressed, discouraged, 276, 279, 323–24, 469, 511–13; description of Cain home in Chestertown, 14; description of his parents, 6; dislike of movies, 196, 222, 329, 345, 420, 435–37; dispute with Gissen, 482–84; drinking and eating too much, 312, 320–21, 337, 354, 442–43 (see also Cain, alcohol, drinking); education, 9–13, 19, 22–29, 30–31, 41–52, 88; end of Hollywood career, 435–38; family,

3–4; as father to Leo and Henrietta, 206, 278; feared becoming ex-writer, 484, 528, 539; feelings of failure, 217; financial situation, income, 104, 115, 171, 193, 223–24, 238–39, 247, 249, 263, 279, 280, 307–08, 315, 320, 323, 327, 365, 366, 384, 426, 435, 442, 447, 459, in Hyattsville: 449, 452, 456, 466, 469, 471, 473–74, 475, 478, 481, 486–87, 507, 528, 537; first attempt to write a play, 131, 134–37; first meeting with Knopf, 185; first meeting with Mencken, 97–98; foe of censorship, 123; friends, neighbors in Maryland, 478–79, 524–26, 540–41; his books as his children, 477, 512; as Hornblow's "kept intellectual," 353–54; hurt by Knopf's rejection of *Mignon*, 474; insecurity, 554; insight into his inability to write screen plays, 261–62; interest in food, 337; interest in labor unions, 90–95, 96, 98–100; interviews with, 353, 432–33, 472, 477, 480, 518–19, 520, 528, 535–36, *PM*, 384–86, 387; invitations for interviews, lectures, etc., 459–60; involved in plagiarism suits, 391–93; Irish heritage of, 3, 298–99; lack of career direction, 24, 30–31; lawsuits against, 443–47; leave of absence from MGM, 365, 367–68, 382; literary status of, 186, 528; literary studies of, 504, 516–17, 519–20, 522; and *Lorraine Cross*, 72–78, 201; love of California, 108, 224–25, 226–29, 252, 437–38, 455; love of music, 34, 152, 164, 264; magazine career, 289–91; memoirs (unpublished), 30, 56, 104, 300, 528–29, 537–38, 539, 542, 554; memorial tribute to, 542–43; move to Beverly Hills, 257–58, 259–60, 264–65; move to California, 217–18; musical evenings, 264–66, 271, 279; at *New Yorker*, 199–204, 205, 206–14; phobia about advances, 277, 308, 321, 372, 426; physical descriptions of, 8, 12, 26–27, 84, 104, 153, 337, 353, 519, 528, 535; political interest, disinterest, 24–25, 161, 316–17, 344, 389, 428–29, 469; position on Communism, 389–90, 411; possibility of working in England, 413, 419; preoccupation with style, 174–75; press conference for *Rainbow's End*, 532–33; proposed committee of Screen Writers Guild to handle plagiarism cases, 330; radio, TV series: "Congressional Investigator" (proposed), 452; reaction to death of Boydie, 74; reaction to death of Florence, 508, 509–10, 520–21; reaction to death of friends, 449–51, 501, 502; reaction to death of Mencken, 449–50, 468–69; reaction to deaths of mother and sisters, 471–72; reaction to Oates's essay on him, 516–17; reaction to professional failures, 136, 275, 276, 475, 476–77, 506–07; reaction to success of *Double Indemnity*, 347–48; reaction to success of *Postman*, 247–49; reading, 10–11, 19, 36, 470; reading Bible, ideas of God, 501–02; realized he was not making a success of serious writing career, 454; received Distinguished Service Award from Univ. of Maryland, 480; recollections re, 9, 22–23, 25, 27, 51, 86, 107–08, 152, 204–05; rejected offer to write for *New Yorker*, 214; relation with editorial writers at *New York World*, 173; relation with father, 6, 8, 38, 39–40, 294–95; relation with mother, 6, 38–39; resisted requests to write autobiography, 503; responded to requests for information on literary friends, 502; resurrection (rediscovery) of, 487–88, 507, 509–21, 522, 532, 533–34, 537; ro-

Cain, James M. (*cont'd*)

mantic affairs, 105, 126–27, 157, 205, 278–79, Kate Cummings, 282, 305–06, 308, 324, 337, 340, 386 (*see also* Cain, marriages); in Sacco-Vanzetti dispute at *New York World*, 166–69; said his work expressed his view of life, 556; at sale of *New York World*, 198–99; screen credits, 289, 292, 329, 420, 435; in Screen Writers Guild, 390, 391–92, 411; self-admitted drunk, 340, 386; self-appraisal, 161; self-doubt, 114; sending money to family, 249, 375, 528; sensitivity, 84, 177; shy, awkward socially, 152; social life, 121, 129, 139, 153–56, 211, 257, 264, in Hollywood, 227–28, 256, 264–65, 353, 437; special feeling for *Postman*, 378–79; speech affectation, 84, 104, 120; squabbles with Knopf, 308, 310, 374, 391, 426, 462–63, 474; sued by Hoffman, 330; sued Universal, 311–12, 320, 325–27, 328, 391; symposium: "Literature and the Cinema," 523, 526; as teacher, 25, 35, 51–52, 54, 55, 56–57, 116, 546, St. John's, 103–04, 107–08, 112–13; theory re Shakespeare's sonnets, 530, 536; theory re voice/homosexuality, 132, 266–67, 283–84; thought movies and fiction should cater to public taste, 419; thought *Past All Dishonor* his best book, 370; thought writing community should support authors in plagiarism cases, 392; tribute to Lawrence, 418; trip East to explain AAA, 398, 401–05; trip to Mexico, 280–82; trip to New York to accept Grand Masters Edgar Award, 522–23; trip with Elina to Europe, 297, 298–99; trips back East, 251–52, 260, 273–76, 279, 286–87, 354, 365, 374–76; unemployed, 223–24, 317; unsettled after split with Elina, 336–38; urge to write plays, 188, 189, 256, 271, 295, 458, 548; view of himself as journalist, 103, 523; views on homosexuality, 287; views on marriage, 110; views on screen credits, 354; visits to family, 84, 103–04, 260, 293, 313, 375; wondered if capable of sustaining relationship with a woman, 413, 417; work career, early, 31–32, 33, 34–35, 36–38, 55–56; worked in coal mines, 96, 98–99; in World War I, 54, 58–59, 60–79, 84; in World War II, 316–40, 343–44, 366–67

—correspondence, 205, 206, 255–56, 432, 447, 507, 514–15, 527, 556; C. Angoff, 259; S. Benson, 255–56, 550–51; brother Boydie, 73–74; Elina, 273, 274, 294, 295–96, 329; C. Fadiman, 343–44; fan letters, 480; W. Gibbs, 289–90; R. Goetz, 509, 510; A. Knopf, 276–77, 297, 302, 338, 419, 420–21, 449, 472; B. Knopf, 306, 307–08, 428; A. Krock, 468; letters to editor, 319, 343, 515; W. Lippmann, 234–35, 236–37, 254–55, 263, 282, 286, 344; Madden, 515–17, 552; M. Markey, 323; H. Mencken, 198, 283–84, 286, 338, 344, 371–72, 408, 411, 450; mother, 388, 463; S. O'Faoláin, 301, 302–03; sister Rosalie, 40, 338, 340, 354, 365, 428, 457, 502, 512, 527; Stallings, 382, 450; Swope, 384, 385, K. White, 480

—friendships, 9, 62, 219–20, 270, 522; P. Goodman, 134–37, 151–56, 157, 158, 187–88, 193–94, 227; B. Knopf, 189–90; Krock, 139–40, 173; C. Laughton, 228–29, 269–70; V. Lawrence, 137–38, 227–28; S. Lewis, 152–56; W. Lippmann, 120–25, 139, 173, 174–75, 472; J. McGuinness, 230; J. Mahin,

260–61; M. Markey, 140, 151, 173, 450–51; H. Mencken, 88–89, 106–07, 108–09, 114, 115, 116, 129–33, 151–56, 192, 546; L. Stallings, 140–51, 173; Swope, 165–66
—health, illness, 58, 279, 338, 453, 456, 471, 478; angina pectoris, 513–14, 520, 522; cholesterol-free diet, 472, 473, 480, 484; operations, 309, 312, 340, 443, 445, 446; stomach, liver, 156, 223, 264, 278, 299, 302, 307, 308–09, 310; TB, 114–17, 131–32; tumor, 499–500; typhoid fever, 89
—journalistic career, 199, 251; *Baltimore American*, 55–56, 57, 84, 87–88; *Baltimore Sun*, 57–58, 84, 85–93, 96, 97, 102, 103; labor reporter, 88, 89, 90–94, 116–17; *New York Herald Tribune*, 251, 253–54, 262–63; *New York World*, 117–25, editorial writer, 159–77, 189, 191, 195–96, 199, 260, 389, 435–36, 523; understanding of role of a newspaper, 169
—marriages: Mary Clough, 62, 84–85, 104–05, 106, 110–11, 126, 127, 156–57; divorce, alimony, 182, 249, 251–52; Florence Macbeth, 413–14, 417; caring for, 456–57, 469, 471–72, 500–01, 507–08; life with, 423–26, 434–35, 441, 442–43, 449, 451, 453, 454–58, 478–81; Aileen Pringle, 341–43, 345–46, 353, 366, 370–71, 372, 385–88, 413, 425, 513; Elina Tyszecka, 105–06, 126–27, 156, 157–58, 186–87, 205–06, 278, 279, 313, 324–25, 327, 328–29
—opinions on: American people, 161; art, 123, 434, 552–53, 556; autobiography, 503; biography, 502–03; books and writers, 545–46; California, 108; career as screenwriter, 289–90; craft of writing, 553–54; Elina, 158; heroes, 339; his physical appearance, 27; his trouble as columnist, 523; his writing, 8, 17, 448, 506, 535–36, 549–50, 551–52, 554, 555–56; Hollywood writers, 239–40, 306–07; Lippmann, 175–77, 199, 319–20; Mencken, 190–92, 193; midlife crises, 469; *Mildred Pierce*, 310; *Mildred Pierce* (film), 373; modern novel, 241–42; movie industry, 221, 418–19; "pure novel," 516; role of writer in war, 318–19; Ross as editor, 211–12; talent for writing, 523; what he stood for as novelist, 485–86; what Hollywood did to his novels, 468; writers and writing, 52, 339, 411–12, 470–71, 516; writing editorials, 160–61
—research, 224, 236, 281–82, 283, 299, 307, 346, 368, 369, 371–72, 376, 385, 431–32; attack on, 381–82; Civil War, 434, 441–42, 451, 475, 476–77; *Magician's Wife*, 499; *Moth*, 427–28, 431–32; trips for, 430–32, 451–52, 460, 463, 531
—story ideas, 52, 224–25, 229, 243, 251, 252–53, 257–59, 263–64, 266–67, 281–82, 283, 290–91, 315, 322, 338, 346, 368, 376, 426–27, 460, 480–81, 484, 486, 507; for plays, 16, 271
—studio jobs, 214, 217–40, 249–50, 251, 279, 285, 286, 289, 296, 310–11, 322–23, 327–28, 329–31, 340, 430, 448; Columbia, 377; end of, 435–38; RKO, 383–85, 413, 417; MGM, 291–93, 344–45, 353, 365; Paramount, 260–62, 376–77; turning point in his career, 330; 20th Century-Fox, 307, 333; Universal, 300–01; Warner Brothers, 303
—subjects, 268, 437; of articles, 102, 122–24, 129, 242, 534, 539–40; of columns, 262; of editorials, 160, 162–64, 170–72, 174, 195–96; Man, 161, 271, 317, 389
—themes, 134–35, 230, 382, 428,

Cain, James M. (*cont'd*)
488; homosexuality, 283–84; incest, 39, 100, 299, 304, 305, 370–71, 421; wish come true, 138, 181, 349, 370, 459, 529, 555–56

—works: anthologized, 313, 321, 338–39; best-sellers, 241, 247, 314; column for *New York American*, 241–42, 243; columns (proposed) 327–28, 367–68; early, 40, 51, 54; first novel, 231–39; historical novels, 322; Introduction to *For Men Only*, 338–39; most important, 336; obituary of *New York World*, 199; original film scripts, 328; paperback editions, 248, 285–86, 367, 442, 447–48, 475, 536; preface to 50th anniversary edition of *Who's Who in America*, 424; published in *New Yorker*, 201, 202; reprint rights, 391, 448; reprint sales, 448, 452, 528; reprints, 170, 179, 248, 285–86, 374, 426, 442; reviews: biography of Mencken, 449–50; reviews: books, 469–71; reviews: music, 106, 164; royalties, 249, 277, 391, 392, 449; sales, 186, 235, 248, 374, 391, 447–48; serial rights, 253; serials made from, 248; sold to film studios, 242–43, 247, 280, 288, 296, 300–01, 302, 303, 332–36, 339–40, 345, 365–66, 466–67; stage versions, 248, 253; used in writing classes, 247; violence, sex in, 547

—works: articles, 14, 95, 117, 123, 239–42, 253, 271–72; *American Mercury*, 14, 20, 22, 74, 84, 106, 108, 109–11, 113–14, 115–16, 117, 120, 129–33, 138, 164, 178, 179, 183, 184, 193, 225, 226, 239–40, 241, 271, 275, 389; "Are Editorials Worth Reading?" 139; "Battle Ground of Coal, The," 94–95, 102; "Editorial Writer, The," 113; "Fit for a Queen, 276*n*;

food, 162–63, 174, 254, 259, 337; "Free Lance for Hollywood, A," 418–19; "Hemp," 138; "Hero, The," 131; "High Dignitaries of State," 115–16; "Influence of Stenography on Literature, The," 253–54; on Lana Turner, 377–78; "Man Merriwell, The," 139, 156; "Opening Gun, The," 392; "Paradise," 226; "Pastor, The," 129–30; "Pathology of Service, The," 130–31; "Pedagogue," 113–14; "Politician: Female," 115–16; profile of John Ford, 424; "Red White and Blue," 138; re proposed AAA, 395–96, 401, 406; on reference books as gifts (solicited), 424; reminiscences, 534–35, 539–40, 542; "Sealing Wax," 202; "Servants of the People," 131; "Solid South, The," 183; "Tribute to a Hero," 241; "Walter Lippmann Had Style," 534–35; "West Virginia: A Mine-field Melodrama," 102–03

—works: collected: Book-of-the-Month club, 517; *Cain X 3*, 517–19, 522; *Everybody Does It* (paperback edition of "Career in C Major" and "The Embezzler"), 448; *Three of a Kind*, 331–32, 347, 427, 433, 436, Cain's preface to, 545

—works: dialogues: in *American Mercury*, 178–79, 182, 191, 217; "Citizenship," 184; in *New York World*, 182–83; *Our Government* (collection), 178, 179, 183–86, 189, 191, 235; reprinted, 184; "Taking of Montfaucon, The" (renamed "The Military Forces"), 184; "Theological Interlude," 178–79; "Trial by Jury," 178–79; "Will of the People," 183–84

—works: novels: *Butterfly, The,* 39, 101, 186, 299, 300, 302, 303–04, 370–71, 374, 375, 376, 381, 384, 387, 419–22, 442, 458, preface to,

419–21, stage version, 481–82, thematic structure, 552, thought his best, 506; *Galatea*, 38, 174, 186, 458–59, 461–62, 475, 499, 511, sale to paperback, 466; *Galloping Domino, The* (based on *7-11*, published as *Sinful Woman*), 442; *Institute, The*, 530, 531, 532, 533, 536–37; *Love's Lovely Counterfeit*, 315, 321, 325, 382, 548, film version: *Slightly Scarlet*, 435, 466–67, 468; *Magician's Wife, The*, 38, 174, 484–99, 505–07, 511, 548; *Mignon*, 37, 463–64, 473–77, 480, 484, 486, 499, 511, 529, rejected by Knopf, 471, structure, 552; *Mildred Pierce*, 38, 174, 218, 305–06, 307–08, 309–10, 312, 313–15, 317, 471, 480–81, 485, film version, 314, 339–40, 345, 348–52, 353, 365, 372–74, 378, 379–80, 435, 548, sales, 314, 315, 426, structure, 552, suit charging plagiarism, 443, 444–47; *Moth, The*, 33, 37, 38, 424, 426–28, 432, 442, 457, abridged version, 448, reviews, 433–34, structure, 552; musical structure of, 552; *Nevada Moon* (retitled *Jealous Woman*), 417–18, 447–48; *Past All Dishonor*, 37, 38, 101, 369–70, 371, 372, 375, 381–84, 387, 419, 420, 422, 442, 463, 475, 476, 485, 487, 549, Cain on, 552, movie options, 517, 528; *Postman Always Rings Twice* (*Bar-B-Que*), 214, 231–39, 242, 243, 277, 308, 310, 317, 420, 434, 475, 485, 488, 504, 528, 546, 548, Cain reread, 485, film version, 253, 260, 339, 348, 352–53, 372, 378–80, 382, 383–84, 391, 435, first line of, 233, 488, impact of, 235, 240–49, Knopf rejected, 474, republished in *Cain X 3*, 517–19, revived as play, 457–58, 462–63, rewritten for stage revival, 462–63, sales, 448, stage version, 253, 260, 262, 267, 269, 270, 272, 273–76, thematic structure, 552; *Rainbow's End*, 531–32, 533, 536, 537; *Serenade*, 38, 174, 284, 286, 317, 322, 348, 430–31, 434, 475, 482, 548, 555, Cain thought plagiarized, 302, 310–12, 325–27, 391, film version, 435, 467–68, Knopf liked, 474, reviews, 159, 286–87, sales, 288, sold to films, 365–66, structure, 552; *Sinful Woman*, 447–48, 475

—works: novels, unpublished, 259, 511–12, 528, 530–31; book on grammar and punctuation (nonfiction), 546; "Bright Gold" feature (proposed), 280; *Cloud 9*, 511; *Cocktail Waitress, The*, 537–39; Don Juan story, 528–30; *Enchanted Isle, The*, 512, retitled *The Mink Coat*, 428; *Kingdom by the Sea*, 33, 39, 511; *Jinghis Quinn*, 511, 539; *Picina, La*, 424, 434; *Pink Buttercup*, 484

—works: plays: *Crashing the Gates* (later *Jubilee*), 134–38; *Give Me One More Day*, 466; *Guest in 701, The*, 458, 464–66; *7-11*, 284–85, 286–87, 293, 294, 295, 296, 321, 338, 442, 466

—works: poems, 75; "Auld Lang Syne," 28–29, 201; "Gridiron Soliloquies," 202

—works, proposed: Civil War novel, to be called *Ghost Riders on the Red River* (later *If Bori Had Blundered*), 376, 434, 441–43, 447, 449, 451, 452, 453–54, 457, 463–64, 471, 473 (see also *Mignon*); movie scripts: *Aida* and *The Traitor*, 249

—works: serials, 258–59; "Beauty, Booty, and Blood" (unpublished), 485; "Double Indemnity," 37, 267–69, 276, 288, 317, 346–48, 488, 548, 555, added 8 million circulation to *Liberty*, 303, anthologized in *Three of a Kind*, 321, film version,

Cain, James M., works (*cont'd*)
331–32, 339, 340, 345, 352–53,
365, 372, 373, 378, 379–80, 382,
418, 435, 447, 467, republished in
Cain X 3, 517–19, thematic structure, 552, TV version, 532, 533;
"Modern Cinderella, A," 293,
295–96, 302, film version: *When Tomorrow Comes*, 296, 300–01, 302,
310–11, 325, 327, 448, retitled *The
Root of His Evil*, 448; "Money and
the Woman" (retitled "The Embezzler"), 301–02, anthologized in
Three of a Kind, 321, republished in
Everybody Does It, 448, novel version: *The Embezzler*, 307–08, sold to
Warner Brothers, 302, 303; "Nevada
Moon" (retitled *Jealous Woman*),
447–48; "Two Can Sing," 279–80,
285, 288, 290, film version, 435, retitled "Career in C Major" and anthologized in *Three of a Kind*, 321
—works: short stories, 226, 452,
460–61; "Baby in the Icebox, The,"
225–26, 229, 231, film version of,
248; "Birthday Party, The," 267;
"Brush Fire," 276*n*, 303, 448; "Career in C Major," 38, 331, reprinted
in *Everybody Does It*, 448; "Cigarette
Girl," 460–61; "Coal Black,"
270–71, 275, 276*n*, 448; "Dead
Man," 448, 469; "Death on the
Beach," 469; "Girl in the Storm,"
301, 303, 338; "Hip, Hip, the Hippo," 261; "Pastorale," 179–80, 181,
186, 224, 229, 271, 448, 469, 488;
"Pay-Off Girl," 452; "Two O'Clock
Blonde," 460–61; "Visitor, The,"
475
—as writer: *Alice in Wonderland* his
guide, 551; approach to storytelling,
230–31, 232; attempt to write about
contemporary people failed (*Institute*), 536–37; attempts to write first
novel, 95, 96, 100–01, 177, 181,
182–83, 186, 225, 547; avoided

profanity in his writing, 136–37; basic principle of narrative construction, 138; career as writer 12–13,
31, 34, 36–38, 88, 93–94, 110,
229, 537, 549, 554–56; characters,
33, 182, 317, 373–74, 422, 517,
529, 547, 554–55; continued writing
after failures, 484–87, 507, 511–12,
514, 528–31, 537–38, 542, 550;
critical confusion re, 545, 547–48,
556; development, 102–03, 110,
173–74, 180, 182; dialogue,
110–11, 129, 185, 204, 234, 256,
292, 325, 334–35, 537, 548–49;
difficulty in writing, 100–01, 229,
233–34, 261, 282, 321, 323, 338,
447, 461, 463, 469, 472, 473, 484,
487, 500, 507, 511–12, 549–50;
emphasis on brevity and conciseness, 108; endings, 271, 275, 381,
427, 458–59, 475, 476, 485–86,
488, 530, 532, 539; failure as playwright, 275, 276, 334–35, 466; failures as screenwriter, 222–23, 230,
239, 328, 334–35, 345, 354, 365,
420, 435–36, 548; fascination with
"low speech," 178, 180, 181, 182,
191, 217, 225; had to pretend to be
someone else, 177, 178, 180–81,
183, 186, 471, 554; influenced by
Hollywood, 436–37, 547–48; influences on, 74, 137, 191 (*see also*
Mencken, H. L.); love-rack principle
of storytelling, 232, 233, 246, 258,
551; most reprinted author in U.S.,
374; motivation, 551; obsession with
accuracy, 101, 173, 431; obsession
with language, 40, 51, 52, 120,
124–25, 546–47; quality of writing
deteriorating, 461, 484; reputation
(as writer), 93–94, 95, 114, 117,
171, 192, 194, 204, 234, 247,
248–49, 276, 299, 300, 313, 422;
rewriting, revising, 268, 309, 369,
506; special approach to historical
fiction, 383; story was everything,

550–51; stylistic limitations, 242, 537; supposed literary influences on, 213; "those who can write must write," 477, 549; title changes, problems, 234, 235, 237–38, 284, 312; as writer of pure novel, 516, 520; writer's block, 276–78, 279, 300, 301, 303 (see also Cain, difficulty in writing); writing in first person, 180, 181, 225, 231, 234, 293, 370, 433–34, 463, 485, 537, 548–50, 554; writing in third person, 229, 303, 307, 485, 506, 511, 538, 550; writing style, 17, 181, 182, 247, 499, 518, 546–47, 548–49; writing with movie sales in mind, 277, 279–80, 315, 321–22, 382, 548

Cain, James W. (father of James M. Cain), 3–6, 8, 11–12, 13, 15, 31, 32, 73, 95, 547; acknowledged in Cain's first book, 185; adroitness at politics, 40; death of, 294–95; definition of tragedy, 551; drinking, 20, 40, 53–54, 58; honorary degree, 13; job at United States Fidelity Guaranty Co., 62, 84, 103; member of Board of Governors of St. John's College, 103; old age, 273, 293; reaction to Jamie's decision to be a writer, 37; reaction to Postman, 246; relation with Jamie, 38, 39–40; tried to help in Jamie's troubles with Elina, 112; at Washington College, 16–22, 25, 28, 52–54, 58–59

Cain, Mary Clough, 26–28, 54; marriage to Cain, 62, 84–85, 104–05, 106, 110–11; divorce and settlement, 157, 251–52; teaching, 31, 84, 85, 98

Cain, Mary Kelly (grandmother of James M. Cain), 3

Cain, P. W. (grandfather of James M. Cain), 3–4

Cain, Rosalie (sister of James M. Cain; later Mrs. Robert McComas), 7–8, 38, 40, 249, 375, 417, 428, 472, 512; Cain's correspondence with, 40, 338, 340, 354, 365, 457, 502, 512, 527

Cain, Rose Mallahan (mother of James M. Cain), 4–6, 8, 11, 37, 62, 77, 124, 246, 435, 453; death of, 471–72; at death of husband, 294; discouraged Cain's singing career, 35; musical ability, 4–5, 6, 9, 39; relation with Cain, 38–39

Cain, Virginia (sister of James M. Cain), 7, 19, 38, 39, 85, 472

Cain family, 27, 30, 31, 37, 38–39, 84, 103, 205, 273; activities, 19; in Annapolis, 5–10, 12–14; in Chestertown, 14–15, 17–18; religion, 6, 20

Cain X 3, 517–19, 522, 528

Caldwell, Erskine: God's Little Acre, 443–44

Callaghan, Morley, 202

Camp, Walter, 4

Camus, Albert, 520

Capone, Al, 226

Capote, Truman, 470

Captivating Mary Carstairs (Harrison), 36

"Career in C Major" (Cain), 38, 331; republished in Everybody Does It, 448

Carmer, Carl, 403

Carmody, John, 518–19, 534

Carnegie, Dale: How to Win Friends and Influence People, 448

Caro, Mae: Nothing to Live For, 444–47

Carroll, Charles, 5

Carroll, Nancy, 293

Carson, Jack, 351

Carter, John, 185

Caruso, Enrico, 266

Casanova, Jacques, 529

Cassidy, Claudia, 462

Cather, Willa, 133, 189–90, 241; Lost Lady, A, 190; My Ántonia, 190; O

Cather, Willa (cont'd)
Pioneers, 189; Professor's House,
The, 129, 190
Cat's Paw, The (Kelland), 261
Chafin, Lafe, 376
Chamlee, Mario, 416
Chandler, Raymond, 333–35, 336,
339, 346, 435, 470, 504, 532, 536,
545, 548; Big Sleep, The, 333
Chase, Samuel, 5
Chastain, Thomas, 528, 531
Cheever, John, 548
Chesterton, G. K., 241
Chicago Tribune, 73, 422, 475–76
Childs, Marquis, 472–73
Christie, Agatha, 347
"Christmas Spirit, The" (O'Hara), 189
Churchill, Allan, 502
Churchill, Winston (American novel-
ist), 6
"Cigarette Girl" (Cain), 460–61
Citizen Kane (film), 347
"Citizenship" (Cain), 184
Clark, Marian, 534, 539
Claxton, Oliver, 200
Cleopatra (film), 262–63
Cline, Leonard, 105, 117, 118
Cloud 9 (Cain) (unpublished), 511
Clough, Mary Rebekah. See Cain, Mary
Clough
"Coal Black" (Cain), 276n, 448
Cobb, Lee J., 532
Coburn, Charles, 447
Cocktail Waitress, The (Cain) (unpub-
lished), 537–39
Cody, Lew, 341
Coffey, Shelby, 534
Cohen, Charles, 31
Cohen, Martin, 466
Cohen, Morris, 392–93
Cohn, Harry, 230
Colbert, Claudette, 262
Cole, Lester, 410
Coleridge, Samuel Taylor, 546
Collier's, 94, 296

Collins, Eileen, 203, 208, 213
Columbia Studios, 229–30, 247, 305,
332, 377
Commins, Saxe, 553
Committee of One Thousand to Abolish
the House Un-American Activities
Committee, 430
Common Sin, The (film script), 365
Commons, John: History of the Labor
Movement, 88
Communism: accusation of, in Cain's
proposed AAA, 397–98, 399, 400,
401–02, 403, 404, 409–11; Cain's
position re, 389–90, 411
Comstock, Anthony, 107
Connelly, Marc, 128, 403, 406; Green
Pastures, 402
Coolidge, Calvin, 127, 138
Cooper, Ethel, 27
Copyright(s), 392, 395, 396, 399, 401,
407; repository for (proposed), 393,
408
Cornwell, John J., 90
Cortina, J. N., 503
Costello, John, 344
Cotten, Joseph, 275
Cousins, Norman, 400
Cowan, Lester, 381, 383
Cowley, Malcolm, 381, 382, 419, 436,
547, 548
Crane, Louise, 25
Crane, Stephen, 17; Red Badge of
Courage, 54, 546
Crashing the Gates (later Jubilee)
(Cain), 134–38, 227
Crawford, Broderick, 487
Crawford, Joan, 350–52, 372–73, 378,
383, 480–81, 499, 506
Crenna, Richard, 532
Critics, 74, 107, 256, 470, 545, 554.
See also Reviews
Cromwell, John, 289
Cronin, Donald, 73, 79
Crosby, Walter W., 31
Crouch, Eddie, 28, 31

Crouse, Russell, 393

Crow, James Francis, 302

Crowther, Bosley, 248, 330, 347, 380, 447, 466–67

Cruising (Walker), 470

Cullen, Victor E., 116, 118

Cummings, Constance, 270, 282, 527, 542

Cummings, Kate, 270, 282, 305–06, 308, 323, 324, 337, 340, 386

Cuppy, Will, 202

Curtis, Jack, 272

Curtiz, Michael, 349, 350, 351–52

Curwood, James Oliver, 96

Dahl, Arlene, 466

Dalmores, Charles, 416

Darnell, Linda, 447

Davis, Bette, 350

Davis, Elmer, 202, 318, 319

Davis, Owen, 376

Davis, Robert Gorham, 422, 444

Day, Clarence, 393

Day, Price, 202

"Dead Man" (Cain), 271, 275, 448, 469

Dean, Alexander, 293

"Death on the Beach" (Cain), 469

Deck, Robin, 526–27

Decker, Bill, 499

Delehanty, Thornton, 399

Delineator (magazine), 133

Dell, 475

Dell, Ethel M., 96

De Mille, Cecil B., 221, 222, 228, 262–63, 320, 341

Dempsey, David, 461

DeSylva, Buddy, 336

DeVoto, Bernard, 444

Dial, 474, 475, 481, 484–85, 486–87, 488, 499, 501, 505–06, 511

Diamond, Maurice, 448

Dickens, Charles, 546

Dictionary of American Biography, 502

Disenchanted, The (Schulberg), 470

Doctor Socrates (film script), 261

Doctorow, E. L., 506; *Ragtime*, 487

Dodgson, Charles L.: *Alice in Wonderland*, 10, 174, 191

Dollar Book Club, 391

Donlevy, Brian, 335

Doran, D. A., 218, 221, 222

Dorsey, George A.: *Why We Behave Like Human Beings*, 153

Dos Passos, John, 409; *Manhattan Transfer*, 107, 129; *Streets of Night*, 107; *Three Soldiers*, 100, 106; *U.S.A.*, 107

"Double Indemnity" (Cain), 37, 267–69, 276, 288, 317, 488, 548, 555; added eight million circulation to *Liberty*, 303; anthologized in *Three of a Kind*, 321; could not pass Hays Office, 331–32; reprinted in *Cain X 3*, 517–19; thematic structure of, 552

Double Indemnity (film version of "Double Indemnity"), 335–36, 339, 340, 345, 352–53, 365, 372, 373, 378, 379–80, 382; premiere, 346–48; television version, 532, 533

Douglas, Kirk, 384

Douglas, Paul, 447, 448

Douglas, William O., 483

Doyle, A. Conan, 339, 546; *Adventures of Sherlock Holmes, The*, 10, 19

Dozier, William, 332, 333, 448

Dramatists Guild, 398

Dreiser, Theodore, 133, 232, 375, 546, 553; *American Tragedy*, 128

Drummond, Roscoe, 409

Dubois, William, 325

Duel in the Sun (Busch), 378

Dunklee, Keith, 524–25

Dunklee, Leona, 524–25, 540

Dunne, Finley Peter, 25

Dunne, Irene, 300, 302

Duvivier, Julien, 289

Echo de Paris, 6

"Editorial Writer, The" (Cain), 113

Eggar, Samantha, 532
Eliot, T. S., 128
Ellen Rogers (Farrell), 313–14
Ellers, Sally, 226
Elmer Gantry (Lewis), 130, 135, 155
"Embezzler, The" (Cain) novel version of "Money and the Woman"), 307–08; republished in *Everybody Does It*, 448. *See also* "Money and the Woman"
Enchanted Isle, The (Cain) (unpub.), 512; retitled *The Mink Coat*, 528
Erskine, John, 398, 400
Esquire, 259, 452, 488
Everybody Does It (Cain), 448; film, originally *Wife, Husband and Friend*, based on "Two Can Sing," 447

Fadiman, Clifton, 314, 318, 339, 343–44, 419
Fairhurst, Charles, 444
Farewell to Arms, A (Hemingway), 241, 470
Farrar, Geraldine, 57, 62
Farrar & Rinehart, 248
Farrell, James T., 317, 338, 374, 399–400, 403, 504; debate with Cain in *SR*, 404–05; *Ellen Rogers*, 313–14
Faulkner, William, 140, 223, 276, 323, 553; *Soldier's Pay*, 128
Fawkes, Guy, 202
Fell, Thomas, 5, 103
Fencing Master, The (play), 415
Ferber, Edna, 128, 406
Ferguson, Harvey, 223, 292
Field, Betty, 376
Fields, W. C., 133–34, 188–89, 269, 539
"Fifth Grand" (Hemingway), 181–82, 448, 469
Films Cain worked on, 221, 223, 230, 261, 285, 289, 291–93, 300–01, 310, 329–31, 340, 345, 354, 376–77, 384, 435. *See also* Cain, James M., studio jobs

Films made from Cain's works, 226, 248, 288, 300–01, 302, 303, 315, 335–36, 346–47, 348–53, 435, 448, 466–68
Fishbein, Morris, 110, 128
"Fit for a Queen" (Cain), 276n
Fitzgerald, F. Scott, 193, 223, 285, 293, 323; *Great Gatsby, The*, 129, 376, 466; Schulberg's novel re, 470; *This Side of Paradise*, 96
Fitzpatrick, Clarke, 57, 103, 246; "1001 Embezzlers," 302
Flanner, Janet ("Genet"), 202
Fleischmann, Raoul, 201, 210–11, 212, 214
Fleming, Rhonda, 384, 466
Flynn, John T., 398
Foch, Ferdinand, 63
Fontaine, Joan, 467–68
For Men Only, 338–39
Forbidden Game (film script), 430
Ford, Ford Madox, 202
Ford, Henry, 171
Ford, John, 424
Fort Apache (film), 424
Fowler, David, 91–92
Foy, Bryan, 303
Frankfurter, Felix, 167
Frankie from Frisco (film script), 340, 345, 354, 365
Franklin, Benjamin, 16
Franklin, J. Harris, 35
Frazier, Suzi, 27
"Free Lance for Hollywood, A" (Cain), 418–19
Freed, Arthur, 250, 354
Freeman, Helen, 135
Friede, Donald, 169–70
Friede, Evelyn, 170
Frings, Ketti: *I Know You*, 391–92
Frohock, W. M., 504
Fuermann, George, 432–33
Fuller, Richard, 312, 533

Gabel, Martin, 431
Gabin, Jean, 289

Gable, Clark, 249, 250, 317, 333

Galatea (Cain), 38, 186, 458–59, 461–62, 466, 475, 499, 511

Gale, Frank, 75–76

Galli-Curci, Amelita, 501

Gallico, Paul, 367, 406, 412

Galloping Domino, The (Cain) (novel; based on *7-11*; published as *Sinful Woman*), 442, 447–48, 475

"Galloping Dominoes" (Cain), 321–22

Gang, Martin, 288, 311–12, 326–27, 328, 387, 393

Gannett, Lewis, 245, 287, 434

Garden City Publishing Company, 391

Garey, Enoch, 103–04, 107, 112–13, 114; *Plattsburgh Manual, The*, 103

Garfield, John, 248, 353, 380, 457–58, 462

Garnett, Tay, 378

Gary, Gene (Hifzi-Bey-Hadzi-Selimovitch), 324

Gatsby (film), 376, 391

Gelder, Robert Van, 314

Geller, James, 204, 214, 235, 242–43, 249, 253, 260, 267, 296, 317, 322; helped Mencken, 255; quit Morris Agency, 323; selling *Mildred Pierce*, 308, 310, 312; showed "Double Indemnity" to studios, 268; sold *Postman* to MGM, 247; sold "Two Can Sing" to 20th Century-Fox, 280

Gershwin, Jerry, 528

Gessner, Bernard, 107, 108

Geyelin, Philip, 523–24

Gibbs, Ethel, 22–23, 27, 53–54

Gibbs, Wolcott, 200, 202, 214, 289–90, 301

Gibney, Sheridan, 429

Gibson, Daniel, 16, 459, 522

Giesler, Jerry, 387

Gilbert, William, 265

Gill, Bob, 23

"Girl in the Storm, The" (Cain), 301, 303, 338

Gissen, Max, 482–84

Give Me One More Day (Cain), 466

Glasgow, Ellen: *Barren Ground*, 129

Glass Heart, The (film script), 384

Glass Key, The (Hammett), 213

God's Little Acre (Caldwell), 443–44

Godseeker, The (Lewis), 155

Goetz, Augustus, 158, 187

Goetz, Ruth Goodman, 133, 152, 187, 194, 227, 275, 299, 472, 523; Cain's correspondence with, 509, 527; on Cain's "new phase," 512; description of Elina, 157–58; on *Institute, The*, 530; memorial tribute to Cain, 542

Goff, Ivan, 468

Gone with the Wind, 383; film, 66

Good Bad Woman, A (play), 123

Good Society, The (Lippmann), 286

Goodhue, Robert, 289

Goodman, Philip, 133–37, 138, 189, 219, 503, 515; break with Mencken, 192, 193; on *New York World*, 196–97, 198, 199; relation with Cain, 151–56, 157, 158, 185, 187–88, 193–94, 227; tried to buy *New York World*, 165–66

Goodman, Ruth. *See* Goetz, Ruth Goodman

Gordon, Ramon, 481–82

Gorney, Jay, 265

Gould, Jay, 118

"Governor, The" (Cain), 313

Grahame, Margot, 286

Grant, Jane, 128

Grant, Robert, 166

Gray, Judd, 232–33

Grayson, Kathryn, 250

Great Gatsby, The (Fitzgerald), 129, 376

Great Train Robbery, The (film), 22, 435

Green Goddess, The (play), 341

Greene, Graham, 483; *Our Man in Havana*, 470

Greene, Tom, 36

Greenfield, Kent, 22

Greenwald, Joseph, 272

Grey, Zane, 96

"Gridiron Soliloquies" (Cain), 202

Griffith, La Nora, 413–14, 417

Griffith, Yeatman, 415

Growth of the Soil, The (Hamsun), 155

Guest in 701, The (Cain), 458, 464–66

Gunther, Henry, 68–69

Gypsy Maid (film script), 329–30

Gypsy Wildcat (film), 330–31, 435, 467

H. L. Mencken (Angoff), 471

Haardt, Sara (later Mrs. Mencken), 194, 273, 342

Haggard, Edith, 249, 252, 254, 255, 259, 261, 267–68, 271, 275, 276

Hale, Ruth, 128

Hall, Jon, 330

Haller, Ernest, 351

Hamburger, Louis, 264

Hamill, Pete, 518

Hammerstein, Oscar, 193–94, 366, 407, 408

Hammerstein, Oscar, II, 406

Hammett, Dashiell, 419, 470, 504, 536, 545; *Glass Key, The*, 213

Hammond, Percy, 274

Hamsun, Knut: *Growth of the Soil, The*, 155

Hand of the Potter, The (play), 232

Hannon, Aleta, 34

Hansen, Harry, 185

Harper's (magazine), 444, 461

Harris, James, 517

Harris, Jed, 273, 274, 295, 296, 343

Harris, William, Jr., 137

Harrison, Henry Sydnor, 40; *Captivating Mary Carstairs*, 36; *Queed*, 36; *V.V's Eyes*, 36

Harte, Bret, 241, 546

Hawthorne, Nathaniel, 397, 546

Hayman, Clifford, 462

Hays Office, 248, 253, 268, 288, 303, 315, 331–32, 333, 335, 339, 348, 352, 365, 378, 379–80, 382

Hayworth, Rita, 377, 448

Hazlitt, Henry, 240–41

Hearst (William Randolph), 242, 253, 263

Heath, Percy, 221

Heaton, John, 118, 124, 173, 174, 198

Heiress, The (play), 187

Helburn, Thelma, 260, 269

Hellinger, Mark, 339

Hemingway, Ernest, 276, 313, 323, 338, 448, 502; *Farewell to Arms, A*, 470; "Fifty Grand," 181–82, 448, 469; "Killers, The," 470; *In Our Time*, 128; *Men Without Women*, 181; *Old Man and the Sea*, 470; supposed influence on Cain, 74, 181, 245, 287, 419–21, 434, 518, 546; *To Have and Have Not*, 287

"Hemp" (Cain), 138

Hergesheimer, Joseph, 342

"Hero, The" (Cain), 131

Heym, Stefan: *Hostages*, 402

Hidden River, The (play), 187

"High Dignitaries of State" (Cain), 115–16

"Hilda Crane" (Raphaelson), 503

Hilton, James, 246

"Hip, Hip, the Hippo" (Cain), 261

Hirshfeld, Samuel, 266–67

Hoblitzel, Raymond, 55

Hoffman, Joseph, 330

Hogan, William, 518

Hollywood Reporter, 275, 397

Hollywood Ten, 289, 390, 397, 410, 411, 429

Hollywood writers, 222–23, 393; Communist influence among, 390, 392, 397. *See also* Authors League, West Coast Guild

Holm, Celeste, 447

Holmes, Geoffrey: *Build My Gallows High*, 384

Holmes, Judson, 343

Hoover, Herbert: *The Challenge of Liberty*, 253

Hopkins, Arthur J., 133

Hopkins, Henry, 9, 283, 337
Hopper, Hedda, 341, 346, 353, 411, 430
Hornblow, Arthur, 340, 345, 353–54, 418
Hornblow, Arthur, Jr., 523
Hossack, Harry F., 72
Hostages (Heym), 402
Hot Saturdays (film script), 223
Houghton Mifflin, 183, 248
How to Win Friends and Influence People (Carnegie), 448
Howard, Bushrod, 10, 11
Howard, Leland, 290
Howard, Roy, 197, 198
Howard, Sidney, 66
Howe, E. W., 129–30
Howells, William Dean, 95–96; *Rise of Silas Lapham, The*, 95
Howes, Melinda, 531, 533
Hughes, Rupert, 386, 398, 408–09, 410, 411
Human Comedy, The (film), 347
Huneker, James, 164
Huston, Walter, 310
Hutchens, John K., 331
Huxley, Aldous, 223, 241, 354, 483; *Those Barren Leaves*, 129
Huxley, Thomas Henry; *Evolution and Ethics*, 78, 130
Hyde, Henry, 94

I Know You (Frings), 391–92
Immoralist, The, (play), 187
In Defense of Women (Mencken), 89, 133
"Influence of Stenography on Literature, The" (Cain), 253–54
Ingersoll, Ralph McAllister, 200, 202, 212
Ingoldsby, William, 4
Institute, The (Cain), 530, 531, 532, 533, 536–37
Irreverent Mr. Mencken, The (Kemler), 449–50

Is Sex Necessary? (Thurber and White), 204
It Can't Happen Here (Lewis), 293

Jack London's Adventure Magazine, 469
Jackson, Joseph E., 382
Jacobs, William, 303
James, Henry: *Wings of the Dove, The*, 392
James M. Cain (Madden), 519–20
"James M. Cain at Twilight Time" (Carmody), 519
"Jason" (Raphaelson), 503
"Jazz Singer, The" (Raphaelson), 503
Jaws (Benchley), 550
Jealous Woman (Cain) (original title: "Nevada Moon"), 447–48
Jeffers, Robinson, 128
Jinghis Quinn (Cain) (unpublished), 511, 539
Johnny O'Clock (film), 384
Johnson, Alva, 202
Johnson, Gerald W., 103, 110
Johnson, Hiram, 88, 109
Johnson, Nunnally, 300, 307, 447
Johnston, Eric, 373
Johnston Office, 380, 383. *See also* Hays Office
Jonas, Robert, 516
Jones, J. S. William, 23–24
Joseph, Robert L., 431, 466
Jubilee (Cain). See *Crashing the Gates*
Julien, Jay, 466
Jun, Rose Marie, 480
Jungle Books (Kipling), 10, 262–63
Junior Miss (Benson), 256
Jurado, Katy, 467

Kahn, E. J., 172; *World of Swope, The*, 502
Kaltenborn, H. V., 398
Kane, H. T., 476
Kaufman, George, 128, 393
Keating, Fred, 286
Keeney, Frank, 91–92

Kelland, Clarence Budington, 398; *Cat's Paw, The*, 261

Kemler, Edgar: *The Irreverent Mr. Mencken*, 449–50

Kent, Frank, 103, 344, 390, 468–69

Keyes, Evelyn, 384

"Killers, The" (Hemingway), 470

Kines, Williams, 55, 56

Kingdom by the Sea (Cain) (unpublished), 33, 39, 511

Kipling, Rudyard: *Jungle Books*, 10, 262–63

Kirby, Rollin, 117, 174, 473

Kirkey, Donald, 354

Kirsch, Robert, 518

Kisielnicki, Carol, 514

Kisielnicki, Ted, 479, 524

Kisielnicki, Thelma, 479, 500, 524, 525, 540–42

Knock on Any Door (Motley), 470

Knopf, Alfred A., 114, 179, 187, 211, 234–38, 243, 268, 322, 372, 381; advertising Cain's works, 288, 314, 433; anthology of Cain's works, 321; Borzoi editions, 128; bought *Mildred Pierce*, 310; Cain's correspondence with, 255, 256, 297, 302, 306, 307–08, 338, 419, 420–21, 428, 449, 472; Cain's squabbles with, 374, 391, 426, 462–63; concern re *Butterfly*, 421; editor of *American Mercury*, 106, 109, 191–92; enthusiastic about *Serenade*, 284; first meeting with Cain, 185; and lawsuits against Cain, 444, 445; liked *Galatea*, 458–59; liked *Past All Dishonor*, 372; at Mencken's funeral, 468; options on Cain's books, 186, 229, 235, 236, 237, 248; postponed publication of *Butterfly*, 381; publishing Cain's first book, 183–85; publishing Chandler, 333; publishing *Love's Lovely Counterfeit*, 321; pushing Cain to produce, 270, 276–77, 370, 371; quarrel with Mencken, 240–41;

rejected *Mignon*, 464, 471, 474; remarried, 513; reprint rights, 286, 448; suggested Book-of-the-Month Club bring out Cain collection, 517; turned down *The Institute*, 531; turned down *Postman*, 474; upset when Cain's work published in paperback, 442

Knopf, Blanche, 133, 183, 189–90, 236, 284, 303, 372; correspondence with Cain, 420–21

Kolmar, Fred, 218, 219

Kopp, Robert, 393

Koshland, William, 463, 511, 512

Kraft Theatre, 487

Kramer, Dale, 200, 502

Krock, Arthur, 117, 118, 119–20, 123–24, 151, 164, 201, 258, 343, 473, 502; break with Mencken, 191; on Cain, 246; Cain's correspondence with, 320, 338, 468; on Cain's music reviews, 162; friendship with Cain, 139–40, 173, 185; go-between in sale of *New York World*, 165; left *New York World*, 166

Kuhn, Gen. Joseph, 62, 66–67, 68, 69

Kuhn, Rene, 398, 400

Kyne, Peter B., 96

Ladd, Alan, 376

Ladies Home Journal, 267, 452

Lalley, Joe, 103

Lamarr, Hedy, 289, 290

Lamott, Kenneth, 518

Lanchester, Elsa, 229, 269

Lange, Jessica, 248

Lanza, Mario, 288, 468

Lardner, John, 347

Lardner, Ring, 180, 200, 225, 338, 434; Cain's indebtedness to, 419, 546, 547; column in *New Yorker*, 209–10; "In the Wake of the News" column, 73; *Treat 'Em Rough*, 74; *You Know Me, Al*, 74

Lardner, Ring, Jr., 392, 410

Last of the Mohicans, The (Cooper), 19

Laughton, Charles, 228–29, 269–70, 539

Laurents, Arthur, 431

Lavery, Emmet, 393, 399, 402, 406, 407, 408, 411

Lawrence, Vincent, 137–38, 227–28, 257, 261, 275, 284, 320, 346, 376, 512; Cain's indebtedness to, 546; death of, 418; influence of, on Cain, 436; *Love Among the Married*, 137; reaction to Cain column, 262–63; reaction to *Postman*, 246; role in evolution of Cain's first novel, 231–34, 237–38; theory of plotting, 506

Lawson, John Howard, 289

Leasing, 391–92, 393, 398, 405

Lee, Charles, 461

Lee, Roland V., 331

Leech, Margaret, 128, 516

Lerman, Oscar, 466

Lerner, Max, 372–73

LeRoy, Mervyn, 291

Levin, Martin, 506

Levy, Benn, 227, 270

Lewis, Carroll, 478–79

Lewis, Frances, 478–79

Lewis, John L., 91, 98

Lewis, Lloyd, 422

Lewis, Martin, 476

Lewis, Oscar, 383

Lewis, Sinclair, 72, 133, 186, 193, 372, 379, 546, 553; alcoholism, 154, 155; *Arrowsmith*, 110, 129, 153; *Babbitt*, 156; *Elmer Gantry*, 135, 155; *Godseeker, The*, 155; *It Can't Happen Here*, 293; *Main Street*, 96, 152; *Man Who Knew Coolidge, The*, 154; relation with Cain, 130, 152–56, 502

Lewis, T. R., 152

Lewis, Wyndham, 202

Liberty (magazine), 249, 280, 303, 448; Cain published in, 268–69, 276, 301

Lindbergh, Charles, 170

Lindsay, Howard, 393

Lindsey, Ben, 128

Linscott, Robert N., 182–83

Linscott, Roger Bourne, 422

Lippmann, Walter, 28, 118, 120–25, 131, 163, 199, 260, 279, 474, 528; appreciated Cain's talent, 171; attitude on imperialism, 319–20; Cain article re, 534–35; Cain's correspondence with, 234–35, 236–37, 254–55, 263, 282, 344; Cain's indebtedness to, 546; defense of Sacco and Vanzetti, 166, 167–68; defense of Scopes, 164; friendship with Cain, 139, 173, 185, 472; *Good Society, The*, 286; on Mencken, 89, 190; *Method of Freedom, The*, 255; as *New York World* failed, 197–98; perfectionist, 174–77; *Public Opinion*, 120; seventieth birthday, 172–73; and Swope, 165–66, 172; *U.S. in World Affairs, The*, 234–35; *U.S. War Aims*, 344

Lipscomb, Thomas, 531–33, 536

Lisser, Joseph, 441

Literature, American, 95–96, 107; Cain's impact on, 234 (*see also* Cain, James M., literary status of); hardboiled school, 422, 444, 504, 520

"Literature and the Cinema" (symposium), 523, 526

Littauer, Kenneth, 290

Little Foxes, The (film), 329

Liveright, Horace, 128, 129

Lloyd, Harold, 228, 261, 270

Lockridge, Richard, 275

Logan, Cain, 534–35

Lolita, 470

London, Jack, 241

Long, Lois, 210

Longstreet, Stephen, 433, 461

Loos, Anita: *Gentlemen Prefer Blondes*, 128

Lorimer, George Horace, 212

Lorraine Cross, The (newspaper), 72–78, 201

Los Angeles Daily News, 319, 327–28

Lost Lady, A (Cather), 190

Love Among the Married (play), 137

"Love Is Where You Find It" (song), 250

Love Me Forever (film), 265

Love's Lovely Counterfeit (Cain), 315, 321, 325, 382, 548; film version: *Slightly Scarlet*, 435, 466–67, 468

Lowell, Abbott, 166

Lowell, Amy, 129

Luce, Clare Boothe, 398

Lucky Baldwin (film script), 307

Ludwig, Emil, 241

Luhn, Harriet, 9

Lynn, Jeffrey, 303

Lyons, Eugene, 398

Macbeth, Charles J., 414–15

Macbeth, Florence. *See* Cain, Florence Macbeth

MacBride, James, 433

McCarey, Leo, 383

McCarthy, Mary, 382

McClain, Joseph H., 522

McClure's magazine, 24–25

McComas, Glenn, 38

McComas, Robert Glenn, 38

McCormick, Mary, 266

McCoy, Horace, 313, 504

MacDonald, Jeanette, 249, 250

MacDonald, John D., 536

Macdonald, Ross, 518

MacDougall, Ranald, 348, 351

McDowell, John, 410

McGerr, Patricia, 522–23

MacGuinness, James, 305, 390, 445

MacGuinness, James Kelvin, 230

McHugh, Vincent, 325

McKinley, William, 24

MacLane, Barton, 291

McManus, Jack, 373

Macmillan (publisher), 236

MacMurray, Fred, 335, 336, 347, 378

McPherson, Bill, 34

McWilliams, Carey, 469, 534

Madden, David, 179, 503–06, 511; *Beautiful Greed, The*, 505, 515–17, 552; *Bijou*, 504n; *James M. Cain*, 519–20, 522; *Pleasure Dome*, 504n; review of *The Institute*, 536, 537; *Suicide's Wife, The*, 504n

Madeira, Edward O., 61, 65, 66, 67, 68, 72, 77

Madly in Love (play), 187

Magician's Wife, The (Cain), 38, 484–99, 505–07, 511, 548; Cain's best writing, 499

Mahin, John Lee, 160, 260–61, 266, 293, 346, 390, 435

Mailer, Norman, 470, 517; *American Dream*, 487–88

Main Street (Lewis), 96, 152

Major and the Minor, The (film), 329, 332

Malcolm, Gilbert, 185, 275, 460, 507; in World War I, 61, 62, 63, 65, 72–78, 87–88

Mallahan, Brigid Ingoldsby (grandmother to James M. Cain), 4

Mallahan, Edwin, 4

Mallahan, Margaret, 4

Mallahan, Mary, 4

Mallahan, Matthew (grandfather to James M. Cain), 4

Mallahan, Rose. *See* Cain, Rose Mallahan

Maltese Falcon, The (film), 335, 347

Maltz, Albert, 348, 410, 429

"Man Merriwell, The" (Cain), 139

Man Who Knew Coolidge, The (Lewis), 154

Manhattan Transfer (Dos Passos), 107, 129

Manhunt, 460–61

Mankiewicz, Herman, 219–20, 223, 393

Mann, Anthony, 468

Mann, Thomas: *Death in Venice*, 129

Manson, Franson, 265

Manwaring, Daniel, 384

March, Alden, 200

March, Joseph, 200

Margolis, Henry, 431

Markey, Gene, 296

Markey, Helen, 430, 450–51

Markey, Marvin, 451

Markey, Morris, 119, 199–200, 247, 324–25, 384; article on H. Julia, 207–09; Cain's correspondence with, 319–20, 323, 423, 450; death of, 450–51; friendship with Cain, 140, 151, 173, 185, 450–51; "Strange Noise of Dr. Beldoon," 209

Marquis, Don, 133

Marshall, Brenda, 303

Marx, Sam, 247

Mason and Lipscomb (publishers; later Mason-Charter), 531–32, 536, 537

Masters, Edgar Lee, 128, 262

Mature, Victor, 310

Maugham, Somerset: The Summing Up, 553

Meaning of Treason, The (West), 92

Men Without Women (Hemingway), 181

Mencken, H. L., 16, 17, 18, 20, 25, 36, 94, 106, 162, 205, 225, 226, 245, 251, 260, 262, 279, 282, 393, 515; acknowledged in Cain's first book, 185; American Language, The, 77, 89, 247, 286; arbiter of American literary taste, 96; at Baltimore Sun, 89; Book of Burlesques, A, 89; Book of Prefaces, A, 89; books about, 449–50; broke with Goodman, 192, 193; Cain on, 190–92, 193; on Cain's AAA proposal, 396; Cain's articles re, 539; and Cain's dialogues, 178, 179; Cain's correspondence with, 283–84, 286, 338, 344, 371–72, 408, 411; Cain's indebtedness to, 546; on Cain's Our Government, 186; column: "Clowns March In, The," 88; column: "Free Lance, The," 89; death of, 449–50, 468, 542; death of wife, 273; defense of

Scopes, 164; did not like Lippmann, 139; as editor, 191–92, 212; editor of Smart Set, 88, 89; friendship with Cain, 88–89, 106–07, 108–10, 114, 115, 116, 117, 129–33, 151–56, 183, 192, 546; friendship with A. Pringle, 342, 343; In Defense of Women, 89, 133; instilled in Cain his obsession with accuracy, 431; liked Love's Lovely Counterfeit, 325; on love, 527; love of music, 106, 193; on marriage, 105; marriage of, 194; meeting with W. Cather, 189–90; mentor to Cain, 77, 95, 97–98; monologues, 190, 211; moved to Hollywood, 255; pleased over Cain's marriage to A. Pringle, 346; pushing careers of young writers, 133; quarrel with Knopf over American Mercury, 240–41; Red-baiting, 286, 389; regard for Cain's talent, 97, 187, 229, 236, 240, 450; requests to Cain for information re, 502; Saturday Night Club, 106, 114, 132–33, 134; style, 88; Sunday Night Club, 114

Mencken, Sara. See Haardt, Sara

Menjou, Adolphe, 312

Merz, Charles, 118, 124, 138n, 173, 185

Method of Freedom, The (Lippmann), 255

Meyers, Henry, 264–65, 266, 271

Meyers, Richard, 286

MGM, 230, 332, 382; Cain working at, 285, 286, 291–93, 344–45, 353, 365; bought Postman, 253, 348, 352–53, 379, 391, 457, 462

Michelson, Charley, 119, 173

Mielziner, Jo, 272

Mignon (Cain), 37, 463–64, 473–77, 480, 484, 499, 511, 529; rejected by Knopf, 471, 474; sales, 475, 481, 486; structure of, 552

Mildred Pierce, 38, 218, 305–06, 307–08, 309–10, 312, 313–15,

Mildred Pierce (cont'd)
317; Cain reread, 485; film version,
314, 339–40, 345, 348–52, 353,
365, 372–74, 378, 379–80, 435,
548; reason for success of, 480–81;
republished in *Cain X 3*, 517–19;
sales, 314, 315, 426; structure of,
552; suit charging plagiarism in,
443, 444–47; TV series failed to materialize, 471
Milestone, Lewis, 220, 246
"Military Forces, The" (Cain). *See*
"Taking of Montfaucon, The"
Miller, Harry: *Through Combat*, 344
Miller, John C., 516
Miller, Merle, 433
Mintz, Sam, 221, 222
Misérables, Les (film), 369
Mizener, Wilson, 220
"Modern Cinderella, A" (Cain) (retitled
The Root of His Evil), 293, 295–96,
302; film version of, 296, 300–01,
302, 311, 448
Moley, Raymond, 344
"Money and the Woman" (Cain) (reti-
tled "The Embezzler"), 301–02,
331; anthologized in *Three of a Kind*,
321; novel version: *The Embezzler*,
307–08; sold to Warner Brothers,
302, 303
Money and the Woman (film version of
same title), 303
Monfort, Alice, 414–15
Monroe, John R., 33–35
Montez, Maria, 329, 366, 467
Montiel, Sarita, 468
Moore, Grace, 265
Moore, James Garfield, 18, 19, 20,
21–22, 240
Moore, Sam, 393
Moran, Jim, 427–28
Morand, Paul, 128
Morehouse, Ward, 450
Morley, Christopher: *Thunder on the
Left*, 129
Morley, Felix, 108, 126

Morris, Mary, 384–85
Morris, William, Agency, 218, 226,
229, 288–89, 295, 302, 308; Cain
broke with, 323
Morrison, Theodore, 444
Morton, Charles, 201
Moth, The (Cain), 8, 33, 37, 38, 424,
426–28, 432, 433–34, 442, 457;
abridged version of, 448; structure
of, 552
Motion picture industry, 423; Cain on,
418–19; in World War II, 317–18,
320
Motley, Willard: *Knock on Any Door*,
470; *We Fished All Night*, 470
Movie Crazy (film), 228, 270
Mumford, Lewis, 128, 483
Murfin, Jane, 292
My Ántonia (Cather), 190
Mystery of Marie La Farge, The
(Saunders), 471
Mystery Writers of America, 522–23

Nash, Ogden, 200–01, 203
Nathan, George Jean, 88, 106, 109,
137, 152, 191, 192, 211; *Bottoms
Up*, 133
Nathan, Robert, 202, 354; *Portrait of
Jenny*, 342
Nation, The, 167, 168, 169, 461, 469,
534; Cain published in, 95, 102–03,
117, 120, 123
Navasky, Vic, 535
Neal, Tom, 248, 462
"Nevada Moon" (Cain) (retitled *Jealous
Woman*), 447–48
Nevada Moon (Cain) (unpublished),
417–18
Nevins, Allan, 118, 124, 173; *Ordeal
of the Union*, 441
New American Library, 444, 448
New Republic, 313, 314, 380
New Theatre, The (magazine), 418
New York American, 241–42
New York Herald Tribune, 199, 234,
245, 249, 346–47, 372, 398–99, 422

New York Times, 79, 166, 167, 185–86, 226, 314, 317, 372; Cain's article on his films and Hays Office, 379–80

New York Times Book Review, 244–45, 404

New York World, 96, 140, 165–70, 196–99, 322, 473; Cain on staff of, 117–25, 126–27; Cain editorial writer on, 159–77, 189, 191, 389, 435–36, 546; Cain's dialogues in, 182–83

New Yorker, The, 119, 202, 249, 255–56, 313, 422, 433, 534–35; Cain at, 199–204, 206–14; Cain published in, 28–29, 164; parody of *Postman* in, 247; "Reporter at Large, A", 151, 200, 207

Newsweek, 380, 381, 480

Newton, Ike, 17, 547

Nichols, Luther, 477

Nicholson, Jack, 248

Nielson, James, 287

Norris, Frank, 241

Norris, Kathleen, 96

North, Sterling, 433

Nothing to Live For (Caro), 444–47

Nugent, Frank, 300

O Pioneers! (Cather), 189

Oates, Joyce Carol, 516–17

Ober, Harold, 374–75, 424, 452, 460, 464, 469, 474

O'Faoláin, Seán, 298–99, 301, 302–03

O'Hara, John, 110, 186, 202, 213–14, 223, 276, 285, 313, 323, 338; "Christmas Spirit, The," 189

Old Man and the Sea (Hemingway), 470

Old Soak, The (play), 133

Olding, Dorothy, 485, 512, 532, 538–39

O'Neill, Eugene, 553; "All God's Chillun Got Wings," 109–10

"Opening Gun, The" (Cain), 392

Ordeal of the Union (Nevins), 441

Ormer, Eric, 383n

Our Government (Cain), 183–85, 189, 191, 235; reviews, 185–86; sales, 186

Our Man in Havana (Greene), 470

Our Town (Wilder), 304

Out of the Past (Tourneur), 384

Outlook, 185

Outside Looking In (Anderson), 135

Owens, Hamilton, 103, 185, 192, 365, 368, 468

Owens, John W., 92

Paca, William, 5

Pallette, Eugene, 300

Palmer, Mitchell, 88

Palmer, Paul, 211, 241, 271, 275, 285–86

Paramount, 230, 332, 335; Cain working at, 214, 218, 219–23, 226, 260–62, 376–77

Parker, Dorothy, 128, 167, 202, 205, 211, 276, 550; "Big Blonde," 339; reaction to *Postman*, 246–47

Parker, James Reid, 202

Parkhill, Forbes, 291

Parks, Bert, 413–14

Parrelly, John, 381

Parsons, Louella, 347, 461

Passage of Arms (Ambler), 470

Past All Dishonor (Cain), 37, 101, 369–70, 371, 372, 375, 381–84, 387, 419, 420, 422, 442, 458, 463, 475, 549; Cain on, 552; Cain reread, 485; considered/rejected for film, 382–83, 487, 517, 528; reviews, 381; success of, 476

Pasternak, Joe, 271

"Pastor, The" (Cain), 129–30

"Pastorale" (Cain), 179–80, 181, 186, 224, 229, 271, 448, 469, 488

"Pathology of Service, The" (Cain), 130–31

Patten, William Gilbert, 139, 156, 179

Patterson, Paul, 103

"Pay-Off Girl" (Cain), 452

Payne, John, 466

Payton, Barbara, 248, 462

Pearl, Raymond, 153

Peck, George, 409–10

"Pedagogue: Old Style" (Cain), 113–14

Pegler, Westbrook, 397

P.E.N. Women, 406

Penguin books, 248

Pennell, Joseph: *The History of Rome Hanks*, 432

Pepe le Moko (film), 289

Perelman, S. J., 202

Perino, Alexander, 337, 432

Perkins, Clarence W., 13–14

Petrillo, James C., 398, 406

Petrocelli, Orlando, 533, 536, 539

Pett, Saul, 461

Philips, Mary, 248, 272, 275

Picina, La (proposed biography of F. Macbeth), 424

Pinero, Sir Arthur Wing, 517

Pink Buttercup, The (Cain) (unpublished), 484

Piper, Alice, 525–26, 540–41, 542

Plattsburgh Manual, The (Garey), 103

Plumes (Stallings), 140

PM, 373–74, 384–85, 387, 433

Pocket Books, 248, 448

Poe, Edgar Allan, 19, 339, 397, 546

"Politician: Female" (Cain), 115–16

Pollack, Arthur, 274

Pollard, Harry, 171

Pomerance, William, 400

Poore, Charles, 381

Poppy (play), 134, 188

Porter, Gene Stratton, 96

Porter, William Sydney, 241

Portrait of Jenny (Nathan), 342

Postman Always Rings Twice (Cain), 214, 231–39, 242, 243, 245, 277, 308, 310, 317, 420, 434, 475, 488, 504, 528, 546, 548; Cain reread, 485; film version, 253, 260, 339, 348, 352–53, 372, 378–80, 382, 383–84, 391, 435; impact of, 235,

244–49; Knopf rejected, 474; originally titled *Bar-B-Que*, 234, 235; paperback editions, 285–86; reaction to, 246; republished in *Cain X 3*, 517–19; revival as play, 457–58, 462–63; sales, 448; sold to MGM, 247; stage version, 262, 267, 269, 270, 272, 273–76; success of, 247–48; thematic structure of, 552

Pound, Ezra, 128

Powell, Dick, 353, 384

Preminger, Otto, 383, 461–62

Presnell, Robert, 303

Price, Byron, 404

Price, Vincent, 468

Pringle, Aileen. *See* Cain, Aileen Pringle

Pringle, Henry F., 202

Professor's House, The (Cather), 129, 190

Public Opinion (Lippmann), 120

Publishers Weekly, 528, 531

Pulitzer, Herbert, 171, 172, 197, 199

Pulitzer, Joseph, 118, 164, 165, 172

Pulitzer, Ralph, 117, 118, 166, 167, 168, 172, 197

Purcell, Gertrude, 265

Queed (Harrison), 36

Radio Writers Guild, 395–96, 399

Raft, George, 335

Raftery, George, 445, 446–47

Ragtime (Doctorow), 487

Rainbow (play), 134, 193–94, 227

Rainbow's End (Cain), 531–52, 533, 536, 537

Rand, Ayn, 398

Random House, 412, 484

Raphaelson, Dorothy ("Dorshka") Wegman, 228, 246, 265, 278, 310

Raphaelson, Samson, 228, 232, 246, 261, 264, 265, 266, 278, 379, 488; on Cain as playwright, 548; Cain felt autobiography justified, 503; Cain visited, critiqued *Guest in 701*, 465–66; Cain wanted to read Civil War novel, 454; Cain's correspondence with, 372, 501; encouraged Cain on *Serenade*, 284; letter read at memorial tribute to Cain, 542–43; on *Mildred Pierce*, 315; *Old Love*, 257; on plays, 256–57; on A. Pringle, 342; short stories, 503; *Young Love*, 257

Rascoe, Burton, 128

Rathbone, Robert, 308–09, 472

Reading, William, 479

Realism, literary, 96, 333, 444

Red Badge of Courage, The (Crane), 54, 546

Red Scare, 88, 93

"Red White and Blue" (Cain), 138

Redbook, 247, 249, 261, 268

Reynolds, Stanley, 92–93

Reston, James, 472

Reviews, 135–36, 159, 545; *Butterfly*, 421–22; *Cain X 3*, 518; films from Cain works, 346–47, 372, 380, 466–67, 468; *Galatea*, 461; *Institute*, 536; *Love's Lovely Counterfeit*, 325; *Magician's Wife*, 506; *Mildred Pierce*, 313–14, 350; *Mildred Pierce* (film), 372; *Mignon*, 475–76; *Moth*, 433–34; movies Cain worked on, 330; *Our Government*, 185–86; *Past All Dishonor*, 381; *Postman Always Rings Twice*, 244–46, 247; *Postman . . .* (film), 380; *Postman . . .* (stage version), 274–75, 462; *Rainbow's End*, 533, 536; *Serenade*, 286–87; *Three of a Kind*, 331

Revnes, Maurice, 223

Rice, Craig, 393

Rice, Elmer, 202, 398, 399, 400, 402, 403, 405, 406

Riffaterre, Virginia, 476

Riggin, Grace, 26, 27

Rise of Silas Lapham, The (Howells), 95

Riskin, Robert, 230–31

RKO, 230, 383–85

Robbins, Henry, 484–85, 486

Roberts, Ben, 468

Robey, Grace, 33–34

Robinson, Casey, 226

Robinson, Edward G., 333, 335, 347, 353, 417–18, 447

Rogers, Will, 119

Romberg, Sigmund, 366

Romero, Cesar, 300

Root of His Evil, The (Cain) (original title "The Modern Cinderella"), 448

Ross, Harold, 128, 151, 220, 502; editor, *New Yorker*, 199–204, 207–14

Ross, Malcolm (Mike), 118, 122, 126, 501

Rovere, Dick, 535

Rubin, Arthur, 383

Rubin, Jack, 292–93

Ruffo, Titta, 416

Ruggles of Red Gap (film), 269

Runyon, Damon, 338

Ruskin, Harry, 378, 379

Russell, Louis, 410

Sacco-Vanzetti case, 159, 166–67, 168, 169, 195

St. John's College, 4, 5, 13, 18, 19, 21, 53, 103, 369; Cain teaching at, 103–04, 107–08, 112–13, 114

Salamanca, Jack, 523, 542

Salisbury, Leah, 458

Sammons, Wheeler, 424

Sargent, Winthrop, 527

Saroyan, William, 313

Saturday Evening Post, 74, 94, 212; Cain published in, 138, 139, 156

Saturday Review, 325, 331, 400–01, 422; Cain-Farrell debate in, 404–05

Saunders, Edith: *The Mystery of Marie La Farge*, 471

Sayre, Joel, 202

Schary, Dore, 383

Scheur, Philip K., 347, 353

Schipa, Tito, 416

Schlesinger, Arthur, Jr., 535
Schorer, Mark, 502
Schulberg, B. P., 219, 220; *The Disenchanted*, 470; *What Makes Sammy Run?*, 350
Schumann-Heink, Ernestine, 57
Schuster, Leonard, 262
Schuster, Lincoln, 118
Scott, Zachary, 351
Scott-Moncrieff (Charles Kenneth Michael), 128
Screen Writer, 392, 408, 418; Cain's AAA material published in, 394–96, 401; Communist propaganda sheet, 411, 430
Screen Writers Guild, 391–92, 395–96, 402, 403, 412; Cain fought Communist takeover in, 428–30; Committee on the Sale of Original Material, 391, 411; Communist dominated, 330, 390, 392, 397, 398, 399, 408, 409, 410–11; Leasing Committee, 392–93; revised form of AAA, 405, 406, 409
Scripps-Howard, 197–98
Scroggs, W. O., 118, 124, 173, 196, 235
"Sealing Wax" (Cain), 202
Sedgwick, Ellery, 94
Seldes, Gilbert, 202
Selznick, David O., 383, 391–92
Serenade (Cain), 38, 159, 284, 286, 317, 322, 339, 348, 430–31, 434, 474, 475, 482, 548, 555; Cain thought plagiarized, 302, 310–12, 325–27, 391; film version, 365–66, 435, 467–68; Knopf liked, 474; reviews, 286–87; sales, 288; structure of, 552; suit charging obscenity in, 443–44
"Servants of the People" (Cain), 131
7-11 (Cain), 284–85, 286–87, 293, 294, 295, 296, 321, 338, 447–48, 466, 475; *Galloping Domino* based on, 442

Seward, William W.: *Skirts of the Dead Night*, 460
Shaffer, Virginia, 105
Shakespeare, William: sonnets, 530, 536
Shanghai Gesture, The (film), 310
Shaw, George Bernard, 403, 408, 517
She Made Her Bed (film version of "Baby in the Icebox"), 226
Sheridan, Ann, 350, 467
Sherlock Holmes (Doyle), 546
Sherrier, Mary, 36
Sherwin, Louis, 185
Sherwood, Robert, 128
Shientag, Bernard, 405
"Short Happy Life of Francis Macomber, The" (Hemingway), 448
Shuster, William, 74
Sign of the Cross (film), 228, 269
Silberman, Jim, 474–75, 484, 486, 511
Sillcox, Louise, 402, 403
Sinclair, Robert, 274, 275
Sinful Woman (Cain) (based on *7-11*; original title *The Galloping Domino*), 442, 447–48, 475
Sirich, Edward, 112–13, 114, 454, 501
Sirich, Marjorie, 114
Sistrom, Joe, 332, 334, 335, 383
Skirts of the Dead Night (Seward), 460
"Skylark" (Raphaelson), 503
Slightly Scarlet (film version of *Love's Lovely Counterfeit*), 466–67, 468
Smart Set, The (magazine), 88, 89, 97, 152
Smith, Bernard, 372, 381
Smith, Harrison, 402
Smith, Marion DeKalb, 52
Smith, William D., 15–16
Smith and Haas, 248
"Snows of Kilimanjaro, The" (Hemingway), 448
Snyder, Ruth, 232–33
Sokolsky, George, 396–97, 398

"Solid South, The" (Cain), 183

Sorenson, Robert, 518

Sousa, John Philip, 56

Sovey, Ramond, 136

Spaeth, Sigmund, 128

Speare, Dorothy, 265

Spectorsky, A. C., 331, 422

Sperling, Milton, 383

Stahl, John, 300–01, 302, 311, 325–27

Stallings, Laurence, 118, 128, 173, 193–94, 220, 291–92; Cain's correspondence with, 382, 450, 477; column: "The First Reader," 119, 140; play: *The Streets Are Guarded*, 367; *Plumes*, 140; relation with Cain, 140–51

Stand Up and Fight (film), 291–92, 329, 435

Standish, Burt L. (pseud.). *See* Patten, William Gilbert

Stanton, William M., 87

Stanwyck, Barbara, 219, 336, 347, 350, 372, 373, 383, 447, 466

Steffens, Lincoln, 25

Steinbeck, John, 287, 313, 338, 374

Steinman, Col. James, 72, 74, 76, 78

Stevens, Ashton, 422

Stone, Thomas, 5

Stout, Rex, 318, 367, 470

Stratton, Samuel, 166

Strauss, Harold, 244–45, 444

Street, Julian, 319

Streets Are Guarded, The (play), 367

Streets of Night (Dos Passos), 107

Stripling, Robert, 410

Stromberg, Hunt, 354

Stryker, Clarence W., 10, 13

Stuart, Mark, 536

Sturgeon, Charles, 312

Subtreasury of American Humor (White and White), 184, 313

Sullivan, Arthur, 265

Sullivan, Barry, 293

Sullivan, Frank, 202, 241

Summing Up, The (Maugham), 553

Sumner, William Graham, 4, 516

Sun Dial, 391

Swanson, Gloria, 341

Swanson, H. N., 323, 332, 333, 374, 383, 384, 418, 424, 435, 448, 506; Cain's correspondence with, 454; critiqued *Guest in 701*, 466; sales, attempted sales of Cain's works to studios, 428, 457, 487, 517, 528

Sweet Love Remembered (play), 187

Swerling, Florence, 265

Swerling, Jo, 265

Swift, Jonathan, 17

Swindell, Larry, 533

Swope, Herbert Bayard, 118, 119, 128, 164, 168, 185, 198, 322, 468; banquet for, 459–60; biography of, 502; Cain's correspondence with, 384, 385; left *New York World*, 172, 196; and Lippmann, 165–66

"Taking of Montfaucon, The" (Cain), (renamed "The Military Forces"), 184–85

Tarbell, Ida, 25

Targ, William, 338–39, 422

Tate, Bessie, 12, 116

Taylor, Deems, 164

Taylor, Dwight, 300, 301, 302, 310–12, 325–26

Taylor, Robert, 291, 317

Taylor, Sam, 261

Tempest, Marie, 415

Ten Commandments, The (film), 221–23

Thackeray, William M.: *Vanity Fair*, 19, 529

Thanatopsis Literary and Inside Straight Club, 127–28, 129

That Was No Hero (film), 285

Thayer, Webster, 166

Theater of Famous Authors, 452

Theatre Guild, 253, 260, 269, 270, 466

"Theological Interlude" (Cain), 179, 184

This Side of Paradise (Fitzgerald), 96

This Week, 267, 488

Thomas, Bob, 351

Thomas, J. Parnell, 412

Thomas, Mostyn, 265, 443

Thompson, Dorothy, 193, 402–03

Thompson, Ralph, 226, 313, 444

Three of a Kind (Cain) (anthology), 321, 331–32, 347, 427, 433, 436; Cain's preface to, 545

Three Soldiers (Dos Passos), 100, 106

Three Weeks (film), 341

Through Combat (Miller), 344

Thurber, James, 200, 204, 209, 247, 263; and Cain, 206–07; *Years with Ross*, 202

Tierney, Gene, 310

Time magazine, 274–75, 314, 325, 380, 381, 422, 506; review of *Moth*, 433–34

Titsworth, Paul, 58

To Have and Have Not (Hemingway), 287

Tourneur, Jacques: *Out of the Past*, 384

Townsend, Charles L., 51–52, 263

Traven, B. (pseud.), 482

Treasure Island (Stevenson), 19; film, 260–61

Treasure of Sierra Madre, The, 482

Treat 'Em Rough (Lardner), 74

"Trial by Jury" (Cain), 178–79

Triangle, 391

"Tribute to a Hero" (Cain), 241

Trumbo, Dalton, 393, 410

Tuchman, Barbara, 516

Turan, Kenneth, 534

Turner, Lana, 248, 353, 373, 377–78, 379, 380, 533

Turney, Catherine, 348

Twain, Mark, 241, 397, 546

20th Century-Fox, 230, 280, 447, 473; Cain working at, 307, 327–28, 329, 332, 333

Twist, John, 468

"Two O'Clock Blonde" (Cain), 460–61

"Two Can Sing" (Cain), 280, 285, 288, 290; film versions: *Everybody Does It; Wife, Husband and Friend*, 300, 435, 447; retitled "Career in C Major" and anthologized in *Three of a Kind*, 321

Tyre, Norman, 393

Tyszecka, Elina Sjosted. *See* Cain, Elina Tyszecka

Tyszecka, Henrietta (later Holmes), 106, 205–06, 218, 278, 316, 324, 325, 371; attempt to reunite Elina and Cain, 513; on Cain's breakup with K. Cummings, 340; death of husband, 343; ill, 293–94; married, child Christine, 329, 343

Tyszecki, Leo, 105, 157, 205–06, 223, 227, 231, 265, 305, 371, 555; attempt to reunite Elina and Cain, 513; on Cain, 254, 256, 258, 278, 323; on Cain's relation with K. Cummings, 282, 340; called Cain, 541; on Elina's role in Cain's success, 336; move to California, 217–18; in World War II, 324

Tyszecki, Victor, 106

United Artists, 331

United Mine Workers, 98

U.S. Army, 79th Infantry Division, 61–62, 67, 68, 71–72, 77, 78–79, 344

U.S. Congress, House Un-American Activities Committee, 410, 412

Universal Studios, 296, 302; Cain working at, 289, 300–01, 329–31; Cain's plagiarism suit against, 311–12, 320, 325–27, 391

U.S. in World Affairs, The (Lippmann), 234–35

U.S. War Aims (Lippmann), 344

U.S.A. (Dos Passos), 107

Van Doren, Carl, 110

Van Dyke, W. S., 291

Van Loon, Hendrik, 128
Van Nostrand, Albert, 504
Vanity Fair (magazine), 226, 235, 239
Velez, Lupe, 285, 286
Verdi, Giuseppe, 403
Victoria Docks at 8, The (film script), 301
Vidal, Gore: *Burr*, 470
Vintage Books, 248
Visconti, Luchino, 248
"Visitor, The" (Cain), 475
Von Auw, Ivan, 474, 482, 507, 511, 512, 528; working with *Magician's Wife*, 485, 486
V.V.'s Eyes (Harrison), 36

Waggner, George, 329–30
Wald, Jerry, 288, 339–40, 350, 365, 366, 383, 467, 475; clairvoyant story suggestion to Cain, 480–81; Company of Artists, 473; and *Mildred Pierce*, 348, 349, 350–52, 372, 379
Walker, Gerald: *Cruising*, 470
Wallace, Richard, 220
Wallis, Hal, 383
Walter Lippmann and His Times, 473
Wanger, Walter, 249, 250, 289
Ward, John, 86
Warner, Jack, 339, 345, 350–51
Warner Brothers, 230, 261, 303, 323, 332, 348, 350; bought *Serenade*, 288, 365–66, 467; sued in Cain *Mildred Pierce* suit, 445, 446, 447
Washington College, Chestertown, Md., 13–22, 24, 51–52, 58–59, 240, 246; Cain declined honors from, 459, 480, 522; football, 18–19, 20–22, 53
Washington Post, 461; *Potomac* edition, 518–19, 534, 537, 539–40, 542
Wasserman, Lew, 351
Watson, Clarence, 93
Watson, Mark, 103
We Fished All Night (Motley), 470
Webb, Kenneth, 406
Weingarten, Larry, 285

Weitzenkorn, Louis, 243
West, Mae, 249
West, Rebecca: *The Meaning of Treason*, 93
"West Virginia: A Mine-field Melodrama" (Cain), 102–03
Weybright, Victor, 444
Wharton, Edith, 546
What Makes Sammy Run? (Schulberg), 350
What Price Glory? (play), 118, 120, 123, 140, 151
Wheeler, Jack, 254
When Tomorrow Comes (film version of "Modern Cinderella"), 302, 310–11, 325, 327, 448
While Rome Burns (Woollcott), 161
Whitaker, Rogers, 207, 213
White, E. B., 202, 205, 213; children's books, 539; and Katharine White: *Subtreasury of American Humor*, 184
White, Florence, 172
White, Katharine, 202, 205, 212, 213, 313, 474; Cain's correspondence with, 469, 480; and E. B. White: *Subtreasury of American Humor*, 184, 313
Whiteman, Paul, 417
Whitwell, Edward, 416, 417
Who's Who in America, 3–4, 10–11, 30, 55, 199, 424; Cain's bible, 502
Why We Behave Like Human Beings (Dorsey), 153
Wife, Husband and Friend (film, based on "Two Can Sing"), 300; remade as *Everybody Does It*, 447
Wild Man from Borneo, The (play), 219
Wilde, Oscar, 556
Wilder, Billy, 230, 332–36, 339, 346–47, 379, 383, 548
Wilder, Isabel, 304, 305
Wilder, Thornton, 242, 304–05, 370; *Bridge of San Luis Rey*, 304, 305; film version of *Bridge . . .*, 331; *Our Town*, 304

Wiley, William, 90–91, 96, 99–100, 299–300
"Will of the People" (Cain), 183–84
Williamson, Thames, 340
Wilson, Carey, 348, 365, 378–79, 554–55
Wilson, Edmund, 306, 329, 352, 381, 382, 419, 436, 547; "Boys in the Back Room, The," 313, 504; Cain's letter to, 555
Wilson, George C., 376
Wilson, Jack, 87–88, 117
Wilson, John, 92
Winchell, Walter, 425
Winesburg, Ohio (Anderson), 96
Wings of the Dove, The (H. James), 392
Winsor, Roy, 452
Witteford, Charles, 533
Wolfe, Nero, 470
Wolfe, Thomas, 276, 487–88, 506, 537; Introduction to *Cain X 3*, 517–18, 519
Wolheim, Louis, 138
Woods, J. M., 91
Woolf, Virginia: *Mrs. Dalloway*, 129
Woollcott, Alexander, 75, 128, 172, 182, 205; *While Rome Burns*, 161

Woollcott, Willie, 134
World of Swope, The (Kahn), 502
World of the 20s, The (Boylan), 170, 171
World Publishing Company, 338
World War I, 54, 58–59, 60–79, 84
World War II, 316–40, 343–44, 366–67
Wright, Harold Bell, 96
Writers Guild, 388
Writers War Board, 367, 390
Wylie, Elinor, 129
Wylie, Philip, 398, 410

Yankwich, Leon, 326–27, 391, 394
Years with Ross (Thurber), 202
You Knew Me, Al (Lardner), 74
Young, Loretta, 300
Young Love (play), 228, 257, 342
Youniss, Dorothy, 525, 526, 533, 534, 540
Youniss, Jim, 525, 526, 542

Zanuck, Darryl F., 328
Zolotow, Maurice: *Billy Wilder*, 230